STATISTICS
FOR
BUSINESS AND ECONOMICS

STATISTICS
FOR
BUSINESS AND ECONOMICS

JAMES T. McCLAVE
Department of Statistics
University of Florida

GEORGE BENSON
Department of Management Sciences
University of Minnesota

DELLEN PUBLISHING COMPANY
San Francisco, California

© Copyright 1978 by Dellen Publishing Company, San Francisco, California

Printed in the United States of America

10 9 8 7 6 5 4 3

Library of Congress Cataloging in Publication Data

McClave, James T.
  Statistics for business and economics.

  Includes index.
  1. Statistics.   2.   Commercial statistics.
I. Benson, P. George, 1946–   joint author.
II. Title.
HA29.M165   519.5   77-17909

ISBN 0–89517–004–3

The figures that appear on the cover and chapter opening pages represent populations in the abstract, statistical sense. The artist, Nan Golub, chose the androgynous silhouettes to illustrate statistical data because they seemed to her to be more interesting than circles, dots, or squares.

CONTENTS

PREFACE

The purpose of this text is to introduce business students to the basic concepts of statistics and to show them how these concepts can be used to aid in decision-making. A common obstacle to achieving this goal seems inherent in the nature of the subject. Students often view statistics as "mathematics," concentrating on the arithmetic and problem solving rather than on the new concepts and their applications to business. As a consequence, they learn how to solve the problems at the ends of chapters, but fail to develop an overview of statistics and its role in business decision-making. Recognizing this situation, we have attempted to present a unified treatment of statistics. Continuity is achieved by showing how one topic relates to another, and how all topics relate to statistical inference.

The text is designed so that the early chapters can be used for a one-quarter (or a one-semester) introductory course for all business undergraduates. The remainder of the text can be used as a second-quarter (semester) follow-up course, with emphasis on special applications such as regression analysis, time series, the analysis of variance, or one of the other methodologies included in the later chapters.

The material is presented in a manner that will permit an instructor to vary the amount of time devoted to particular topics. Sections that are not prerequisite to succeeding sections and chapters are marked "(Optional)." For example, an instructor who wishes to devote more time at the beginning of the course to descriptive statistics might wish to cover all topics in Chapters 2, 3, and 4. In contrast, an instructor who wishes to move rapidly into statistical inference might omit the optional sections (2.2, 2.3, and 2.5) and devote only one or two lectures to these chapters.

We have included several features in this text that will make it different from most introductory business statistics texts currently available. These features, which assist the student in achieving an overview of statistics and an understanding of its relevance in the solution of business problems, are as follows:

1. Case Studies Many important concepts are emphasized by the inclusion of case studies, which consist of brief summaries of actual business applications of the concepts and are often drawn directly from the business literature. These case studies allow the student to see business applications of important statistical concepts immediately after the introduction of the concepts. The case studies also help to answer by example the often asked questions, "Why should I study statistics? Of what relevance is statistics to business?" Finally, the case studies constantly remind the student that each concept is related to the dominant theme—statistical inference.

2. Where we've been . . . Where we're going . . . The first page of each chapter is a "unification" page. Our purpose is to allow the student to see how the chapter fits into the scheme of statistical inference. First, we briefly show how the material presented in previous chapters helps us to achieve our goal (Where we've been). Then, we indicate what the next chapter (or chapters) contributes to the overall objective (Where we're going). This feature allows us to point out that we are constructing the foundation block by block, with each chapter an important component in the structure of statistical inference. Furthermore, this feature provides a series of brief resumés of the material covered as well as glimpses of future topics.

3. Many Examples and Exercises We believe that most students learn by doing. Therefore, many examples and exercises are a necessity in an introductory statistics text. We have included two types:

a. Simple mechanical examples and exercises with manufactured data. Examples of this type are used to convey concepts to the student rapidly. Relevance to business applications is of secondary importance for these examples. They portray situations that can be described in a few words and are unhampered by a barrage of background information designed to make them "practical," but which often detracts from instructional objectives. Mechanical exercises have the same advantage: With a minimum of labor they enable a student to recheck his or her ability to comprehend a concept or a definition.

b. Realistic business statistics examples and exercises that allow the student to see applications of statistics to business problems.

Answers for most of the exercises are included at the end of the text.

4. On Your Own . . . The chapters end with an exercise entitled "On Your Own . . . ." The intent of this exercise is to give the student some hands-on experience with a business application of the statistical concepts introduced in the chapter. In most cases, the student is required to collect, analyze, and interpret data relating to some business phenomenon.

5. A Simple, Clear Style We have tried to achieve a simple and clear writing style. Subjects that are tangential to our objective have been avoided, even though some may be of academic interest to those well-versed in statistics. We have not taken an encyclopedic approach in the presentation of material.

6. An Extensive Coverage of Multiple Regression Analysis and Model Building This topic represents one of the most useful statistical tools for the solution of business problems. Although an entire text could be devoted to regression modeling, we feel that we have presented a coverage that is understandable, usable, and much more comprehensive than the presentations in other introductory business statistics texts. We devote three chapters to discussing the major types of inferences that can be derived from a regression analysis, showing how these results appear in computer printouts and, most important, selecting multiple regression models to be used in an analysis. Thus, the instructor has the choice of a one-chapter coverage of simple regression, a two-chapter treatment of simple and multiple regression, or a complete three-chapter coverage of simple regression, multiple regression, and model building. The following chapter on time series analysis is closely tied to the three chapters on multiple regression analysis, and presents an introduction to forecasting based on time-dependent data. This extensive coverage of such useful statistical tools will provide added evidence to the student of the relevance of statistics to the solution of business problems.

7. Footnotes and Appendix A   Although the text is designed for students with a noncalculus background, footnotes explain the role of calculus in various derivations. Footnotes are also used to inform the student about some of the theory underlying certain results. Appendix A presents some useful counting rules for the instructor who wishes to place greater emphasis on probability. Consequently, we think the footnotes and Appendix A provide an opportunity for flexibility in the mathematical and theoretical level at which the material is presented.

Many individuals contributed their time and skills to this text. We acknowledge Frank Dietrich for his invaluable assistance in reviewing the early drafts of the manuscript and for providing several of the case studies used in the text. We also want to thank Ron Shiffler for his many helpful comments, particularly with regard to the exercises. The assistance of Kirk Pierret, who contributed many exercises and helped in the preparation of the solutions at the end of the text, is deeply appreciated. We thank Marlin Eby and James Lackritz, who spent many hours researching and writing some of our more realistic exercises. Finally, we acknowledge Ann Kennedy and Jackie Host for a superb job of transforming our scribbles, inserts, and masses of symbols into typed copy.

ACKNOWLEDGMENTS

The authors and the publisher would like to thank the following for their careful reviews of the rough manuscript. This text is much improved due to their efforts.

Larry M. Austin
Texas Tech University
Lubbock, Texas

Francis J. Brewerton
Middle Tennessee State University
Murfreesboro, Tennessee

Robert W. Brobst
University of Texas at Arlington
Arlington, Texas

Edward R. Clayton
Virginia Polytechnic Institute and State University
Blacksburg, Virginia

Dileep Dhavale
University of Northern Iowa
Cedar Falls, Iowa

Douglas A. Elvers
University of North Carolina
Chapel Hill, North Carolina

Warren M. Holt
Southeastern Massachusetts University
North Dartmouth, Massachusetts

Ross H. Johnson
Madison College
Harrisonburg, Virginia

Martin Labbe
State University of New York College at New Paltz
New Paltz, New York

Philip Levine
William Patterson College
Wayne, New Jersey

Eddie M. Lewis
University of Southern Mississippi
Hattiesburg, Mississippi

Edward J. McDonnell
Los Angeles City College
Los Angeles, California

William M. Partlan
Fordham College
Bronx, New York

Patrick Shannon
Boise State University
Boise, Idaho

Donald N. Steinnes
University of Minnesota at Duluth
Duluth, Minnesota

Virgil F. Stone
Texas A and I University
Kingsville, Texas

Chipei Tseng
Northern Illinois University
De Kalb, Illinois

M. Michael Umble
University of Georgia
Athens, Georgia

Charles F. Warnock
Colorado State University
Fort Collins, Colorado

William J. Weida
United States Air Force Academy
Colorado Springs, Colorado

Douglas A. Wolfe
Ohio State University
Columbus, Ohio

STATISTICS
FOR
BUSINESS AND ECONOMICS

WHERE WE'RE GOING . . .

Statistics? Is it a field of study, a group of numbers that summarize some business operation, or, as the title of a recent book (Tanur et al., 1972) suggests, "a guide to the unknown"? We will attempt to answer this question in Chapter 1. Throughout the remainder of the text, we will show you how statistics can be used to aid in making business decisions.

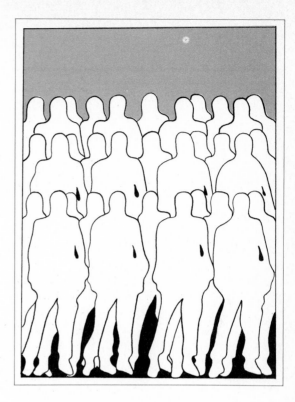

1

WHAT IS STATISTICS?

What does statistics mean to you? Does it bring to mind batting averages, the Dow Jones Average, unemployment figures, numerical distortions of facts (lying with statistics!), or simply a college requirement you have to complete? We hope to convince you that statistics is a meaningful, useful science with a broad, almost limitless scope of application to business and economic problems. We also want to show that statistics lie only when they are misapplied. Finally, our objective is to paint a unified picture of statistics to leave you with the impression that your time was well-spent studying a subject that will prove useful to you in many ways.

Statistics means "numerical descriptions" to most people. The Dow Jones Average, monthly unemployment figures, and the fraction of women executives in a particular industry all represent statistical descriptions of large sets of data collected on some phenomenon. Most often the purpose of calculating these numbers goes beyond the description of the particular set of data. Frequently, the data are regarded as a sample selected from some larger set of data. For example, a sampling of unpaid accounts for a large merchandiser would allow you to calculate an estimate of the average value of unpaid accounts. This estimate could be used as an audit check on the total value of all unpaid accounts held by the merchandiser. So, the applications of statistics to business can be divided into two broad areas: (1) describing large masses of data and (2) making inferences (estimates, decisions, predictions, etc.) about some set of data based on sampling. Let us examine some case studies that illustrate applications of statistics in business.

CASE STUDY 1.1

The employment status (employed or unemployed) of each individual in the United States work force is a set of measurements that is of interest to economists, business people, and sociologists because it characterizes the employment situation in our country. These measurements provide information on the social and economic health of our society. Each month the United States Census Bureau samples about 60,000 homes in order to estimate the percentage of unemployed people in the labor force. Thus, a statistical inference (the estimate) serves as a monthly indicator of the nation's economic welfare.

CASE STUDY 1.2

Two sets of data of interest to a firm's marketing department are (1) the set of taste-preference scores given by consumers to their product and their competitors' products when all brands are clearly labeled and (2) the taste-preference scores given by the same set of consumers when all brand labels have been removed and the consumers' only means of product identification is taste. With such information the marketing department should be able to determine whether taste preference arose because of perceived physical differences in the products or as a result of the consumers' image of the brand (brand image is, of course, largely a result of a firm's marketing efforts). Such a determination should help the firm develop marketing strategies for their product.

A study using these two sets of data was conducted by Ralph Allison and Kenneth Uhl (1965) in an effort to determine whether beer drinkers could distinguish among major brands of unlabeled beer. A sample of 326 beer drinkers was randomly selected from the set of beer drinkers identified as males who drank beer at least three times a week. During the first week of the study each of the 326 participants was given a six-pack of unlabeled beer containing three major brands and was asked to taste-rate each beer on a scale from 1 (poor) to 10 (excellent). During the second week the same set of drinkers was given a six-pack containing six major brands. This time, however, each bottle carried its usual label. Again, the drinkers were asked to taste-rate each beer from 1 to 10. From a statistical analysis of the two sets of data yielded by the study, Allison and Uhl concluded that the 326 beer drinkers studied could not distinguish among brands by taste on an overall basis. This result enabled them to infer statistically that such was also the case for beer drinkers in general. Their results also indicated that brand labels and their associations did significantly influence the tasters' evaluations. These findings suggest that physical differences in the products have less to do with their success or failure in the marketplace than the image of the brand in the consumers' minds. As to the benefits of such a study, Allison and Uhl note, "to the extent that product images, and their changes, are believed to be a result of advertising . . . the ability of firms' advertising programs to influence product images can be more thoroughly examined."

CASE STUDY 1.3   A problem frequently faced by the management training specialist is the lack of management enthusiasm for and interest in in-plant training programs. Since most training programs involve classroom participation by the trainee, a data set of interest to the management training specialist is the total number of class absences per trainee.

Robert J. House (1962) used a data set to help him study the effects of certain changes in the management training program of a large engineering firm on the enthusiasm for and acceptance of the program by management trainees. The courses offered by the Management Training Department of the firm had very few completion requirements, were very permissive in nature, and offered very little challenge or stimulation to participants. Consequently, many trainees did not attend class regularly and, in general, the training program was looked upon with apathy.

In an attempt to find a teaching method that would help rectify this situation, a course with higher standards and more authoritative teaching was given to two classes of fifty-one and fifty-three trainees, respectively, and the rate of absences in each class was compared to the rate of absences in a class of forty-nine trainees that had taken the same course (i.e., the same course content) under the old teaching policies. A comparison of the rates of absences indicated that the rate of absences under the new teaching system was significantly lower than under the old system. From this result, it can be **inferred** that the revised teaching method should increase class attendance in future courses as well.

The attendance result, along with others noted in the study, prompted the conclusion that the new teaching policies evoked a higher level of acceptance of and enthusiasm for the management training program. Thus, instead of having to speculate informally about the effectiveness of the new training policies, the statistical analysis of the study enabled the Management Training Department to assess their impact formally.

During the 1950's, the United Airlines Maintenance Base at San Francisco was responsible for the maintenance and overhaul of all United Airlines aircraft (Hunz, 1956). Their storeroom received, stored, and distributed all the parts needed for maintenance of the aircraft. To control the stock of spare parts and to determine the value of parts on-hand, counts of the number of each item in stock, called *inventory counts,* were taken. It was the responsibility of the Auditing Division of United Airlines to verify the accuracy of the inventory counts. Thus, a set of data of interest to the accountants of the Auditing Division was the presence or absence of a counting error in counting the stock of each item in the storeroom's physical inventory. The accountants did not verify the accuracy of the counts by recounting all the inventory item groups, but by sampling a small number of these groups and recounting them. If they found a large number of discrepancies between the original counts and their test counts, they inferred that many of the rest of the item counts (those not sampled and recounted) were also in error and concluded that the original inventory counts were unacceptable and would have to be done again. If they found only a small number of discrepancies, they inferred that most of the item counts not rechecked were accurate and concluded that the original inventory counts were satisfactory. Prior to the use of this inferential statistical procedure the Auditing Division verified inventory counts by recounting *all* the items in stock. The inferential procedure enabled them to do the same quality verification work as before, but at a substantial reduction in work-hours.

Why study statistics in a business program? The quantification of business research and business operations (quality control, statistical auditing, forecasting, etc.) has been truly astounding over the past several decades. Econometric modeling, market surveys, and the creation of indices like the Consumer Price Index all represent relatively recent attempts to quantify economic behavior. It is extremely important that today's business graduate be able to understand the methods and language of statistics, since the alternative is to be swamped by a flood of numbers that are more confusing than enlightening to the untutored mind. The business student should develop a discerning sense of rational thought that will distill the information contained in these numbers, so it may be used to make intelligent decisions, inferences, and generalizations. We believe that the study of statistics is essential to the ability to operate effectively in the modern business environment.

**1.2
THE ELEMENTS
OF STATISTICS**

Although applications of statistics abound in almost every area of human endeavor, there are certain elements common to all statistical problems. The foundation of every statistical problem is a population:

DEFINITION 1.1
The population is a set of data that characterizes some phenomenon (in our situation, some business phenomenon).

Our definition of population is broader than the usual one. We are not just referring to a group of people. For example, the employment status of every person in the United States labor force is a population, as is the weekly profit figure for the entire time (past and future) a firm is in business. Other examples of populations are the number of errors on each page in an accountant's ledger and the daily Dow Jones Average, past and future. Thus, we think of a population as being a large — perhaps infinitely large — collection of measurements.

The second element of a statistical problem is the **sample**:

DEFINITION 1.2

The **sample** is a set of data selected from a population.

The sample is a subset (part of) the population. The collections of daily Dow Jones Averages for the past 5 years, the monthly unemployment figures for the past 18 months, the weekly sales of a firm over the past year, and the number of errors per page on 10 pages of a 100 page ledger all represent samples of the respective populations.

The usefulness of the sample is clarified by considering the third element of a statistical problem — the **inference**:

DEFINITION 1.3

A **statistical inference** is a decision, estimate, prediction, or generalization about the population based on information contained in a sample.

That is, we use the information in the smaller set of measurements (the sample) to make decisions, predictions, or generalizations about the large or whole set of measurements (the population). For example, we might use the number of accounting errors in a 10 page sample of a ledger to estimate the number of errors on all 100 pages of the ledger. Or we could use the past 18 months' unemployment figures to predict the next month's employment rate. We might try to infer this year's total sales from last year's weekly sales figures. Finally, we could predict the Dow Jones Average a year from now based on the sample of daily Dow Jones Averages over the past 5 years. In each case we are employing the information in a sample to make inferences about the corresponding population.

The preceding definitions identify three of the four elements of a statistical problem. The fourth, and perhaps the most important, is the topic of Section 1.3.

EXERCISES

1.1. A television station was interested in determining the effects of television advertising on the purchase of products advertised. It surveyed 2,452 Davenport, Iowa residents and asked: "Have you ever purchased the product that sponsors (some specific) program?" Identify the population, sample, and type of statistical inference to be made for this problem.

1.2. The checking of all vendors' accounts payable invoices for errors that would cost a company money is a costly and time-consuming procedure. A method has been developed, based on sampling of accounts payable, for effectively and economically checking for vendors' errors without making a 100% check of all invoices. Identify the population, sample, and type of statistical inference to be made for this problem.

1.3. To compute their yearly income, trading stamp companies must determine their liability for unredeemed stamps. This requires them to estimate the fraction of unredeemed stamps. Davidson et al. (1967) have developed a method for estimating this fraction by studying the time lapse between the issue and redemption of a sample of stamps. Identify the population, sample, and type of statistical inference to be made for this problem.

1.3
STATISTICS:
WITCHCRAFT
OR SCIENCE?

We have identified the primary objective of statistics as making inferences about a population based on information contained in a sample. However, inference-making constitutes only part of our story. We also want to measure and report the **reliability** of each inference made—this is the fourth element of a statistical problem.

The measure of reliability that accompanies an inference separates the science of statistics from the art of fortune-telling. A palm reader, like a statistician, may examine a sample (your hand) and make inferences about the population (your life). However, no measure of reliability can be attached to the reader's inferences. On the other hand, we will always be sure to assess the reliability of our statistical inferences. For example, if we use a sample of previous profit figures to predict a firm's future profits, we will give a **bound** on our **prediction error**. This bound is simply a number that the error of our prediction is not likely to exceed. Thus, the uncertainty of our prediction is measured by the size of the bound on the prediction errors. In general, the reliability of our statistical inferences will be discussed at length throughout this text. For now, we simply want you to realize that an inference is incomplete without a measure of its reliability.

We conclude with a summary of the elements of a statistical problem:

FOUR ELEMENTS COMMON TO ALL STATISTICAL PROBLEMS

1. The population of interest, with a procedure for sampling the population.
2. The sample and analysis of the information in the sample.
3. The inferences about the population, based on information contained in the sample.
4. A measure of reliability for the inference.

SUPPLEMENTARY
EXERCISES

1.4. What is a statistical inference?
1.5. A car and truck dealer who was interested in determining the number of customized vans to order from the manufacturer for sale next fall, conducted a telephone

survey of 100 homes in the community in order to estimate what the local demand for vans would be. Identify the four elements common to any statistical problem in the context of the dealer's survey.

1.6. A manufacturer of record turntables with automatic tone arms received many customer complaints about the jerkiness of its product's tone arm movement. As a result, the manufacturer decided to institute a quality control program in the assembly plant. It was decided that if 3% or more of a day's production of turntables were defective, there must be a serious assembly error somewhere on the production line and it should be located and corrected. Instead of the costly procedure of testing all turntables produced each day, it was decided to estimate the fraction defective in a day's production by choosing thirty turntables at random from the day's production and testing them. The number of defectives found would be used to estimate the fraction of the day's production that were assembled improperly. Identify the four elements to any statistical problem in the context of this quality control problem.

The next three exercises are designed to examine your current thinking on the subject of reliability. We will formally address this subject in subsequent chapters.

1.7. Refer to Case Study 1.1. Suppose you were asked to assess the reliability of the monthly estimate of the percentage of unemployed workers in the labor force. What information do you think would help you in making your assessment?

1.8. Refer to Case Study 1.3. Suppose you were responsible for deciding whether or not to revise your firm's in-plant management training program. If a study such as House's (1962) were conducted in your plant, you would obviously be very interested in the results. Suppose such a study was conducted and, like the House study, it indicated that the rate of classroom absences was significantly lower under the new teaching system than under the old system. In considering this result you would certainly want to know how reliable it was. What information do you think would help you in measuring the reliability of the study?

1.9 Refer to Exercise 1.3. Suppose you were an accountant for a trading stamp company and were responsible for preparing the firm's end-of-year income statement. You would be interested in knowing the firm's liability for unredeemed stamps. Suppose the firm's statistician estimated the fraction of stamps unredeemed out of all those sold during the year to be $1/12$. Suppose also that the statistician failed to give you an indication of the reliability of this estimate (a very serious oversight for a statistician to make). Since the reliability of your income statement would depend on the reliability of the statistician's estimate, you would be more than passively interested in knowing the reliability of the estimate. What information would help you measure the reliability of the statistician's estimate?

ON YOUR OWN . . .

If you could start your own business right now, what kind would it be? Identify a set of business data that would be of interest to you and your firm. Is the data set you identified a sample or a population? How could you use this data set to help your business operate more efficiently?

REFERENCES

Allison, R. I., & Uhl, K. P. "Influence of beer brand identification on taste perception." *Journal of Marketing Research,* Aug. 1965, 36–39.

Careers in statistics, American Statistical Association and the Institute of Mathematical Statistics, 1974.

Davidson, H. J., Neter, J., & Petras, A. S. "Estimating the liability for unredeemed stamps." *Journal of Accounting Research,* 1967, *5,* 186–207.

House, R. J. "An experiment in the use of management training standards." *Journal of the Academy of Management,* 1962, *5.*

Hunz, E. "Application of statistical sampling to inventory audits." *The Internal Auditor,* 1956, *13,* 38.

Tanur, J. M., Mosteller, F., Kruskal, W. A., Link, R. F., Pieters, R. S., & Rising, G. R. *Statistics: A guide to the unknown.* San Francisco: Holden-Day, 1972.

Willis, R. E., & Chervany, N. L. *Statistical analysis and modeling for management decision-making.* Belmont, Ca.: Wadsworth, 1974. Chapter 1.

WHERE WE'VE BEEN . . .

By examining typical examples of the use of statistics in business, we listed four elements that are common to every business statistical problem: a population, a sample, an inference, and a measure of the reliability of the inference. The last two elements identify the goal of statistics—using sample data to make an inference (a decision, estimate, or prediction) about a population.

WHERE WE'RE GOING . . .

Before we make an inference, we must be able to describe a data set. Graphical methods that provide a compact description of a data set are the topic of this chapter.

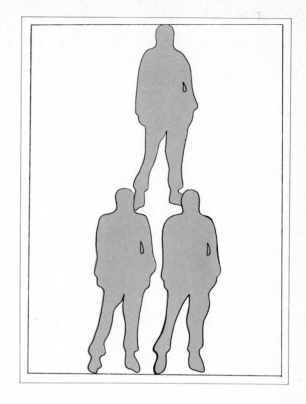

2

GRAPHICAL DESCRIPTIONS OF DATA

Before we can use the information in a sample to make inferences about a population, we must be able to extract the relevant information from the sample. That is, we need methods to summarize and describe the sample measurements. For example, if we look at last year's sales for a sample of 100 companies, we are unlikely to extract much information by looking at the set of 100 sales figures. We would get a clearer picture of the data by calculating the average sales for all 100 companies, by determining the highest and lowest company sales, by drawing a graph showing the average monthly sales over the 12 month period, or, in general, by employing some summarizing technique that will extract relevant information from the data and, at the same time, allow us to obtain a clearer understanding of the sample.

In this chapter we will first define two different types of business data, and then present some graphical methods for describing data of each type. You will see that graphical methods for describing data are intuitively appealing descriptive techniques and that they can be used to describe either a sample or a population. However, as we will begin to demonstrate in Chapters 3 and 4, numerical methods for describing data are the keys that unlock the door to population inference-making.

As you will subsequently see, some of the descriptive measures discussed in this chapter are primarily of interest for describing large data sets. If statistical inference is your goal, only Sections 2.1 and 2.4 are essential. For this reason, Sections 2.2, 2.3, and 2.5 are marked "optional."

2.1 TYPES OF BUSINESS DATA

Although the number of business phenomena that can be measured is almost limitless, business data can generally be classified as one of two types: quantitative or qualitative.

DEFINITION 2.1
Quantitative data are observations that are measured on a numerical scale.

The most common type of business data is quantitative data, since many business phenomena are measured on numerical scales. Examples of quantitative business data are:

1. The daily Dow Jones Average
2. The monthly unemployment percentage
3. Last year's sales for a sample of firms
4. The number of women executives in an industry

The measurements in these examples are all numerical.

All data that are not quantitative are qualitative:

DEFINITION 2.2
If each measurement in a data set falls into one and only one of a set of categories, the data set is called qualitative.

Qualitative data are observations that are categorical rather than numerical. Examples of qualitative business data are:

1. The political party affiliations of a sample of business executives. Each executive would have one and only one political party affiliation.
2. The brand of gasoline last purchased by each person in a sample of automobile owners. Again, each measurement would fall into one and only one category.
3. The state in which each firm in a sample of firms in the United States has its highest yearly sales.

Notice that each of the examples has nonnumerical, or qualitative, measurements.

As you would expect, the methods used for summarizing the information in a sample of measurements depends on the type of business data being collected. We will devote the remainder of this chapter to the presentation of graphical methods for describing quantitative and qualitative data sets.

EXERCISES

2.1. Classify the following examples of business data as either qualitative or quantitative:

    a. The brand of pocket calculators purchased by twenty business statistics students.
    b. The list price of pocket calculators purchased by twenty business statistics students.
    c. The number of automobiles purchased over the past 5 years by the head of the household in a sample of fifty households.
    d. The month indicated by each of a sample of business firms as the month during which it had the highest sales.
    e. The depth of tread remaining on each tire in a sample of automobile tires after 20,000 miles of wear.

2.2. Classify the following examples of business data as either qualitative or quantitative:

    a. The brand of stereo speaker that each of a sample of twenty-five college students indicated they preferred.
    b. The loss (in dollars) incurred in each of the last 5 years by a department store as a result of shoplifting.
    c. The color of interior house paint (other than white) that each of the five largest manufacturers of paint says generates the most sales revenue for their firm.

2.3. Classify the following examples of business data as either qualitative or quantitative:

    a. The number of corporate mergers during each of the last 15 years.
    b. The change in the Consumer Price Index during each of the last 6 months.
    c. The length of time before each of a sample of thirty dry cell batteries goes dead.
    d. The American automobile manufacturer that each of a sample of twenty-five service station mechanics indicated as producing the most reliable cars.

2.2
GRAPHICAL
METHODS FOR
DESCRIBING
QUALITATIVE
DATA:
THE BAR GRAPH
(OPTIONAL)

As we noted in Section 2.1, a qualitative observation falls into one and only one of a group of categories. For example, suppose a women's clothing store located in the downtown area of a large city wants to open a branch in the suburbs. To obtain some information about the geographical distribution of its present customers, the store manager conducts a survey in which each customer is asked to identify her place of residence with regard to the city's four quadrants: northwest (NW), northeast (NE), southwest (SW), and southeast (SE). Out-of-town customers are excluded from the survey.

The results of the survey—the responses of a sample of $n = 30$ resident customers —might appear as in Table 2.1. (Note that the symbol n is used here and throughout the text to represent the sample size, i.e., the number of measurements in a sample.) You can see that each of the thirty measurements falls in one and only one of the four possible categories representing the four quadrants of the city.

TABLE 2.1
CUSTOMER RESIDENT
SURVEY:
$n = 30$

CUSTOMER	RESIDENCE	CUSTOMER	RESIDENCE	CUSTOMER	RESIDENCE
1	NW	11	NW	21	NE
2	SE	12	SE	22	NW
3	SE	13	SW	23	SW
4	NW	14	NW	24	SE
5	SW	15	SW	25	SW
6	NW	16	NE	26	NW
7	NE	17	NE	27	NW
8	SW	18	NW	28	SE
9	NW	19	NW	29	NE
10	SE	20	SW	30	SW

A natural and useful summarizing technique for qualitative data is to tabulate the **frequency** or **relative frequency** of each category.

DEFINITION 2.3
The **frequency** for a category is the total number of measurements that fall in the category. The frequency for a particular category, say category i, will be denoted by the symbol f_i.

DEFINITION 2.4
The **relative frequency** for a category is the frequency of that category divided by the total number of measurements, i.e., the relative frequency for category i is

$$\text{Relative frequency} = \frac{f_i}{n}$$

where

$n = $ Total number of measurements

$f_i = $ Frequency for the ith category

The frequency for a category is the total number of measurements in that category, while the relative frequency for a category is the **proportion** of measurements in the category. Table 2.2 shows the frequency and relative frequency for the customer residences listed in Table 2.1. Note that the sum of the frequencies should always equal the total number of measurements in the sample and the sum of the relative frequencies should always equal 1 (except for rounding errors, as in Table 2.2).

TABLE 2.2
FREQUENCIES AND RELATIVE FREQUENCIES FOR CUSTOMER RESIDENCE SURVEY

CATEGORY	FREQUENCY	RELATIVE FREQUENCY
NE	5	$5/30 = .167$
NW	11	$11/30 = .367$
SE	6	$6/30 = .200$
SW	8	$8/30 = .267$
Total	30	1

A common method for graphically presenting the frequencies or relative frequencies for qualitative data is the **bar chart**. For this type of chart the frequencies (or relative frequencies) are represented by a bar—one bar for each category. The height of the bar for a given category is proportional to the category frequency (or relative frequency). Usually, the bars are placed in a vertical position with the base of the bar located on the horizontal axis of the graph. The order of the bars on the horizontal axis is unimportant. Both a frequency bar chart and a relative frequency bar chart are shown in Figure 2.1 for the customer residence example.

CASE STUDY 2.1   George E. Delehanty (1966) examined the impact on occupation structure of the introduction of electronic data-processing techniques and equipment into the large clerical operations of five large life insurance companies. He used a series of relative frequency bar charts to illustrate the changing pattern of one of the companies'

FIGURE 2.1
BAR CHARTS FOR CUSTOMER RESIDENCE EXAMPLE

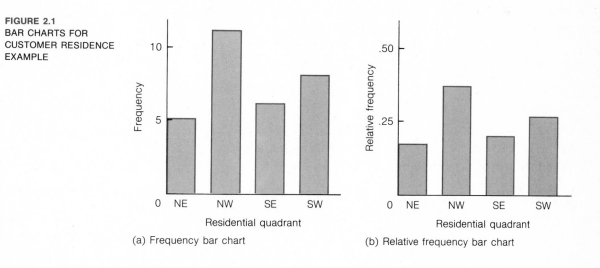

(a) Frequency bar chart

(b) Relative frequency bar chart

FIGURE 2.2
BAR CHARTS
DESCRIBING
COMPANY B'S HOME
OFFICE WORK FORCE
BY GRADE

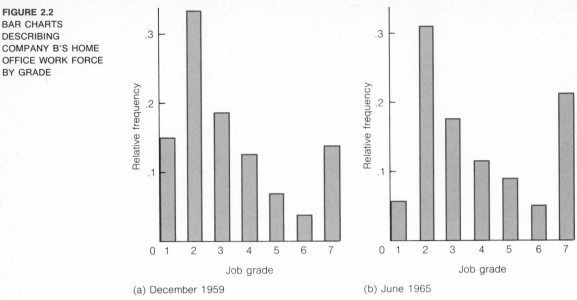

(a) December 1959

(b) June 1965

Source: Delehanty (1966).

(referred to as company B) work force distribution. Two of these bar charts are presented in Figure 2.2. The firm's various occupational levels are characterized by salary classes and are referred to as "job grades." The workers with the lowest salaries are included in job grade 1. Notice how between December 1959 and June 1965 the proportion of workers in the lower job grades (1, 2, 3, and 4) decreased, while the proportion of workers in the higher grades (5, 6, and 7) increased. The bar charts of Figure 2.2 effectively illustrate this change. The reader can easily detect the change in firm B's occupation structure without having to dig through a morass of numbers.

Based on the information in Figure 2.2, other data about company B, and information about the four other life insurance companies studied, Delehanty concluded (subject to certain qualifications discussed in the article) that "adaptation to punched-card and computer data processing has been associated with reduced requirements for low level clerical workers and increased requirements for higher level clerical manpower." He continues, "Higher levels of staff, technicians, and top management have generally experienced sharp increases in employment."

EXERCISES

2.4. A questionnaire sent to the chief executives of some of the country's largest industrial corporations and commercial banking companies by *Fortune* magazine revealed the following information concerning their main career emphasis:

MAIN CAREER EMPHASIS	FREQUENCY
Legal	109
Financial	202
Marketing, distribution	223
Engineering, research and development	59
Production operations	149
General management	42
Other	30

Source: "A Group Profile of the *Fortune* 500 Chief Executive."
Fortune, May 1976.

Construct a relative frequency bar chart for these data.

2.5. Suppose the following table contains the number of housing starts per month in your state during a 7 month interval last year:

MONTH	NUMBER OF HOUSING STARTS
February	1,562
March	1,433
April	1,381
May	1,430
June	1,527
July	1,391
August	1,542

a. Construct a relative frequency bar chart for these data.
b. Do you think the bar chart is an effective way to organize and present these data to someone? Why or why not? If not, can you think of a better way?

**2.3
GRAPHICAL
METHODS FOR
DESCRIBING
QUALITATIVE
DATA:
THE PIE CHART
(OPTIONAL)**

A second method of graphing qualitative data sets—the pie chart—is often used in newspaper and magazine articles to depict budgets and other economic information. A complete circle (the pie) represents the total number of measurements. This is partitioned into a number of slices, one slice for each category. The size of a slice is proportional to the relative frequency of a particular category. For example, since a complete circle spans 360°, if the relative frequency for a category is .30, the slice assigned to that category is 30% of 360 or (.30)(360) = 108°. See Figure 2.3.

Figure 2.4 shows a pie chart for the customer residence data of Section 2.2. Notice that the sizes of the slices are proportional to the relative frequencies assigned to the four categories. A compass and calculator are needed if the pie chart is to be precisely drawn, thus making it somewhat inconvenient to draw. However, even if

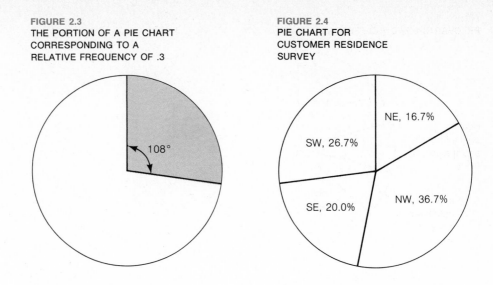

FIGURE 2.3
THE PORTION OF A PIE CHART
CORRESPONDING TO A
RELATIVE FREQUENCY OF .3

FIGURE 2.4
PIE CHART FOR
CUSTOMER RESIDENCE
SURVEY

we only approximate the size of the wedges, the pie chart provides a useful picture of a qualitative data set.

CASE STUDY 2.2   In the February 2, 1976, issue of *Time* magazine an article appeared that discussed President Gerald Ford's proposed federal budget for the fiscal year 1977 (October 1, 1976–September 30, 1977). Data were presented that allow the reader to compare the 1967, 1972, and 1977 budgets. The pie chart offers a convenient method for comparing these budgets, as shown in Figure 2.5. Figure 2.5(a) describes the $158.3 billion budget of 1967, Figure 2.5(b) describes the $231.9 billion budget of 1972, and Figure 2.5(c) shows the approximate breakdown for the estimated budget of 1977. These pie charts reflect the changing pattern of the budget over the years. For example, notice the defense budget. In 1967, at the height of the Viet Nam war, 43.6% of the total budget went for defense. In 1972, this had fallen to 33.4%, and for 1977 it is estimated to be only 25.6%. This is illustrated in Figure 2.5 by the shrinking pie wedge labeled ''defense.'' Notice, however, that while the defense budget as a percentage of the total budget has been shrinking, the total number of dollars allocated to defense has been growing.

EXERCISES   **2.6.** The market for pocket calculators is divided among manufacturers as follows:

MANUFACTURER	MARKET SHARE
A	46%
B	38%
C	10%
D	5%
Others	1%

Construct a pie chart to describe the distribution of the market for pocket calculators.

FIGURE 2.5
PIE CHARTS DEPICTING FEDERAL BUDGETS

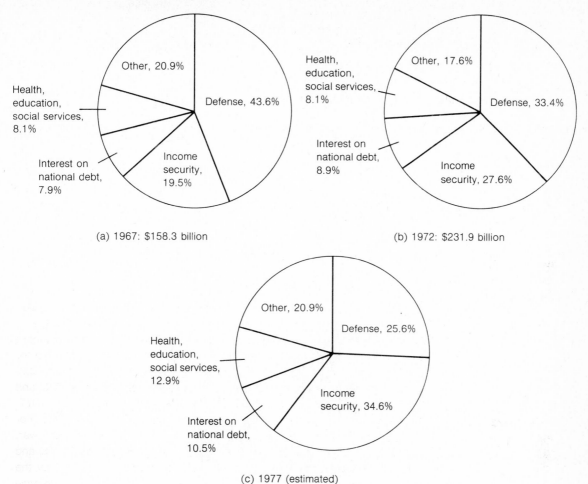

(a) 1967: $158.3 billion

(b) 1972: $231.9 billion

(c) 1977 (estimated)

2.7. A sample of 500 business executives was selected, and each reported his or her political affiliation. The results were as follows:

POLITICAL PARTY	FREQUENCY	RELATIVE FREQUENCY
Republican	290	.58
Democrat	180	.36
Independent	30	.06

Source: "A Group Profile of the *Fortune* 500 Chief Executive." *Fortune,* May 1976.

Construct a pie chart to describe this sample.

2.8. The following pie chart appeared in *Fortune* magazine:

AT WHAT AGE TODAY'S CHIEF EXECUTIVE OFFICERS GOT THEIR JOBS

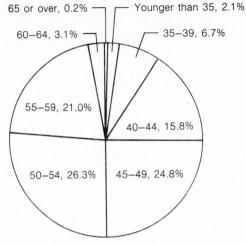

Source: "A Group Profile of the *Fortune* 500 Chief Executive," *Fortune,* May 1976. Joe Argenziano for *Fortune* magazine.

    a.   What is the pie chart attempting to portray?

    b.   How does the pie chart accomplish this portrayal?

    c.   What does the pie chart tell you about the phenomenon it is portraying?

    d.   Why might the pie chart have been used instead of a relative frequency bar chart?

    e.   Do pie charts and relative frequency bar charts convey the same information? Explain.

2.9. Refer to Exercise 2.8. The pie chart below appeared in the same *Fortune* article. Repeat parts a, b, and c of Exercise 2.8 for this pie chart.

HOLDINGS BY THE CHIEF EXECUTIVES IN THEIR OWN COMPANIES

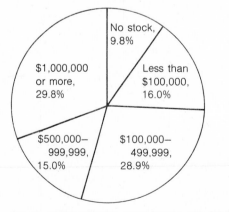

Source: "A Group Profile of the *Fortune* 500 Chief Executive." *Fortune,* May 1976. Joe Argenziano for *Fortune* magazine.

2.4
GRAPHICAL METHODS FOR DESCRIBING QUANTITATIVE DATA: THE FREQUENCY HISTOGRAM AND POLYGON

Quantitative data sets are those which consist of numerical measurements. Thus, a quantitative sample is simply a list of numerical values. Most business data are quantitative, so methods for summarizing quantitative data are especially important. In this section, we will present one of the most useful graphical methods for summarizing this type of data.

The **histogram** (often called a **frequency distribution**) is the most popular graphical technique for depicting quantitative data. The histogram is very similar to the bar chart for qualitative data presented in Section 2.2. To introduce the histogram we will use a sample of thirty companies from the 1975 *Fortune* 500 (the top 500 companies in sales for calendar year 1975). The measurement we will be interested in is the earnings per share (E/S) for these thirty companies. The earnings per share is computed by dividing the year's total net profit by the total number of shares of common stock outstanding. This figure is of interest to the economic community because it reflects the economic health of the company. The earnings per share figures for the sample of thirty companies are shown (to the nearest cent) in Table 2.3.

The first step in constructing the histogram for quantitative data is to form **measurement classes**. These are intervals on the numerical scale of the measurements. The lower boundary of the first measurement class should be located immediately preceding the smallest measurement, and the upper boundary of the last measurement class should be located at a point following the largest measurement. All measurement classes must be of equal length, and the boundaries must be chosen so that no measurements fall on the boundaries. Finally, the number of measurement classes usually will range from five to twenty, with a smaller number of measurement classes corresponding to a small set of measurements, and a larger number of measurement classes corresponding to a large set of measurements.

TABLE 2.3
EARNINGS PER SHARE FOR SAMPLE OF THIRTY COMPANIES FROM THE 1975 *FORTUNE* 500

COMPANY	E/S	COMPANY	E/S	COMPANY	E/S
1	1.97	11	0.60	21	4.02
2	3.20	12	1.15	22	6.06
3	4.44	13	2.02	23	3.37
4	3.65	14	1.74	24	2.75
5	3.81	15	9.70	25	8.29
6	5.63	16	5.21	26	4.55
7	7.60	17	3.16	27	3.77
8	5.36	18	1.06	28	1.71
9	2.47	19	4.25	29	1.93
10	5.15	20	2.06	30	1.65

We construct six measurement classes for the earnings per share data, as shown in Table 2.4. The smallest measurement is 0.60, so we begin the first class at 0.595. The length of each class is 1.52, so that the last (sixth) class ends at 9.715; the largest measurement in the sample is 9.70. Note that each boundary falls on a 0.005 value (one significant digit more than the measurements), which guarantees that no measurement will fall on a class boundary.

	MEASUREMENT CLASS	FREQUENCY	RELATIVE FREQUENCY
TABLE 2.4	0.595–2.115	10	10/30 = .333
MEASUREMENT	2.115–3.635	5	5/30 = .167
CLASSES,	3.635–5.155	8	8/30 = .267
FREQUENCIES, AND	5.155–6.675	4	4/30 = .133
RELATIVE	6.675–8.195	1	1/30 = .033
FREQUENCIES FOR	8.195–9.715	2	2/30 = .067
THE EARNINGS PER			
SHARE DATA	Total	30	1.0

The final step in the construction of the histogram is to plot the measurement classes on a horizontal axis and the frequency (or relative frequency) of each class on a vertical axis. Unlike the bar chart, the frequency (or relative frequency) is not plotted as a vertical line over a single point, but instead as a rectangle with a base width equal to that of the measurement class and a height equal to the frequency (or relative frequency). Both the frequency and relative frequency histograms for the earnings per share data are shown in Figure 2.6.

The steps for constructing histograms for quantitative data sets are summarized below:

HOW TO CONSTRUCT A HISTOGRAM

1. Arrange the data in increasing order, from smallest to largest measurement.

2. Divide the interval from the smallest to the largest measurement into between five and twenty equal subintervals, making sure that:

    a. Each measurement falls into one and only one measurement class

    b. No measurement falls on a measurement class boundary

Use a small number of measurement classes if you have a small amount of data; use a larger number of classes for large amounts of data.

3. Compute the frequency (or relative frequency) of measurements in each measurement class.

4. Using a vertical axis of about three-fourths the length of the horizontal axis, plot each frequency (or relative frequency) as a rectangle over the corresponding measurement class.

By looking at a histogram (say, the relative frequency histogram in Figure 2.6), you can see two important facts. First, note the total area under the histogram, and then note the proportion of the total area that falls over a particular interval of the x-axis. You will see that the proportion of the total area that falls above an interval is

FIGURE 2.6
HISTOGRAMS FOR
EARNINGS PER SHARE
DATA

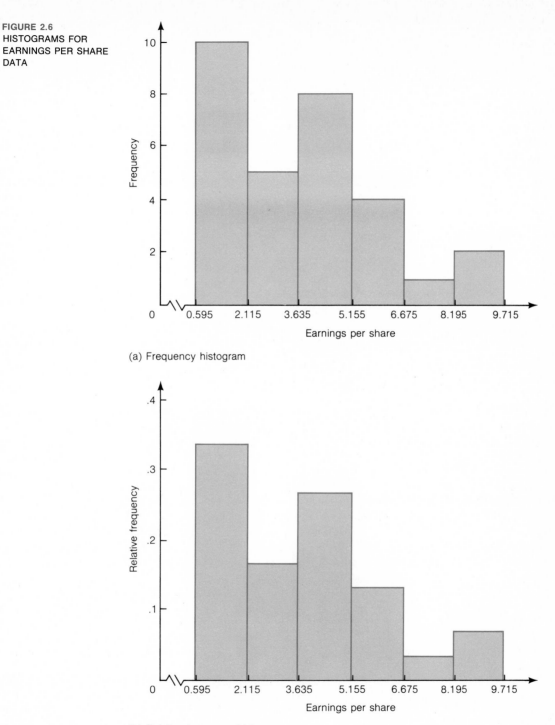

(a) Frequency histogram

(b) Relative frequency histogram

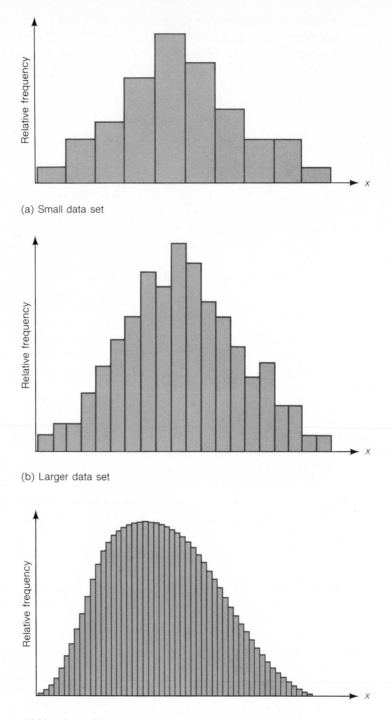

(a) Small data set

(b) Larger data set

(c) Very large data set

equal to the relative frequency of measurements falling in the interval.* For example, the relative frequency for the class interval 0.595–2.115 is .333. Consequently, the rectangle above the interval contains .333 of the total area under the histogram.

Second, you can imagine the appearance of the relative frequency histogram for a very large set of data (say, a population). As the number of measurements in a data set is increased, you can obtain a better description of the data by decreasing the width of the class intervals. When the class intervals become small enough, a relative frequency histogram will (for all practical purposes) appear as a smooth curve (see Figure 2.7).

Another method of graphing the frequencies (or relative frequencies) for the measurement classes is the frequency (or relative frequency) polygon. To construct the frequency polygon, we form measurement classes precisely as for the frequency histogram. We then place a dot at the midpoint of each measurement class at a height equal to the frequency of the class. Then, neighboring dots are connected by straight lines. The first and last dot are connected by a line segment to the horizontal axis at a point one-half class interval width below the lowest measurement class and above the highest measurement class, respectively.

CASE STUDY 2.3   Robert R. Sterling and Raymond Radosevich (1969) examined the hypothesis that accountants generally agree on the book value of a depreciable asset, but do not agree on its current market value. A questionnaire was prepared in which the installment purchase of a depreciable asset was described and the respondent was asked to determine the market value of the asset. The questionnaire also contained a series of questions relating to the book value of the asset. These questions enabled Sterling and Radosevich to calculate a book value for the asset for each of the respondents. The questionnaire was mailed to a random sample of 500 Certified Public Accountants (CPA's) in the United States; 114 and 99 usable book value and market value responses, respectively, were returned.

The frequency distributions of book values and market values obtained from the returned questionnaires appear in Figure 2.8. In both histograms, the intervals from $150 to $200 and $600 to $650 include all responses less than $200 and greater than $600, respectively. The histograms suggest disagreement among the CPA's as to both the book value and the market value of the asset. Thus, Sterling and Radosevich rejected the hypothesis that accountants tend to agree on book values and to disagree on market values.

Note that decisions based on a visual comparison of histograms are risky because they are subject to an unknown probability of error. For example, we might wonder whether disagreement among the CPA's really exists or whether the difference we see in the histograms is due to random variation that would be present from sample to sample. We will begin to answer questions of this type in Chapter 8.

*Some histograms are constructed with all class intervals equal except the first and last, which are open-ended. The proportionality between area and relative frequency will not hold for these histograms. We will restrict our attention to histograms that possess equal-sized class intervals, because later we will want to draw a correspondence between relative frequency histograms and probability distributions.

FIGURE 2.8
FREQUENCY
HISTOGRAMS FOR
BOOK AND MARKET
VALUES AS ASSESSED
BY CPA'S

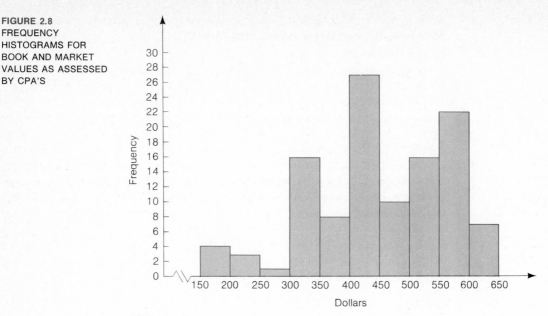

(a) Book values

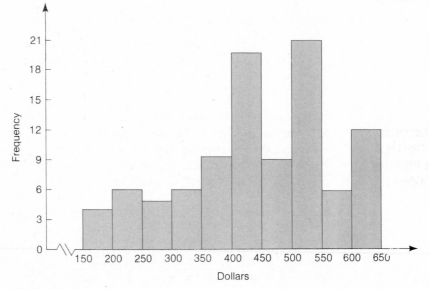

(b) Market values

2.10. The annual incomes for a random sample of thirty steelworkers are recorded. They are presented below in thousands of dollars:

10.1	8.1	13.0	11.2	9.9	13.6
11.2	9.7	12.6	10.3	11.0	12.3
8.7	9.4	8.9	10.6	10.4	10.9
10.5	10.2	11.8	12.5	12.1	12.0
13.2	9.7	12.4	14.5	10.5	9.7

Construct a relative frequency histogram for these data.

2.11. A large company is interested in determining the length of service of people presently in their employ. A sample of twenty-five employees is chosen, and the length of service is recorded for each employee in the sample. The data are as follows (the units are years):

2.1	1.4	4.5	6.6	1.3
15.6	11.6	6.8	1.5	2.9
3.4	8.7	0.5	7.7	6.4
0.7	3.9	8.2	8.0	5.5
10.3	3.0	3.9	4.1	4.3

Construct a relative frequency histogram for these data.

2.12. Sixteen economists were asked to project the percent change in the Consumer Price Index between now (September) and January 1 next year. The following are their projections:

+1%	+6%	−1%	+3%
+4%	+7%	+6%	+0%
+2%	−1%	+12%	−2%
−5%	+5%	+4%	+5%

    a. Construct a relative frequency histogram for these data.
    b. How might you summarize these sixteen predictions without using a graph or a table?

2.5
DISTORTING
THE TRUTH
WITH PICTURES
(OPTIONAL)

While it may be true in telling a story that "a picture is worth a thousand words," it is also true that pictures can be used to convey a colored and distorted message to the viewer. So the old adage applies: "Let the buyer (reader) beware." Examine relative frequency histograms and, in general, all graphical descriptions with care.

We will mention a few of the pitfalls to watch for when analyzing a chart or graph. But first we should mention the time series graph, which is often the object of distortion. This type of graph records the behavior of some business variable over time, with the business variable plotted on the vertical axis and the time plotted on the horizontal axis. Examples of business variables commonly graphed as time series abound: economic indices, profit, sales, supply, demand, etc. We will treat the subject of time series more completely in Chapter 14. For now, we will simply use some time series graphs to demonstrate several ways pictures may be distorted.

FIGURE 2.9
FIRM A'S MARKET
SHARE FROM
1970 TO 1975
—PACKED
VERTICAL AXIS

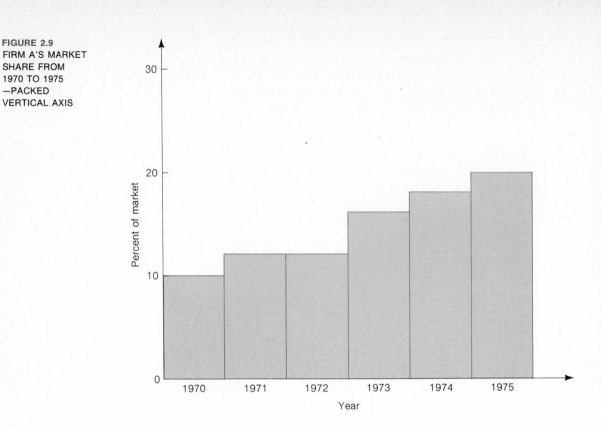

One common way to change the impression conveyed by a graph is to change the scale on the vertical axis, the horizontal axis, or both. For example, if you want to show that the change in firm A's market share over time is moderate, you should pack in a large number of units per inch on the vertical axis. That is, make the distance between successive units on the vertical scale small, as shown in Figure 2.9. You can see that a change in the firm's market share over time is barely apparent.

If you want to use the same data to make the changes in firm A's market share appear large, you should increase the distance between successive units on the vertical axis. That is, you stretch the vertical axis by graphing only a few units per inch, as shown in Figure 2.10. The telltale sign of stretching is a long vertical axis, but this is often hidden by starting the vertical axis at some point above 0, as shown in Figure 2.11(a). Or, the same effect can be achieved by using a broken line for the vertical axis, as shown in Figure 2.11(b).

Stretching the horizontal axis (increasing the distance between successive units) may also lead you to incorrect conclusions. For example, Figure 2.12(a) depicts the change in the Gross National Product (GNP) from mid-1974 to the first quarter of 1976. If you increase the size of the horizontal axis, as in Figure 2.12(b), the change in the GNP over time seems to be less pronounced.

The changes in categories indicated by a bar graph can also be emphasized or deemphasized by stretching or shrinking the vertical axis. Another method of achieving visual distortion with bar graphs is by making the width of the bars proportional to their height. For example, look at the bar chart in Figure 2.13(a), which depicts the percentage of a year's total automobile sales attributable to each of the four major manufacturers. Now suppose we make the width as well as the height grow as the market share grows. This is shown in Figure 2.13(b). The reader may tend to equate the *area* of the bars with the relative market share of each manufacturer. In fact, the true relative market share is proportional only to the height of the bars.

We have presented only a few of the ways that graphs can be used to convey misleading pictures of business phenomena. However, the lesson is clear. Examine all graphical descriptions of data with care. Particularly, check the axes and the size of the units on each axis. Ignore the visual changes and concentrate on the actual numerical changes indicated by the graph or chart.

FIGURE 2.10
FIRM A'S MARKET
SHARE FROM
1970 TO 1975
—STRETCHED
VERTICAL AXIS

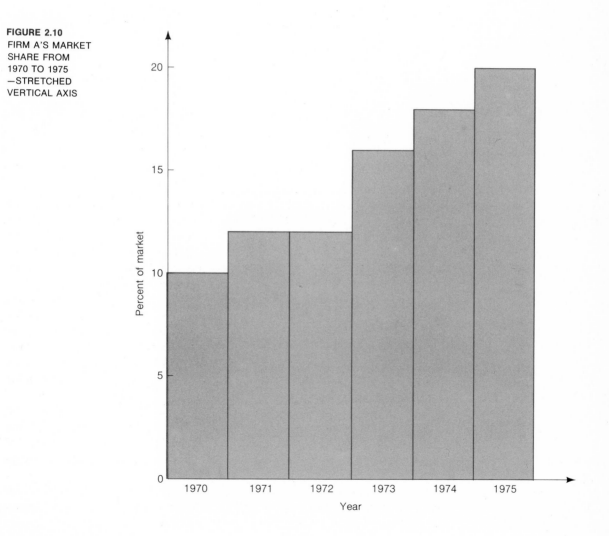

FIGURE 2.11
CHANGES IN MONEY
SUPPLY FROM
FEBRUARY TO APRIL
1976

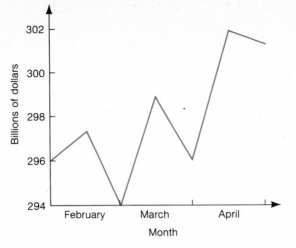

(a) Vertical axis started at a point greater than 0

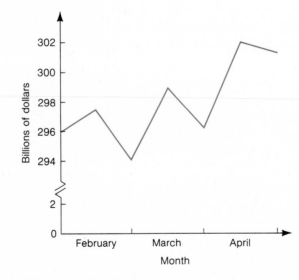

(b) Gap in vertical axis

FIGURE 2.12
GROSS NATIONAL
PRODUCT FROM
MID-1974 TO THE
FIRST QUARTER
OF 1976

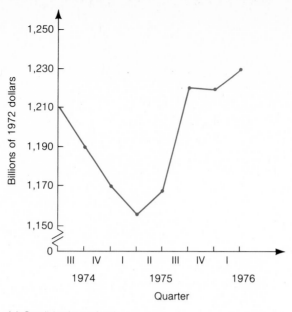

(a) Small horizontal axis

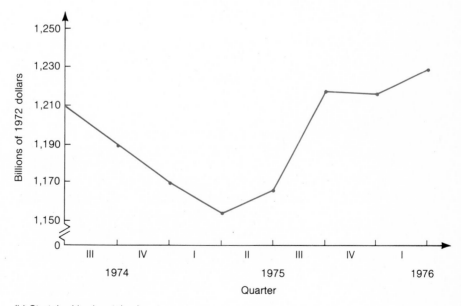

(b) Stretched horizontal axis

FIGURE 2.13
RELATIVE SHARE OF
THE AUTOMOBILE
MARKET FOR EACH OF
FOUR MAJOR
MANUFACTURERS

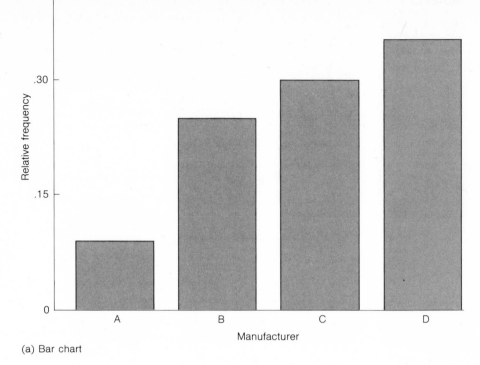

(a) Bar chart

(b) Width of bars grows with height

SUMMARY   Business data can be classified as one of two types: qualitative or quantitative. In a qualitative data set each observation falls into one of a set of categories, while in a quantitative data set each observation is measured on a numerical scale.

Since we want to use sample data to make inferences about the population from which it is drawn, it is important for us to be able to describe the data. Graphical methods are important and useful tools for describing both types of data. The bar chart and pie chart are useful graphical methods for describing qualitative data. The histogram is a graphical technique used to describe quantitative data sets.

Our ultimate goal is to use the sample to make inferences about the population. We must be wary of using graphical techniques to accomplish this goal, since they do not lend themselves to a measure of the reliability for an inference. Therefore, we need to develop numerical measures to describe a data set. This is the purpose of the next two chapters.

SUPPLEMENTARY
EXERCISES

[*Note: Starred (*) exercises refer to optional sections in this chapter.*]

2.13.   Classify the following examples of business data as either qualitative or quantitative:

a.   The style of music preferred by a sample of thirty radio listeners.
b.   The length of time it takes each of fifteen telephone installers to hook up a wall telephone.
c.   The population of each of a sample of ten cities in the United States.

*2.14.   A questionnaire sent to the chief executives of the country's 500 largest industrial corporations and commercial banking companies by *Fortune* magazine revealed the following information concerning their educational backgrounds:

LEVEL OF EDUCATION	PERCENT
High school or less	4.5
Attended college	9.3
College graduate	27.9
Postgraduate study	18.6
Master's degree	24.2
Doctorate	15.5

Source: "A Group Profile of the *Fortune* 500 Chief Executive." May 1976.

Construct a relative frequency bar chart for the data.

*2.15.   Construct a pie chart for the data in Exercise 2.14.

2.16. The following is a list of the lengths (in inches) of a sample of twenty golf tees produced by a machine designed to produce tees 1.5 inches in length:

1.55	1.52	1.48	1.49	1.50
1.51	1.50	1.53	1.54	1.52
1.51	1.50	1.50	1.49	1.51
1.51	1.53	1.47	1.50	1.51

Construct a relative frequency histogram for the data.

*2.17. In experimenting with a new technique for imprinting paper napkins with designs, names, etc., Royal Imprints, Inc., discovered that four different results were possible:

A. Imprint successful
B. Imprint smeared
C. Imprint off-center to the left
D. Imprint off-center to the right

To test the reliability of the technique, they imprinted 1,000 napkins and obtained the results shown in the graph (letters defined as above).

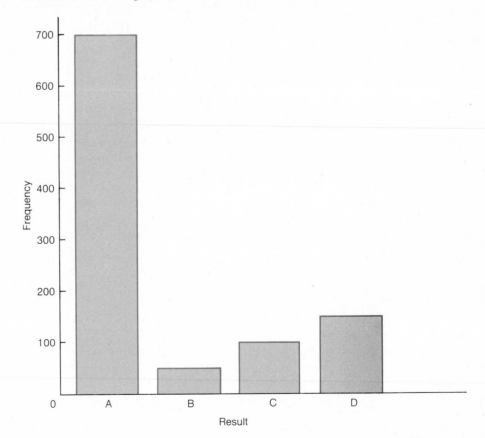

a. What type of graphical tool is the figure?

b. What information does the graph convey to you?

c. From the information provided by the graph how might you numerically describe the reliability of the printing technique?

*2.18. For a recent Friday, six of the major luxury hotels in Atlanta reported that the following number of rooms were occupied:

HOTEL	NUMBER OF ROOMS OCCUPIED
Hyatt Regency	702
Atlanta Hilton	811
Peachtree Plaza	902
Marriott	698
Fairmont	409
Omni International	500

a. Construct a relative frequency bar chart for these data.

b. Is it possible to determine which hotel had the greatest percentage of its rooms filled on that Friday? Explain.

c. What other information about the hotels would make the above data more meaningful?

2.19. Before choosing a community in which to test market its new product, company Z wanted to obtain family income profiles for each prospective test-market community. One such profile is shown here.

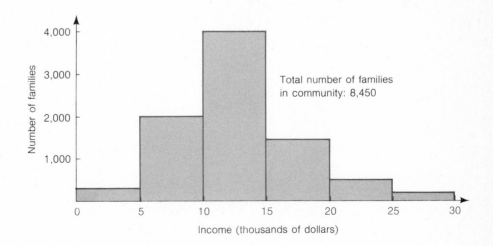

a. What type of graphical method has been used to portray the community's income profile?

b. Does the graph describe a data set that is a sample or a population? Explain.

c. Describe what the graph tells you about the income structure of the community.

*2.20. REGIONAL SHARE OF SINGLE-FAMILY HOUSING STARTS IN THE UNITED STATES

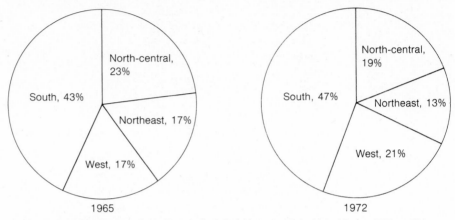

1965   1972

Source: United States Bureau of the Census, *Statistical Abstracts of the United States 1973,* p. 684.

a. What type of graphical tool is shown here?

b. What are the figures attempting to describe?

c. If you were given the *number* of housing starts for each region in 1965 and 1972, how would you construct the figures?

d. What information can be obtained by comparing the two figures?

2.21. Use one of the graphical methods presented in this chapter to depict the following data set:

1972 MONTHLY RENT OF RENTER-
OCCUPIED HOUSING UNITS

RENT ($)	PERCENT OF RENTERS IN EACH RENT CLASS
Less than 40	6
40–59	11
60–79	17
80–99	15
100–119	12
120–149	17
150 or more	22

Source: United States Bureau of the Census,
Statistical Abstracts of the United States 1973.

2.22. Construct relative frequency histograms for the two data sets shown below. Compare the histograms to observe the change in the labor force between 1960 and 1972.

FEMALE WORK FORCE
AGED 25 AND OVER
(IN THOUSANDS)

AGE	1960	1972
25–34	4,159	6,525
35–44	5,325	6,024
45–54	5,150	6,550
55–64	2,964	4,224

Source: United States Bureau of the Census, *Statistical Abstracts of the United States 1973.*

2.23. How might you use the data given below to shed new light on the female work force comparisons made in Exercise 2.22?

TOTAL NUMBER OF FEMALES
AGED 25 AND OVER
(IN THOUSANDS)

AGE	1960	1972
25–34	11,639	13,792
35–44	12,326	11,632
45–64	10,393	12,236
55–64	8,036	10,113

Source: United States Bureau of the Census, *Statistical Abstracts of the United States 1973.*

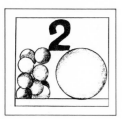

ON YOUR OWN . . .

Utilizing the data sources listed below, sources suggested by your instructor, or your own resourcefulness, find two real business-oriented data sets: one quantitative and one qualitative. Describe both data sets graphically using one or more of the graphical techniques presented in this chapter. These data sets and your graphs will be referred to in ''On Your Own'' sections in later chapters, so choose data sets of interest to you and be sure to keep copies of the data sets and your graphs. (See page 36.)

SUGGESTED DATA SOURCES

Board of Governors of the Federal Reserve System. *Federal Reserve Bulletin* (monthly).

Business Week (magazine).

Forbes (magazine).

Fortune (magazine).

United States Bureau of the Census. *Census of manufacturers.*

United States Bureau of the Census. *County business patterns.*

United States Bureau of the Census. *County and city data book.*

United States Bureau of the Census. *Statistical abstracts of the United States* (yearly).

United States Department of Commerce, Office of Business Economics. *Business statistics.*

United States Department of Commerce, Office of Business Economics. *Survey of current business* (monthly).

United States Department of Labor. *Monthly Labor Review.*

United States Department of Labor, Bureau of Labor Statistics. *Employment and earnings.*

United States Department of Labor, Bureau of Labor Statistics. *National survey of professional, administrative, technical, and clerical pay.*

Wall Street Journal (daily).

Your state's statistical abstract.

GUIDES TO FINDING DATA

Business Periodical Index.

Coman. *Sources of business information.*

Houser & Leonard. *Government statistics for business use.*

United States Bureau of the Census. *Directory of non-federal statistics for states and local areas.*

Wall Street Journal Index.

Your local chamber of commerce.

REFERENCES

Brunner, J. A., & Brunner, G. A. "Are voluntarily unlisted telephone subscribers really different?" *Journal of Marketing Research,* Feb. 1971, *8,* 121–124.

Chou, Ya-lun. *Statistical analysis.* 2d ed. New York: Holt, Rinehart, and Winston, 1975. Chapter 2.

Delehanty, G. E. "Office automation and the occupation structure." *Industrial Management Review,* Spring 1966, 99–109.

Huff, D. *How to lie with statistics.* New York: Norton, 1954.

Lapin, L. L., *Statistics for modern business decisions.* New York: Harcourt Brace Jovanovich, 1973. Chapter 2.

Neter, J., Wasserman, W. & Whitmore, G. A. *Fundamental statistics for business and economics.* 4th ed. Boston: Allyn and Bacon, 1973. Chapter 3.

Sterling, R. R., & Radosevich, R. "A valuation experiment." *Journal of Accounting Research,* Spring 1969, 90–95.

As we noted in Chapter 1, the goal of this course is to teach you how to use sample data to make inferences (decisions, estimates, or predictions) about a population data set. The first step in arriving at this goal is to learn how to describe a data set—either a population or a sample. As you learned in Chapter 2, graphical methods are advantageous because they convey a rapid and easily understood description of data sets.

WHERE WE'RE GOING . . .

There is a major drawback to using a graphical descriptive method—a graph or chart of sample data—for making an inference about a population from which a sample was selected. Namely, it is difficult to provide a measure of the reliability of the inference. How similar will the graphical description of the sample data be to the corresponding figure for the population? To answer this question statisticians use one or more numbers to create a mental image of a data set. These numbers, called *numerical descriptive measures,* are the topics of Chapters 3 and 4. As we will subsequently learn in Chapter 9, a sample numerical descriptive measure can be used to make an inference about the corresponding descriptive measure of the population from which the sample was selected. Most important, we will be able to provide a measure of reliability for this inference.

3

NUMERICAL MEASURES
OF
CENTRAL TENDENCY

Now that we have presented some graphical techniques for summarizing and describing data sets, we turn to numerical methods for accomplishing this objective. When we speak of a data set, we refer to either a sample or a population. If statistical inference is our goal, we will wish ultimately to use sample numerical descriptive measures to make inferences about the corresponding measures for a population.

As you will see, there are a large number of numerical methods available to describe data sets. Most of these methods measure one of two data characteristics:

1. The central tendency of the set of measurements, i.e., the tendency of the data to cluster or to center about certain numerical values.
2. The variability of the set of measurements, i.e., the spread of the data.

In this chapter, we will concentrate on measures of central tendency. In Chapter 4, we will discuss measures of variability.

3.1 THE MODE: A MEASURE OF CENTRAL TENDENCY

The **mode** is a measure of central tendency that is primarily useful for describing quantitative data sets:

DEFINITION 3.1
The **mode** is the measurement that occurs most frequently in the data set.

Whether the data are categorical or numerical in nature, the mode shows where the data tend to concentrate.

Because it emphasizes data concentration, the mode has applications in marketing as well as in the description of large data sets collected by state and federal agencies. For example, a retailer of men's clothing would be interested in the modal neck size and sleeve length of potential customers. A supermarket manager is interested in the cereal brand with the largest share of the market, i.e., the modal brand. The modal income class of the laborers in the United States is of interest to the Labor Department. Thus, the mode provides a useful measure of central tendency for many business applications.

Unless the data set is rather large, the mode for a quantitative data set may not be very meaningful. For example, again consider the earnings per share measurements for the sample of thirty *Fortune* 500 companies we used in the previous chapter. If you were to reexamine these data (presented in Table 2.3), you would find that none of the thirty measurements is duplicated in this sample. Thus, strictly speaking, all thirty measurements are modes for this sample. Obviously, this information is of no practical use for data description. We can calculate a more meaningful mode by constructing a relative frequency histogram for the data. The interval containing the most measurements is called the **modal class** and the mode is taken to be the midpoint of this class interval.* Figure 3.1 shows the frequency histogram for the thirty

*There are several definitions for the mode of a relative frequency histogram. Our definition is one of the simplest, but it is adequate for an introductory discussion of the mode.

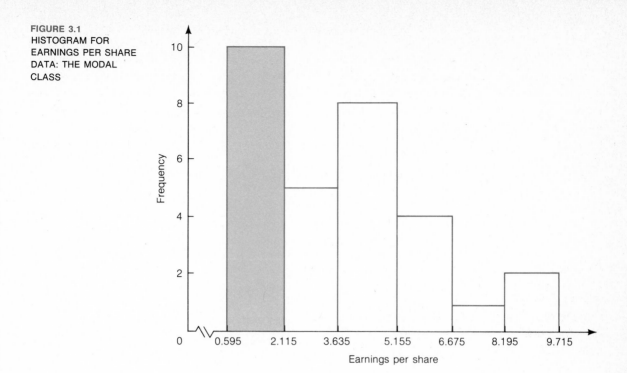

FIGURE 3.1
HISTOGRAM FOR EARNINGS PER SHARE DATA: THE MODAL CLASS

earnings per share measurements. The modal class, the one corresponding to the interval 0.595–2.115 (shaded in Figure 3.1), lies to the left side of the distribution. In the sense that the mode measures data concentration, it provides a measure of central tendency of the data.

3.2
THE ARITHMETIC MEAN: A MEASURE OF CENTRAL TENDENCY FOR QUANTITATIVE DATA

The most popular and best understood measure of central tendency for a quantitative data set is the arithmetic mean (or simply, the mean):

> **DEFINITION 3.2**
> The mean of a set of quantitative data is equal to the sum of the measurements divided by the number of measurements contained in the data set.

Or, in nontechnical terms, the mean is the average value of the data set.

Before calculating the mean (or other numerical descriptive measures) of data sets we will present some shorthand notation that will simplify our calculation instructions. Remember that such notation is used for one reason only—to avoid having to repeat the same verbal descriptions over and over. If you mentally substitute the verbal definition of a symbol each time you read it, you will soon become accustomed to its use.

We will denote the measurements of a data set as follows:

$$x_1, x_2, x_3, \ldots, x_n$$

where x_1 is the first measurement in the data set, x_2 is the second measurement in the data set, x_3 is the third measurement in the data set, . . . , and x_n is the nth (and last) measurement in the data set. Thus, if we have five measurements in a set of data, we will write

$$x_1, x_2, x_3, x_4, x_5$$

to represent the measurements. If the actual numbers are

$$5, 3, 8, 5, 4$$

we have $x_1 = 5$, $x_2 = 3$, $x_3 = 8$, $x_4 = 5$, and $x_5 = 4$.

To calculate the mean of a set of measurements, we must sum them and divide by n, the number of measurements in the set. The sum of measurements $x_1, x_2, \ldots, x_n$ is

$$x_1 + x_2 + \cdots + x_n$$

To shorten the notation for this sum, we will let

$$x_1 + x_2 + \cdots + x_n = \sum_{i=1}^{n} x_i$$

where $\sum$ is the symbol for summation. Verbally translate $\sum_{i=1}^{n} x_i$ as follows: "The sum of the measurements, whose typical member is x_i, beginning with the member x_1 and ending with the member x_n." The typical member will always appear following the $\sum$, the subscript of the first member of the summation will always appear below the $\sum$ symbol, and the subscript of the last member of the summation will always appear above the $\sum$. For example,

$$\sum_{i=2}^{5} x_i = x_2 + x_3 + x_4 + x_5$$

where the typical element x_i follows the $\sum$ symbol, the first element to appear in the sum is identified by the subscript 2 (shown below the $\sum$ symbol), and the last element to appear in the sum is denoted by the 5 (shown above the $\sum$ symbol).

Finally, we will denote the mean of a sample of measurements by $\bar{x}$ (read "x-bar"), and represent the formula for its calculation as follows:*

$$\bar{x} = \frac{\sum_{i=1}^{n} x_i}{n}$$

---

*Note: We omit the formula for calculating the mean for grouped data (data presented in a relative frequency table). The reader interested in this special topic should consult the references included at the end of this chapter.

EXAMPLE 3.1   Calculate the mean of the following five sample measurements:

5, 3, 8, 5, 6

Solution   Using the definition of sample mean and the shorthand notation, we find

$$\bar{x} = \frac{\sum_{i=1}^{5} x_i}{5} = \frac{5 + 3 + 8 + 5 + 6}{5} = \frac{27}{5} = 5.4$$

The mean of this sample is 5.4.

EXAMPLE 3.2   In the period 1974–1976 electric utility stocks paid substantial dividends and were regarded by many to be an excellent investment for income purposes. The dividend rate, given as a percentage of market price on December 31, 1975, is shown below for sixteen electric utilities selected at random from the listings of the New York Stock Exchange. Suppose you had invested equal amounts of money in these utilities. Calculate the mean percent dividend for these sixteen stocks.

Tucson Gas and Electric	7.8
Detroit Edison	10.9
Niagara Mohawk Power	9.5
Pennsylvania Power and Light	9.1
Allegheny Power System	8.6
Florida Power	7.1
Minnesota Power and Light	8.5
Pacific Gas and Electric	9.1
Carolina Power and Light	8.0
Indianapolis Power and Light	8.9
Union Electric	9.6
South Carolina Electric and Gas	9.0
Northern States Power	7.4
Duke Power	7.2
Gulf States Utilities	8.2
Texas Utilities	5.9

Solution   The mean return per unit of capital invested is

$$\bar{x} = \frac{\sum_{i=1}^{16} x_i}{16} = \frac{7.8 + 10.9 + \cdots + 5.9}{16} = \frac{134.8}{16} = 8.425\%$$

Glancing at the data set, you can see that the smallest dividend rate is 5.9, the largest is 10.9, and the mean, 8.425%, falls near the middle of this data set. Investing equal amounts of money in each of these sixteen utilities would spread the risk and return a mean dividend of 8.425%.

The sample mean will play an important role in accomplishing our objective of making inferences about populations based on sample information. For this reason it is important to use a different symbol when we want to discuss the mean of a population of measurements, i.e., the mean of the entire set of measurements in which we are interested. We use the Greek letter μ ("mu") for the population mean. We will adopt a general policy of using Greek letters to represent population numerical descriptive measures and Roman letters to represent corresponding descriptive measures for the sample.

$$\bar{x} = \text{Sample mean} \qquad \mu = \text{Population mean}$$

The sample mean $\bar{x}$ will often be used to estimate (make an inference about) the population mean μ. For example, the population of all 500 earnings per share measurements for the 1975 *Fortune* 500 has a mean $\mu = 2.96$. Our sample of thirty earnings per share measurements has a mean $\bar{x} = 3.74$. If, as is usually the case, we did not have access to the population of measurements, we could use $\bar{x}$ as an estimator or approximator for μ. Then we would need to know something about the reliability of our inference. That is, we would need to know how accurately we might expect $\bar{x}$ to estimate μ. In Chapter 9, we will find that this accuracy depends on two factors:

1. The size of the sample—the larger the sample, the more accurate the estimate will tend to be

2. The variability or spread of the data—all other factors remaining constant, the more variable the data, the less accurate the estimate

In summary, the mean provides a valuable measure of the central tendency for a set of measurements. It is a very common tool in business and economic research, and therefore, the mean will be the focus of much of our discussion of inferential statistics.

CASE STUDY 3.1

The most outstanding characteristic of the general hotel reservation system is the option of the prospective guest, without penalty, to change or cancel his reservation or even to "no-show" (fail to arrive without notice). Overbooking (taking reservations in excess of the hotel capacity) is practiced widely throughout the industry as a compensating economic measure. This has motivated our research into the problem of determining policies for overbooking which are based on some set of rational criteria.

So says Marvin Rothstein (1974) in an article that appeared in the journal for the American Institute for Decision Sciences. In this paper Rothstein introduces a method for scientifically determining hotel booking policies and applies it to the booking problems of the 133 room Sheraton Pocono Inn at Stroudsburg, Pennsylvania.

From the Sheraton Pocono Inn's records the number of reservations, walk-ins (people without reservations who expect to be accommodated), cancellations, and no-shows were tabulated for each day during the period August 1–28, 1971. The Inn's records for this period included approximately 3,100 guest histories. From the tabulated data the mean or average number of room reservations per day for each of the 7 days of the week were computed. These appear in Table 3.1. In applying his booking policy decision method to the Sheraton's data, Rothstein used the means listed in Table 3.1 to help portray the Inn's demand for rooms.

TABLE 3.1
MEAN NUMBER OF
ROOM RESERVATIONS,
AUGUST 1–28, 1971,
133 ROOMS

SUNDAY	MONDAY	TUESDAY	WEDNESDAY	THURSDAY	FRIDAY	SATURDAY
138	126	149	160	150	150	169

The mean of Saturday reservations during the period August 1–28, 1971, is 169. This may be interpreted as an estimate of μ, the mean number of rooms demanded via reservations (walk-ins also contribute to the demand for rooms) on a Saturday during 1971. If the reservation data for all Saturdays during 1971 had been tabulated, μ could have been computed. But, since only the August data is available, it was used to estimate μ. Can you think of some problems associated with using August's data to estimate the mean for the entire year?

3.3
THE MEDIAN: ANOTHER MEASURE OF CENTRAL TENDENCY FOR QUANTITATIVE DATA

Another important measure of central tendency is the **median** of a set of measurements:

DEFINITION 3.3
The **median** of a data set is a number such that half the measurements fall below the median and half fall above.

The median is of most value in describing large data sets. If the data set is characterized by a relative frequency histogram (see Figure 3.2), the median is the point on the x-axis such that half the area under the histogram lies above the median and half lies

FIGURE 3.2
LOCATION OF
THE MEDIAN

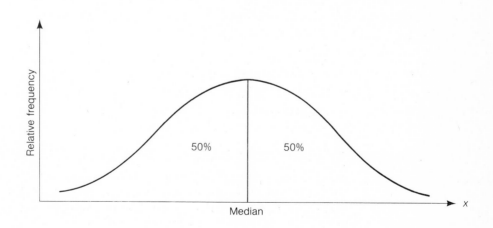

below. [*Note:* In Section 2.4 we observed that the relative frequency associated with a particular interval on the *x*-axis is proportional to the amount of area under the histogram that lies above the interval.]

For a small, or even a large but finite, number of measurements, there may be many numbers that satisfy the property indicated in Figure 3.2. For this reason, we will arbitrarily calculate the median of a data set as follows:

CALCULATING A MEDIAN

1. If the number of measurements in a data set is odd, the median is the middle number when the measurements are arranged in ascending (or descending) order of magnitude.
2. If the number of measurements is even, the median is the mean of the two middle measurements when the measurements are arranged in ascending (or descending) order of magnitude.

EXAMPLE 3.3

Consider the following sample of $n = 7$ measurements:

5, 7, 4, 5, 9, 6, 2

a. Calculate the median of this sample.
b. Eliminate the last measurement (the 2) and calculate the median of the remaining $n = 6$ measurements.

Solution

a. The 7 measurements in the sample arranged in ascending order are

2, 4, 5, 5, 6, 7, 9

Since the number of measurements is odd, the median is the middle measurement. Thus, the median of this sample is 5.
b. After removing the 2 from the set of measurements, our sample arranged in ascending order appears as follows:

4, 5, 5, 6, 7, 9

Now the number of measurements is even, and so we average the middle two measurements. The median is $(5 + 6)/2 = 5.5$.

The median often provides information about the sample and/or population that the mean does not. In particular, the median is less sensitive than the mean to extremely large or small measurements. For example, if you were interested in computing a measure of central tendency of the incomes of a company's employees, the mean might be misleading. If all blue- and white-collar employees' incomes are included in the data set, the high incomes of a few executives will influence the mean more than the median. Thus, the median will provide a more accurate picture of the typical income for the company. Similarly, the median yearly sales for a sample of companies would locate the middle of the sales data. However, a few companies with very large yearly sales would greatly influence the mean, making it deceptively large. That is, the mean could exceed a vast majority of the sample measurements, making it a misleading measure of central tendency.

For a numerical example, we have arranged the earnings per share data for the sample of thirty 1975 *Fortune* 500 companies in ascending order. The result is Table 3.2.

TABLE 3.2
EARNINGS PER SHARE DATA IN ASCENDING ORDER

0.60	2.47	4.44
1.06	2.75	4.55
1.15	3.16	5.15
1.65	3.20	5.21
1.71	3.37	5.36
1.74	3.65	5.63
1.93	3.77	6.06
1.97	3.81	7.60
2.02	4.02	8.29
2.06	4.25	9.70

The median equals the average of the fifteenth and sixteenth measurements: $(3.37 + 3.65)/2 = 3.51$. Note that the median is smaller than the mean (3.74) for this sample. This fact indicates that the data is skewed to the right, i.e., that the measurements tend to tail off to the right. This is because the mean is affected more than

FIGURE 3.3
EARNINGS PER SHARE DATA: MODAL CLASS, MEAN, AND MEDIAN

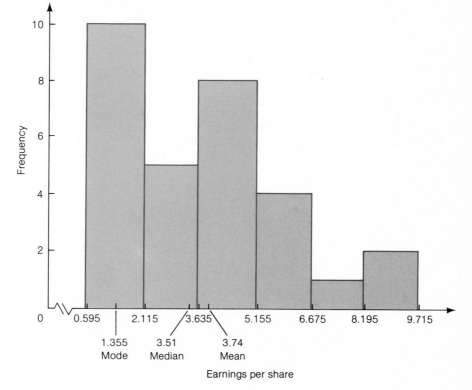

Earnings per share

the median by extreme (large or small) observations. Consequently, if a distribution tails out in one direction, the mean will shift toward this tail. This skewness is evident in Figure 3.3, where we show the mode, mean, and median for the earnings per share data.

The comparison of mean and median gives us a general method for detecting skewness in data sets:

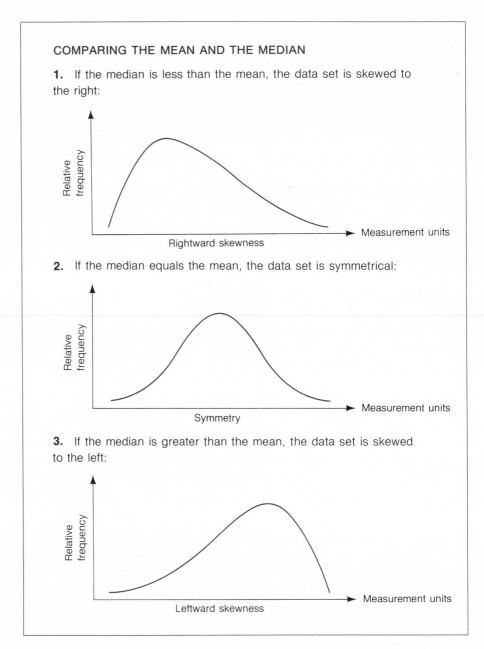

COMPARING THE MEAN AND THE MEDIAN

1. If the median is less than the mean, the data set is skewed to the right:

2. If the median equals the mean, the data set is symmetrical:

3. If the median is greater than the mean, the data set is skewed to the left:

CASE STUDY 3.2   George T. Milkovich, Anthony J. Annoni, and Thomas A. Mahoney (1972) explain the delphi technique as follows:

> The delphi technique, a set of procedures originally developed by the Rand Corporation in the late 1940's, is designed to obtain the most reliable consensus of opinion of a group of experts. Essentially, the delphi is a series of intensive interrogations of each individual expert (by a series of questionnaires) concerning some primary question interspersed with controlled feedback. The procedures are designed to avoid direct confrontation of the experts with one another.
>
> The interaction among the experts is accomplished through an intermediary who gathers the data requests of the experts and summarizes them along with the experts' answers to the primary question. This mode of controlled interaction among the experts is a deliberate attempt to avoid the disadvantages associated with more conventional use of experts such as in round table discussions or direct confrontation of opposing views. The developers of the delphi argue the procedures are more conducive to independent thought and allow more gradual formulation to a considered opinion.

This article presents a study of the usefulness of the delphi procedure in projecting labor requirements in a low profit margin national retail firm. Seven company executives formed the panel of experts. Five questionnaires submitted at approximately 8-day intervals were used to interrogate the seven experts. On the second through fifth questionnaires, they were each asked the primary question: "How many buyers will the firm need 1 year from now?" Their individual responses, along with the median response of the group for each questionnaire appear in Table 3.3.

TABLE 3.3
PROJECTED DEMAND
FOR BUYERS

QUESTIONNAIRE	EXPERTS							MEDIAN
	A	B	C	D	E	F	G	
2	55	35	33	35	55	33	32	35
3	45	35	41	35	41	34	32	35
4	45	38	41	35	41	34	34	38
5	45	38	41	35	45	34	34	38

Note that the median response increased from 35 on questionnaire number 2 to 38 on questionnaires 4 and 5. This increase indicates an upward shift in the distribution of the experts' estimates as to the number of buyers the firm would need a year from now.

One of the conclusions of the study was that the delphi technique provided closer estimates of the actual number of buyers (37) needed by the firm 1 year later than did other more conventional estimating techniques.

EXERCISES   **3.1.** To help evaluate the need for increased early morning service from Harriet Avenue to downtown Burnsville, the Metropolitan Transit Authority sampled 8 days last month and recorded the number of people boarding the 7:30 AM downtown express. The following are the results of the sample:

April 1: 30	April 15: 45	April 28: 36
April 8: 42	April 18: 42	April 29: 41
April 11: 38	April 25: 35	

Find the mean and median of this data set.

3.2. [*Note:* The purpose of this exercise is to aid in the interpretation of summation notation.] Refer to Exercise 3.1. Express each of the following sums in summation notation:

    a. The sum of all eight sample observations
    b. The sum of the first five sample observations
    c. The sum of the last three sample observations

3.3. The following is a list of the amount (rounded to the nearest dollar) spent on groceries during a 2 week period last January by a sample of ten consumers:

$60	$ 85	$147	$99	$81
55	111	182	77	85

Find the mean and median for this data set.

3.4. Refer to Exercise 3.3. If each of the consumers had spent exactly $10 more on groceries than listed in Exercise 3.3, how would the sample mean and median that you computed in Exercise 3.3 be affected? What is the effect on the sample mean and median of adding a constant to each of the sample measurements?

SUMMARY

Numerical methods for describing quantitative data sets can be grouped as follows:
1. Measures of central tendency
2. Measures of variability

In this chapter we presented several numerical measures of central tendency.

    The **mode** is the most frequently observed member of the data set. The **mean** is the average of the data, obtained by summing the *n* measurements in the data set and dividing by *n*. The **median** is a number in the data set chosen so that half the measurements in the data set fall below the median and half fall above. The relationship between the mean and median provides information about the **skewness** of the frequency distribution. For making inferences about the population, the sample mean will usually be preferred to the other measures of central tendency.

SUPPLEMENTARY EXERCISES

3.5. A company is considering producing and marketing loose-leaf notebooks in a large city. To help decide whether such an expansion of its product line would be profitable the firm needs an estimate of the yearly demand for loose-leaf notebooks. Accordingly, the marketing department randomly chose forty-nine bookstores, stationary stores, and business users of loose-leaf notebooks in the city and asked them how many loose-leaf notebooks they purchased last year. The following are the results of the survey:

155	491	871	480	711	506	415
401	499	666	450	995	466	211
262	512	302	299	806	489	581
425	331	410	284	606	706	433
555	500	338	690	570	333	203
398	777	844	301	459	327	636
452	351	476	521	300	519	402

In its current form this data set cannot be conveniently used as input to the firm's decision-making process. Summary measures are needed.

    a. Depict the above data set in a histogram.
    b. Compute the mean, median, and mode of the data set and locate them on the histogram.

[*Note:* Knowing the number of stores in the city, the firm could use the sample mean and the price per unit to estimate the gross sales. How we can attach a measure of reliability to this estimate will be explained in Chapter 9.]

3.6. Before purchasing stock in an electronics firm, the management of a mutual fund wants information concerning the price movements of the firm's stock during the past year. Thirty days of the past year were randomly selected and the closing price (to the nearest dollar) was recorded for each day:

$31	$27	$40	$43	$48	$33
28	28	39	36	49	26
44	29	42	35	32	28
50	34	47	29	50	28
32	37	29	30	28	29

The mutual fund's management has decided it should purchase the stock only if the mean closing price for last year is $41 or more.

    a. Define the terms *mean, median,* and *mode* in the context of this problem.
    b. Construct a relative frequency histogram for the data.
    c. Compute the mean, median, and mode for the above data set and locate them on the histogram.
    d. Do you think the mutual fund should purchase the firm's stock? [*Note:* Simply looking at the sample and using your intuition could lead you to an erroneous conclusion. We will learn how to use the sample mean to make decisions about a population mean in Chapters 9 and 10.]

REFERENCES

Dyckman, T. R., & Thomas, L. J. *Fundamental statistics for business and economics.* Englewood Cliffs, N.J.: Prentice-Hall, 1977. Chapter 3.

Mendenhall, W. *Introduction to probability and statistics.* 4th ed. North Scituate, Mass.: Duxbury, 1975. Chapter 3.

Milkovich, G. T., Annoni, A. J., & Mahoney, T. A. "The use of the delphi procedures in manpower forecasting." *Management Science,* Dec. 1972, *19,* Part I, 381–388.

Pfaffenberger, R. C., & Patterson, J. H. *Statistical methods for business and economics.* Homewood, Ill.: Richard Irwin, 1977. Chapter 2.

Rothstein, M. "Hotel overbooking as a Markovian sequential decision process." *Decision Sciences,* July 1974, *5,* 389–405.

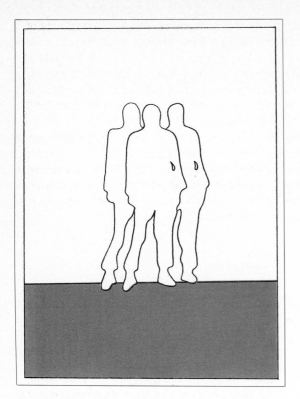

4

NUMERICAL MEASURES
OF
VARIABILITY

Because data description is an essential prerequisite to a study of statistical inference, we have considered two methods for accomplishing this task. Graphical methods for describing data sets were presented in Chapter 2. Three numerical descriptive measures, which create a mental image of the data, were presented in Chapter 3. These measures—the mode, the mean, and the median—locate the center of a distribution of data.

Not only do we want to locate the center of a data set, we need to know something about the spread or variation of the data. For example, it is not enough to know the mean gain that you might expect from a business venture. You would want to know something about the variability of gains associated with similar ventures, because the greater the variability, the greater the risk. Several numerical descriptive measures of data variability are presented in this chapter.
Given the mean and one of these measures of data variability, you will be able to visualize the relative frequency distribution for a data set. Although description of this sample data may be of interest in some cases, our ultimate goal is to find a method for describing the unknown data set, the population.

In Chapter 3 we presented some methods for measuring the central tendency of a quantitative data set. However, central tendency tells only part of the story. Our information is incomplete without a measure of the **variability or spread** of the data set. Note that in describing a data set, we refer to either the sample or the population. Ultimately (in Chapter 9), we will use the sample numerical descriptive measures (statistics) to make inferences about the corresponding descriptive measures for the population from which the sample was selected.

If you examine the two histograms in Figure 4.1, you will notice that both hypothetical data sets are symmetric, with equal modes, medians, and means. However, data set 1 in Figure 4.1(a) has measurements spread evenly over the measurement classes, while data set 2 in Figure 4.1(b) has most of its measurements clustered about the center. For this reason, a measure of variability is needed, along with a measure of central tendency, to describe a data set.

4.1
THE RANGE

Perhaps the simplest measure of the variability of a quantitative data set is its **range**:

DEFINITION 4.1
The **range** of a data set is equal to the largest measurement minus the smallest measurement.

The range measures the spread of the data by measuring the distance between the smallest and largest measurements. For example, stock A may vary in price during a given year from \$32 to \$36, while stock B may vary from \$10 to \$58, as shown in Figure 4.2. The range in price of stock A is \$36−\$32 = \$4, while that for stock B is \$58−\$10 = \$48. A comparison of ranges tells us that the price of stock B was much more variable than the price of stock A.

FIGURE 4.1

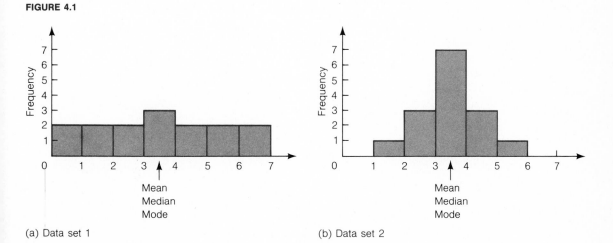

(a) Data set 1

(b) Data set 2

FIGURE 4.2
RANGES OF STOCK
PRICES FOR TWO
COMPANIES

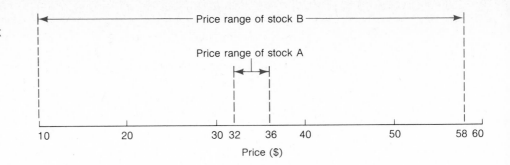

The range is not always a satisfactory measure of variability. For example, suppose we are comparing the profit margin (as percent of total bid price) per construction job for 100 construction jobs for each of two cost estimators working for a large construction company. We find that the profit margins range from −10% (loss) to +40% (profit) for both cost estimators and therefore that the ranges for the two data sets, 40% − (−10%) = 50% are equal. Because of this, we might be inclined to conclude that there is little or no difference in the performance of the two estimators.

But, suppose the histograms for the two sets of 100 profit margin measurements appear as shown in Figure 4.3. Although the ranges are equal and all central tendency measures are the same for these two symmetric data sets, there is an obvious difference between the two sets of measurements. The difference is that estimator B's profit margins tend to be more stable, i.e., to pile up or to cluster about the center of the data set. In contrast, estimator A's profit margins are spread rather evenly over the range, indicating a higher incidence of some high profit margins, but also a higher risk of losses. Thus, even though the ranges are equal, the profit margin record of estimator A is more variable than that of estimator B, indicating a distinct difference in their cost estimating characteristics. We therefore need to develop more informative numerical measures of variability than the range.

FIGURE 4.3
PROFIT MARGIN
HISTOGRAMS FOR TWO
COST ESTIMATORS

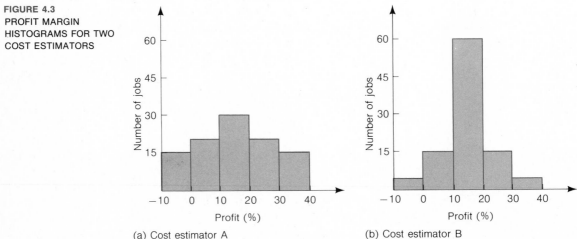

(a) Cost estimator A

(b) Cost estimator B

You will recall from Case Study 3.2 that the delphi technique is a set of procedures that may be used to obtain a consensus opinion from a group of experts through a series of questionnaires. Case Study 3.2 illustrated the use of the median as a measure of central tendency for the distribution of expert opinions elicited by the questionnaires. As a measure of variability of the data (i.e., the opinions), Milkovich et al. (1972) used the range. Table 3.3, showing the experts' opinions, is repeated here as Table 4.1, with the range of the distribution of opinions of each questionnaire shown at the right.

The range of 23 on the second questionnaire indicates that at that time the experts' opinions were widely dispersed. The decrease in the range to 11 following the fourth questionnaire indicates that as the experts received more information about the firm's needs and learned about each others' opinions, the variability in the distribution of their opinions decreased. Milkovich et al. noted that the decrease in the range was an indication that the experts' opinions were converging.

TABLE 4.1
PROJECTED DEMAND
FOR BUYERS

QUESTIONNAIRE	A	B	C	D	E	F	G	MEDIAN	RANGE
				EXPERTS					
2	55	35	33	35	55	33	32	35	23
3	45	35	41	35	41	34	32	35	13
4	45	38	41	35	41	34	34	38	11
5	45	38	41	35	45	34	34	38	11

4.2 VARIANCE AND STANDARD DEVIATION

Recall that we represent the n measurements in a sample by the symbols $x_1, x_2, \ldots, x_n$ and we represent their mean by $\bar{x}$. What would be the interpretation of $x_1 - \bar{x}$? It is the distance between the first sample measurement, x_1, and the sample mean, $\bar{x}$. If we were to calculate this distance for *every* measurement in the sample, we would create a set of distances from the mean:

$$x_1 - \bar{x}, x_2 - \bar{x}, x_3 - \bar{x}, \ldots, x_n - \bar{x}$$

What information do these distances contain? If they tend to be large, the interpretation is that the data are spread out or highly variable. If the distances are mostly small, the data are clustered around the mean $\bar{x}$, and therefore do not exhibit much variability. As a simple example, consider the two samples in Table 4.2, which each have five measurements (we have ordered the numbers for convenience). You will note that both samples have a mean of 3. However, a glance at the distances shows

TABLE 4.2

	SAMPLE 1	SAMPLE 2
Measurements	1, 2, 3, 4, 5	2, 3, 3, 3, 4
Mean	$\bar{x} = \dfrac{1 + 2 + 3 + 4 + 5}{5} = \dfrac{15}{5}$ $= 3$	$\bar{x} = \dfrac{2 + 3 + 3 + 3 + 4}{5} = \dfrac{15}{5}$ $= 3$
Distances from $\bar{x}$	$1 - 3, 2 - 3, 3 - 3, 4 - 3, 5 - 3$ or $-2, \quad -1, \quad 0, \quad 1, \quad 2$	$2 - 3, 3 - 3, 3 - 3, 3 - 3, 4 - 3$ or $-1, \quad 0, \quad 0, \quad 0, \quad 1$

FIGURE 4.4
DISTANCES FROM THE
MEAN FOR TWO
DATA SETS

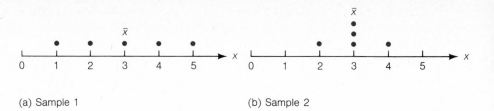

(a) Sample 1   (b) Sample 2

that sample 1 has greater variability, i.e., has more large distances from $\bar{x}$ than sample 2, which is clustered around $\bar{x}$. You can see this clearly by looking at these distances in Figure 4.4. Thus, the distances provide information about the variability of the sample measurements.

The next step is to condense the information into a single numerical measure of variability. Simply averaging the distances from $\bar{x}$ will not help. For example, in samples 1 and 2 the negative and positive distances cancel, so that the average distance is 0. Since this is true for any data set, i.e., the average distance from the mean is always 0, we gain no information by averaging the distances from $\bar{x}$.

There are two methods for dealing with the fact that positive and negative distances from the mean cancel. The first is to treat all the distances as though they were positive, ignoring the sign of the negative distances. We will not pursue this line of thought because the resulting measure of variability (the mean of the absolute values of the distances) is difficult to interpret. A second method of eliminating the minus signs associated with the distances is to square them. The quantity we can calculate from the squared distances will provide a meaningful description of the variability of a data set.

To use the squared distances calculated from a data set, we first calculate the **sample variance:**

DEFINITION 4.2

The **sample variance** for a sample of n measurements is equal to the sum of the squared distances from the mean divided by $(n - 1)$. In symbols, using s^2 to represent the sample variance,

$$s^2 = \frac{\displaystyle\sum_{i=1}^{n} (x_i - \bar{x})^2}{n - 1}$$

Referring to the two samples in Table 4.2, you can calculate the variance for sample 1 as follows:

$$s^2 = \frac{(1 - 3)^2 + (2 - 3)^2 + (3 - 3)^2 + (4 - 3)^2 + (5 - 3)^2}{5 - 1}$$

$$= \frac{4 + 1 + 0 + 1 + 4}{4} = 2.5$$

The second step in finding a meaningful measure of data variability is to calculate the **standard deviation** of the data set:

> **DEFINITION 4.3**
> The **sample standard deviation**, s, is defined as the positive square root of the sample variance, s^2. Thus,
> $$s = \sqrt{s^2} = \sqrt{\frac{\sum_{i=1}^{n} (x_i - \bar{x})^2}{n - 1}}$$

The corresponding quantity, the **population standard deviation**, will be denoted by σ ("sigma"). The **population variance** will therefore be denoted by σ^2. The symbols for the variances and standard deviations are summarized below:

> s^2 = Sample variance
>
> σ^2 = Population variance
>
> s = Sample standard deviation
>
> σ = Population standard deviation

Notice that in contrast to the variance, the standard deviation is expressed in the original units of measurement. For example, if the original measurements are in dollars, the standard deviation will be expressed in dollars. Second, you may wonder why we use the divisor $(n - 1)$ instead of n when calculating the sample variance. This is because by using the divisor $(n - 1)$ you obtain a better estimate of σ^2 than you do by dividing the sum of the squared distances by n. Since we will ultimately want to use sample statistics to make inferences about the corresponding population parameters, $(n - 1)$ is preferred to n when defining the sample variance.

EXAMPLE 4.1 Calculate the standard deviation of the following sample: 2, 3, 3, 3, 4.

Solution For this set of data, $\bar{x} = 3$. Then,

$$s = \sqrt{\frac{(2 - 3)^2 + (3 - 3)^2 + (3 - 3)^2 + (3 - 3)^2 + (4 - 3)^2}{5 - 1}}$$

$$= \sqrt{\frac{2}{4}} = \sqrt{0.5} = 0.71$$

Example 4.1 may have raised two thoughts in your mind. First, calculating s^2 and s can be very tedious if $\bar{x}$ is a number that contains a large number of significant figures or if there are a large number of measurements in a data set. Second, we have not explained how a sample standard deviation can be used to describe the variability of a data set. Fortunately, we have an easier method for calculating s^2 and s and this method will be explained in Section 4.3. The interpretation of s will be the subject of Section 4.4.

4.3 CALCULATION FORMULAS FOR VARIANCE AND STANDARD DEVIATION

As the number of measurements in the sample becomes larger, the sample variance becomes more difficult to calculate. We must calculate the distance between each measurement and the mean, square it, sum the squared distances, and finally divide by $(n - 1)$. Fortunately, there is a shortcut formula for computing the sample variance:

SHORTCUT FORMULA FOR SAMPLE VARIANCE

$$s^2 = \frac{(\text{Sum of squares of sample measurements}) - \dfrac{(\text{Sum of sample measurements})^2}{n}}{n - 1}$$

$$= \frac{\displaystyle\sum_{i=1}^{n} x_i^2 - \dfrac{\left(\displaystyle\sum_{i=1}^{n} x_i\right)^2}{n}}{n - 1}$$

Note that the formula requires only the sum of the sample measurements, $\sum_{i=1}^{n} x_i$, and the sum of the squares of the sample measurements, $\sum_{i=1}^{n} x_i^2$. Be careful when you calculate these two sums. Rounding the values x^2 that appear in $\sum_{i=1}^{n} x_i^2$ or rounding the quantity $\left(\sum_{i=1}^{n} x_i\right)^2 \Big/ n$, can lead to substantial errors in the calculation of s^2.

EXAMPLE 4.2

Use the shortcut formula to compute the variance of these two samples of five measurements each.

Sample 1:   1, 2, 3, 4, 5   Sample 2:   2, 3, 3, 3, 4

Solution

We first work with sample 1. The two quantities needed are

$$\sum_{i=1}^{5} x_i = 1 + 2 + 3 + 4 + 5 = 15$$

and

$$\sum_{i=1}^{5} x_i^2 = 1^2 + 2^2 + 3^2 + 4^2 + 5^2 = 1 + 4 + 9 + 16 + 25 = 55$$

Then the sample variance for sample 1 is

$$s^2 = \frac{\sum\limits_{i=1}^{5} x_i^2 - \dfrac{\left(\sum\limits_{i=1}^{5} x_i\right)^2}{5}}{5 - 1} = \frac{55 - \dfrac{(15)^2}{5}}{4} = \frac{55 - 45}{4} = \frac{10}{4} = 2.5$$

Similarly, for sample 2 we get

$$\sum_{i=1}^{5} x_i = 2 + 3 + 3 + 3 + 4 = 15$$

and

$$\sum_{i=1}^{5} x_i^2 = 2^2 + 3^2 + 3^2 + 3^2 + 4^2 = 4 + 9 + 9 + 9 + 16 = 47$$

Then the variance for sample 2 is

$$s^2 = \frac{\sum\limits_{i=1}^{5} x_i^2 - \dfrac{\left(\sum\limits_{i=1}^{5} x_i\right)^2}{5}}{5 - 1} = \frac{47 - \dfrac{(15)^2}{5}}{4} = \frac{47 - 45}{4} = \frac{2}{4} = 0.5$$

Note that these results agree with our calculations in the previous section.

EXAMPLE 4.3
The earnings per share measurements for a sample of thirty companies in the 1975 *Fortune* 500 are repeated here. Calculate the sample variance, s^2, and the standard deviation, s, for these measurements.

1.97	0.60	4.02	3.20	1.15	6.06
4.44	2.02	3.37	3.65	1.74	2.75
3.81	9.70	8.29	5.63	5.21	4.55
7.60	3.16	3.77	5.36	1.06	1.71
2.47	4.25	1.93	5.15	2.06	1.65

Solution
The calculation of the sample variance, s^2, would be very tedious for this sample if we tried to use the formula

$$s^2 = \frac{\sum\limits_{i=1}^{30} (x_i - \bar{x})^2}{30 - 1}$$

because it would be necessary to compute all thirty squared distances from the mean. However, for the shortcut formula we need only compute

$$\sum_{i=1}^{30} x_i = 1.97 + 4.44 + \cdots + 1.65 = 112.33$$

and

$$\sum_{i=1}^{30} x_i^2 = (1.97)^2 + (4.44)^2 + \cdots + (1.65)^2 = 560.7373$$

Then

$$s^2 = \frac{\displaystyle\sum_{i=1}^{30} x_i^2 - \frac{\left(\displaystyle\sum_{i=1}^{30} x_i\right)^2}{30}}{30 - 1} = \frac{560.7373 - \dfrac{(112.33)^2}{30}}{29} = 4.8323$$

Notice that we retained four decimal places in the calculation of s^2 to reduce rounding errors, even though the original data was accurate to only two decimal places.[*]
   The standard deviation is

$$s = \sqrt{s^2} = \sqrt{4.8323} = 2.20$$

4.1. Given the following information about two data sets of interest, compute $\bar{x}$, the sample variance, and the standard deviation for each.

    a. $n = 30$, $\displaystyle\sum_{i=1}^{n} x_i^2 = 2{,}000$, $\displaystyle\sum_{i=1}^{n} x_i = 150$

    b. $n = 100$, $\displaystyle\sum_{i=1}^{n} x_i^2 = 10{,}000$, $\displaystyle\sum_{i=1}^{n} x_i = 950$

4.2. For each of the following data sets compute $\displaystyle\sum_{i=1}^{n} x_i$, $\displaystyle\sum_{i=1}^{n} x_i^2$, and $\left(\displaystyle\sum_{i=1}^{n} x_i\right)^2$:

    a. 11, 5, 3, 4, 2
    b. 2, 6, 0, 0, 2
    c. 100, 4, 12, 100
    d. −1, 0, −4, −2, −3
    e. 0, 0, 0, 0, 10

4.3. Compute $\bar{x}$, s^2, and s for each of the data sets in Exercise 4.2.

4.4. Compute $\bar{x}$, s^2, and s for each of the following data sets:

    a. 1, 5, 0, 2, 5, 7, 1
    b. 1, 2, 0, 0, 5, 4
    c. 10, 8, 12, 2
    d. 3, 4, 10, 2

4.5. Compute $\bar{x}$, s^2, and s for each of the following data sets:

    a. 1, 1, 20, 20, 8
    b. 2, 100, 104, 2

[*]The accuracy of the original data has nothing to do with the degree of accuracy used in computing s^2 and s. Theoretically, s^2 and s should be computed without rounding error, but this is often impossible in practice.

c. $-1, -3, -2, 0, -3, -3$
d. $\frac{1}{5}, \frac{1}{5}, \frac{1}{5}, \frac{2}{5}, 0.2, \frac{4}{5}$

4.6. A service station decided to conduct a survey of service records to determine the length of time (in months) between customer oil changes. A random sample of the station records produced the following times between oil changes:

6	6	24	8	6
6	6	16	6	12
18	8	4	12	12

Compute the sample mean, variance, and standard deviation.

4.7. In Exercise 4.6, if the individual who changed the oil in his or her car every 24 months had instead changed it every 18 months, would the sample variance increase or decrease? Why? If instead of every 24 or 18 months, the person had changed the oil every 6 months, how would the resulting sample variance compare to the sample variances when the oil was changed every 24 months? Every 18 months?

4.4 INTERPRETING THE STANDARD DEVIATION

As we have seen, if we are comparing the variability of two samples selected from a population, the sample with the larger standard deviation is the more variable of the two. Thus, we know how to interpret the standard deviation on a relative or comparative basis, but we have not explained how it provides a measure of variability for a single sample.

One way to interpret the standard deviation as a measure of variability of a data set would be to answer questions such as the following: "How many measurements are within 1 standard deviation of the mean?" "How many measurements are within 2 standard deviations?" For a specific data set, we can answer the questions by counting the number of measurements in each of the intervals. However, if we are interested in obtaining a general answer to these questions, the problem is more difficult.

TABLE 4.3
AIDS TO INTERPRETATION OF A STANDARD DEVIATION

1. A rule (from Chebyshev's theorem) that applies to any sample of measurements, regardless of the shape of the frequency distribution:

- **a.** It is possible that none of the measurements will fall within 1 standard deviation of the mean ($\bar{x} - s$ to $\bar{x} + s$).
- **b.** At least $\frac{3}{4}$ of the measurements will fall within 2 standard deviations of the mean ($\bar{x} - 2s$ to $\bar{x} + 2s$).
- **c.** At least $\frac{8}{9}$ of the measurements will fall within 3 standard deviations of the mean ($\bar{x} - 3s$ to $\bar{x} + 3s$).

2. A rule of thumb that applies to samples with frequency distributions that are mound-shaped:

- **a.** Approximately 68% of the measurements will fall within 1 standard deviation of the mean ($\bar{x} - s$ to $\bar{x} + s$).
- **b.** Approximately 95% of the measurements will fall within 2 standard deviations of the mean ($\bar{x} - 2s$ to $\bar{x} + 2s$).
- **c.** Essentially all the measurements will fall within 3 standard deviations of the mean ($\bar{x} - 3s$ to $\bar{x} + 3s$).

FIGURE 4.5
HISTOGRAM OF A
MOUND-SHAPED
SAMPLE

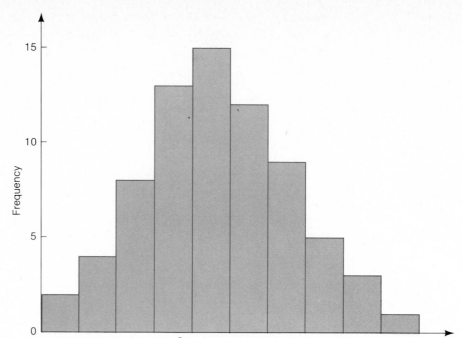

Sample measurements

In Table 4.3 we present two sets of answers to the questions of how many measurements fall within 1, 2, and 3 standard deviations of the mean. The first set, which applies to *any* sample, is derived from a theorem proved by the Russian mathematician Chebyshev. The second set, which applies only to mound-shaped samples, is based upon empirical evidence that has accumulated over time. The frequency histogram of a mound-shaped sample is approximately symmetric, with a clustering of measurements about the midpoint of the distribution (the mean, median, and mode should all be about the same), tailing off rapidly as we move away from the center of the histogram. Thus, the histogram will have the appearance of a mound or bell, as shown in Figure 4.5. The percentages given for the various intervals in Table 4.3 provide remarkably good approximations even when the distribution of the data is slightly skewed or asymmetric.*

EXAMPLE 4.4 The earnings per share data for a sample of thirty companies from the 1975 *Fortune* 500 is repeated again here.

1.97	0.60	4.02	3.20	1.15	6.06
4.44	2.02	3.37	3.65	1.74	2.75
3.81	9.70	8.29	5.63	5.21	4.55
7.60	3.16	3.77	5.36	1.06	1.71
2.47	4.25	1.93	5.15	2.06	1.65

*Note that the rule of thumb in Table 4.3 not only applies to normal distributions of data, but also applies very well to mound-shaped distributions of large data sets and to distributions that possess a moderate degree of skewness.

We have previously shown that the mean and standard deviation of these data are 3.74 and 2.20, respectively. Calculate the fraction of the thirty measurements in the intervals $\bar{x} \pm s$, $\bar{x} \pm 2s$, and $\bar{x} \pm 3s$, and compare the results with those in Table 4.3.

Solution

We first form the interval

$$(\bar{x} - s, \bar{x} + s) = (3.74 - 2.20, 3.74 + 2.20) = (1.54, 5.94)$$

A check of the measurements shows that twenty-three measurements are within this 1 standard deviation interval around the mean. This represents $^{23}\!/_{30} \approx 77\%$ of the sample measurements.

The next interval of interest is

$$(\bar{x} - 2s, \bar{x} + 2s) = (3.74 - 4.40, 3.74 + 4.40) = (-0.66, 81.4)$$

All but two measurements are within this interval, so approximately 93% are within 2 standard deviations of $\bar{x}$.

Finally, the 3 standard deviation interval around $\bar{x}$ is

$$(\bar{x} - 3s, \bar{x} + 3s) = (3.74 - 6.60, 3.74 + 6.60) = (-2.86, 10.34).$$

All the measurements fall within 3 standard deviations of the mean.

These 1, 2, and 3 standard deviation percentiles (77, 93, and 100) agree fairly well with the approximations of 68%, 95%, and 100% presented in Table 4.3 for mound-shaped distributions. If you look at the frequency histogram for this data set in Figure 2.6, you will note that the distribution is not really mound-shaped, nor is it extremely skewed. Thus, we get reasonably good results from the mound-shaped approximations. Of course, we know from Table 4.3 that no matter what the shape of the distribution, we would expect at least 75% and 89% ($^{8}\!/_{9}$) within 2 and 3 standard deviations, respectively, of $\bar{x}$.

EXAMPLE 4.5

The aids for interpreting the value of a standard deviation (Table 4.3) can be put to an immediate practical use as a check on the calculation of a standard deviation. Suppose you have a data set for which the smallest measurement is 20 and the largest is 80. You have calculated the standard deviation of the data set to be

$$s = 190$$

How can you use Table 4.3 to provide a rough check on your calculated value of s?

Solution

The larger the number of measurements in a data set, the greater will be the tendency for very large or very small measurements (extreme values) to appear in the data set. But from Table 4.3 you know that most of the measurements (approximately 95% if the distribution is mound-shaped) will be within 2 standard deviations of the mean. And, regardless of how many measurements are in the data set, almost all of them will fall within 3 standard deviations of the mean (see Figure 4.6). Consequently, we would expect the range to be equal to somewhere between 4 and 6 standard deviations, i.e., between $4s$ and $6s$. For the given data set, the range is

$$\begin{aligned} \text{Range} &= \text{Largest measurement} - \text{Smallest measurement} \\ &= 80 - 20 = 60 \end{aligned}$$

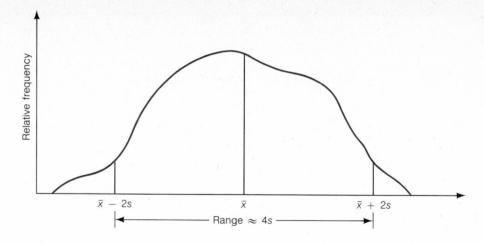

FIGURE 4.6
THE RELATION
BETWEEN THE RANGE
AND THE STANDARD
DEVIATION

Then if we let the range equal 6s, we obtain

$$\text{Range} = 6s$$
$$60 = 6s$$
$$s = 10$$

Or, if we let the range equal 4s, we obtain a larger (and more conservative) value for s, namely,

$$\text{Range} = 4s$$
$$60 = 4s$$
$$s = 15$$

Now you can see that it does not make much difference whether you let the range equal 4s (which is more realistic for most data sets) or 6s (which is reasonable for large data sets). It is clear that your calculated value, $s = 190$, is too large, and you should check your calculations.

CASE STUDY 4.2   The degree of sensitization on the part of a firm to the needs and wants of its consumers is frequently an important factor in determining the firm's overall success. Jean Namias (1964) presents a procedure for achieving such sensitivity. The procedure uses the rate of consumer complaints about a product to determine when and when not to conduct a search for specific causes of consumer complaints. For simplification we will discuss Namias' paper as if the procedure described used the number of complaints per 10,000 units of a product sold to determine when and when not to conduct a search for specific causes of consumer complaints. The details of the procedure are discussed in Case Study 4.3.

Namias' procedure, given our simplification, makes use of the **distribution** of the number of consumer complaints received about a product per 10,000 units of the product sold. To visualize such a distribution imagine that a company produces its product in lots of 10,000 units and keeps track of the number of complaints received about items in each lot. What the company's complaint records will show is a series of numbers, perhaps 100, 96, 145, 201, etc., each of which is the number of complaints received about a particular lot of 10,000 units. This series of numbers is a quantitative data set from which a relative frequency histogram can be drawn. The histogram constructed from this data set is a representation of the distribution of interest, i.e., the distribution of the number of consumer complaints received about a product per 10,000 units of the product sold. The variance and standard deviation of this distribution are measures of the variation in the number of consumer complaints received. Namias determined that this distribution was mound-shaped. Accordingly, it can be said that approximately 95% of the time the number of complaints about a product will be within 2 standard deviations of the mean number of complaints. It is upon this fact, as we shall see in Case Study 4.3, that Namias' procedure for determining when it would be worthwhile to conduct a search for specific causes of consumer complaints is founded.

If it could not have been determined that the distribution of the number of complaints was mound-shaped, it could only have been said that at least 75% of the time the number of complaints about a product will be within 2 standard deviations of the mean number of complaints.

EXERCISES

4.8. As a result of government pressure, automobile manufacturers in the United States are deeply involved in research to improve their products' gas mileage. One manufacturer, hoping to achieve 20 miles per gallon on one of its full-size models, measured the mileage obtained by thirty test versions of the model with the following results (rounded to the nearest mile for convenience):

20	20	22	21	20	17
18	21	21	18	20	21
19	21	19	23	21	20
25	19	22	17	21	24
20	17	16	19	18	20

a. If the manufacturer would be satisfied with a (population) mean of 20 miles per gallon, how would it react to the above test data?

b. Compute $\bar{x}$, s^2, and s for the data set.

c. What percentage of the measurements would you expect to find in the intervals $\bar{x} \pm s$, $\bar{x} \pm 2s$, and $\bar{x} \pm 3s$?

d. Count the number of measurements that actually fall within the intervals of part c and express each interval count as a percentage of the total number of measurements. Compare these results with the results of part c.

4.9. Refer to Example 4.5. Use Table 4.3 to check your calculation of s in Exercise 4.8.

4.10. Audience sizes at concerts given by the Jacksonville Symphony over the past 2 years were recorded and found to have a sample mean of 3,125 and a sample standard deviation of 25. Calculate $\bar{x} \pm s$, $\bar{x} \pm 2s$, and $\bar{x} \pm 3s$. What fraction of the recorded audience sizes of the past 2 years would be expected to fall in each of these intervals?

4.11. A manufacturer of citizen-band radios, disturbed because retailers were complaining that they were not receiving new shipments of radios as fast as they had been promised, decided to run a check on the current radio distribution network. Each of the fifty warehouses owned by the manufacturer throughout the country had been instructed to maintain at least 200 radios in stock at all times so that a supply would always be readily available for retailers. The manufacturer checked the inventories of twenty of these warehouses and obtained the following counts (number of radios in stock):

50	15	40	202	240
203	150	0	135	195
200	25	300	410	250
100	0	205	130	90

a. What is the mean number of radios in stock for the twenty warehouses checked?

b. Compute s^2 and s for the data set.

c. What percentage of the measurements would you expect to find in the intervals $\bar{x} \pm s$, $\bar{x} \pm 2s$, and $\bar{x} \pm 3s$?

d. Count the number of measurements that actually fall within the intervals of part c and express each interval count as a percentage of the total number of measurements. Compare these results with the results of part c.

4.12. Use Table 4.3 to check your calculation of s in Exercise 4.11.

4.13. If the frequency distribution of audience sizes in Exercise 4.10 were known to be mound-shaped, what fraction of the recorded audience sizes would be expected to fall within each of the intervals calculated in that exercise?

4.14. A producer of alkaline batteries was interested in obtaining a statistical description of the shelf-life of the battery it manufactures. Twenty-five batteries were selected at random as they came off the assembly line and their shelf-lives were tested. The following are the lifetimes of the twenty-five batteries rounded to the nearest month:

24	21	24	20	19
25	27	24	30	21
23	24	24	19	24
26	22	25	24	24
25	23	28	23	25

a. Compute $\bar{x}$, s^2, and s for this data set.

b. What percentage of the measurements would you expect to find in the intervals $\bar{x} \pm s$, $\bar{x} \pm 2s$, and $\bar{x} \pm 3s$?

c. Count the number of measurements that actually fall within the intervals of part b and express each interval count as a percentage of the total number of measurements. Compare these results with the results of part b.

4.15. Use Table 4.3 to check your calculation of s in Exercise 4.14.

4.16. Given a data set with a largest value of 900 and a smallest value of 50, what would you estimate the standard deviation to be? Explain the logic behind the procedure you used to estimate the standard deviation.

4.17. A boat dealer has determined that the frequency distribution of the number of outboard motor sales per month over the last 5 years is mound-shaped, with a sample mean of 25 and a sample variance of 4. Approximately what percentage of the recorded monthly sales figures of the past 5 years would be expected to fall above $\bar{x} + 2s$? Below $\bar{x} - 2s$? Above $\bar{x} + 3s$?

4.18. For each of the past 30 workdays Royal Imprints, Inc., has recorded the number of decorative felt placemats produced. The most produced in 1 day was 92; the least was 60. Estimate the standard deviation in number of placemats produced during the 30 day period.

**4.5
MEASURES OF
RELATIVE
STANDING**

As we have seen, numerical measures of central tendency and variability describe the general nature of a data set (either a sample or a population). We may also be interested in describing the relative quantitative location of a particular measurement within a data set. Descriptive measures of the relationship of a measurement to the rest of the data are called **measures of relative standing.**

One measure of relative standing is its **percentile ranking:**

DEFINITION 4.4

Let $x_1, x_2, \ldots, x_n$ be a set of n measurements arranged in order of magnitude. The *p*th **percentile** is a number x such that $p\%$ of the measurements fall below the *p*th percentile and $(100 - p)\%$ fall above it.

**FIGURE 4.7
RELATIVE FREQUENCY
DISTRIBUTION FOR
YEARLY SALES OF
OIL COMPANIES**

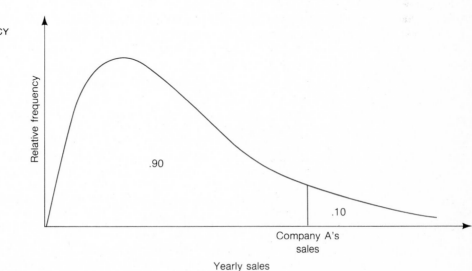

For example, if oil company A reports that its yearly sales are in the 90th percentile of all companies in the industry, the implication is that 90% of all oil companies have yearly sales less than company A's, with only 10% having yearly sales exceeding company A's. This is demonstrated in Figure 4.7.

Another measure of relative standing in popular use is the z-score. As you can see in Definition 4.5, the z-score makes use of the mean and standard deviation of the data set in order to specify the location of a measurement:

DEFINITION 4.5
The sample z-score for a measurement x is

$$z = \frac{x - \bar{x}}{s}$$

The population z-score for a measurement x is

$$z = \frac{x - \mu}{\sigma}$$

Note that the z-score is calculated by subtracting $\bar{x}$ (or μ) from the measurement x and then dividing the result by s (or σ). The final result, the z-score, represents the distance between a given measurement x and the mean expressed in standard deviations.

EXAMPLE 4.6   Suppose a sample of 200 steelworkers is taken, and the annual income of each is determined. The mean and standard deviation are

$$\bar{x} = \$14{,}000 \qquad s = \$2{,}000$$

Suppose Joe Smith's annual income is $12,000. What is his sample z-score?

Solution   Joe Smith's annual income lies below the mean income of the 200 steelworkers (Figure 4.8). We compute

$$z = \frac{x - \bar{x}}{s} = \frac{\$12{,}000 - \$14{,}000}{\$2{,}000} = -1.0$$

which tells us that Joe Smith's annual income is 1.0 standard deviation *below* the sample mean, or, in short, his sample z-score is -1.0.

The numerical value of the z-score reflects the relative standing of the measurement. A large positive z-score implies that the measurement is larger than almost all

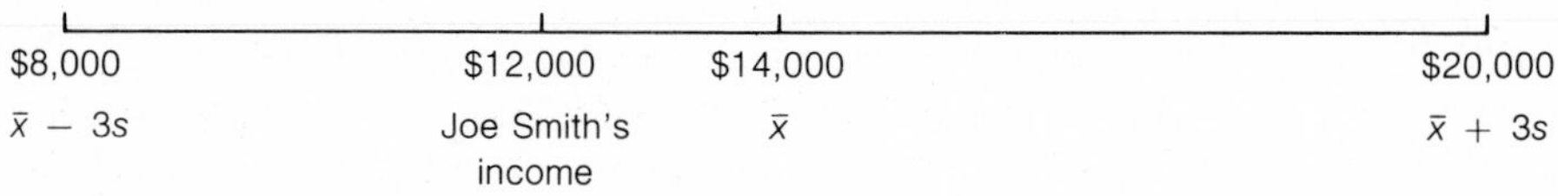

FIGURE 4.8
ANNUAL INCOME
OF STEELWORKERS

$8,000	$12,000	$14,000	$20,000
$\bar{x} - 3s$	Joe Smith's income	$\bar{x}$	$\bar{x} + 3s$

CHAPTER 4   NUMERICAL MEASURES OF VARIABILITY

other measurements, while a large negative z-score indicates that the measurement is smaller than almost every other measurement. If a z-score is 0 or near 0, the measurement is located in the midsection of the sample or population.

We can be more specific if we know that the frequency distribution of the measurements is mound-shaped. In this case, the following interpretation of the z-scores can be given:

INTERPRETATION OF z-SCORES FOR MOUND-SHAPED DISTRIBUTIONS OF DATA

1. Approximately 68% of the measurements will have a z-score between -1 and 1.
2. Approximately 95% of the measurements will have a z-score between -2 and 2.
3. All or almost all the measurements will have a z-score between -3 and 3.

Note that the above interpretation of z-scores is identical to that given in Table 4.3 for samples from mound-shaped distributions. The statement that a measurement falls in the interval $(\mu - \sigma)$ to $(\mu + \sigma)$ is identical to the statement that a measurement has a population z-score between -1 and 1, since all measurements between $(\mu - \sigma)$ and $(\mu + \sigma)$ are within 1 standard deviation of μ (see Figure 4.9).

We will end this section with an example that indicates how the z-scores may be used to accomplish our primary objective: the use of sample information to make inferences about the population.

FIGURE 4.9
POPULATION z-SCORES
FOR A MOUND-SHAPED
DISTRIBUTION

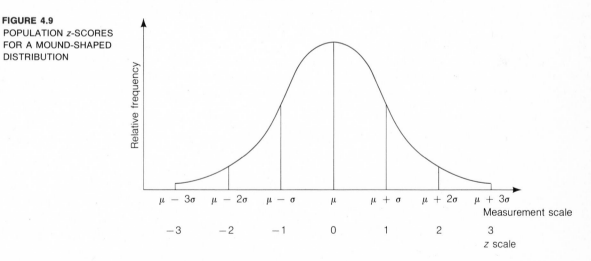

EXAMPLE 4.7

Suppose a female bank executive believes that her salary is low as a result of sex discrimination. To try to substantiate her belief, she collects information on the salaries of her male counterparts in the banking business. She finds a mean salary of

$17,000 with a standard deviation of $1,000. Her salary is $13,500. Does this information substantiate her claim of sex discrimination?

Solution

The analysis might proceed as follows: First, we calculate the z-score for the woman's salary with respect to the sample of her male counterparts. Thus,

$$z = \frac{\$13,500 - \$17,000}{\$1,000} = -3.5$$

The implication is that the woman's salary is 3.5 standard deviations *below* the mean of the male salary distribution. Furthermore, if a check of the male salary data shows that the frequency distribution is mound-shaped, we can infer that very few salaries in this distribution should have a z-score less than -3, as shown in Figure 4.10. Therefore, a z-score of -3.5 either represents a measurement from a distribution different from the male salary distribution, or it represents a very unusual (highly improbable) measurement for the male salary distribution.

   Well, which of the two situations do you think prevails? Do you think the woman's salary is simply an unusually low one in the distribution of salaries, or do you think her claim of salary discrimination is justified? Most people would probably conclude that her salary does not come from the male salary distribution. However, the careful investigator should require more information before inferring sex discrimination as the cause. We would want to know more about the sample collection technique the woman used, and more about her competence at her job. Also, perhaps other factors, like the length of employment, should be considered in the analysis.

   The above exemplifies an approach to statistical inference that might be called the rare event approach. An experimenter hypothesizes a specific frequency distribution to describe a population of measurements. Then a sample of measurements is drawn from the population. If the experimenter finds it unlikely that the sample came from the hypothesized distribution, the hypothesis is concluded to be false. Thus, in Example 4.7 the woman believes her salary reflects sex discrimination. She hypothesizes that her salary should be just another measurement in the distribution of her male counterparts' salaries if no discrimination exists. However, it was so unlikely

FIGURE 4.10
MALE SALARY
DISTRIBUTION

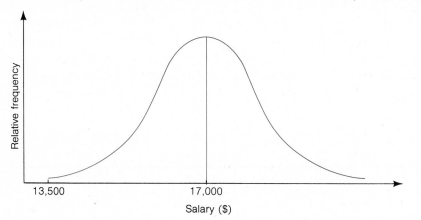

that the sample (in this case, her salary) came from the male frequency distribution that she rejects that hypothesis, concluding that the distribution from which her salary was drawn is different from the distribution for the males.

This rare event approach to inference-making will be further discussed in later chapters. Proper application of the approach requires a knowledge of probability, the subject of our next chapter.

CASE STUDY 4.3   Now we will finish the discussion begun in Case Study 4.2 of a method proposed by Jean Namias (1964) to determine when and when not to conduct a search for specific causes of consumer complaints.

The rate of consumer complaints about a product may change or vary as a result of merely chance or fate, or it may be due to some specific cause, such as a decline in the quality of the product. Concerning the former, Namias (1964) says:

> In any operation or production process, variability in the output or product will occur, and no two operational results may be expected to be exactly alike. Complete constancy of consumer rates of complaint is not possible, for the vagaries of fate and chance operate even within the most rigid framework of quality or operation control.

Namias provides a decision rule with which to determine when the observed variation in the rate of consumer complaints is due to chance and when it is due to specific causes. If the observed rate is 2 standard deviations or less away from the mean rate of complaint, it is attributed to chance. If the observed rate is farther than 2 standard deviations above the mean rate, it is attributed to a specific problem in the production or distribution of the product. The reasoning is that if there are no problems with the production and distribution of the product, 95% of the time the rate of complaint should be within 2 standard deviations of the mean rate. If the production and distribution process were operating normally, it would be very unlikely for a rate higher than 2 standard deviations above the mean to occur. Instead, it is more likely that the high complaint rate is caused by abnormal operation of the production and/or distribution process, i.e., something specific is wrong with the process.

Namias only recommends searching for the cause (or causes) if the observed variation in the rate of complaints is determined by the rule to be the result of a specific cause (or causes). The degree of variability due to chance must be tolerated. Namias says,

> As long as the results exhibit chance variability, the causes are common, and there is no need to attempt to improve the product by making specific changes. Indeed this may only create more variability, not less, and it may inject trouble where none existed, with waste of time and money . . . . On the other hand, time and money are again wasted through failure to recognize specific conditions when they arise. It is therefore economical to look for a specific cause when there is more variability than is expected on the basis of chance alone.

Namias collected data from the records of a beverage company for a 2 week period to demonstrate the effectiveness of the rule. Consumer complaints concerned primarily chipped bottles that looked dangerous. For one of the firm's brands the mean complaint rate was determined to be 26.01 and the rate 2 standard deviations above the mean was determined to be 48.78 complaints per 10,000 bottles sold. The complaint rate observed during the 2 weeks under study was 93.12 complaints per 10,000 bottles sold. Since 93.12 is many more than 2 standard deviations above the mean rate, it was concluded that the high rate of complaints must have been caused by some specific problem in the production or distribution of the particular brand of beverage and that a search for the problem would probably be worthwhile. The problem was traced to rough handling of the bottled beverage in the warehouse by newly hired workers. As a result, a training program for new workers was instituted.

EXERCISES

4.19. What do we mean by the 75th percentile of a quantitative data set?

4.20. What is another name for the 50th percentile?

4.21. In each of the following compute x's z-score and note whether your result is a sample z-score or a population z-score:

    a. $x = 20$, $s = 5$, $\bar{x} = 30$

    b. $x = 100$, $\mu = 99$, $\sigma = 2$

    c. $\mu = 45$, $\sigma = 5$, $x = 30$

    d. $x = 21$, $\bar{x} = 21$, $s = 3$

4.22. In 1975 Westinghouse Electric fell in the 96th percentile of the distribution of sales of the 500 largest industrial corporations (according to *Fortune** magazine's rankings). Explain how this locates Westinghouse in the sales distribution.

4.23. A parking lot owner's accountant determined the owner's receipts for each of 100 randomly chosen days from the past year. The mean and standard deviation for the 100 days were $310 and $20, respectively. Yesterday's receipts amounted to $370.

    a. Find the sample z-scores for yesterday's receipts.

    b. How many standard deviations away from the mean are yesterday's receipts?

    c. Would you consider yesterday's receipts to be unusually high? Why or why not?

4.24. Refer to Exercise 4.22. Northwestern Steel and Wire fell below the 10th percentile of the sales distribution. Explain how this locates Northwestern in the sales distribution.

4.25. The mean and standard deviation of the gross weekly income distribution of Royal Imprints' 120 employees were determined to be $170 and $10, respectively.

    a. Approximately what percentage of the employees would be expected to have incomes over $190 per week? Under $160 per week? Over $200 per week?

*''A Group Profile of the *Fortune* 500 Chief Executive.'' *Fortune,* May 1976.

b. If you were employed by Royal Imprints and your weekly income was $185, what would your z-score be and how many standard deviations would your salary be away from the mean salary?

4.26. The 1975 mean earnings per share, μ, for 500 firms in *Fortune's** list of the 500 largest industrial corporations is $2.96. The largest and smallest earnings per share figures among the 500 listed are $23.23 and $-$27.68, respectively.

a. Estimate σ, the standard deviation of the earnings per share distribution of the 500 firms.

b. Find the approximate z-score for each of the following firms' 1975 earnings per share figures:

Honeywell	$ 3.96
Getty Oil	13.71
Rath Packing	-5.49
Minnesota Mining and Manufacturing	2.29
Rockwell International	2.96
Chrysler	-4.33

c. Approximately how many standard deviations away from the mean are each of the earnings per share figures in part b?

4.27. It is known that the frequency distribution of the number of citizen-band radios sold each week by a large department store in Atlanta is mound-shaped with a mean of 35 and a variance of 9.

a. Approximately what percentage of the measurements in the frequency distribution should fall in the interval 32–38? 26–44?

b. If the z-score for last week's sales was -1.33, how many radios did the store sell?

c. If it is known that a rival department store has a mound-shaped frequency distribution of the number of citizen-band radios sold each week with a mean of 35 and a standard deviation of 2, for which store is it more likely that more than 41 radios will be sold in a week? Why?

4.28. Refer to Exercise 4.25. It is known that the weekly gross income distribution is mound-shaped.

a. Approximately what percentage of the employees would be expected to have incomes over $190 per week? Under $160 per week? Over $200 per week?

b. If you and a friend both worked at Royal Imprints and your income was $160 per week and hers was $195 per week, how many standard deviations apart are your two incomes?

c. If you randomly chose an employee of Royal Imprints, is it more likely that his or her gross income is over $190 per week or under $145 per week? Why?

*"A Group Profile of the *Fortune* 500 Chief Executive." *Fortune,* May 1976.

The numerical description of a set of data requires more than a measure of central tendency. The **variability** of the data set must also be described. The **range, absolute deviation, variance, and standard deviation** all represent numerical measures of variability. Of these, the variance and standard deviation are in most common use, especially when the ultimate objective is to make inferences about a population.

The mean and standard deviation may be used to make statements about the fraction of measurements in a given interval. For example, we know that at least 75% of the measurements in a data set will lie within 2 standard deviations of the mean. If the frequency distribution of the data set is mound-shaped, approximately 95% of the measurements will lie within 2 standard deviations of the mean.

Measures of relative standing provide still another dimension on which to describe a data set. The objective of these measures is to describe the location of a specific measurement relative to the rest of the data set. By doing so, you can construct a mental image of the relative frequency distribution. **Percentiles** and *z-scores* are important examples of measures of relative standing.

The **rare event** concept of statistical inference means that if the chance that a particular sample came from a hypothetical population is very small, we can either conclude that the sample is extremely rare or that the hypothesized population is not the one from which the sample was drawn. The more unlikely it is that the sample came from the hypothesized population, the more strongly we favor the conclusion that the hypothesized population is not the true one. We need to be able to assess accurately the rarity of a sample, and this requires a knowledge of probability, the subject of our next chapter.

SUPPLEMENTARY EXERCISES

4.29. Compute $\sum_{i=1}^{n} x_i^2$, $\sum_{i=1}^{n} x_i$, and $\left(\sum_{i=1}^{n} x_i\right)^2$ for each of the following data sets:

a.   10, 0, 1, 4, 5
b.   15, 15, 2, 6, 8
c.   −1, 2, 0, −4, −8, 10
d.   100, 0, 0, 1

4.30. Compute s^2 and s for each of the data sets in Exercise 4.29.

4.31. Compute s^2 for each of the following data sets:

a. $\sum_{i=1}^{n} x_i^2 = 246$, $\sum_{i=1}^{n} x_i = 45$, $n = 15$

b. $\sum_{i=1}^{n} x_i^2 = 543$, $\sum_{i=1}^{n} x_i = 106$, $n = 25$

c. $\sum_{i=1}^{n} x_i^2 = 65$, $\sum_{i=1}^{n} x_i = 9$, $n = 7$

4.32. For each of the following data sets, compute $\bar{x}$, s, and s^2:

a.   11, 2, 2, 1, 9
b.   22, 9, 21, 15

c. 1, 0, 1, 10, 11, 11, 0

d. 4, 4, 4, 4

4.33. For each of the following data sets, compute $\bar{x}$, s, and s^2:

a. 5, 6, 6, 5, 6, 5

b. -1, 4, -3, 0, -3, -1

c. $\frac{4}{5}$, 0.8, 0.4, $\frac{1}{5}$

4.34. What is the best measure of the variability of a quantitative data set? Why?

4.35. In reference to a measurement or observation, what is a measure of relative standing?

4.36. How does a z-score locate a measurement within a set of measurements? Explain in words.

4.37. One hundred management trainees were given an examination in basic accounting. Their test scores were found to have a mean and variance of 80 and 36, respectively.

a. Approximately what percentage of the test scores would be expected to fall in the interval 74–86?

b. If a grade of 68 was required to pass the test, approximately what percentage of the trainees would be expected to fail?

4.38. Rework Exercise 4.37 assuming that the distribution of test scores was determined to be mound-shaped.

4.39. The following is a list of the number of defective bottles produced by a particular bottle-making machine each hour during the last 10 hours:

2, 6, 4, 5, 8, 10, 1, 3, 6, 6

a. Determine the mean, median, mode, range, variance, and standard deviation of this data set.

b. Which of the measures in part a are measures of variability and which are measures of central tendency?

4.40. Refer to Example 4.5. As a check on your calculation of s in Exercise 4.39, use the range of the data in that exercise to approximate s.

4.41. Refer to Exercise 4.39. In what units is each of your answers to part a?

4.42. A sample of twenty economists were asked to project what the prime interest rate of a well-known New York bank would be at the start of the second quarter next year. The following are their projections:

0.07	0.06	0.06	0.11	0.08
0.09	0.11	0.09	0.09	0.08
0.07	0.07	0.07	0.07	0.09
0.07	0.07	0.10	0.08	0.06

Compute $\bar{x}$, s, and s^2 for this data set.

4.43. Refer to Exercise 4.42. What fraction of the projections would be expected to fall in the intervals $\bar{x} \pm s$, $\bar{x} \pm 2s$, and $\bar{x} \pm 3s$? Count the number of projections that in fact fall in these intervals and compare this count with the number that were expected.

4.44. Refer to Exercises 4.42 and 4.43. What is the z-score for a projection of 0.10?

4.45. The vice president in charge of sales for the conglomerate you work for has asked you to evaluate the sales records of two of the firm's divisions. You note that the range of monthly sales for division A over the last 2 years is $50,000 and the range for division B is only $30,000. You compute each division's mean monthly sales for the same time period and discover that both divisions have a mean of $110,000. Assume that is all the information you have about the division's sales records. Would you be willing to say which one of the divisions has a more consistent sales record? Why or why not?

4.46. Refer to Exercise 4.45. Estimate the standard deviation of the monthly sales distribution of division B.

4.47. Refer to Exercise 4.46. Based on your estimate of the monthly sales standard deviation of division B, would you say it is more likely that its sales next month will be over $120,000 or under $90,000?

4.48. Refer to Exercise 4.47. Is it possible for division B's sales next month to be over $160,000? Explain.

4.49. Philadelphia, Pennsylvania, falls in the 34th percentile of the population distribution of the world's 130 largest cities.* Describe Philadelphia's location within the population distribution.

4.50. The manufacturers of an amazing new gadget claim in an advertisement for sales personnel that their first-year salespeople earn an average of $25,000. You call their main office and demand to know the standard deviation of first-year salespeople's incomes. The assistant personnel manager's secretary tells you the standard deviation is $6,000. What can be said about the fraction of the manufacturer's salespeople who make between $7,000 and $43,000 during their first year?

4.51. Refer to Exercise 4.50. If we assume that the first-year salespeople's salaries have a mound-shaped frequency distribution, what percentage of the salespeople would you expect to make more than $37,000 during the first year? Less than $25,000?

4.52. Refer to Exercise 4.50. After graduating from school you become one of the manufacturer's salespeople. During your first year on the road you make only $4,000, and you decide to complain to the company by writing a letter. Which of the statements below would be valid and could be used in your letter? Explain why they are valid. If any of the statements are invalid, explain why they are invalid.

    a. Since the probability of a first-year salesperson making only $4,000 is so small (according to the data, μ and σ, given by the company), my lack of success proves conclusively that your company has made false advertising claims or has made an error.

    b. My first-year sales, although not great, are typical of first-year salespeople.

*According to *Reader's Digest 1975 Almanac and Yearbook*.

c.   Since the probability of making this little money is so small, it might be that your company has made an error in the calculation of μ and/or σ.

d.   Another way to explain my lack of success is that I might be one of those extremely few salespeople who are not successful in their first year.

e.   According to the information given and Table 4.3, the fraction of people whose sales are $4,000 or under is exactly $\frac{1}{9}$.

f.   It could be that σ, the population standard deviation, is actually much smaller than $6,000 (i.e., $\mu = \$25,000$, but σ is much smaller than $6,000).

4.53.   Refer to Exercise 4.50. Suppose your income was $40,000 a year. Use a z-score to locate your income in the distribution of first-year salespeople's incomes.

4.54.   Refer to Exercise 4.50. Suppose the income z-score of one of the first-year salespeople was 2.5. What was the person's income?

4.55.   Compute the range for each of the data sets in Exercise 4.32.

4.56.   A local automobile dealer pays $2,500 for a particular model car, will not sell it to a customer for less than $2,900, and, as a result of competition across the street, cannot sell it for more than $3,300. If the dealer sells ten cars of this particular model, what is the range within which his total profit from the ten cars sold can fall?

4.57.   Suppose you used the following formula as a measure of the variability (V) of a data set:

$$V = \frac{\sum\limits_{i=1}^{n}(x_i - \bar{x})}{n}$$

What information can be learned about the variability of a data set using this formula? Using the data of Exercise 4.29, find V.

4.58.   Many firms use on-the-job training to teach their employees computer programming. Suppose you work in the Personnel Department of a firm that just finished training a group of its employees to program and you have been requested to review the performance of one of the trainees on the final test that was given to all trainees. The mean and standard deviation of the test scores are 80 and 5, respectively, and the distribution of scores is mound-shaped.

a.   The employee in question scored 65 on the final test. Compute the employee's z-score.

b.   Approximately what percentage of the trainees will have z-scores equal to or less than the employee of part a?

c.   If a trainee were arbitrarily selected from those who had taken the final test, is it more likely that he or she would score 90 or above, or 65 or below?

4.59.   Chebyshev's theorem (mentioned in Table 4.3) states that at least $1 - (1/K^2)$ of a set of measurements will lie within K standard deviations of the mean of the data set. Use Chebyshev's theorem to state the fraction of a set of measurements that will lie within

a.   2 standard deviations of the mean μ ($K = 2$)

b.   3 standard deviations of the mean

c.   1.5 standard deviations of the mean

4.60. Seven workdays were sampled in June and the number of machine break-downs per day in the woodworking shop of a furniture company were recorded. This procedure was repeated in August after the firm had replaced ten of its oldest machines. The data are listed here.

JUNE	AUGUST
8	0
3	3
0	4
0	11
10	3
4	3
9	2

a. Which month exhibits more variability in the number of machines that break down per day as measured by the range? As measured by s^2? In this case, which measure, s^2 or the range, do you feel better represents the variability of the data sets? Explain.

b. Add 3 to each of the numbers of breakdowns per day in June and re-compute s^2 for June. Compare your result with that obtained in part a. What is the effect on s^2 of adding a constant to each of the sample measurements?

c. Multiply each of the numbers of breakdowns per day in June by 3 and recompute s^2 for June. Compare your result with that obtained in part a. What is the effect on s^2 of multiplying each sample measurement by a constant?

ON YOUR OWN . . .

1. Find the variance, standard deviation, and range of the quantitative data set you found for the "On Your Own" section in Chapter 2.

2. Use Table 4.3 to describe the distribution of this data set.

3. Count the actual number of observations that fall within 1, 2, and 3 standard deviations of the mean of the data set and compare these counts with the description of the data set you developed above.

REFERENCES

Hamburg, M. *Statistical analysis for decision making.* 2d ed. New York: Harcourt Brace Jovanovich, 1977. Chapter 1.

Huntsberger, D. V., Billingsley, P., & Croft, D. J. *Statistical inference for management and economics.* Boston: Allyn and Bacon, 1975. Chapter 3.

Mendenhall, W., & Reinmuth, J. E. *Statistics for management and economics.* 2d ed. North Scituate, Mass.: Duxbury, 1974. Chapter 3.

Milkovich, G. T., Annoni, A. J., & Mahoney, T. A. "The use of the delphi procedures in manpower forecasting." *Management Science,* Dec. 1972, *19,* Part I, 381–388.

Namias, J. "A method to detect specific causes of consumer complaints." *Journal of Marketing Research,* Aug. 1964, 63–68.

We identified inference from a sample to a population as the goal of statistics, and then, in Chapters 2–4, we considered how an inference about a population may be phrased. To do this, we had to be able to describe a set of measurements using graphical and numerical descriptive methods.

WHERE WE'RE GOING . . .
Now that we know how to phrase an inference about a population, we turn to the problem of making the inference. What is it that permits us to make the inferential jump from sample to population and then to give a measure of reliability for the inference? As you will subsequently see, the answer is *probability*. This chapter is devoted to a study of probability—what it is and some of the basic concepts of the theory that surrounds it.

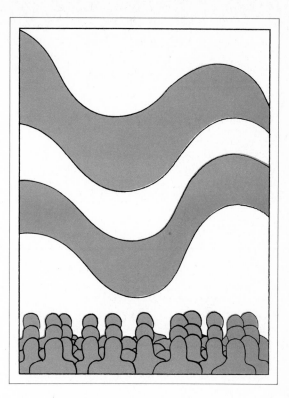

5
PROBABILITY

You will recall that statistics is concerned with decisions about a population based on sample information. Understanding how this will be accomplished is easier if you understand the relationship between population and sample. This understanding is enhanced by reversing the statistical procedure of making inferences from sample to population. In this chapter we assume the population *known* and calculate the chances of obtaining various samples from the population. Thus, probability is the "reverse" of statistics: In probability we use the population information to infer the probable nature of the sample.

Probability plays an important role in decision-making. To illustrate, suppose you have an opportunity to invest in an oil exploration company. Past records show that for ten out of ten previous oil drillings (a sample of the company's experiences), all ten resulted in dry wells. What do you conclude? Do you think the chances are better than 50–50 that the company will hit a producing well? Should you invest in this company? We think your answer to these questions will be an emphatic "No." If the company's exploratory prowess is sufficient to hit a producing well 50% of the time, a record of ten dry wells out of ten drilled is an event that is just too **improbable.** Do you agree?

As another illustration, suppose you are playing poker with what your opponents assure you is a well-shuffled deck of cards. In three consecutive 5 card hands, the person on your right is dealt 4 aces. Based on this sample of three deals, do you think the cards are being adequately shuffled? Again, we think your answer will be "No" and that you will reach this conclusion because dealing three hands of 4 aces is just too **improbable** assuming that the cards were properly shuffled.

Note that the decisions concerning the potential success of the oil drilling company and the decision concerning the card shuffling were both based on probabilities, namely the probabilities of certain sample results. Both situations were contrived so that you could easily conclude that the probabilities of the sample results were small. Unfortunately, the probabilities of many observed sample results are not so easy to evaluate. For these cases we will need the assistance of a theory of probability.

**5.1
EVENTS,
SAMPLE SPACES,
AND PROBABILITY**

All or most of the sets of data that are of interest to the business community are generated by some **experiment:**

> **DEFINITION 5.1**
> An **experiment** is the process of making an observation or taking a measurement.

Our definition of experiment is broader than that used in the physical sciences, where we might picture test-tubes, microscopes, etc. Examples of statistical experiments in business are recording whether a customer prefers one of two brands of coffee (say, brand A or brand B), measuring the change in the Dow Jones Average from one day to the next, recording the weekly sales of a business firm, and counting the number of errors on a page of an accountant's ledger.

An experimental outcome is called an event:

DEFINITION 5.2

An event is an outcome of the experiment.

Thus, if the experiment is to observe the up face following the toss of a die, three examples of events are observing an even number, observing a number less than 4, and observing a 6. If the experiment is counting the number of errors on a page of an accountant's ledger, three examples of events are observing no errors, observing less than five errors, and observing more than ten errors. Our goal is to be able to calculate the probability that a particular event occurs when an experiment is performed.

The calculation of event probabilities is made easier by listing the most basic outcomes of the experiment:

DEFINITION 5.3

A simple event is an event that cannot be decomposed into two or more other events.

In Table 5.1 we present three examples of experiments and their simple events. We will commence with simple coin and dice examples because they are most likely

TABLE 5.1
EXPERIMENTS AND THEIR SIMPLE EVENTS

a. Experiment: Observe the up face on a coin
Simple events: 1. Observe a head
2. Observe a tail
b. Experiment: Observe the up face on a die
Simple events: 1. Observe a 1
2. Observe a 2
3. Observe a 3
4. Observe a 4
5. Observe a 5
6. Observe a 6
c. Experiment: Observe the up faces on two coins
Simple events: 1. Observe H_1, H_2
2. Observe H_1, T_2
3. Observe T_1, H_2
4. Observe T_1, T_2
(where H_1 means "Head on coin 1," H_2 means "Head on coin 2," etc.)

to be familiar to you. Experiment a in Table 5.1 is to observe the result of the toss of a single coin. You will undoubtedly agree that the most basic possible outcomes of this experiment are Observe a head and Observe a tail. Experiment b in Table 5.1 is to observe the result of tossing a single die. Note that the events Observe a 1, Observe a 2, etc., cannot be further decomposed into more basic events. Therefore, they are simple events. However, the event Observe an even number can be decomposed into Observe a 2, Observe a 4, and Observe a 6. Thus, Observe an even number is not a simple event. The reasoning is similar for experiment c in Table 5.1.

Simple events possess an important property. If the experiment is conducted once, you can observe one and only one simple event. For example, if you toss a coin and observe a head, you cannot observe a tail on the same toss. If you toss a die and observe a 2, you cannot also observe a 6. Such events are said to be **mutually exclusive.** That is, for a single experiment, only one of the simple events can occur. To demonstrate that this property does not hold for all events, consider the event Observe an even number. It is possible for us to Observe an even number *and* Observe a 2 on the same toss.

The collection of all the simple events of an experiment is called the **sample space:**

DEFINITION 5.4
The **sample space** of an experiment is the collection of all its simple events.

For example, there are six simple events associated with experiment b in Table 5.1. This set of six simple events comprise the sample space for the experiment. Similarly, for experiment c in Table 5.1, there are four simple events in the sample space.

A graphical method, called the **Venn diagram,** is useful for presenting the sample space and its simple events. The sample space is shown as a closed figure, labeled S. This figure contains a set of points, called **sample points,** with each point representing a simple event. Figure 5.1 shows the Venn diagram for each of the three experiments in Table 5.1. Note that the number of sample points in a sample space S is equal to the number of simple events associated with the respective experiment: two for experiment a, six for experiment b, and four for experiment c.

Now that we have defined the terms *simple event* and *sample space,* we are prepared to define the **probabilities of simple events.** The probability of a simple event is a number that measures the likelihood that the event will occur when the experiment is performed. This number is usually taken to be the relative frequency of the occurrence of a simple event in a very long series of repetitions of an experiment. Or, when this information is not available, we select the number based upon experience. For example, if we are assigning probabilities to the two simple events in the coin toss experiment (Observe a head and Observe a tail), we might reason that if we toss a balanced coin a very large number of times, the simple events Observe a head and Observe a tail will occur with the same relative frequency of .5. Thus, the probability of each simple event is .5.

FIGURE 5.1
VENN DIAGRAMS FOR
THE THREE
EXPERIMENTS FROM
TABLE 5.1

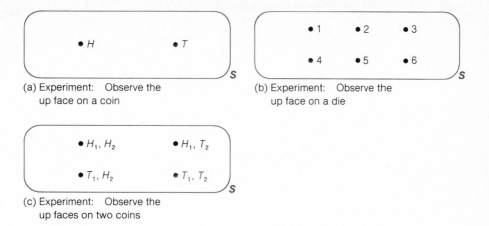

(a) Experiment: Observe the
up face on a coin

(b) Experiment: Observe the
up face on a die

(c) Experiment: Observe the
up faces on two coins

In other cases we may choose the probability based on general information about the experiment. For example, if the experiment is observing whether a business venture succeeds or fails (the simple events), we may assess the probability of success by considering the personnel managing the venture, the general state of the economy at the time, the success of similar ventures, and any other information deemed pertinent.* If we finally decide that the venture has an 80% chance of succeeding, we assign a probability of .8 to the simple event Success. We hope that .8 is a reasonably accurate measure of the likelihood of the occurrence of the simple event Success. If it is not, we may be misled on any decisions based on this probability or based on any calculations in which it appears.

No matter how you assign the probabilities to simple events, the probabilities assigned must obey two rules:

---

1. All simple event probabilities *must* lie in the interval 0–1. (Of course, a simple event probability *may* be equal to 0 or equal to 1.)
2. The probabilities of all the simple events within a sample space must sum to 1.

To find the probability of any event, you should recall that an event is any outcome of an experiment. Let us examine this statement in greater detail. Consider the die tossing experiment and the event Observe an even number. Notice that you could just as easily define this event by saying "Observe a 2, Observe a 4, or Observe a 6," since the event will occur if and only if one of these three simple events occurs. Consequently, you can think of the event Observe an even number as the collection of the three simple events Observe a 2, Observe a 4, and Observe a 6. This event, which we will denote by the symbol A, can be represented in a Venn diagram by a closed figure

*For a text that deals in detail with subjective evaluation of probabilities, see Winkler (1972).

FIGURE 5.2
DIE TOSS EXPERIMENT
WITH EVENT
A = OBSERVE AN
EVEN NUMBER

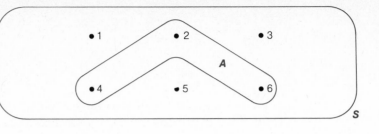

inside the sample space S. This closed figure A will contain the simple events that comprise event A, as shown in Figure 5.2.

To summarize, we have demonstrated that an event can be defined in words or it can be defined as a specific set of simple events. This leads us to the following definition of an event:

DEFINITION 5.5
An event is a specific collection of simple events.

How do you decide which simple events belong to the set associated with an event A? Test each simple event in the sample space S. If event A occurs when a particular simple event occurs, then that simple event is in the event A. For example, in the die toss experiment, the event Observe an even number (event A) will occur if the simple event Observe a 2 occurs. By the same reasoning, the simple events Observe a 4 and Observe a 6 are in event A.

Now return to our original objective—finding the probability of any event. Consider the problem of finding the probability of observing an even number (event A) in the single toss of a die. You will recall that A will occur if one of the three simple events, toss a 2, 4, or 6, occurs. Since two or more simple events cannot occur at the same time, we can easily calculate the probability of event A by summing the probabilities of the three simple events. We would attach a probability equal to $\frac{1}{6}$ to each of the simple events (if the die is fair), so the probability of observing an even number (event A), denoted by the symbol $P(A)$, would be

$$P(A) = P(\text{Observe a 2}) + P(\text{Observe a 4}) + P(\text{Observe a 6})$$

$$= \frac{1}{6} + \frac{1}{6} + \frac{1}{6} = \frac{1}{2}$$

This example leads us to a general procedure for finding the probability of an event A:

The probability of an event A is calculated by summing the probabilities of the simple events in A.

CHAPTER 5 PROBABILITY

Thus, we can summarize the steps for calculating the probability of any event:*

STEPS FOR CALCULATING PROBABILITIES OF EVENTS

1. Define the experiment.
2. List the simple events.
3. Assign probabilities to the simple events.
4. Determine the collection of simple events contained in the event of interest.
5. Sum the simple event probabilities to get the event probability.

EXAMPLE 5.1

Consider the experiment of tossing two coins. Assume both coins are fair:

a. List the simple events and assign them reasonable probabilities.
b. Consider the events

$$A = \{\text{Observe exactly one head}\} \qquad B = \{\text{Observe at least one head}\}$$

and calculate $P(A)$ and $P(B)$.

Solution

a. The simple events are

$$H_1, H_2 \qquad H_1, T_2 \qquad T_1, H_2 \qquad T_1, T_2$$

where H_1 denotes Observe a head on coin 1, H_2 denotes Observe a head on coin 2, etc. If both coins are fair, we can again use the concept of relative frequency in a long series of experimental repetitions to conclude that each simple event should be assigned a probability of $1/4$.

b. We use a Venn diagram to show the events $A = \{\text{Observe exactly one head}\}$ and $B = \{\text{Observe at least one head}\}$ (Figure 5.3). Then, we may calculate the probabilities by adding the appropriate simple event probabilities:

$$P(A) = P(H_1, T_2) + P(T_1, H_2) = \frac{1}{4} + \frac{1}{4} = \frac{1}{2}$$

$$P(B) = P(H_1, H_2) + P(H_1, T_2) + P(T_1, H_2) = \frac{1}{4} + \frac{1}{4} + \frac{1}{4} = \frac{3}{4}$$

FIGURE 5.3
VENN DIAGRAM OF
THE TWO-COIN TOSS

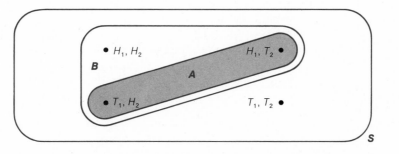

*A thorough treatment of this topic can be found in the text by W. Feller (1957).

EXAMPLE 5.2   A bank wishes to divide its service windows into two groups corresponding to the type of customer account: commercial or personal. One problem facing the bank is deciding how to apportion the service windows to the categories of service. At this stage of our study, we do not have the tools to solve this problem, but we can say that one of the important factors affecting the solution is the proportion of the two types of customers that enter the bank at a particular time. To illustrate, what is the probability that an incoming customer will have a commercial account? What is the probability that the next two customers will have commercial accounts? What is the probability for the general case of k customers? Explain how you might attempt to solve this problem. [*Note:* For this example we use the term *customer* to refer only to people who seek teller service.]

Solution   The experiment corresponding to the entrance of a single customer is identical to the coin tossing experiment illustrated in Figure 5.1(a). A customer has either a commercial (consider this a head) or a personal (consider this a tail) account, and there are no other possible outcomes. Consequently, there are two simple events corresponding to the sample space:

Experiment: Observe the type of account a single customer has
Simple events: 1. $C = \{$The customer has a commercial account$\}$
2. $P = \{$The customer has a personal account$\}$

The difference between this problem and the coin tossing problem becomes apparent when we attempt to assign probabilities to the two simple events. What probability should we assign to the simple event C? Some people might say .5, as for the coin tossing experiment, but you can see that finding the probability of simple event C, $P(C)$, is not so easy. Suppose that a check of the bank's records showed that 95% of their accounts were personal. Then, at first glance, it would appear that $P(C)$ is .05. But this may not be correct, because the probability will depend upon how frequently the two types of customers use the accounts—i.e., how many times per week, on the average, they seek banking service. So, the important point to note is that here is a case where equal probabilities are not assigned to the simple events. How can we find these probabilities? A good procedure might be to monitor the system for a period of time, and ask incoming customers which type of service they desire. Then the proportions of the two types of customers could be used to approximate the probabilities of the two simple events.

The experiment corresponding to the entrance of the next two customers is identical to the experiment of Example 5.1, tossing two coins, except that the probability that a single customer possesses a commerical account is not .5. We will learn how to find the probabilities of the simple events for this experiment, or for the general case of k customers, in Section 5.5.

EXAMPLE 5.3   You have the capital to invest in two of four ventures, each of which requires approximately the same amount of investment capital. Unknown to you, two of the investments will eventually fail and two will be successful. You research the four ventures because you think that your research should increase your probability of a successful choice over a purely random selection, and eventually decide on two. What is the lower limit of your probability of selecting the two best out of four? That is, if you used no information and selected two ventures at random, what is the probability that you would select the two successful ventures? At least one?

Solution

Denote the two successful enterprises as S_1 and S_2 and the two failing enterprises as F_1 and F_2. The experiment involves a random selection of two out of the four ventures and each possible pair of ventures represents a simple event. The six simple events that make up the sample space are

1. S_1, S_2 4. S_2, F_1
2. S_1, F_1 5. S_2, F_2
3. S_1, F_2 6. F_1, F_2

The next step is to assign probabilities to the simple events. If we assume that the choice of any one pair is as likely as any other, then the probability of each simple event is $\frac{1}{6}$. Now check to see which simple events result in the choice of two successful ventures. Only one such simple event exists, namely, S_1, S_2. Therefore, the probability of choosing two successful ventures out of the four is

$$P(S_1, S_2) = \frac{1}{6}$$

The event of selecting at least one of the two successful ventures includes all the simple events except F_1, F_2.

$P(\text{Select at least one success})$

$$= P(S_1, S_2) + P(S_1, F_1) + P(S_1, F_2) + P(S_2, F_1) + P(S_2, F_2)$$

$$= \frac{1}{6} + \frac{1}{6} + \frac{1}{6} + \frac{1}{6} + \frac{1}{6} = \frac{5}{6}$$

Therefore, the worst that you could do in selecting two ventures out of four may not be too bad. The probability of selecting two successful ventures will be at least $\frac{1}{6}$ and the probability of selecting at least one successful venture out of two is at least $\frac{5}{6}$.

The preceding examples have one thing in common: The number of simple events in each of the sample spaces was small and hence the simple events were easy to identify and list. How can we manage this when the simple events run into the thousands or millions? For example, suppose you sample five people from a group of 1,000. Then each different sample of five people would represent a simple event. How can you determine the number of simple events associated with this sampling experiment?

One method of determining the number of simple events for a complex experiment is to develop a counting system. Start by examining a simple version of the experiment. For example, see if you can develop a system for counting the number of samples of two people from a total of four (this is exactly what was done in Example

5.3). If the people are represented by the symbols C_1, C_2, C_3, and C_4, the simple events could be listed in the following pattern:

$$C_1, C_2 \qquad C_2, C_3 \qquad C_3, C_4$$
$$C_1, C_3 \qquad C_2, C_4$$
$$C_1, C_4$$

Note the pattern and now try a more complex situation, say, sampling three people out of five. List the simple events and observe the pattern. Finally, see if you can deduce the pattern for the general case. Perhaps you can program a computer to produce the matching and counting for the number of samples of five selected from a total of 1,000.

A second method of determining the number of simple events for an experiment is to use **combinatorial mathematics**. This branch of mathematics is concerned with developing counting rules for given situations. For example, there is a simple rule for finding the number of different samples of five people selected from 1,000. This rule is given by the formula

$$\binom{N}{n} = \frac{N!}{n!(N-n)!}$$

where N is the number of elements in the population; n is the number of elements in the sample; and the factorial symbol (!) means that, say, $n! = n(n-1)(n-2)\cdots 3 \cdot 2 \cdot 1$. Thus, $5! = 5 \cdot 4 \cdot 3 \cdot 2 \cdot 1$. (The quantity 0! is defined to be equal to 1.)

EXAMPLE 5.4

Find the number of different samples when selecting two elements from a group of four.

Solution

For this example, $N = 4$, $n = 2$, and

$$\binom{4}{2} = \frac{4!}{2!2!} = \frac{4 \cdot 3 \cdot 2 \cdot 1}{(2 \cdot 1)(2 \cdot 1)} = 6$$

You can see that this agrees with the number of simple events obtained above and in Example 5.3.

EXAMPLE 5.5

Suppose that you plan to invest equal amounts of money in each of five common stocks. If you have chosen twenty stocks from which to make the selection, how many different samples of five stocks can be selected from the twenty?

Solution

For this example, $N = 20$ and $n = 5$. Then the number of different samples of five that can be selected from the twenty stocks is

$$\binom{20}{5} = \frac{20!}{5!(20-5)!} = \frac{20!}{5!15!}$$

$$= \frac{20 \cdot 19 \cdot 18 \cdots 3 \cdot 2 \cdot 1}{(5 \cdot 4 \cdot 3 \cdot 2 \cdot 1)(15 \cdot 14 \cdot 13 \cdots 3 \cdot 2 \cdot 1)} = 15,504$$

The symbol $\binom{N}{n}$, meaning the number of combinations of N elements taken n at a time, is just one of a large number of counting rules that have been developed by combinatorial mathematicians. If you are interested in learning more about combinatorial mathematics, you will find a few of the basic counting rules in Appendix A. Others can be found in the reference books listed at the end of this chapter.

EXERCISES

5.1. If the experiment is Observe the direction of the change in price of IBM stock at the close of business tomorrow relative to its price today, list the simple events.

5.2. A cigarette manufacturer has decided to market two new brands. An analysis of current market conditions and a review of the firm's past successes and failures with new brands has led the manufacturer to believe that the probability of a new brand succeeding (i.e., turning a profit) in its first year is .4. Thus, the simple events and the probabilities of their occurrence in this marketing experiment are as follows ($S_1 = $ Brand 1 succeeds, $F_1 = $ Brand 1 fails, etc.):

SIMPLE EVENTS	PROBABILITIES
S_1, S_2	.16
S_1, F_2	.24
F_1, S_2	.24
F_1, F_2	.36

Find the probability of each of the following events:

$A = \{$Both new brands are successful in the first year$\}$

$B = \{$At least one new brand is successful in the first year$\}$

5.3. A buyer for a large metropolitan department store must choose two firms from the four available to supply the store's fall line of men's slacks. The buyer has not dealt with any of the four firms before and considers their products equally attractive. Unknown to the buyer, two of the four firms are having serious financial problems that may result in their not being able to deliver the fall line of slacks as soon as promised. If the probability of the buyer selecting a particular firm from among the four is the same for each firm, the following are the simple events and their probabilities for this buying experiment ($G_1 = $ Firm 1 in good financial condition, $P_1 = $ Firm 1 in poor financial condition, etc.):

SIMPLE EVENTS	PROBABILITIES
G_1, G_2	$\frac{1}{6}$
G_1, P_1	$\frac{1}{6}$
G_1, P_2	$\frac{1}{6}$
G_2, P_1	$\frac{1}{6}$
G_2, P_2	$\frac{1}{6}$
P_1, P_2	$\frac{1}{6}$

Find the probability of each of the following events:

A = {Buyer selects two firms in good financial condition}

B = {Buyer selects at least one firm in poor financial condition}

5.4. A firm's accounting department claims the firm will make a profit in the first quarter of the year in one of the following ranges, with probability as noted:

PROFIT RANGE ($)	PROBABILITY
Under 75,000	.10
75,000–99,999	.15
100,000–124,999	.25
125,000–149,999	.35
150,000–174,999	.10
175,000 or over	.05

Find the probability of each of the following events:

A = {The firm makes $99,999 or less}

B = {The firm makes over $149,999}

C = {The firm makes between $100,000 and $149,999}

5.5. Suppose you are assigned to study the automobile traffic patterns on an interstate highway. You plan to observe the next six cars passing your observation point and record the state for which they are licensed. Describe the sample space for your experiment.

5.6. What specific information would you need to help you assess the probability that the Consumer Price Index will rise next month?

**5.2
COMPOUND
EVENTS**

Events can often be viewed as a composition of two or more other events. These events, called **compound events,** can be formed (composed) in two ways.

DEFINITION 5.6
The **union** of two events A and B is the event that occurs if either A or B or both occur on a single performance of the experiment. We will denote the union of events A and B by the symbol $A \cup B$.

DEFINITION 5.7
The **intersection** of two events A and B is the event that occurs if both A and B occur on a single performance of the experiment. We will write $A \cap B$ for the intersection of events A and B.

EXAMPLE 5.6   Consider the die toss experiment. Define the following events:

$$A = \{\text{Toss an even number}\}$$
$$B = \{\text{Toss a number less than or equal to 3}\}$$

a. Describe $A \cup B$ for this experiment.

b. Describe $A \cap B$ for this experiment.

c. Calculate $P(A \cup B)$ and $P(A \cap B)$ assuming the die is fair.

Solution

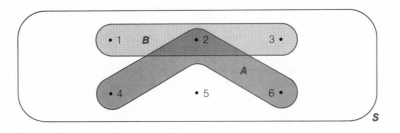

a. The union of A and B is the event that occurs if we observe either an even number, a number less than or equal to 3, or both on a single throw of the die. Consequently, the simple events in the event $A \cup B$ are those for which A occurs, B occurs, or both A and B occur. Testing the simple events in the entire sample space, we find that the collection of simple events in the union of A and B is

$$A \cup B = \{1, 2, 3, 4, 6\}$$

b. The intersection of A and B is the event that occurs if we observe **both** an even number and a number less than or equal to 3 on a single throw of the die. Testing the simple events to see which imply the occurrence of **both** events A and B, we see that the intersection contains only one simple event:

$$A \cap B = \{2\}$$

In other words, the intersection of A and B is the simple event Observe a 2.

c. Recalling that the probability of an event is the sum of the simple events of which the event is composed, we have

$$P(A \cup B) = P(1) + P(2) + P(3) + P(4) + P(6)$$
$$= \frac{1}{6} + \frac{1}{6} + \frac{1}{6} + \frac{1}{6} + \frac{1}{6} = \frac{5}{6}$$

and

$$P(A \cap B) = P(2) = \frac{1}{6}$$

5.3 COMPLEMENTARY EVENTS

A very useful concept in the calculation of event probabilities is the notion of complementary events:

DEFINITION 5.8
The **complement** of any event A is the event that A does not occur. We will denote the complement of A by A^c.

FIGURE 5.4
VENN DIAGRAM OF COMPLEMENTARY EVENTS

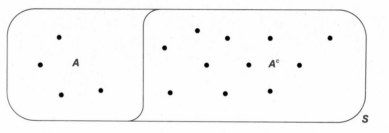

Since an event A is a collection of simple events, the simple events included in A^c are just those that are not in A. Figure 5.4 demonstrates this. You will note from the figure that all simple events in S are included in *either* A or A^c, and that *no* simple event is in both A and A^c. This leads us to conclude that the probabilities of an event and its complement must sum to 1:

The sum of the probabilities of complementary events equals 1, i.e.,

$$P(A) + P(A^c) = 1$$

In many probability problems it will be easier to calculate the probability of the complement of the event of interest rather than the event itself. Then, since

$$P(A) + P(A^c) = 1$$

we can calculate $P(A)$ by using the relationship

$$P(A) = 1 - P(A^c)$$

EXAMPLE 5.7

Consider the experiment of tossing two fair coins. Calculate the probability of event $A = \{$Observing at least one head$\}$ by using the complementary relationship.

Solution

We know that the event $A = \{$Observing at least one head$\}$ consists of the simple events

$$A = \{H_1, H_2; \quad H_1, T_2; \quad T_1, H_2\}$$

FIGURE 5.5
COMPLEMENTARY
EVENTS IN THE TOSS
OF TWO COINS

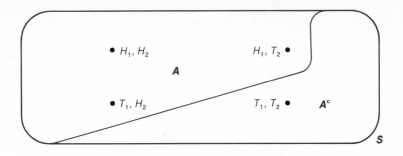

The complement of A is defined as the event that occurs when A does not occur. Therefore,

$$A^c = \{\text{Observe no heads}\} = \{T_1, T_2\}.$$

This complementary relationship is shown in Figure 5.5. Assuming the coins are balanced,

$$P(A^c) = P(T_1, T_2) = \frac{1}{4}$$

and

$$P(A) = 1 - P(A^c) = 1 - \frac{1}{4} = \frac{3}{4}$$

EXERCISES

5.7. a. Give an example of a compound event that is the union of two or more events.
  b. Give an example of a compound event that is the intersection of two events.
  c. Give an example of a compound event that is also a simple event.

5.8. Three coins are tossed and the following events are defined:

$A = \{\text{Observe exactly one head}\}$
$B = \{\text{Observe exactly two heads}\}$
$C = \{\text{Observe exactly two tails}\}$

Assume that the coins are balanced. Then calculate the following probabilities by summing the probabilities of the appropriate simple events:

  a. $P(A \cup B)$ b. $P(A \cap B)$ c. $P(A \cap C)$ d. $P(B \cap C)$

5.9. After completing an inventory of three warehouses, a golf club shaft manufacturer described its stock of 12,246 shafts with the following percentages:

		TYPE OF SHAFT		
		Regular	Stiff	Extra stiff
	#1	19%	8%	3%
WAREHOUSE	#2	14%	8%	2%
	#3	28%	18%	0

Suppose a shaft is selected at random from the 12,246 currently in stock and the warehouse number and type of shaft are observed.

    a. List all the simple events for this experiment.
    b. What is the set of all simple events called?
    c. Let C be the event that the shaft selected is from warehouse #3. Find $P(C)$ by summing the probabilities of the simple events in C.
    d. Let F be the event that the shaft chosen is an extra stiff type. Find $P(F)$.
    e. Let A be the event that the shaft selected is from warehouse #1. Find $P(A)$.
    f. Let D be the event that the shaft selected is a regular type. Find $P(D)$.
    g. Let E be the event that the shaft selected is a stiff type. Find $P(E)$.

5.10. The athletic ticket office at the University of Minnesota described the 30,000 tickets remaining for the Gopher's final two home games with the following table of percentages:

		SEATING AREA		
		East side	West side	End zone
OPPONENT	Iowa	30%	21%	35%
	Ohio State	0	4%	10%

Suppose a ticket is selected at random from the 30,000 remaining.

    a. List all the simple events for this experiment.
    b. What is the set of all simple events called?
    c. Let A be the event that the ticket chosen is for the Iowa game. Find $P(A)$.
    d. Let B be the event that the ticket chosen is for the Ohio State game. Find $P(B)$.
    e. Let C be the event that the ticket chosen is for the east side. Find $P(C)$.
    f. Let D be the event that the ticket chosen is for the west side. Find $P(D)$.
    g. Let E be the event that the ticket chosen is for the end zone. Find $P(E)$.

5.11. A large research and development corporation, interested in providing an in-house continuing education program for its employees, compiled the following percentages describing its 5,000 employees' current education level:

	HIGHEST DEGREE OBTAINED			
	High school diploma	Bachelor's	Master's	Ph.D.
MALES	5%	20%	12%	11%
FEMALES	18%	15%	14%	5%

Suppose an employee is selected at random from the firm's 5,000 employees and the following events are defined:

A = {Employee chosen was a male}

B = {Employee chosen was a female}

C = {Highest degree obtained by the chosen employee is Ph.D.}

D = {Highest degree obtained by the chosen employee is Master's}

E = {Highest degree obtained by the chosen employee is Bachelor's}

F = {Highest degree obtained by the chosen employee is high school diploma}

Describe the characteristics of an employee portrayed by the following events:

a. $A \cup C$ b. $B \cup F$ c. $A \cap D$ d. $E \cap B$

5.12. Refer to Exercise 5.11. Find the probabilities of the following events by summing the probabilities of the appropriate simple events:

a. A, B, C, D, E, F b. $A \cup B$ c. $B \cap C$

d. $A \cap F$ e. $A \cap B$ f. $C \cap D$

5.13. Whether purchases are made by cash or credit card is of concern to merchandisers, because they must pay a certain percentage of the sale value to the credit agency. To better understand the relationship between types of purchase (credit or cash) and types of merchandise, a department store analyzed 10,000 sales and placed them in the categories shown in the table.

| | | TYPE OF MERCHANDISE | | | |
		Women's wear	Men's wear	Sportswear	Household
TYPE OF	Cash	4%	7%	12%	7%
PURCHASE	Credit card	37%	11%	4%	18%

Suppose that a single sale is selected at random from the 10,000 and the following events are defined:

A = {Sale was paid by credit card}

B = {Merchandise purchased was women's wear}

C = {Merchandise purchased was men's wear}

D = {Merchandise purchased was sportswear}

Describe the characteristics of a sale that implied the following events:

a. $A \cup B$ b. $B \cup C$ c. $B \cap A$ d. $C \cap A$

5.14. Refer to Exercise 5.13. Find the probabilities of the following events by summing the probabilities of the appropriate simple events:

a. A, B, C, D b. $A \cup B$ c. $B \cup C$ d. $B \cap A$ e. $C \cap A$

5.15. Refer to Exercise 5.13. The following events are defined:

$A = \{\text{Sale was paid by credit card}\}$

$B = \{\text{Merchandise purchased was women's wear}\}$

a. Describe the events A^c and B^c.
b. Find $P(A^c)$.
c. Find $P(B^c)$.
d. Find the probability that the sale was neither in men's wear nor women's wear.
e. Find the probability that the sale was *not* a credit card purchase in the sportswear department.

5.16. Refer to Exercise 5.9. Describe the characteristics of a golf club shaft portrayed by the following events:

a. $A \cap F$ b. $C \cup E$ c. $C \cap D$ d. $A \cup F$ e. $A \cup D$

5.17. Refer to Exercise 5.9. Find the probabilities of the following events:

a. $A \cup C$ b. $A \cap F$ c. $C \cup E$ d. $C \cap F$ e. $D \cap E$

5.18. Refer to Exercise 5.9. Describe the characteristics of the golf club shaft portrayed by the following events:

a. $A \cup E$ b. $A \cap E$ c. $C \cap A$ d. $C \cup F$

5.19. Refer to Exercise 5.10. Find the probabilities of the following events:

a. $A \cap E$ b. $B \cup D$ c. $B \cap C$
d. $B \cup E$ e. $C \cup D$ f. $D \cap E$

5.20. Refer to Exercise 5.10. The following events are defined:

$A = \{\text{Ticket selected was for the Iowa game}\}$

$C = \{\text{Ticket selected was for the east side}\}$

a. Describe the events A^c and C^c.
b. Find $P(A^c)$.
c. Find $P(C^c)$.
d. Find the probability that the ticket chosen was not for the Ohio State game or the Iowa game.
e. Find the probability that the ticket chosen was not for the east side.
f. Find the probability that the ticket chosen was not for the Ohio State game on the east side.

**5.4
CONDITIONAL
PROBABILITY**

The probabilities we assign to the simple events of an experiment are measures of our belief that they will occur when the experiment is performed. When we assign these probabilities, we should make no assumptions other than those contained in or implied by the definition of the experiment. However, at times we will want to make assumptions other than those implied by the experimental description, and these extra assumptions may alter the probabilities we assign to the simple events of an experiment.

For example, we have shown that the probability of observing an even number (event A) on a toss of a fair die is $\frac{1}{2}$. However, suppose you are given the information that on a particular throw of the die the result was a number less than or equal to 3 (event B). Would you still believe that the probability of observing an even number on that throw of the die is equal to $\frac{1}{2}$? If you reason that making the assumption that B has occurred reduces the sample space from six simple events to three simple events (namely, those contained in event B), the reduced sample space is as shown in Figure 5.6.

FIGURE 5.6
REDUCED SAMPLE
SPACE FOR THE DIE
TOSS EXPERIMENT
—GIVEN THAT
EVENT B HAS
OCCURRED

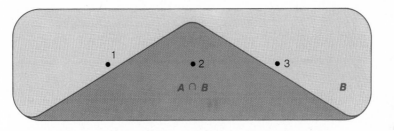

Since the only even number of the three numbers in the reduced sample space B is the number 2 and since the die is fair, we conclude that the probability that A occurs given that B occurs is one in three, or $\frac{1}{3}$. We will use the symbol $P(A|B)$ to represent the probability of event A given that event B occurs. For the die toss example,

$$P(A|B) = \frac{1}{3}$$

To get the probability of event A given that event B occurs, we proceed as follows: We divide the probability of the part of A that falls within the reduced sample space B, namely $P(A \cap B)$, by the total probability of the reduced sample space, namely $P(B)$. Thus, for the die toss example where event $A = \{$Observe an even number$\}$ and event $B = \{$Observe a number less than or equal to 3$\}$, we find

$$P(A|B) = \frac{P(A \cap B)}{P(B)} = \frac{P(2)}{P(1) + P(2) + P(3)} = \frac{\frac{1}{6}}{\frac{3}{6}} = \frac{1}{3}$$

This formula for $P(A|B)$ is true in general:

To find the conditional probability that event A occurs given that event B occurs, divide the probability that *both* A and B occur by the probability that B occurs, that is,

$$P(A|B) = \frac{P(A \cap B)}{P(B)}$$

EXAMPLE 5.8

Suppose you are interested in the probability of the sale of a large piece of earth-moving equipment. A single prospect is contacted. Let F denote the fact that the buyer has sufficient money (or credit) to buy the product and let F^c denote the complement to F (the event that the prospect does not have the financial capability to buy the product). Similarly, let B denote the fact that the buyer wishes to buy the product and let B^c be the complement of that event. Then the four simple events associated with the experiment are shown in Figure 5.7, and their probabilities are given in Table 5.2.

TABLE 5.2
PROBABILITIES OF
CUSTOMER DESIRE
TO BUY AND
ABILITY TO FINANCE

| | | DESIRE | |
		To buy, B	Not to buy, B^c
ABLE TO	Yes, F	.2	.1
FINANCE	No, F^c	.4	.3

Find the probability that a single prospect will buy given that the prospect is able to finance the purchase.

Solution

Suppose you consider the large collection of prospects for the sale of your product and randomly select one person from this collection. What is the probability that the person selected will buy the product? In order to buy the product, the customer must be both financially able and have the desire to buy, so this probability would correspond to the entry in Table 5.2 below B and next to F or $P(B \cap F) = .2$. This is called the **unconditional probability** of the event $B \cap F$.

In contrast, suppose you know that the prospect selected has the financial capability for purchasing the product. Now you are seeking the probability that the customer will buy given (the condition) that the customer has the financial ability to pay. This probability, the **conditional probability** of B given that F has occurred and denoted by the symbol $P(B|F)$, would be determined by considering only the simple events in the reduced sample space containing the simple events $B \cap F$ and $B^c \cap F$, i.e., simple events that imply the prospect is financially able to buy (this subspace is shaded in Figure 5.8). From our definition of conditional probability,

$$P(B|F) = \frac{P(B \cap F)}{P(F)}$$

where $P(F)$ is the sum of the probabilities of the two simple events corresponding to $B \cap F$ and $B^c \cap F$ (given in Table 5.2). Then

$$P(F) = P(B \cap F) + P(B^c \cap F) = .2 + .1 = .3$$

FIGURE 5.7
SAMPLE SPACE FOR
CONTACTING A SALES
PROSPECT

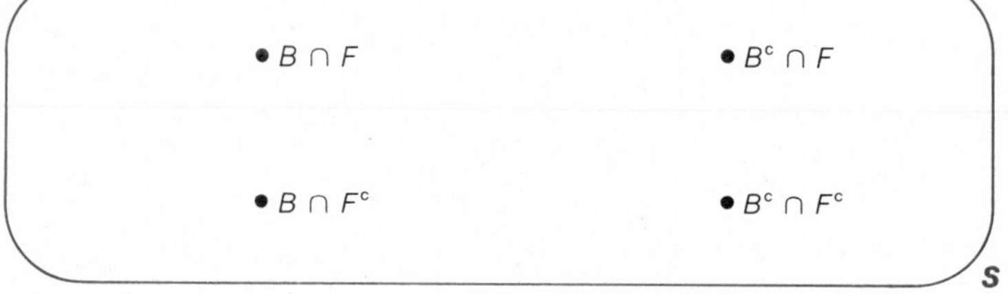

CHAPTER 5   PROBABILITY

FIGURE 5.8
SUBSPACE (SHADED)
CONTAINING SAMPLE
POINTS IMPLYING A
FINANCIALLY ABLE
PROSPECT

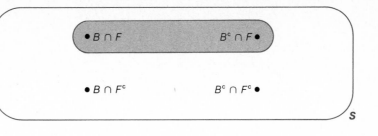

and the conditional probability that a prospect buys, given that the prospect is financially able, is

$$P(B|F) = \frac{P(B \cap F)}{P(F)} = \frac{.2}{.3} = .667$$

As we would expect, the probability that the prospect will buy, knowing that he or she is financially able, is higher than the unconditional probability of selecting a prospect who will buy.

EXAMPLE 5.9

The investigation of consumer product complaints by the Federal Trade Commission has generated much interest by manufacturers in the quality of their products. A manufacturer of an electromechanical kitchen aid conducted an analysis of a large number of consumer complaints and found that they fell into the six categories shown in Table 5.3. If a consumer complaint is received, what is the probability that the cause of the complaint was product appearance given that you know that the complaint originated prior to the end of the guarantee period?

**TABLE 5.3
DISTRIBUTION OF
PRODUCT COMPLAINTS**

	REASON FOR COMPLAINT		
	Electrical	Mechanical	Appearance
DURING GUARANTEE PERIOD	18%	13%	32%
AFTER GUARANTEE PERIOD	12%	22%	3%

Solution

Let A represent the event that the cause of a particular complaint was product appearance and let B represent the event that the complaint occurred prior to the termination of the guarantee period. Checking Table 5.3, you can see that $(18 + 13 + 32) = 63\%$ of the complaints occur prior to the termination of the guarantee time. Hence, $P(B) = .63$. The percentage of complaints that were caused by appearance, A, *and* occurred prior to the termination time, B, is 32%. Therefore, $P(A \cap B) = .32$.

Using these probability values, we can calculate the conditional probability $P(A|B)$ that the cause of a complaint is appearance given that the complaint occurred prior to the termination of the guarantee time:

$$P(A|B) = \frac{P(A \cap B)}{P(B)} = \frac{.32}{.63} = .51$$

Consequently, you can see that slightly more than half of the complaints that occurred prior to guarantee time were due to scratches, dents, or other imperfections in the surface of the kitchen devices.

You will see in later chapters that conditional probability plays a key role in many business applications of statistics. For example, we may be interested in the probability that a particular stock gains 10% during the next year. We may estimate this probability (a statistical problem) by using information like the past performance of the stock, the general state of the economy at present, etc. However, our probability estimate may change drastically if we assume the Gross National Product will increase by 10% in the next year. We would then be estimating the *conditional probability* that our stock gains 10% in the next year given that the GNP gains 10% in the same year. Thus, the probability of any event that is calculated or estimated based on an assumption that some other event occurs concurrently is a conditional probability.

CASE STUDY 5.1   In his doctoral dissertation Alfred A. Kuehn (1958) examined sequential purchase data to gain some insight into consumer brand switching. He analyzed the frozen orange juice purchases of approximately 600 Chicago families during 1950–1952. The data were collected by the *Chicago Tribune* Consumer Panel. Kuehn was interested in determining the influence of a consumer's last four orange juice purchases on the next purchase. Thus, sequences of five purchases were analyzed.

Table 5.4 contains a summary of the data collected for Snow Crop brand orange juice and part of Kuehn's analysis of the data. In the column labeled "Previous Purchase Pattern" an S stands for the purchase of Snow Crop by a consumer and an O stands for the purchase of a brand other than Snow Crop. Thus, for example, SSSO is used to represent the purchase of Snow Crop three times in a row followed

TABLE 5.4 OBSERVED APPROXIMATE PROBABILITY OF PURCHASING SNOW CROP, GIVEN THE FOUR PREVIOUS BRAND PURCHASES	PREVIOUS PURCHASE PATTERN S = Snow Crop O = Other brand	SAMPLE SIZE	FREQUENCY	OBSERVED APPROXIMATE PROBABILITY OF PURCHASE
	SSSS	1,047	844	.806
	OSSS	277	191	.690
	SOSS	206	137	.665
	SSOS	222	132	.595
	SSSO	296	144	.486
	OOSS	248	137	.552
	SOOS	138	78	.565
	OSOS	149	74	.497
	SOSO	163	66	.405
	OSSO	181	75	.414
	SSOO	256	78	.305
	OOOS	500	165	.330
	OOSO	404	77	.191
	OSOO	433	56	.129
	SOOO	557	86	.154
	OOOO	8,442	405	.048

by the purchase of some other brand of frozen orange juice. The column labeled "Sample Size" lists the number of occurrences of the purchase sequences in the first column. The column labeled "Frequency" lists the number of times the associated purchase sequence in the first column led to the next purchase (i.e., the fifth purchase in the sequence) being Snow Crop.

The column labeled "Observed Approximate Probability of Purchase" contains the relative frequency with which each sequence of the first column led to the next purchase being Snow Crop. These relative frequencies, which give approximate probabilities, are computed for each sequence of the first column by dividing the frequency of the sequence by the sample size of the sequence. Notice that these approximate probabilities are really conditional probabilities. For the sequences of five purchases analyzed, each of the entries in the fourth column is the approximate probability that the next purchase is Snow Crop, given that the previous four purchases were as noted in the first column. For example, .806 is the approximate probability that the next purchase will be Snow Crop given that the previous four purchases were also Snow Crop.

An examination of the approximate probabilities in the fourth column indicates that both the most recent brand purchased and the number of times a brand is purchased have an effect on the next brand purchased. It appears that the influence on the next brand of orange juice purchased by the second most recent purchase is not as strong as the most recent purchase, but is stronger than the third most recent purchase. In general, it appears that the probability of a particular consumer purchasing Snow Crop the next time he or she buys orange juice is inversely related to the number of consecutive purchases of another brand he or she bought since last purchasing Snow Crop, and is directly proportional to the number of Snow Crop purchases among the four purchases.

Kuehn, of course, goes on to conduct a more formal statistical analysis of these data, which we will not pursue here. We simply want you to see that probability is a basic tool for making inferences about populations using sample data.

5.5 PROBABILITIES OF UNIONS AND INTERSECTIONS

Since unions and intersections of events are themselves events, we can always calculate their probabilities by adding the probabilities of the simple events that compose them. However, if we know the probabilities of certain events related to the union or intersection, sometimes it is simpler to use different formulas to calculate their probabilities.

The union of two events will often contain many simple events, since the union occurs if either one or both of the events occur. By studying the Venn diagram in Figure 5.9, you can see that the probability of the union of two events A and B can

FIGURE 5.9
VENN DIAGRAM OF UNION

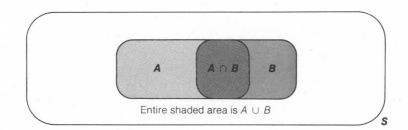

Entire shaded area is $A \cup B$

be obtained by summing $P(A)$ and $P(B)$ and subtracting the probability corresponding to $A \cap B$. Therefore, the formula for calculating the probability of the union of two events is given below:

ADDITIVE RULE OF PROBABILITY
The probability of the union of events A and B is the sum of the probabilities of events A and B minus the probability of the intersection of events A and B, i.e.,

$$P(A \cup B) = P(A) + P(B) - P(A \cap B)$$

Note that we must subtract the intersection, because when we add the probabilities of A and B the intersection probability is counted twice.

EXAMPLE 5.10

Consider the die toss experiment. Define the events

$A = \{$Observe an even number$\}$

$B = \{$Observe a number less than or equal to 3$\}$

Assuming the die is fair, calculate the probability of the union of A and B by using the additive rule of probability.

Solution

The formula for the probability of a union requires that we calculate the following:

$$P(A) = P(2) + P(4) + P(6) = \frac{1}{6} + \frac{1}{6} + \frac{1}{6} = \frac{3}{6}$$

$$P(B) = P(1) + P(2) + P(3) = \frac{1}{6} + \frac{1}{6} + \frac{1}{6} = \frac{3}{6}$$

$$P(A \cap B) = P(2) = \frac{1}{6}$$

Now we can calculate the probability of $A \cup B$.

$$P(A \cup B) = P(A) + P(B) - P(A \cap B) = \frac{3}{6} + \frac{3}{6} - \frac{1}{6} = \frac{5}{6}$$

If two events A and B do not intersect, i.e., when $A \cap B$ contains no simple events, we call the events A and B mutually exclusive events:

DEFINITION 5.9
Events A and B are mutually exclusive if $A \cap B$ contains no simple events.

FIGURE 5.10
VENN DIAGRAM OF
MUTUALLY EXCLUSIVE
EVENTS

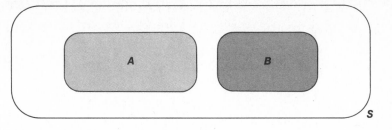

Figure 5.10 shows a Venn diagram of two mutually exclusive events. The events A and B have no simple events in common, i.e., A and B cannot occur simultaneously, and $P(A \cap B) = 0$. Thus, we have the following important relationship:

> If two events A and B are mutually exclusive, the probability of the union of A and B equals the sum of the probabilities of A and B, i.e.,
>
> $$P(A \cup B) = P(A) + P(B)$$

Now we will develop a formula for calculating the probability of an intersection. Actually, we have already developed the formula in another context. You will recall that the formula for calculating the conditional probability of A given B is

$$P(A|B) = \frac{P(A \cap B)}{P(B)}$$

If we turn this formula around by multiplying both sides of the equation by $P(B)$, we get a formula for the probability of the intersection of events A and B:

> **MULTIPLICATIVE RULE OF PROBABILITY**
>
> $$P(A \cap B) = P(B)P(A|B) = P(A)P(B|A)$$

The expression on the right of the above equation is obtained by multiplying both sides of

$$P(B|A) = \frac{P(A \cap B)}{P(A)}$$

by $P(A)$.

Before working an example, we emphasize that the intersection often contains only a few simple events, and then the probability is easy to calculate by summing the appropriate simple event probabilities. However, the formula for calculating intersection probabilities plays a very important role in an area of business statistics known as **Bayesian statistics.** (More complete discussions of Bayesian statistics are contained in the references at the end of the chapter.)

EXAMPLE 5.11   Suppose an investment firm is interested in the following events:

A = {Common stock in XYZ Corporation gains 10% next year}

B = {Gross National Product gains 10% next year}

The firm has assigned the following probabilities on the basis of available information:

$$P(A|B) = .8 \qquad P(B) = .3$$

That is, the investment company believes the probability is .8 that the XYZ common stock will gain 10% in the next year *assuming that* the GNP gains 10% in the same time period. In addition, the company believes the probability is only .3 that the GNP will gain 10% in the next year. Use the formula for calculating the probability of an intersection to calculate the probability that XYZ common stock *and* the GNP gain 10% in the next year.

Solution   We want to calculate $P(A \cap B)$. The formula is

$$P(A \cap B) = P(B)P(A|B) = (.3)(.8) = .24$$

Thus, the probability, according to this investment firm, is .24 that both XYZ common stock and the GNP will gain 10% in the next year.

In the previous section we showed that the probability of an event A may be substantially altered by the assumption that the event B has occurred. However, this will not always be the case. In some instances the assumption that event B has occurred will not alter the probability of event A at all. When this is true, we call events A and B **independent:**

DEFINITION 5.10
Events A and B are **independent** if the assumption that B has occurred does not alter the probability that A has occurred, i.e.,

$$P(A|B) = P(A)$$

When events A and B are **independent** it will also be true that

$$P(B|A) = P(B)$$

Events that are not independent are said to be **dependent.**

EXAMPLE 5.12   If in the die toss experiment we decide to change the definition of event B to {Observe a number less than or equal to 4}, but let event A remain an even number, are events A and B independent (assuming a fair die)?

FIGURE 5.11

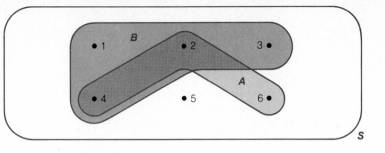

Solution

The Venn diagram for this experiment is shown in Figure 5.11. We first calculate

$$P(A) = \frac{1}{2}$$

$$P(B) = P(1) + P(2) + P(3) + P(4) = \frac{4}{6} = \frac{2}{3}$$

$$P(A \cap B) = P(2) + P(4) = \frac{2}{6} = \frac{1}{3}$$

Now assuming B has occurred, the conditional probability of A is

$$P(A|B) = \frac{P(A \cap B)}{P(B)} = \frac{1/3}{2/3} = \frac{1}{2} = P(A)$$

Thus, assuming the occurrence of event B does not alter the probability of observing an even number—it remains $\frac{1}{2}$. Therefore, the events A and B are independent. Note that if we turn the events around and calculate the conditional probability of B given A, our conclusion is the same:

$$P(B|A) = \frac{P(A \cap B)}{P(A)} = \frac{1/3}{1/2} = \frac{2}{3} = P(B)$$

EXAMPLE 5.13

Refer to the consumer product complaint study in Example 5.9. The percentages of complaints of various types in the pre- and post-guarantee periods are shown in Table 5.3. Define the following events:

$A = \{\text{Cause of complaint is product appearance}\}$

$B = \{\text{Complaint occurred during the guarantee term}\}$

Are A and B independent events?

Solution

Events A and B are independent if $P(A|B) = P(A)$. We calculated $P(A|B)$ in Example 5.9 to be .51, and from Table 5.3 we can see that

$$P(A) = .32 + .03 = .35$$

Therefore, $P(A|B)$ is not equal to $P(A)$, and A and B are not independent events.

We will make three final points about independence. The first is that the property of independence, unlike the mutually exclusive property, cannot be shown on or gleaned from a Venn diagram. In general, the only way to check for independence is by performing the calculations of the probabilities in the definition.

The second point concerns the relationship between the mutually exclusive and independence properties. Suppose that events A and B are mutually exclusive, as shown in Figure 5.10. Are these events independent or dependent? That is, does the assumption that B occurs alter the probability of the occurrence of A? It certainly does, because if we assume that B has occurred, it is impossible for A to have occurred simultaneously. Thus, mutually exclusive events are dependent events.

The third point is that the probability of the intersection of independent events is very easy to calculate. Referring to the formula for calculating the probability of an intersection, we find

$$P(A \cap B) = P(B)P(A|B)$$

Thus, since $P(A|B) = P(A)$ when A and B are independent, we have the following useful rule:

If events A and B are **independent**, the probability of the intersection of A and B equals the product of the probabilities of A and B, i.e.,

$$P(A \cap B) = P(A)P(B)$$

In the die toss experiment, we showed in Example 5.12 that the events $A = \{$Observe an even number$\}$ and $B = \{$Observe a number less than or equal to 4$\}$ are independent if the die is fair. Thus,

$$P(A \cap B) = P(A)P(B) = \left(\frac{1}{2}\right)\left(\frac{2}{3}\right) = \frac{1}{3}$$

This agrees with the result

$$P(A \cap B) = P(2) + P(4) = \frac{2}{6} = \frac{1}{3}$$

that we obtained in the example.

EXAMPLE 5.14   In Example 5.2, a bank considered the problem of apportioning its service windows according to two types of accounts: personal or commercial. In the example, we attempted the smaller problem of finding the probability that one, two, or, in general, k customers arriving at the bank possessed a commercial account. We are now ready to find the probability that both of two customers arriving at the bank possess commercial accounts. Suppose that a study of arriving customers showed that 20% of arriving customers intend to utilize their commercial accounts at the bank.

a. If two customers arrive at the bank, what is the probability that they will both utilize a commercial account?

b. If k customers arrive at the bank, what is the probability that all will utilize commercial accounts?

Solution

a. Let C_1 be the event that customer 1 will utilize a commercial account and let C_2 be a similar event for customer 2. The event that *both* customers will utilize commercial accounts is the intersection $C_1 \cap C_2$. Then, since it is not unreasonable to assume that the service requirements of the customers would be independent of one another, the probability that both will utilize commercial accounts is

$$P(C_1 \cap C_2) = P(C_1)P(C_2)$$
$$= (.2)(.2) = (.2)^2 = .04$$

b. Let C_i represent the event that the ith customer will utilize a commercial account. Then the event that all three of three arriving customers will utilize a commercial account is the intersection of the events $C_1 \cap C_2$ (from part a) along with the event C_3. Assuming independence of the events, C_1, C_2 and C_3, we have

$$P(C_1 \cap C_2 \cap C_3) = P(C_1 \cap C_2)P(C_3)$$
$$= (.2)^2(.2) = (.2)^3 = .008$$

Noting the pattern, you can see that the probability that all k out of k arriving customers will utilize a commercial account is the probability of $C_1 \cap C_2 \cap \cdots \cap C_k$, or

$$P(C_1 \cap C_2 \cap \cdots \cap C_k) = (.2)^k \qquad \text{for} \quad k = 1, 2, 3, \ldots$$

EXERCISES

5.21. Three coins are tossed and the following events are defined:

$A = \{$Observe at least one head$\}$

$B = \{$Observe exactly two heads$\}$

$C = \{$Observe exactly two tails$\}$

$D = \{$Observe at most one head$\}$

$E = \{$Observe at least two tails$\}$

Using the formulas of this section calculate the following:

a. $P(A \cup B)$ b. $P(A \cap B)$ c. $P(A \cup C)$

d. $P(C \cap A)$ e. $P(A^c \cap C)$ f. $P(D \cap E)$

5.22. Use the events defined in Exercise 5.21 to find the following:

a. $P(B|A)$ b. $P(C|D)$ c. $P(C|E)$

5.23. Given that $P(R) = \frac{1}{3}$, $P(S) = \frac{1}{3}$, and that events R and S are mutually exclusive, find $P(R|S)$ and $P(S|R)$.

5.24. Two dice are tossed and the following events are defined:

$A = \{$Sum of the numbers showing is an odd number$\}$

$B = \{$Sum of the numbers showing is 8, 9, 11, *or* 12$\}$

Are events A and B independent? Why?

5.25. A soft drink bottler has two quality control inspectors independently check each case of soft drinks for chipped or cracked bottles before the cases leave the bottling plant. Having observed the work of the two trusted inspectors over several years, the bottler has determined that the probability of a defective case getting by the first inspector is .05 and the probability of a defective case getting by the second inspector is .10. What is the probability that a defective case gets by both inspectors?

5.26. A company is considering advertising its product in two magazines, A and B. Thirty percent of its potential customers subscribe to magazine A, 40% to B, and 15% to both A and B.

    a.   What percentage of the potential customers subscribe to A or B? To both A and B?

    b.   If a potential customer is chosen at random and that customer subscribes to magazine A, what is the probability that the customer also subscribes to magazine B?

5.27. A fast-food restaurant chain with 700 outlets in the United States describes the geographic location of its restaurants with the following table of percentages:

		REGION			
		NE	SE	SW	NW
POPULATION OF CITY	Under 10,000	5%	6%	3%	0
	10,000–100,000	10%	15%	12%	5%
	Over 100,000	25%	4%	5%	10%

A restaurant is to be chosen at random from the 700 to test market a new style of chicken.

    a.   Given the restaurant chosen is in a city with population over 100,000, what is the probability that it is located in the northeast?

    b.   Given the restaurant chosen is in the southeast, what is the probability that it is located in a city with population under 10,000?

5.28. Refer to Exercise 5.27. If the restaurant selected is located in the southwest, what is the probability that the city it is in has a population under 100,000?

5.29. Refer to Exercise 5.27. If the restaurant selected is located in the northwest, what is the probability that the city it is in has a population over 10,000?

5.30. Refer to Exercise 5.27. The following events are defined:

$A = \{$Population of city where chosen restaurant is located is over 100,000$\}$

$B = \{$Chosen restaurant is located in the northeast$\}$

Are A and B independent events? Explain.

5.31. The following table of percentages describes the 1,000 apartment units in a large suburban apartment complex:

| | | APARTMENT SIZE | | |
		One bedroom	Two bedroom	Three bedroom
LOCATION WITHIN BUILDING	First floor	5%	30%	10%
	Second floor	25%	20%	10%

The manager of the complex is considering installing new carpets in all the apartments. Before doing so he wants to wear-test the brand in which he is interested for 6 months in one of the 1,000 apartments. He plans to choose one apartment at random from the 1,000 and install a test carpet.

    a. What is the probability that he will choose a first floor, two bedroom apartment?

    b. Given that he chooses a second floor apartment, what is the probability that the apartment has three bedrooms?

    c. Given that he chooses a one bedroom apartment, what is the probability that the apartment is on the second floor?

5.32. Refer to Exercise 5.31. Given that the apartment selected is on the first floor, what is the probability that it has two or three bedrooms?

5.33. Refer to Exercise 5.31. What is the probability that the manager will select a second floor, one bedroom apartment?

5.34. Refer to Exercise 5.31. The following events are defined:

    $A = \{$Apartment selected has one bedroom$\}$

    $B = \{$Apartment selected is located on the first floor$\}$

Are events A and B independent? Explain.

5.35. Refer to Exercise 5.31. The following events are defined:

    $C = \{$Apartment selected has three bedrooms$\}$

    $D = \{$Apartment selected has two bedrooms$\}$

Are events C and D independent? Explain.

**5.6
RANDOM
SAMPLING**

How a sample is selected from a population is of vital importance in statistical inference because the probability of an observed sample will be used to infer the characteristics of the sampled population. To illustrate, suppose you deal yourself 4 cards from a deck of 52 cards and all 4 cards are aces. Do you conclude that your deck is an ordinary bridge deck, containing only 4 aces, or do you conclude that the deck is stacked with more than 4 aces? It depends on how the cards were drawn. If the 4 aces were always placed at the top of a standard bridge deck, drawing 4 aces is not unusual—it is certain. On the other hand, if the cards are thoroughly mixed, drawing 4 aces in a sample of 4 cards is highly improbable. The point, of course, is that in order to use the observed sample of 4 cards to draw inferences about the population (the deck of 52 cards), you need to know how the sample was selected from the deck.

One of the simplest and most frequently employed sampling procedures produces what is known as a random sample:

DEFINITION 5.11
If n elements are selected from a population in such a way that every sample combination in the population has an equal probability of being selected, the n elements are said to be a **random sample**. *

If a population is not too large and the elements can be marked on slips of paper, poker chips, etc., you can physically mix the slips of paper or chips and remove n elements from the total. Then the elements that appear on the slips or chips selected would indicate the population elements to be included in the sample. Such a procedure would not guarantee a random sample, because it is often difficult to achieve a thorough mix, but it provides a reasonably good approximation to random sampling.

Most samplers use a table of random numbers (see Table I in Appendix B). Random number tables are constructed in such a way that every number occurs with equal (approximately) probability. To use a table of random numbers, we number the N elements in the population from 1 to N. Then we turn to Table I and haphazardly select a number in the table. Proceeding from this number across the rows or down the column (either will do), remove and record n numbers from the table. Use only the necessary number of digits in each random number to identify the element to be included in the sample. We illustrate this procedure with an example below.

EXAMPLE 5.15

Suppose you wish to randomly sample five households (we will keep the number in the sample small to simplify our example) from a population of 100,000 households. Use Table I to select a random sample.

Solution

First, number the households in the population from 1 to 100,000. Then, turn to a page of Table I, say, the first page. A reproduction of part of the first page of Table I is shown in Figure 5.12. Now, commence with the random number that appears in the third row, second column. This number is 48360. Proceed down the second column to obtain the remaining four random numbers. The five selected random numbers are shaded in Figure 5.12. Using the first five digits to represent the households from 1 to 99,999 and the number 00000 to represent household 100,000, you can see that the households numbered

| 48,360 | 93,093 | 39,975 | 6,907 | 72,905 |

should be included in your sample.

---

*Strictly speaking, this is a simple random sample. There are many different types of random samples. The simple random sample is the most common.

FIGURE 5.12
REPRODUCTION OF
PART OF
TABLE I, APPENDIX B

ROW \ COLUMN	1	2	3	4	5	6
1	10480	15011	01536	02011	81647	91646
2	22368	46573	25595	85393	30995	89198
3	24130	48360	22527	97265	76393	64809
4	42167	93093	06243	61680	07856	16376
5	37570	39975	81837	16656	06121	91782
6	77921	06907	11008	42751	27756	53498
7	99562	72905	56420	69994	98872	31016
8	96301	91977	05463	07972	18876	20922
9	89579	14342	63661	10281	17453	18103
10	85475	36857	53342	53988	53060	59533
11	28918	69578	88231	33276	70997	79936
12	63553	40961	48235	03427	49626	69445
13	09429	93969	52636	92737	88974	33488
14	10365	61129	87529	85689	48237	52267
15	07119	97336	71048	08178	77233	13916

SUMMARY

We have developed some of the basic tools of probability that enable us to assess the probability of various sample outcomes given a specific population structure. Although many of the examples we presented were of no practical importance, they accomplished their purpose if you now understand the concepts and definitions necessary for a basic understanding of probability.

In the next several chapters we will present probability models that can be used to solve practical business problems. You will see that for most applications, we will need to make inferences about unknown aspects of these probability models, i.e., we will need to apply inferential statistics to the problem.

SUPPLEMENTARY EXERCISES

5.36. A manufacturer has decided to market a new product. As a result, one of the following will happen:

1. The product will be financially very successful for the firm.
2. The product will be only a moderate financial success.
3. The firm will lose money on the new product.
4. Introduction of the product will prove so costly as to force the firm out of business.

Describe the complement of the following events:

$A = $ {Product will at least be moderately successful}

$B = $ {Product will not be a big financial success}

5.37. It has been determined by the Marketing and Accounting Department that the probabilities of the outcomes listed in Exercise 5.36 are as follows:

1. $\frac{1}{8}$
2. $\frac{8}{16}$
3. $\frac{5}{16}$
4. $\frac{1}{16}$

Calculate $P(A)$, $P(B)$, $P(A^c)$, $P(A \cap B)$, $P(A \cup B)$, and $P(A|B)$.

5.38. Refer to Exercise 5.36. Suppose you disagree with the probabilities assessed by the Marketing and Accounting Department in Exercise 5.37. You believe they should be as follows:

1. $\frac{1}{8}$
2. $\frac{9}{16}$
3. $\frac{3}{16}$
4. $\frac{3}{32}$

What basic error have you made in the assignment of these probabilities? Correct the probability assigned to event 4 and repeat Exercise 5.37 with these revised probabilities.

5.39. An advertising agency was interested in whether one of its client's advertisements in the latest issue of a nutritional magazine was noticed by readers of the magazine. Accordingly, it asked 1,500 of the magazine's subscribers who said they had read the latest issue whether they had noticed the advertisement. The following table of percentages describes their responses:

		NOTICED THE AD	DID NOT NOTICE THE AD
	Under 30	25%	5%
AGE GROUP	30–50	20%	15%
	Over 50	10%	25%

Suppose one of the 1,500 readers is chosen at random.

   a. List all the simple events for this experiment.
   b. What is the set of simple events in part a called?
   c. For each of the simple events in part a, find the probability that it will occur.

5.40. Refer to Exercise 5.39. The following events are defined:

   A = {Reader questioned was under 30}

   B = {Reader questioned was between 30 and 50}

   C = {Reader questioned noticed the advertisement}

   D = {Reader questioned did not notice the advertisement}

Describe a reader portrayed by the following events:

   a. $A \cap C$ b. $B \cup D$ c. $A \cap B$

5.41. Refer to Exercise 5.39. Find the probabilities of the following events:

   a. $A \cup C$ b. $A \cap D$ c. $B \cup C$ d. $C \cap D$ e. $D \cup C$

5.42. Refer to Exercise 5.39. The following events are defined:

   E = {Reader questioned was over 50}

   F = {Reader questioned was over 50 *and* did not notice the advertisement}

Describe the following events:
   a. E^c b. F^c

5.43. Refer to Exercise 5.39. Show that

$$P(B^c) = 1 - P(B)$$

5.44. What are the two rules that probabilities assigned to simple events must obey?

5.45. How are simple events and compound events related?

5.46. A stock market analyst believes that the probability of a certain stock's price staying the same *or* decreasing by the close of business today is .72. What should the analyst's assessment be of the probability of the stock's price increasing by the close of business? Why?

5.47. Construct a Venn diagram to represent the following stock of forty-five pocket calculators on-hand in a small bookstore:

    40   have square root option
    15   have percent option
    10   have percent option and square root option

5.48. Refer to Exercise 5.47. A calculator is chosen at random from the store's stock of forty-five calculators:

    a.   What is the probability that it will not have a percent option?
    b.   What is the probability that it will have a percent or a square root option?

5.49. Recall that $P(A \cup B) = P(A) + P(B) - P(A \cap B)$. Use a Venn diagram to find a general expression for $P(A \cup B \cup C)$.

5.50. Refer to Exercise 5.47. Another bookstore in town has the following stock of calculators:

    45   have square root option
    30   have percent option
    10   have a memory
    25   have a square root and a percent option
     5   have a square root option and a memory
     3   have a percent option and a memory
     2   have all three options

Use the result of Exercise 5.49 to deduce the number of calculators in the store's inventory.

5.51. Refer to Exercise 5.50. A calculator is chosen at random from the store's stock.

    a.   What is the probability that the chosen calculator has all three options?
    b.   What is the probability that the chosen calculator has either a memory or a square root option?

5.52. Refer to Exercise 5.50. If a calculator is chosen at random from the store's stock and you know it has a square root option, what is the probability that it also has a percent option?

5.53. Explain why the following statement is or is not valid: If an individual is chosen at random from all United States citizens living in the fifty states, the probability that this individual lives in New Hampshire is $\frac{1}{50}$.

5.54. Your firm has decided to market two new products. The manager of the Marketing Department believes the probability of product A being accepted by the public and product B not being accepted is .3, of product B being accepted and product A not being accepted is .4, and of both products A and B being accepted is .2. Given these probabilities the manager has concluded that the probability of both products failing is .01. Do you agree with this conclusion? Explain.

5.55. Suppose only two daily newspapers are available in your town—a local paper and one from a nearby city—and that 1,000 people in town subscribe to a daily paper. Assume that 65% of the people in town who subscribe to a daily newspaper subscribe to the local paper and 40% of those who subscribe to a daily paper subscribe to the city paper.

    a.   Use a Venn diagram to describe the population of newspaper subscribers.
    b.   If one of the 1,000 subscribers is chosen at random, what is the probability that he or she subscribes to both newspapers?

5.56. Refer to Exercise 5.11 (in Section 5.3). The table of percentages describing the education level of the corporation's 5,000 employees is repeated below:

| | HIGHEST DEGREE OBTAINED | | | |
	High school diploma	Bachelor's	Master's	Ph.D.
MALES	5%	20%	12%	11%
FEMALES	18%	15%	14%	5%

Suppose an employee is chosen at random from the firm's 5,000 employees.

    a.   Given that the person selected is a woman, what is the probability that the highest degree she has obtained is a Master's?
    b.   Given that the person selected has a Ph.D., what is the probability that the person selected is a woman?

5.57. Refer to Exercise 5.56. The following events are defined:

$A = \{$Person selected is a male$\}$

$B = \{$Person selected is a female$\}$

Are A and B independent events? Explain.

5.58. Refer to Exercise 5.27 (in Section 5.5). The table of percentages describing the location of a fast-food restaurant chain's franchises is reproduced below:

| | | REGION | | | |
		NE	SE	SW	NW
POPULATION OF CITY	Under 10,000	5%	6%	3%	0%
	10,000–100,000	10%	15%	12%	5%
	Over 100,000	25%	4%	5%	10%

A restaurant is chosen at random from the 700 to test market a new style of chicken. The following new events are defined:

$A = \{$Chosen restaurant is located in the southeast$\}$

$B = \{$Chosen restaurant is located in city of population under 10,000$\}$

$C = \{$Chosen restaurant is located in city of population over 10,000$\}$

$D = \{$Chosen restaurant is in the northeast$\}$

a. Find $P(A|B)$.　　　　b. Find $P(B|A)$.

c. Find $P(A|C)$.　　　　d. Find $P(C|D)$.

5.59. Refer to Exercise 5.58. Show that the following is true:

$$P(A \cap B) = P(A)P(B|A) = P(B)P(A|B) = .06$$

5.60. How can you show that two events are mutually exclusive?

5.61. Given that $P(A \cap B) = .4$ and $P(A|B) = .8$, find $P(B)$.

5.62. Are mutually exclusive events also dependent events? Explain.

5.63. The corporations in the highly competitive razor blade industry do a tremendous amount of advertising each year. Corporation G gave a supply of the three top name brands, G, S, and W, to a consumer and asked him to use them and rank them in order of preference. The corporation was, of course, hoping the consumer would prefer its brand and rank it first, thereby giving them some material for a consumer interview advertising campaign. If the consumer did not prefer one blade more than any other, but was still required to rank the blades, what is the probability that:

a. The consumer ranked brand G first?

b. The consumer ranked brand G last?

c. The consumer ranked brand G last and brand W second?

d. The consumer ranked brand W first, brand G second, and brand S third?

5.64. A manufacturer of 35 mm cameras knows that a shipment of thirty cameras sent to a large discount store contains six defective cameras. The manufacturer also knows that the store will choose two of the cameras at random, test them, and accept the shipment if neither is defective.

a. What is the probability that the first camera chosen by the store will be defective?

b. Given that the first camera chosen passed inspection, what is the probability that the second camera chosen will fail inspection?

c. What is the probability that the shipment will be accepted?

5.65. The probability that a mini-computer salesperson sells a computer to a prospective customer on the first visit to the customer is .4. If the salesperson fails to make the sale on the first visit, the probability that the sale will be made on the second visit is .65. The salesperson never visits a prospective customer more than twice. What is the probability that the salesperson will make a sale to a particular customer?

5.66. Use a Venn diagram to show that

$$P(A \cap B^c) = P(A) - P(A \cap B)$$

5.67. A fair coin is flipped twenty times and twenty heads are observed. In such cases it is often said that a tail is due on the next flip. Is this statement true or false? Explain.

ON YOUR OWN . . .

Obtain a standard bridge deck of 52 cards and think of the cards as the 52 items your firm produces each day. Let the 4 aces and 4 kings in the deck represent defective items.

a. If one item is randomly sampled from a day's production, what is the probability of its being defective?

b. Shuffle the cards, draw one, and record whether it is a defective item. Then replace the card and repeat the process. After each draw, recalculate the proportion of the draws that have resulted in a defective item. Construct a graph with the proportion of defectives on the *y*-axis and the number of draws on the *x*-axis. Notice how the proportion defective stabilizes as the number of draws increases.

c. Draw a horizontal line on the graph in part b at a height equal to the probability you calculated in part a. Compare the calculated proportion of defectives to this probability. As the number of draws is increased, does the calculated proportion of defectives more closely approach the actual probability of drawing a defective?

REFERENCES

Feller, W. *An introduction to probability theory and its applications.* Vol. I. New York: Wiley, 1957. Chapters 1, 4, and 5.

Harnett, D. L. *Introduction to statistical methods.* Reading, Mass.: Addison-Wesley, 1970. Chapter 2.

Kuehn, A. A. "An Analysis of the Dynamics of Consumer Behavior and Its Implications for Marketing Management." Unpublished doctoral dissertation, Graduate School of Industrial Administration, Carnegie Institute of Technology, 1958.

Parzen, E. *Modern probability theory and its applications.* New York: Wiley, 1960. Chapters 1 and 2.

Winkler, R. L. *An introduction to Bayesian inference and decision.* New York: Holt, Rinehart, and Winston, 1972. Chapter 2.

Winkler, R. L., & Hays, W. L. *Statistics: Probability, inference, and decision.* 2d ed. New York: Holt, Rinehart, and Winston, 1975. Chapters 1 and 2.

By illustration we indicated in Chapter 5 how probability would be used to make an inference from an observed sample about the sampled population. We also noted that probability would be used to measure the reliability of the inference.

WHERE WE'RE GOING . . .
Most experimental events in Chapter 5 were described in words or denoted by capital letters. In real life, most sample observations are numerical—in other words, data. In this chapter, we will learn that business data are observed values of random variables. We will study several important random variables and will learn how to find the probabilities of specific numerical outcomes.

6
DISCRETE RANDOM VARIABLES

You may have noticed that most of the examples of business experiments given in Chapter 5 generated quantitative (numerical) data. This is frequently true; observations on many types of phenomena are numerical measurements. The Consumer Price Index, unemployment rate, number of sales made in a week, and yearly profit of a company are all examples of numerical measurements of some business phenomena. Thus, most business experiments have simple events that correspond to values of some numerical variable.

DEFINITION 6.1
A random variable is a rule that assigns one (and only one) numerical value to each simple event of an experiment.*

The term *random variable* is more meaningful than just the term *variable,* because the adjective *random* indicates that the experiment may result in one of the several possible values of the variable, according to the random outcome of the experiment. For example, if the experiment is to count the number of customers who use the drive-up window of a bank each day, the random variable (the number of customers) will vary from day to day, partly because of the random phenomena that influence whether customers use the drive-up window. Thus, the possible values of this random variable range from zero to the maximum number of customers the window could possibly serve in a day.

We will define two different types of random variables, discrete and continuous, in Section 6.1. Then we will spend the remainder of this chapter discussing specific types of discrete random variables and the aspects that make them important to the business statistician.

6.1
TWO TYPES OF RANDOM VARIABLES

Assigning one unit of probability to the simple events in a sample space, and consequently to the values of a random variable, is not always as easy as the examples in Chapter 5 may lead you to believe. If the number of simple events is finite, the job is easy. If the number of simple events is infinite but you can list them in order (we call this countable), the task is still not too difficult. But if the simple events are numerical and correspond to the infinitely large number of points contained in a line interval, the task is impossible. Why? Because you cannot assign a small portion of probability to each of the simple events in this infinitely large set—the sum of the probabilities will exceed 1 (the sum will be infinitely large). The consequences of this mathematical fact are important. We will have to use two different probability models, depending on whether the number of simple events in a sample space (or equivalently, the values that a random variable can assume) are countable or they correspond to the infinitely large number of points contained in one or more intervals on a line.

*By *experiment,* we mean an experiment that yields random outcomes (as defined in Chapter 5).

DEFINITION 6.2
Random variables that can assume a countable number of values are called discrete.

DEFINITION 6.3
Random variables that can assume values corresponding to any of the points contained in one or more intervals on a line are called continuous.

Examples of discrete random variables are:

1. The number of sales made by a salesperson in a given week: $x = 0, 1, 2, \ldots$ [*Note:* Theoretically, x could become very large.]

2. The number of people in a sample of 500 who favor a particular product over all competitors: $x = 0, 1, 2, \ldots, 499, 500$.

3. The number of bids received in a bond offering: $x = 0, 1, 2, \ldots$ [*Note:* Theoretically, x could become very large.]

4. The number of errors on a page of an accountant's ledger: $x = 0, 1, 2, \ldots$

5. The number of customers waiting to be served in a restaurant at a particular time: $x = 0, 1, 2, \ldots$

Note that each of the examples of discrete random variables begins with the words "the number of . . . ." This is very common, since the discrete random variables most frequently observed in business are counts.

Examples of continuous random variables are:

1. The length of time between arrivals at a hospital clinic: $0 \leq x \leq \infty$ (infinity).

2. For a new apartment complex, the length of time from completion until a specified number of apartments are rented: $0 \leq x \leq \infty$.

3. The amount of carbonated beverage loaded into a 12 ounce can in a can filling operation: $0 \leq x \leq 12$.

4. The depth at which a successful oil drilling venture first strikes oil.

5. The weight of a food item bought in a supermarket.

In Section 6.2 we will discuss how to find the probability distribution for a discrete random variable. Then, several discrete random variables that play important roles in business decisions will be presented in subsequent sections. Probability distributions for some useful continuous random variables will be the subject of Chapter 7.

EXERCISES

6.1. What is a random variable?

6.2. How do discrete and continuous random variables differ?

6.3. Which of the following describe continuous random variables and which describe discrete random variables?

    a. The time required to complete a certain task.
    b. The number of people who attend a play at the civic center.
    c. The number of cars recalled by an automobile manufacturer next year.
    d. The actual weight of the contents of a 1 pound bag of sugar.
    e. The number of invoices containing arithmetic errors.

6.4. Give two examples of a business-oriented discrete random variable. Do the same for a continuous random variable.

6.5. If you were the manager of a clothing store, what are two examples of discrete random variables that would be of interest to you?

6.6. If you were a stockbroker, what is an example of a continuous random variable that would be of interest to you?

6.2 PROBABILITY DISTRIBUTION FOR DISCRETE RANDOM VARIABLES

Since a random variable assigns a numerical value to each of the simple events associated with an experiment, a complete description of a random variable requires that we specify its probability distribution. Note that each simple event is assigned one and only one value of the random variable, and hence, the values of the random variable represent mutually exclusive events.

> **DEFINITION 6.4**
> The probability distribution of a discrete random variable is a graph, table, or formula that specifies the probability associated with each possible value the random variable can assume.

To illustrate, consider the example below.

EXAMPLE 6.1

Recall the experiment of tossing two coins (Chapter 5), and let x be the number of heads observed. Find the probability distribution for the random variable x, assuming the two coins are fair.

Solution

Recall from Chapter 5 that the sample space and simple events for this experiment are as shown in Figure 6.1, and the probability associated with each of the four simple

FIGURE 6.1
VENN DIAGRAM FOR THE TWO-COIN TOSS EXPERIMENT

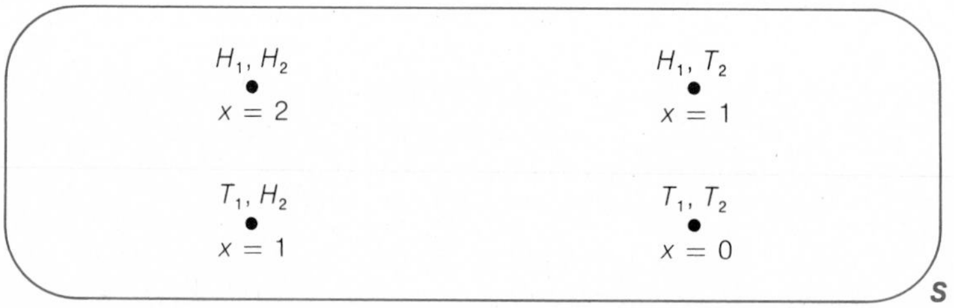

H_1, H_2
•
$x = 2$

H_1, T_2
•
$x = 1$

T_1, H_2
•
$x = 1$

T_1, T_2
•
$x = 0$

S

FIGURE 6.2
PROBABILITY
DISTRIBUTION:
GRAPHICAL FORM

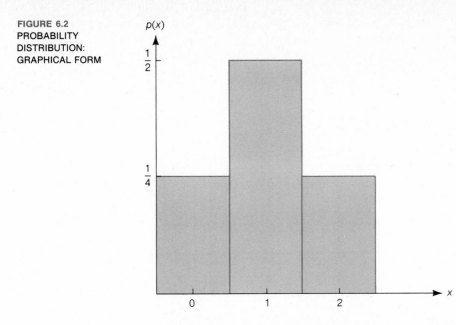

events is $\frac{1}{4}$. The random variable x can assume values 0, 1, 2. Then identifying the probabilities of the simple events associated with each of these values of x, we have

$$P(x = 0) = P(T_1, T_2) = \frac{1}{4}$$

$$P(x = 1) = P(T_1, H_2) + P(H_1, T_2) = \frac{1}{4} + \frac{1}{4} = \frac{1}{2}$$

$$P(x = 2) = P(H_1, H_2) = \frac{1}{4}$$

We will denote the probability distribution of x by the symbol $p(x)$. Then, for this example we have $p(0) = \frac{1}{4}$, $p(1) = \frac{1}{2}$, and $p(2) = \frac{1}{4}$. Table 6.1 shows the probability distribution of x in tabular form and Figure 6.2 shows it in graphical form.

TABLE 6.1
PROBABILITY
DISTRIBUTION:
TABULAR FORM

x	$p(x)$
0	$\frac{1}{4}$
1	$\frac{1}{2}$
2	$\frac{1}{4}$

We could also present the probability distribution for x as a formula, but this would unnecessarily complicate a very simple example. We will give the formulas for the probability distributions of discrete random variables later in this chapter.

Example 6.1 illustrates how the probability distribution for a discrete random variable can be derived, but for many practical examples of business random variables, the task is much more difficult. Fortunately, experiments and associated discrete random variables with identical characteristics are found in many different areas of business. That is, although the data may be collected in an area of accounting, marketing, economics, or management, for all practical purposes the data represent observed values of the same type of random variable. This fact simplifies the problem for the business statistician. All that must be done is to define the nature of these often repeated experiments, define the type of random variable, and give the probability distribution of the random variable. Two requirements must be satisfied by all probability distributions for discrete random variables:

REQUIREMENTS FOR THE PROBABILITY DISTRIBUTION OF A DISCRETE RANDOM VARIABLE x

$$p(x) \geq 0 \quad \text{for all values of } x$$
$$\sum_{\text{All } x} p(x) = 1$$

In Sections 6.4–6.7 we will describe four important types of discrete random variables, give their probability distributions, and explain where and how they can be applied in business. (Mathematical derivations of the probability distributions will be omitted, but these details can be found in the references at the end of the chapter.)

But first, in Section 6.3, we will discuss some descriptive measures of these sometimes complex probability distributions. Since probability distributions are analogous to the relative frequency distributions of Chapter 3, it should be no surprise that the mean and standard deviation are useful descriptive measures.

EXERCISES

6.7. A die is tossed. Let x be the number of spots observed on the upturned face of the die.

    a. Find the probability distribution of x and display it in tabular form.
    b. Display the probability distribution of x in graphical form.

6.8. It is known that for each of two stocks it is equally likely for the stocks to increase, remain the same, or decrease in price by the close of business tomorrow. If only these two stocks are observed and x represents the number of stocks that increase in price by the close of business tomorrow, find the probability distribution for x and display it in tabular form. (Assume the stocks are independent.)

6.9. A building contractor believes the probability distribution of the number of new four bedroom homes he will be requested to build next fall is that shown in the table at the top of page 121.

    a. Display the probability distribution in graphical form.
    b. According to the contractor's beliefs, what is the probability that he will be requested to build no more than five homes?
    c. More than seven?

MARKET DEMAND	
x = Number of homes	$p(x)$
0	.01
1	.02
2	.05
3	.08
4	.10
5	.15
6	.18
7	.24
8	.10
9	.05
10	.02
	1.00

6.10. Suppose the product development manager for your firm plans to market two new products. She thinks it is possible that both will fail consumer market tests, it is more likely that one will pass, and even more likely that neither will fail the market tests. Let x represent the number of the two new products that pass market tests. Display in tabular form a possible representation of the product manager's probability distribution for x.

6.3 EXPECTED VALUES OF DISCRETE RANDOM VARIABLES

If a discrete random variable x were observed a very large number of times and if the data generated were arranged in a relative frequency distribution, the relative frequency distribution would be indistinguishable from the probability distribution for the random variable. Thus, the probability distribution for a random variable is a theoretical model for the relative frequency distribution of a population. To the extent that the two distributions are equivalent (and we will assume they are) the probability distribution for x possesses a mean μ and a variance σ^2 that are identical to the corresponding descriptive measures for the population. The purpose of this section is to explain how you can find the mean value—or expected value, as it is called—for a random variable. We will illustrate the procedure with an example.

Examine the probability distribution for x (the number of heads observed in the toss of two coins) in Figure 6.3. Try to locate the mean of the distribution intuitively. We may reason that the mean μ of this distribution is equal to 1 as follows: In a large number of experiments, we should observe 0 heads $\frac{1}{4}$ of the time, 1 head $\frac{1}{2}$ of the time, and 2 heads $\frac{1}{4}$ of the time. Thus, the average number of heads is

$$\mu = 0\left(\frac{1}{4}\right) + 1\left(\frac{1}{2}\right) + 2\left(\frac{1}{4}\right)$$

$$= 0 + \frac{1}{2} + \frac{1}{2} = 1$$

Note that to get the population mean of the random variable x, we multiply each possible value of x by its probability $p(x)$, and then we sum this product over all

FIGURE 6.3
PROBABILITY
DISTRIBUTION FOR
A TWO-COIN TOSS

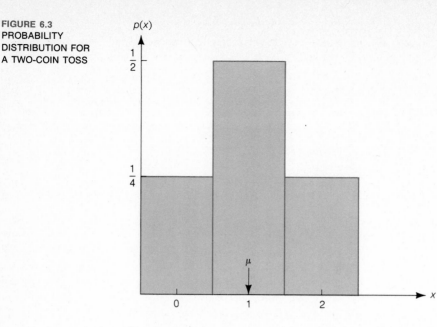

possible values of x. Another term often used as a substitute for the **mean of** x is the expected value of x, denoted $E(x)$:

DEFINITION 6.5
The expected value of a discrete random variable x is
$$\mu = E(x) = \sum_{\text{All } x} x\, p(x)$$

EXAMPLE 6.2

Suppose you work for an insurance company and you sell a $10,000 whole life insurance policy at an annual premium of $290. Actuarial tables show that the probability of death during the next year for a person of your customer's age, sex, health, etc., is .001. What is the expected gain (amount of money made by the company) for a policy of this type?

Solution

The experiment is to observe whether the customer survives the upcoming year. The probabilities associated with the two simple events, Live and Die, are .999 and .001, respectively. The random variable you are interested in is the gain, x, which can assume the following values:

GAIN x	SIMPLE EVENT	PROBABILITY
$290	Customer lives	.999
$290 − $10,000	Customer dies	.001

If the customer lives, the company gains the $290 premium as profit. If the customer dies, the gain is negative because the company must pay $10,000, for a net "gain" of $(290 − 10,000). The expected gain is therefore

$$\mu = E(x) = \sum_{\text{All } x} x\, p(x)$$

$$= (290)(.999) + (290 - 10,000)(.001)$$

$$= 290(.999 + .001) - 10,000(.001)$$

$$= 290 - 10 = \$280$$

In other words, if the company were to sell a very large number of 1 year $10,000 policies to customers possessing the characteristics described above, it would (on the average) net $280 per sale in the next year.

We want to measure the variability as well as the central tendency of a probability distribution. The population variance σ^2 is defined as the average squared distance of the x measurements from the population mean μ. This quantity is also called the expected value of the squared distance from the mean, i.e., $\sigma^2 = E[(x - \mu)^2]$:

DEFINITION 6.6
The variance of a discrete random variable x is

$$\sigma^2 = E[(x - \mu)^2] = \sum_{\text{All } x} (x - \mu)^2\, p(x)$$

Thus, to calculate the average of $(x - \mu)^2$, we multiply all possible values of $(x - \mu)^2$ by $p(x)$ and then sum over all possible x values.* The standard deviation σ is defined as the square root of the variance σ^2.

EXAMPLE 6.3   Suppose you invest a fixed sum of money in each of five business ventures. Assume you know that 70% of such ventures are successful, the outcomes of the ventures are independent of one another, and the probability distribution for the number x of successful ventures out of five is:

x	$p(x)$
0	.002
1	.029
2	.132
3	.309
4	.360
5	.168

---

*It can be shown that $E[(x - \mu)^2] = E(x^2) - \mu^2$, where $E(x^2) = \sum_{\text{All } x} x^2\, p(x)$. Note the similarity between this expression and the shortcut formula $\sum_{i=1}^{n} (x_i - \bar{x})^2 = \sum_{i=1}^{n} x^2 - \left(\sum x\right)^2 / n$ given in Chapter 4.

a. Find $\mu = E(x)$.

b. Find $\sigma = \sqrt{E[(x - \mu)^2]}$.

c. Graph $p(x)$. Locate μ and the interval $\mu \pm 2\sigma$ on the graph. Explain how μ and σ can be used to describe $p(x)$.

Solution

a. Applying the formula,

$$\mu = E(x) = \sum_{\text{All } x} x\, p(x)$$

$$= 0(.002) + 1(.029) + 2(.132) + 3(.309) + 4(.360) + 5(.168)$$

$$= 3.50$$

b. Now we calculate the variance of x:

$$\sigma^2 = E[(x - \mu)^2] = \sum_{\text{All } x} (x - \mu)^2\, p(x)$$

$$= (0 - 3.5)^2(.002) + (1 - 3.5)^2(.029) + (2 - 3.5)^2(.132)$$

$$+ (3 - 3.5)^2(.309) + (4 - 3.5)^2(.360) + (5 - 3.5)^2(.168)$$

$$= 1.05$$

Thus, the standard deviation is

$$\sigma = \sqrt{\sigma^2} = \sqrt{1.05} = 1.02$$

c. The graph of $p(x)$ is shown in Figure 6.4. Note that the mean μ and the interval $\mu \pm 2\sigma$ are shown on the graph. We can use μ and σ to describe the probability distribution $p(x)$ in the same way that we used $\bar{x}$ and s to describe a relative frequency distribution in Chapter 4. Note particularly that $\mu = 3.5$ locates the center of the probability distribution. If the investment is made in the five ventures, we expect to obtain a number x of successes near 3.5. Similarly, $\sigma = 1.02$ measures the spread of the probability distribution $p(x)$. Since this distribution is a theoretical relative frequency distribution that is moderately mound-shaped (see Figure 6.4), we expect (see Table 4.3) at least 75% and, more likely, near 95% of observed x values to fall in the interval $\mu \pm 2\sigma$, i.e., between 1.46 and 5.54. Compare this with the actual probability that x falls in the interval $\mu \pm 2\sigma$. From Figure 6.4 you can see that this probability includes the sum of $p(x)$ for all values of x except $p(0) = .002$ and $p(1) = .029$. Therefore, 96.9% of the probability distribution lies within 2 standard deviations of the mean. This percentage is consistent with Table 4.3.

CASE STUDY 6.1

The June 1, 1977 business section of the Orlando, Florida, *Sentinel Star* featured the following headline: "Red Lobster to Fight Tax Claim." According to the *Sentinel Star,* the Red Lobster Inns of America, a national seafood chain, has decided to take the state of Florida to court. The dispute concerns the 4% sales tax levied on most purchases in the state and mainly focuses on the state's "bracket collection system." According to the bracket system, a merchant must collect 1¢ for sales between 10¢ and 25¢, 2¢ for sales from 26¢ to 50¢, 3¢ for sales between 51¢ and 75¢, and 4¢ for

FIGURE 6.4
GRAPH OF p(x) FOR
EXAMPLE 6.3

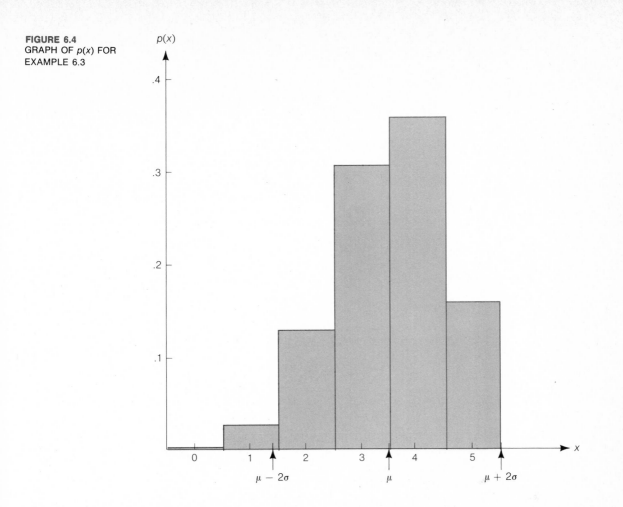

sales between 76¢ and 99¢. Red Lobster contends that if this system is followed, merchants will always collect more than 4%. That is, if a sale is made for $10.41, 4% will be collected on the $10, but more than 4% will be collected on the 41¢. This, they contend, will amount to more than 4% on the total sale and therefore is not consistent with the 4% tax required by law.

Concrete evidence supplied by the state of Florida tax records do indeed support the contention that the amount of tax collected using the bracket system exceeds the 4% specified by law. It appears that the state sales tax receipts exceeded expected revenue (based on 4%) by $9.5 million.

What percent sales tax should the state expect to receive using the bracket system for computing the tax? (As noted, the tax on the whole dollar portion of the sale will be 4%.) Using the formula for calculating expected values, you can show (see Exercise 6.86) that the expected percent tax paid on the cents portion of a sale is 4.6%.

6.11. Given the probability distribution:

x	p(x)
2	.1
3	.2
4	.2
5	.3
10	.2

a. Find μ.
b. Graph $p(x)$ and locate μ on the graph.

6.12. Given the probability distribution:

x	p(x)
0	.2
10	.3
20	.3
30	.2

a. Find μ.
b. Graph $p(x)$ and locate μ on the graph.

6.13. Given the following probability distribution, compute μ:

x	p(x)
−4	.05
−3	.07
−2	.10
−1	.15
0	.26
1	.15
2	.10
3	.07
4	.05

6.14. A company's marketing and accounting departments have determined that if the company markets its newly developed line of party favors, the following probability distribution will describe the contribution of the new line to the firm's profit during the next 6 months:

Profit contribution	p(Profit contribution)
−$5,000*	.3
$10,000	.4
$30,000	.3

*A negative profit is a loss.

The company has decided it should market the new line of party favors if the expected contribution to profit for the next 6 months is over $10,000. Based on the probability distribution, will the company market the new line?

6.15. Given the following probability distribution, compute μ, σ^2, and σ for the random variable x:

x	$p(x)$
0.5	.05
1.5	.20
2.5	.25
4.5	.35
6.5	.10
7.5	.02
8.5	.03

a. Graph $p(x)$. Locate μ and the interval $\mu \pm 2\sigma$ on the graph.
b. What is the probability that x will fall within the interval $\mu \pm 2\sigma$?

6.16. Refer to Exercise 6.13. Compute σ^2 and σ for the random variable x. Graph $p(x)$. Locate μ and the interval $\mu \pm 2\sigma$ on the graph. What is the probability that x will fall within the interval $\mu \pm 2\sigma$?

6.17. A buyer for a large department store wants to project the required inventory for men's ten-speed bicycles next spring. Experience has shown that demand (x) has approximately the probability distribution shown.

DEMAND x = Number of bicycles	$p(x)$
40	.01
60	.06
80	.16
100	.24
120	.23
140	.15
160	.10
180	.05

a. Find $E(x)$.
b. Find $E[(x - \mu)^2]$.
c. Find σ.
d. Graph $p(x)$ and locate μ and the interval $\mu \pm 2\sigma$ on the graph.
e. Based on the above information, how many bicycles would you order for next spring? Explain the reasoning behind your decision.

6.18. Describe the difference between the meanings of the symbols μ and $\bar{x}$.

6.19. You have decided to purchase either stock A or stock B. Discuss how the variance of the daily closing price for each stock might be used to help you evaluate the relative risk involved in investing in one stock rather than the other.

6.20. In the context of the following sentence from Section 6.3, discuss what is meant by the phrase "a theoretical model": "Thus, the probability distribution for a random variable is a theoretical model for the relative frequency distribution of a population."

6.4
THE BINOMIAL RANDOM VARIABLE

A common source of business data is an opinion or preference survey. Many of these surveys result in dichotomous responses, i.e., responses that admit one of two possible alternatives, such as Yes–No. The number of Yes responses (or No responses) will usually have a binomial probability distribution. For example, suppose a random sample of consumers is selected from the totality of potential consumers of a particular product. The number of consumers in the sample who prefer the product to its competition is a random variable that has a binomial probability distribution.

All experiments that have the characteristics of the coin tossing experiments of Chapter 5 and the preceding sections of this chapter yield binomial random variables. Imagine an experiment that is equivalent to tossing a coin n times. Although the coin may not be balanced, you are interested in observing the number of heads, x, in the n tosses. For such an experiment, x is a binomial random variable. In general, to decide whether a discrete random variable has a binomial probability distribution, check it against the characteristics listed below.

CHARACTERISTICS OF A BINOMIAL RANDOM VARIABLE

1. The experiment consists of n identical trials.
2. There are only two possible outcomes on each trial. We will denote one outcome by S (for Success) and the other by F (for Failure).
3. The probability of S remains the same from trial to trial. This probability will be denoted by p, and the probability of F will be denoted by q. Note that $p + q = 1$.
4. The trials are independent.
5. The binomial random variable x is the number of S's in n trials.

EXAMPLE 6.4

For each of the following examples, decide whether x is a binomial random variable:

a. You randomly select three bonds out of a possible ten for an investment portfolio. Unknown to you, eight of the ten will maintain their present value, and the other two will lose value due to a change in their ratings. Let x be the number of the three bonds you select that lose value.

b. Before marketing a new product on a large scale, many companies conduct a consumer preference survey to determine whether the product is likely to be successful. Suppose a company develops a new diet soda, and then conducts a taste-preference survey with 100 randomly chosen consumers stating their preference among the new soda and the two leading sellers. Let x be the number of the 100 who choose the new brand over the two others.

c. Some surveys are conducted using a method of sampling other than simple random sampling (defined in Chapter 5). For example, suppose a television cable company is trying to decide whether to establish a branch in a particular city. The company plans to conduct a survey to determine the fraction of households in the city that would use the cable television service. The sampling method is to choose a city block at random, and then to survey every household on that block. This sampling technique is called **cluster sampling**. Suppose ten blocks are sampled in this manner, producing a total of 124 household responses. Let x be the number of the 124 households that would use the cable television service.

Solution

a. In checking the binomial characteristics, a problem arises with independence (characteristic 4 in the box). Suppose the first bond you picked was one of the two that will lose value. This reduces the chances that the second bond you pick will lose value, since now only one of the nine remaining bonds are in that category. Thus, the choices you make are dependent, and therefore x, the number of the three bonds you select that lose value, is *not* a binomial random variable.

b. Surveys that produce dichotomous responses and use random sampling techniques are classical examples of binomial experiments. In our example, each randomly selected consumer either states a preference for the new diet soda or does not. The sample of 100 consumers is a very small proportion of the totality of potential consumers, so the response of one would be, for all practical purposes, independent of another. Thus, x is a binomial random variable.

c. This example is a survey with dichotomous responses (Yes or No to the cable service), but the sampling method is not simple random sampling. Again, the binomial characteristic of independent trials would very probably not be satisfied. The responses of households within a particular block almost surely would be dependent, since households within a block tend to be similar with respect to income, race, and general interests. Thus, the binomial model would not be satisfactory for x if the cluster sampling technique were employed.

The probability distribution for the binomial random variable is shown (in formula form) below:

THE BINOMIAL PROBABILITY DISTRIBUTION

$$p(x) = \binom{n}{x} p^x q^{n-x} \qquad (x = 0, 1, 2, \ldots, n)$$

where

$p = $ Probability of a success on a single trial

$q = 1 - p$

$n = $ Number of trials

$x = $ Number of successes in n trials

$$\binom{n}{x} = \frac{n!}{x!(n-x)!}$$

As noted in Chapter 5, the symbol 5! means $5 \cdot 4 \cdot 3 \cdot 2 \cdot 1 = 120$. Similarly, $n! = n(n - 1)(n - 2) \cdots 3 \cdot 2 \cdot 1$, and, remember, $0! = 1$.

The mean, variance, and standard deviation for the binomial variable x are shown below:

MEAN, VARIANCE, AND STANDARD DEVIATION FOR A BINOMIAL RANDOM VARIABLE

$$\text{Mean:} \quad \mu = np$$

$$\text{Variance:} \quad \sigma^2 = npq$$

$$\text{Standard deviation:} \quad \sigma = \sqrt{npq}$$

As we demonstrated in Chapters 3 and 4, the mean and standard deviation provide measures of the central tendency and variability, respectively, of a distribution. Thus, we can use μ and σ to obtain a rough visualization of the probability distribution for x when the calculation of the probabilities is too tedious. To illustrate the use of the binomial probability distribution, consider the example below.

EXAMPLE 6.5

A machine that produces stampings for automobile engines is malfunctioning and producing 10% defectives. The defective and nondefective stampings proceed from the machine in a random manner. If five stampings are randomly collected, find the probability that three of them are defective.

Solution

Let $p = .1$ be the probability that a single stamping will be defective and let x equal the number of defectives in $n = 5$ trials. Then

$$q = 1 - p = 1 - .1 = .9$$

and

$$p(x) = \binom{n}{x} p^x q^{n-x} = \binom{5}{x} (.1)^x (.9)^{5-x}$$

$$= \frac{5!}{x!(5 - x)!} (.1)^x (.9)^{5-x} \qquad (x = 0, 1, 2, 3, 4, 5)$$

To find the probability of $x = 3$ defectives in a sample of $n = 5$, substitute $x = 3$ into the formula for $p(x)$ to obtain

$$p(3) = \frac{5!}{3!(5 - 3)!} (.1)^3 (.9)^{5-3} = \frac{5!}{3!2!} (.1)^3 (.9)^2$$

$$= \frac{5 \cdot 4 \cdot 3 \cdot 2 \cdot 1}{(3 \cdot 2 \cdot 1)(2 \cdot 1)} (.1)^3 (.9)^2$$

$$= .0081$$

EXAMPLE 6.6

Refer to Example 6.5 and find the values of $p(0)$, $p(1)$, $p(2)$, $p(4)$, and $p(5)$. Graph $p(x)$. Calculate the mean μ and standard deviation σ. Locate μ and the interval $\mu - 2\sigma$ to $\mu + 2\sigma$ on the graph. If the experiment were repeated many times, what proportion of the x observations would fall within the interval $\mu - 2\sigma$ to $\mu + 2\sigma$?

Solution

Again, $n = 5$, $p = .1$, and $q = .9$. Then, substituting into the formula for $p(x)$:

$$p(0) = \frac{5!}{0!(5-0)!}(.1)^0(.9)^{5-0} = \frac{5 \cdot 4 \cdot 3 \cdot 2 \cdot 1}{(1)(5 \cdot 4 \cdot 3 \cdot 2 \cdot 1)}(1)(.9)^5$$

$$= .59049$$

$$p(1) = \frac{5!}{1!(5-1)!}(.1)^1(.9)^{5-1} = 5(.1)(.9)^4$$

$$= .32805$$

$$p(2) = \frac{5!}{2!(5-2)!}(.1)^2(.9)^{5-2} = (10)(.1)^2(.9)^3$$

$$= .07290$$

$$p(4) = \frac{5!}{4!(5-4)!}(.1)^4(.9)^{5-4} = 5(.1)^4(.9)$$

$$= .00045$$

$$p(5) = \frac{5!}{5!(5-5)!}(.1)^5(.9)^{5-5} = (.1)^5$$

$$= .00001$$

The graph of $p(x)$, appearing as a probability histogram, is shown in Figure 6.5 [$p(3)$ is taken from Example 6.4 to be .0081].

To calculate the values of μ and σ, substitute $n = 5$ and $p = .1$ into the following formulas:

$$\mu = np = (5)(.1) = .5$$
$$\sigma = \sqrt{npq} = \sqrt{(5)(.1)(.9)} = \sqrt{.45} = .67$$

To find the interval $\mu - 2\sigma$ to $\mu + 2\sigma$, we calculate

$$\mu - 2\sigma = .5 - 2(.67) = -.84 \qquad \mu + 2\sigma = .5 + 2(.67) = 1.84$$

If the experiment were repeated a large number of times, what proportion of the x observations would fall within the interval $\mu - 2\sigma$ to $\mu + 2\sigma$? You can see from Figure 6.5 that all observations equal to 0 or 1 will fall within the interval. The probabilities corresponding to these values are .5905 and .3280, respectively. Consequently, you would expect $.5905 + .3280 = .9185$, or approximately 91.9%, of the observations to fall within the interval $\mu - 2\sigma$ to $\mu + 2\sigma$. This again emphasizes that for most probability distributions, observations rarely fall more than 2 standard deviations from μ.

FIGURE 6.5
THE BINOMIAL
DISTRIBUTION:
$n = 5$, $p = .1$

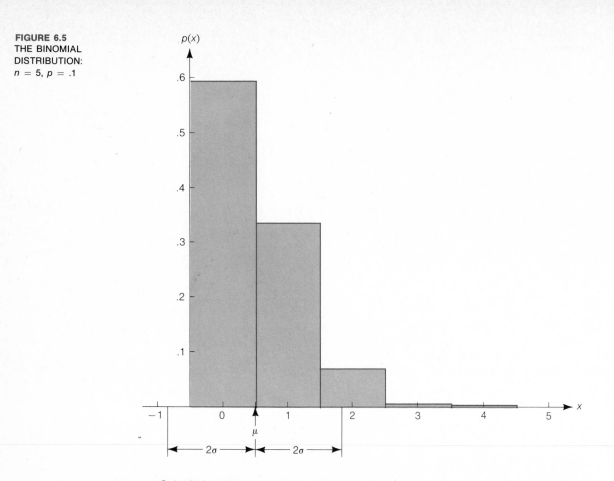

Calculating all the binomial probabilities is tedious when n is large. You can often avoid this calculation by using Table II in Appendix B, part of which is shown in Figure 6.6. Because we will have greater use for the sums of the binomial probabilities than for the probabilities corresponding to specific values of x, the entries in Table II are the cumulative sums

$$P(x \leq k) = p(0) + p(1) + p(2) + \cdots + p(k)$$

for values of k equal to 0, 1, 2, . . . , $(n - 1)$. Note that all entries at $k = n$ would be 1.000 [$P(x \leq n) = 1$, so we omit this row from the binomial tables.]

The part of Table II shown in Figure 6.6 corresponds to $n = 10$ trials. Values of p are shown across the top row and values of a number k are shown at the left. To find $P(x \leq 2)$ for $n = 10$ and $p = .1$, see the column corresponding to $p = .1$ and the row corresponding to $k = 2$. The recorded value is

$$P(x \leq 2) = .930$$

You can also use Table II to find the probabilities associated with specific values of x. Remember that the entries in the table are the sums of the binomial probabilities

CHAPTER 6 DISCRETE RANDOM VARIABLES

FIGURE 6.6
REPRODUCTION OF PART OF TABLE II, APPENDIX B

b. $n = 10$

k \ p	0.01	0.05	0.10	0.20	0.30	0.40	0.50	0.60	0.70	0.80	0.90	0.95	0.99
0	.904	.599	.349	.107	.028	.006	.001	.000	.000	.000	.000	.000	.000
1	.996	.914	.736	.376	.149	.046	.011	.002	.000	.000	.000	.000	.000
2	1.000	.988	.930	.678	.383	.167	.055	.012	.002	.000	.000	.000	.000
3	1.000	.999	.987	.879	.650	.382	.172	.055	.011	.001	.000	.000	.000
4	1.000	1.000	.998	.967	.850	.633	.377	.166	.047	.006	.000	.000	.000
5	1.000	1.000	1.000	.994	.953	.834	.623	.367	.150	.033	.002	.000	.000
6	1.000	1.000	1.000	.999	.989	.945	.828	.618	.350	.121	.013	.001	.000
7	1.000	1.000	1.000	1.000	.998	.988	.945	.833	.617	.322	.070	.012	.000
8	1.000	1.000	1.000	1.000	1.000	.998	.989	.954	.851	.624	.264	.086	.004
9	1.000	1.000	1.000	1.000	1.000	1.000	.999	.994	.972	.893	.651	.401	.096

from $x = 0$ to $x = k$. Therefore, to find the probability that x is exactly 2 for $n = 10$ and $p = .1$, go to Table II and subtract the entry in row 1 from the entry in row 2 in the column corresponding to $p = .1$. That is,

$$p(2) = \sum_{x=0}^{2} p(x) - \sum_{x=0}^{1} p(x)$$
$$= .930 - .736 = .194$$

EXAMPLE 6.7

Suppose a poll of twenty employees is taken in a large company. The purpose is to determine x, the number who favor unionization. Suppose that 60% of all the company's employees favor unionization.

a. Find the mean and standard deviation of x.
b. Use Table II to find the probability that $x < 10$.
c. Use Table II to find the probability that $x > 12$.
d. Use Table II to find the probability that $x = 11$.

Solution

a. The number of employees polled is presumably small compared with the total number of employees in this company. Thus, we may treat x, the number of the twenty who favor unionization, as a binomial random variable. The value of p is the fraction of the total employees who favor unionization, i.e., $p = .6$. Therefore, we calculate the mean and variance:

$$\mu = np = 20(.6) = 12$$
$$\sigma^2 = npq = 20(.6)(.4) = 4.8$$

The standard deviation is then

$$\sigma = \sqrt{4.8} = 2.19$$

b. The tabulated value is

$$P(x \le 9) = .128$$

c. To find the probability

$$P(x > 12) = \sum_{x=13}^{20} p(x)$$

we use the fact that for all probability distributions, $\sum_{\text{All } x} p(x) = 1$. Therefore,

$$P(x > 12) = 1 - P(x \le 12)$$

$$= 1 - \sum_{x=0}^{12} p(x)$$

Consulting Table II, we find the entry in row $k = 12$, column $p = .6$ to be .584. Thus,

$$P(x > 12) = 1 - .584 = .416$$

d. To find the probability that exactly eleven employees favor unionization, recall that the entries in Table II are cumulative probabilities and use the relationship

$$P(x = 11) = [p(0) + p(1) + \cdots + p(10) + p(11)]$$
$$- [p(0) + p(1) + \cdots + p(9) + p(10)]$$
$$= P(x \le 11) - P(x \le 10)$$

Then

$$P(x = 11) = .404 - .245 = .159$$

The probability distribution for x in this example is shown in Figure 6.7. Note that the interval $\mu \pm 2\sigma = (7.6, 16.4)$.

CASE STUDY 6.2

Arthur A. Brown, Frank T. Hulswit, and John D. Kettelle (1956) were asked by a large firm to study, and perhaps determine reasons for and solutions to, its lack of growth over the prior 5 years. In their article, Brown et al. refer to the firm as "Penstock Press, a large commercial printing company."

The primary concern of the study was Penstock's sales operations. Accordingly, Brown et al. conducted an experiment to study the sales-effectiveness of Penstock's salespeople. The salespeople were instructed to increase their sales efforts toward all of Penstock's customers, but in particular toward sixty of the larger customers, for a 4 month experimental period. At the end of the 4 month period it was determined that the probability of a customer making a genuinely positive response to the increased sales effort merely by chance was .25. Of Penstock's sixty large customers, it was noted that twenty-four made what appeared to be genuinely positive responses. But before concluding that the increased sales effort toward the sixty large customers had paid off, Brown et al. felt it was important to determine how likely it would be for twenty-four or more of the sixty customers to make positive responses merely by chance. Assuming that the probability of a positive response occurring by chance (.25) is the same for each of the sixty customers, and that the response of one customer

FIGURE 6.7
THE BINOMIAL
PROBABILITY
DISTRIBUTION FOR x
IN EXAMPLE 6.7:
$n = 20, p = .6$

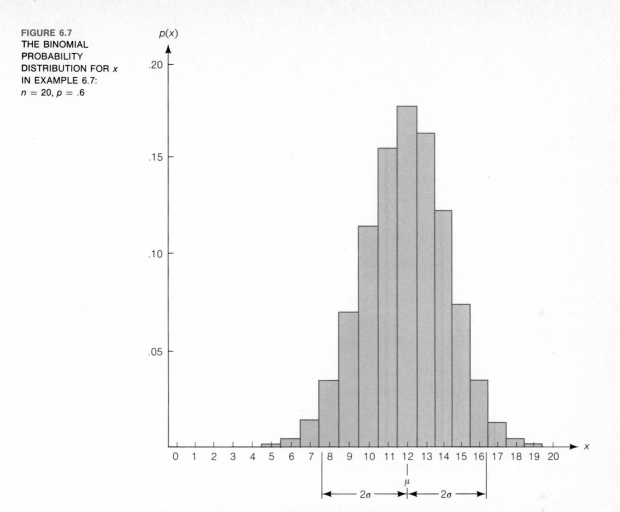

does not affect that of another, the number of positive responses observed has a binomial probability distribution. Accordingly, the probability of twenty-four or more positive responses from the sixty customers can be determined as follows:

$$P(x \geq 24, n = 60, p = .25) = \sum_{x=24}^{60} \binom{60}{x} .25^x (.75)^{60-x} = .004$$

(Due to the size of n, the number of customers in the experiment, it would be unrealistic to try to compute the above probability by hand. If you had access to binomial tables for $n = 60$ and $p = .25$, the probability could be found using the tables. Otherwise it would be necessary to use a computer or an approximation such as the one we will discuss in Section 7.5.) The fact that the probability of observing twenty-four or more genuinely positive responses from the sixty customers merely by chance is only .004 indicates that in actually observing twenty-four such responses either a very rare event has occurred or the responses were in fact genuine and the increased sales effort did influence the increase in sales.

Brown et al. (1956) concluded that the number of positive responses could not be explained by chance, but they in fact "implied deliberate continuing business from the customers," i.e., genuine responses. The authors noted that this conclusion was supported by Penstock's salespeople.

6.21. Compute the following:

a. $\dfrac{5!}{2!(5-2)!}$ b. $\dbinom{6}{3}$ c. $\dbinom{4}{0}$

6.22. Given that x is a binomial random variable, $n = 5$, and $p = .2$, calculate the values for $p(x)$, $x = 0, 1, 2, 3, 4, 5$. Graph $p(x)$.

6.23. Given that x is a binomial random variable, compute $p(x)$ for each of the following cases:

a. $n = 4$, $x = 2$, $p = .5$
b. $n = 3$, $x = 3$, $q = .9$
c. $n = 2$, $x = 0$, $p = .3$

6.24. Given that x is a binomial random variable, $n = 5$, and $p = .3$:

a. Display $p(x)$ in tabular form.
b. Compute the mean and variance of x.
c. Graph $p(x)$ and locate $E(x)$ and the interval $\mu \pm 2\sigma$ on the graph.
d. What is the probability that x falls within the interval $\mu \pm 2\sigma$?

6.25. Given that x is a binomial random variable, $n = 6$, and $p = .5$:

a. Display $p(x)$ in tabular form.
b. Compute the mean and variance of x.
c. Graph $p(x)$ and locate $E(x)$ and the interval $\mu \pm 2\sigma$ on the graph.
d. What is the probability that x falls within the interval $\mu \pm 2\sigma$?

6.26. Use the results of Exercise 6.25 to find the following probabilities:

a. $P(x \le 2)$ b. $P(x \le 4)$ c. $P(x < 3)$

6.27. Given that x is a binomial random variable, $n = 15$, and $p = .3$, use Table II to find the following probabilities:

a. $P(x \le 2)$ b. $P(x \ge 5)$ c. $P(x \le 14)$
d. $P(x < 10)$ e. $P(x > 10)$ f. $P(x = 10)$

6.28. Your firm's accountant believes that 10% of the company's invoices contain arithmetic errors. To check this theory the accountant randomly samples twenty-five invoices and finds that seven contain errors. What is the probability that of the twenty-five invoices written, seven or more contain errors? What assumptions do you have to make to solve this problem using the methodology of this chapter?

6.29. A problem of great concern to a manufacturer is the cost of repair and replacement required under a product's guarantee agreement. Assume it is known that 10% of all electronic pocket calculators purchased are returned for repair while their guarantee is still in effect. If a firm purchased twenty-five pocket calculators for its salespeople, what is the probability that five or more of these calculators will need repair while their guarantees are still in effect?

6.30. Suppose you are a purchasing officer for a company. You have purchased 50,000 electrical switches and have been guaranteed by the supplier that the shipment will contain no more than 0.1% defectives. To check the shipment, you randomly sample 500 switches, test them, and find that four are defective. Calculate μ and σ for this sample of 500. Based on this evidence, do you think the supplier has complied with the guarantee? Explain. [*Hint:* Use μ and σ for $p = .001$ to see if a value of x as large as 4 is probable.]

6.31. Most firms utilize sampling plans to control the quality of manufactured items ready for shipment or the quality of items that have been purchased. To illustrate the use of a sampling plan, suppose you are shipping electrical fuses in lots, each containing 10,000 fuses. The plan specifies that you will randomly sample twenty-five fuses from each lot and accept (and ship) the lot if the number of defective fuses, x, in the sample is less than 3. If $x \geq 3$, you will reject the lot and hold it for a complete reinspection. What is the probability of accepting a lot ($x = 0$, 1, or 2) if the actual fraction defective in the lot is:

a. 1   b. .8   c. .5
d. .2   e. .05   f. 0

Construct a graph showing $P(A)$, the probability of lot acceptance, as a function of lot fraction defective, p. This graph is called the **operating characteristic curve** for the sampling plan.

6.32. Refer to Exercise 6.31. Suppose the sampling plan called for sampling $n = 25$ fuses and accepting a lot if $x \leq 3$. Calculate the quantities specified in Exercise 6.31 and construct the operating characteristic curve for this sampling plan. Compare this curve with the curve obtained in Exercise 6.31. (Note how the curve characterizes the ability of the plan to screen bad lots from shipment.)

6.33. After a costly study, a market analyst claims that 12% of all consumers in a particular sales region prefer a certain noncarbonated beverage. To check the validity of this figure, you decide to conduct a survey in the region. You randomly sample $n = 400$ consumers and find that $x = 31$ prefer the beverage. Compute μ and σ for x. Based on a sample of 400, is it likely that you will observe a value of $x \leq 31$? Explain. Do the results of your survey agree with the 12% estimate given by the market analyst?

6.5 THE POISSON RANDOM VARIABLE (OPTIONAL)

A type of probability distribution useful in describing the number of events that will occur in a specific period of time or in a specific area or volume is the **Poisson distribution** (named after the eighteenth century physicist and mathematician, Siméon Poisson). Typical examples of random variables for which the Poisson probability distribution provides a good model are:

1. The number of industrial accidents in a given manufacturing plant per month observed by a plant safety supervisor.

2. The number of noticeable surface defects (scratches, dents, etc.) found by quality inspectors on a new automobile (or any manufactured product).

3. The parts per million of some toxicant found in the water or air emission from a manufacturing plant (a random variable of great interest to both the business community and the Environmental Protection Agency).

4. The number of arithmetic errors per 100 invoices (or per 1,000 invoices, etc.) in the accounting records of a company.

5. The number of customer arrivals per unit time at a service counter (a service station, a hospital clinic, a supermarket checkout counter, etc.).

6. The number of death claims per day received by an insurance company.

7. The number of breakdowns of an electronic computer per month.

The characteristics of the Poisson random variable are usually rather difficult to verify for practical examples. The examples given above satisfy them well enough that the Poisson distribution provides a good model in many instances. As with all probability models, the real test of the adequacy of the Poisson model is in whether it provides a reasonable approximation to reality, that is, whether empirical data support it.

CHARACTERISTICS OF A POISSON RANDOM VARIABLE

1. The experiment consists of counting the number of times a particular event occurs during a given unit of time, or in a given area or volume (or weight, distance, or any other unit of measurement).

2. The probability that an event occurs in a given unit of time, area, or volume is the same for all the units.

3. The number of events that occur in one unit of time, area, or volume is independent of the number that occur in other units.

4. The mean (or expected) number of events in each unit will be denoted by the Greek letter lambda, λ.

The probability distribution, mean, and variance for a Poisson random variable are shown at the top of page 139.*

In Table III of Appendix B you will find values of $e^{-\lambda}$ for various values of λ. These will aid in calculating Poisson probabilities.

---

*The Poisson probabilities are good approximations to the binomial probabilities when n is large and p is small (say, $np \leq 7$). To illustrate with a relatively small value of n, if $n = 25$ and $p = .05$, the exact value (to three places) of the binomial probability $p(2)$ is .231. The Poisson approximation is .224. The approximations are much better for $n > 100$ (see Exercise 6.42).

> PROBABILITY DISTRIBUTION, MEAN, AND VARIANCE FOR A
> POISSON RANDOM VARIABLE
>
> $$p(x) = \frac{\lambda^x e^{-\lambda}}{x!} \qquad (x = 0, 1, 2, \ldots)$$
>
> $$\mu = \lambda \qquad \sigma^2 = \lambda$$
>
> where
>
> λ = Mean number of events during the given time period
>
> $e = 2.71828 \ldots$

EXAMPLE 6.8

Suppose the number x of a company's absent employees on Mondays has (approximately) a Poisson probability distribution. Furthermore, assume that the average number of Monday absentees is 2.5.

a. Find the mean and standard deviation of x, the number of absent employees on Monday.
b. Find the probability that exactly five employees are absent on a given Monday.
c. Find the probability that two or more employees are absent on a Monday.

Solution

a. The mean and variance of a Poisson random variable are both equal to λ. Thus, for this example

$$\mu = \lambda = 2.5 \qquad \sigma^2 = \lambda = 2.5$$

Then the standard deviation is

$$\sigma = \sqrt{2.5} = 1.58$$

b. We want the probability that exactly five employees are absent on Monday. The probability distribution for x is

$$p(x) = \frac{\lambda^x e^{-\lambda}}{x!}$$

Then, since $\lambda = 2.5$, $x = 5$, and $e^{-2.5} = .082085$ (from Table III),

$$p(5) = \frac{(2.5)^5 e^{-2.5}}{5!} = \frac{(2.5)^5 (.082085)}{5 \cdot 4 \cdot 3 \cdot 2 \cdot 1} = .067$$

c. To find the probability that two or more employees are absent on Monday, we need to find

$$P(x \geq 2) = p(2) + p(3) + p(4) + \cdots = \sum_{x=2}^{\infty} p(x)$$

FIGURE 6.8
POISSON
PROBABILITY
DISTRIBUTION FOR x
IN EXAMPLE 6.8

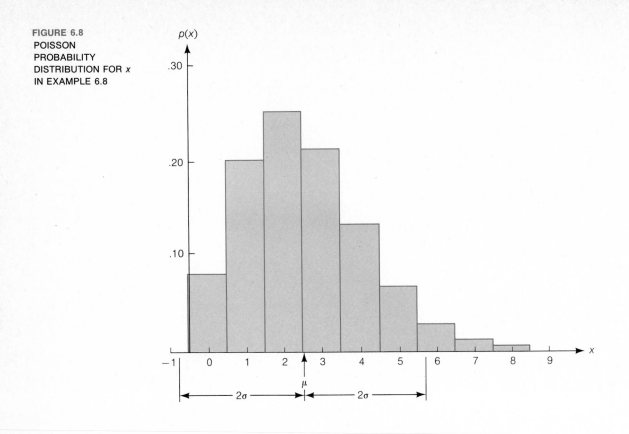

Rather than attempting to calculate this very long summation, we use the complementary event:

$$P(x \geq 2) = 1 - P(x \leq 1) = 1 - [p(0) + p(1)]$$

$$= 1 - \frac{(2.5)^0 \, e^{-2.5}}{0!} - \frac{(2.5)^1 \, e^{-2.5}}{1!}$$

$$= 1 - \frac{1(.082085)}{1} - \frac{2.5(.082085)}{1}$$

$$= 1 - .287 = .713$$

According to our Poisson model, the probability that two or more employees are absent on a Monday is .713.

The probability distribution for x in the example is shown in Figure 6.8 for x values between 0 and 9. The mean $\mu = 2.5$ and the interval $\mu \pm 2\sigma = (-.7, 5.7)$ are indicated.

EXERCISES

6.34. Give examples of two random variables of interest to a banker for which the Poisson probability distribution provides a good model.

6.35. Given that x is a random variable for which a Poisson probability distribution provides a good characterization, compute the following:

    a. $P(x \leq 3)$, when $\lambda = 2$ b. $P(x = 0)$, when $\lambda = 5$

    c. $P(x \geq 1)$, when $\lambda = 1$ d. $P(x = 0)$, when $\lambda = 10$

6.36. Given that x is a random variable for which a Poisson probability distribution with $\lambda = 2$ provides a good characterization:

    a. Graph $p(x)$ for $x = 0, 1, 2, \ldots , 9$.

    b. Find μ and σ for x, and locate μ and the interval $\mu \pm 2\sigma$ on the graph.

    c. What is the probability that x will fall within the interval $\mu \pm 2\sigma$?

6.37. Given that x is a random variable for which a Poisson probability distribution with $\lambda = 5$ provides a good characterization:

    a. Graph $p(x)$ for $x = 0, 1, 2, \ldots , 9$.

    b. Find μ and σ for x, and locate μ and the interval $\mu \pm 2\sigma$ on the graph.

    c. What is the probability that x will fall within the interval $\mu \pm 2\sigma$?

6.38. The safety supervisor at a large manufacturing plant believes the expected number of industrial accidents per month to be 3.4. What is the probability of exactly two accidents occurring next month? Three or more? What assumptions do you need to make to solve this problem using the methodology of this chapter?

6.39. As a check on the quality of the wooden doors produced by a company, its owner requested that each door undergo inspection for defects before leaving the plant. The plant's quality control inspector found that on the average 1 square foot of door surface contains 0.5 minor flaw. Subsequently, 1 square foot of each door's surface was examined for flaws. The owner decided to have all doors reworked that were found to have two or more minor flaws in the square foot of surface that was inspected. What is the probability that a door will fail inspection and be sent back for reworking? What is the probability that a door will pass inspection?

6.40. The probability distribution of x, the number of people who arrive at a cashier's counter in a bank during a specified period of time, often possesses (approximately) a Poisson probability distribution. Knowing the mean arrival rate, λ, the Poisson probability distribution can be used to aid in the design of the customer service facility. Suppose you estimate that the mean number of arrivals per minute for cashier service at a bank is one person per minute. What is the probability that in a given minute, the number of arrivals will equal three or more? Can you tell the bank manager that the number of arrivals will rarely exceed three per minute?

6.41. The Environmental Protection Agency (EPA) issues standards on air and water pollution that vitally affect the safety of consumers and the operations of industry. For example, the EPA states that manufacturers of vinyl chloride and similar compounds must limit the amount of these chemicals in plant air emissions to 10 parts per million. Suppose you represent one of the manufacturers and you know that the mean emission of vinyl chloride for your plant is 4 parts per million. If the parts per million of vinyl chloride in air follows a Poisson probability distribution and x is the parts per million for a particular sample, what is the standard deviation of x for your plant? If the mean parts per million for your plant is really equal to 4, is it likely that a sample would yield a value of x that would exceed the EPA limits? Explain.

6.42. When n is large, p is small, and $np \leq 7$, the Poisson probability distribution provides a good approximation to the binomial probability distribution. Since we provide exact binomial probabilities (Table II in Appendix B) for relatively small values of n, you can investigate the adequacy of the approximation for $n = 25$. Use Table II to find $p(0)$, $p(1)$, and $p(2)$ for $n = 25$ and $p = .05$. Calculate the corresponding Poisson approximations using $\lambda = \mu = np$. (Note that these approximations are reasonably good for n as small as 25. To use the approximation, we would prefer that $n \geq 100$.)

6.43. The probability that a health insurance company must pay a major medical claim for a policy is .001. If a group of 1,000 policyholders represents a random sample from all possible policyholders, what is the probability that the insurance company will have to pay at least one major medical claim in this sample? [*Hint:* See Exercise 6.42.]

6.6 THE HYPERGEOMETRIC RANDOM VARIABLE (OPTIONAL)

The **hypergeometric probability distribution** provides a realistic model for some types of enumerative (count) data. The characteristics of the hypergeometric distribution are listed below:

CHARACTERISTICS OF A HYPERGEOMETRIC RANDOM VARIABLE

1. The experiment consists of randomly drawing n elements without replacement from a set of N elements, r of which are S's (for Success) and $(N - r)$ of which are F's (for Failure).

2. The hypergeometric random variable x is the number of S's in the draw of n elements.

Note that both the hypergeometric and binomial characteristics stipulate that each draw or trial results in one of two outcomes. The basic difference between these random variables is that the hypergeometric trials are dependent, while the binomial trials are independent. The draws are dependent because the probability of drawing an S (or an F) is dependent upon what occurred on preceding draws.

To illustrate the dependence between trials, we note that the probability of drawing an S on the first draw is r/N. Then, the probability of drawing an S on the second draw depends on the outcome of the first. It will be either $(r - 1)/(N - 1)$ or $r/(N - 1)$, depending on whether the first draw was an S or an F. Consequently, the results of the draws represent dependent events.

For example, suppose we define x as the number of women hired in a random selection of three applicants from a total of six men and four women. This random variable satisfies the characteristics of a hypergeometric random variable with $N = 10$ and $n = 3$. The possible outcomes on each trial are either selection of a female (S) or selection of a male (F). Another example of a hypergeometric random variable is the number x of defective television picture tubes in a random selection of $n = 4$ from a shipment of $N = 8$ tubes. And, as a third example, suppose $n = 5$ stocks are randomly selected from a list of $N = 15$ stocks. Then, the number x of the five selected companies that pay regular dividends to stockholders is a hypergeometric random variable.

PROBABILITY DISTRIBUTION, MEAN, AND VARIANCE OF THE
HYPERGEOMETRIC RANDOM VARIABLE

$$p(x) = \frac{\binom{r}{x}\binom{N-r}{n-x}}{\binom{N}{n}} \qquad [x = \text{Maximum}[0, n - (N - r)], \ldots, \text{Minimum}(r, n)]$$

$$\mu = \frac{nr}{N} \qquad \sigma^2 = \frac{r(N-r)n(N-n)}{N^2(N-1)}$$

where

N = Total number of elements

r = Number of S's in the N elements

n = Number of elements drawn

x = Number of S's drawn in the n elements

EXAMPLE 6.9

Suppose, as we mentioned earlier, an employer randomly selects three new employees from a total of ten applicants, six men and four women. Let x be the number of women who are hired.

a. Find the mean and standard deviation of x.

b. Find the probability that no women are hired.

Solution

a. Since x is a hypergeometric random variable with $N = 10$, $n = 3$, and $r = 4$, the mean and variance are

$$\mu = \frac{nr}{N} = \frac{(3)(4)}{10} = 1.2$$

$$\sigma^2 = \frac{r(N-r)n(N-n)}{N^2(N-1)} = \frac{4(10-4)3(10-3)}{(10)^2(10-1)}$$

$$= \frac{(4)(6)(3)(7)}{(100)(9)} = .56$$

The standard deviation is

$$\sigma = \sqrt{.56} = .75$$

FIGURE 6.9
PROBABILITY
DISTRIBUTION FOR *x*
IN EXAMPLE 6.9

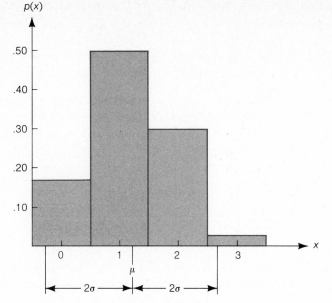

b. The probability that no women are selected by the employer, assuming the selection is truly random, is

$$P(x = 0) = p(0) = \frac{\binom{4}{0}\binom{10 - 4}{3 - 0}}{\binom{10}{3}}$$

$$= \frac{\dfrac{4!}{0!(4 - 0)!}\dfrac{6!}{3!(6 - 3)!}}{\dfrac{10!}{3!(10 - 3)!}} = \frac{(1)(20)}{120}$$

$$= \frac{1}{6}$$

The entire probability distribution for x in the example is shown in Figure 6.9. The mean $\mu = 1.2$ and the interval $\mu \pm 2\sigma = (-.3, 2.7)$ are indicated. You can see that if this random variable were observed over and over again for a large number of times, most of the values of x would fall within the interval $\mu \pm 2\sigma$.

EXERCISES

6.44. How do binomial and hypergeometric random variables differ? In what respects are they similar?

6.45. Given that x is a hypergeometric random variable, $N = 6$, $n = 3$, and $r = 4$, compute the following:

    a. $P(x = 1)$ b. $P(x = 0)$ c. $P(x = 3)$ d. $P(x \geq 4)$

6.46. Given that x is a hypergeometric random variable, compute $p(x)$ for each of the following cases:

  a. $N = 5$, $n = 3$, $r = 4$, $x = 1$
  b. $N = 10$, $n = 5$, $r = 3$, $x = 3$
  c. $N = 3$, $n = 2$, $r = 2$, $x = 2$
  d. $N = 4$, $n = 2$, $r = 2$, $x = 0$

6.47. Given that x is a hypergeometric random variable, $N = 10$, $n = 5$, and $r = 6$:

  a. Display the probability distribution for x in tabular form.
  b. Compute the mean and variance of x.
  c. Graph $p(x)$ and locate μ and the interval $\mu \pm 2\sigma$ on the graph.
  d. What is the probability that x will fall within the interval $\mu \pm 2\sigma$?

6.48. Given that x is a hypergeometric random variable, $N = 12$, $n = 8$, and $r = 7$:

  a. Display the probability distribution for x in tabular form.
  b. Compute μ and σ for x.
  c. Graph $p(x)$ and locate μ and the interval $\mu \pm 2\sigma$ on the graph.
  d. What is the probability that x will fall within the interval $\mu \pm 2\sigma$?

6.49. Use the results of Exercise 6.48 to find the following probabilities:

  a. $P(x = 1)$ b. $P(x = 4)$ c. $P(x \le 4)$
  d. $P(x \ge 5)$ e. $P(x < 3)$ f. $P(x \ge 8)$

6.50. Defective alternators have been mistakenly installed in three of the last six truck engines to emerge from an assembly line. It is not known which engines contain the defective alternators. If three of the six engines are randomly selected, what is the probability that each contains a defective alternator? None contain a defective alternator? More than one contain a defective alternator?

6.51. Five individuals apply for two vacancies in the shipping department of your plant. Two of the five people have superior credentials. You have been instructed to choose randomly two of the five applicants to fill the open positions. What is the probability that you will choose the two individuals with the superior credentials? At least one of the individuals with the superior credentials?

6.52. Suppose you are purchasing cases of wine (twelve bottles per case) and that periodically you select a test case to determine the adequacy of the sealing process. To do this, you randomly select and test three bottles in the case. If a case contains one spoiled bottle of wine, what is the probability that it will appear in your sample?

6.53. If you are purchasing small lots of a manufactured product and it is very costly to test a single item, it may be desirable to test a sample of items from the lot rather than every item in the lot. Such a sampling plan would be based upon a hypergeometric probability distribution. For example, suppose that each lot contains ten items. You decide to sample four items per lot and reject the lot if you observe one or more defectives. If the lot contains one defective item, what is the probability that you will accept the lot? What is the probability that you will accept the lot if it contains four defective items?

Another common discrete random variable that has many business applications is the geometric random variable. Like the binomial random variable, it arises naturally from a discussion of a coin tossing experiment (whether the coin is balanced or unbalanced). But instead of tossing the coin a fixed number of times and observing the number x of heads, we toss the coin and count the number x of tosses until the first head appears. Like the binomial experiment, we assume that the tosses are independent of each other. The geometric random variable has the characteristics listed below:

CHARACTERISTICS OF THE GEOMETRIC RANDOM VARIABLE

1. The experiment consists of a sequence of independent trials.
2. Each trial results in one of two outcomes. We denote one of them by S and the other by F.
3. The probability of S remains the same from trial to trial. We will denote this probability by p.
4. The geometric random variable x is defined to be the number of trials until the first S is observed.

The probability distribution for the geometric random variable provides a good model for the length of time a customer must wait for some type of servicing. For this application, the time must be measured in whole units (minutes, hours, etc.). Then, x is equal to the number of time units a customer must wait until he or she is served.

The number of job applicants interviewed by an employer until the first suitable prospect is found is another discrete random variable that might be modeled by a

---

PROBABILITY DISTRIBUTION, MEAN, AND VARIANCE OF A GEOMETRIC RANDOM VARIABLE

$$p(x) = q^{x-1}p \qquad (x = 1, 2, 3, 4, \ldots)$$

$$\mu = \frac{1}{p} \qquad \sigma^2 = \frac{q}{p^2}$$

where

$p = $ Probability of an S outcome

$q = 1 - p$

$x = $ Number of trials until the first S is observed.

---

geometric probability distribution. Or, for a sequence of independent drillings for oil, x could represent the number of drillings until the first successful well is hit.

EXAMPLE 6.10   Let x be the number of days until the closing price of a certain stock shows a gain over the previous day's closing price. Assume that x is a geometric random variable, with p, the probability of a gain in price from one day to the next, equal to .5.

a. Find the mean and standard deviation of x.
b. Find the probability that more than 2 days pass before a gain in price from one day to the next is observed.

Solution   **a.** The mean and variance for this geometric random variable are

$$\mu = \frac{1}{p} = \frac{1}{.5} = 2 \qquad \sigma^2 = \frac{q}{p^2} = \frac{.5}{(.5)(.5)} = 2$$

Then the standard deviation is

$$\sigma = \sqrt{\sigma^2} = \sqrt{2} = 1.41$$

FIGURE 6.10
PROBABILITY
DISTRIBUTION FOR x
IN EXAMPLE 6.10

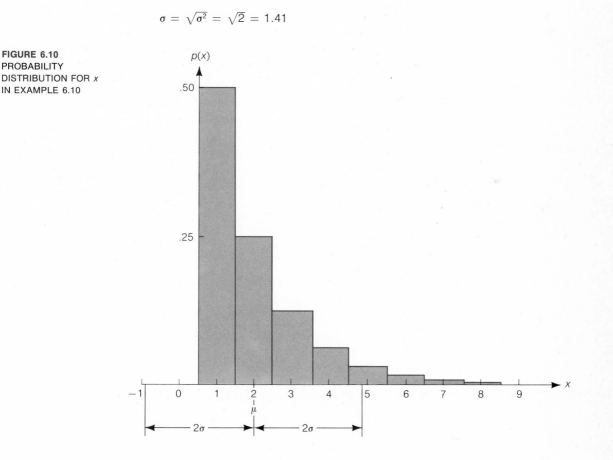

b. To find the probability that more than 2 days pass before a gain in price is observed, we must find

$$P(x > 2) = p(3) + p(4) + p(5) + \cdots$$

Since this sum is never-ending, we turn to the complementary event:

$$P(x > 2) = 1 - P(x \le 2)$$
$$= 1 - [p(1) + p(2)]$$

Now,

$$p(1) = q^{1-1}p^1 = (.5)^0(.5)^1 = .5$$
$$p(2) = q^{2-1}p^1 = (.5)^1(.5)^1 = .25$$

Thus,

$$P(x > 2) = 1 - [.5 + .25] = .25$$

There is a .25 probability that more than 2 days will pass before the stock shows a gain in its closing price from one day to the next.

The probability distribution for x in this example is shown in Figure 6.10. The expected value of x and the interval $\mu \pm 2\sigma$ are indicated. Note that the geometric probabilities will always show $p(x)$ decreasing as x increases.

EXERCISES

6.54. Give two business-oriented examples of geometric random variables.

6.55. Given that x is a geometric random variable and $p = .1$, compute the following:

    a. $P(x = 2)$ b. $P(x = 4)$ c. $P(x \le 3)$

    d. $P(x > 4)$ e. $P(x = 1)$ f. $P(x \ge 2)$

6.56. Given that x is a geometric random variable and $p = .4$:

    a.   Graph $p(x)$, $x = 1, 2, \ldots, 7$.

    b.   Compute the mean and variance of x. Locate μ and the interval $\mu \pm 2\sigma$ on the graph.

    c.   What is the probability that x will fall within the interval $\mu \pm 2\sigma$?

6.57. An oil company has determined that the probability of striking oil on any particular drilling is .2. Accordingly, what is the probability that it would drill four dry wells before striking oil on the fifth drilling?

6.58. The personnel office of a large research and development firm has determined that the probability of any particular job applicant being qualified for the existing opening on the company's technical staff is .10. What is the probability that the personnel office will not find a qualified applicant until the third person interviewed? What is the probability that the first person interviewed will qualify?

6.59. If the probability that a customer will be served by a clerk during any given minute he or she is in the store is .3, what is the probability that the customer will have to wait 4 or more minutes to be served?

SUMMARY   In the business world, observations taken on discrete random variables (those that can assume a countable number of values) often have the characteristics of **a binomial, Poisson, hypergeometric, or geometric random variable.** In this chapter we gave the identifying characteristics for each of these random variables, indicated some business data for which the probability models would be appropriate, and gave the formulas for their probability distributions, means, and variances.

Using the probability distribution for a random variable, we were able to calculate the probabilities of specific sample observations. When the probabilities were difficult to calculate, the means and standard deviations provided numerical descriptive measures that enabled us to visualize the probability distributions and thereby to make some very approximate probability statements about their behavior.

SUPPLEMENTARY
EXERCISES

[*Note: Starred (*) exercises refer to optional sections in this chapter.*]

6.60. Given that x is a binomial random variable, compute $p(x)$ for each of the following cases:

 a. $n = 3$, $x = 1$, $p = .1$
 b. $n = 5$, $x = 4$, $p = .5$
 c. $n = 2$, $x = 0$, $p = .4$

*6.61. Given that x is a hypergeometric random variable, compute $p(x)$ for each of the following cases:

 a. $N = 6$, $n = 4$, $r = 3$, $x = 2$
 b. $N = 5$, $n = 2$, $r = 2$, $x = 2$
 c. $N = 7$, $n = 4$, $r = 4$, $x = 3$

*6.62. Given that x is a geometric random variable, compute $p(x)$ for each of the following cases:

 a. $p = .2$, $x = 3$ b. $p = .5$, $x = 4$ c. $p = .9$, $x = 2$

*6.63. Given that x is a Poisson random variable, compute $p(x)$ for each of the following cases:

 a. $\lambda = 2$, $x = 3$ b. $\lambda = 1$, $x = 4$ c. $\lambda = .5$, $x = 2$

6.64. Which of the following describe discrete random variables and which describe continuous random variables?

 a. The number of damaged inventory items
 b. The average monthly sales revenue generated by a salesperson over the past year
 c. The number of square feet of warehouse space a company rents
 d. The length of time a firm must wait before its copying machine is fixed

6.65. An important function in any business is long-range planning. Additions to a firm's physical plant, for example, cannot be achieved overnight; their construction must be planned years in advance. Anticipating a substantial growth in sales over the next 5 years, a printing company is planning today for the warehouse space it will need 5 years hence. It obviously cannot be certain exactly how many square feet of storage space it will need in 5 years, but the company can project its needs using a probability distribution such as the following:

x = Square feet of storage space needed	p(x)
10,000	.05
15,000	.15
20,000	.35
25,000	.25
30,000	.15
35,000	.05

What is the expected number of square feet of storage space the printing company will need in 5 years?

6.66. Suppose it is known that 5% of all radios produced by a manufacturer have defective tuning mechanisms. Your store receives a large shipment of the radios from which you choose ten radios to inspect. You have decided not to accept the shipment if you discover one or more defective radios. Before inspecting the ten radios, what is the probability that you will not accept the shipment?

*6.67.** If 20% of the finished products coming off an assembly line are defective, what is the probability that more than three randomly selected finished products would have to be inspected before a defective product is found?

6.68. The state highway patrol has determined that one out of every six calls for help originating from roadside call boxes is a hoax. Five calls for help have been received and five tow trucks dispatched. What is the probability that none of the calls was a hoax? That only three of the callers really needed assistance? What assumptions do you have to make in order to solve this problem?

6.69. Refer to Exercise 6.68. If the highway patrol answers 10,000 calls for help next year and each call costs the patrol about $20 (labor, gas, etc.), approximately how much money will be wasted answering false alarms?

*6.70.** By mistake a manufacturer of tape recorders includes three defective recorders in a shipment of ten going out to a small retailer. The retailer has decided to accept the shipment of recorders only if none are found to be defective. Upon receipt of the shipment the retailer examines only five of the recorders. What is the probability that the shipment will be rejected? If the retailer inspects six of the recorders, what is the probability that the shipment will be accepted?

*6.71.** Refer to Exercise 6.68. The highway patrol has determined that the expected number of calls for help per hour is 1.1. What is the probability that in the next hour more than two calls for help will be received? Exactly three calls?

*6.72.** You have determined that one out of five customers that enter your furniture store make a purchase. What is the probability that of the first four customers in a day the fourth is the initial customer to make a purchase?

6.73. A wholesale office equipment outlet claims that on an average it sells 2.5 typewriters per day. If it has only five typewriters in stock at the close of business today and does not expect to receive a shipment of new typewriters until some time after the close of business tomorrow, what is the probability that the outlet's current supply of typewriters will not be sufficient to meet tomorrow's demand?

6.74. If the probability of a customer responding to one of your marketing department's mail questionnaires is .6, what is the probability that of twenty questionnaires mailed, more than fifteen will be returned?

6.75. Of the eight families in a particular neighborhood, six have incomes over $20,000 and two have incomes under $20,000. If four of these eight families are randomly selected to participate in a taste test for a newly developed type of instant breakfast food, what is the probability that three of the chosen families have an income over $20,000? What is the probability that at least one family with an income under $20,000 is chosen?

6.76. Large bakeries typically have fleets of delivery trucks. It was determined by one such bakery that the expected number of delivery truck breakdowns per day was 1.5. What is the probability that there will be exactly two breakdowns today and exactly three tomorrow? Less than two today and more than two tomorrow? Assume that the number of breakdowns is independent from day to day.

6.77. A sales manager has determined that a salesperson makes a sale to 70% of the retailers visited. If the salesperson visits five retailers today and twenty tomorrow, what is the probability that he or she makes exactly four sales today *and* more than ten tomorrow?

6.78. Refer to Exercise 6.77. If the salesperson visits four retailers today and five tomorrow, what is the probability that in these two days he or she will make exactly two sales?

6.79. A large cigarette manufacturer has determined that the probability of a new brand of cigarettes obtaining a large enough market share to make production profitable is .3. If over the next 3 years this manufacturer introduces one new brand a year, what is the probability that at least one new brand will obtain sufficient market share to make its production profitable? What is the probability that all three new brands will obtain sufficient market share? What assumptions do you have to make in order to solve this problem?

6.80. If it is known that 5% of the finished products coming off an assembly line are defective, what is the probability that one of the next four products coming off the line is defective? What assumptions do you have to make to solve this problem using the methodology of this chapter?

6.81. Given that x is a random variable for which a Poisson probability distribution with $\lambda = 3$ provides a good characterization, compute the following:

    a. $P(x = 1)$ b. $P(x = 3)$ c. $P(x = 0)$

    d. $P(x = 5)$ e. $P(x \le 2)$ f. $P(x \ge 2)$

*6.82. Given that x is a geometric random variable and that $p = .2$, compute the following:

a. $P(x = 2)$ b. $P(x = 2, 3, \text{ or } 4)$ c. $P(x \leq 2)$

d. $P(x = 5)$ e. $P(x > 4)$ f. $P(x = 1, 2, \text{ or } 5)$

*6.83. Given that x is a geometric random variable and that $p = .5$:

a. Graph $p(x)$ for $x = 1, 2, \ldots, 7$.
b. Compute μ and σ for $p(x)$. Locate μ and the interval $\mu \pm 2\sigma$ on the graph.
c. What is the probability that x will fall within the interval $\mu \pm 2\sigma$?

*6.84. A small life insurance company has determined that on the average it receives five death claims per day. What is the probability that the company will receive three claims or less on a particular day? Exactly five claims? If x equals the number of claims per day, what assumptions must you make to find these probabilities?

6.85. Suppose you are an airport manager. In looking over your records for the past year, you note that 60% of the time the 8:10 PM flight from Atlanta is 20 or more minutes late. If you assume that the probability of the 8:10 PM flight being 20 or more minutes late on each day during the upcoming 5 day period is .6, what is the probability that the plane will be more than 20 minutes late exactly three times in the next 5 days? At least three times in the next 5 days?

6.86. [*Warning:* This exercise is realistic, but the computations involved are tedious.] Refer to Case Study 6.1—the Red Lobster sales tax problem. Let $x = 0, 1, 2, \ldots, 99$ be the number of cents (exceeding whole dollars) involved in a sale, and assume that the sales tax is assessed using the bracket system listed in the table.

Values of x	Tax (¢)
0, 1, . . . , 9	0
10, 11, . . . , 25	1
26, 27, . . . , 50	2
51, 52, . . . , 75	3
76, 77, . . . , 99	4

Suppose that x has a probability distribution $p(x) = .01$, $x = 0, 1, 2, \ldots, 99$ (an assumption that might be fairly accurate for restaurant sales). Find the expected value of the percentage of tax paid on the cents portion of a sale. [*Hint:* You can write the percent tax—call it y—for each value of x. You also know the probabilities associated with each value of x and, consequently, each value of y. Then the expected percentage of tax paid is $E(y) = \sum y\, p(y)$.]

ON YOUR OWN . . .

To control the quality of incoming or outgoing large lots of manufactured items, manufacturers employ a quality control lot acceptance sampling plan. For example, if each lot consists of 1,000 items, the plan will call for the selection of a random sample of n items (n is usually small) from each lot. The items in each sample are carefully inspected, the number of defectives recorded, and the lot considered to be of acceptable quality if the number of defectives is less than or equal to some specified number, a. The number a is called the **acceptance number** for the plan.

To illustrate, simulate sampling from a large lot of items that contain 10% defectives. Place ten poker chips (or marbles, etc.) in a bowl and mark one of the ten as defective. Randomly select a sample of five items from a lot by selecting a chip from the ten, replacing it, and repeating the process four more times. Count the number of times, x, that you observe the defective chip. This process is equivalent to selecting a random sample of $n = 5$ items from a large lot containing 10% defectives.

If you choose $a = 1$ as the acceptance number for the plan, then you will accept only lots for which $x \leq 1$.

By choosing n and a, you change the ability of a sampling plan to screen out bad lots. To investigate the properties of a sampling plan with $n = 5$ and $a = 1$, simulate the process of sampling from $N = 100$ lots.

a. Collect the 100 values of x obtained from the simulation and construct a relative frequency histogram for x. Note that this histogram is an approximation to $p(x)$. Estimate the proportion of lots that will be accepted by the plan by dividing the number of lots accepted by 100.

b. Calculate the exact values of $p(x)$ for $n = 5$ and $p = .1$, and compare these with the results of part a.

REFERENCES

Brown, A. A., Hulswit, F. T., & Kettelle, J. D. "A study of sales operations." *Operations Research*, June 1956, *4*, 296–308.

Hamburg, M. *Statistical analysis for decision making*. 2d ed. New York: Harcourt Brace Jovanovich, 1977. Chapter 3.

Hogg, R. V., & Craig, A. T. *Introduction to mathematical statistics*. 3d ed. New York: Wiley, 1970. Chapters 1 and 3.

Lapin, L. L. *Statistics for modern business decisions*. New York: Harcourt Brace Jovanovich, 1973. Chapter 5.

Mendenhall, W. *Introduction to probability and statistics*. 4th ed. North Scituate, Mass.: Duxbury, 1975. Chapters 5 and 6.

Parzen, E. *Modern probability theory and its applications*. New York: Wiley, 1960. Chapters 3, 4, 6, and 7.

Willis, R. E., & Chervany, N. L. *Statistical analysis and modeling for management decision-making*. Belmont, Ca.: Wadsworth, 1974. Chapter 5.

Wonnacott, T. H., & Wonnacott, R. J. *Introductory statistics for business and economics*. New York: Wiley, 1972. Chapter 4.

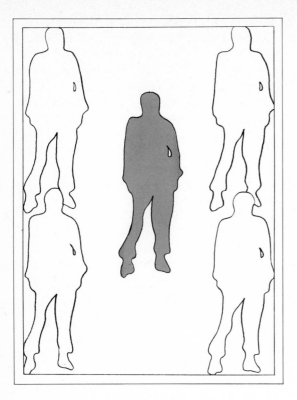

WHERE WE'VE BEEN . . .

Because numerical data represent observed values of random variables, we needed to find the probabilities associated with specific sample observations. As noted in Chapter 6, this task depends upon whether a random variable is .discrete or continuous. The probability theory of Chapter 5 provided the mechanism for finding the probabilities associated with discrete random variables. Finding and describing this set of probabilities—the probability distribution for a discrete random variable—was the subject of Chapter 6.

WHERE WE'RE GOING . . .

Since business data are derived from observations on continuous as well as discrete random variables, we need to know probability distributions associated with continuous random variables and also how to use the mean and standard deviation to describe these distributions. Chapter 7 will address this problem and, in particular, will introduce the normal probability distribution. As you will subsequently see, the normal probability distribution is one of the most useful distributions in business statistics.

7

CONTINUOUS RANDOM VARIABLES

In this chapter we will consider some continuous random variables that are prevalent in business. Recall that a continuous random variable is one that can assume any value within some interval or intervals on a line. For example, the length of time between a consumer's purchase of new automobiles, the thickness of sheets of steel produced in a rolling mill, and the length of time between charges of a pocket calculator are all continuous random variables. The methodology we employ to describe continuous random variables will necessarily be somewhat different from that used to describe discrete random variables. We will first discuss the general form of continuous probability distributions, and then we will present three specific types that are used in making business decisions. The normal probability distribution, which plays a basic and important role in both the theory and applications of statistics, is essential to the study of most of the subsequent chapters. The other two distributions, the uniform and the exponential, have business applications, but a study of these topics is optional.

7.1 CONTINUOUS PROBABILITY DISTRIBUTIONS

The graphical form of the probability distribution for a continuous random variable x will be a smooth curve that might appear as shown in Figure 7.1. This curve, a function of x, is denoted by the symbol $f(x)$ and is variously called a **probability density function**, a **frequency function**, or a **probability distribution**.

The areas under a probability distribution correspond to probabilities for x. For example, the area A between the two points a and b, as shown in Figure 7.1, is the probability that x assumes a value between a and b ($a < x < b$). Because areas over intervals represent probabilities, it follows that the total area under a probability distribution, the probability assigned to all values of x, should equal 1. Note that probability distributions for continuous random variables will possess different shapes

FIGURE 7.1
A PROBABILITY DISTRIBUTION $f(x)$ **FOR A CONTINUOUS RANDOM VARIABLE** x

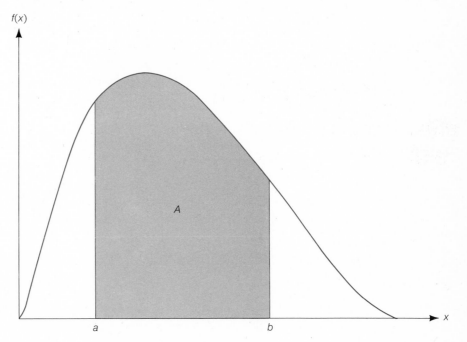

depending on the relative frequency distributions of real data that the probability distribution is supposed to model.

The areas under most probability distributions are obtained by the use of the calculus* or other numerical methods. Because this is often a difficult procedure, we will give the areas for some of the most common probability distributions in tabular form in Appendix B. Then, to find the area between two values of x, say $x = a$ and $x = b$, you will simply have to consult the appropriate table.

For each of the continuous random variables presented in this chapter, we will give the formula for the probability distribution along with its mean and standard deviation. These two numbers, μ and σ, will enable you to make some approximate probability statements about a random variable even when you do not have access to a table of areas under the probability distribution.

7.2
THE NORMAL
DISTRIBUTION

One of the most commonly observed continuous random variables has a **bell-shaped** probability distribution, as shown in Figure 7.2. It is known as a **normal random variable** and its probability distribution is called a **normal distribution**.

You will see during the remainder of this text that the normal distribution plays a very important role in the science of statistical inference. Many business phenomena generate random variables with probability distributions that are very well approximated by a normal distribution. For example, the percentage of monthly gain (or loss) of a stock's price may be a normal random variable, and the probability distribution for the yearly sales of a corporation might be approximated by a normal probability distribution. The normal distribution might also provide an accurate model for the probability distribution of the weights of loads of produce shipped to a supermarket. You can determine the adequacy of the normal approximation to an existing population of data by comparing the relative frequency distribution of a sample of the data (200 or 300 measurements, or more) to the normal probability distribution.

FIGURE 7.2
A NORMAL
PROBABILITY
DISTRIBUTION

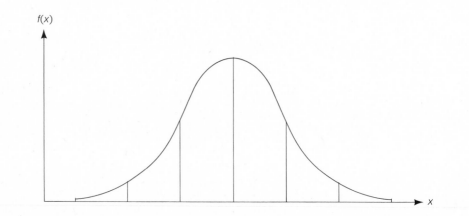

*Students with knowledge of the calculus should note that the probability that x assumes a value in the interval $a < x < b$ is $P(a < x < b) = \int_a^b f(x)\,dx$, assuming the integral exists. Similar to the requirements for a discrete probability distribution, we require $f(x) \geq 0$ and $\int_{-\infty}^{\infty} f(x)\,dx = 1$.

FIGURE 7.3
SEVERAL NORMAL
DISTRIBUTIONS,
WITH DIFFERENT
MEANS AND STANDARD
DEVIATIONS

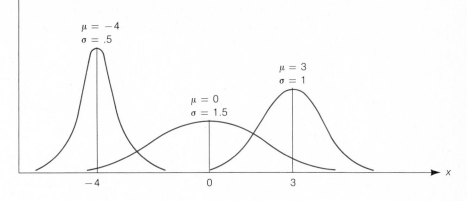

The normal distribution is perfectly symmetric about its mean μ, as can be seen in the examples in Figure 7.3. Its spread is determined by the value of its standard deviation, σ.

The formula for the normal probability distribution is shown below:

PROBABILITY DISTRIBUTION FOR A NORMAL RANDOM VARIABLE x

$$f(x) = \frac{1}{\sigma\sqrt{2\pi}} e^{-(1/2)[(x-\mu)/\sigma]^2}$$

where

μ = Mean of the normal random variable x

σ^2 = Variance of the normal random variable x

π = 3.1416 . . .

e = 2.71828 . . .

Note that the mean μ and variance σ^2 appear in this formula, so that no separate formulas for μ and σ^2 are necessary. To graph the normal curve we will have to know the numerical values of μ and σ.

Computing the area over intervals under the normal probability distribution is a difficult task.* Consequently, we will use the computed areas listed in Table IV of

---

*The student with knowledge of the calculus should note that there is not a closed-form expression for $P(a < x < b) = \int_a^b f(x)\,dx$ for the normal probability distribution. The value of this definite integral can be obtained to any desired degree of accuracy by approximation procedures. For this reason, it is tabulated for the user.

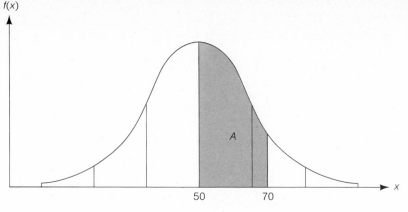

FIGURE 7.4
NORMAL FREQUENCY
FUNCTION:
$\mu = 50, \sigma = 15$

Appendix B. Since there are an infinitely large number of normal curves—one for each pair of values for μ and σ—we have formed a single table that will apply to any of these normal curves. This is done by constructing the table of areas as a function of the z-score (presented in Section 4.5). The population z-score for a measurement was defined as the *distance* between the measurement and the population mean, divided by the population standard deviation. Thus, the z-score gives the distance between a measurement and the mean in units equal to the standard deviation. In symbolic form, the z-score for the measurement x is

$$z = \frac{x - \mu}{\sigma}$$

To illustrate the use of Table IV, suppose we know that the length of time between charges of a pocket calculator has a normal distribution, with a mean of 50 hours and a standard deviation of 15 hours. If we were to observe the length of time that elapses before the need for the next charge, what is the probability that this measurement will assume a value between 50 and 70 hours? This probability is the area under the normal probability distribution between 50 and 70, as shown in the shaded area, A, of Figure 7.4.

The first step in finding the area A is to calculate the z-score corresponding to the measurement 70. We calculate

$$z = \frac{x - \mu}{\sigma} = \frac{70 - 50}{15} = \frac{20}{15} = 1.33$$

Thus, the measurement, 70, is 1.33 standard deviations away from the mean, 50. The second step is to refer to Table IV (a partial reproduction of this table is shown in Figure 7.5). Note that z-scores are listed in the left-hand column of the table. To find the area corresponding to a z-score of 1.33, we first locate the value 1.3 in the left-hand column. Since this column lists z values to one decimal place only, we refer to the top row of the table to get the second decimal place, .03. Finally, we locate the

FIGURE 7.5
REPRODUCTION OF PART OF TABLE IV, APPENDIX B

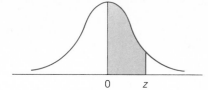

z	.00	.01	.02	.03	.04	.05	.06	.07	.08	.09
0.0	.0000	.0040	.0080	.0120	.0160	.0199	.0239	.0279	.0319	.0359
0.1	.0398	.0438	.0478	.0517	.0557	.0596	.0636	.0675	.0714	.0753
0.2	.0793	.0832	.0871	.0910	.0948	.0987	.1026	.1064	.1103	.1141
0.3	.1179	.1217	.1255	.1293	.1331	.1368	.1406	.1443	.1480	.1517
0.4	.1554	.1591	.1628	.1664	.1700	.1736	.1772	.1808	.1844	.1879
0.5	.1915	.1950	.1985	.2019	.2054	.2088	.2123	.2157	.2190	.2224
0.6	.2257	.2291	.2324	.2357	.2389	.2422	.2454	.2486	.2517	.2549
0.7	.2580	.2611	.2642	.2673	.2704	.2734	.2764	.2794	.2823	.2852
0.8	.2881	.2910	.2939	.2967	.2995	.3023	.3051	.3078	.3106	.3133
0.9	.3159	.3186	.3212	.3238	.3264	.3289	.3315	.3340	.3365	.3389
1.0	.3413	.3438	.3461	.3485	.3508	.3531	.3554	.3577	.3599	.3621
1.1	.3643	.3665	.3686	.3708	.3729	.3749	.3770	.3790	.3810	.3830
1.2	.3849	.3869	.3888	.3907	.3925	.3944	.3962	.3980	.3997	.4015
1.3	.4032	.4049	.4066	.4082	.4099	.4115	.4131	.4147	.4162	.4177
1.4	.4192	.4207	.4222	.4236	.4251	.4265	.4279	.4292	.4306	.4319
1.5	.4332	.4345	.4357	.4370	.4382	.4394	.4406	.4418	.4429	.4441

number where the row labeled $z = 1.3$ and the column labeled .03 meet. This number represents the area between the mean, μ, and the measurement that has a z-score of 1.33:

$$A = .4082$$

Or, the probability that the calculator operates between 50 and 70 hours before needing a charge is .4082.

EXAMPLE 7.1   Suppose you have a normal random variable x with $\mu = 50$ and $\sigma = 15$. Find the probability that x will fall within the interval $30 < x < 50$.

Solution   The solution to this example can be seen from Figure 7.6. Note that both $x = 30$ and $x = 70$ lie the same distance from the mean, $\mu = 50$; $x = 30$ lies below the mean and $x = 70$ lies above it. Then, because the normal curve is symmetric about the mean, the area representing the probability that x falls between $x = 30$ and $\mu = 50$ is equal to the area representing the probability that it falls between $\mu = 50$ and $x = 70$. The probability (from Table IV) is .4082 (obtained in the previous discussion).

FIGURE 7.6
NORMAL PROBABILITY
DISTRIBUTION:
$\mu = 50$, $\sigma = 15$

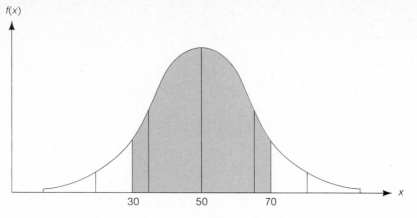

Because $x = 30$ lies to the left of the mean, the corresponding z-score should be negative and of the same numerical value as the z-score corresponding to $x = 70$. Checking, we obtain

$$z = \frac{x - \mu}{\sigma} = \frac{30 - 50}{15} = -1.33$$

In finding areas (probabilities) under the normal curve, it is easier to show the location of the z-scores rather than the corresponding values of x. For example, the z-scores corresponding to $x = 30$ and $x = 70$ are located on the distribution of z-scores at the points shown in Figure 7.7. The distribution of z-scores, known as a **standard normal distribution**, will always have a mean equal to 0 and a standard deviation equal to 1.

FIGURE 7.7
A DISTRIBUTION
OF z-SCORES
(A STANDARD NORMAL
DISTRIBUTION)

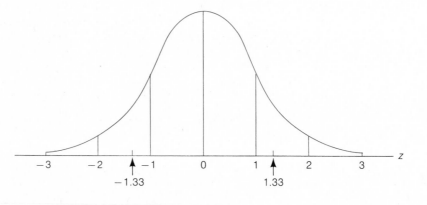

EXAMPLE 7.2

Use Table IV to determine the area to the right of the z-score 1.64 for the standard normal distribution, i.e., find $P(z \geq 1.64)$.

FIGURE 7.8
STANDARD NORMAL
DISTRIBUTION:
$\mu = 0$, $\sigma = 1$

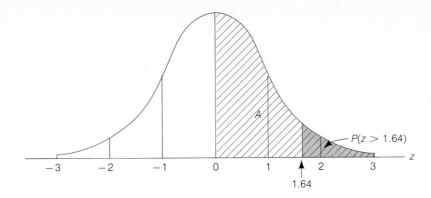

Solution   The probability that a normal random variable will fall more than 1.64 standard deviations to the right of its mean is indicated in Figure 7.8. Because the normal distribution
is symmetric, half of the total probability (.5) lies to the right of the mean and half to
the left. Therefore, the desired probability is

$$P(z > 1.64) = .5 - A$$

where A is the area between $\mu = 0$ and $z = 1.64$, as shown in the figure. Referring
to Table IV, the area A corresponding to $z = 1.64$ is .4495. So,

$$P(z > 1.64) = .5 - A = .5 - .4495 = .0505$$

EXAMPLE 7.3   Find the total area to the right of $z = -.74$ in the standard normal distribution. This
area is $P(z > -.74)$.

Solution   The standard normal distribution is shown in Figure 7.9, with the area to the right of
$-.74$, $P(z > -.74)$, shaded. Note that we have divided the total shaded area corresponding to $P(z > -.74)$ into two parts: the area to the left of $z = 0$, A_1, and the
area to the right of $z = 0$, A_2. Whenever the desired area overlaps the mean, it is
necessary to make this division and to find the areas separately in Table IV. The area
A_2 is easy to find, since it is all the area to the right of the mean. Thus, $A_2 = .5$. The

FIGURE 7.9
STANDARD NORMAL
DISTRIBUTION:
$\mu = 0$, $\sigma = 1$

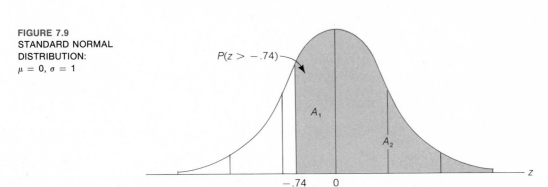

area A_1 is the area between $z = 0$ and $z = -.74$. Therefore, we can find A_1 directly from Table IV (remember, we ignore the sign of the z value). We find $A_1 = .2704$. Then the total area, A, to the right of $z = -.74$ is the sum of the areas A_1 and A_2:

$$P(z > -.74) = A_1 + A_2 = .2704 + .5 = .7704$$

EXAMPLE 7.4   Find the total area to the right of $z = 1.96$ and to the left of $z = -1.96$. To put this in probabilistic terminology, find the probability that a normal random variable lies more than 1.96 standard deviations away from the mean.

Solution   The requested probability $P(z > 1.96 \text{ or } z < -1.96)$ is the sum of the two areas A_1 and A_2 shown in Figure 7.10. Because the normal distribution is symmetric, the areas lying to the right of $z = 1.96$ and to the left of $z = -1.96$ must be equal. Therefore, $A_1 = A_2$.

Checking Table IV, we find the area corresponding to $z = 1.96$ to be .4750. This is the area between $z = 0$ and $z = 1.96$. Therefore,

$$A_2 = .5 - .4750 = .0250$$

And, because of the symmetry of the normal distribution,

$$P(z > 1.96 \text{ or } z < -1.96) = A_1 + A_2 = .0250 + .0250 = .0500$$

**FIGURE 7.10
STANDARD NORMAL
DISTRIBUTION:**
$\mu = 0, \sigma = 1$

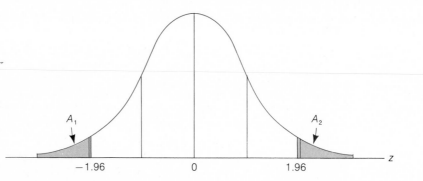

EXAMPLE 7.5   Suppose an automobile manufacturer introduces a new model, which has an advertised mean in-city mileage of 27 miles per gallon. Although such advertisements never report any measure of variability from car to car, suppose you write the manufacturer for the details of the tests, and you find that the standard deviation is 3 miles per gallon.

The information leads you to formulate a probability model for the random variable x, the in-city mileage for this car model. You believe that the probability distribution of x can be approximated by a normal distribution, with a mean of 27 and a standard deviation of 3.

a.   If you were to buy this model of automobile, what is the probability that you would purchase one that averages less than 20 miles per gallon for in-city driving?

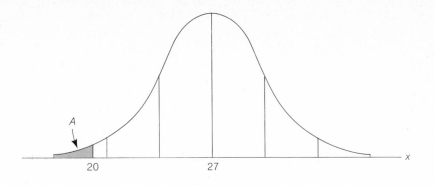

FIGURE 7.11
NORMAL PROBABILITY
DISTRIBUTION FOR x
IN EXAMPLE 7.5:
$\mu = 27$ MILES PER
GALLON,
$\sigma = 3$ MILES PER
GALLON

A

20   27 x

b. Suppose you purchase one of these new models and it does get less than 20 miles per gallon for in-city driving. Should you conclude that your probability model is incorrect?

Solution

a. The probability model proposed for x, the in-city mileage, is shown in Figure 7.11. We are interested in finding the area, A, to the left of 20, since this area corresponds to the probability that a measurement chosen from this distribution falls below 20. Or, in other words, if this model is correct, the area A represents the fraction of cars that can be expected to get less than 20 miles per gallon for in-city driving. To find A, we first calculate the z value corresponding to $x = 20$. That is,

$$z = \frac{x - \mu}{\sigma} = \frac{20 - 27}{3} = -\frac{7}{3} = -2.33$$

We now drop the negative sign, look up 2.33 in Table IV, and find that the corresponding area is .4901. This is the area between $z = 0$ and $z = -2.33$, so we find

$$A = .5 - .4901 = .0099 \simeq .01$$

According to this probability model, you should have only about a 1% chance of purchasing a car of this make with an in-city mileage under 20 miles per gallon.

b. Now you are asked to make an inference based on a sample—the car you purchased. You are getting less than 20 miles per gallon for in-city driving. What do you infer? We think you will agree that one of two possibilities is true:

The probability model is correct, and you simply were unfortunate to have purchased one of the cars in the 1% that get less than 20 miles per gallon in the city.
The probability model is incorrect. That is, if the manufacturers meant that the in-city mileage for the cars has a normal distribution with a mean equal to 27 and $\sigma = 3$, the claim is false.

You have no way of knowing which possibility is the correct one, but certainly the evidence points to the second one. We are again relying on the rare event approach to statistical inference that we introduced earlier. The basic idea is that the sample (one measurement in this case) was so unlikely to have been drawn from the proposed probability model that it casts serious doubt on the model. We would be inclined to believe that the model is somehow in error. Perhaps the assumption of a normal distribution is unwarranted, or the mean of 27 is an overestimate, or the standard deviation of 3 is an underestimate, or some combination of these errors was made. At any rate, the form of the actual probability model certainly merits further investigation.

CASE STUDY 7.1   Frederick S. Hillier (1963) described several ways that a business firm can easily, but effectively, evaluate risky investment projects. He noted that up to the time of his writing,

> such procedures as have been suggested for dealing with risk have tended to be either quite simplified or somewhat theoretical. Thus, these procedures have tended to provide management with only a portion of the information required for a sound decision, or they have assumed the availability of information which is almost impossible to obtain.

In one of his approaches to handling risk, Hillier assumes that the cash flow from an investment to the firm in the ith future year after the investment is made is normally distributed, and shows that the present worth, P, of the proposed investment is, therefore, normally distributed with mean μ_P and variance σ_P^2. He points out that by describing P with a probability distribution as he has done, management is provided with information about P and, as a result, with some basis upon which to evaluate the risk of the investment decision.

Hillier provides an example of how management can evaluate the risk of an investment by assuming its present worth is normally distributed:

> Suppose that, on the basis of the forecasts regarding prospective cash flow from a proposed investment of $10,000, it is determined that $\mu_P = \$1,000$ and $\sigma_P = \$2,000$. Ordinarily, the current procedure would be to approve the investment since $\mu_P > 0$. However, with additional information available ($\sigma_P = \$2,000$) regarding the considerable risk of the investment, the executive can analyze the situation further. Using widely available tables for the normal distribution, he could note that the probability that $P < 0$, so that the investment won't pay, is 0.31. Furthermore, the probability is 0.16, 0.023, and 0.0013, respectively, that the investment will lose the present worth equivalent of at least $1,000, $3,000, and $5,000, respectively. Considering the financial status of the firm, the executive can use this and similar information to make his decision. Suppose, instead, that the executive is attempting to choose between this investment and a second investment with $\mu_P = \$500$ and $\sigma_P = \$500$. By conducting a similar analysis for the second investment, the executive can decide whether the greater expected earnings of the first investment justifies the greater risk. A useful technique for making this comparison is to superimpose the drawing of the probability distribution of P for the second investment upon the corresponding drawing for the first investment. This same approach generalizes to the comparison of more than two investments.

EXERCISES   **7.1.** Use Table IV to calculate the area under the standard normal frequency function between the following pairs of z-scores:

   a. $z = 0$ and $z = 2$ b. $z = 0$ and $z = 1.5$
   c. $z = 0$ and $z = 3$ d. $z = 0$ and $z = .5$

7.2. Repeat Exercise 7.1 for each of the following pairs of z-scores:

   a. $z = -1$ and $z = 1$ b. $z = -2$ and $z = 2$
   c. $z = -.5$ and $z = .5$ d. $z = -3$ and $z = 3$

7.3. Repeat Exercise 7.1 for each of the following pairs of z-scores:

   a. $z = -1.5$ and $z = 1$ b. $z = -.5$ and $z = .75$
   c. $z = -2$ and $z = -1$ d. $z = -3$ and $z = 1.5$
   e. $z = .5$ and $z = 3.5$ f. $z = 2$ and $z = -.5$

7.4. Use Table IV to find each of the following:

   a. $P(z \geq 2)$ b. $P(z \leq -2)$ c. $P(z \geq 1.96)$
   d. $P(z \geq 0)$ e. $P(z \leq -.5)$ f. $P(z \leq -1.96)$

7.5. Use Table IV to find each of the following:

   a. $P(-1 \leq z \leq 1)$ b. $P(-1.96 \leq z \leq 1.96)$
   c. $P(-1.645 \leq z \leq 1.645)$ d. $P(-3 \leq z \leq 3)$

7.6. Find a value of z, call it z_0, such that:

   a. $P(z \geq z_0) = .05$ b. $P(z \geq z_0) = .025$
   c. $P(z \leq z_0) = .025$ d. $P(z \geq z_0) = .0228$

7.7. Given that the random variable x is best described by a normal distribution with $\mu = 30$ and $\sigma = 5$, find the z-score that corresponds to each of the following x values:

   a. $x = 25$ b. $x = 30$ c. $x = 37.5$
   d. $x = 10$ e. $x = 50$ f. $x = 32$

7.8. Refer to Exercise 7.7. How many standard deviations away from the mean of x are each of the following x values?

   a. $x = 10$ b. $x = 32.5$ c. $x = 30$ d. $x = 60$

7.9. Find a value of z, call it z_0, such that:

   a. $P(z \leq z_0) = .0013$ b. $P(-z_0 \leq z \leq z_0) = .95$
   c. $P(-z_0 \leq z \leq z_0) = .90$ d. $P(-z_0 \leq z \leq z_0) = .6826$
   e. $P(-z_0 \leq z \leq 0) = .0596$

7.10. Given that the continuous random variable x has a normal probability distribution with mean 100 and variance 64, draw a rough sketch (i.e., graph) of the frequency function of x. Locate μ and the interval $\mu \pm 2\sigma$ on the graph. Find the following probabilities:

   a. $P(\mu - 2\sigma \leq x \leq \mu + 2\sigma)$ b. $P(x \geq 108)$
   c. $P(x \leq 92)$ d. $P(92 \leq x \leq 116)$
   e. $P(92 \leq x \leq 96)$ f. $P(76 \leq x \leq 124)$

7.11. A fast-food chain advertises a "quarter-pound" hamburger. Suppose the amount of ground beef that goes into the hamburgers is normally distributed with a mean of .25 pound and a standard deviation of .02 pound. What is the probability of a customer getting less than .25 pound of ground beef in a hamburger? More than .3 pound of ground beef?

7.12. Testing has shown that a new washing machine has a length of life that is normally distributed with mean equal to 3.10 years and a standard deviation equal to .54 year. If the washers are guaranteed for 2 years, what percentage will fail before the end of the guarantee time?

7.13. A company that sells annuities must base the annual payout on the probability distribution of the length of life of the participants in the plan. Suppose the probability distribution of participants in the plan is approximately a normal distribution with $\mu = 68$ years and $\sigma = 3.5$ years.

    a. What proportion of the plan participants would receive payments beyond age 70?
    b. Age 75?

7.14. The board of examiners that administers the real estate brokers' examination in a certain state found that the mean score on the test was 435 and the standard deviation was 72. If the board wants to set the passing score so that only the best 30% of all applicants pass, what is the passing score? Assume the scores are normally distributed.

7.15. The distribution of the demand (in number of units per unit time) for a product can often be approximated by a normal probability distribution. For example, a bakery has found that the demand for its standard loaf of white bread is 7,200 loaves per day with a standard deviation of 300 loaves. Based on cost considerations, the company has decided that its best strategy is to produce a sufficient number of loaves so that it will fully supply demand on 94% of all days.

    a. How many loaves of bread should the company produce?
    b. Based on the production in part a, what percentage of days will the company be left with more than 500 loaves of unsold bread?

7.16. A machine for filling quart milk cartons can be adjusted so that the mean of the distribution of fills (in ounces) is equal to some predetermined mean value, μ, with a standard deviation equal to .6 ounce. If the distribution of fills is approximately normal:

    a. What percentage of the cartons will contain less than 32 ounces if μ is set at 32 ounces?
    b. If μ is set at 33 ounces?
    c. What setting should the dairy choose for μ if the management wants to underfill (less than 32 ounces) only 5% of all cartons?

**7.3
THE UNIFORM
DISTRIBUTION
(OPTIONAL)**

Perhaps the simplest of all the continuous probability distributions is the uniform distribution. The frequency function has a rectangular shape, as shown in Figure 7.12. Note that the possible values of x consist of all points on the real line between point c and point d. The height of $f(x)$ is constant in that interval, and equals $1/(d - c)$.

FIGURE 7.12
THE UNIFORM
PROBABILITY
DISTRIBUTION

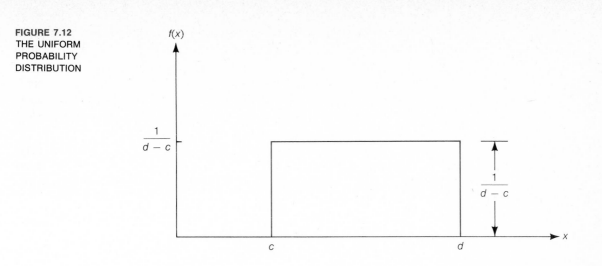

Therefore, the total area under $f(x)$ is given by

Total area of a rectangle $=$ (Base)(Height)

$$= (d - c)\left(\frac{1}{d - c}\right) = 1$$

The uniform probability distribution provides a model for continuous random variables that are **evenly distributed** over a certain interval. That is, a uniform random variable is one that is just as likely to assume a value in one interval as it is to assume a value in any other interval of equal size. There is no clustering of values around any value; instead, there is an even spread over the entire region of possible values.

The uniform distribution is sometimes referred to as the **randomness distribution,** since one way of generating a uniform random variable is to perform an experiment in which a point is **randomly** selected on the horizontal axis between the points c and d. If we were to repeat this experiment infinitely often, we would create a uniform probability distribution like that shown in Figure 7.12. The random selection of points on a line can also be used to generate random numbers such as those in Table I of Appendix B. Recall that random numbers are selected in such a way that every number would have an equal probability of selection. Therefore, random numbers are realizations of a uniform random variable. (Random numbers were used to draw random samples in Section 5.6.)

The formulas for the uniform probability distribution, its mean, and standard deviation are shown at the top of page 168.

Suppose that the interval $a < x < b$ lies within the domain of x, i.e., it falls within the larger interval $c < x < d$. Then the probability that x assumes a value within the interval $a < x < b$ is the area of the rectangle over the interval, namely $(b - a)/(c - d)$.*

*The student with knowledge of the calculus should note that $P(a < x < b) = \int_a^b f(x)\, dx = \int_a^b 1/(c - d)\, dx = (b - a)/(c - d)$.

PROBABILITY DISTRIBUTION, MEAN, AND STANDARD
DEVIATION OF A UNIFORM RANDOM VARIABLE x

$$f(x) = \frac{1}{d - c} \qquad (c \leq x \leq d)$$

$$\mu = \frac{c + d}{2} \qquad \sigma = \frac{d - c}{\sqrt{12}}$$

EXAMPLE 7.6

Suppose the research department of a steel manufacturer believes that one of the company's rolling machines is producing sheets of steel of varying thickness. The thickness is a uniform random variable with values between 150 and 200 millimeters. Any sheets less than 160 millimeters thick must be scrapped, since they are unacceptable to buyers.

a. Calculate the mean and standard deviation of x, the thickness of the sheets produced by this machine. Then graph the probability distribution, and show the mean on the horizontal axis. Also show 1 and 2 standard deviation intervals around the mean.

b. Calculate the fraction of steel sheets produced by this machine that have to be scrapped.

Solution

a. To calculate the mean and standard deviation for x, we substitute 150 and 200 millimeters for c and d, respectively, in the formulas. Thus,

$$\mu = \frac{c + d}{2} = \frac{150 + 200}{2} = 175 \text{ millimeters}$$

and

$$\sigma = \frac{d - c}{\sqrt{12}} = \frac{200 - 150}{\sqrt{12}} = \frac{50}{3.464} = 14.43$$

FIGURE 7.13
THE FREQUENCY
FUNCTION FOR x
IN EXAMPLE 7.6

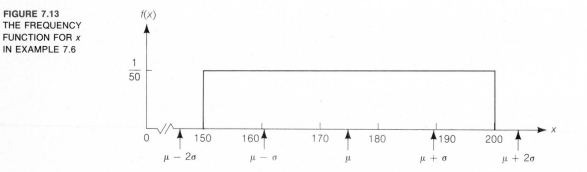

The uniform probability distribution is

$$f(x) = \frac{1}{d - c} = \frac{1}{200 - 150} = \frac{1}{50}$$

The graph of this function is shown in Figure 7.13. The mean and 1 and 2 standard deviation intervals around the mean are shown on the horizontal axis.

b. To find the fraction of steel sheets produced by the machine that have to be scrapped, we must find the probability that x, the thickness, is less than 160 millimeters. As indicated in Figure 7.14, we need to calculate the area under the frequency function $f(x)$ between the points $x = 150$ and $x = 160$. This is the area of a rectangle with base $160 - 150 = 10$ and height $\frac{1}{50}$. The fraction that has to be scrapped is then

$$P(x < 160) = (\text{Base})(\text{Height}) = (10)\left(\frac{1}{50}\right) = \frac{1}{5}$$

That is, 20% of all the sheets made by this machine must be scrapped.

FIGURE 7.14
THE PROBABILITY
THAT THE SHEET
THICKNESS, x, IS
BETWEEN 150 AND
160 MILLIMETERS

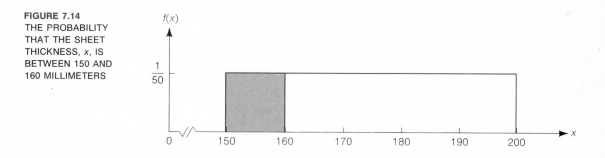

EXERCISES

7.17. Suppose that x is a random variable best described by a uniform probability distribution with $c = 10$ and $d = 30$.

    a. Find $f(x)$.
    b. Find the mean and variance for x.
    c. Graph $f(x)$ and locate μ and the interval $\mu \pm 2\sigma$ on the graph. Note that the probability that x assumes a value within the interval $\mu \pm 2\sigma$ is equal to 1.

7.18. Refer to Exercise 7.17. Find the following:

    a. $P(10 \leq x \leq 15)$ b. $P(20 \leq x \leq 30)$ c. $P(x \geq 20)$
    d. $P(x \leq 14)$ e. $P(x \leq 5)$ f. $P(0 \leq x \leq 18)$
    g. $P(x \geq 35)$

7.19. Suppose that x is a random variable best described by a uniform probability distribution with $c = 1$ and $d = 2$.

    a. Find $f(x)$.
    b. Find the mean and variance of x.

7.20. The manager of a local soft drink bottling company believes that when a new beverage-dispensing machine is set to dispense 7 ounces, it in fact dispenses an amount at random anywhere between 6.5 and 7.5 ounces inclusive.

  a. Is the amount dispensed by the beverage machine a discrete or a continuous random variable? Explain.

  b. Graph the frequency function for x, the amount of beverage the manager believes is dispensed by the new machine when it is set to dispense 7 ounces.

  c. Find the mean and standard deviation for the distribution graphed in part b, and locate the mean and the interval $\mu \pm 2\sigma$ on the graph.

7.21. Refer to Exercise 7.20. Find the following probabilities:

  a. $P(x \geq 7)$ b. $P(6.5 \leq x \leq 7.5)$ c. $P(x \leq 6.75)$

  d. $P(x > 7.25)$ e. $P(x < 6)$ f. $P(6.5 \leq x \leq 7.25)$

7.22. Refer to Exercises 7.20 and 7.21. What is the probability that each of the next six bottles filled by the new machine will contain more than 7.25 ounces of beverage? Assume that the amount of beverage dispensed in one bottle is independent of the amount dispensed in another bottle.

7.23. An assembly line foreman believes the proportion, x, of generators assembled improperly on his line each day is best described by a uniform distribution with $c = .01$ and $d = .05$.

  a. Graph the probability distribution for x.

  b. Compute the mean and variance of x.

  c. Locate the interval $\mu \pm 2\sigma$ on the graph.

  d. According to the foreman's distribution of p, 25% of the time x should be greater than what value?

7.24. Refer to Exercise 7.23. Find a in each of the following:

  a. $P(x \geq a) = .5$ b. $P(x \geq a) = .75$

  c. $P(x \leq a) = .2$ d. $P(x \leq a) = 0$

  e. According to the foreman's distribution of x, what is the probability that more than 4% or less than 2% of the generators produced tomorrow by his assembly line will be defective?

7.4 THE EXPONENTIAL DISTRIBUTION (OPTIONAL)

Another important probability distribution that is useful for describing business data is the **exponential probability distribution**. Some business phenomena with frequency functions that might be well approximated by the exponential distribution are the length of time between emergency arrivals at a hospital, or the length of time between the filing of claims in a small insurance office. Note that in each of these examples, the measurements are the lengths of time between certain events. For this reason, the exponential distribution is sometimes called the **waiting time distribution**.

The formula for the exponential probability distribution is shown below, along with the mean and standard deviation of this frequency function:

PROBABILITY DISTRIBUTION, MEAN, AND STANDARD DEVIATION FOR AN EXPONENTIAL RANDOM VARIABLE x

$$f(x) = \lambda\, e^{-\lambda x} \qquad (x > 0)$$

$$\mu = \frac{1}{\lambda} \qquad \sigma = \frac{1}{\lambda}$$

Unlike the normal frequency function, which has a shape determined by the values of the two quantities μ and σ, the shape of the exponential distribution is governed by a single quantity, λ. Further, it is a probability distribution with the property that its mean equals its standard deviation. Exponential distributions corresponding to $\lambda = .5, 1$, and 2 are shown in Figure 7.15.

**FIGURE 7.15
EXPONENTIAL
FREQUENCY FUNCTION**

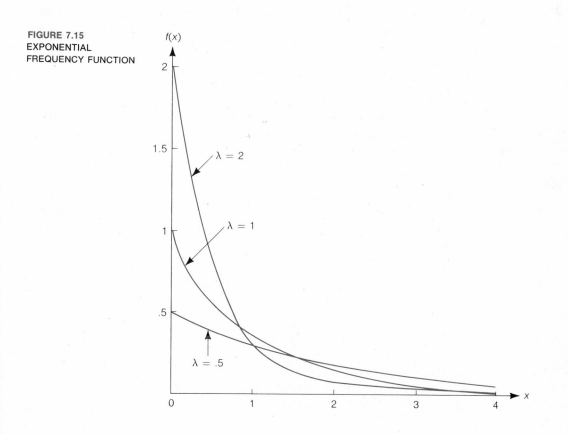

FIGURE 7.16
THE AREA, *A*, TO
THE RIGHT OF A
NUMBER, *a*, FOR AN
EXPONENTIAL
FREQUENCY FUNCTION

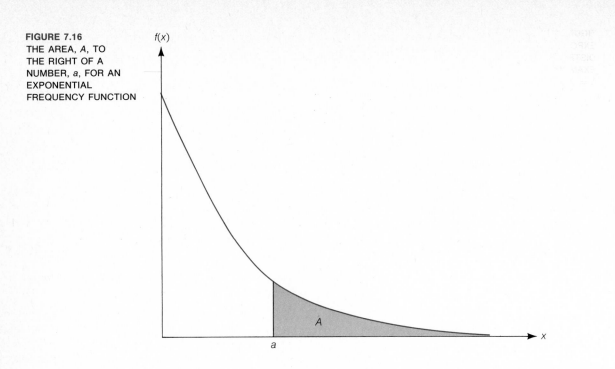

To calculate probabilities for exponential random variables, we need to be able to find areas under the exponential probability distribution. Suppose we want to find the area, *A*, to the right of some number, *a*, as shown in Figure 7.16. This area can be calculated by using the following formula:

FINDING THE AREA, *A*, TO THE RIGHT OF A NUMBER, *a*, FOR AN EXPONENTIAL FREQUENCY FUNCTION

$$A = P(x \geq a) = e^{-\lambda a}$$

Use Table III in Appendix B to find the value of $e^{-\lambda a}$ after substituting the appropriate numerical values for λ and *a*.

EXAMPLE 7.7   Suppose the length of time (in days) between sales for an automobile salesperson is modeled as an exponential random variable with $\lambda = .5$. What is the probability that the salesperson goes more than 5 days without a sale?

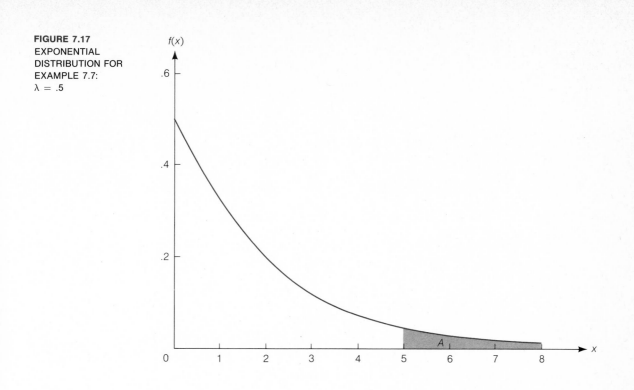

FIGURE 7.17
EXPONENTIAL
DISTRIBUTION FOR
EXAMPLE 7.7:
$\lambda = .5$

Solution

The probability we want is the area, A, to the right of $a = 5$ in Figure 7.17. To find this probability, use the formula given for area:

$$A = e^{-\lambda a} = e^{-(.5)(5)} = e^{-2.5}$$

Referring to Table III, we find

$$A = e^{-2.5} = .082085$$

That is, our model indicates that the automobile salesperson has a probability of about .08 of going more than 5 days without a sale.

EXAMPLE 7.8

A microwave oven manufacturer is trying to determine the length of warranty period it should attach to its magnetron tube, the most critical component in the oven. Preliminary testing has shown that the length of life (in years), x, of a magnetron tube has an exponential probability distribution with $\lambda = .16$.

a. Find the mean and standard deviation for x.
b. Suppose a warranty period of 5 years is attached to the magnetron tube. What fraction of tubes must the manufacturer plan to replace, assuming the exponential model with $\lambda = .16$ is correct?
c. Find the probability that the life of a magnetron tube will fall within the interval $\mu - 2\sigma$ to $\mu + 2\sigma$.

FIGURE 7.18
FREQUENCY FUNCTION
FOR EXAMPLE 7.8;
EXPONENTIAL
DISTRIBUTION:
$\lambda = .16$

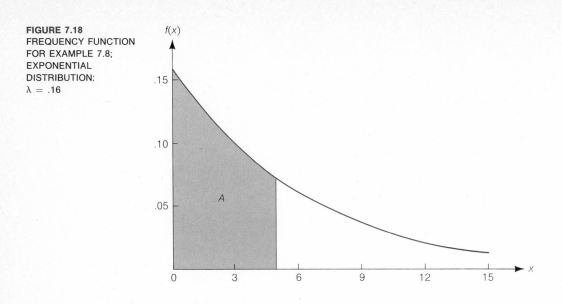

Solution

a. Using the formulas for the mean and standard deviation for an exponential random variable, we find

$$\mu = \frac{1}{\lambda} = \frac{1}{.16} = 6.25 \text{ years}$$

Also, since $\mu = \sigma$, $\sigma = 6.25$ years.

b. To find the fraction of tubes that will have to be replaced before the 5 year warranty period expires, we need to find the area between 0 and 5 under the frequency function. This area, A, is shown in Figure 7.18. To find the required probability, we recall the formula

$$P(x > a) = e^{-\lambda a}$$

Using this formula, we can find

$$P(x > 5) = e^{-\lambda(5)} = e^{-(.16)(5)} = e^{-.80} = .449329$$

(see Table III). To find the area A, we use the complementary relationship:

$$P(x \le 5) = 1 - P(x > 5) = 1 - .449329 = .550671$$

So, approximately 55% of the magnetron tubes will have to be replaced during the 5 year warranty period.

c. We would expect the probability that the life of a magnetron tube, x, falls within the interval $\mu - 2\sigma$ to $\mu + 2\sigma$ to be quite large (near .95 if we think the approximation in Table 4.3 might apply). A graph of the exponential distribution showing the interval $\mu - 2\sigma$ to $\mu + 2\sigma$ is shown in Figure 7.19. Since the point $\mu - 2\sigma$ lies below $x = 0$, we only need to find the area between $x = 0$ and $a = \mu + 2\sigma = 6.25 + 2(6.25) = 18.75$.

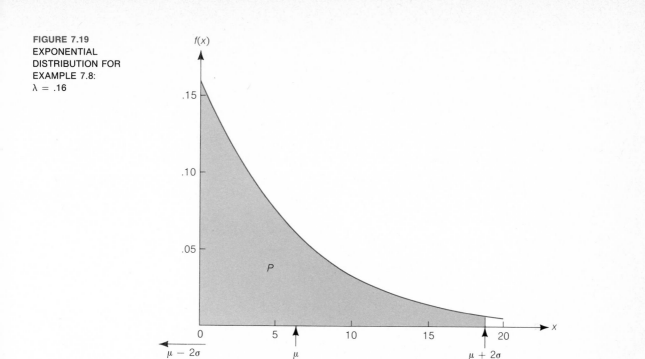

FIGURE 7.19
EXPONENTIAL
DISTRIBUTION FOR
EXAMPLE 7.8:
$\lambda = .16$

This area, P, which is indicated in Figure 7.19, is

$$P = 1 - P(x > 18.75)$$
$$= 1 - e^{-\lambda(18.75)} = 1 - e^{-(.16)(18.75)}$$
$$= 1 - e^{-3}$$

Checking Table III for the value of e^{-3}, we find $e^{-3} = .049787$. Therefore, the probability that the life, x, of a magnetron tube falls within the interval $\mu - 2\sigma$ to $\mu + 2\sigma$ is

$$P = 1 - e^{-3}$$
$$= 1 - .049787 = .950213$$

You can see that this probability agrees very well with Table 4.3, even though this probability distribution is not mound-shaped (it is strongly skewed to the right).

CASE STUDY 7.2   In a discussion about the reliability of computer software, G. J. Schick (1974) says the following:

> Custom software . . . is expensive to develop and requires extensive testing—the goal being to certify that the software is in error-free condition, ready to support the mission for which it was designed. Similar economies should also be expected from an integrated statistical software test program. Traditionally, there are never enough time or resources to test all possible branches and data combinations in a computer program of reasonable size.

Current practice is to design and develop a software system and then to test it to detect errors, until the amount of time and expense required to discover remaining errors is too great to justify further testing. . . . In principle, few large real-time computer programs ever have been tested completely and unequivocally in the sense that every logical data path has been successfully executed under every logical combination for the data at hand for all possible options. One management objective would be to test every logical path in the computer program at least once with some kind of numerical check. At the present state of the art, such a degree of testing is neither feasible nor realistic. In practice, the contractor must be willing to release and the customer willing to accept a level of risk associated with a program that has been less than completely checked.

In finding and correcting errors in a computer program (debugging) and determining the program's reliability, Schick and others have noted the importance of the distribution of the time until the next program error is found. If this distribution is assumed to be exponential, with

$$f(x) = \lambda\, e^{-\lambda x} \qquad (x > 0, \quad \lambda > 0)$$

then, as Schick points out, its mean, $1/\lambda$, would be the average time required to find the next error.

In his article, Schick describes a method relative to software reliability for estimating the parameter, λ, of the exponential distribution. Using computer debugging data supplied by the United States Navy, Schick demonstrates how this estimation procedure and the exponential distribution can be used to estimate the reliability of a computer program. [*Note:* The model used by Schick to represent the distribution for the time until the next error is based on the exponential distribution, but it is slightly more complicated because he assumes that λ varies. For our purposes, however, nothing is lost by assuming the distribution he uses to be exponential.]

After twenty-six program errors were found, Schick estimated λ to be .042. Accordingly, $1/\lambda = 23.8$ days. This means that the average time it would take to find the next (twenty-seventh) error would be about 24 days. Thus, the probability of it taking, say, 60 or more days to find the next error is

$$P(x \geq 60) = e^{-(.042)(60)} = .08046$$

Over the next 290 days, five more errors were detected. Since this is a rate of about one error every 60 days and since $P(x \geq 60) \simeq .08$, it seems unlikely that an exponential distribution with $\lambda = .042$ is an appropriate representation of the distribution for the time until the next error. Based on the number of new errors found and the length of time it took to find them, Schick reestimated λ. He found $\lambda = .0036$. Thus, $1/\lambda = 278$ days, meaning that on an average the next error (thirty-second) would not occur for 278 days. At this point, the length of time and, therefore, the cost required to find any remaining program errors may be prohibitive. Debugging should probably be discontinued. A buyer of the computer program could be told that on an average the program should operate error-free for 278 days.

EXERCISES

7.25. Give two examples of business phenomena with probability distributions that might be well approximated by an exponential distribution.

7.26. Given that x has an exponential distribution with $\lambda = 2$, find the following probabilities:

    a. $P(x > 1)$ b. $P(x > .5)$ c. $P(x > 4)$ d. $P(x > .25)$

7.27. Given that x has an exponential distribution with $\lambda = 1.5$, find the following probabilities:

    a. $P(x \leq 2)$ b. $P(x \leq 4)$ c. $P(x \leq 1)$ d. $P(x \leq .5)$

7.28. Suppose the random variable x is best approximated by an exponential probability distribution with $\lambda = 3$. Find the mean and variance of x. Find the probability that x will assume a value within the interval $\mu \pm 2\sigma$.

7.29. The shelf-life of a product is a random variable that is related to consumer acceptance and, ultimately, to sales and profit. Suppose the shelf-life of bread is best approximated by an exponential distribution with mean equal to 2 days. What fraction of the loaves stocked today would you expect to still be saleable (i.e., not stale) 3 days from now?

7.30. The length of time between breakdowns of an essential piece of equipment is an important factor in deciding on the amount of auxiliary equipment needed to assure continuous service. A machine room foreman believes the time between breakdowns of a particular electrical generator is best approximated by an exponential distribution with mean equal to 10 days.

    a. What is the standard deviation of this exponential distribution?

    b. Assuming the foreman has correctly characterized the distribution for the time between breakdowns and that the generator broke down today, what is the probability that the generator will break down again within the next 14 days?

    c. What is the probability that the generator will operate for more than 20 days without a breakdown?

7.31. The probability distribution of the length of service time is important in the design of service facilities, and it has a definite effect on sales. Suppose the time an individual has to wait in line to be served at a fast-food hamburger franchise is assumed to have an exponential distribution with mean equal to 1 minute. What is the probability that an individual would have to wait more than 2 minutes before being served? Less than 30 seconds?

7.32. The probability distribution for the length of life (in miles of driving) of a particular make of automobile transmission, driven under normal conditions, is approximately exponential with a mean of 90,000 miles (i.e., $\mu = 9$ in units of 10,000 miles). If the transmission is guaranteed for 12,000 miles, what percentage of the transmissions will have to be replaced under the guarantee?

7.33. The length of time between arrivals at a hospital clinic and the length of clinical service time are two random variables that play an important role in designing a clinic and deciding how many physicians and nurses are needed for its operation. The probability distributions of both the length of time between arrivals and the length of service time are often approximately exponential. If the mean time between arrivals for patients at a clinic is 4 minutes:

    a.   What is the probability that a particular interarrival time (the time between the arrival of two patients) is less than 1 minute?

    b.   What is the probability that the next four interarrival times are all less than 1 minute?

    c.   What is the probability that an interarrival time will exceed 10 minutes?

7.34. The following is a sample of the length of time between arrivals (rounded to the nearest minute) at the emergency room of a hospital:

1	10	3	3	9	7	1	4	3
14	6	4	5	7	9	5	1	9
13	4	2	6	12	5	1	10	5
8	3	23	11	14	18	15	12	1
4	22	26	37	3	8	19	5	8
18	16	28	31	21				

    a.   Draw a relative frequency histogram for the above data. Does it appear that an exponential distribution could be used to characterize the length of time between arrivals? Explain.

    b.   If you were asked to model the length of time between arrivals for this emergency room, discuss how you would estimate λ.

**7.5
APPROXIMATING
A BINOMIAL
DISTRIBUTION
WITH A NORMAL
DISTRIBUTION**

When a discrete random variable can assume a large number of values, the calculation of its probabilities may become very tedious. To contend with this problem, we provide tables in Appendix B to give the probabilities for some values of n and the parameters of the discrete probability distributions, but these tables are by necessity incomplete. For example, the binomial table (Table II) can be used only for $n = 5, 10,$ 15, 20, or 25. To avoid this limitation, we seek approximation procedures for calculating the probabilities associated with discrete random variables.

When n is large, the normal probability distribution provides a good approximation to the probability histogram of the binomial random variable. To show how this approximation works, we refer to Example 6.7, in which we used the binomial distribution to model the number x of twenty employees who favor unionization. We assumed that 60% of all the company's employees favored unionization. The mean and standard deviation of x were found to be $\mu = 12$ and $\sigma = 2.19$. The binomial distribution for $n = 20$ and $p = .6$ is shown in Figure 7.20, and the approximating normal distribution with a mean $\mu = 12$ and standard deviation $\sigma = 2.19$ is superimposed.

As part of Example 6.7, we used Table II to find the probability that $x < 10$. This probability, which is shaded in Figure 7.20, was found to equal .128. To find the normal approximation, we first note that $P(0 \le x < 10)$ corresponds to the area to the left of $x = 9.5$ on the normal curve in the figure. We use $x = 9.5$ rather than $x = 9$ or $x = 10$ so that all the binomial probability corresponding to $x = 9$ is included in the

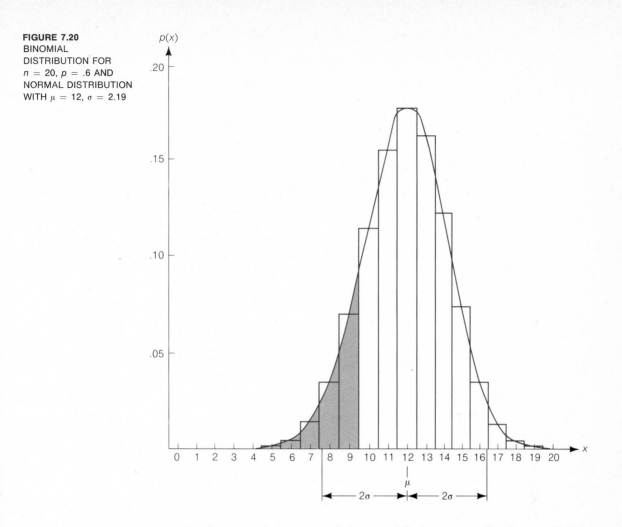

FIGURE 7.20
BINOMIAL
DISTRIBUTION FOR
$n = 20$, $p = .6$ AND
NORMAL DISTRIBUTION
WITH $\mu = 12$, $\sigma = 2.19$

approximating normal curve area, but none of that corresponding to $x = 10$ is included. We thus calculate

$$z = \frac{x - \mu}{\sigma} = \frac{9.5 - 12}{2.19} = -1.14$$

From Table IV of Appendix B we find that the area between $z = 0$ and $z = -1.14$ is .3729. Thus, the approximating normal probability is the area to the left of $x = 9.5$, or

$$P(x \le 9) \approx .5 - .3729 = .1271$$

You can see that the approximation differs only slightly from the exact value, .128.

You may be wondering how large n should be before the normal distribution provides an adequate approximation to the binomial. We will, as a rule of thumb, require that the interval $\mu \pm 3\sigma$ lie completely within the range of values for x, i.e., within the interval from 0 to n. In the example above, $\mu \pm 3\sigma = 12 \pm 3(2.19) = 12 \pm 6.57 = (5.43, 18.57)$. This lies within the interval from 0 to 20, so the normal approximation should be adequate.

EXAMPLE 7.9

The pocket calculator has become relatively inexpensive because its solid-state circuitry is stamped by machine, thus making mass production feasible. A problem with anything that is mass-produced is quality control. The process must somehow be monitored to be sure the rate of defective items is kept at an acceptable level.

One method of dealing with this problem is **lot acceptance sampling**, in which a sample of the items produced is selected, and each item in the sample is carefully tested. The lot of items is then accepted or rejected, based upon the number of defectives in the sample. For example, suppose a manufacturer of calculators chooses 200 stamped circuits from the day's production and determines x, the number of defective circuits in the sample. Suppose that up to a 6% rate of defectives is considered acceptable for the process.

a. Find the mean and standard deviation of x, assuming a 6% defective rate.
b. Use the normal approximation to determine the probability that twenty or more defectives are observed in the sample of 200 circuits, i.e., that $x \geq 20$.

Solution

a. The random variable x is binomial, with $n = 200$ and the fraction defective $p = .06$. Thus,

$$\mu = np = 200(.06) = 12$$
$$\sigma = \sqrt{npq} = \sqrt{200(.06)(.94)} = \sqrt{11.28} = 3.36$$

Note that

$$\mu \pm 3\sigma = 12 \pm 3(3.36) = 12 \pm 10.08 = (1.92, 22.08)$$

FIGURE 7.21
NORMAL APPROXIMATION TO THE BINOMIAL DISTRIBUTION WITH $n = 200$, $p = .06$

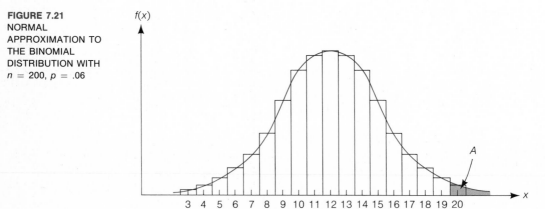

CHAPTER 7 CONTINUOUS RANDOM VARIABLES

lies completely within the range from 0 to 200, so that the normal probability distribution should provide an adequate approximation to this binomial distribution.

b. To find the approximating area corresponding to $x \geq 20$, refer to Figure 7.21. Note that we want to include all of the binomial probability histogram from 20 to 200, inclusive. But in order to include the entire rectangle corresponding to $x = 20$, we must begin the approximating area at $x = 19.5$. Thus, our z value is

$$z = \frac{x - \mu}{\sigma} = \frac{19.5 - 12}{3.36} = \frac{7.5}{3.36} = 2.23$$

Referring to Table IV of Appendix B, the area to the right of the mean corresponding to $z = 2.23$ (see Figure 7.22) is .4871. So, the area A is

$$A = .5 - .4871 = .0129$$

Thus, the normal approximation to the binomial probability is

$$P(x \geq 20) = .0129$$

In other words, the probability is extremely small that twenty or more defectives will be observed in a sample of 200 circuits, *if in fact the true defective rate is 6%*. If the manufacturer were to observe $x \geq 20$, the likely reason is that the process is producing more than the acceptable 6% defectives.

FIGURE 7.22
STANDARD NORMAL
DISTRIBUTION

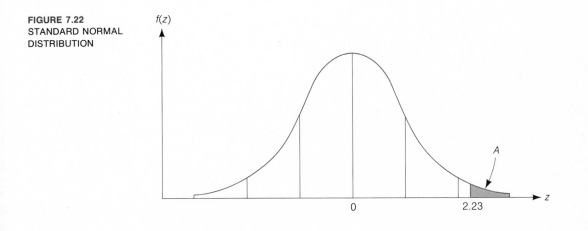

7.35. Why might you want to use a normal distribution to approximate a binomial distribution?

7.36. Under what circumstances is it appropriate to approximate a binomial distribution with a normal distribution?

7.37. Suppose that x is a binomial random variable with $p = .5$ and $n = 20$.

    a. Would it be appropriate to approximate the probability distribution of x with a normal distribution? Explain.

    b. Assuming that a normal distribution provides an adequate approximation to the distribution of x, what are the mean and variance of the approximating normal distribution?

    c. Use Table II of Appendix B to find the exact value of $P(8 \leq x \leq 10)$.

    d. Use the normal approximation to find $P(8 \leq x \leq 10)$.

7.38. Assume that x is a binomial random variable with $n = 25$ and $p = .4$. Use Table II of Appendix B and the normal approximation to find the exact and approximate values, respectively, for the following probabilities:

    a. $P(x \leq 10)$ b. $P(x \geq 12)$ c. $P(x \geq 15)$

7.39. Assume that x is a binomial random variable with $n = 50$ and $p = .4$. Use a normal approximation to find the following:

    a. $P(x \leq 40)$ b. $P(25 \leq x \leq 30)$ c. $P(x \geq 20)$

7.40. It is against the law to discriminate against job applicants because of race, religion, sex, or age. Forty percent of the individuals who apply for an accountant's position in a large corporation are over 45 years of age. If the company decides to choose fifty of a very large number of applicants for closer credential screening, claiming that the selection will be random and not age-biased, what is the probability that less than fifteen of those chosen are over 45 years of age? (Assume that the applicant pool is large enough so that x, the number over 45 in the sample, has a binomial probability distribution.)

7.41. The local pizza shop has determined that the probability of a delivery order taken on April 1 being a hoax is .3. Suppose that each phony order costs the pizza shop $6. If today is April 1 and the shop takes ninety delivery orders, what is the probability that it will lose more than $180 today on phony orders?

7.42. An advertising agency was hired to introduce a new product. It claimed that after its campaign, 30% of all consumers were familiar with the product. To check the claim, the manufacturer of the product surveyed 2,000 consumers. Of this number, 527 consumers had learned about the product through sources attributable to the campaign. What is the probability that as few as 527 (i.e., 527 or less) would have learned about the product if the campaign was really 30% effective?

7.43. A credit card company claims that 80% of all clothing purchases in excess of $10 are made with credit cards. A random check of 100 clothing purchases in excess of $10 showed that seventy-three had been made with credit cards. If 80% of all clothing purchases in excess of $10 are made with credit cards and if x is the number in a sample of 100 that make credit card purchases, find:

    a. $P(x \leq 73)$ b. $P(75 \leq x \leq 85)$

7.44. To check on the effectiveness of a new production process, 700 photoflash devices were randomly selected from a large number that had been produced. If the process actually produces 6% defectives, what is the probability that:

  a. More than fifty defectives appear in the sample of 700?
  b. The number of defectives in the sample of 700 is forty-five or less?

7.45. A manufacturer of pencils has 5 gross (1 gross = 12 dozen) randomly chosen from each day's production and inspected for defects (chips, cracks, etc.). The manufacturer is willing to tolerate up to a 10% defective rate in the production process. If the process defective rate is more than 10%, the process is considered out of control.

  a. Assuming that 10% of all pencils produced are defective, what is the probability of observing eighty or more defectives in a day's sample?
  b. Is it likely that the process is in control if 100 defective pencils are observed in a day's sample? Explain.

SUMMARY

Many **continuous random variables** in business applications have probability distributions that are well approximated by the **normal, uniform,** or **exponential probability distributions**. In this chapter we showed the graphical shape of these probability distributions, gave their means and variances, and pointed out some practical applications of each of these probability models. In addition, we showed that the normal probability distribution provides a good approximation for the binomial distribution when n is sufficiently large.

SUPPLEMENTARY EXERCISES

[*Note: Starred (*) exercises refer to optional sections in this chapter.*]

*7.46. Assume that x is a random variable best described by a uniform distribution with $c = 20$ and $d = 100$.

  a. Find $f(x)$.
  b. Find the mean and standard deviation of x.
  c. Graph the probability distribution for x and locate its mean and the interval $\mu \pm 2\sigma$ on the graph.
  d. Find $P(x \leq 50)$.
  e. Find $P(x \geq 90)$.
  f. Find $P(x \leq 100)$.
  g. Find $P(\mu - \sigma \leq x \leq \mu + \sigma)$.
  h. Find $P(x > 100)$.

*7.47. Given that x has an exponential distribution with $\lambda = .25$, find:

  a. $P(x \leq 1)$ b. $P(x > 1)$ c. $P(x = 1)$
  d. $P(x \leq 8)$ e. $P(4 \leq x \leq 12)$

7.48. Use Table IV of Appendix B to calculate the area under the standard normal frequency function between the following pairs of z-scores:

    a. -1.96 and 1.96 b. -1.645 and 1.645 c. -3 and 3

    d. -3 and 2 e. 1 and 3 f. -1.5 and 3

7.49. Use Table IV of Appendix B to find the following probabilities:

    a. $P(z \geq .5)$ b. $P(z \leq .5)$

    c. $P(z \geq -2.5)$ d. $P(-2.75 \leq z \leq -.25)$

7.50. Find a value of z, call it z_0, such that

    a. $P(z \geq z_0) = .5$ b. $P(z \leq z_0) = .5199$

    c. $P(z \geq z_0) = .3300$ d. $P(z_0 \leq z \leq .59) = .5845$

7.51. The random variable x has a normal distribution with $\mu = 80$ and $\sigma = 10$. Find the following probabilities:

    a. $P(x \leq 75)$ b. $P(x \geq 90)$ c. $P(60 \leq x \leq 70)$

    d. $P(x > 75)$ e. $P(x = 75)$ f. $P(x \leq 105)$

7.52. Assume that x is a binomial random variable with $n = 50$ and $p = .6$. Find the following probabilities:

    a. $P(x \leq 35)$ b. $P(10 \leq x \leq 30)$

    c. $P(x \geq 40)$ d. $P(20 \leq x \leq 33)$

7.53. Suppose the present value of a risky investment is approximately normally distributed with mean \$10,000 and standard deviation \$4,000. What is the probability that the present value of the investment is less than \$1,000? Greater than \$20,000?

7.54. After extensive testing of a new low-tar cigarette, a tobacco company concluded that the number of milligrams of tar yielded by each cigarette had a probability distribution that was approximately normal with $\mu = 8$ and $\sigma = 1.9$ milligrams.

    a. What is the probability that one of the new low-tar cigarettes will yield more than 10 milligrams of tar?

    b. If two of the new low-tar cigarettes are chosen at random and tested, what is the probability that both will yield less than 6 milligrams of tar?

7.55. Golf balls that do not meet a manufacturer's shape specifications are referred to as being "out of round" and may be sold as rejects. Assume that 10% of the balls produced by a particular machine are out of round. What is the probability that of the next 200 balls produced by the machine, twenty-five or more are out of round?

7.56. A firm believes the internal rate of return for its proposed investment can best be described by a normal distribution with mean 15% and standard deviation 3%. What is the probability that the internal rate of return for the investment will be:

    a. Greater than 20% or less than 10%?

    b. At least 6%?

    c. More than 16.5%?

*7.57. Blending feeders are used to break up tobacco that has been aged in tightly packed hogsheads. One cigarette manufacturer determined that the time between breakdowns for each of its blending feeders is best represented by an exponential distribution with mean equal to 100 hours of operation. Given that a particular feeder was just repaired and put back into service, what is the probability that it will not break down for at least 50 more hours? What is the probability that it will break down within the next 100 hours?

7.58. A loan officer in a large bank has been assigned to screen sixty loan applications during the next week. If her past record indicates that she turns down 20% of the applicants, what is the probability that forty-one or more of the sixty applications will be approved? What is the probability that between forty-five and fifty of the applications will be approved?

*7.59. Assume the length of the active life of baking yeast has an exponential distribution with mean equal to 6 months. Suppose the expiration date marked on a package of yeast is based on a life of 7 months. What is the probability that a package of the yeast will lose its potency before its expiration date?

7.60. The length of time required to assemble a photoelectric cell is normally distributed with mean equal to 18.1 minutes and $\sigma = 1.3$ minutes. What is the probability that it will require more than 20 minutes to assemble a cell?

7.61. It is quite common for the standard deviation of a random variable to increase proportionally as the mean increases. When this occurs, the coefficient of variation,

$$CV = \frac{\sigma}{\mu}$$

the ratio between σ and μ, is the proportionality constant. To illustrate, the error (in dollars) in assessing the value of a house increases as the house increases in value. Suppose that long experience with assessors in a given region has shown that the coefficient of variation is .08 and that the probability distribution of assessed valuations on the same house by many different assessors is approximately normal with a mean we will call the "true value" of the house. Suppose the true value of your house is $50,000 and it is being assessed for taxation purposes. What is the probability that the assessor will assess your house in excess of $55,000?

7.62. According to the United States Labor Department, the median income in the United States is in the neighborhood of $14,000 per year. Since this figure will vary somewhat over time, assume that the median is exactly $14,000. If 1,000 people are randomly sampled from the population of workers, what is the probability:

    a. That more than half have incomes less than $14,000 per year?
    b. That fewer than 480 have incomes less than $14,000 per year?
    c. That the number of incomes, x, in the sample of 1,000 is within the interval $475 \leq x \leq 525$?

*7.63. The number of serious accidents in a manufacturing plant has (approximately) a Poisson probability distribution with a mean of 2 serious accidents per month.

a. If an accident occurs today, what is the probability that the next serious accident will not occur within the next month? [*Note:* If x, the number of events per unit time, has a Poisson distribution with mean λ, then it can be shown that the time between adjacent pairs of events has an exponential probability distribution with mean $1/\lambda$.]

b. What is the probability that more than one accident will occur within the next month?

*7.64. The Poisson probability distribution, like the binomial, can be approximated by a normal probability distribution. This approximation, using $\mu = \lambda$ and $\sigma = \sqrt{\lambda}$, will be good when λ is large (large enough so that the distance between $x = 0$ and λ is at least $3\sigma = 3\sqrt{\lambda}$). The number of union complaints per unit time at a particular manufacturing plant has a Poisson probability distribution with $\mu = 40$ complaints per month. Use the normal approximation to the Poisson probability distribution to find:

a. The probability that the number of complaints in a given month will be less than thirty-five.

b. The probability that the number of complaints in a given month exceeds forty.

c. What is the probability that in each of 3 succeeding months, the number of complaints exceeds forty?

7.65. A company has a lump-sum incentive plan for salespeople that is dependent upon their level of sales. If they sell less than $100,000 per year, they receive a $1,000 bonus; from $100,000 to $200,000, they receive $5,000; and above $200,000, they receive $10,000. If the annual sales per salesperson has approximately a normal distribution with $\mu = \$180,000$ and $\sigma = \$50,000$:

a. Find p_1, the proportion of salespeople who receive a $1,000 bonus.

b. Find p_2, the proportion of salespeople who receive a $5,000 bonus.

c. Find p_3, the proportion of salespeople who receive a $10,000 bonus.

d. What is the mean value of the bonus payout for the company? [*Hint:* See the definition for the expected value of a random variable in Chapter 6.]

7.66. The probability distribution of the number of people per month who open a savings account in a large banking system is approximately normally distributed with $\mu = 1,280$ and $\sigma = 265$.

a. If the bank gives a $10 gift to each new account holder, what portion of the time will the bank's payout for gifts exceed $15,000 per month?

b. What is the bank's mean monthly payout for gifts?

7.67. Contrary to our intuition, very reliable decisions concerning the proportion of a large group of consumers favoring a particular product or a particular social issue can be based upon relatively small samples. For example, suppose the target population of consumers contains 50,000,000 people and that we wish to decide whether the proportion of consumers, p, in the population that favor some product (or issue) is as large as some value, say .2. Suppose you randomly select a sample as small as 1,600 from the 50,000,000 and you observe 400 (or 25%) of the consumers in the sample who favor the new product. How would this sample result produce sufficient evidence to conclude that p (the proportion of consumers favoring the product in the population of 50,000,000) is at least as large as .2?

7.68. Eighty 10 pound bags of sugar were randomly sampled from the stock of a local sugar wholesaler and weighed. The following are the results rounded to the nearest tenth of a pound:

10.2	10.2	9.6	9.9	10.0	10.0	10.0	10.1
10.4	9.9	9.6	10.0	9.9	10.1	9.9	9.9
9.8	10.0	10.4	10.0	9.7	9.9	10.2	9.8
9.9	10.3	10.0	10.0	9.8	9.8	10.1	9.9
10.1	9.9	10.2	9.8	10.0	10.1	9.5	10.0
10.0	10.1	10.1	10.1	10.2	10.5	9.9	10.1
9.5	9.9	9.7	9.9	9.9	10.1	9.9	10.3
10.1	10.1	9.8	10.0	10.0	10.0	9.7	10.0
10.0	10.2	10.0	10.1	10.3	9.8	10.0	10.2
9.6	9.9	9.8	10.0	9.8	10.2	10.0	9.9

Construct a relative frequency histogram for these data and suggest a continuous probability distribution that could be used to approximate the weight distribution of the wholesaler's stock of 10 pound bags of sugar.

ON YOUR OWN . . .

For large values of n the computational effort involved in working with the binomial probability distribution is considerable. Fortunately, in many instances the normal distribution provides a good approximation to the binomial distribution. This exercise was designed to enable you to demonstrate to yourself how well the normal distribution approximates the binomial distribution.

a. Let the random variable x have a binomial probability distribution with $n = 10$ and $p = .5$. Using the binomial distribution, find the probability that x takes on a value in each of the following intervals: $\mu \pm \sigma$, $\mu \pm 2\sigma$, and $\mu \pm 3\sigma$.
b. Find the probabilities requested in part a using a normal approximation to the given binomial distribution.
c. Determine the magnitude of the difference between each of the three probabilities as determined by the binomial distribution and by the normal approximation.
d. Letting x have a binomial distribution with $n = 20$ and $p = .5$, repeat parts a, b, and c. Notice that the probability estimates provided by the normal distribution are more accurate for $n = 20$ than for $n = 10$.

REFERENCES

Dyckman, T. R., & Thomas, L. J. *Fundamental statistics for business and economics.* Englewood Cliffs, N.J.: Prentice-Hall, 1977. Chapter 8.

Hillier, F. S. "The derivation of probabilistic information for the evaluation of risky investments. *Management Science,* Apr. 1963, *9,* 443–457.

Hogg, R. V., & Craig, A. T. *Introduction to mathematical statistics.* 3d ed. New York: Wiley, 1970. Chapters 1 and 3.

Lindgren, B. W. *Statistical theory.* 3d ed. New York: Macmillan, 1976. Chapters 2 and 3.

Mood, A. M., Graybill, F. A., & Boes, D. C. *Introduction to the theory of statistics.* 3d ed. New York: McGraw-Hill, 1974. Chapter 3.

Neter, J., Wasserman, W., & Whitmore, G. A. *Fundamental statistics for business and economics.* 4th ed. Boston: Allyn and Bacon, 1973. Chapter 7.

Schick, G. J. "The search for a software reliability model." *Decision Sciences,* Oct. 1974, *5,* 529.

Winkler, R. L., & Hays, W. *Statistics: Probability inference, and decision.* 2d ed. New York: Holt, Rinehart, and Winston, 1975. Chapter 3.

WHERE WE'VE BEEN . . .

We have learned in earlier chapters that the objective of most statistical investigations is inference—that is, making decisions about or estimating some numerical descriptive measure (a parameter) of a population based on sample data. To actually make the decision or estimate the population parameter, we use the sample data to compute sample statistics (Chapters 3 and 4) such as the sample mean or variance.

WHERE WE'RE GOING . . .

Because sample measurements are observed values of random variables, the value we compute for a sample statistic will vary in a random manner from sample to sample. In other words, since sample statistics are computed from random variables, they themselves are random variables, and they have probability distributions that are either discrete or continuous, as discussed in Chapters 6 and 7. Since the value of a statistic may lead to either a "good" or a "poor" inference, we need to know its probability distribution. This probability distribution, called the *sampling distribution* because it characterizes the distribution of values of the statistic over a very large number of samples, is the topic of this chapter. Particularly, we will discuss why many sampling distributions tend to be approximately normal, and you will see how sampling distributions can be used to evaluate the accuracy of parameter estimates.

8

SAMPLING DISTRIBUTIONS

In Chapters 6 and 7 we assumed that we knew the probability distribution of a random variable, and based on this knowledge, we were able to compute the mean, variance, and probability that the random variable assumed specific values. However, in most practical business applications, this information will not be available. To illustrate, in Example 6.7 we calculated the probability that the binomial random variable x (the number of twenty polled employees who favor unionization) assumed specific values. To do this, it was necessary to assume some value for p (the proportion of the employees in the population who favor unionization). Thus, for the purposes of illustration we assumed $p = .6$, but, in all likelihood, the exact value of p would be unknown. In fact, the probable purpose of taking the poll was to estimate p. Similarly, when we modeled the in-city gas mileage of a certain automobile model in Example 7.5, we used the normal probability distribution with an *assumed* mean and standard deviation of 27 and 3 miles per gallon, respectively. In reality, the true mean and standard deviation are unknown quantities that would have to be estimated.

Numerical quantities that describe probability distributions are called **parameters**. Thus, p (the probability of a success in a binomial experiment), and μ and σ (the mean and standard deviation of a normal distribution) are examples of parameters.

DEFINITION 8.1
Numerical descriptive measures of a population are called **parameters**.

We will often use the information contained in a sample to make inferences about the parameters of a population. In order to make such inferences, we must compute **sample statistics** that will aid in making these inferences:

DEFINITION 8.2
A **sample statistic** is a quantity calculated from the observations in a sample.

Some examples of useful sample statistics we have already discussed are the sample mean, sample median, sample variance, and sample standard deviation.

Before we can use these and other sample statistics to make inferences about population parameters, we have to be able to evaluate their properties. How can we decide which sample statistic contains the most information about a population parameter? The purpose of this chapter is to answer this question.

8.1
INTRODUCTION TO SAMPLING DISTRIBUTIONS

If you wish to estimate a parameter of a population—say, the population mean μ—there are a number of sample statistics that can be used for the estimate. Two possible candidates are the sample mean and the sample median. Which will provide the better estimate?

You can see that there is no exact answer to this question, because the statistics are calculated from sample measurements that are observed values of random variables. That is, the sample measurements represent the outcome of a random sampling experiment and we never know in advance the exact values of the sample measurements. For one sample, the sample median might be closer to the population mean; for the next sample, the sample mean might be closer than the median. Consequently, we cannot compare two sample statistics by examining the values they assume for a single sample. We need to regard the sample statistics as random variables (random outcomes of the sampling process) so that we can make probability statements about their behavior.

The probability distribution for a statistic based on a random sample of n measurements could be generated in the following way: For purposes of illustration, we will suppose we are sampling from a population with $\mu = 10$ and $\sigma = 5$, the sample statistic is $\bar{x}$, and the sample size is $n = 25$. Draw a single random sample of twenty-five measurements from the population and suppose that $\bar{x} = 9.8$. Return the measurements to the population and try again. That is, draw another random sample of $n = 25$ measurements and see what you obtain for an outcome. Now, perhaps, $\bar{x} = 11.4$. Replace these measurements, draw another sample of $n = 25$ measurements, calculate $\bar{x}$, etc. If this sampling process were repeated over and over again an infinitely large number of times, you would generate an infinitely large number of values of $\bar{x}$ that could be arranged in a relative frequency distribution. This distribution, which would appear as shown in Figure 8.1, is the probability distribution (or **sampling distribution,** as it is commonly called) of the statistic $\bar{x}$:

DEFINITION 8.3
The **sampling distribution** of a sample statistic calculated from a sample of n measurements is the probability distribution of the statistic.

In actual practice, the sampling distribution of a statistic is obtained mathematically or by simulating the sampling on a computer using the procedure described above.

FIGURE 8.1
SAMPLING DISTRIBUTION FOR $\bar{x}$ BASED ON A SAMPLE OF $n = 25$ MEASUREMENTS

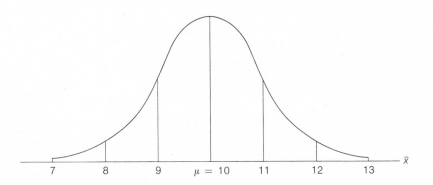

FIGURE 8.2
TWO SAMPLING
DISTRIBUTIONS FOR
ESTIMATING THE
POPULATION
VARIANCE σ^2

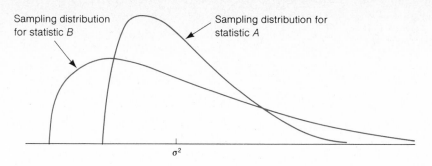

If $\bar{x}$ has been calculated from a sample of $n = 25$ measurements selected from a population with mean $\mu = 10$ and standard deviation $\sigma = 5$, the sampling distribution (Figure 8.1) provides all the information you may wish to know about its behavior. For example, the probability that you will draw a sample of twenty-five measurements and obtain a value of $\bar{x}$ in the interval $9 \leq \bar{x} \leq 10$, will be the area under the sampling distribution over that interval. Note that you need not know the actual value of μ in order to use the information that a sampling distribution provides about a statistic. All you need to know is the position of the sampling distribution relative to μ.

Since the properties of a statistic are typified by its sampling distribution, it follows that to compare two statistics, you compare their sampling distributions. For example, if you have two statistics, A and B, for estimating the same parameter (for purposes of illustration, suppose the parameter is the population variance σ^2) and if their sampling distributions are as shown in Figure 8.2, you would choose statistic A in preference to statistic B. You would make this choice because the sampling distribution for statistic A centers over σ^2 and has less spread (variation) than the sampling distribution for statistic B. When you draw a single sample in a practical sampling situation, the odds are higher that statistic A will fall nearer σ^2.

Remember that in practice we will not know the numerical value of the unknown parameter σ^2, so we will not know whether statistic A or statistic B is closer to σ^2 for particular samples. We have to rely on our theoretical knowledge of the sampling distributions to choose the best sample statistic, and then use it sample after sample.

To show how two statistics can be compared, we will generate approximations to the sampling distributions for two statistics in the example below.

EXAMPLE 8.1   Suppose we perform the following experiment: Take a sample of eleven measurements from the uniform distribution shown in Figure 8.3. Calculate the two sample statistics

$$\bar{x} = \text{Sample mean} = \frac{\sum x_i}{11}$$

$$m = \text{Median} = \text{Sixth sample measurement when the eleven measurements are arranged in ascending order}$$

In this particular example we *know* that the population mean is $\mu = .5$. The objective will be to find out which sample statistic contains more information about μ. We use

FIGURE 8.3
UNIFORM FREQUENCY
FUNCTION FROM
0 TO 1

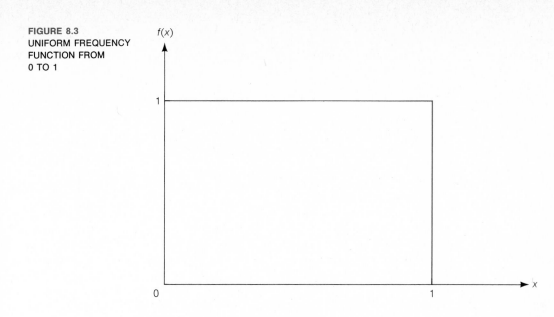

a computer to generate 1,000 samples, all with $n = 11$ observations. Then, we compute $\bar{x}$ and m for each sample. Our problem is to find the resulting approximate sampling distributions of $\bar{x}$ and m.

Solution

The first ten of the 1,000 samples generated are presented in Table 8.1. For each of the 1,000 samples we compute the sample mean $\bar{x}$ and the sample median m. For example, the first computer-generated sample from the uniform distribution (arranged in ascending order) contained the following measurements: .125, .138, .139, .217, .419, .506, .516, .757, .771, .786, .919. The sample mean, $\bar{x}$, and median, m, computed for this sample are

$$\bar{x} = \frac{.125 + .138 + \cdots + .919}{11} = .481$$

$$m = \text{Sixth ordered measurement} = .506$$

TABLE 8.1
FIRST TEN SAMPLES
OF $n = 11$
MEASUREMENTS FROM
A UNIFORM
DISTRIBUTION

SAMPLE	MEASUREMENTS										
1	.217	.786	.757	.125	.139	.919	.506	.771	.138	.516	.419
2	.303	.703	.812	.650	.848	.392	.988	.469	.632	.012	.065
3	.383	.547	.383	.584	.098	.676	.091	.535	.256	.163	.390
4	.218	.376	.248	.606	.610	.055	.095	.311	.086	.165	.665
5	.144	.069	.485	.739	.491	.054	.953	.179	.865	.429	.648
6	.426	.563	.186	.896	.628	.075	.283	.549	.295	.522	.674
7	.643	.828	.465	.672	.074	.300	.319	.254	.708	.384	.534
8	.616	.049	.324	.700	.803	.399	.557	.975	.569	.023	.072
9	.093	.835	.534	.212	.201	.041	.889	.728	.466	.142	.574
10	.957	.253	.983	.904	.696	.766	.880	.485	.035	.881	.732

FIGURE 8.4

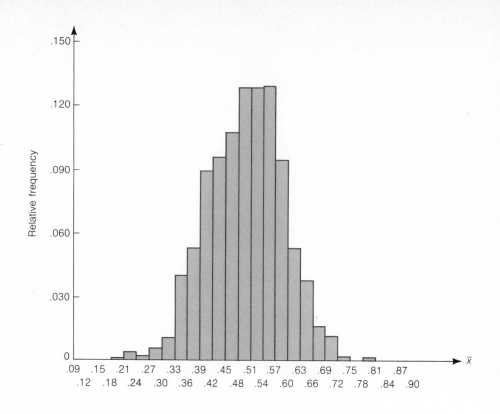

(a) Sampling distribution of $\bar{x}$ (based on 1,000 samples of $n = 11$ measurements)

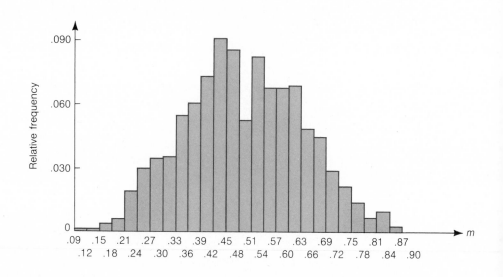

(b) Sampling distribution of m (based on 1,000 samples of $n = 11$ measurements)

The relative frequency histograms for $\bar{x}$ and m for the 1,000 samples of size $n = 11$ are shown in Figure 8.4.

You can see that the values of $\bar{x}$ tend to cluster around μ to a greater extent than do the values of m. Thus, on the basis of the observed sampling distributions, we conclude that $\bar{x}$ contains more information about μ than m does—at least for samples of $n = 11$ measurements from the uniform distribution.

As noted earlier, we will not always have to simulate repeated sampling on a computer to find sampling distributions. Many sampling distributions can be derived mathematically, but the theory necessary to do this is beyond the scope of this text. Consequently, when we need to know the properties of a statistic, we will present its sampling distribution and describe its properties. Several of the important properties we look for in sampling distributions are discussed in the next section.

8.2 PROPERTIES OF SAMPLING DISTRIBUTIONS: UNBIASEDNESS AND MINIMUM VARIANCE

We have already stressed that valuable information about a sample or population is contained in the two descriptive measures: mean and standard deviation. Similarly, the means and standard deviations of sampling distributions help us decide which sample statistic contains the most information about a population parameter.

As a first consideration, we would like the sampling distribution to center over the parameter we wish to estimate. One way to express centrality is in terms of the mean of the sampling distribution. Consequently, we say that a statistic is **unbiased** if its sampling distribution has a mean equal to the parameter it is intended to estimate. When this situation occurs, the sampling distribution of the statistic will be centered over the parameter as shown in Figure 8.5(a). If the mean of a sampling distribution is not equal to the parameter it is intended to estimate, the statistic is said to be **biased**. The sampling distribution for a biased statistic is shown in Figure 8.5(b).

DEFINITION 8.4

If a sample statistic has a sampling distribution with a mean equal to the population parameter the statistic is intended to estimate, the statistic is said to be an **unbiased** estimator of the parameter.

If the mean of the sampling distribution is not equal to the parameter, the statistic is said to be a **biased** estimator of the parameter.

The standard deviation of a sampling distribution measures another important property of statistics—the spread of the estimates generated by repeated sampling. Suppose two statistics, A and B, are both unbiased estimators of the population parameter called θ (theta). Note that θ could be any parameter, such as μ, σ^2, σ, etc. Since the means of the two sampling distributions are the same, we turn to their standard deviations in order to decide which will provide estimates that fall closer

FIGURE 8.5
SAMPLING
DISTRIBUTIONS OF
UNBIASED AND
BIASED ESTIMATORS

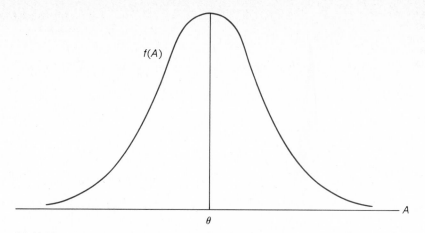

$f(A)$

θ

(a) Unbiased sample statistic for the parameter θ

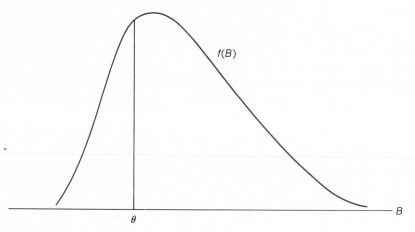

$f(B)$

θ

(b) Biased sample statistic for the parameter θ

to the unknown estimated population parameter. Naturally, we will choose the sample statistic that has the smallest standard deviation among all unbiased statistics. Figure 8.6 depicts sampling distributions for A and B. Note that the standard deviation of the distribution of A is smaller than the standard deviation for B, indicating that over a large number of samples, the values of A cluster more closely around the unknown population parameter than do the values of B.

In summary, to make an inference about a population parameter, use the sample statistic with a sampling distribution that is unbiased and has a small standard deviation (usually smaller than other unbiased sample statistics). How to find this sample statistic will not concern us, because the "best" statistic for estimating particular parameters is a matter of record. We will simply present an unbiased estimator with

FIGURE 8.6
SAMPLING
DISTRIBUTIONS OF
TWO UNBIASED
ESTIMATORS

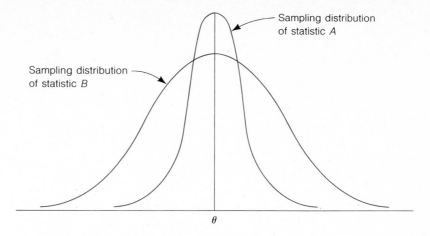

its standard deviation for each population parameter we consider. [*Note:* The standard deviation of the sampling distribution of a statistic is usually called the standard error of the statistic.]

8.3
THE CENTRAL
LIMIT THEOREM

Estimating the mean useful life of automobiles, the mean monthly sales for all automobile dealers in a large city, and the mean breaking strength of a new plastic are practical problems with something in common. In each we are interested in making an inference about the mean μ of some population. Because many practical business problems involve estimating μ, it is particularly important to have a sample statistic that is a good estimator of μ. As we mentioned in Chapter 3, the sample mean $\bar{x}$ is,

FIGURE 8.7
UNIFORM SAMPLED
POPULATION

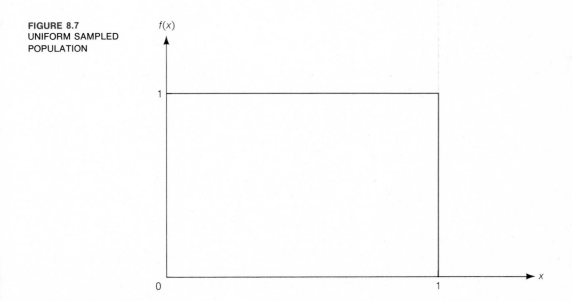

in general, the best estimator of μ. The following important theorem provides information about the sampling distribution for this useful statistic:

THE CENTRAL LIMIT THEOREM
For large sample sizes, the mean $\bar{x}$ of a sample from a population with mean μ and standard deviation σ has a sampling distribution that is approximately normal, **regardless of the probability distribution of the sampled population.** The larger the sample size, the better will be the normal approximation to the sampling distribution of $\bar{x}$.

Not only will the sampling distribution of $\bar{x}$ be approximately normal, it will always be unbiased (i.e., $E(\bar{x}) = \mu$) with a standard deviation of $\sigma/\sqrt{n}$, where n is the sample size. These properties are summarized below:

PROPERTIES OF THE SAMPLING DISTRIBUTION OF $\bar{x}$

1. The mean of the sampling distribution is equal to the mean of the sampled population, i.e., $\mu_{\bar{x}} = E(\bar{x}) = \mu$.
2. The standard deviation of the sampling distribution is equal to the standard deviation of the sampled population divided by the square root of the sample size, i.e., $\sigma_{\bar{x}} = \sigma/\sqrt{n}$.
3. The sampling distribution of $\bar{x}$ is approximately normal for large sample sizes. *

For example, suppose the sampled population has the uniform probability distribution shown in Figure 8.7. The mean and standard deviation of this probability distribution are $\mu = .5$ and $\sigma = .29$ (see Section 7.3 for the formulas for μ and σ). Now suppose a sample of eleven measurements is selected from this population. The sampling distribution of the sample mean for samples of size 11 will also have a mean of .5, with a standard deviation

$$\sigma_{\bar{x}} = \frac{\sigma}{\sqrt{n}} = \frac{.29}{\sqrt{11}} = .09$$

(That is, the standard error of $\bar{x}$ is $\sigma/\sqrt{n} = .09$.)

Recall that in Example 8.1 we generated 1,000 samples of $n = 11$ measurements each. The relative frequency histogram for the 1,000 sample means is shown in Figure 8.8, and the normal probability distribution with a mean of .5 and standard deviation

---

* Also, because of the central limit theorem, the sum of the identically distributed independent random variables, $\sum_{i=1}^{n} x_i$, will have a sampling distribution that will be approximately normal for large samples. This distribution will have a mean equal to $n\mu$ and a variance equal to $n\sigma^2$.

FIGURE 8.8
RELATIVE FREQUENCY
HISTOGRAM FOR $\bar{x}$
IN 1,000 SAMPLES,
WITH NORMAL
FREQUENCY FUNCTION
SUPERIMPOSED

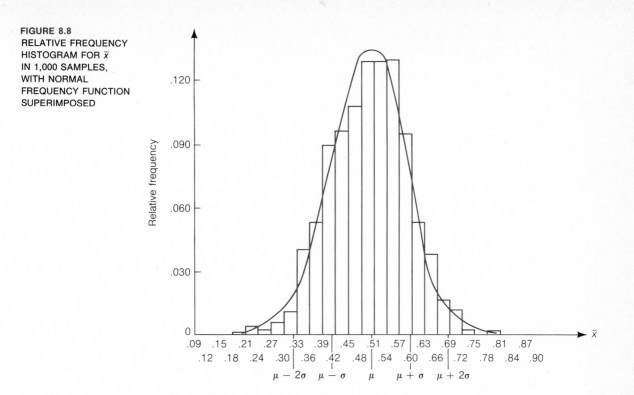

.09 is superimposed. You can see that this normal probability distribution approximates the computer-generated sampling distribution very well, even though the sample size is only $n = 11$.

EXAMPLE 8.2

A manufacturer of automobile batteries claims that the mean life of its best battery is 54 months, with a standard deviation of 6 months. Suppose a consumer group decides to check the claim by purchasing a sample of fifty of these batteries and subjecting them to tests that determine their lives.

a. Assuming the manufacturer's claim is true, describe the sampling distribution of the mean of a sample of fifty batteries.

b. Assuming the manufacturer's claim is true, what is the probability the consumer group's sample has a mean life of 52 or fewer months?

Solution

a. Even though we have no information about the shape of the probability distribution of the lives of the batteries, we can use the central limit theorem to deduce that the sampling distribution for a sample mean of fifty batteries is approximately normally distributed. Furthermore, the mean of this sampling distribution is the same as the

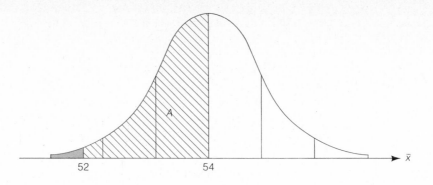

mean of the sampled population, which is $\mu = 54$ months, according to the manufacturer's claim. Finally, the standard deviation of the sampling distribution is given by

$$\sigma_{\bar{x}} = \frac{\sigma}{\sqrt{n}} = \frac{6}{\sqrt{50}} = .85 \text{ months}$$

Note that we used the claimed standard deviation of the sampled population, $\sigma = 6$ months. Thus, if we assume the claim is true, the sampling distribution for the mean life of the fifty batteries sampled is as shown in Figure 8.9.

b. If the manufacturer's claim is true, the probability that the consumer group observes a mean battery life of 52 or fewer months for their sample of fifty batteries, $P(\bar{x} \leq 52)$, is equivalent to the shaded area in Figure 8.9. Since the sampling distribution is approximately normal, we can find this area by computing the z value:

$$z = \frac{\bar{x} - \mu_{\bar{x}}}{\sigma_{\bar{x}}} = \frac{\bar{x} - \mu}{\sigma_{\bar{x}}} = \frac{52 - 54}{.85} = -2.35$$

where $\mu_{\bar{x}}$, the mean of the sampling distribution of $\bar{x}$, is equal to μ, the mean of the lives of the sampled population.

The area A shown in Figure 8.9 between $\bar{x} = 52$ and 54 is found in Table IV of Appendix B to be .4906, so the area to the left of 52 is

$$P(\bar{x} \leq 52) = .5 - A = .5 - .4906 = .0094$$

Thus, the probability the consumer group will observe a sample mean of 52 or less is only .0094 if the manufacturer's claim is true. If the fifty tested batteries do result in a mean of 52 or fewer months, the consumer group will have strong evidence that the manufacturer's claim is untrue, because such an event is very unlikely to occur if the claim is true. (This is still another application of the rare event approach to statistical inference.)

In addition to providing a very useful approximation for the sampling distribution of a sample mean, the central limit theorem offers an explanation for the fact that many relative frequency distributions of data are mound-shaped. Many of the macroscopic measurements we take in business research are really means or sums of many microscopic phenomena. For example, a year's sales of a company is the total of the many individual sales the company made during the year. Thus, the year's sales for a sample of similar companies may have a mound-shaped relative frequency distribution. Similarly, the length of time a construction company takes to complete a house might be viewed as the total of the time each of the large number of distinct jobs necessary to build the house takes to complete. The monthly profit of a firm can be viewed as the mean profit of all the transactions of the firm for that month. If we adopt viewpoints like these, the central limit theorem offers some explanation for the frequent occurrence of mound-shaped distributions in nature.

CASE STUDY 8.1   In the winter of 1976, National Car Rental Systems, Inc., commissioned USAC Properties, Inc. [the performance testing/endorsement arm of the United States Automobile Club (USAC)] to conduct a survey of the general condition of the cars rented to the public by Hertz, Avis, National, and Budget Rent-A-Car.* National was interested in comparing the condition of the cars they rented with those of the other leading car-rental companies.

It was decided that teams of USAC officials would evaluate each company's cars on appearance and cleanliness, accessory performance, mechanical functions, and vehicle safety using a demerit point system designed specifically for this survey. Each car would start with a score of 100 points and would lose points for each discrepancy noted by the inspectors.

If all the cars in each company's fleet were inspected and graded, one measure of the overall condition of each company's cars would be the mean of all scores received by each company. Such a survey, however, besides being virtually impossible to conduct logistically, would not yield results of sufficient consequence to justify its cost. It was therefore decided that the mean score each company would receive if all their cars were inspected (referred to below as a company's *fleet mean score*) would have to be estimated. Accordingly, ten major airports were randomly chosen and ten cars from each company were randomly rented for inspection from each airport by USAC officials, i.e., a sample size $n = 100$ cars from each company's fleet was drawn and inspected. In the analysis of USAC's inspection results, each company's mean score, $\bar{x}$, was used to estimate the company's unknown fleet mean score. (The use of a sample mean to estimate a population mean will be discussed in detail in Chapter 9.) As we have seen in this chapter, $\bar{x}$ is a random variable with a sampling distribution that has a mean equal to the mean of the population from which the sample yielding $\bar{x}$ was drawn. Thus, in the context of this case, the mean of the sampling distribution of $\bar{x}$ is the unknown fleet mean score. Since the sample size used by USAC was 100, the statisticians who evaluated USAC's inspection results were able to invoke the central limit theorem and assume the sampling distribution of $\bar{x}$ to be approximately normally distributed. This assumption enabled comparisons of fleet mean scores for Hertz, Avis, National, and Budget Rent-A-Car to be made using the conventional large-sample testing procedures that will be presented in Chapter 9.

*Information by personal communication with Rajiv Tandon, Corporate Vice President of Management Information Systems, National Car Rental Systems, Inc., Minneapolis, Minn.

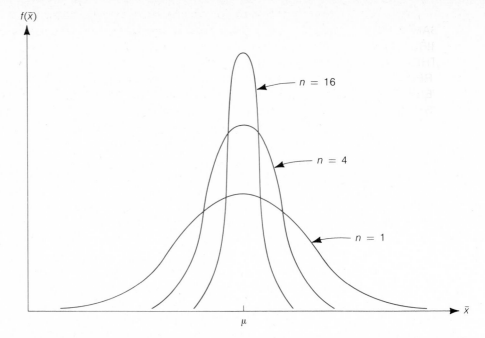

FIGURE 8.10
THREE SAMPLING
DISTRIBUTIONS FOR $\bar{x}$

$f(\bar{x})$

$n = 16$

$n = 4$

$n = 1$

μ

$\bar{x}$

8.4

**THE RELATION
BETWEEN
SAMPLE SIZE
AND A
SAMPLING
DISTRIBUTION**

Suppose you draw two random samples from a population—one sample containing $n = 5$ observations and the second containing $n = 10$—and you want to compute $\bar{x}$ for each sample and use these statistics to estimate the population mean μ. Intuitively, it would seem that the $\bar{x}$ based on the sample of ten measurements would contain more information about μ than the $\bar{x}$ based on $n = 5$. (After all, the sample of $n = 10$ may have cost twice as much to collect as the sample containing $n = 5$.) But, how is this larger sample size reflected in the sampling distribution of a statistic?

For the statistics you will encounter in this text, the variance of the sampling distribution of a statistic will be inversely proportional to the sample size.* Or, you can say that the standard deviation of the sampling distribution is proportional to $1/\sqrt{n}$. (This relationship can be seen in the standard deviation of a sample mean $\bar{x}$ that is equal to $\sigma/\sqrt{n}$.) So, to reduce the standard deviation of the sampling distribution of a statistic by $\frac{1}{2}$, you will need 4 times as many observations in your sample ($1/\sqrt{n} = 1/\sqrt{4} = \frac{1}{2}$). Or, to reduce the standard deviation to $\frac{1}{3}$ its original value, you will need 9 times as many observations.

The sampling distributions for the sample mean $\bar{x}$, based on random samplings from a normally distributed population, are shown in Figure 8.10 for $n = 1$, 4, and 16 observations. The curve for $n = 1$ represents the probability distribution for the population. Those for $n = 4$ and $n = 16$ are sampling distributions for $\bar{x}$. Note how the distributions contract (variation decreases) for $n = 4$ and $n = 16$. The standard deviation for $\bar{x}$ based on $n = 16$ measurements is $\frac{1}{2}$ the corresponding standard deviation for the distribution based on $n = 4$ measurements.

*Note that this is not true of all statistics, but it is true for most.

8.5

THE SAMPLING DISTRIBUTION FOR THE DIFFERENCE BETWEEN TWO STATISTICS

Quite often we will want to compare the proportion of people or objects in one population that possess some special attribute with the proportion in another. For example, we might want to compare the proportion of defective glass bottles that emerge from two glass-blowing processes, or we might want to compare the proportions of consumers who prefer product #1 versus those who prefer product #2. Or, we might want to compare the means of two populations, say, the mean return from one type of investment with the mean return from another. All three of these problems will utilize a comparison of the corresponding sample statistics. For example, to estimate the difference in the means of two populations, we use the difference between the means, $\bar{x}_1$ and $\bar{x}_2$, of independent random samples selected from the two populations. How close will the difference in the sample means, $(\bar{x}_1 - \bar{x}_2)$, lie to the actual difference in the population means? To answer this question, we need to know something about the sampling distribution of the quantity $(\bar{x}_1 - \bar{x}_2)$.

We cannot completely specify the form of the sampling distribution for the difference between two statistics without considering particular cases, but we can say something about the mean, variance, and standard deviation of the sampling distribution.* We will give formulas for these quantities that will always apply and then demonstrate their uses with an example.

Suppose you wish to estimate the difference between two population parameters, θ_1 and θ_2. You have an unbiased statistic for estimating θ_1 (call it A) and another unbiased statistic for estimating θ_2 (call it B). Then, because these estimates are unbiased, it follows that $E(A) = \theta_1$ and $E(B) = \theta_2$ (i.e., the mean of the sampling distribution of A is θ_1 and the mean of the sampling distribution of B is θ_2). Further, assume that the variance of the sampling distribution of A is σ_A^2 and the variance of B is σ_B^2. Then it can be shown (the proof is omitted here) that the mean and variance of the sampling distribution of $(A - B)$, assuming A and B are independent, are

$$\mu_{(A-B)} = E(A - B) = \theta_1 - \theta_2$$
$$\sigma_{(A-B)}^2 = \sigma_A^2 + \sigma_B^2$$

We will illustrate the use of these formulas with the example below.[†]

EXAMPLE 8.3

Suppose you have two populations of investment returns that have means μ_1 and μ_2 and variances σ_1^2 and σ_2^2, respectively. Independent random samples of n_1 and n_2 observations are selected from the two populations: n_1 from population 1 and n_2 from population 2. The sample means $\bar{x}_1$ and $\bar{x}_2$ are computed from the samples. Find the expected value and standard deviation of the sampling distribution for the difference in two sample means, $(\bar{x}_1 - \bar{x}_2)$.

---

*The theory of statistics provides information on the form of the sampling distribution for the following class of statistics: The sums or differences of any number of normally distributed random variables will have a sampling distribution that is normally distributed. The random variables need not be independent of each other.

†Although it is not relevant to our discussion, it also can be shown that the variance of the sum of two independent statistics A and B is $\sigma_{(A+B)}^2 = \sigma_A^2 + \sigma_B^2$.

FIGURE 8.11
SAMPLING
DISTRIBUTION
FOR $(\bar{x}_1 - \bar{x}_2)$

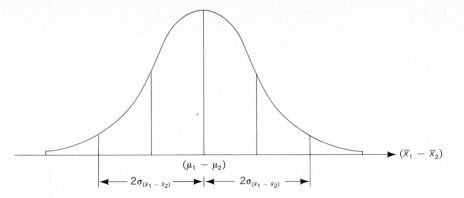

Solution

Since we know from Section 8.3 that $E(\bar{x}_1) = \mu_1$ and $E(\bar{x}_2) = \mu_2$, it follows that the mean of the sampling distribution of $(\bar{x}_1 - \bar{x}_2)$ is

$$E(\bar{x}_1 - \bar{x}_2) = E(\bar{x}_1) - E(\bar{x}_2) = \mu_1 - \mu_2$$

Recall that the variance of the mean $\bar{x}$ of a random sample of n observations is σ^2/n (where σ^2 is the variance of the sampled population). It follows that the variance of the sample means $\bar{x}_1$ and $\bar{x}_2$ are

$$\sigma^2_{\bar{x}_1} = \frac{\sigma^2_1}{n_1} \qquad \text{and} \qquad \sigma^2_{\bar{x}_2} = \frac{\sigma^2_2}{n_2}$$

Then, using the formula for the variance of the difference of two independent statistics,

$$\sigma^2_{(\bar{x}_1 - \bar{x}_2)} = \sigma^2_{\bar{x}_1} + \sigma^2_{\bar{x}_2} = \frac{\sigma^2_1}{n_1} + \frac{\sigma^2_2}{n_2},$$

and the standard deviation of the sampling distribution for $(\bar{x}_1 - \bar{x}_2)$ is

$$\sigma_{(\bar{x}_1 - \bar{x}_2)} = \sqrt{\frac{\sigma^2_1}{n_1} + \frac{\sigma^2_2}{n_2}}$$

It can be shown that the sampling distribution for $(\bar{x}_1 - \bar{x}_2)$ will be approximately normal for large values of n_1 and n_2. Therefore, for large samples, the sampling distribution for $(\bar{x}_1 - \bar{x}_2)$ will appear as shown in Figure 8.11.

SUMMARY

Many practical business problems require that an inference be made about some population **parameter** (call it θ). If we want to make this inference on the basis of information in a sample, we will need to compute a **sample statistic** that contains information about θ. The amount of information a sample statistic contains about θ is reflected by its **sampling distribution**, the probability distribution of the sample statistic. In particular, we want a sample statistic that is an **unbiased** estimator of θ and has a smaller variance than any other unbiased sample statistic.

When the population parameter of interest is the mean μ, the sample mean provides an unbiased estimator with a standard deviation of $\sigma/\sqrt{n}$. In addition, the **central limit theorem** assures us that the sampling distribution for the mean of a large sample will be approximately normally distributed, no matter what the shape of the relative frequency distribution of the sampled population.

The sample size is related to the amount of information in a sample that is relevant to some population parameter. For example, the standard deviation of the sampling distribution of the sample mean $\bar{x}$ will be inversely proportional to the square root of the sample size (i.e., $1/\sqrt{n}$).

The sampling distributions for all the many statistics that can be computed from sample data could be discussed in detail, but this would delay discussion of the practical objective of this course—the role of statistical inference in business decision-making. Consequently, we will comment further on the sampling distributions of statistics when we use them as estimators or decision-makers in the following chapters.

EXERCISES

8.1. The table contains fifty random samples of random digits, $x = 0, 1, 2, 3, \ldots$, 9, where $p(x) = \frac{1}{10}$. Each sample contains $n = 6$ measurements.

SAMPLE	SAMPLE	SAMPLE	SAMPLE
8,1,8,0,6,6	7,6,7,0,4,3	4,4,5,2,6,6	0,8,4,7,6,9
7,2,1,7,2,9	1,0,5,9,9,6	2,9,3,7,1,3	5,6,9,4,4,2
7,4,5,7,7,1	2,4,4,7,5,6	5,1,9,6,9,2	4,2,3,7,6,3
8,3,6,1,8,1	4,6,6,5,5,6	8,5,1,2,3,4	1,2,0,6,3,3
0,9,8,6,2,9	1,5,0,6,6,5	2,4,5,3,4,8	1,1,9,0,3,2
0,6,8,8,3,5	3,3,0,4,9,6	1,5,6,7,8,2	7,8,9,2,7,0
7,9,5,7,7,9	9,3,0,7,4,1	3,3,8,6,0,1	1,1,5,0,5,1
7,7,6,4,4,7	5,3,6,4,2,0	3,1,4,4,9,0	7,7,8,7,7,6
1,6,5,6,4,2	7,1,5,0,5,8	9,7,7,9,8,1	4,9,3,7,3,9
9,8,6,8,6,0	4,4,6,2,6,2	6,9,2,9,8,7	5,5,1,1,4,0
3,1,6,0,0,9	3,1,8,8,2,1	6,6,8,9,6,0	4,2,5,7,7,9
0,6,8,5,2,8	8,9,0,6,1,7	3,3,4,6,7,0	8,3,0,6,9,7
8,2,4,9,4,6	1,3,7,3,4,3		

a. Use the 300 random digits to construct a relative frequency histogram for the data. This relative frequency distribution should approximate $p(x)$.

b. Calculate the mean of the 300 digits. This will give an accurate estimate of μ (the mean of the population) and should be very near to the $E(x)$, which is 4.5.

c. Calculate s^2 for the 300 digits. This should be close to the variance of x, $\sigma^2 = 8.25$.

d. Suppose you intend to make an inference about the mean μ using the median of a sample of $n = 6$ measurements. To see how well the sample median will estimate μ, calculate the median m for each of the fifty samples. Construct a relative frequency histogram for the sample medians to see how close they lie to the mean of $\mu = 4.5$. Calculate the mean and standard deviation of the fifty medians.

e. Calculate $\bar{x}$ for each of the fifty samples. Construct a relative frequency histogram for the sample means to see how close they lie to the mean of $\mu = 4.5$. Calculate the mean and standard deviation of the fifty means.

8.2. To see the effect of sample size on the standard deviation of the sampling distribution of a statistic, refer to Exercise 8.1 and combine pairs of samples (moving down the columns of the table) to obtain twenty-five samples of $n = 12$ measurements. Calculate the median for each sample.

  a. Construct a relative frequency histogram for the twenty-five medians. Compare this with the histogram prepared for Exercise 8.1, part d, which is based on samples of $n = 6$ digits.

  b. Calculate the mean and standard deviation of the twenty-five medians. Compare the standard deviation of this sampling distribution with the standard deviation of the sampling distribution in Exercise 8.1, part d. What relationship would you expect to exist between the two standard deviations?

8.3. Refer to Exercise 8.2. Repeat the exercise, but use the means of the samples rather than the medians.

8.4. Suppose a sample of $n = 50$ items is drawn from a population of manufactured products and the weight x of each item is recorded. Prior experience has shown that the weight has a probability distribution with $\mu = 6$ ounces and $\sigma = 2.5$ ounces. Then $\bar{x}$, the sample mean, will be approximately normally distributed (because of the central limit theorem).

  a. Calculate $\mu_{\bar{x}}$ and $\sigma_{\bar{x}}$.

  b. What is the probability that the manufacturer's sample has a mean weight of between 5.75 and 6.25 ounces?

  c. What is the probability that the manufacturer's sample has a mean weight of less than 5.5 ounces?

  d. How would the sampling distribution of $\bar{x}$ change if the sample size n were increased from 50 to, say, 100?

8.5. The distribution of the number of barrels of oil produced by a particular oil well each day for the past 3 years has a mean of 400 and a variance of 5,625.

  a. Describe the sampling distribution of the mean number of barrels produced per day for samples of 40 production days drawn from the past 3 years.

  b. What is the probability that the sample mean will be greater than 425? Less than 400?

8.6. Refer to Exercise 8.5. If it was not known that the mean number of barrels produced per day was 400, describe how you might use the sample mean to estimate μ? Explain the reasoning behind your procedure.

8.7. To determine whether a metal lathe producing machine bearings is properly adjusted, a random sample of twenty-five bearings is collected and the diameter of each is measured. If the standard deviation of the diameter of the machine bearings measured over a long period of time is .001 inch, what is the probability that the mean $\bar{x}$ of the sample of twenty-five bearings will lie within .0001 inch of the population mean diameter of the bearings?

8.8. Refer to Exercise 8.7. Suppose the mean diameter of the bearings produced by the machine is supposed to be .5 inch. The company decides to use the sample mean (from Exercise 8.7) to decide whether the process is in control, i.e., whether it is producing bearings with a mean diameter of .5 inch. The machine will be considered out of control if the mean of the sample of $n = 25$ diameters is less than .4994 inch or larger than .5006 inch. If the true mean diameter of the bearings produced by the machine is .501 inch, what is the probability that the test will fail to imply that the process is out of control?

8.9. Over the last month a large supermarket chain received many consumer complaints about the quantity of chips in 9 ounce bags of a particular brand of potato chips. Suspecting that the complaints were merely the result of the potato chips settling to the bottom of the bags during shipping, but wanting to be able to assure its customers they were getting their money's worth, the chain decided to examine the next shipment of chips received by their largest store. Sixteen 9 ounce bags were randomly selected from the shipment, their contents weighed, and the sample mean weight computed. The chain's management decided that if the sample mean were less than 8.6 ounces, the shipment would be refused and a complaint registered with the potato chip company. Assume the distribution of weights of the contents of the potato chip bags in question has a mean of 8.5 ounces and a standard deviation of .6 ounce.

  a. What is the probability that the supermarket chain's investigation will not lead to refusal of the shipment?
  b. What assumption(s) did you have to make in order to answer part a? Justify the assumptions.

8.10. Suppose you wish to purchase a case of expensive wine. You plan to open two bottles for immediate use and you will keep the remaining bottles if the two are acceptable. Suppose there are ten bottles in the case, and, unknown to you, the condition of the wine in the bottles is as shown below (1 = good, 0 = bad):

BOTTLE	1	2	3	4	5	6	7	8	9	10
CONDITION	1	0	0	1	1	1	1	1	0	1

Since you are only interested in the ten bottles in the case, the collection of ten 0 or 1 responses is the population of interest to you.

  a. If you randomly sample two bottles from the case, how many different samples (different pairs of bottles) could you select? List them.
  b. Suppose you are going to accept the case only if both bottles in the sample are good. Identify all samples containing two good bottles. What is the probability that you will accept the case? [*Hint:* See the definition of a random sample, Section 5.6.]
  c. Let x equal the number of good bottles in the sample of $n = 2$. Construct the sampling distribution of x.

8.11. As part of a company's quality control program, it is a common practice to monitor the quality characteristics of a product over time. For example, the amount of alkali in soap might be monitored by randomly selecting from the production process and analyzing $n = 5$ test quantities of soap each hour. The mean, $\bar{x}$, of the sample would be plotted against time on a control chart as shown below:

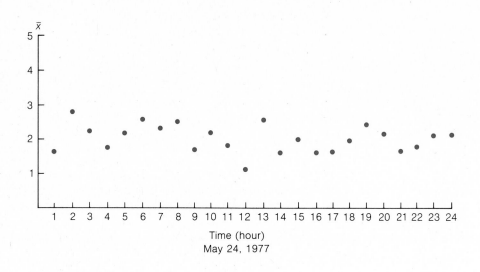

Time (hour)
May 24, 1977

If the process is in control, $\bar{x}$ should assume a distribution about a process mean μ with standard deviation σ. The control chart below shows a horizontal line to locate the process mean and two lines, located $3\sigma_{\bar{x}}$ above and below μ, which are called control limits:

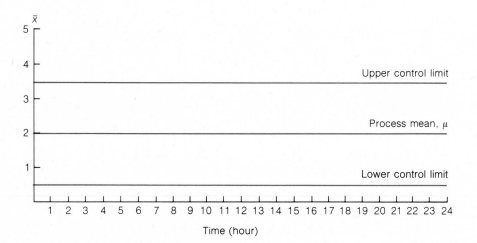

Time (hour)

If $\bar{x}$ falls within the control limits, the process is deemed to be in control. If $\bar{x}$ is outside the limits, the monitor flashes a warning and suggests that something is wrong with the process. Suppose for the soap process that experience has shown $\mu = 2\%$ and $\sigma = 1\%$.

    a.   If $n = 5$, how far away from μ should you locate the upper and lower control limits?

    b.   If the process is in control, what is the probability that $\bar{x}$ will fall outside the control limits? State any assumptions you must make in reaching a solution.

SUPPLEMENTARY EXERCISES

*8.12.   A building contractor has decided to purchase a load of factory-reject aluminum siding as long as the average number of flaws per piece of siding in a sample of size thirty-five from the factory's reject pile is 2.1 or less. If it is known that the number of flaws per piece of siding in the factory's reject pile has a Poisson probability distribution with a mean of 2.5, find the probability that the contractor will not purchase a load of siding. [*Hint:* If x is a Poisson random variable with mean λ, then σ_x^2 also equals λ.]

8.13.   In purchasing supplies for your manufacturing process, you can purchase a particular part from one of two suppliers, A or B. The parts are in short supply, but you think you can buy somewhere between 20,000–25,000 from A and 40,000–50,000 from B. Given this information, within what range would you expect the total number of parts to fall? [*Hint:* To solve this practical problem, you have to make some assumptions about the probability distributions of x_A and x_B, the numbers of parts you will be able to purchase from suppliers A and B. Suppose you interpret the statement that x_A will lie "somewhere between 20,000–25,000" to mean that the probability distribution of A appears as follows:

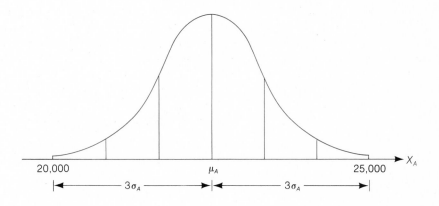

That is, assume μ_A falls in the middle of the interval $20,000 \leq x_A \leq 25,000$ and the interval spans $6\sigma_A$, where σ_A is the standard deviation of the probability distribution of x_A. Then $6\sigma_A = 5{,}000$ and $\sigma_A = 833.3$. Now, find σ_B, μ_A, μ_B, and the interval shown below:

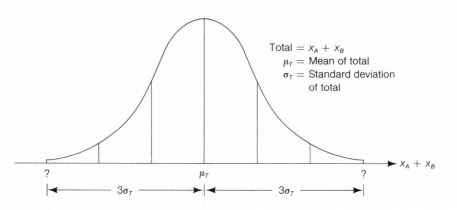

8.14. The following is a very useful result concerning the mean and variance of some sampling distributions: Suppose that c is a constant and x is a statistic with mean μ and variance σ^2. Then it can be shown (the proof is omitted here) that the mean and variance of cx are

$$E(cx) = c\,E(x) = c\mu$$
$$\sigma_{cx}^2 = c^2\sigma^2$$

Application: If you draw a random sample of n people from a large population of consumers and x is the number in the sample who favor some proposal (favor a particular product, etc.), then x is a binomial random variable with mean $\mu = np$ and variance $\sigma^2 = npq$ (from Chapter 6). The proportion of people in the sample who favor the proposal, x/n, is used to estimate the population proportion, p.

    a. Use the information above to show that the sampling distribution for the sample proportion x/n has a mean equal to p and a standard deviation equal to $\sqrt{p(1-p)/n}$.

    b. Let each person in the population who favors the proposal be represented by a 1 and each person who does not by a 0. Then the entire population of consumers can be viewed as a collection of 1's and 0's, x will equal the sum of the 1's and 0's in the sample of n, and x/n will be the sample average. What will be the approximate form of the sampling distribution of the sample proportion when the sample size n is large? Why?

    c. Suppose you select a random sample of 1,600 consumers from a large population that (unknown to you) contains 20% ($p = .2$) who prefer your product over its competitors. What is the probability that your sample proportion will differ from the population proportion ($p = .2$) by more than .01?

ON YOUR OWN . . .

To better understand the central limit theorem and sampling distribution, consider the following experiment: Toss four identical coins and record the number of heads observed. Then repeat this experiment four more times, so that you end up with a total of five observations for the random variable x, the number of heads when four coins are tossed.

Now, derive and graph the probability distribution for x, assuming the coins are balanced. Note that the mean of this distribution is $\mu = 2$ and the standard deviation is $\sigma = 1$. This probability distribution represents the one from which you are drawing a random sample of five measurements.

Next, calculate the mean $\bar{x}$ of the five measurements, i.e., calculate the mean number of heads you observed in five repetitions of the experiment. Although you have repeated the basic experiment five times, you have only one observed value of $\bar{x}$. To derive the probability distribution or sampling distribution of $\bar{x}$ empirically, you have to repeat the entire process (of tossing four coins five times) many times. Do it 100 times.

The approximate sampling distribution of $\bar{x}$ can be derived theoretically by making use of the central limit theorem. We expect at least an approximate normal probability distribution, with a mean $\mu = 2$ and a standard deviation

$$\sigma_{\bar{x}} = \frac{\sigma}{\sqrt{n}} = \frac{1}{\sqrt{5}} = .45$$

Count the number of your 100 $\bar{x}$'s that fall in each of the following intervals:

Interval	Interval	Interval	Interval	Interval	Interval
⟵ 1 ⟶	⟵ 2 ⟶	⟵ 3 ⟶	⟵ 4 ⟶	⟵ 5 ⟶	⟵ 6 ⟶

	1.10	1.55	2	2.45	2.90	
	$\mu - 2\sigma_{\bar{x}}$	$\mu - \sigma_{\bar{x}}$	μ	$\mu + \sigma_{\bar{x}}$	$\mu + 2\sigma_{\bar{x}}$	

Use the normal probability distribution with $\mu = 2$ and $\sigma_{\bar{x}} = .45$ to calculate the expected number of the 100 $\bar{x}$'s in each of the intervals. How closely does the theory describe your experimental results?

REFERENCES

Hogg, R. V., & Craig, A. T. *Introduction to mathematical statistics.* 3d ed. London: Macmillan, 1971. Chapter 4.

Lindgren, B. W. *Statistical theory.* 3d ed. New York: Macmillan, 1976. Chapter 2.

Neter, J., Wasserman, W., & Whitmore, G. A. *Fundamental statistics for business and economics.* 4th ed. Boston: Allyn and Bacon, 1973. Chapters 9–11.

Winkler, R. L., & Hays, W. *Statistics: Probability, inference, and decision.* 2d ed. New York: Holt, Rinehart, and Winston, 1975. Chapter 5.

WHERE WE'VE BEEN . . .
In the preceding chapters we learned that populations are characterized by numerical descriptive measures (called *parameters*), and that decisions about their values are based on sample statistics computed from sample data. Since statistics vary in a random manner from sample to sample, inferences based on them will be subject to uncertainty. This property is reflected in the sampling (probability) distribution of a statistic.

WHERE WE'RE GOING . . .
This chapter puts all the preceding material to practice. That is, we will estimate or make decisions about population means or proportions based on a single sample selected from a population. Most important, we will use the sampling distribution of a sample statistic to assess the uncertainty associated with an inference.

9

ESTIMATION AND A TEST OF AN HYPOTHESIS: SINGLE SAMPLE

The estimation of the mean gas mileage for a new car model, the testing of a claim that a certain brand of television tube has a mean life of 5 years, and the estimation of the mean yearly sales for companies in the steel industry are business problems with a common element. In each case we are interested in making an inference about the mean of a population. This important problem constitutes the primary topic of this chapter.

We will concentrate on two types of inferences about a population parameter: **estimation of the parameter and tests of hypotheses, or claims, about the parameter.** You will see that different techniques are used for making inferences, depending upon whether a sample contains a large or small number of measurements. Regardless, our objectives remain the same. We want to make the best use of the information in the sample to make an inference and to assess its reliability.

In Sections 9.1 and 9.2 we consider large-sample methods for estimation and tests of hypotheses about population means. The small-sample analogs of these two topics are covered in Section 9.3. Finally, we consider large-sample inferences about a binomial proportion in Section 9.4.

9.1 LARGE-SAMPLE ESTIMATION OF A POPULATION MEAN

Suppose that a large credit corporation wants to estimate the average amount of money owed by its delinquent creditors, i.e., creditors who are more than 2 months behind in payment. To accomplish this objective, the company plans to sample 100 of their delinquent accounts and to use the sample mean, $\bar{x}$, of the amounts overdue to estimate the mean of *all* delinquent accounts, μ. Further, they plan to use the sampling distribution of the sample mean to assess the accuracy of their estimate. How will this be accomplished?

Recall that for large samples the sampling distribution of the sample mean is approximately normal, as shown in Figure 9.1. Now, suppose you plan to take a sample of $n = 100$ measurements, and calculate the following interval:

$$\bar{x} \pm 2\sigma_{\bar{x}} = \bar{x} \pm \frac{2\sigma}{\sqrt{n}}$$

FIGURE 9.1
SAMPLING
DISTRIBUTION OF $\bar{x}$

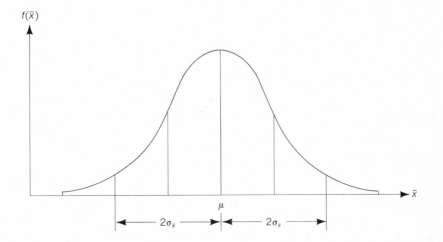

That is, you will form an interval 2 standard deviations around the sample mean. What are the chances (answer before you have drawn your sample) that this interval will enclose μ, the population mean?

To answer this question, refer to Figure 9.1. If the 100 measurements yield a value of $\bar{x}$ that falls between the two lines shown in color, i.e., within 2 standard deviations of μ, the interval $\bar{x} \pm 2\sigma_{\bar{x}}$ will contain μ. If $\bar{x}$ falls outside either of these boundaries, the interval $\bar{x} \pm 2\sigma_{\bar{x}}$ will not contain μ. Since the area under the normal curve (the sampling distribution for $\bar{x}$) between these boundaries is about .95 (more precisely, from Table IV of Appendix B, the area is .9544), we know that the interval $\bar{x} \pm 2\sigma_{\bar{x}}$ will contain μ with a probability approximately equal to .95.

To illustrate, suppose that the sum and the sum of squares of the debits for the sample of 100 delinquent accounts are

$$\sum_{i=1}^{n} x_i = \$23,300$$

$$\sum_{i=1}^{n} (x_i - \bar{x})^2 = 801,900$$

First calculate the sample statistics:

$$\bar{x} = \frac{\sum_{i=1}^{100} x_i}{n} = \frac{23,300}{100} = \$233$$

$$s = \sqrt{\frac{\sum_{i=1}^{100} (x_i - \bar{x})^2}{n - 1}} = \sqrt{\frac{801,900}{99}} = \$90$$

To form the 2 standard deviation interval around $\bar{x}$, we calculate

$$\bar{x} \pm 2\sigma_{\bar{x}} = 233 \pm 2\left(\frac{\sigma}{\sqrt{100}}\right)$$

But now we face a problem. You can see that without knowing the standard deviation, σ, of the original population, i.e., the standard deviation of the amounts of *all* delinquent accounts, we cannot calculate this interval. However, since we have a large sample ($n = 100$ measurements), we can approximate the interval by using the sample standard deviation, s, to approximate σ. Thus,

$$\bar{x} \pm 2\left(\frac{\sigma}{\sqrt{100}}\right) \simeq \bar{x} \pm 2\left(\frac{s}{\sqrt{100}}\right)$$

$$= 233 \pm 2\left(\frac{90}{10}\right) = 233 \pm 18$$

That is, we estimate the mean amount of deliquency for all accounts to fall within the interval ($215, $251).

FIGURE 9.2
INTERVAL
ESTIMATORS FOR θ:
TEN SAMPLES

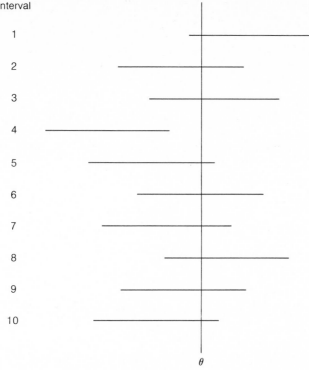

Can we be sure that μ, the true mean amount due, is within the interval ($215, $251)? We cannot be certain, but we can be reasonably confident that it is. This confidence is derived from the knowledge that if we were to repeatedly draw samples of 100 accounts from this delinquent group and form a 2 standard deviation interval around $\bar{x}$ each time, 95% of the intervals would contain μ. We have no way of knowing (without looking at all the delinquent accounts) whether our sample interval is one of the 95% that contain μ or one of the 5% that do not, so we simply state that we are 95% confident our interval ($215, $251) contains μ. Thus, we have given an interval estimate of the mean delinquency per account and have given a measure of the reliability of the estimate.

The foregoing is an example of how an interval can be used to estimate a population parameter. This is a common statistical practice, because when we use an interval estimator, we can usually assess the level of confidence we have that the interval actually contains the true value of the parameter. Figure 9.2 shows what happens when a number of samples are drawn from a population and a confidence interval for a parameter, say θ, is calculated from each. The location of θ is indicated by the vertical line in the figure. Ten confidence intervals, corresponding to ten samples, are shown as horizontal line segments. Note that the confidence intervals move from sample to sample—sometimes containing θ and other times missing θ. If our confidence level is 95%, then in the long-run, 95% of our sample confidence intervals will contain θ.

FIGURE 9.3
LOCATING $z_{\alpha/2}$ ON
THE STANDARD
NORMAL CURVE

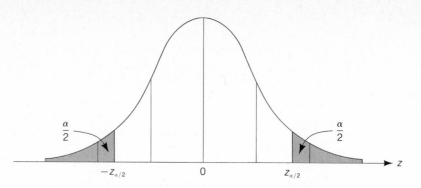

Suppose you wish to choose a **confidence coefficient** other than .95. Notice in Figure 9.1 that the confidence coefficient .95 is equal to the total area under the sampling distribution, less .05 of the area, which is divided equally between the two tails. Using this idea, we can construct a confidence interval with any desired confidence coefficient by increasing or decreasing the area (call it α) assigned to the tails of the sampling distribution (see Figure 9.3). For example, if we place $\alpha/2$ in each tail and if $z_{\alpha/2}$ is the z value such that the area $\alpha/2$ will lie to its right, then the confidence interval with confidence coefficient $(1 - \alpha)$ is

$$\bar{x} \pm z_{\alpha/2}\sigma_{\bar{x}}$$

To illustrate, for a confidence coefficient of .90, $(1 - \alpha) = .90$, $\alpha = .10$, $\alpha/2 = .05$, and $z_{.05}$ is the z value that locates .05 in one tail of the sampling distribution. Recall that Table IV of Appendix B gives the areas between the mean and a specified z value. Since the total area to the right of the mean is .50, $z_{.05}$ will be the z value corresponding to an area to the right of the mean equal to .450. This z value is $z_{.05} = 1.645$. Confidence coefficients used in practice (in published articles) range from .90 to .99. The most common confidence coefficients with corresponding values of α and $z_{\alpha/2}$ are shown in Table 9.1.

TABLE 9.1
COMMONLY USED
VALUES OF $z_{\alpha/2}$

CONFIDENCE LEVEL $100(1 - \alpha)$	α	$\alpha/2$	$z_{\alpha/2}$
90%	.10	.05	1.645
95%	.05	.025	1.96
99%	.01	.005	2.576

LARGE-SAMPLE $100(1 - \alpha)$ PERCENT CONFIDENCE INTERVAL FOR μ

$$\bar{x} \pm z_{\alpha/2}\sigma_{\bar{x}}$$

where $z_{\alpha/2}$ is the z value with an area $\alpha/2$ to its right (see Figure 9.3) and $\sigma_{\bar{x}} = \sigma/\sqrt{n}$. The parameter σ is the standard deviation of the sampled population and n is the sample size.

EXAMPLE 9.1

Unoccupied seats on flights cause the airlines to lose revenue. Suppose a large airline wants to estimate its average number of unoccupied seats per flight over the past year. To accomplish this, the records of 225 flights are randomly selected from the files, and the number of unoccupied seats are noted for each of the sampled flights. The sample mean and standard deviation are

$$\bar{x} = 11.6 \text{ seats} \qquad s = 4.1 \text{ seats}$$

Estimate μ, the mean number of unoccupied seats per flight during the past year, using a 90% confidence interval.

Solution

The general form of the 90% confidence interval for a population mean is

$$\bar{x} \pm z_{\alpha/2}\sigma_{\bar{x}} = \bar{x} \pm z_{.05}\sigma_{\bar{x}}$$
$$= \bar{x} \pm 1.645\left(\frac{\sigma}{\sqrt{n}}\right)$$

For the 225 records sampled, we have

$$11.6 \pm 1.645\left(\frac{\sigma}{\sqrt{225}}\right)$$

Since we do not know the value of σ (the standard deviation of the number of unoccupied seats per flight for all flights of the year), we use our best approximation, the sample standard deviation, s. Then the 90% confidence interval is, approximately,

$$11.6 \pm 1.645\left(\frac{4.1}{\sqrt{225}}\right) = 11.6 \pm 0.45$$

or, from 11.15 to 12.05. That is, the airline can be 90% confident that the mean number of unoccupied seats per flight was between 11.15 and 12.05 during the sampled year.

CASE STUDY 9.1

The following quotations have been extracted from the December 13, 1976 issue of *Business Week:*

"We're dancing to the tune of the customer as never before," says J. Janvier Wetzel, vice-president for sales promotion at Los Angeles-based Broadway Department Stores. "With population growth down to a trickle compared with its previous level, we're no longer spoiled with instant success every time we open a new store. Traditional department stores are locked in the biggest competitive battle in their history."

The nation's retailers are becoming uncomfortably aware that today's operating environment is vastly different from that of the 1960s. Population growth is slowing, a growing singles market is emerging, family formations are coming at later ages, and more women are embarking on careers. Of the 71 million households in the U.S. today, the dominant consumer buying segment is families headed by persons over 45. But by 1980 this group will have lost its majority status to the 25 to 40 year-old group. Merchants must now reposition their stores to attract these new customers.

To do so retailers are using market research to ferret out new purchasing attitudes and lifestyles and then translating this into customer buying segments. . . . department stores are taking a hard look at some of the basics of their business by . . . spending heavily for far more elaborate market research. Data on demographics, psychographics (measurement of attitudes), and lifestyle are being fed into retailers' computers so they can make marketing decisions based on actual spending patterns and estimate their inventory needs with less risk.

In order to stock their various departments with the type and style of goods that appeal to their potential group of customers, a downtown department store should be interested in estimating the average age of downtown shoppers, not shoppers in general. Suppose a downtown department store questions forty-nine downtown shoppers concerning their age (the offer of a small gift certificate may help convince shoppers to respond to such questions). The sample mean and standard deviation are found to be 40.1 and 8.6, respectively. The store could then estimate the mean age of all downtown shoppers, μ, via a 95% confidence interval as follows:

$$\bar{x} \pm 1.96\left(\frac{s}{\sqrt{n}}\right) = 40.1 \pm 1.96\left(\frac{8.6}{\sqrt{49}}\right)$$

$$= 40.1 \pm 2.4$$

Thus, the department store should gear its sales to the segment of consumers with average age between 37.7 and 42.5.

EXERCISES

9.1. Explain what is meant by the statement, "We are 95% confident that our interval estimate contains μ."

9.2. Refer to Case Study 9.1. A department store, interested in determining the average age of the customers of its contemporary apparel department, questioned sixty-four of the department's customers. It was found that the average age of the sixty-four people questioned was 28.2 and the sample standard deviation was 8 years. Estimate μ, the average age of the department's customers, using a 95% confidence interval.

9.3. To estimate the average rate of fuel consumption of their snowmobiles, a manufacturer tested thirty-six of them and obtained the following results: $\bar{x} = 20.3$ miles per gallon, $s = 2$ miles per gallon. Estimate the average rate of fuel consumption of all snowmobiles produced using a 90% confidence interval.

9.4. Refer to Exercise 9.3. To be able to continue marketing their snowmobiles, the manufacturer must produce snowmobiles that do not exceed the 78 decibel noise limit recently set by the government. In order to determine the average decibel level of the snowmobiles it currently has in stock, forty-nine are randomly selected, run at full throttle, and their noise levels measured. The sample statistics, expressed in decibels, are: $\bar{x} = 75$ decibels, $s = 14$ decibels. Estimate the average decibel level of the snowmobiles the manufacturer currently has in stock using a 99% confidence interval.

9.2
LARGE-SAMPLE TEST OF AN HYPOTHESIS ABOUT A POPULATION MEAN

Suppose building specifications in a certain city require that the average breaking strength of residential sewer pipe be more than 2,400 pounds per foot of length (i.e., per lineal foot). Each manufacturer who wants to sell pipe in this city must demonstrate that its product meets the specification. Note that we are again interested in making an inference about the mean, μ, of a population. However, in this example we are less interested in estimating the value of μ than we are in testing an **hypothesis** about its value. That is, we want to decide whether or not the mean breaking strength of the pipe exceeds 2,400 pounds per lineal foot.

When a researcher tries to establish an hypothesis, it is called the **research hypothesis** or **alternative hypothesis**. He or she must define a **null hypothesis,** the direct opposite of the research hypothesis, and attempt to gain support for the research (or alternative) hypothesis by producing evidence to show that the null hypothesis is false. In our example, the sewer pipe manufacturer must show that the mean breaking strength of its pipe exceeds 2,400 pounds per lineal foot, i.e., $\mu > 2,400$. Therefore, the null and research hypotheses are:

Null hypothesis (H_0): $\mu = 2,400$ (i.e., the manufacturer's pipe does not meet specifications)

Research (alternative) hypothesis (H_a): $\mu > 2,400$ (i.e., the manufacturer's pipe does meet specifications)

Next, we need a procedure for using the information in the sample to decide which hypothesis is true. Since we are testing hypotheses about a population mean, μ, it is reasonable to use the sample mean, $\bar{x}$, to decide between the two hypotheses. Specifically, we will reject the null hypothesis H_0 in favor of the research hypothesis H_a when the sample mean $\bar{x}$ strongly indicates that μ exceeds 2,400 pounds per lineal foot.

A convenient measure of the distance between $\bar{x}$ and 2,400 is the z-score:

$$z = \frac{\bar{x} - 2,400}{\sigma_{\bar{x}}} = \frac{\bar{x} - 2,400}{\sigma/\sqrt{n}}$$

FIGURE 9.4
THE SAMPLING DISTRIBUTION OF $\bar{x}$, ASSUMING $\mu = 2,400$

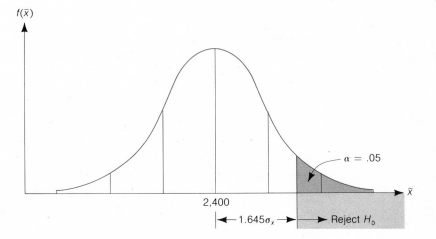

How large a z-score will be required before you decide to reject the null hypothesis? If you examine Figure 9.4, you will note that the chance of observing $\bar{x}$ more than 1.645 standard deviations above 2,400 is only .05, **if in fact the true mean μ is 2,400.** Thus, if the sample mean is more than 1.645 standard deviations above 2,400, either H_0 is true and a relatively rare event has occurred (.05 probability) or H_a is true and the population mean exceeds 2,400. Deciding that the research hypothesis is true when it is false is called a **Type I decision error.** As indicated in Figure 9.4, the risk of making a Type I error, that is, deciding in favor of the research hypothesis when in fact the null hypothesis is true, is denoted by the symbol α. That is,

$$\alpha = P(\text{Type I error})$$
$$= P(\text{Rejecting the null hypothesis} \,|\, \text{Null hypothesis is true})$$

In our example,

$$\alpha = P(z > 1.645 \,|\, \mu = 2,400) = .05$$

We summarize the elements of the test below.

SUMMARY OF A TEST OF AN HYPOTHESIS

$$H_0: \quad \mu = 2,400 \qquad H_a: \quad \mu > 2,400$$

$$\text{Test statistic:} \quad z = \frac{\bar{x} - 2,400}{\sigma_{\bar{x}}}$$

$$\text{Rejection region:} \quad z > 1.645 \qquad \text{for} \quad \alpha = .05$$

To illustrate the use of the test, suppose we tested fifty sections of sewer pipe and found the mean and standard deviation for these fifty measurements to be

$$\bar{x} = 2,460 \text{ pounds per lineal foot} \qquad s = 200 \text{ pounds per lineal foot}$$

As in the case of estimation, we can use s to approximate σ when s is calculated from a large set of sample measurements.

The test statistic is

$$z = \frac{\bar{x} - 2,400}{\sigma_{\bar{x}}} = \frac{\bar{x} - 2,400}{\sigma/\sqrt{n}} \approx \frac{\bar{x} - 2,400}{s/\sqrt{n}}$$

Substituting $\bar{x} = 2,460$, $n = 50$, and $s = 200$, we have

$$z \approx \frac{2,460 - 2,400}{200/\sqrt{50}} = \frac{60}{28.28} = 2.12$$

Therefore, the sample mean lies $2.12\sigma_{\bar{x}}$ above the hypothesized value of μ, 2,400, as shown in Figure 9.5. Since this value of z exceeds 1.645, it falls in the rejection region. That is, we reject the null hypothesis that $\mu = 2,400$ and accept the research

FIGURE 9.5
LOCATION OF THE
TEST STATISTIC FOR
A TEST OF THE
HYPOTHESIS
H_0: $\mu = 2,400$

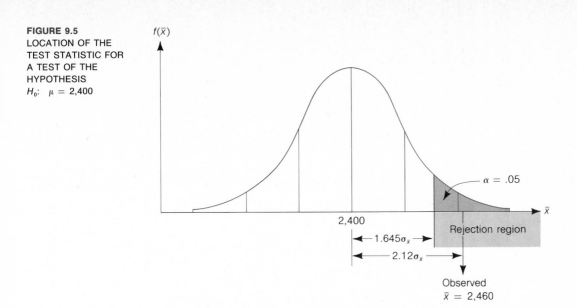

hypothesis, $\mu > 2,400$. Thus, it appears that the company's pipe has a mean strength that exceeds 2,400 pounds per lineal foot.

How much faith can be placed in this conclusion? What is the probability that our statistical test could lead us to reject the null hypothesis (and conclude that the company's pipe met the city's specifications) when in fact the null hypothesis was true? The answer is "$\alpha = .05$." That is, we selected the level of risk, α, of making a Type I error when we constructed the test. Thus, the chances are only 1 in 20 that our test could lead us to conclude the manufacturer's pipe satisfied the city's specifications when in fact this conclusion was false.

Now suppose the sample data had not indicated that the sewer pipe met the city's specifications, i.e., what would we have concluded if $z \leq 1.645$? Well, we would have stated the evidence in the sample was not sufficient to support the research hypothesis at the $\alpha = .05$ **level of significance**. Note that we carefully avoid stating that the null hypothesis is true, for then we would be risking a second type of error—concluding the null hypothesis is true (the pipe fails to meet specifications) when in fact the research hypothesis is true (the pipe does meet specifications). We call this a **Type II error**. The probability of committing a Type II error is usually denoted by the symbol β (beta).

Table 9.2 summarizes the four possible situations that might arise when an hypothesis is tested. The two possible states of nature correspond to the two columns of the table; that is, either H_0 is true or H_a is true. The two rows of the table indicate the two possible conclusions that can be reached; either H_0 is true or H_a is true. The two kinds of decisions are shown in the body of the table. Either the research hypothesis or the null hypothesis can be accepted. In either case, there are two types of risk: the risk of making a Type I error, measured by α, and the risk of making a Type II error, measured by β. Note that a Type I error can be made *only* when the research hypothesis is accepted (which occurs when the null hypothesis is rejected) and a Type II error can be made *only* when the null hypothesis is accepted. Not too surprisingly, the measures of these two types of risk, α and β, are related.

TABLE 9.2
CONCLUSIONS AND
CONSEQUENCES FOR
A TEST OF
AN HYPOTHESIS

		TRUE STATE OF NATURE	
		H_0 true	H_a true
CONCLUSION	H_0 true	Correct decision	Type II error (probability β)
	H_a true	Type I error (probability α)	Correct decision

You can see in Figure 9.6 that α is decreased by moving the rejection region farther out into the tail of the sampling distribution. By doing so, the rejection region becomes smaller and the acceptance region becomes larger. What happens to β as the acceptance region becomes larger?

Since β is the probability of accepting H_0, given that some alternative value of the parameter is true, β is the probability that the test statistic falls in the acceptance region. And, the larger the acceptance region, the larger will be the value of β. So, the relationship between α and β is what you might expect intuitively: As you decrease one type of risk (say, the risk α of falsely accepting H_a), you increase the other (the risk β of falsely accepting H_0). Fortunately, we can reduce both types of risk by increasing the sample size. The more information you have in the sample, the greater will be the ability of the test statistic to reach the correct decision.

In theory, we could consider the probabilities of the two types of risk, α and β, the possible financial losses attached to the Type I and II errors and choose the rejection region so as to minimize the expected loss. In practice, β is difficult to calculate for many tests, and it is impossible to specify a meaningful alternative to the null hypothesis for others. In short, the theory does not always work. So as an introduction to tests of hypotheses, we suggest the following procedure: Select the null hypothesis as the opposite of the research hypothesis (the one you want to support). Then, if you reject the null hypothesis and accept the research hypothesis, you will know the probability of having made an incorrect decision. It will be α and you can choose this value as large or small as you wish prior to the selection of your sample. If the test statistic does not fall in the rejection region, *do not* accept the null hypothesis unless you know β. Withhold judgment and seek a larger sample size to lead you closer to a decision. Or, estimate the parameter using a confidence interval. This will give an interval estimate of its true value and give you a measure of the reliability of your inference.

FIGURE 9.6
REDUCING α REDUCES THE REJECTION REGION AND ENLARGES THE ACCEPTANCE REGION

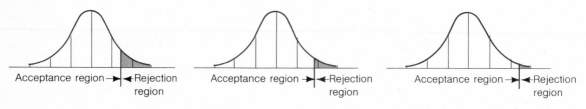

EXAMPLE 9.2   Sewer pipe produced by another manufacturer was submitted to the city for testing. A sampling of the strengths of seventy sections of pipe gave

$$\bar{x} = 2,430 \qquad s = 190$$

Do these statistics, calculated from the sample data, present sufficient evidence to indicate that the manufacturer's pipe meets the city's specifications?

Solution   As in our earlier discussion, the elements of the test are

$$H_0: \quad \mu = 2,400 \qquad H_a: \quad \mu > 2,400$$

Test statistic: $z = \dfrac{\bar{x} - 2,400}{\sigma_{\bar{x}}} = \dfrac{\bar{x} - 2,400}{\sigma/\sqrt{n}} \approx \dfrac{\bar{x} - 2,400}{s/\sqrt{n}}$

Rejection region: $z > 1.645 \qquad$ for $\quad \alpha = .05$

Substituting the sample statistics into the test statistic, we have

$$z \approx \frac{\bar{x} - 2,400}{s/\sqrt{n}} = \frac{2,430 - 2,400}{190/\sqrt{70}} = 1.32$$

In other words, the sample mean of 2,430, although greater than 2,400, is only $1.32\sigma_{\bar{x}}$ above that value (see Figure 9.7). Therefore, the sample does not provide sufficient evidence to conclude that the sewer pipe meets the city's strength specifications.

Although the value of the sample mean $\bar{x}$ could be used as a test statistic to test an hypothesis about a population mean μ, you can see that it is easier to use the z statistic. In fact, for the above examples, we based the decision to either reject or not reject the null hypothesis on the computed value of z. That is, saying you will reject H_0 in Example 9.2 if $\bar{x}$ lies more than $1.645\sigma_{\bar{x}}$ above $\mu = 2,400$ is the same as saying you will reject H_0 if $z > 1.645$.

FIGURE 9.7
LOCATION OF THE
TEST STATISTIC FOR
EXAMPLE 9.2

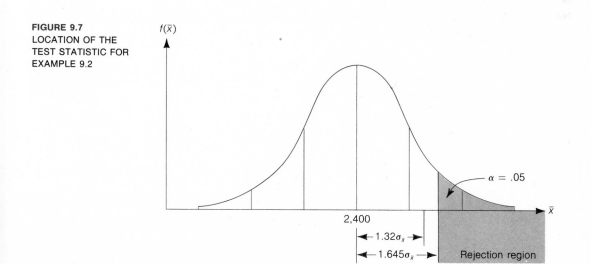

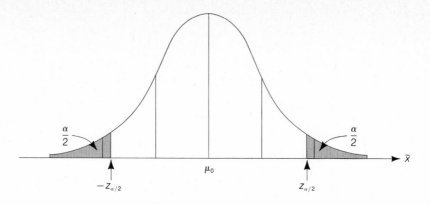

The research hypothesis for Example 9.2, namely that $\mu > 2{,}400$ pounds per lineal foot, leads to a **one-tailed (or one-sided)** statistical test because we rejected the null hypothesis only for large values of z (values in the upper tail of the z distribution). But some statistical investigations seek to show that μ is *either* larger or smaller than some specified value. This type of research (alternative) hypothesis, for example, H_a: $\mu > 2{,}400$ *or* $\mu < 2{,}400$, will be supported for large positive or large negative values of z. Thus, the rejection region will be located in both tails of the z distribution, splitting α between the two tails (see Figure 9.8). Such a statistical test is said to be **two-sided or two-tailed.** The value of z, denoted by the symbol $z_{\alpha/2}$, that places half of α in the upper tail of the z distribution, can be obtained from the table of areas under the normal curve (Table IV of Appendix B).

EXAMPLE 9.3

A manufacturer of cereal wants to test the hypothesis that a filling machine is set to load boxes with a mean load of $\mu = 12$ ounces per box. If the mean load either exceeds 12 ounces per box or is less than this amount, the manufacturer wants to detect the situation. Suppose that 100 boxes of cereal are filled and weighed and that $\bar{x}$ and s were calculated to be

$$\bar{x} = 11.8 \text{ ounces} \qquad s = 0.5 \text{ ounce}$$

Test to see whether the data indicate that the mean filling weight, μ, differs from 12 ounces. Use $\alpha = .05$.

Solution

The elements of the test are

H_0: $\mu = 12$

H_a: $\mu \neq 12$ $\qquad$ (i.e., $\mu > 12$ or $\mu < 12$)

Test statistic: $z = \dfrac{\bar{x} - 12}{\sigma_{\bar{x}}}$

Rejection region: $z > 1.96$ $\qquad$ or $\qquad$ $z < -1.96$ $\quad$ (see Figure 9.9)

FIGURE 9.9
TWO-TAILED
REJECTION REGION:
$\alpha = .05$

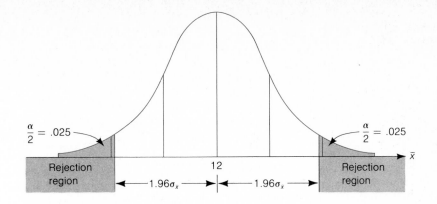

Note that $z = 1.96$ was chosen for the rejection region because $P(z > 1.96) = .025$. (This value is obtained from Table IV of Appendix B.) We now calculate

$$z = \frac{\bar{x} - 12}{\sigma_{\bar{x}}} = \frac{\bar{x} - 12}{\sigma/\sqrt{n}} = \frac{11.8 - 12}{\sigma/\sqrt{100}}$$

$$\approx \frac{11.8 - 12}{s/10} = \frac{-.2}{.5/10} = -4$$

You can see in Figure 9.9 that the calculated z value, -4, is well into the lower-tail rejection region and there is ample evidence to indicate that the mean filling level, μ, differs from 12 ounces. It appears that on the average, the machine is underfilling the boxes. How reliable is this conclusion? We know that the test statistic will erroneously reject the null hypothesis only 5% of the time (because $\alpha = .05$). Therefore, we are reasonably confident that this statistical test has led us to a correct conclusion.

LARGE-SAMPLE TEST OF AN HYPOTHESIS ABOUT μ

One-tailed test	Two-tailed test
H_0: $\mu = \mu_0$*	H_0: $\mu = \mu_0$*
H_a: $\mu < \mu_0$	H_a: $\mu \neq \mu_0$
(or H_a: $\mu > \mu_0$)	

Test statistic: $z = \dfrac{\bar{x} - \mu_0}{\sigma_{\bar{x}}}$ Test statistic: $z = \dfrac{\bar{x} - \mu_0}{\sigma_{\bar{x}}}$

Rejection region: $z < -z_\alpha$ Rejection region: $z < -z_{\alpha/2}$
   (or $z > z_\alpha$)   or $z > z_{\alpha/2}$

where α is chosen so that   where $z_{\alpha/2}$ is chosen so that
$$P(z > z_\alpha) = \alpha$$ $$P(z > z_{\alpha/2}) = \frac{\alpha}{2}$$

*Note: μ_0 is the symbol for the numerical value assigned to μ under the null hypothesis.

As we have indicated by the preceding examples, a large-sample statistical test of an hypothesis concerning a population mean can either be one-tailed or two-tailed, depending on the nature of the research (alternative) hypothesis we wish to support. A summary of the test is given in the box. The two possible conclusions resulting from the sample data are also given.

POSSIBLE CONCLUSIONS FOR A TEST OF AN HYPOTHESIS

1. If the calculated z-score falls in the rejection region, conclude that the research hypothesis is true. The probability that an incorrect decision (rejecting H_0 when it is true) has been made is α.

2. If the calculated z-score does not fall in the rejection region, state that the data do not provide evidence to support the research hypothesis. (The null hypothesis should not be accepted unless the probability β of a Type II error is calculated. This is not easy to do for most sampling distributions.)

EXERCISES

9.5. What is the difference between a research hypothesis and a null hypothesis?

9.6. Define each of the following:

a. Type I error   b. Type II error   c. α d. β

9.7. In the hypothesis testing, who or what determines the size of the rejection region?

9.8. If you test an hypothesis and reject the null hypothesis in favor of your research hypothesis, does your test prove that the research hypothesis is correct? Explain.

9.9. When do you risk making a Type I error? A Type II error?

9.10. For each of the following rejection regions, sketch the sampling distribution for z and indicate the location of the rejection region:

a. $z > 1.96$ b. $z > 1.645$ c. $z > 2.576$ d. $z < -1.29$
e. $z < -1.645$ or $z > 1.645$ f. $z < -2.576$ or $z > 2.576$

9.11. If the rejection region is defined as in Exercise 9.10, what is the probability that a Type I error will be made in each case?

9.12. A large automobile manufacturer claims that its new luxury model will travel an average of 18 miles on a gallon of gas. To test the manufacturer's claim, a consumer magazine test drove thirty-six of the luxury models and determined the gas mileage for each. The following statistics were then obtained:

$$\bar{x} = 17.2 \text{ miles per gallon} \qquad s = 1.8 \text{ miles per gallon}$$

Do these statistics support the manufacturer's claim? Let $\alpha = .05$.

9.13. The University of Minnesota uses thousands of fluorescent light bulbs each year. The brand of bulb it currently uses has a mean life of 900 hours. A manufacturer claims that its new brand of bulbs, which are cheaper than the brand the university currently uses, has a mean life of more than 900 hours. The university has decided to purchase the new brand if, when tested, the test evidence supports the manufacturer's claim at the .05 significance level. Suppose sixty-four bulbs were tested with the following results:

$$\bar{x} = 920 \text{ hours} \qquad s = 80 \text{ hours}$$

Will the University of Minnesota purchase the new brand of fluorescent bulbs?

9.14. A manufacturer of fishing line claims that the mean breaking strength of a competitor's 20 pound line is really less than 20 pounds. A sample of forty pieces of the competitor's 20 pound line has been drawn and each piece tested. The following results were obtained:

$$\bar{x} = 19.6 \text{ pounds} \qquad s = 0.8 \text{ pound}$$

Does the evidence support the manufacturer's claim at the .10 significance level?

9.15. A machine is set to produce nails with a mean length of 1 inch. Nails that are too long or too short do not meet the customer's specifications and must be rejected. To avoid producing too many rejects, the nails produced by the machine are sampled from time to time and tested as a check to see whether the machine is still operating properly, i.e., producing nails with a mean length of 1 inch. Suppose fifty nails have been sampled, and $\bar{x} = 1.02$ inches and $s = 0.04$ inch. At the .01 significance level, does the sample evidence indicate that the machine is producing nails with a mean not equal to 1 inch, i.e., is the production process out of control?

9.3 SMALL-SAMPLE INFERENCES ABOUT A POPULATION MEAN

One of the items of interest to an investor in the stock market is the amount a company's annual earnings per share will increase or decrease over the next year. Recall that earnings per share is computed by dividing the total annual earnings of the company by the total number of shares of stock outstanding. One way of trying to project the change in earnings per share is to ask the opinion of several experts, thus obtaining a sample of projections for the particular company. Then, this sample of opinions can be used to make an inference about the mean projected earnings per share, μ, of all stock analysts. However, time and cost restrictions would probably limit the sample of opinions to a small number, so that the large-sample inferential techniques of Sections 9.1 and 9.2 may not be applicable.

Many inferences in business must be made on the basis of very limited information, i.e., **small samples.** When making an inference about a population mean μ, small samples have two immediate problematic effects:

PROBLEM 1

The shape of the sampling distribution of the sample mean $\bar{x}$ now depends on the shape of the population that is sampled. We can no longer assume that the sampling distribution of $\bar{x}$ is approximately normal, because the central limit theorem applies only to large samples.

PROBLEM 2

Although it is still true that $\sigma_{\bar{x}} = \sigma/\sqrt{n}$, we can no longer use the sample standard deviation s to approximate σ when we need to estimate $\sigma_{\bar{x}}$. The approximation may be very unsatisfactory when the sample size is small.

Solution to Problem 1	The sampling distribution of $\bar{x}$ will be approximately normal even for small samples if we assume that the population being sampled is approximately normal.

Solution to Problem 2

Instead of using the statistic

$$z = \frac{\bar{x} - \mu}{\sigma_{\bar{x}}} = \frac{\bar{x} - \mu}{\sigma/\sqrt{n}}$$

which requires knowledge of, or a good approximation to, σ, we use the statistic

$$t = \frac{\bar{x} - \mu}{s/\sqrt{n}}$$

which replaces the population standard deviation σ by the sample standard deviation s.

The distribution of the t statistic in repeated sampling was discovered by W. S. Gosset, a scientist in the Guinness brewery, who published his discovery in 1908 under the pen name of Student. The main result of Gosset's work is that if we are sampling from a normal distribution, the t statistic will have a sampling distribution very much like that of the z statistic: mound-shaped, symmetric, with mean zero. The primary difference between the sampling distributions of t and z is that the t distribution is more variable than the z, which follows intuitively when you realize that t contains two random quantities ($\bar{x}$ and s), while z contains only one ($\bar{x}$).

The actual increase in variability in the sampling distribution of t depends on the sample size n. A convenient way of expressing this dependence is to say that the t statistic has $(n - 1)$ **degrees of freedom.** Recall that the quantity $(n - 1)$ is the divisor that appears in the formula for s^2. This number plays a key role in the sampling distribution of s^2 and will appear in discussions of other statistics in later chapters. Particularly, the smaller the number of degrees of freedom associated with the t statistic, the more variable will be its sampling distribution.

In Figure 9.10 we show both the sampling distribution of z and the sampling distribution of a t statistic with 4 degrees of freedom (df). You can see that the increased variability of the t statistic means that the t value, t_α, that locates an area α in the upper tail of the t distribution will be larger than the corresponding value z_α. Values of t that will be used in forming small-sample confidence intervals for μ and rejection regions

FIGURE 9.10
STANDARD NORMAL (z)
DISTRIBUTION AND
t DISTRIBUTION
WITH 4 df

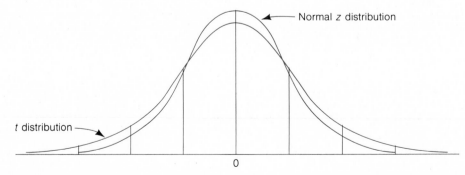

Normal z distribution

t distribution

0

CHAPTER 9 ESTIMATION AND A TEST OF AN HYPOTHESIS: SINGLE SAMPLE

FIGURE 9.11
REPRODUCTION OF
PART OF
TABLE V, APPENDIX B

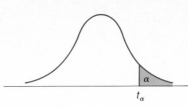

DEGREES OF FREEDOM	$t_{.100}$	$t_{.050}$	$t_{.025}$	$t_{.010}$	$t_{.005}$
1	3.078	6.314	12.706	31.821	63.657
2	1.886	2.920	4.303	6.965	9.925
3	1.638	2.353	3.182	4.541	5.841
4	1.533	2.132	2.776	3.747	4.604
5	1.476	2.015	2.571	3.365	4.032
6	1.440	1.943	2.447	3.143	3.707
7	1.415	1.895	2.365	2.998	3.499
8	1.397	1.860	2.306	2.896	3.355
9	1.383	1.833	2.262	2.821	3.250
10	1.372	1.812	2.228	2.764	3.169
11	1.363	1.796	2.201	2.718	3.106
12	1.356	1.782	2.179	2.681	3.055
13	1.350	1.771	2.160	2.650	3.012
14	1.345	1.761	2.145	2.624	2.977
15	1.341	1.753	2.131	2.602	2.947

for small-sample tests of hypotheses about μ are given in Table V of Appendix B. A partial reproduction of this table is shown in Figure 9.11. Note that t_α values are listed for degrees of freedom from 1 to 29, where α refers to the tail area to the right of t_α. For example, if we want the t value with an area of .025 to its right and 4 df, we look in the table under the column $t_{.025}$ for the entry in the row corresponding to 4 df. This entry is $t_{.025,4} = 2.776$, as shown in Figure 9.12. The corresponding standard normal z-score is $z_{.025} = 1.96$.

FIGURE 9.12
THE $t_{.025}$ VALUE IN
A t DISTRIBUTION
WITH 4 df AND THE
CORRESPONDING
$z_{.025}$ VALUE

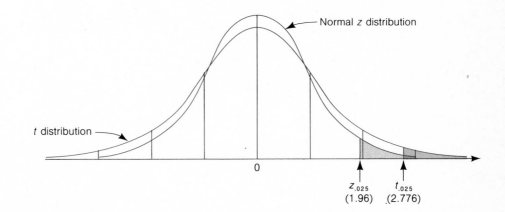

Normal z distribution

t distribution

$z_{.025}$ (1.96) $t_{.025}$ (2.776)

Note that the last row of Table V, where df = infinity, contains the standard normal z values. This follows from the fact that as the sample size n grows very large, s becomes closer to σ, and thus t becomes closer in distribution to z. In fact, when df = 29, there is little difference between corresponding tabulated values of z and t. Thus, we choose the arbitrary cutoff of $n = 30$ (df = 29) to distinguish between the large- and small-sample inferential techniques.

Returning to the projected earnings per share example, suppose we can get a sample of five expert opinions about next year's earnings per share for a stock. We calculate the mean and standard deviation of these five projections to be

$$\bar{x} = \$2.63 \qquad s = \$0.72$$

If we know that last year's earnings were $2.01 per share, is there enough evidence to indicate that the mean expert projection, μ, exceeds last year's figure?

The type of inference desired is a test of an hypothesis. Since we want to show that the mean expert projection for this year exceeds last year's earnings per share, we will test the null hypothesis that $\mu = \$2.01$ against the alternative hypothesis that $\mu > \$2.01$. Thus, the elements of the test are

Null hypothesis H_0: $\mu = \$2.01$

Research hypothesis H_a: $\mu > \$2.01$

Since σ is unknown and the sample is small ($n = 5$), we use the t statistic:

Test statistic: $t = \dfrac{\bar{x} - \mu_0}{s/\sqrt{n}} = \dfrac{\bar{x} - 2.01}{s/\sqrt{n}}$

Assumption: The relative frequency distribution of the population of projected earnings per share is approximately normal.

Note that we must assume the normality of our population in order to use the t statistic. If we want to test at the $\alpha = .05$ level, the rejection region will be

Rejection region: $t > t_{.05,4} = 2.132$ \qquad where \quad df $= n - 1 = 4$

This rejection region is shown in Figure 9.13.

FIGURE 9.13
REJECTION REGION
FOR PROJECTED
EARNINGS PER SHARE
TEST

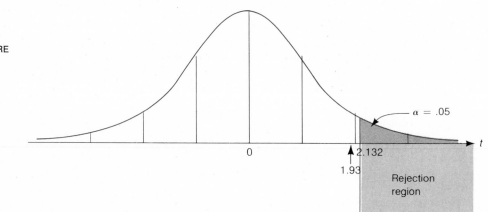

We now calculate

$$t = \frac{\bar{x} - 2.01}{s/\sqrt{n}} = \frac{2.63 - 2.01}{.72/\sqrt{5}}$$

$$= \frac{.62}{.72/2.24} = 1.93$$

Since the value of t, 1.93, calculated from the sample data does not exceed the tabulated value of 2.132, we cannot conclude that the mean projection of all experts exceeds last year's earnings of $2.01.

We summarize the technique for conducting a small-sample test of an hypothesis about a population mean below.

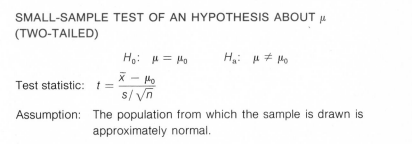

SMALL-SAMPLE TEST OF AN HYPOTHESIS ABOUT μ
(TWO-TAILED)

$$H_0: \quad \mu = \mu_0 \qquad H_a: \quad \mu \neq \mu_0$$

Test statistic: $\quad t = \dfrac{\bar{x} - \mu_0}{s/\sqrt{n}}$

Assumption: The population from which the sample is drawn is approximately normal.

Rejection region: $\quad t < -t_{\alpha/2, n-1} \qquad$ or $\qquad t > t_{\alpha/2, n-1}$

EXAMPLE 9.4

A major car manufacturer wants to test a new engine to see whether it meets new air pollution standards. The mean emission, μ, of all engines of this type must be less than 20 parts per million of carbon. Ten engines are manufactured for testing purposes, and the mean and standard deviation of the emissions for this sample of engines are determined to be

$$\bar{x} = 17.1 \text{ parts per million} \qquad s = 3.0 \text{ parts per million}$$

Do the data supply sufficient evidence to allow the manufacturer to conclude that this type of engine meets the pollution standard? Assume that the manufacturer is willing to risk a Type I error with probability equal to $\alpha = .01$.

Solution

The manufacturer wants to establish the research hypothesis that the mean emission level, μ, for all engines of this type is less than 20 parts per million. The elements of this small-sample one-tailed test are

$$H_0: \quad \mu = 20 \qquad H_a: \quad \mu < 20$$

Test statistic: $\quad t = \dfrac{\bar{x} - 20}{s/\sqrt{n}}$

Assumption: The relative frequency distribution of the population of emission levels for all engines of this type is approximately normal.

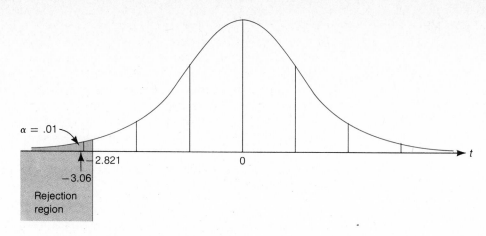

FIGURE 9.14
REJECTION REGION
FOR EXAMPLE 9.4

Rejection region: For $\alpha = .01$ and df $= n - 1 = 9$, the one-tailed rejection region (see Figure 9.14) is $t < -t_{.01,9} = -2.821$

We now calculate the test statistic.

$$t = \frac{\bar{x} - 20}{s/\sqrt{n}} = \frac{17.1 - 20}{3.0/\sqrt{10}} = -3.06$$

Since the calculated t falls in the rejection region (see Figure 9.14), the manufacturer concludes that $\mu < 20$ parts per million and the new engine type meets the pollution standard. Are you satisfied with the reliability associated with this inference? The probability is only $\alpha = .01$ that the test would support the research hypothesis when in fact it was false.

We may also use the t distribution to form a small-sample confidence interval for a population mean μ, **if the population is approximately normally distributed**. Recall that the large-sample confidence interval for μ is

$$\bar{x} \pm z_{\alpha/2}\sigma_{\bar{x}} = \bar{x} \pm z_{\alpha/2}\left(\frac{\sigma}{\sqrt{n}}\right)$$

where $100(1 - \alpha)$ percent is the desired confidence level. To form the small-sample confidence interval, replace σ by s and $z_{\alpha/2}$ by $t_{\alpha/2,n-1}$ (remember, the degrees of freedom must be specified for the tabulated t value).

SMALL-SAMPLE CONFIDENCE INTERVAL FOR μ

$$\bar{x} \pm t_{\alpha/2,n-1}\left(\frac{s}{\sqrt{n}}\right)$$

Assumption: The relative frequency distribution of the sampled population is approximately normal.

EXAMPLE 9.5

When food prices began their rapid increase in the early 1970s, some of the major television networks began periodically to purchase a grocery basket full of food at supermarkets around the country. They always bought the same items at each store so they could compare food prices. Suppose you want to estimate the mean price for a grocery basket in a specific geographical region of the country. You purchase the specified items at a random sample of twenty supermarkets in the region. The mean and standard deviation of the costs at the twenty supermarkets are

$$\bar{x} = \$26.84 \qquad s = \$2.63$$

Form a 95% confidence interval for the mean cost, μ, of a grocery basket for this region.

Solution

If we assume that the distribution of costs for the grocery basket at all supermarkets in the region is approximately normal, we can use the t statistic to form the confidence interval. For a confidence level of 95%, we need the tabulated value of t with df $= n - 1 = 19$:

$$t_{\alpha/2, n-1} = t_{.025, 19} = 2.093$$

Then the confidence interval is

$$\bar{x} \pm t_{.025, 19}\left(\frac{s}{\sqrt{n}}\right) = 26.84 \pm 2.093\left(\frac{2.63}{\sqrt{20}}\right)$$

$$= 26.84 \pm 1.23 = (25.61, 28.07)$$

Thus, we are reasonably confident that the interval from $25.61 to $28.07 contains the true mean cost, μ, of the grocery basket. This is because, if we were to employ our interval estimator on repeated occasions, 95% of the intervals constructed would contain μ.

We have emphasized throughout this section that the assumption of a normally distributed population is necessary for making small-sample inferences about μ when using the t statistic. While many business phenomena do have approximately normal distributions, it is also true that many business phenomena have distributions that are not normal or even mound-shaped. Empirical evidence acquired over the years has shown that the t distribution is rather insensitive to moderate departures from normality. That is, the use of the t statistic when sampling from mound-shaped populations generally produces credible results; however, for cases in which the distribution is distinctly nonnormal, **nonparametric methods** should be used. Nonparametric statistics are the subject of Chapter 16.

EXERCISES

9.16. In what ways are the distributions of the z statistic and t statistic alike? How do they differ?

9.17. Let t_0 be a particular value of t. Use Table V of Appendix B to find t_0 values such that the following statements are true:

a. $P(t \geq t_0) = .025$ where $n = 10$
b. $P(t \geq t_0) = .01$ where $n = 5$
c. $P(t \leq t_0) = .005$ where $n = 20$
d. $P(t \leq t_0) = .05$ where $n = 12$

9.18. In any bottling process, a manufacturer will lose money if the bottles contain either more or less than is claimed on the label. Accordingly, bottlers pay close attention to the amount of their product being dispensed by bottle-filling machines. Suppose a quality control inspector for a catsup company is interested in testing whether the mean number of ounces of catsup per family-size bottle is 20 ounces. The inspector samples nine bottles, measures the weight of their contents, and finds that $\bar{x} = 19.7$ ounces and $s = 0.3$ ounce. Does the sample evidence indicate that the catsup-dispensing machine is in need of adjustment? Test at an $\alpha = .05$ level of significance.

9.19. Refer to Exercise 9.18. Find a 90% confidence interval for the mean number of ounces of catsup being dispensed.

9.20. A cigarette manufacturer advertises that its new low-tar cigarette "contains on average no more than 4 milligrams of tar." You have been asked to test the claim using the following sample information: $n = 25$, $\bar{x} = 4.16$ milligrams, $s = 0.30$ milligram. Does the sample information disagree with the manufacturer's claim? Test using $\alpha = .05$.

9.21. Refer to Exercise 9.20. Find a 90% confidence interval for the mean amount of tar in the manufacturer's new low-tar brand.

9.22. A company purchases large quantities of naphtha in 50 gallon drums. Because the purchases are on-going, small shortages in the drums can represent a sizable loss to the company. The weights of the drums vary slightly from drum to drum, so the weight of the naphtha is determined by removing it from the drums and measuring it. Suppose the company samples the contents of twenty drums, measures the naphtha in each, and calculates $\bar{x} = 49.70$ gallons and $s = 0.32$ gallon. Do the sample statistics provide sufficient evidence to indicate that the mean fill per 50 gallon drum is less than 50 gallons? Use $\alpha = .10$.

9.23. Refer to Exercise 9.22. Find a 90% confidence interval for the mean number of gallons of naphtha per drum.

9.24. Suppose you want to estimate the mean percentage of gain in per share value for growth-type mutual funds over a specific 2 year period. Ten mutual funds are randomly selected from the population of all the commonly listed funds. The percentage gain figures are shown below:

12.1	-3.7	7.6	6.8	-2.3
4.6	8.4	18.1	9.2	3.0

Find a 90% confidence interval for the mean percentage of gain for the population of funds.

9.25. A random sampling of twelve market analysts gave the following forecasts for the price change (in dollars) over a 6 month period of a particular steel stock:

0	3	12	−4	10	7
6	5	5	−1	4	3

Suppose the mean of the population of forecasts for all market analysts is an accurate measure of the actual gain that the stock will experience. Estimate the mean forecast gain using a 95% confidence interval. [*Note:* Although it is clear that the population of forecasts will not be normal, assume the distribution will be adequately approximated by a normal distribution.]

9.26. A problem that occurs with certain types of mining is that some byproducts tend to be mildly radioactive and these products sometimes get into our freshwater supply. The EPA (1976) has issued regulations concerning a limit on the amount of radioactivity in supplies of drinking water. Particularly, the maximum level for naturally occurring radiation is 5 picocuries per liter of water. A random sample of twenty-four water specimens from a city's water supply produced the sample statistics $\bar{x} = 3.9$ picocuries per liter and $s = 4.0$ picocuries per liter.

    a. Do these data provide sufficient evidence to indicate that the mean level of radiation is safe (below the maximum level set by the EPA)? Test using $\alpha = .01$.

    b. Why should you want to use a small value of α for the test in part a?

9.4 LARGE-SAMPLE INFERENCES ABOUT A BINOMIAL PROBABILITY

Many market studies are conducted by companies with the objective of determining the fraction of buyers of a particular product that prefer the company's brand. For example, a tobacco company may conduct a market study by sampling and interviewing 1,000 smokers to determine their brand preference. The objective of the survey is to estimate the proportion of all smokers who smoke the company's brand. The number x of the 1,000 sampled who smoke the company's brand is a binomial random variable (see Section 6.4 for a description of the binomial experiment). The probability p that a smoker prefers the company's brand is the parameter to be estimated.

How would you estimate the probability p of success in a binomial experiment? One logical answer is to use the proportion of successes in the sample. That is, we can estimate p by calculating

$$\hat{p} \text{ (read ``p hat'')} = \frac{\text{Number of successes in the sample}}{\text{Number of trials}}$$

$$= \frac{x}{n}$$

Thus, if 313 of the 1,000 smokers were found to smoke the company's brand, we would estimate the proportion p of all smokers who prefer their brand to be

$$\hat{p} = \frac{x}{n} = \frac{313}{1,000} = .313$$

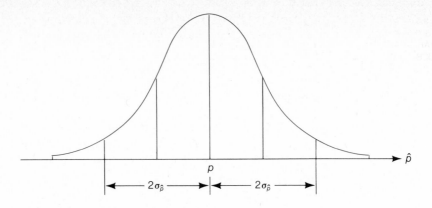

**FIGURE 9.15
SAMPLING
DISTRIBUTION OF $\hat{p}$**

To determine the reliability of the estimator $\hat{p}$, we need to know its sampling distribution. That is, if we were to draw samples of 1,000 smokers over and over again, each time calculating a new estimate $\hat{p}$, what would the frequency distribution of all the $\hat{p}$'s be? The answer lies in viewing $\hat{p}$ as the average or mean number of successes per trial over the n trials. The central limit theorem tells us that the relative frequency distribution of the sample mean for *any* population is approximately normal for large samples. The sampling distribution of $\hat{p}$ has the characteristics indicated in Figure 9.15 and listed below:

SAMPLING DISTRIBUTION OF $\hat{p}$

1. The mean of the sampling distribution of $\hat{p}$ is p, i.e., $\hat{p}$ is an unbiased estimator of p.
2. The standard deviation of the sampling distribution of $\hat{p}$ is $\sqrt{pq/n}$, i.e., $\sigma_{\hat{p}} = \sqrt{pq/n}$, where $q = 1 - p$.
3. For large samples, the sampling distribution of $\hat{p}$ is approximately normal.

The fact that the sampling distribution of $\hat{p}$ is approximately normal for large samples allows us to form confidence intervals and test hypotheses about p in a manner which is completely analogous to that used for large-sample inferences about μ:

LARGE-SAMPLE CONFIDENCE INTERVALS FOR p

$$\hat{p} \pm z_{\alpha/2}\sigma_{\hat{p}} = \hat{p} \pm z_{\alpha/2}\sqrt{pq/n} \qquad \text{where} \quad q = 1 - p$$

TABLE 9.3
VALUES OF pq FOR SEVERAL DIFFERENT p VALUES

p	pq
.5	.25
.6 or .4	.24
.7 or .3	.21
.8 or .2	.16
.9 or .1	.09

Thus, if 313 of 1,000 smokers smoke the company's brand, a 95% confidence interval for the proportion of all smokers who prefer the company's brand is

$$\hat{p} \pm z_{\alpha/2}\sigma_{\hat{p}} = .313 \pm 1.96\sqrt{pq/1,000}$$

where $q = 1 - p$. Just as we needed an approximator for σ in calculating a large-sample confidence interval for μ, we now need an approximation for p. As Table 9.3 shows, the approximation for p need not be especially accurate, because the value of pq needed for the confidence interval is relatively insensitive to changes in p. Therefore, we can use $\hat{p}$ to approximate p. Keeping in mind that $\hat{q} = 1 - \hat{p}$, we substitute these values into the formula for the confidence interval:

$$\hat{p} \pm 1.96\sqrt{pq/1,000} \approx \hat{p} \pm 1.96\sqrt{\hat{p}\hat{q}/1,000}$$
$$= .313 \pm 1.96\sqrt{(.313)(.687)/1,000} = .313 \pm .029$$
$$= (.284, .342)$$

The company can be 95% confident that the interval from 28.4% to 34.2% contains the true percentage of all smokers who prefer one of its brands. That is, in repeated construction of confidence intervals, 95% of all samples would produce confidence intervals that enclose p.

Tests of hypotheses concerning p are also analogous to those for population means (large samples).

LARGE-SAMPLE TEST OF AN HYPOTHESIS ABOUT p (TWO-TAILED)

H_0: $p = p_0$ (p_0 = hypothesized p value) H_a: $p \neq p_0$

Test statistic: $z = \dfrac{\hat{p} - p_0}{\sigma_{\hat{p}}}$

Rejection region: $z < -z_{\alpha/2}$ or $z > z_{\alpha/2}$

EXAMPLE 9.6

The reputations (and hence, sales) of many businesses can be severely damaged by shipments of manufactured items that contain an unusually large percentage of defectives. For example, a manufacturer of flashbulbs for cameras may want to be reasonably certain that less than 5% of its bulbs are defective. Suppose 300 bulbs are randomly selected from a very large shipment, each is tested, and ten defective bulbs are found. Does this provide sufficient evidence for the manufacturer to conclude that the fraction defective in the entire shipment is less than .05? Use $\alpha = .01$.

FIGURE 9.16
REJECTION REGION
FOR EXAMPLE 9.6

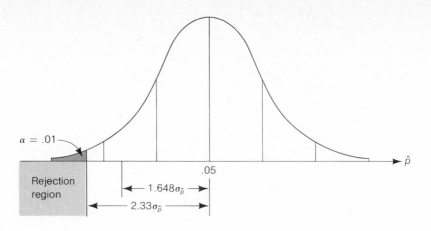

$\alpha = .01$

Rejection region

.05

$\leftarrow 1.648\sigma_{\hat{p}} \rightarrow$

$\leftarrow \quad 2.33\sigma_{\hat{p}} \quad \rightarrow$

$\hat{p}$

Solution

The objective of the sampling is to determine whether there is sufficient evidence to indicate that p is less than .05. Consequently, we will test the null hypothesis that $p = .05$ against the alternative hypothesis that $p < .05$. The elements of the test are

$$H_0: \quad p = .05 \qquad H_a: \quad p < .05$$

Test statistic: $\quad z = \dfrac{\hat{p} - .05}{\sigma_{\hat{p}}}$

Rejection region: $\quad z < -z_{.01} = -2.33 \quad$ (see Figure 9.16)

We now calculate the test statistic:

$$z = \frac{\hat{p} - .05}{\sigma_{\hat{p}}} = \frac{(10/300) - .05}{\sqrt{pq/n}} = \frac{.033 - .05}{\sqrt{pq/300}}$$

We must approximate pq, so we use $\hat{p}\hat{q}$ to get

$$z \approx \frac{-.017}{\sqrt{(.033)(.967)/300}} = \frac{-.017}{.0103} = -1.648$$

As shown on Figure 9.16, the calculated z value does not fall in the rejection region. The manufacturer cannot conclude with 99% confidence that the shipment contains fewer than 5% defective bulbs.

By increasing the size of the sample, and thereby providing more information about p, the flashbulb manufacturer might find support for the research hypothesis. Without this information, it is uncertain whether the fraction defective is less than .05. Or, the manufacturer might wish to accurately estimate p using a confidence interval based on a sample of flashbulbs that is larger than 300.

The confidence interval and test of an hypothesis for p in Example 9.6 are based on the assumption that the sample size n is large enough so that $\hat{p}$ will have a sampling distribution (according to the central limit theorem) that is approximately normal.

As a rule of thumb, this condition will be satisfied if the interval $\hat{p} \pm 3\sigma_{\hat{p}}$ does not contain 0 or 1.*

Small-sample estimators and test procedures are also available for p. These are omitted from our discussion, because most surveys conducted in business use samples that are large enough to employ the large-sample estimators and tests presented in this section.

EXERCISES

9.27. Explain the meaning of the phrase "$\hat{p}$ is an unbiased estimator of p."

9.28. Given $\hat{p} = .45$ and $n = 64$, construct a 95% confidence interval for p.

9.29. Given $\hat{p} = .9$ and $n = 100$, construct a 90% confidence interval for p.

9.30. A tire manufacturer interested in estimating the proportion of defective automobile tires it produces, tested a sample of 490 tires and found twenty-seven to be defective. Find a 95% confidence interval for p, the true fraction of defective tires produced by the firm.

9.31. Interested in how well their new computer billing operation is working, a company statistician samples 400 bills that are ready for mailing and checks them for errors. Twenty-four are found to contain at least one error. Find a 90% confidence interval for p, the true proportion of bills that contain errors.

9.32. A producer of frozen orange juice claims that 20% of all orange juice drinkers prefer its product. To test the validity of this claim, a competitor samples 200 orange juice drinkers and finds that only thirty-three prefer the producer's brand. Does the sample evidence refute the producer's claim? Test at the $\alpha = .10$ level of significance.

9.33. Last year a local television station determined that 70% of the people who watch news at 11:00 PM watch its station. The station's management believes that the current audience share may have changed. In an attempt to determine whether the audience share had in fact changed, the station questioned a random sample of eighty local viewers and found that sixty watched its news show. Does the sample evidence support the management's belief? Test at the $\alpha = .10$ level of significance.

9.34. Shoplifting is an escalating problem for retailers. According to *U.S. News and World Report* (Feb. 21, 1977), one New York City store randomly selected 500 shoppers and observed them while they were in the store. One in twelve was seen stealing. How accurate is this estimate? Find a 95% confidence interval for p, the proportion of all the store's customers who are shoplifters.

**9.5
DETERMINING
THE
SAMPLE SIZE**

When an experiment is planned with the purpose of estimating a population parameter —say, a mean μ or a binomial probability p—the required reliability of the estimate and the number of measurements to be included in the sample must be determined. How can this sample size be selected?

To answer this question, we use the knowledge acquired in Section 8.4 about the relation between the sample size and the variance of the sampling distribution of a

---

*This requirement is equivalent to that given in Section 7.5 for a normal distribution to provide an adequate approximation to a binomial distribution, although the requirement was stated in terms of the binomial random variable x rather than the sample fraction of successes, $\hat{p}$.

statistic. Since the variance will decrease inversely proportional to the sample size, we can force the statistic to fall (with a specified probability) as close to the population parameter as we please by choosing a sufficiently large value for the sample size. For example, since the standard deviation of the sampling distribution of $\bar{x}$ (see Figure 9.17) is $\sigma_{\bar{x}} = \sigma/\sqrt{n}$, we can make $\sigma_{\bar{x}}$ as small as we please by choosing a sufficiently large value for the sample size n.

Recall that in Section 9.1 we estimated the mean overdue amount for all delinquent accounts in a large credit corporation. A sample of 100 delinquent accounts produced an estimate $\bar{x}$ that was within $18 of the true mean amount due, μ, for all delinquent accounts. Suppose the corporation wanted μ estimated to within $5 with 95% confidence. How large a sample would be required?

For the sample size $n = 100$, we found an approximate 95% confidence interval to be

$$\bar{x} \pm 2\sigma_{\bar{x}} \approx \$233 \pm \$18$$

If we now want our estimator $\bar{x}$ to be within $5 of μ, we must have

$$2\sigma_{\bar{x}} = 5$$

or

$$\frac{2\sigma}{\sqrt{n}} = 5$$

The necessary sample size is found by solving the above equation for n. To do this, we need an approximation for σ. For our example, the appropriate approximation is the standard deviation of the 100 accounts, $s = 90$. Thus,

$$\frac{2\sigma}{\sqrt{n}} \approx \frac{2s}{\sqrt{n}}$$

$$= \frac{2(90)}{\sqrt{n}} = 5$$

$$\sqrt{n} = \frac{2(90)}{5} = 36$$

$$n = (36)^2 = 1,296$$

FIGURE 9.17

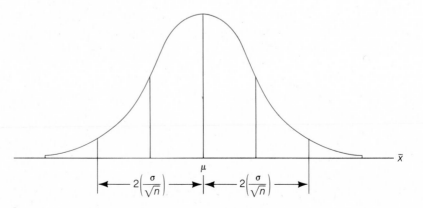

CHAPTER 9 ESTIMATION AND A TEST OF AN HYPOTHESIS: SINGLE SAMPLE

The company will have to sample approximately 1,300 delinquent accounts in order to estimate the mean overdue amount μ to within \$5 with about 95% confidence. [*Note:* This could include the 100 contained in the pilot sample.]

A similar argument follows if we want to determine the sample size necessary for estimating a binomial probability to within a given bound B with a specified confidence level. The general equations for determining the sample size to estimate both μ and p are given below:

SAMPLE SIZE DETERMINATION WITH $100(1 - \alpha)$ PERCENT CONFIDENCE

For estimating μ to within a bound B with probability $(1 - \alpha)$, solve the following for n:

$$z_{\alpha/2}\left(\frac{\sigma}{\sqrt{n}}\right) = B$$

The solution is

$$n = \frac{z_{\alpha/2}^2 \sigma^2}{B^2}$$

- -

For estimating p to within a bound B with probability $(1 - \alpha)$, solve the following for n:

$$z_{\alpha/2}\sqrt{pq/n} = B$$

The solution is

$$n = \frac{z_{\alpha/2}^2 pq}{B^2}$$

EXAMPLE 9.7

Refer to Example 9.6 in which a flashbulb manufacturer was making an inference about the fraction defective in a shipment. Suppose the manufacturer wants to estimate the true fraction p to within 1% (i.e., $B = .01$) with 99% confidence. How large a sample would be needed (assume the true p value is near .05)?

Solution

Since we want the error of estimation to be less than $B = .01$ with probability .99, we must have $\alpha = 1 - .99 = .01$. Then, $z_{\alpha/2} = z_{.005} = 2.575$. Substituting these values into the formula for n,

$$n = \frac{z_{\alpha/2}^2 pq}{B^2} = \frac{(2.575)^2(.05)(.95)}{(.01)^2}$$

$$= 3,149.5 \approx 3,150$$

Thus, an extremely large sample—about 3,150 bulbs—must be tested if the manufacturer wants to be 99% sure the estimate of the fraction defective will fall within 1% of the true value of p. (A cost–benefit analysis would be required before we could know whether such accuracy is worth the cost of the sampling.)

9.35. If you want to estimate the proportion of operating automobiles that are equipped with air pollution devices, approximately how large a sample would be required to estimate p to within .02 with probability equal to .95? [*Hint:* Since you do not have prior knowledge about p, choose $p = .5$ to find the sample size. This will give a value for n that is at least as large as required.]

9.36. Suppose a department store wants to estimate μ, the average age of the customers in its contemporary apparel department, correct to within 2 years with probability equal to .95. Approximately how large a sample would be required? [*Note:* The management does not know σ, but guesses that the age of its customers ranges from 15 to 45. If you take this range to equal 4σ, you will have a conservative approximation to σ that can be used to calculate n.]

9.37. The EPA standards on the amount of suspended solids that can be discharged into rivers and streams is a maximum of 60 milligrams per liter daily, with a maximum monthly average of 30 milligrams per liter. Suppose you want to test a randomly selected sample of n water specimens and to estimate the mean daily rate of pollution produced by a mining operation. If you want your estimate correct to within 1 milligram with probability equal to .95, how many water specimens would you have to include in your sample? Assume prior knowledge indicates that pollution readings in water samples taken during a day are approximately normally distributed with a standard deviation equal to 5 milligrams.

9.38. Suppose you are a retailer and you want to estimate the proportion of your customers who are shoplifters. You decide to select a random sample of shoppers and check closely to determine whether they steal any merchandise while in the store. Suppose that experience suggests the percentage of shoplifters is near 5%. How many customers should you include in your sample if you want to estimate the proportion of shoplifters in your store correct to within .02?

The objective of statistics is to make inferences about a population based on information in a sample. In this chapter we have presented several methods for accomplishing this objective.

The inference-making techniques we discussed are **estimation and hypothesis testing**. Estimation of a population parameter is accomplished by using an interval estimate with a probability of coverage (**confidence level**) that is fixed by the experimenter at a high level (usually .90, .95, or .99). On the other hand, when a specific **research (alternative) hypothesis** is tested about a parameter, the probability α of falsely rejecting the **null hypothesis** and accepting the research hypothesis is chosen to be small. Thus, we try to minimize the chance of error in both of these inference-making procedures.

One of the most important parameters about which inferences are made is the population mean μ. The sample mean $\bar{x}$ is used for making the inference, but the method depends on the **sample size**. When the sample size is large (we have arbitrarily specified $n > 30$ as large), the standard normal z statistic is used. The t **statistic** is employed when σ is unknown and a small sample is drawn from a normally (or approximately normally) distributed population.

Another important parameter in business applications is the binomial proportion p. This probability of success is estimated by the sample fraction of success, $\hat{p}$, and the z statistic is again used to form confidence intervals or to test an hypothesis. The sample size necessary for estimating a population mean μ or a binomial proportion p can be determined by specifying the confidence level and the desired bound on the estimate.

SUPPLEMENTARY EXERCISES

9.39. Let t_0 be a particular value of t. Use Table V of Appendix B to find the values such that the following statements are true:

    a. $P(t \leq t_0) = .10$ where $n = 23$
    b. $P(t \geq t_0) = .005$ where $n = 3$
    c. $P(t \leq -t_0$ or $t \geq t_0) = .05$ where $n = 7$
    d. $P(t \leq -t_0$ or $t \geq t_0) = .01$ where $n = 24$

9.40. If the rejection of the null hypothesis of a particular test would cause your firm to go out of business, would you want α to be small or large? Explain.

9.41. A company is interested in estimating the mean number of days of sick leave, μ, taken by all its employees. The firm's statistician selects at random 100 personnel files and notes the number of sick days taken by each employee. The following sample statistics are computed:

$$\bar{x} = 12.2 \text{ days} \qquad s = 10 \text{ days}$$

    a. Estimate μ using a 90% confidence interval.
    b. How many personnel files would the statistician have to select in order to estimate μ to within 2 days with 99% confidence?
    c. Do the data support the research hypothesis that μ, the mean number of sick days taken by the employees, is greater than 10.9 days? Test at an $\alpha = .05$ level of significance.

9.42. A sample of 300 transistors are tested and twelve are found to be defective. Find a 95% confidence interval for p, the true fraction defective.

9.43. Refer to Exercise 9.42. Approximately how many transistors would need to be sampled in order to estimate p to within .01 with probability equal to .95?

9.44. In confirming the reliability of a bank's records, auditing firms sometimes ask a sample of the bank's customers to confirm the accuracy of their savings account balances as reported by the bank. Suppose an auditing firm is interested in estimating the proportion of a bank's savings accounts on whose balances the bank and the customer disagree. Of 200 savings account customers questioned by the auditors, fifteen said their balance disagreed with that reported by the bank.

    a. Estimate the actual proportion of the bank's savings accounts on whose balances the bank and customer disagree using a 95% confidence level.
    b. The bank claims that the true fraction of accounts on which there is disagreement is .05. You, as an auditor, doubt this claim. Test the bank's claim at the .10 significance level.

9.45. Refer to Exercise 9.44. How many savings account customers should the auditors question if they want to estimate p to within .02 with probability equal to .95?

9.46. The EPA sets a limit of 5 parts per million on PCB (a dangerous substance) in water. A major manufacturing firm producing PCB for electrical insulation discharges small amounts from the plant. The company management, attempting to control the PCB in its discharge, has given instructions to halt production if the mean amount of PCB in the effluent exceeds 3 parts per million. A random sampling of fifty water specimens produced the following statistics: $\bar{x} = 3.1$ parts per million, $s = 0.5$ part per million.

    a. Do these statistics provide sufficient evidence to halt the production process? Use $\alpha = .01$.

    b. If you were the plant manager, would you want to use a large or a small value for α for the test in part a?

9.47. Failure to meet payments on student loans guaranteed by the government has been a problem for both the banks and the United States government. A random sample of $n = 1,000$ loans to college students in one region of the United States indicates that 273 loans are in default. Find a 95% confidence interval for the proportion of all student loans in the region that are in default.

9.48. A large mail-order company has placed an order for 5,000 electric can openers with a supplier on condition that no more than 2% of the can openers will be defective. To check the shipment, the company tests a random sample of 400 of the can openers and finds eleven are defective. Does this provide sufficient evidence to indicate that the proportion of defective can openers in the shipment exceeds 2%? Test using $\alpha = .05$.

9.49. Refer to Exercise 9.48. Suppose the company wants to estimate the proportion, p, of defective can openers in the shipment correct to within .04 with probability equal to .95. Approximately how large a sample would be required?

ON YOUR OWN . . .

Choose a population pertinent to your major area of interest that has an unknown mean (or, if the population is binomial, that has an unknown proportion of success). For example, a marketing major may be interested in the proportion of consumers who prefer a particular product. An advertising major might want to estimate the proportion of the television viewing audience who regularly watch a particular program. An economics major may want to estimate the mean monthly expenditure of college students on food.

    Define the parameter you want to estimate and conduct a **pilot study** to obtain an initial estimate of the parameter of interest, and more importantly, an estimate of the variability associated with the estimator. A pilot study is a small experiment (perhaps twenty to thirty observations) used to gain some information about the population of interest. The purpose is to help plan more elaborate future experiments. Based upon the results of your pilot study, determine the sample size necessary to estimate the parameter to within a reasonable bound (of your choice) with a 95% confidence interval.

REFERENCES

Environmental Protection Agency. *Environment Midwest,* Sept.–Oct. 1976, Region V.

Hamburg, M. *Statistical analysis for decision making.* 2d ed. New York: Harcourt Brace Jovanovich, 1977. Chapters 6 and 7.

Mendenhall, W., & Reinmuth, J. E. *Statistics for management and economics.* 2d ed. North Scituate, Mass.: Duxbury, 1974. Chapters 8 and 9.

Willis, R. E., & Chervany, N. L. *Statistical analysis and modeling for management decision-making.* Belmont, Ca.: Wadsworth, 1974. Chapters 8 and 11.

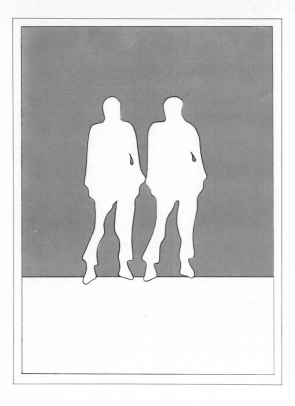

WHERE WE'VE BEEN . . .
The two methods for making statistical
inferences, estimation and tests of hypotheses,
were presented in Chapter 9. Confidence
intervals and tests of hypotheses based on single
samples were used to make inferences about
sampled populations. Particularly, we gave
confidence intervals and tests of hypotheses
concerning a population mean μ and a binomial
proportion p, and learned how to select the
sample size necessary to obtain a specified
amount of information concerning a parameter.

WHERE WE'RE GOING . . .
Now that we have learned to make inferences
about a single population, it is natural that we
would want to compare two populations. We may
want to compare the mean costs per pound in
the manufacture of two drugs, the mean lives of
two industrial products, or the mean gains that
might be expected from two investment strategies. How to decide whether mean differences
exist and how to estimate the mean difference
will be the subject of this chapter.

10

TWO SAMPLES: ESTIMATION AND TESTS OF HYPOTHESES

10.1

LARGE-SAMPLE INFERENCES ABOUT THE DIFFERENCE BETWEEN TWO POPULATION MEANS: INDEPENDENT SAMPLING

Suppose a chain of department stores is considering two suburbs of a large city as alternatives for locating a new store. The final decision about which location to choose is to be based on a comparison of the mean incomes of families living in the two suburbs.* The store is to be located in the suburb that has the highest mean income per household.

Let μ_1 represent the mean income of families in suburb 1 and μ_2 represent the mean incomes of families in suburb 2. Then our objective is to make an inference about $(\mu_1 - \mu_2)$, the difference between the mean incomes for the two suburbs.

Suppose that independent random samples of 100 households are randomly selected from each suburb and the mean incomes $\bar{x}_1$ and $\bar{x}_2$ are calculated for the two samples. An intuitively appealing estimator for $(\mu_1 - \mu_2)$ is the difference between the sample means, $(\bar{x}_1 - \bar{x}_2)$. The performance of this estimator in repeated sampling is summarized by the properties of its sampling distribution (see Figure 10.1).[†] Since the shape of the sampling distribution is approximately normal for large samples, we

---

PROPERTIES OF THE SAMPLING DISTRIBUTION OF $(\bar{x}_1 - \bar{x}_2)$

1. The sampling distribution of $(\bar{x}_1 - \bar{x}_2)$ is approximately normal for large samples.

2. The mean of the sampling distribution of $(\bar{x}_1 - \bar{x}_2)$ is $(\mu_1 - \mu_2)$.

3. If the two samples are independent, the standard deviation of the sampling distribution is

$$\sigma_{(\bar{x}_1 - \bar{x}_2)} = \sqrt{\frac{\sigma_1^2}{n_1} + \frac{\sigma_2^2}{n_2}}$$

where σ_1^2 and σ_2^2 are the variances of the two populations being sampled, and n_1 and n_2 are the respective sample sizes.

FIGURE 10.1
SAMPLING DISTRIBUTION OF $(\bar{x}_1 - \bar{x}_2)$

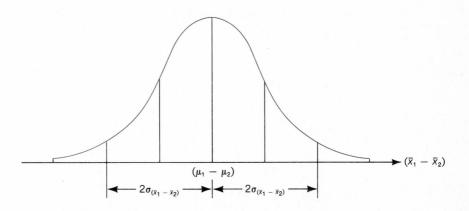

*Assume the incomes within a suburb are moderately homogeneous and hence the distributions are not heavily skewed. For this case, the mean would be a satisfactory measure of central tendency for the data.
[†] The sampling distribution for $(\bar{x}_1 - \bar{x}_2)$ for large samples was discussed in Section 8.5.

can use the z statistic to make inferences about $(\mu_1 - \mu_2)$, just as we did for a single mean. The procedures for forming confidence intervals and testing hypotheses are summarized below. Note the similarity of these procedures to their counterparts for a single mean (Sections 9.1 and 9.2).

LARGE-SAMPLE CONFIDENCE INTERVAL FOR $(\mu_1 - \mu_2)$

$$(\bar{x}_1 - \bar{x}_2) \pm z_{\alpha/2}\sigma_{(\bar{x}_1 - \bar{x}_2)} = (\bar{x}_1 - \bar{x}_2) \pm z_{\alpha/2}\sqrt{\frac{\sigma_1^2}{n_1} + \frac{\sigma_2^2}{n_2}}$$

Assumptions: The two samples are randomly selected in an independent manner from the two populations. The sample sizes, n_1 and n_2, are large enough so that $\bar{x}_1$ and $\bar{x}_2$ each have approximately normal sampling distributions and so that s_1^2 and s_2^2 provide good approximations to σ_1^2 and σ_2^2. This will be true if $n_1 \geq 30$ and $n_2 \geq 30$.

LARGE-SAMPLE TEST OF AN HYPOTHESIS FOR $(\mu_1 - \mu_2)$ (TWO-TAILED)

$$H_0: \quad (\mu_1 - \mu_2) = D_0 \qquad H_a: \quad (\mu_1 - \mu_2) \neq D_0$$

where

D_0 = Hypothesized difference between the means*

Test statistic: $z = \dfrac{(\bar{x}_1 - \bar{x}_2) - D_0}{\sigma_{(\bar{x}_1 - \bar{x}_2)}}$

where

$$\sigma_{(\bar{x}_1 - \bar{x}_2)} = \sqrt{\frac{\sigma_1^2}{n_1} + \frac{\sigma_2^2}{n_2}}$$

Rejection region: $z < -z_{\alpha/2}$ $\qquad$ or $\qquad$ $z > z_{\alpha/2}$

Assumptions: Same as for the large-sample confidence interval above.

For example, suppose the means and standard deviations for the samples of households from the two suburbs are as follows:

SUBURB 1	SUBURB 2
$\bar{x}_1 = \$18{,}750$	$\bar{x}_2 = \$15{,}150$
$s_1 = \$3{,}200$	$s_2 = \$2{,}700$
$n_1 = 100$	$n_2 = 100$

*Often, $D_0 = 0$.

Then to form a 95% confidence interval for the difference $(\mu_1 - \mu_2)$ between the true mean suburban incomes, we calculate

$$(\bar{x}_1 - \bar{x}_2) \pm 1.96\sqrt{\frac{\sigma_1^2}{n_1} + \frac{\sigma_2^2}{n_2}} = (18,750 - 15,150) \pm 1.96\sqrt{\frac{\sigma_1^2}{100} + \frac{\sigma_2^2}{100}}$$

To complete the calculations for this confidence interval we must estimate σ_1^2 and σ_2^2. Since the samples are both relatively large, the sample variances s_1^2 and s_2^2 will provide reasonable approximations. Thus, our interval is approximately

$$3,600 \pm 1.96\sqrt{\frac{(3,200)^2}{100} + \frac{(2,700)^2}{100}} = 3,600 \pm 837 = (2,763, 4,437)$$

Using this estimation procedure, a confidence interval will enclose the difference in population means, $(\mu_1 - \mu_2)$, 95% of the time. Therefore, we are reasonably confident that the mean income of households in suburb 1 is between $2,763 and $4,437 higher than the mean income of households in suburb 2. Based on this information, the department store chain should build the new store in suburb 1.

EXAMPLE 10.1

The management of a restaurant wants to determine whether a new advertising campaign has increased its mean daily income (gross). The income for 50 business days prior to the campaign's beginning were recorded. After conducting the advertising campaign and allowing a 20 day period for the advertising to take effect, the restaurant management recorded the income for 30 business days. These two samples will allow the management to make an inference about the effect of the advertising campaign on the restaurant's daily income. A summary of the results of the two samples is shown below:

BEFORE CAMPAIGN	AFTER CAMPAIGN
$n_1 = 50$	$n_2 = 30$
$\bar{x}_1 = \$1,255$	$\bar{x}_2 = \$1,330$
$s_1 = \$215$	$s_2 = \$238$

Do these samples provide sufficient evidence for the management to conclude that the mean income has been increased by the advertising campaign? Test using $\alpha = .05$.

Solution

We can best answer this question by a test of an hypothesis. Defining μ_1 as the mean daily income before the campaign and μ_2 as the mean daily income after the campaign, we will attempt to support the research (alternative) hypothesis that $\mu_2 > \mu_1$ [i.e., that $(\mu_1 - \mu_2) < 0$]. Thus, we will test the null hypothesis, $(\mu_1 - \mu_2) = 0$, rejecting this hypothesis if $(\bar{x}_1 - \bar{x}_2)$ equals a large negative value. The elements of the test are as follows:

H_0: $(\mu_1 - \mu_2) = 0$ \qquad (i.e., $D_0 = 0$)

H_a: $(\mu_1 - \mu_2) < 0$ \qquad (i.e., $\mu_1 < \mu_2$)

Test statistic: $z = \dfrac{(\bar{x}_1 - \bar{x}_2) - D_0}{\sigma_{(\bar{x}_1 - \bar{x}_2)}} = \dfrac{(\bar{x}_1 - \bar{x}_2) - 0}{\sigma_{(\bar{x}_1 - \bar{x}_2)}}$

Rejection region: $z < -z_\alpha = -1.645$ \quad (see Figure 10.2)

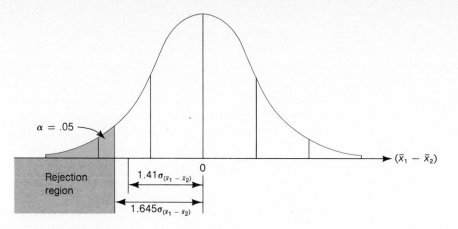

FIGURE 10.2
REJECTION REGION
FOR ADVERTISING
CAMPAIGN EXAMPLE

$\alpha = .05$

Rejection
region

$1.41\sigma_{(\bar{x}_1 - \bar{x}_2)}$

0

$1.645\sigma_{(\bar{x}_1 - \bar{x}_2)}$

$(\bar{x}_1 - \bar{x}_2)$

We now calculate

$$z = \frac{(\bar{X}_1 - \bar{X}_2) - 0}{\sigma_{(\bar{x}_1 - \bar{x}_2)}} = \frac{(1{,}255 - 1{,}330)}{\sqrt{\dfrac{\sigma_1^2}{n_1} + \dfrac{\sigma_2^2}{n_2}}}$$

$$\approx \frac{-75}{\sqrt{\dfrac{s_1^2}{n_1} + \dfrac{s_2^2}{n_2}}} = \frac{-75}{\sqrt{\dfrac{(215)^2}{50} + \dfrac{(238)^2}{30}}} = \frac{-75}{53.03} = -1.41$$

As you can see in Figure 10.2, the calculated z value does not fall in the rejection region. The samples do not provide sufficient evidence, at the $\alpha = .05$ significance level, for the restaurant management to conclude that the advertising campaign has increased the mean daily income.

EXAMPLE 10.2   Find a 95% confidence interval for the difference in mean daily incomes before and after the advertising campaign of Example 10.1 and discuss the implications of the confidence interval.

Solution   The 95% confidence interval for $(\mu_1 - \mu_2)$ is

$$(\bar{X}_1 - \bar{X}_2) \pm z_{\alpha/2}\sqrt{\frac{\sigma_1^2}{n_1} + \frac{\sigma_2^2}{n_2}}$$

Once again, we will substitute s_1^2 and s_2^2 for σ_1^2 and σ_2^2, because these quantities will provide good approximations to σ_1^2 and σ_2^2 for samples as large as $n_1 = 50$ and $n_2 = 30$. Then, the 95% confidence interval for $(\mu_1 - \mu_2)$ is

$$(1{,}255 - 1{,}330) \pm 1.96\sqrt{\frac{(215)^2}{50} + \frac{(238)^2}{30}} = -75 \pm 103.94$$

Thus, we estimate the difference in mean daily income to fall in the interval $-\$178.94$ to $\$28.94$. In other words, we estimate that μ_2, the mean daily income *after* the advertising campaign, could be larger than μ_1, the mean daily income *before* the campaign, by as much as $\$178.94$ per day or it could be less than μ_1 by $\$28.94$ per day.

Now what should the restaurant management do? You can see that the sample sizes collected in the experiment were not large enough to detect a difference in $(\mu_1 - \mu_2)$. To be able to detect a difference (if in fact a difference exists), the management will have to repeat the experiment and increase the sample sizes. This will reduce the width of the confidence interval for $(\mu_1 - \mu_2)$. The restaurant management's best estimate of $(\mu_1 - \mu_2)$ is the point estimate $(\bar{x}_1 - \bar{x}_2) = -\$75$. Thus, the management must decide whether the cost of conducting the advertising campaign is overshadowed by a possible gain in mean daily income estimated at $75 (but which might be as large as $178.94 or could be as low as $-\$28.94$). Based on this analysis, the management will decide whether to continue the experiment or reject the new advertising program as a poor investment.

EXERCISES

10.1. Describe the sampling distribution of $(\bar{x}_1 - \bar{x}_2)$.

10.2. A large supermarket chain is interested in determining whether a difference exists between the mean shelf-life (in days) of brand S bread and brand H bread. Random samples of fifty freshly baked loaves of each brand were tested, with the following results:

BRAND S	BRAND H
$\bar{x}_1 = 4.1$	$\bar{x}_2 = 5.2$
$s_1 = 1.2$	$s_2 = 1.4$

Is there sufficient evidence to conclude that a difference does exist between the mean shelf-lives of brand S and brand H? Test at the $\alpha = .05$ level.

10.3. Construct a 90% confidence interval for $(\mu_1 - \mu_2)$ in Exercise 10.2. Give an interpretation of your confidence interval.

10.4. An experiment has been conducted to compare the productivity of two machines. Machine 1 produced an average of 51.4 items per hour with a standard deviation of $s_1 = 2.1$ for 35 randomly selected hours during the past 2 weeks. Machine 2 produced an average of 49.5 items per hour with a standard deviation of $s_2 = 1.8$ for 45 randomly selected hours during the past 2 weeks.

    a. Describe the two populations being investigated.

    b. Do the samples provide sufficient evidence at the .10 significance level to conclude that, on the average, machine 1 produces more items per hour than machine 2?

    c. How reliable is your response to part b?

10.5. Construct a 95% confidence interval for $(\mu_1 - \mu_2)$ in Exercise 10.4. Would a 99% confidence interval be narrower or wider than the one you constructed? Why?

10.6. Two manufacturers of corrugated fiberboard each claim that the strength of their product tests on the average at more than 360 pounds per square inch. As a result of consumer complaints, a consumer products testing firm believes that firm A's product is stronger than firm B's. To test its belief, 100 fiberboards were chosen randomly from firm A's inventory and 100 were chosen from firm B's inventory. The following are the results of tests run on the samples:

A	B
$\bar{x}_1 = 365$	$\bar{x}_2 = 352$
$s_1 = 23$	$s_2 = 41$

Does the sample information support the consumer products testing firm's belief? Test at the .05 significance level.

10.7. What assumptions did you make in conducting the test in Exercise 10.6? Do you think such assumptions could comfortably be made in practice? Why or why not?

10.8. Refer to Exercise 10.6. Does the sample information support firm A's claim that the mean strength of its corrugated fiberboard is more than 360 pounds per square inch? Test at a significance level of .10.

10.2
SMALL-SAMPLE INFERENCES ABOUT THE DIFFERENCE BETWEEN TWO POPULATION MEANS: INDEPENDENT SAMPLING

Suppose a television network wanted to determine whether major sports events or first-run movies attract more viewers in the prime-time hours. It selected twenty-eight prime-time evenings; of these, thirteen had programs devoted to major sports events and the remaining fifteen had first-run movies. The number of viewers (estimated by a television viewer rating firm) was recorded for each program. If μ_1 is the mean number of sports viewers per evening of sports programming and μ_2 is the mean number of movie viewers per evening, we want to detect a difference between μ_1 and μ_2—if such a difference exists. Therefore, we want to test the null hypothesis

$$H_0: \ (\mu_1 - \mu_2) = 0$$

against the alternative hypothesis

$$H_a: \ (\mu_1 - \mu_2) \neq 0 \quad \text{(i.e., either} \quad \mu_1 > \mu_2 \quad \text{or} \quad \mu_2 > \mu_1)$$

Since the sample sizes are small, estimates of σ_1^2 and σ_2^2 will be unreliable and the z test statistic will be inappropriate for the test. But, as in the case of a single mean (Section 9.3), we can construct a Student's t statistic. This statistic (formula to be given subsequently) has the familiar t distribution described in Chapter 9. To use the

FIGURE 10.3
ASSUMPTIONS FOR THE TWO-SAMPLE t: (1) NORMAL POPULATIONS, (2) EQUAL VARIANCES

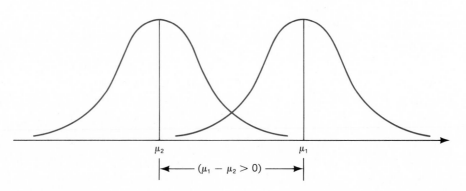

t statistic, both sampled populations must be approximately normally distributed with equal population variances, and the random samples must be selected independently of each other. The normality and equal variances assumptions would imply relative frequency distributions for the populations that would appear as shown in Figure 10.3. Will these assumptions be satisfied for the television viewing problem? We think the variation of the two populations of numbers of viewers will approximately satisfy these assumptions.

Since we assume the two populations have equal variances ($\sigma_1^2 = \sigma_2^2 = \sigma^2$), it is reasonable to use the information contained in both samples to construct a pooled sample estimator of σ^2 for use in the t statistic. Thus, if s_1^2 and s_2^2 are the two sample variances (both estimating the variance σ^2 common to both populations), the pooled estimator of σ^2, denoted as s_p^2, is

$$s_p^2 = \frac{(n_1 - 1)s_1^2 + (n_2 - 1)s_2^2}{(n_1 - 1) + (n_2 - 1)}$$

$$= \frac{(n_1 - 1)s_1^2 + (n_2 - 1)s_2^2}{n_1 + n_2 - 2}$$

or

$$s_p^2 = \frac{\overbrace{\sum_{i=1}^{n_1} (x_i - \bar{x}_1)^2}^{\substack{\text{From} \\ \text{sample 1}}} + \overbrace{\sum_{i=1}^{n_2} (x_i - \bar{x}_2)^2}^{\substack{\text{From} \\ \text{sample 2}}}}{n_1 + n_2 - 2}$$

Recall that the term *degrees of freedom* was defined in Section 9.3 as 1 less than the sample size for each sample, i.e., $(n_1 - 1)$ and $(n_2 - 1)$. The degrees of freedom associated with this pooled variance, s_p^2, is its denominator, i.e., $(n_1 - 1) + (n_2 - 1) = n_1 + n_2 - 2$.

To obtain the small-sample test statistic for testing H_0: $(\mu_1 - \mu_2) = D_0$, substitute the pooled estimate of σ^2 into the formula for the two-sample z statistic (Section 10.1) to obtain

$$t = \frac{(\bar{x}_1 - \bar{x}_2) - D_0}{\sqrt{s_p^2 \left(\dfrac{1}{n_1} + \dfrac{1}{n_2}\right)}}$$

It can be shown that this statistic, like the t statistic of Chapter 9, follows a t distribution with $(n_1 + n_2 - 2)$ degrees of freedom.

We will use the television viewer example to outline the final steps for this t test: The hypothesized difference in mean number of viewers is $D_0 = 0$. The rejection region will be two-tailed and will be based on a t distribution with $(n_1 + n_2 - 2)$ or $(13 + 15 - 2) = 26$ df. Letting $\alpha = .05$, the rejection region for the test would be

$$t < -t_{\alpha/2, n_1 + n_2 - 2} \qquad \text{or} \qquad t > t_{\alpha/2, n_1 + n_2 - 2}$$

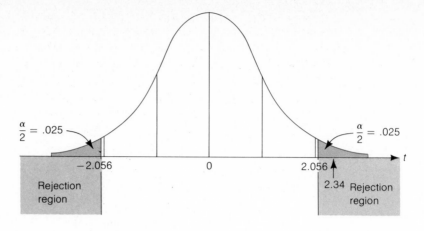

The value for $t_{.025,26}$ given in Table V of Appendix B is 2.056. Thus, the rejection region for the television example is

$$t < -2.056 \qquad \text{or} \qquad t > 2.056$$

This rejection region is shown in Figure 10.4.

Now, suppose the television network's samples produce the results shown below:

SPORTS	MOVIE
$n_1 = 13$	$n_2 = 15$
$\bar{x}_1 = 6.8$ million	$\bar{x}_2 = 5.3$ million
$s_1 = 1.8$ million	$s_2 = 1.6$ million

[*Note:* Although the sample estimates of variance are not equal, the assumption that the population variances are equal may still be valid. We will present a method for checking this assumption statistically in Section 10.3.]

We first calculate

$$s_p^2 = \frac{(n_1 - 1)s_1^2 + (n_2 - 1)s_2^2}{n_1 + n_2 - 2} = \frac{(13 - 1)(1.8)^2 + (15 - 1)(1.6)^2}{13 + 15 - 2}$$

$$= \frac{74.72}{26} = 2.87$$

Then,

$$t = \frac{(\bar{x}_1 - \bar{x}_2) - D_0}{\sqrt{s_p^2 \left(\frac{1}{n_1} + \frac{1}{n_2}\right)}} = \frac{(6.8 - 5.3) - 0}{\sqrt{2.87\left(\frac{1}{13} + \frac{1}{15}\right)}}$$

$$= \frac{1.5}{.64} = 2.34$$

Since the observed value of t, $t = 2.34$, falls in the rejection region (see Figure 10.4), the samples provide sufficient evidence to indicate that the mean number of viewers differ for major sports events and first-run movies shown in prime time. Or, we say that the test results are statistically significant at the $\alpha = .05$ level of significance. Because the rejection was in the positive or upper tail of the t distribution, the indication is that the mean number of viewers for sports events exceeds that for movies.

The same t statistic can also be used to construct confidence intervals for the difference between population means. Both the confidence interval and the test of hypothesis procedures are summarized below.

SMALL-SAMPLE CONFIDENCE INTERVAL FOR $(\mu_1 - \mu_2)$

$$(\bar{x}_1 - \bar{x}_2) \pm t_{\alpha/2, n_1 + n_2 - 2} \sqrt{s_p^2 \left(\frac{1}{n_1} + \frac{1}{n_2} \right)}$$

where

$$s_p^2 = \frac{(n_1 - 1)s_1^2 + (n_2 - 1)s_2^2}{n_1 + n_2 - 2}$$

Assumptions: 1. Both sampled populations have relative frequency distributions that are approximately normal.
2. The population variances are equal.
3. The samples are randomly and independently selected from the populations.

SMALL-SAMPLE TEST OF AN HYPOTHESIS FOR $(\mu_1 - \mu_2)$
(TWO-TAILED)

$$H_0: \ (\mu_1 - \mu_2) = D_0 \qquad H_a: \ (\mu_1 - \mu_2) \neq D_0$$

$$\text{Test statistic:} \quad t = \frac{(\bar{x}_1 - \bar{x}_2) - D_0}{\sqrt{s_p^2 \left(\frac{1}{n_1} + \frac{1}{n_2} \right)}}$$

Assumptions: Same as for the small-sample confidence interval for $(\mu_1 - \mu_2)$ above.

Rejection region: $t < -t_{\alpha/2, n_1 + n_2 - 2}$ $\qquad$ or $\qquad$ $t > t_{\alpha/2, n_1 + n_2 - 2}$

EXAMPLE 10.3

Suppose you want to estimate the difference in annual operating costs for automobiles with rotary engines and those with standard engines. You find eight owners of cars with rotary engines and twelve owners of cars with standard engines, who have purchased their cars within the last 2 years and are willing to participate in the experiment. Each of the twenty owners keeps accurate records of the amount spent on operating his or her car (including gasoline, oil, repairs, etc.) for a 12 month period. All costs are recorded on a per 1,000 mile basis to adjust for differences in mileage driven during the 12 month period. The results are summarized below:

ROTARY	STANDARD
$n_1 = 8$	$n_2 = 12$
$\bar{x}_1 = \$56.96$	$\bar{x}_2 = \$52.73$
$s_1 = \$4.85$	$s_2 = \$6.35$

Estimate the true difference $(\mu_1 - \mu_2)$ between the mean operating cost per 1,000 miles of cars with rotary and standard engines. Use a 90% confidence level.

Solution

The objective of this experiment is to obtain a 90% confidence interval for $(\mu_1 - \mu_2)$. To use the small-sample confidence interval for $(\mu_1 - \mu_2)$, you will have to make the following assumptions:

1. The operating cost per 1,000 miles is normally distributed for cars with both rotary and standard engines. Since these costs are actually averages (because we observe them on a per 1,000 mile basis), the central limit theorem lends credence to this assumption.

2. The variance in cost is the same for the two types of cars. Under these circumstances, we might expect the variation in costs from automobile to automobile to be about the same for both types of engines.

3. The samples are randomly and independently selected from the two populations. We have randomly chosen twenty different owners for the two samples in such a way that the cost measurement for one owner is not dependent upon the cost measurement for any other owner. Therefore, this assumption would be valid.

The first step in performing the test is to calculate the pooled estimate of variance:

$$s_p^2 = \frac{(n_1 - 1)s_1^2 + (n_2 - 1)s_2^2}{n_1 + n_2 - 2}$$

$$= \frac{(8 - 1)(4.85)^2 + (12 - 1)(6.35)^2}{8 + 12 - 2}$$

$$= 33.7892$$

Then, the 90% confidence interval for $(\mu_1 - \mu_2)$, the difference in mean operating costs for the two types of automobiles, is

$$(\bar{x}_1 - \bar{x}_2) \pm t_{\alpha/2, n_1 + n_2 - 2} \sqrt{s_p^2 \left(\frac{1}{n_1} + \frac{1}{n_2} \right)}$$

$$= (56.96 - 52.73) \pm t_{.05, 18} \sqrt{33.7892 \left(\frac{1}{8} + \frac{1}{12} \right)}$$

$$= 4.23 \pm 1.734(2.653) = 4.23 \pm 4.60$$

$$= (-0.37, 8.83)$$

This means that we estimate the difference in mean operating costs between cars with rotary engines and those with standard engines to fall in the interval from $-\$0.37$ to $\$8.83$. In other words, we estimate the mean operating costs for rotary engines to be anywhere from $\$0.37$ less than to $\$8.83$ more than the operating costs per 1,000 miles for standard engines. Although the sample means seem to suggest that rotary cars cost more to operate, there is insufficient evidence to indicate that $(\mu_1 - \mu_2)$ differs from zero, because the interval includes zero as a possible value for $(\mu_1 - \mu_2)$. To show a difference in mean operating costs (if it exists), you will have to increase the sample sizes and, thereby, narrow the width of the confidence interval for $(\mu_1 - \mu_2)$.

The two-sample t statistic is a powerful tool for comparing population means when the assumptions are satisfied. It has also been shown to retain its usefulness when the sampled populations are only approximately normally distributed. And, when the sample sizes are equal, the assumption of equal population variances can be relaxed. That is, when $n_1 = n_2$, σ_1^2 and σ_2^2 can be quite different and the test statistic will still have (approximately) a Student's t distribution. When the experimental situation does not satisfy the assumptions, other statistical tests are available. These nonparametric statistical tests are described in Chapter 16.

EXERCISES

10.9. To use the t statistic to test for differences in the means of two populations, what assumptions must be made about the two populations? About the two samples?

10.10. In the t tests of this section, σ_1^2 and σ_2^2 are assumed to be equal. Thus, we say $\sigma_1^2 = \sigma_2^2 = \sigma^2$. Why is a pooled estimator of σ^2 used instead of either s_1^2 or s_2^2?

10.11. In Section 10.1 a z statistic was used to test hypotheses about the difference between two population means. In this section we are also concerned with testing hypotheses about the difference between two populations means, but we do so via a t statistic. Explain.

10.12. A manufacturing company is interested in determining whether there is a significant difference between the average number of units produced per day by two different machine operators. A random sample of ten daily outputs was selected for each operator from the outputs over the past year. The data on number of items produced per day is shown below:

OPERATOR 1	OPERATOR 2
$n_1 = 10$	$n_2 = 10$
$\bar{x}_1 = 35$	$\bar{x}_2 = 31$
$s_1^2 = 17.2$	$s_2^2 = 19.1$

Do the samples provide sufficient evidence at the .05 significance level to conclude that a difference does exist between the mean daily outputs of the machine operators?

10.13. Find a 90% confidence interval for $(\mu_1 - \mu_2)$ in Exercise 10.12. Explain clearly the meaning of your confidence interval.

10.14. The management of a chain of movie theaters believes the average total weekend attendance at the Ocala theater is greater than that at the Burnsville theater.

Independent random samples of weekend attendence figures were drawn from the accounting records. The following data were obtained from the samples:

OCALA	BURNSVILLE
$n_1 = 16$	$n_2 = 17$
$\bar{x}_1 = 855$ people	$\bar{x}_2 = 750$ people
$s_1^2 = 1{,}684$	$s_2^2 = 1{,}439$

Does the sample evidence support the management's belief? Test at the .05 significance level.

10.15. Construct a 95% confidence interval for $(\mu_1 - \mu_2)$ in Exercise 10.14.

10.16. Suppose you are the personnel manager for a company and you suspect a difference in the mean length of work time lost due to sickness for two types of employees: those who work at night versus those who work during the day. Particularly, you suspect that the mean time lost for the night shift exceeds the mean for the day shift. To check your theory, you randomly sample the records for ten employees for each shift category and record the number of days lost due to sickness within the past year. The data are shown below:

NIGHT SHIFT, 1		DAY SHIFT, 2	
21	2	13	18
10	19	5	17
14	6	16	3
33	4	0	24
7	12	7	1
$\bar{x}_1 = 12.8$		$\bar{x}_2 = 10.4$	
$\sum\limits_{i=1}^{n} x_i^2 = 2{,}436$		$\sum\limits_{i=1}^{n} x_i^2 = 1{,}698$	

a. Calculate s_1^2 and s_2^2.

b. Show that the pooled estimate of the common population standard deviation, σ, is 8.86. Look at the range of the observations within each of the two samples. Does it appear that the estimate, 8.86, is a reasonable value for σ?

c. If μ_1 and μ_2 represent the mean number of days per year lost due to sickness for the night and day shifts, respectively, test the null hypothesis H_0: $\mu_1 = \mu_2$ against the alternative H_a: $\mu_1 > \mu_2$. Use $\alpha = .05$. Do the data provide sufficient evidence to indicate that $\mu_1 > \mu_2$?

d. What assumptions must be satisfied so that the t test from part c is valid?

10.17. Suppose your plant purifies its waste and discharges the water into a local river. An EPA inspector has collected water specimens of the discharge of your plant and also water specimens in the river upstream from your plant. Each water specimen is divided into five parts, the bacteria count is read on each, and the mean count for each specimen is reported. The average bacteria count readings for each of six specimens are reported below for the two locations.

PLANT DISCHARGE	UPSTREAM
30.1	29.7
36.2	30.3
33.4	26.4
28.2	27.3
29.8	31.7
34.9	32.3

a.   Why would the bacteria count readings shown above tend to be approximately normally distributed?
b.   Do the data provide sufficient evidence to indicate that the mean of the bacteria count for the discharge exceeds the mean of the count upstream? Use $\alpha = .05$.

**10.3
COMPARING TWO
POPULATION
VARIANCES:
INDEPENDENT
RANDOM
SAMPLES**

Suppose you want to use the two-sample t statistic to compare the mean productivity of two paper mills. However, you are concerned that the assumption of equal variances of the productivity for the two plants may be unrealistic. It would be helpful to have a statistical procedure to check the validity of this assumption.

The common statistical procedure for comparing population variances σ_1^2 and σ_2^2 makes an inference about the ratio, σ_1^2/σ_2^2, using the ratio of the sample variances, s_1^2/s_2^2. Thus, we will attempt to support the research hypothesis that the ratio σ_1^2/σ_2^2 differs from 1 (i.e., the variances are unequal) by testing the null hypothesis that the ratio equals 1 (i.e., the variances are equal).

$$H_0: \quad \frac{\sigma_1^2}{\sigma_2^2} = 1 \qquad (\sigma_1^2 = \sigma_2^2)$$

$$H_a: \quad \frac{\sigma_1^2}{\sigma_2^2} \neq 1 \qquad (\sigma_1^2 \neq \sigma_2^2)$$

We will use the test statistic

$$F = \frac{s_1^2}{s_2^2}$$

To establish a rejection region for the test statistic, we need to know how s_1^2/s_2^2 is distributed in repeated samples. That is, we need to know the sampling distribution of s_1^2/s_2^2. As you will subsequently see, the sampling distribution of s_1^2/s_2^2 is based upon two of the assumptions already required for the t test, namely:

1. The two sampled populations are normally distributed.
2. The samples are randomly and independently selected from their respective populations.

FIGURE 10.5
AN F DISTRIBUTION
WITH 7 AND 9 df

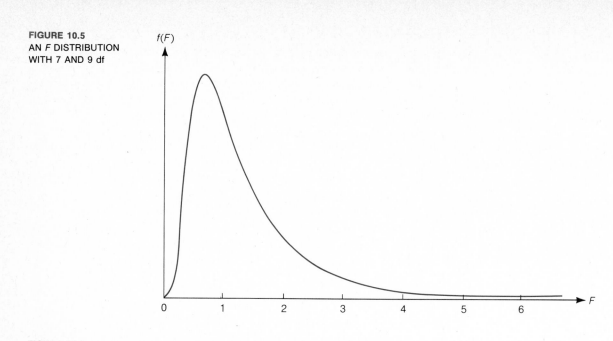

FIGURE 10.6
REPRODUCTION OF PART OF TABLE VI, APPENDIX B: $\alpha = .05$

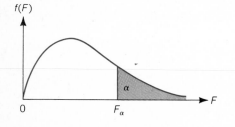

		NUMERATOR DEGREES OF FREEDOM							
ν_2	ν_1 1	2	3	4	5	6	7	8	9
1	161.4	199.5	215.7	224.6	230.2	234.0	236.8	238.9	240.5
2	18.51	19.00	19.16	19.25	19.30	19.33	19.35	19.37	19.38
3	10.13	9.55	9.28	9.12	9.01	8.94	8.89	8.85	8.81
4	7.71	6.94	6.59	6.39	6.26	6.16	6.09	6.04	6.00
5	6.61	5.79	5.41	5.19	5.05	4.95	4.88	4.82	4.77
6	5.99	5.14	4.76	4.53	4.39	4.28	4.21	4.15	4.10
7	5.59	4.74	4.35	4.12	3.97	3.87	3.79	3.73	3.68
8	5.32	4.46	4.07	3.84	3.69	3.58	3.50	3.44	3.39
9	5.12	4.26	3.86	3.63	3.48	3.37	3.29	3.23	3.18
10	4.96	4.10	3.71	3.48	3.33	3.22	3.14	3.07	3.02
11	4.84	3.98	3.59	3.36	3.20	3.09	3.01	2.95	2.90
12	4.75	3.89	3.49	3.25	3.11	3.00	2.91	2.85	2.80
13	4.67	3.81	3.41	3.18	3.03	2.92	2.83	2.77	2.71
14	4.60	3.74	3.34	3.11	2.96	2.85	2.76	2.70	2.65

DENOMINATOR DEGREES OF FREEDOM

When these assumptions are satisfied and when the null hypothesis is true (i.e., $\sigma_1^2 = \sigma_2^2$), the sampling distribution of $F = s_1^2/s_2^2$ is the F distribution with $(n_1 - 1)$ and $(n_2 - 1)$ degrees of freedom, respectively. The shape of the F distribution will depend upon the degrees of freedom associated with s_1^2 and s_2^2, i.e., $(n_1 - 1)$ and $(n_2 - 1)$. An F distribution with 7 and 9 df is shown in Figure 10.5. As you can see, the distribution is skewed to the right.

We need to be able to find F values corresponding to the tail areas of this distribution in order to establish the rejection region for our test of hypothesis, because when the population variances are unequal, we expect the ratio F of the sample variances to either be very large or very small. The upper-tail F values can be found in Tables VI and VII of Appendix B. Table VI is partially reproduced in Figure 10.6. It gives F values that correspond to $\alpha = .05$ upper-tail areas for different degrees of freedom. The columns of Tables VI and VII correspond to various degrees of freedom for the numerator sample variance, s_1^2, while the rows correspond to the degrees of freedom for the denominator sample variance, s_2^2. Thus, if the numerator degrees of freedom is 7 and the denominator degrees of freedom is 9, we look in the seventh column and ninth row to find the $F_{.05,7,9} = 3.29$. As shown in Figure 10.7, $\alpha = .05$ is the tail area to the right of 3.29 in the F distribution with 7 and 9 df. That is, if $\sigma_1^2 = \sigma_2^2$, the probability that the F statistic will exceed 3.29 is $\alpha = .05$.

Suppose we want to compare the variability in production for two paper mills and that we have obtained the following results:

SAMPLE 1	SAMPLE 2
$n_1 = 13$ days	$n_2 = 18$ days
$\bar{x}_1 = 26.3$ production units	$\bar{x}_2 = 19.7$ production units
$s_1 = 8.2$ production units	$s_2 = 4.7$ production units

FIGURE 10.7
AN F DISTRIBUTION FOR 7 AND 9 df:
$\alpha = .05$

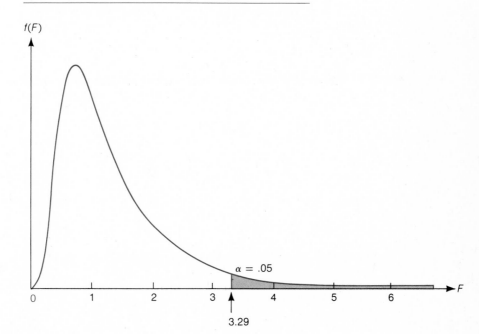

To form the rejection region for a two-tailed F test we want to make certain that the upper tail is used, because only the upper-tail values of F are shown in Tables VI and VII. To accomplish this, **we will always place the larger sample variance in the numerator of the F test statistic.** This has the effect of doubling the tabulated value for α, since we double the probability that the F ratio will fall in the upper tail by always placing the larger sample variance in the numerator. That is, we make the test two-tailed by putting the larger variance in the numerator rather than establishing rejection regions in both tails.

Thus, for our production example, we have a numerator s_1^2 with df $= n_1 - 1 = 12$ and a denominator s_2^2 with df $= n_2 - 1 = 17$. Therefore, the test statistic will be

$$F = \frac{\text{Larger sample variance}}{\text{Smaller sample variance}} = \frac{s_1^2}{s_2^2}$$

and we will reject H_0: $\sigma_1^2 = \sigma_2^2$ for $\alpha = .10$ when the calculated value of F exceeds the tabulated value:

$$F_{.05, n_1 - 1, n_2 - 1} = F_{.05, 12, 17} = 2.38 \quad \text{(see Figure 10.8)}$$

Now, what do the data tell us? We calculate

$$F = \frac{s_1^2}{s_2^2} = \frac{(8.2)^2}{(4.7)^2} = 3.04$$

and compare it to the rejection region shown in Figure 10.8. You can see that the F value 3.04 falls in the rejection region, and therefore, the data provide sufficient evidence to indicate that the population variances differ. Consequently, we would

FIGURE 10.8
REJECTION REGION FOR PRODUCTION EXAMPLE
F DISTRIBUTION

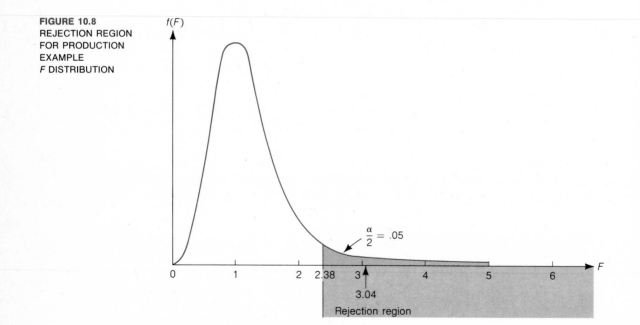

be reluctant to use the two-sample t statistic to compare the population means, since the assumption of equal population variances is apparently untrue.

What would you have concluded if the value of F calculated from the samples had not fallen in the rejection region? Would you conclude that the null hypothesis of equal variances is true? No, because then you risk the possibility of a Type II error (accepting H_0 when H_a is true) without knowing the value of β, the probability of accepting H_0: $\sigma_1^2 = \sigma_2^2$ when in fact it is false. Since we will not consider the calculation of β for specific alternatives in this text, when the F statistic does not fall in the rejection region, we simply conclude that insufficient sample evidence exists to refute the null hypothesis that $\sigma_1^2 = \sigma_2^2$.

The F test for equal population variances is summarized below:

F TEST FOR EQUAL POPULATION VARIANCES (TWO-TAILED)

$$H_0: \quad \frac{\sigma_1^2}{\sigma_2^2} = 1 \qquad \text{or} \qquad \sigma_1^2 = \sigma_2^2$$

$$H_a: \quad \frac{\sigma_1^2}{\sigma_2^2} \neq 1 \qquad \text{or} \qquad \sigma_1^2 \neq \sigma_2^2$$

Test statistic: $\quad F = \dfrac{\text{Larger sample variance}}{\text{Smaller sample variance}} = \dfrac{s_1^2}{s_2^2}$

where we number the samples so that $s_1^2 > s_2^2$

Assumptions: 1. Both sampled populations are normally distributed.
2. The samples are random and independent.

Rejection region: $\quad F > F_{\alpha/2, n_1 - 1, n_2 - 1}$

where

$n_1 - 1 = $ df larger (numerator) sample variance

$n_2 - 1 = $ df smaller (denominator) sample variance

EXAMPLE 10.4

Refer to Example 10.3, in which we used the two-sample t statistic to compare the mean operating cost of cars with rotary and standard engines. Use the F test to check the assumption that the population variances are equal. Use $\alpha = .10$.

Solution

The elements of the test are as follows:

$$H_0: \quad \frac{\sigma_1^2}{\sigma_2^2} = 1 \qquad H_a: \quad \frac{\sigma_1^2}{\sigma_2^2} \neq 1$$

Test statistic: $\quad F = \dfrac{\text{Larger sample variance}}{\text{Smaller sample variance}} = \dfrac{s_2^2}{s_1^2}$

To find the rejection region, we proceed as follows: The numerator degrees of freedom are df $= n_2 - 1$; the denominator degrees of freedom are df $= n_1 - 1$. Thus, from Table VI we find the rejection region:

$$F > F_{\alpha/2, n_2-1, n_1-1} = F_{.05, 12-1, 8-1}$$
$$= F_{.05, 11, 7} \approx 3.60$$

(Since no tabled value is given for a numerator df $= 11$, we average the entries at 10 and 12 to obtain $F_{.05, 11, 7} \approx 3.60$.)

We now calculate

$$F = \frac{s_2^2}{s_1^2} = \frac{(6.35)^2}{(4.85)^2} = 1.71$$

This F value is not in the rejection region. Therefore, there is insufficient evidence at the $\alpha = .10$ level to refute the assumption of equal population variances.

The following example shows that the F statistic is sometimes used to compare population variances in their own right, rather than just to check the validity of an assumption.

EXAMPLE 10.5

Suppose an investor wants to compare the risks associated with two different stocks, where the risk of a given stock is measured by the variation in daily price changes. Suppose we obtain a random sample of twenty-five daily price changes for stock 1 and twenty-five for stock 2. The sample results are summarized below:

STOCK 1	STOCK 2
$n_1 = 25$	$n_2 = 25$
$\bar{x}_1 = .250$	$\bar{x}_2 = .125$
$s_1 = .76$	$s_2 = .46$

Compare the risks associated with the two stocks by testing the null hypothesis that the variances of the price changes for the stocks are equal. Use $\alpha = .10$.

Solution

$H_0: \dfrac{\sigma_1^2}{\sigma_2^2} = 1$ $H_a: \dfrac{\sigma_1^2}{\sigma_2^2} \neq 1$

Test statistic: $F = \dfrac{\text{Larger sample variance}}{\text{Smaller sample variance}} = \dfrac{s_1^2}{s_2^2}$

Assumptions: 1. The changes in daily stock prices have relative frequency distributions that are approximately normal.
2. The stock samples are randomly and independently selected from a set of daily stock reports.

Rejection region: $F > F_{\alpha/2, n_1-1, n_2-1} = F_{.05, 24, 24} = 1.98$

We calculate

$$F = \frac{s_1^2}{s_2^2} = \frac{(.76)^2}{(.46)^2} = 2.73$$

The calculated F exceeds the rejection value of 1.98. Therefore, we conclude that the variances of daily price changes differ for the two stocks. It appears that the risk, as measured by the variance of daily price changes, is greater for stock 1 than for stock 2. How much reliability can we place in this inference? Only one time in ten (since $\alpha = .10$), on the average, would this statistical test lead us to conclude erroneously that σ_1^2 and σ_2^2 were different when in fact they were equal.

EXERCISES

10.18. Under what conditions is the sampling distribution of s_1^2/s_2^2 an F distribution?

10.19. Use Tables VI and VII of Appendix B to find each of the following F values:

a. $F_{.05,8,7}$ b. $F_{.01,15,20}$ c. $F_{.05,12,5}$ d. $F_{.01,5,25}$

10.20. In Exercise 10.14 the management of a chain of theaters was concerned with whether there was a difference in the mean total weekend attendance at two different theaters. Two independent random samples yielded the following data concerning attendance at the two theaters:

OCALA	BURNSVILLE
$n_1 = 16$	$n_2 = 17$
$\bar{x}_1 = 855$ people	$\bar{x}_2 = 750$ people
$s_1^2 = 1,684$	$s_2^2 = 1,439$

In order to run the hypothesis test required in Exercise 10.14, you had to assume $\sigma_1^2 = \sigma_2^2$. Use an F test to check that assumption. Let $\alpha = .10$. Explain the significance of your result.

10.21. In Exercise 10.12 a manufacturing company was interested in determining whether a significant difference existed between the mean number of units produced per hour by two different machine operators. Two independent random samples yielded the following data:

OPERATOR 1	OPERATOR 2
$n_1 = 10$	$n_2 = 10$
$\bar{x}_1 = 35$ units	$\bar{x}_2 = 31$ units
$s_1^2 = 17.2$	$s_2^2 = 19.1$

In order to conduct the hypothesis test required in Exercise 10.12 you had to assume $\sigma_1^2 = \sigma_2^2$. Use an F test with $\alpha = .10$ to check that assumption. Explain the significance of your result.

10.22. Suppose your firm has been experimenting with two different physical arrangements of its assembly line. It has been determined that both arrangements yield approximately the same average number of finished units per day. To obtain an arrangement that produces greater process control you suggest that the arrangement with the smallest variance in the number of finished units produced per day be permanently adopted. Two independent random samples yield the following results:

ASSEMBLY LINE 1	ASSEMBLY LINE 2
$n_1 = 21$ days	$n_2 = 21$ days
$s_1^2 = 1,432$	$s_2^2 = 3,761$

Do the samples provide sufficient evidence at the .10 significance level to conclude that the variances of the two arrangements differ? If so, which arrangement would you choose? If not, what would you suggest the firm do?

10.23. The quality control department of a paper company measures the brightness (a measure of reflectance) of finished paper on a periodic basis throughout the day. Two instruments that are available to measure the paper specimens are subject to error, but they can be adjusted so that the mean readings for a control paper specimen are the same for both instruments. Suppose you are concerned about the precision of the two instruments, namely that instrument 2 is less precise than instrument 1. To check this theory, five measurements of a single paper sample are made on both instruments. The data are shown below:

INSTRUMENT 1	INSTRUMENT 2
29	26
28	34
30	30
28	32
30	28

Do the data provide sufficient evidence to indicate that instrument 2 is less precise than instrument 1? Test using $\alpha = .05$.

10.4

TWO-SAMPLE INFERENCES ABOUT THE DIFFERENCE BETWEEN TWO POPULATION MEANS: PAIRED DIFFERENCE EXPERIMENTS

Suppose you want to compare the mean daily sales of two discotheque lounges located in the same city. If you were to record the lounges' total sales for each of 12 days (2 work weeks), the results might appear as shown in Table 10.1.

Test the null hypothesis that the mean daily sales, μ_1 and μ_2, for the two discotheques are equal against the research hypothesis that they differ, i.e.,

$$H_0: \ \mu_1 - \mu_2 = 0 \qquad H_a: \ \mu_1 - \mu_2 \neq 0$$

Using the two-sample t statistic (Section 10.2) we would calculate

$$s_p = \sqrt{\frac{(n_1 - 1)s_1^2 + (n_2 - 1)s_2^2}{n_1 + n_2 - 2}} = 174.35$$

and

$$t = \frac{(\bar{x}_1 - \bar{x}_2) - 0}{s_p \sqrt{\left(\frac{1}{n_1} + \frac{1}{n_2}\right)}} = \frac{(449.67 - 422.33)}{174.35 \sqrt{\frac{1}{12} + \frac{1}{12}}}$$

$$= \frac{27.34}{71.18} = .39$$

This small t value will not lead to rejection of H_0 when compared to the t distribution with $n_1 + n_2 - 2 = 22$ df, even if α were chosen as large as .20 ($t_{\alpha/2, n_1 + n_2 - 2} = t_{.10, 22} = 1.321$). Thus, we might conclude that insufficient evidence exists to infer that there is a difference in mean daily sales for the two discotheques.

TABLE 10.1
DAILY SALES
FOR TWO DISCOS

DAY	DISCO 1	DISCO 2
1 (Monday)	$253	$226
2 (Tuesday)	327	311
3 (Wednesday)	335	306
4 (Thursday)	483	434
5 (Friday)	635	594
6 (Saturday)	691	657
7 (Monday)	231	213
8 (Tuesday)	291	275
9 (Wednesday)	358	333
10 (Thursday)	446	427
11 (Friday)	644	609
12 (Saturday)	702	683
	$\bar{x}_1 = \$449.67$	$\bar{x}_2 = \$422.33$
	$s_1 = \$176.69$	$s_2 = \$172.01$

However, if you examine the data in Table 10.1 more closely, you will find this conclusion difficult to accept. The sales of disco 1 exceed those of disco 2 *for every one of the 12 days.* This, in itself, is strong evidence to indicate that μ_1 differs from μ_2, and we will subsequently confirm this fact. Why, then, was the t test unable to detect this difference?

The cause of this apparent inconsistency with the test result is that the two-sample t is inappropriate, because the assumption of independent samples is invalid. If you examine the pairs of daily sales, you will note that the sales of the two discotheques tend to rise and fall together over the days of the week. This pattern suggests a very strong daily dependence between the two samples and a violation of the assumption of independence required for the two-sample t test of Section 10.2. In this particular situation, note the **large variation within samples** (reflected by the large value of s_p^2) in comparison to the **small difference between the sample means.** Because s_p^2 was so large, the t test was unable to detect the difference between μ_1 and μ_2.

Now, consider a valid method to analyze the data of Table 10.1. We add to this table a column of differences between the daily sales of the discotheques, to form Table 10.2. We can regard these daily differences in sales as a random sample of all

TABLE 10.2
DAILY SALES AND
DIFFERENCES FOR
TWO DISCOS

DAY	DISCO 1	DISCO 2	DIFFERENCE (DISCO 1 − DISCO 2)
1	$253	$226	$27
2	327	311	16
3	335	306	29
4	483	434	49
5	635	594	41
6	691	657	34
7	231	213	18
8	291	275	16
9	358	333	25
10	446	427	19
11	644	609	35
12	702	683	19

$$\bar{x}_D = \$27.33$$
$$s_D = \$10.66$$

daily differences, past and present. Then we can use this sample to make inferences about the mean of the population of differences, μ_D, which is equal to the difference $(\mu_1 - \mu_2)$, i.e., the mean of the population (sample) of differences equals the difference between the population (sample) means. Thus, our test becomes

$$H_0: \quad \mu_D = 0 \qquad (\text{i.e.,} \quad \mu_1 - \mu_2 = 0)$$
$$H_a: \quad \mu_D \neq 0 \qquad (\text{i.e.,} \quad \mu_1 - \mu_2 \neq 0)$$

The test statistic is a one-sample t, since we are now analyzing a single sample of differences:

$$\text{Test statistic:} \quad t = \frac{\bar{x}_D - 0}{s_D/\sqrt{n_D}}$$

where

$\bar{x}_D$ = Sample mean of differences

s_D = Sample standard deviation of differences

n_D = Number of differences

Assumptions: 1. The population of differences in daily sales is approximately normally distributed.

2. The sample differences are randomly selected from a population of differences.

To find the rejection region, we choose $\alpha = .05$, so

$$t < -t_{.025,n_D-1} \qquad \text{or} \qquad t > t_{.025,n_D-1}$$

Referring to Table V of Appendix B, we find the t value corresponding to $\alpha/2 = .025$ and $n_D - 1 = 12 - 1 = 11$ df to be $t_{.025,11} = 2.201$. Thus, the null hypothesis is rejected if $t < -2.201$ or $t > 2.201$. Note that the number of degrees of freedom has decreased from $n_1 + n_2 - 2 = 22$ to 11 by using the **paired difference experiment** rather than the two independent random samples design.

Now calculate

$$t = \frac{\bar{x}_D - 0}{s_D / \sqrt{n_D}} = \frac{27.33}{10.66 / \sqrt{12}} = 8.88$$

Because this value of t falls in the rejection region, we conclude that the difference in mean daily sales for the two discotheques differs from zero. The fact that $\bar{x}_1 - \bar{x}_2 = \bar{x}_D = \$27.33$ strongly suggests that the mean daily sales for disco 1 exceeds the mean daily sales for disco 2.

This kind of experiment, in which observations are paired and the differences analyzed, is called a **paired difference experiment**. In many cases a paired difference experiment can provide more information about the difference between population means than an independent samples experiment. The differencing removes the variability due to the dimension on which the observations are paired. For example, in the discotheque example the day to day variability in daily sales is removed by analyzing the differences between the discotheques' daily sales. The removal of the variability due to this extra dimension is called **blocking**, and the paired difference experiment is a simple example of a **randomized block experiment**. In our example, the days represent the blocks.

Some other examples for which the paired difference experiment might be appropriate are the following:

1. To compare the performance of two automobile salespeople we might test a hypothesis about the difference $(\mu_1 - \mu_2)$ in their respective mean monthly sales. If we randomly choose n_1 months of salesperson 1's sales and independently choose n_2 months of salesperson 2's sales, the month to month variability caused by the seasonal nature of new car sales might inflate s_p and prevent the two-sample t statistic from detecting a difference between μ_1 and μ_2, even when a difference actually exists. However, by taking the difference in monthly sales for the two salespeople for each of n months, the month to month variability (seasonal variation) in sales can be eliminated and the probability of detecting a difference in $(\mu_1 - \mu_2)$, if a difference exists, is increased.

2. Suppose you want to estimate the difference $(\mu_1 - \mu_2)$ in mean price between two major brands of premium gasoline. If you were to choose two independent random samples of stations for each brand, the variability in price due to geographical location may be large. To eliminate this source of variability, you could choose pairs of stations, one station for each brand, in close geographical proximity and use the sample of differences between the prices of the brands to make an inference about $(\mu_1 - \mu_2)$.

3. Suppose a college placement center wants to estimate the difference $(\mu_1 - \mu_2)$ in mean starting salaries for men and women graduates who seek jobs through the center. If it independently samples men and women, the starting salaries may vary due to their different college majors and differences in grade-point averages. To eliminate these sources of variability, the placement center could match male and female job-seekers according to their majors and grade-point averages. Then the differences between the starting salaries of each pair in the sample could be used to make an inference about $(\mu_1 - \mu_2)$.

If we used the paired difference experiment for these examples, we would use one of the inferential procedures summarized below:

PAIRED DIFFERENCE TEST OF AN HYPOTHESIS (TWO-TAILED)

H_0: $\mu_D = D_0$ $(\mu_1 - \mu_2 = D_0)$

H_a: $\mu_D \neq D_0$ $(\mu_1 - \mu_2 \neq D_0)$

Test statistic: $t = \dfrac{\bar{x}_D - D_0}{s_D / \sqrt{n_D}}$

Assumptions: 1. The relative frequency distribution of the population of differences is normal.

2. The differences are randomly selected from the population of differences.

Rejection region: $t < -t_{\alpha/2, n_D - 1}$ or $t > t_{\alpha/2, n_D - 1}$

PAIRED DIFFERENCE CONFIDENCE INTERVAL

$\bar{x}_D \pm t_{\alpha/2, n_D - 1} (s_D / \sqrt{n_D})$

Assumption: Same as for the paired difference test (above).

EXAMPLE 10.6

A paired difference experiment is conducted to compare the starting salaries of male and female college graduates who find jobs. Pairs are formed by choosing a male and a female with the same major and similar grade-point averages. Suppose a random sample of ten pairs is formed in this manner and the starting annual salary of each

TABLE 10.3

PAIR	MALE	FEMALE	DIFFERENCE (MALE − FEMALE)
1	$ 8,300	$ 7,800	$ 500
2	10,500	10.600	−100
3	9.400	8,800	600
4	7,500	7,500	0
5	12,500	11,600	900
6	6,800	7,000	−200
7	8,500	8,200	300
8	10,200	9,100	1,100
9	7,400	7,200	200
10	8,200	7,500	700

person is recorded. The results are shown in Table 10.3. Test to see whether there is evidence that the mean starting salary, μ_1, for males exceeds the mean starting salary, μ_2, for females. Use $\alpha = .05$.

Solution

The elements of the paired difference test are

$$H_0: \quad \mu_D = 0 \qquad (\mu_1 - \mu_2 = 0)$$
$$H_a: \quad \mu_D > 0 \qquad (\mu_1 - \mu_2 > 0)$$

Note that we propose a one-sided research hypothesis, since we are interested in determining whether the data indicate that μ_1 exceeds μ_2, i.e., mean male starting salaries exceed mean female starting salaries.

Test statistic: $\quad t = \dfrac{\bar{x}_D - 0}{s_D / \sqrt{n_D}}$

Assumption: The relative frequency distribution for the population of differences is normal.

Since the test is upper-tailed, we reject when

$$t > t_{\alpha, n_D - 1} = t_{.05, 9} = 1.833$$

as shown in Figure 10.9.

We now calculate, using x_{Di} to represent the ith difference measurement,

$$\sum_{i=1}^{10} x_{Di} = 500 + (-100) + \cdots + 700 = 4,000$$

and

$$\sum_{i=1}^{10} x_{Di}^2 = 3,300,000$$

FIGURE 10.9
REJECTION REGION
FOR EXAMPLE 10.6

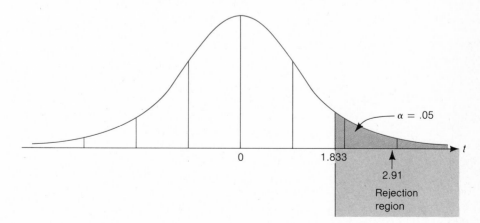

Then,

$$\bar{x}_{\mathrm{D}} = \frac{\sum_{i=1}^{10} x_{\mathrm{D}i}}{10} = \frac{4{,}000}{10} = 400$$

$$s_{\mathrm{D}}^2 = \frac{\sum_{i=1}^{n_{\mathrm{D}}} (x_{\mathrm{D}i} - \bar{x}_{\mathrm{D}})^2}{n_{\mathrm{D}} - 1} = \frac{\sum_{i=1}^{10} x_{\mathrm{D}i}^2 - \left(\sum_{i=1}^{10} x_{\mathrm{D}i}\right)^2 \Big/ 10}{9}$$

$$= \frac{3{,}300{,}000 - (4{,}000)^2/10}{9} = 188{,}888.89$$

$$s_{\mathrm{D}} = \sqrt{s_{\mathrm{D}}^2} = 434.61$$

Substituting these values into the formula for the test statistic, we find that

$$t = \frac{\bar{x}_{\mathrm{D}} - 0}{s_{\mathrm{D}}/\sqrt{n_{\mathrm{D}}}} = \frac{400}{434.61/\sqrt{10}} = \frac{400}{137.44} = 2.91$$

As you can see in Figure 10.9, the calculated t falls in the rejection region. Thus, we conclude at the $\alpha = .05$ level of significance that the mean starting salary for males exceeds the mean starting salary for females.

One measure of the amount of information about $(\mu_1 - \mu_2)$ gained by using a paired difference experiment rather than an independent samples experiment in Example 10.6 is the relative widths of the confidence intervals obtained by the two methods. A 95% confidence interval for $(\mu_1 - \mu_2)$ using the paired difference experiment is

$$\bar{x}_{\mathrm{D}} \pm t_{\alpha/2, n_{\mathrm{D}} - 1} \frac{s_{\mathrm{D}}}{\sqrt{n_{\mathrm{D}}}} = 400 \pm t_{.025, 9} \frac{434.61}{\sqrt{10}}$$

$$= 400 \pm 2.262 \frac{434.61}{\sqrt{10}}$$

$$= 400 \pm 310.88$$

$$\approx 400 \pm 311$$

$$= (\$89, \$711)$$

If we analyzed the same data as though it were an independent samples experiment,[*] we would first calculate the following quantities:

MALES	FEMALES
$\bar{x}_1 = \$8{,}930$	$\bar{x}_2 = \$8{,}530$
$s_1^2 = 3{,}009{,}000$	$s_2^2 = 2{,}331{,}222.22$

[*]This is only done to provide a measure of the increase in the amount of information obtained by a paired design in comparison to an unpaired design. Actually, if an experiment is designed using pairing, an unpaired analysis would be invalid because the assumption of independent samples would not be satisfied.

Then

$$s_p^2 = \frac{(n_1 - 1)s_1^2 + (n_2 - 1)s_2^2}{n_1 + n_2 - 2} = \frac{9(3,009,000) + 9(2,331,222.22)}{18}$$

$$= 2,670,111.11$$

$$s_p = \sqrt{s_p^2} = 1,634.05$$

The 95% confidence interval is

$$(\bar{x}_1 - \bar{x}_2) \pm t_{\alpha/2, n_1 + n_2 - 2} \, s_p \sqrt{\frac{1}{n_1} + \frac{1}{n_2}} = 400 \pm t_{.025, 10 + 10 - 2} \, 1,634.05 \sqrt{\frac{1}{10} + \frac{1}{10}}$$

$$= 400 \pm (2.101)(1,634.05) \sqrt{\frac{1}{10} + \frac{1}{10}}$$

$$= 400 \pm 1,535.35$$

$$\approx 400 \pm 1,535$$

$$= (-\$1,135, \$1,935)$$

The confidence interval for the independent sampling experiment is about five times wider than for the corresponding paired difference confidence interval. Blocking out the variability due to differences in majors and grade-point averages significantly increases the information about the difference in mean male and female starting salaries by providing a much more accurate (smaller confidence interval for the same confidence coefficient) estimate of $(\mu_1 - \mu_2)$.

You may wonder whether conducting a paired difference experiment is always superior to an independent samples experiment. The answer is: Most of the time, but not always. We sacrifice half of the degrees of freedom in the t statistic when a paired difference design is used instead of an independent samples design. This is a loss of information, and unless this loss is more than compensated for by the reduction in variability obtained by blocking (pairing), the paired difference experiment will result in a net loss of information about $(\mu_1 - \mu_2)$. Thus, we should be convinced that the pairing will significantly reduce variability before performing the paired difference experiment. Most of the time this will happen.

One final note: The pairing of the observations is determined *before* the experiment is performed (that is, by the *design* of the experiment). A paired difference experiment is *never* obtained by pairing the sample observations after the measurements have been acquired. Such is the stuff of which statistical lies are made!

CASE STUDY 10.1   Procedures to maintain comparable salaries between federal white-collar workers and those in the private sector are mandated by federal law. William M. Smith (1976) has discussed one statistical mechanism used in complying with this law. An annual survey, the *National Survey for Professional, Administrative, Technical, and Clerical Pay,* is conducted by the Bureau of Labor Statistics. Salary information is collected for approximately eighty-five work-level categories ranging from clerical to administrative positions in twenty occupations.

The design of the survey resembles a paired difference design, because the occupation and experience of employees in the private and government sectors are matched as closely as possible before a comparison is made. Test statistics like the paired difference t can be used to compare the mean salaries for the two sectors (see Exercise 10.28). Then, if the data indicate that the mean salaries differ for certain levels, the need for an adjustment is indicated.

Smith points out that presidential or legislative intervention often prevents the adjustments indicated by the data from being enacted. However, the results of the survey are valuable as a salary guide for the private sector and to those performing general economic analyses.

EXERCISES

10.24. Frequently, a paired difference experiment provides more information about the difference between two population means than an independent random samples experiment. Explain. Also explain when it may not.

10.25. A manufacturer of automobile shocks was interested in comparing the durability of its shocks with that of the biggest competitor. To make the comparison, one of the manufacturer's and one of the competitor's shocks were randomly selected and installed on the rear wheels of each of six cars. After the cars had been driven 20,000 miles, the strength of each test shock was measured, coded, and recorded. The following are the results of the examination:

CAR NUMBER	MANUFACTURER'S	COMPETITOR'S
1	8.8	8.4
2	10.5	10.1
3	12.5	12.0
4	9.7	9.3
5	9.6	9.0
6	13.2	13.0

a. Do the data present sufficient evidence to conclude that there is a difference in the mean strength of the two types of shocks after 20,000 miles of use? Let $\alpha = .05$.

b. What assumptions are necessary in order to apply a paired difference analysis to the data?

c. Construct a 95% confidence interval for $(\mu_1 - \mu_2)$. Interpret the meaning of your confidence interval.

10.26. Suppose the data in Exercise 10.25 are based on independent random samples.

a. Do the data provide sufficient evidence to indicate a difference between the mean strengths for the two types of shocks? Let $\alpha = .05$.

b. Construct a 95% confidence interval for $(\mu_1 - \mu_2)$. Interpret your result.

c. Compare the confidence intervals you obtained in Exercises 10.25 and part b of this exercise. Which is larger? To what do you attribute the difference in size? Assuming in each case that the appropriate assumptions are met, which interval provides you with more information about $(\mu_1 - \mu_2)$? Explain.

d. Are the results of an unpaired analysis valid when the data have been collected from a paired experiment?

10.27. A company has five plants that each produce the same product. The number of units produced at one of the plants on a randomly selected day was recorded. This was done for all five plants. After the physical arrangement of the assembly line at each plant was modified, the sampling procedure was repeated. The sampling results are contained in the following table:

PLANT NUMBER	BEFORE	AFTER
1	90	93
2	94	96
3	91	92
4	85	88
5	88	90

a. Are the the two samples independent? Explain.

b. Do the data present sufficient evidence to conclude that there is a difference in the mean daily output of the company's plants before and after the change in their assembly line structure?

c. Construct a 90% confidence interval for $(\mu_1 - \mu_2)$. Interpret the interval.

10.28. In Case Study 10.1 we discussed the *National Survey for Professional, Administrative, Technical, and Clerical Pay,* which is conducted annually to determine whether federal pay scales are commensurate with private sector salaries. Recall that the government and private workers in the study are matched as closely as possible before the salaries are compared. Suppose that the following represent annual salaries for twelve pairs of individuals in the sample matched on job level and experience:

PAIR	PRIVATE	GOVERNMENT
1	$12,500	$11,750
2	22,300	20,900
3	14,500	14,800
4	32,300	29,900
5	20,800	21,500
6	19,200	18,400
7	15,800	14,500
8	17,500	17,900
9	23,300	21,400
10	42,100	43,200
11	16,800	15,200
12	14,500	14,200

a. Use these data to place a 99% confidence interval on the difference between the mean salaries of the private and government sectors.

b. What assumptions are necessary for the validity of the procedure you used in part a?

**10.5
INFERENCES
ABOUT THE
DIFFERENCE IN
PROPORTIONS:
INDEPENDENT
BINOMIAL
EXPERIMENTS**

Suppose that a manufacturer of campers wants to compare the potential market for its products in the northeastern United States to the market in the southeastern United States. Such a comparison would help the manufacturer decide where to concentrate sales efforts. The company randomly chooses 1,000 households in the northeastern United States (NE) and 1,000 households in the southeastern United States (SE) and determines whether each household plans to buy a camper within the next 5 years. The objective is to use this sample information to make an inference about the difference $(p_1 - p_2)$ between the proportion p_1 of *all* households in the NE and the proportion p_2 of all households in the SE who plan to purchase a camper within 5 years.

The two samples represent independent binomial experiments (see Section 6.4 for the characteristics of binomial experiments), with the binomial random variables x_1 and x_2 being the numbers of the 1,000 sampled households in each area that indicate they will purchase a camper within 5 years. The results of the sample can be summarized as follows:

NE	SE
$n_1 = 1,000$	$n_2 = 1,000$
$x_1 = 42$	$x_2 = 24$

We can now calculate the *sample* proportions $\hat{p}_1$ and $\hat{p}_2$ of the households in the NE and SE, respectively, who are prospective buyers:

$$\hat{p}_1 = \frac{x_1}{n} = \frac{42}{1,000} = .042 \qquad \hat{p}_2 = \frac{x_2}{n} = \frac{24}{1,000} = .024$$

The difference between the sample proportions, $(\hat{p}_1 - \hat{p}_2)$, makes an intuitively appealing estimator of the difference between the population parameters, $(p_1 - p_2)$. For our example, the estimate is

$$(\hat{p}_1 - \hat{p}_2) = .042 - .024 = .018$$

To judge the reliability of the estimator $(\hat{p}_1 - \hat{p}_2)$, we must observe its performance in repeated sampling from the two populations. That is, we need to know the sampling distribution of $(\hat{p}_1 - \hat{p}_2)$. Properties of the sampling distribution are given in the box. Remember that $\hat{p}_1$ and $\hat{p}_2$ can be viewed as means of the number of successes in the respective samples, so that the central limit theorem will apply when the sample sizes are large.

Since the distribution of $(\hat{p}_1 - \hat{p}_2)$ in repeated sampling is approximately normal, we can use the z statistic to form confidence intervals for $(p_1 - p_2)$ or to test a hypothesis about $(p_1 - p_2)$. For the camper example, a 95% confidence interval for the difference $(p_1 - p_2)$ is

$$(\hat{p}_1 - \hat{p}_2) \pm 1.96\sigma_{(\hat{p}_1 - \hat{p}_2)} = (\hat{p}_1 - \hat{p}_2) \pm 1.96\sqrt{\frac{p_1 q_1}{n_1} + \frac{p_2 q_2}{n_2}}$$

The quantities $p_1 q_1$ and $p_2 q_2$ must be estimated in order to complete the calculation of the standard deviation, $\sigma_{(\hat{p}_1 - \hat{p}_2)}$, and hence of the confidence interval. In Section 9.4 we showed that the value of pq is relatively insensitive to the value chosen

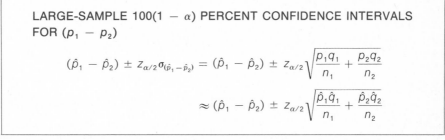

PROPERTIES OF THE SAMPLING DISTRIBUTION OF $(\hat{p}_1 - \hat{p}_2)$

1. If the sample sizes n_1 and n_2 are large (see Section 7.5 for a clearer meaning of large), the sampling distribution of $(\hat{p}_1 - \hat{p}_2)$ is approximately normal.

2. The mean of the sampling distribution of $(\hat{p}_1 - \hat{p}_2)$ is $(p_1 - p_2)$,* i.e.,

$$E(\hat{p}_1 - \hat{p}_2) = p_1 - p_2$$

Thus, $(\hat{p}_1 - \hat{p}_2)$ is an unbiased estimator of $(p_1 - p_2)$.

3. The standard deviation of the sampling distribution of $(\hat{p}_1 - \hat{p}_2)$* is

$$\sigma_{(\hat{p}_1 - \hat{p}_2)} = \sqrt{\frac{p_1 q_1}{n_1} + \frac{p_2 q_2}{n_2}}$$

---

to approximate p. Therefore, $\hat{p}_1 \hat{q}_1$ and $\hat{p}_2 \hat{q}_2$ will provide satisfactory estimates to approximate $p_1 q_1$ and $p_2 q_2$, respectively. Then,

$$(\hat{p}_1 - \hat{p}_2) \pm 1.96 \sqrt{\frac{p_1 q_1}{n_1} + \frac{p_2 q_2}{n_2}} \approx (\hat{p}_1 - \hat{p}_2) \pm 1.96 \sqrt{\frac{\hat{p}_1 \hat{q}_1}{n_1} + \frac{\hat{p}_2 \hat{q}_2}{n_2}}$$

$$= (.042 - .024)$$

$$\pm 1.96 \sqrt{\frac{(.042)(.958)}{1,000} + \frac{(.024)(.976)}{1,000}}$$

$$= .018 \pm .016$$

$$= (.002, .034)$$

Thus, we estimate the difference $(p_1 - p_2)$ to fall in the interval (.002, .034). It appears that there are between 0.2% and 3.4% more households in the NE than in the SE who plan to purchase campers in the next 5 years. The confidence coefficient associated with our interval estimate is .95.

The general forms for confidence intervals and for testing hypotheses about the difference $(p_1 - p_2)$ between binomial probabilities are given below:

LARGE-SAMPLE $100(1 - \alpha)$ PERCENT CONFIDENCE INTERVALS FOR $(p_1 - p_2)$

$$(\hat{p}_1 - \hat{p}_2) \pm z_{\alpha/2} \sigma_{(\hat{p}_1 - \hat{p}_2)} = (\hat{p}_1 - \hat{p}_2) \pm z_{\alpha/2} \sqrt{\frac{p_1 q_1}{n_1} + \frac{p_2 q_2}{n_2}}$$

$$\approx (\hat{p}_1 - \hat{p}_2) \pm z_{\alpha/2} \sqrt{\frac{\hat{p}_1 \hat{q}_1}{n_1} + \frac{\hat{p}_2 \hat{q}_2}{n_2}}$$

---

*The mean and variance of the sampling distribution of $(\hat{p}_1 - \hat{p}_2)$ can be derived using the formulas given in Section 8.5.

LARGE-SAMPLE TEST OF AN HYPOTHESIS ABOUT $(p_1 - p_2)$
(TWO-TAILED)

$$H_0: \ (p_1 - p_2) = D_0 \qquad H_a: \ (p_1 - p_2) \neq D_0$$

where D_0 is the hypothesized value of $(p_1 - p_2)$

Test statistic: $\quad z = \dfrac{(\hat{p}_1 - \hat{p}_2) - D_0}{\sigma_{(\hat{p}_1 - \hat{p}_2)}}$

Rejection region: $\quad z < -z_{\alpha/2} \qquad$ or $\qquad z > z_{\alpha/2}$

EXAMPLE 10.7

A consumer agency wants to determine whether there is a difference between the proportions of the two leading automobile models that need major repairs (more than $300) within 2 years of their purchase. A sample of 400 2 year owners of model 1 are contacted, and a sample of 500 2 year owners of model 2 are contacted. The numbers x_1 and x_2 of owners who report that their cars needed major repairs within the first 2 years are 53 and 78, respectively. Test the null hypothesis that no difference exists between the proportions in population 1 and 2 needing major repairs against the alternative that a difference does exist. Use $\alpha = .10$.

Solution

If we define p_1 and p_2 as the true proportions of model 1 and model 2 owners, respectively, whose cars need major repairs within 2 years, the elements of the test are

$$H_0: \ (p_1 - p_2) = 0 \qquad H_a: \ (p_1 - p_2) \neq 0$$

Test statistic: $\quad z = \dfrac{(\hat{p}_1 - \hat{p}_2) - 0}{\sigma_{(\hat{p}_1 - \hat{p}_2)}}$

Rejection region ($\alpha = .10$): $\quad z > z_{\alpha/2} = z_{.05} = 1.645 \qquad$ or

$$z < -z_{\alpha/2} = -z_{.05} = -1.645 \quad \text{(see Figure 10.10)}$$

FIGURE 10.10
REJECTION REGION
FOR EXAMPLE 10.7

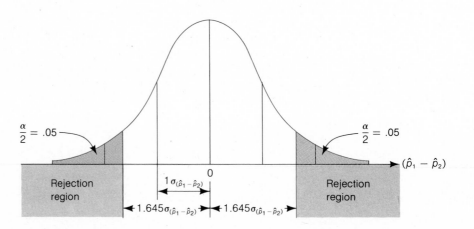

We now calculate

$$z = \frac{(\hat{p}_1 - \hat{p}_2) - 0}{\sigma_{(\hat{p}_1 - \hat{p}_2)}} = \frac{(\hat{p}_1 - \hat{p}_2)}{\sqrt{\dfrac{p_1 q_1}{n_1} + \dfrac{p_2 q_2}{n_2}}}$$

$$\approx \frac{(\hat{p}_1 - \hat{p}_2)}{\sqrt{\dfrac{\hat{p}_1 \hat{p}_1}{n_1} + \dfrac{\hat{p}_2 \hat{p}_2}{n_2}}} = \frac{(53/400) - (78/500)}{\sqrt{\dfrac{(53/400)(347/400)}{400} + \dfrac{(78/500)(422/500)}{500}}}$$

$$= \frac{-.0235}{.0235} = -1.0$$

The samples provide insufficient evidence at the $\alpha = .10$ significance level to detect a difference between the fractions of the two models that need repairs within 2 years. Even though 2.35% more sampled owners of model 2 needed major repairs, this difference is only 1 standard deviation ($z = -1$) from the hypothesized difference of zero between the true fractions.

EXERCISES

10.29. Describe the sampling distribution of $(\hat{p}_1 - \hat{p}_2)$.

10.30. What are the characteristics of a binomial experiment?

10.31. The quantities $\hat{p}_1$ and $\hat{p}_2$ have been defined to be x_1/n and x_2/n, respectively. What assumptions do we make about x_1 and x_2?

10.32. Explain why the central limit theorem is important in finding an approximate distribution for $(\hat{p}_1 - \hat{p}_2)$. See Section 8.5.

10.33. Explain how knowing the sampling distribution of $(\hat{p}_1 - \hat{p}_2)$ can help us measure the reliability of the estimator $(\hat{p}_1 - \hat{p}_2)$.

10.34. Moving companies (home movers, etc.) are required by the government to publish a Carrier Performance Report each year. One of the descriptive statistics they must include in this report is the percentage of shipments on which a $50 or greater claim for loss or damage was filed in the previous year. Suppose company A and company B each decide to estimate this figure by sampling their records, and they obtain the following data:

	COMPANY A	COMPANY B
Total shipments delivered	9,542	6,631
Number of shipments on which a claim of $50 or greater was filed	1,653	501

a. Estimate the true proportion of shipments on which a claim of $50 or greater was made against company A. Use an estimate that reflects its reliability.

b. Repeat part a for company B.

c. Use a 95% confidence interval to estimate the true difference in the proportion of claims made against company A and company B.

10.35. Refer to Exercise 10.34. Test the null hypothesis that no difference exists between the true percentage of claims made against company A and company B against the alternative hypothesis that a difference does exist. Use $\alpha = .05$. Do your test results indicate that one carrier is superior to the other? If so, which one? Explain how you arrived at your conclusion.

10.36. If α were set at .01 in Exercise 10.35, would you be less likely or more likely to reject the null hypothesis? Explain.

10.37. Suppose a firm switches its table salt container from a cylinder (expensive) to a rectangular box (inexpensive). The firm samples 1,000 households nationwide, both before and after the switch, to estimate the percentage of households that purchase its brand of salt. The following results are obtained:

	BEFORE	AFTER
Sample size	1,000	1,000
Number of households using firm's brand	475	305

a. Estimate the true difference in the percentage of households using the firm's salt before and after the packaging switch. Use a 90% confidence interval.

b. Interpret the confidence interval of part a. Be sure you clearly express the reliability of the interval.

10.38. Refer to Exercise 10.37. The firm's vice president in charge of sales claims the switch to the box has seriously hurt the market share. Does the sample evidence support this claim at the .05 significance level?

10.39. The Reserve Mining Company of Minnesota commissioned a team of physicians to study the breathing patterns of its miners who were exposed to taconite dust. The physicians compared the breathing of 307 miners who had been employed in Reserve's Babbit, Minnesota, mine for more than 20 years with thirty-five Duluth area men with no history of exposure to taconite dust. The physicians concluded that "there is no significant difference in respiratory symptoms or breathing ability between the group of men who have worked in the taconite industry for more than 20 years and a group of men of similar smoking habits but without exposure to taconite dust." Using the statistical procedures you have learned in this chapter, design an hypothesis test (give H_0, H_a, test statistics, etc.) that would have been appropriate for use in the physicians' study. [Source: Associated Press, *Minneapolis Tribune,* Feb. 20, 1977.]

10.40. Refer to Exercise 10.39. Suppose the physicians determined that sixty-one of the 307 miners had breathing irregularities, and that five of the thirty-five Duluth men had breathing irregularities. Test to see whether these data indicate that a higher proportion of breathing irregularities exists among those who have been exposed to taconite dust than among those who have not been exposed.

**10.6
DETERMINING
THE
SAMPLE SIZE**

You can find the appropriate sample size to estimate the difference between a pair of parameters with a specified degree of reliability by using the method described in Section 9.5. That is, to estimate the difference between a pair of parameters correct to within B units with probability $(1 - \alpha)$, let $z_{\alpha/2}$ standard deviations of the sampling distribution of the estimator equal B. Then solve for the sample size. To do this, you have to solve the problem for a specific ratio between n_1 and n_2. Most often, you will want to have equal sample sizes, i.e., $n_1 = n_2 = n$. We will illustrate the procedure with two examples.

EXAMPLE 10.8

The sales manager for a chain of supermarkets wants to determine whether store location, management, etc., produce a difference in the mean meat purchase per customer (zero purchases to be excluded) at two different stores. The estimate of the difference in mean meat purchase per customer is to be correct to within $2.00 with probability equal to .95. If the two sample sizes are to be equal, find $n_1 = n_2 = n$, the number of customer meat sales to be randomly selected from each store.

Solution

To solve the problem, you have to know something about the variation in the dollar amount of meat sales per customer. Suppose you know that the sales have a range of approximately $30 at each store. Then you could approximate $\sigma_1 = \sigma_2 = \sigma$ by letting the range equal 4σ, and

$$4\sigma \approx \$30$$

$$\sigma \approx \$7.50$$

The next step is to solve the equation

$$z_{\alpha/2}\sqrt{\frac{\sigma_1^2}{n_1} + \frac{\sigma_2^2}{n_2}} = B$$

for n, where $n = n_1 = n_2$. Since we want the estimate to lie within $B = \$2.00$ of $(\mu_1 - \mu_2)$ with probability equal to .95, $z_{\alpha/2} = z_{.025} = 1.96$. Then, letting $\sigma_1 = \sigma_2 = 7.5$ and solving for n, we have

$$1.96\sqrt{\frac{(7.5)^2}{n} + \frac{(7.5)^2}{n}} = 2.00$$

$$1.96\sqrt{\frac{2(7.5)^2}{n}} = 2.00$$

$$n = 108.01 \approx 108$$

Consequently, you will have to randomly sample 108 meat sales per store to estimate the difference in mean meat sales per customer correct to within $2.00.

EXAMPLE 10.9

A production supervisor suspects a difference exists between the proportions of defective items produced by two different machines. Experience has shown that the proportion defective for the two machines is in the neighborhood of .03. If the supervisor wants to estimate the difference in the proportions correct to within .005 with probability .95, how many items must be randomly sampled from the production of each machine? (Assume that you want $n_1 = n_2 = n$.)

Solution

For the specified level of reliability, $z_{\alpha/2} = z_{.025} = 1.96$. Then, letting $p_1 = p_2 = .03$ and $n_1 = n_2 = n$, the required sample size per machine is found by solving the following equation for n:

$$z_{\alpha/2}\sqrt{\frac{p_1 q_1}{n_1} + \frac{p_2 q_2}{n_2}} = B$$

$$1.96\sqrt{\frac{(.03)(.97)}{n} + \frac{(.03)(.97)}{n}} = .005$$

$$1.96\sqrt{\frac{2(.03)(.97)}{n}} = .005$$

$$n = 8{,}943.2$$

You can see that this may be a tedious sampling procedure. If the supervisor insists on estimating $(p_1 - p_2)$ correct to within .005 with probability equal to .95, approximately 9,000 items will have to be inspected for each machine.

EXERCISES

10.41. An article in the *Wall Street Journal* (June 6, 1977) stated that soaring prices on new cars have created a swing toward automobile loans in excess of 36 months. In fact, several large automobile finance companies indicate the percentage of long-term loans (in excess of 36 months, with most at 48 months) has increased from less than 10% in 1976 to somewhere near 50% in 1977. Suppose you plan to survey potential buyers in your sales region to estimate the proportion of buyers in the over 40 age group who favor 48 month automobile loans and the proportion in the 40 and under age group who favor the 48 month automobile loans. If you intend to select random samples of the same size from each of these two groups:

    a. Approximately how many potential automobile buyers should be included in your samples to estimate the difference in proportions correct to within .05 with probability equal to .95?

    b. Suppose you want to obtain individual estimates for the proportions in the two age groups. Will the sample size found in part a be large enough to provide estimates of each proportion correct to within .05 with probability equal to .95?

10.42. Suppose you are interested in the growth rate of dividends. Consider investing $1,000 in a stock and suppose you want to estimate the dividend rate on your $1,000 investment at the end of 5 years. Particularly, you want to compare two types of stocks, electrical utilities and oil companies. To conduct your study, you plan to randomly select n oil stocks and n electrical utility stocks. For each stock, you will check the records, calculate the number of shares of stock you could have purchased 5 years ago for $1,000, and then calculate the dividend rate (in percent) that the stock would be paying today on your $1,000 investment. Suppose you think the dividend rates will vary over a range of roughly 25%. To obtain an approximate value for σ_1 and σ_2, let $\sigma_1 = \sigma_2 = \sigma$ and let the range be 4σ. Then the range is $25 \approx 4\sigma$ and $\sigma \approx 6.25$. How large should n be if you want to estimate the difference in the mean rate of dividend return correct to within 3%?

10.43. A television manufacturer wants to compare with a competitor the proportions of its best sets that need repair within 1 year. If it is desired to estimate the difference in proportions to within .05 with 90% confidence, ar:d if the manufacturer plans to sample twice as many buyers of its sets as buyers of the competitor's sets, how many buyers of each brand must be sampled? Assume the proportion of sets that need repair will be about .2 for both brands.

SUMMARY

We have presented various techniques for using the information in two samples to make inferences about the difference between population parameters. As you would expect, we are able to make reliable inferences with fewer assumptions about the sampled populations when the sample sizes are large. When we cannot take large samples from the populations, the **two-sample t statistic** permits us to use the limited sample information to make inferences about the **difference between means** when the assumptions of normality and equal population variances are at least approximately true. The **paired difference experiment** offers the possibility of increasing the information about $(\mu_1 - \mu_2)$ by pairing similar observational units to control variability. In designing a paired difference experiment, we expect that the reduction in variability will more than compensate the loss in degrees of freedom.

Two other inferential procedures for making comparisons between population parameters were presented in this chapter. The **F test** was used to compare two population variances, σ_1^2 and σ_2^2. This test is useful in checking the assumption of equal population variances, an assumption that is essential to the independent samples t test (and confidence interval) for a comparison of two population means. The F test can also be used to compare the variances of two populations when these variances assume practical importance as a measure of risk, error, etc.

This chapter concluded with a comparison of two binomial parameters, p_1 and p_2. Practical examples of such comparisons are numerous; they frequently appear in the analysis of business surveys. A company might want to compare the proportion of consumers who prefer a new product A to a new (or old) product B. Or, the comparison might occur in a production setting when a manufacturer wants to compare the fraction of defectives that emerges from two production lines.

SUPPLEMENTARY EXERCISES

10.44. List the assumptions necessary for each of the following inferential techniques:

    a. Large-sample inferences about the difference $(\mu_1 - \mu_2)$ between population means using a two-sample z statistic.

    b. Small-sample inferences about $(\mu_1 - \mu_2)$ using an independent samples design and a two-sample t statistic.

    c. Small-sample inferences about $(\mu_1 - \mu_2)$ using a paired difference design and a single-sample t statistic to analyze the differences.

    d. Large-sample inferences about the difference $(p_1 - p_2)$ between binomial proportions using a two-sample z statistic.

10.45. To compare the rate of return an investor can expect on tax-free municipal bonds with the rate of return on taxable bonds, an investment advisory firm randomly samples ten bonds of each type and computes the annual rate of return over the past 3 years for each bond. The rate of return is then adjusted for taxes, assuming the investor is in a 30% tax bracket. The mean and standard deviations for the adjusted returns are as follows:

TAX-FREE BONDS	TAXABLE BONDS
$\bar{x}_1 = 7.8\%$	$\bar{x}_2 = 7.3\%$
$s_1 = 1.1\%$	$s_2 = 1.0\%$

    a. Test to see whether there is a difference in the mean rate of return between tax-free and taxable bonds for investors in the 30% tax bracket. Use $\alpha = .05$.

    b. What assumptions were necessary for the validity of the procedure you used in part a?

10.46. Refer to Exercise 10.45. Test the assumption that the two population variances are the same. Use $\alpha = .10$.

10.47. Advertising companies often try to characterize the average user of a client's product so that the advertisements can be targeted at particular segments of the buying community. Suppose a new movie is about to be released and an advertising company wants to determine whether to aim the advertisements at people under 25 years old or those over 25. They plan to arrange an advance showing of the movie to a number of individuals from each group and then to obtain an opinion about the movie from each individual. How many individuals should be included in each sample if the advertising company wants to estimate the difference in the proportions of those who like and dislike the movie to within .05 with 90% confidence? Assume the sample size for each group will be the same and about half of each group will like the movie.

10.48. A consumer protection agency wants to compare the work of two electrical contractors in order to evaluate their safety records. The agency plans to inspect residences in which each of these contractors has done the wiring in order to estimate the differences in the proportion of residences that are electrically deficient. Suppose the proportions of deficient work are expected to be about .10 for both contractors. How many homes should be inspected in order to estimate the difference in proportions to within .05 with 90% confidence?

10.49. Management training programs are often instituted in order to teach supervisory skills and thereby increase productivity. Suppose a company psychologist administers a set of examinations to each of ten supervisors before such a training program begins and then administers similar examinations at the end of the program. The examinations are designed to measure supervisory skills, with higher scores indicating increased skill. The results of the tests are shown on page 285.

SUPERVISOR	BEFORE TRAINING PROGRAM	AFTER TRAINING PROGRAM
1	63	78
2	93	92
3	84	91
4	72	80
5	65	69
6	72	85
7	91	99
8	84	82
9	71	81
10	80	87

Test to see whether the data indicate that the training program is effective. Use $\alpha = .10$.

10.50. Two banks, bank 1 and bank 2, each independently sampled forty and fifty of their business accounts, respectively, and determined the number of the bank's services (loans, checking, savings, investment counseling, etc.) each sampled business was using. Both banks offer the same services. A summary of the data supplied by the samples is listed below:

BANK 1	BANK 2
$\bar{x}_1 = 2.2$	$\bar{x}_2 = 1.8$
$s_1 = 1.15$	$s_2 = 1.10$

Do the samples yield sufficient evidence to conclude that the average number of services used by bank 1's business customers is significantly greater (at the $\alpha = .10$ level) than the average number of services used by bank 2's business customers?

10.51. Find a 99% confidence interval for $(\mu_1 - \mu_2)$ in Exercise 10.50. Does the interval include zero? Interpret the confidence interval.

10.52. Radio stations sometimes conduct prize giveaways in an attempt to increase their share of the listening audience. Suppose a station manager calls 300 randomly selected households in a city, and finds that sixty-five have members who regularly listen to the station. The station then conducts a 2 month promotional contest and follows it with a survey of 500 randomly chosen households. The survey shows that 154 households have members who regularly listen to the station.

    a. Use a 90% confidence interval to estimate the difference between the before and after proportions of those who regularly listen to the station.

    b. Place a 95% confidence interval on the proportion of those who listen to the station after the promotion is over.

10.53. Suppose you have been offered similar jobs in two different locales. To help in deciding which job to accept, you would like to compare the cost of living in the two cities. One of your primary concerns is the cost of housing, so you obtain a copy of a newspaper from each locale and begin to study the housing prices in the classified advertisements. One convenient method for getting a general idea of prices is to compute the prices on a per square foot basis. This is done by dividing the price of the house by the heated area (in square feet) of the house. Random samples of sixty-three advertisements in locale 1 and seventy-eight in locale 2 produce the following results:

LOCALE 1	LOCALE 2
$\bar{x}_1 = 23.40 per square foot	$\bar{x}_2 = 25.20 per square foot
$s_1 = 2.50 per square foot	$s_2 = 2.80 per square foot

Is there evidence that the mean housing price per square foot differs in the two locales?

10.54. Refer to Exercise 10.53. You also want to compare food prices in the two locales. You develop a list of fifteen food items of various types and obtain prices from the newspaper advertisements for a supermarket chain that has a store in each locale. The results are shown below:

FOOD ITEM	LOCALE 1	LOCALE 2
1	$2.49	$2.55
2	0.35	0.37
3	5.12	5.05
4	1.33	1.52
5	0.78	0.85
6	3.03	2.98
7	0.25	0.35
8	4.16	4.29
9	3.83	3.75
10	2.93	3.11
11	1.03	1.25
12	2.13	2.05
13	6.25	6.25
14	2.14	2.30
15	1.98	1.97

a. Do these data provide sufficient evidence to indicate a difference between the mean food prices in the two locales?
b. Can you think of a better way to design the above experiment?

10.55. Some power plants are located near rivers or oceans so that the water can be used for cooling the condensers. As part of an environmental impact study, suppose a power company wants to estimate the mean difference in water temperature between the discharge of its plant and the off-shore waters. How many sample measurements must be taken at each site in order to estimate the true mean difference to within $0.2°C$ with 95% confidence? Assume the range in readings will be about $4°C$ at each site and the same number of readings are to be taken at each site.

10.56. The use of preservatives by food processors has become a controversial issue. Suppose two preservatives are extensively tested and determined safe for use in meats. A processor wants to compare the preservatives for their effects on retarding spoilage. Suppose fifteen cuts of fresh meat are treated with preservative A and fifteen with B, and the number of hours until spoilage begins is recorded for each of the thirty cuts of meat. The results are summarized below:

PRESERVATIVE A	PRESERVATIVE B
$\bar{x}_1 = 106.4$ hours	$\bar{x}_2 = 96.5$ hours
$s_1 = 10.3$ hours	$s_2 = 13.4$ hours

a. Is there evidence of a difference in mean spoilage rate between the two preservatives at the $\alpha = .05$ level?

b. Can you recommend an experimental design that the processor could have used to reduce the variability in the data?

10.57. Refer to Exercise 10.56. Place a 95% confidence interval on the difference between the mean spoilage rates for the two preservatives.

10.58. An economist wants to investigate the difference in unemployment rates between an urban industrial community and a university community in the same state. She interviews 525 potential members of the work force in the industrial community and 375 in the university community. Of these, forty-seven and twenty-two, respectively, are unemployed. Use a 95% confidence interval to estimate the difference in unemployment rates in the two communities.

10.59. A careful auditing is essential to all businesses, large and small. Suppose a firm wants to compare the performance of two auditors it employs. One measure of auditing performance is error rate, so the firm decides to sample 200 pages at random from the work of each auditor and carefully examine each page for errors. Suppose the number of pages on which at least one error is found is seventeen for auditor A and twenty-five for auditor B. Test to see whether these data indicate a difference in the true error rates for the two auditors. Use $\alpha = .01$.

10.60. Since tourism is the largest industry in the state of Florida, the economy of the state depends heavily on the number of tourists who visit Florida annually and on the mean amount of money tourists spend while they are in the state. Suppose a study is conducted during 2 consecutive years, say 1976 and 1977, to compare the mean expenditure of tourists in Florida. Random samples of 325 and 375 tourists (a family is treated as one tourist) are selected in 1976 and 1977, respectively, and the total expenditure in the state is recorded for each. The results are summarized below:

1976	1977
$\bar{x}_1 = \$676$	$\bar{x}_2 = \$853$
$s_1 = \$554$	$s_2 = \$715$
$n_1 = 325$	$n_2 = 375$

a. Form a 90% confidence interval for the difference in mean expenditure per tourist in 1976 and 1977.

b. What assumptions are necessary for the validity of the procedure in part a?

10.61. When new instruments are developed to perform chemical analyses of products (food, medicine, etc.), they are usually evaluated with respect to two criteria: accuracy and precision. *Accuracy* refers to the ability of the instrument to identify correctly the nature and amounts of a product's components. *Precision* refers to the consistency with which the instrument will identify the components of the same material. Thus, a large variability in the identification of a single sample of a product indicates a lack of precision. Suppose a pharmaceutical firm is considering two brands of an instrument that is designed to identify the components of certain drugs. As part of a comparison of precision, ten test-tube samples of a well-mixed batch of a drug are selected and then five are analyzed by instrument A and five by instrument B. The data shown below are the percentages of the primary component of the drug given by the instruments:

INSTRUMENT A	INSTRUMENT B
43	46
48	49
37	43
52	41
45	48

Do these data provide evidence of a difference in the precision of the two machines? Use $\alpha = .10$.

10.62. A large department store plans to renovate one of its floors, with one of the results being an increase in floor space for one department. The management has narrowed the decision about which department to enlarge to two departments: mens' clothing and sporting goods. The final decision will be based on mean sales, with the department having the greater mean to be enlarged. The last 12 months' sales data are shown below:

MONTH	MENS' CLOTHING	SPORTING GOODS
1	$15,726	$17,533
2	11,243	10,895
3	22,325	19,449
4	23,494	21,500
5	12,676	18,925
6	13,492	21,426
7	15,525	16,774
8	15,799	16,223
9	16,449	16,135
10	16,993	17,834
11	19,832	18,429
12	32,434	34,565

a. Use these data to form a 95% confidence interval for the mean difference in monthly sales for the two departments.

b. On the basis of the confidence interval formed in part a, can you make a recommendation to the store management as to which department should be enlarged?

c. What assumptions are necessary to make valid the procedure you used in part a?

10.63. Many college and university professors have been accused of "grade promotion" over the past several years. This means they assign higher grades now than in the past, even though students' work is of the same caliber. If grade promotion has occurred, the mean grade-point average of today's students should exceed the mean of 10 years ago. To test the grade promotion theory at one university, a business professor randomly selects seventy-five business majors who are graduating with the present class and fifty who graduated 10 years ago. The results are shown below:

10 YEARS AGO	PRESENT
$\bar{x}_1 = 2.82$	$\bar{x}_2 = 3.04$
$s_1 = .43$	$s_2 = .38$
$n_1 = 50$	$n_2 = 75$

Test to see whether the data support the hypothesis of grade promotion in the business school of this university. Use $\alpha = .05$.

10.64. Smoke detectors are highly recommended safety devices for early fire detection in homes and businesses. It is extremely important that the devices are not defective. Suppose that 100 brand A smoke detectors are tested and twelve fail to emit a warning signal. Subjected to the same test, fifteen out of ninety brand B detectors fail to operate. Form a 90% confidence interval to estimate the difference in the fraction of defective smoke detectors produced by the two companies. Interpret this confidence interval.

10.65. The federal government is interested in determining whether salary discrimination exists between men and women in the private sector. Suppose random samples of fifteen women and twenty-two men are drawn from the population of first-level managers in the private sector. The information is summarized below:

WOMEN	MEN
$\bar{x}_1 = 18,400$	$\bar{x}_2 = 19,700$
$s_1 = 2,300$	$s_2 = 3,100$
$n_1 = 15$	$n_2 = 22$

a. Do these data provide sufficient evidence to indicate the mean salary of male first-level managers exceeds the mean salary of females in that position?

b. What assumptions are necessary for the validity of the test used in part a?

10.66. Refer to Exercise 10.65. Conduct a test to see whether the data indicate that the assumption of equal salary variances is false.

10.67. An automobile manufacturer wants to estimate the difference in the mean miles per gallon rating for two models of cars that the company produces. If the range of ratings is expected to be about 6 miles per gallon for each model, how many cars for each type must be tested in order to estimate the difference in means to within 0.5 mile per gallon with 95% confidence?

ON YOUR OWN . . .

Many stock market indices, like the Dow Jones Average, act both as indicators of stock market trends and as economic indicators. One way of comparing economic conditions at the end of two consecutive years would be to estimate the difference in mean closing price of all stocks on the New York Stock Exchange. Below we have outlined two methods of sampling to estimate the difference in mean closing price on the last day of market operations for two consecutive years, say 1976 and 1977.

Method 1 (two independent samples)
Step 1. Obtain lists of the closing prices of all stocks on the New York Stock Exchange for the last operating days of 1976 and 1977. (Any library will have these available.)
Step 2. Using a table of random numbers, randomly choose fifteen stocks from the 1976 list and record the closing price of each.
Step 3. Again refer to a table of random numbers and choose a second (independent) sample of fifteen closing prices from the 1977 list.
Step 4. Using the two samples of closing prices, form a 95% confidence interval for the true difference in mean closing prices for the two years.

Method 2 (paired samples)
Step 1. Same as method 1.
Step 2. Same as method 1.
Step 3. Obtain the closing prices for the *same stocks in 1977 as those used in 1976.*
Step 4. Using this set of paired observations, form a 95% confidence interval for the true mean difference in closing prices for the two years.

Before actually collecting any data, state which method you think will provide more information (and why). Then, to compare the two methods, first perform the entire experiment outlined in method 1. After you have completed this, obtain the closing prices for the *same* 1977 stocks as the 1976 stocks analyzed, and complete step 4 of method 2.

Which method provided a shorter confidence interval and thus more information on this performance of the experiment? Does this agree with your preliminary answer?

REFERENCES

Hamburg, M. *Statistical analysis for decision making.* 2d ed. New York: Harcourt Brace Jovanovich, 1977. Chapter 6.

Mendenhall, W. *Introduction to probability and statistics,* 4th ed. North Scituate, Mass.: Duxbury, 1975. Chapter 8.

Neter, J., Wasserman, W. & Whitmore, G. A. *Fundamental statistics for business and economics.* 4th ed. Boston: Allyn and Bacon, 1973. Chapter 14.

Smith, W. M. ''Federal pay procedures and the comparability survey.'' *Monthly Labor Review,* Aug. 1976, 27–31.

Winkler, R. L., & Hays, W. L. *Statistics: Probability, inference, and decision.* 2d ed. New York: Holt, Rinehart, and Winston, 1975. Chapter 6.

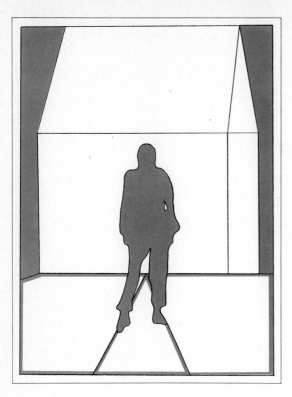

11

SIMPLE LINEAR REGRESSION

WHERE WE'VE BEEN . . .

The answers to many questions that arise in business require knowledge about the mean of a population or about the difference between two population means. Means play an important role in estimating the long-term consequences of business actions. If a new observation is selected from a population, the mean is often used as the predicted (or forecast) value. Estimating and testing hypotheses about means, or the difference between two means, based on random sampling from populations were the subjects of Chapters 9 and 10.

WHERE WE'RE GOING . . .

For many business phenomena, estimating a population mean (or the difference between two means) using the methods of Chapters 9 and 10 is inefficient, because many business variables are related and therefore contribute information about each other. For example, suppose you want to predict the assessed value of a house in a particular community. Using the methods of Chapter 9, you could select a random sample of houses from the community and use the mean of their assessed values to predict the assessed value of the house of interest to you. But using this procedure would ignore the information contained in easily observed variables that are related to assessed house value, namely the square feet of floor space, number of bathrooms, age of the house, etc. In this chapter we will consider the problem of relating the mean value of a single dependent variable y (for example, assessed house value) to a single independent variable x (say, square feet of floor space) using a linear relationship. We will also discuss how to measure the strength of the relationship between y and x, and how to use x to estimate the mean value of y or to predict some future value of y. The more complex problem of relating y to many independent variables will be the topic of Chapter 12.

Much business research is devoted to the topic of **modeling,** i.e., trying to describe how variables are related. For example, an econometrician might be interested in modeling the relationship between the GNP and the current rate of unemployment. An advertising agency might want to know the relationship between a firm's sales revenue and the amount spent on advertising. And an investment firm may be interested in relating the performance of the stock market to the current discount rate of the Federal Reserve Board.

One method of modeling the relationship between variables is called **regression analysis**—this important topic is the subject of Chapters 11–13. In this chapter, we will discuss a simple **linear (straight-line) model** for the relationship between two variables, the **least squares method** of fitting regression models using sample data, how to make inferences about the model, and how to use the model for predictions.

| 11.1 PROBABILISTIC MODELS | An important consideration in merchandising a product is the amount of money spent on advertising. Suppose you want to model the monthly sales revenue of an appliance store as a function of the monthly advertising expenditure. The first question to be answered is this: Do you think an exact relationship exists between these two variables? That is, do you think the exact value of sales revenue can be predicted if the advertising expenditure is specified? We think you will agree with us that this is not possible for several reasons. Sales depend on many variables other than advertising expenditure; for example, time of year, state of the general economy, inventory, and price structure. However, even if many variables are included in the model (the topic of Chapter 12), it is still unlikely that we can *exactly* predict the monthly sales. There will almost certainly be some variation in sales due strictly to **random phenomena** that cannot be modeled or explained. We will refer to all unexplained variations in sales—caused by important but unincluded variables or by unexplainable random phenomena—as **random error.** |

If we construct a model that hypothesizes an exact relationship between variables, it is called a **deterministic model.** For example, if we believe that monthly sales revenue y will be exactly ten times the monthly advertising expenditure x, we write

$$y = 10x$$

This represents a deterministic relationship between the variables y and x.

On the other hand, if we believe that the model should be constructed to allow for random error, then we hypothesize a **probabilistic model.** This includes both a deterministic component and a random error component. For example, if we hypothesize that the sales y is related to advertising x by

$$y = 10x + \text{Random error}$$

we are hypothesizing a **probabilistic** relationship between y and x. Note that the deterministic component of this probabilistic model is $10x$.

As you will subsequently see, the random error will play an important role in testing hypotheses or finding confidence intervals for the deterministic portions of the model and will enable us to estimate the magnitude of the error of prediction when the model is used to predict some value of y to be observed in the future.

We begin with the simplest of probabilistic models—the straight-line model. Fitting this model to a set of data is often called a **regression analysis** or **regression modeling**. The elements of the straight-line model are summarized in the box below.

THE STRAIGHT-LINE MODEL

$$y = \beta_0 + \beta_1 x + \varepsilon$$

where

y = Dependent variable (variable to be modeled)

x = Independent* variable (variable used as a predictor of y)

ε (epsilon) = Random error component

β_0 (beta zero) = y-intercept of the line, i.e., point at which the line intercepts or cuts through the y-axis (see Figure 11.1)

β_1 (beta one) = Slope of the line, i.e., amount of increase (or decrease) in the deterministic component of y for every 1 unit increase in x (see Figure 11.1)

Note that we use Greek symbols, β_0 and β_1, to represent the y-intercept and slope of the model. They are population parameters with numerical values that will be known only if we have access to the entire population of (x, y) measurements.

It is helpful to think of regression modeling as a five step procedure:

Step 1. Hypothesize the deterministic component of the probabilistic model.
Step 2. Use sample data to estimate unknown parameters in the model.
Step 3. Specify the probability distribution of the random error term, and estimate any unknown parameters of this distribution.
Step 4. Statistically check the usefulness of the model.
Step 5. When satisfied that the model is useful, use it for prediction, estimation, etc.

---

*The word *independent* should not be interpreted in a probabilistic sense, as defined in Chapter 5. The phrase *independent variable* is used in regression analysis to refer to a predictor variable for the response y.

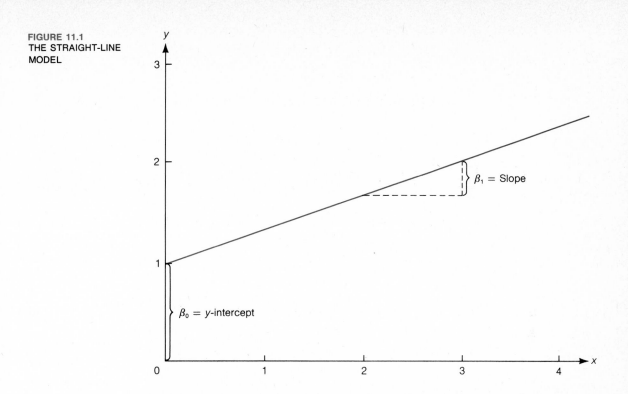

FIGURE 11.1
THE STRAIGHT-LINE
MODEL

In this chapter we will skip step 1 (which is difficult) and deal only with the straight-line model. Chapters 12 and 13 will discuss how to build more complex models.

EXERCISES

11.1. In each case graph the line that passes through the points.

a. (0, 2) and (2, 6)   b. (0, 4) and (2, 6)
c. (0, −2) and (−1, −6)   d. (0, −4) and (3, −7)

11.2. The equation for a straight line (deterministic) is

$$y = \beta_0 + \beta_1 x$$

If the line passes through the point (0, 1), then $x = 0$, $y = 1$ must satisfy the equation, i.e.,

$$1 = \beta_0 + \beta_1(0)$$

Similarly, if the line passes through the point (2, 3), then $x = 2$, $y = 3$ must satisfy the equation, i.e.,

$$3 = \beta_0 + \beta_1(2)$$

Use these two equations to solve for β_0 and β_1, and find the equation of the line that passes through the points (0, 1) and (2, 3).

11.3. Find the equations of the lines passing through the points listed in Exercise 11.1.

11.4. Plot the following lines:

a. $y = 3 + 2x$ b. $y = 1 + x$

c. $y = -2 + 3x$ d. $y = 5x$

e. $y = 4 - 2x$

11.5. Give the slope and y-intercept for each of the lines defined in Exercise 11.4.

11.2
FITTING
THE MODEL:
LEAST SQUARES
APPROACH

Suppose an appliance store conducts a 5 month experiment to determine the effect of advertising on sales revenue. The results are shown in Table 11.1 (the number of measurements and the measurements themselves are unrealistically simple to avoid arithmetic confusion in this initial example). The straight-line model is hypothesized to relate sales revenue y to advertising expenditure x. That is,

$$y = \beta_0 + \beta_1 x + \varepsilon$$

The question is this: How can we best use the information in the sample of five observations in Table 11.1 to estimate the unknown y-intercept β_0 and slope β_1?

TABLE 11.1

MONTH	ADVERTISING EXPENDITURE x, hundreds of dollars	SALES REVENUE y, thousands of dollars
1	1	1
2	2	1
3	3	2
4	4	2
5	5	4

FIGURE 11.2
SCATTERGRAM FOR
DATA IN TABLE 11.1

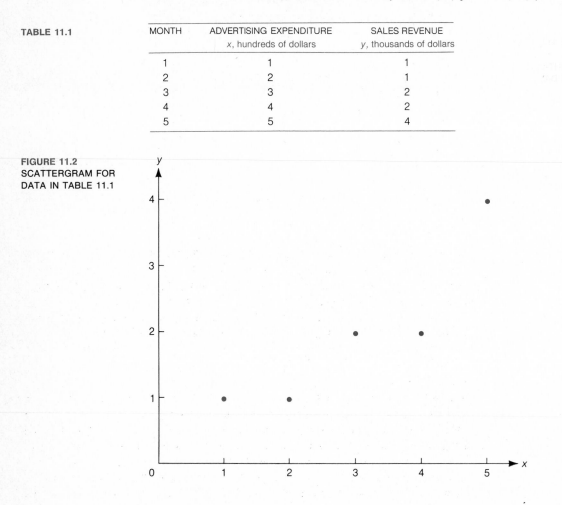

To gain some information on the approximate values of these parameters, it is helpful to plot the sample data. Such a plot, called a scattergram, locates each of the five data points on a graph as shown in Figure 11.2. Note that the scattergram suggests a general tendency for y to increase as x increases. If you place a ruler on the scattergram, you will see that a line may be drawn through three of the five points, as shown in Figure 11.3. To obtain the equation of this visually fitted line, note that the line intersects the y-axis at $y = -1$, so the y-intercept is -1. Also, y increases exactly 1 unit for every 1 unit increase in x, indicating that the slope is $+1$. Therefore, the equation is

$$\tilde{y} = -1 + 1(x) = -1 + x$$

where $\tilde{y}$ is used to denote the predicted y from the visual model.

To evaluate the visual model in Figure 11.3 quantitatively, we compare the observed and predicted values in Table 11.2. Note that the last two columns contain the differences and squared differences, respectively, between the observed and predicted values of the dependent variable. These differences, called errors or deviations, are the vertical distances between observed and predicted values (shown in color in

FIGURE 11.3
VISUAL
STRAIGHT-LINE FIT
TO THE DATA

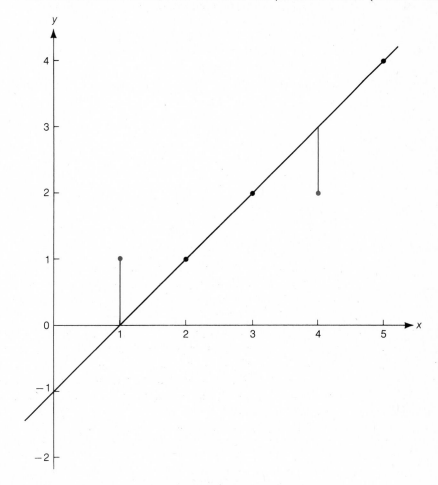

Figure 11.3). Note that the sum of the errors (SE) equals 0 and the sum of the squared errors (SSE), which gives emphasis to large deviations of the points from the line, is equal to 2.

x	y	$\hat{y} = -1 + x$	$(y - \bar{y})$		$(y - \bar{y})^2$
1	1	0	$(1 - 0) =$	1	1
2	1	1	$(1 - 1) =$	0	0
3	2	2	$(2 - 2) =$	0	0
4	2	3	$(2 - 3) =$	-1	1
5	4	4	$(4 - 4) =$	0	0
			Sum of errors (SE) $=$	0	Sum of Squared errors (SSE) $= 2$

You can see by shifting the ruler around the graph that it is possible to find many lines for which SE $= 0$, but it can be shown that there is one (and only one) line for which the SSE is a minimum. This line, called the least squares line or least squares prediction equation, is given by

$$\hat{y} = -.1 + .7x$$

and is shown in Figure 11.4. The observed and predicted values of y, along with the deviations and squares of deviations, are shown in Table 11.3. Note that SE $= 0$, a

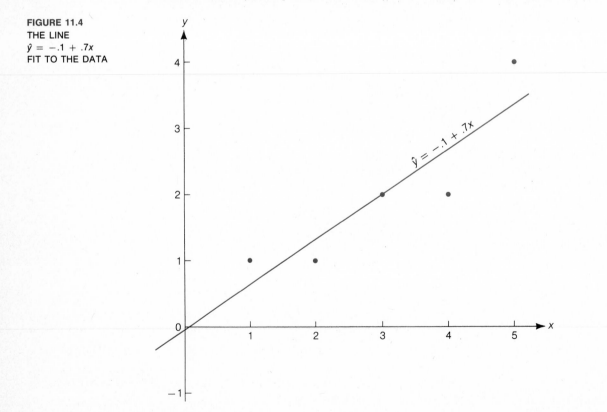

FIGURE 11.4
THE LINE
$\hat{y} = -.1 + .7x$
FIT TO THE DATA

$\hat{y} = -.1 + .7x$

CHAPTER 11 SIMPLE LINEAR REGRESSION

TABLE 11.3	x	y	$\hat{y} = -.1 + .7x$	$(y - \hat{y})$	$(y - \hat{y})^2$
COMPARING OBSERVED	1	1	.6	$(1 - .6) = \quad .4$	0.16
AND PREDICTED	2	1	1.3	$(1 - 1.3) = -.3$	0.09
VALUES FOR THE	3	2	2.0	$(2 - 2.0) = 0$	0.00
LEAST SQUARES	4	2	2.7	$(2 - 2.7) = -.7$	0.49
MODEL	5	4	3.4	$(4 - 3.4) = \quad .6$	0.36
				SE $= 0$	SSE $= 1.10$

property of all least squares lines, and that SSE $= 1.10$. No other line can be found that will produce an SSE as small as 1.10.

DEFINITION 11.1
The least squares line is one that has a smaller SSE than any other straight-line model.

The formulas for computing the y-intercept and slope for the least squares line are given below.

FORMULAS FOR THE LEAST SQUARES LINE*

Slope: $\hat{\beta}_1 = \dfrac{SS_{xy}}{SS_{xx}}$

y-intercept: $\hat{\beta}_0 = \bar{y} - \hat{\beta}_1\bar{x}$

where

$$SS_{xy} = \sum_{i=1}^{n} x_i y_i - \frac{\left(\sum_{i=1}^{n} x_i\right)\left(\sum_{i=1}^{n} y_i\right)}{n}$$

$$SS_{xx} = \sum_{i=1}^{n} x_i^2 - \frac{\left(\sum_{i=1}^{n} x_i\right)^2}{n}$$

n = Sample size

---

*Students who are familiar with the calculus should note that the values of β_0 and β_1 that minimize SSE $= \sum_{i=1}^{n} (y_i - \hat{y}_i)^2$ are obtained by setting the two partial derivatives $\partial SSE/\partial\beta_0$ and $\partial SSE/\partial\beta_1$ equal to zero. The solutions to these two equations yield the formulas shown in the box. Furthermore, we denote the *sample* solutions to the equations by $\hat{\beta}_0$ and $\hat{\beta}_1$, where the ^(hat) denotes that these are sample estimates of the true population intercept β_0 and slope β_1.

TABLE 11.4
PRELIMINARY
COMPUTATIONS
FOR THE
ADVERTISING–SALES
EXAMPLE

x_i	y_i	x_i^2	$x_i y_i$
1	1	1	1
2	1	4	2
3	2	9	6
4	2	16	8
5	4	25	20
Totals $\sum x_i = 15$	$\sum y_i = 10$	$\sum x_i^2 = 55$	$\sum x_i y_i = 37$

Preliminary computations for finding the least squares line for the advertising–sales example are contained in Table 11.4. We can now calculate*

$$SS_{xy} = \sum x_i y_i - \frac{\left(\sum x_i\right)\left(\sum y_i\right)}{5} = 37 - \frac{(15)(10)}{5}$$

$$= 37 - 30 = 7$$

$$SS_{xx} = \sum x_i^2 - \frac{\left(\sum x_i\right)^2}{5} = 55 - \frac{(15)^2}{5}$$

$$= 55 - 45 = 10$$

Then, the slope of the least squares line is

$$\hat{\beta}_1 = \frac{SS_{xy}}{SS_{xx}} = \frac{7}{10} = .7$$

and the y-intercept is

$$\hat{\beta}_0 = \bar{y} - \hat{\beta}_1 \bar{x} = \frac{\sum y_i}{5} - \hat{\beta}_1 \frac{\left(\sum x_i\right)}{5}$$

$$= \frac{10}{5} - (.7)\frac{(15)}{5}$$

$$= 2 - (.7)(3) = 2 - 2.1 = -.1$$

The least squares line is thus

$$\hat{y} = \hat{\beta}_0 + \hat{\beta}_1 x = -.1 + .7x$$

As we have already seen in Table 11.3, the SSE for this model is 1.10.

To summarize, we have defined the best-fitting straight line to be one that satisfies the least squares criterion, that is, the sum of the errors will equal zero and the sum of the squared errors will be smaller than for any other straight-line model. This line is called the least squares line, and its equation is called the least squares prediction equation.

*Since summations will be used extensively from this point on, we will omit the limits on $\sum$ when the summation includes all the measurements in the sample, i.e., when the symbol is $\sum_{i=1}^{n}$, we will write $\sum$.

11.6. Use the method of least squares to fit a straight line to the following six data points:

x	1	2	3	4	5	6
y	1	2	2	3	5	5

a. What are the least squares estimates of β_0 and β_1?
b. Plot the data points and graph the least squares line. Does the line pass through the data points?

11.7. Use the method of least squares to fit a straight line to the following five data points:

x	−2	−1	0	1	2
y	4	3	3	1	−1

a. What are the least squares estimates of β_0 and β_1?
b. Plot the data points and graph the least squares line. Does the line pass through the data points?

11.8. A car dealer is interested in modeling the relationship between the number of cars sold by the firm each week and the number of salespeople who work on the showroom floor. The dealer believes the relationship between the two variables can best be described by a straight line. The sample data shown in the table were supplied by the car dealer.

WEEK OF	NUMBER OF CARS SOLD y	NUMBER OF SALESPEOPLE ON DUTY x
January 30	20	6
June 3	18	6
March 2	10	4
October 26	6	2
February 7	11	3

a. Construct a scattergram for the data.
b. Assuming the relationship between the variables is best described by a straight line, use the method of least squares to estimate the y-intercept and slope of the line.
c. Plot the least squares line on your scattergram.
d. According to your least squares line, approximately how many cars should the dealer expect to sell in a week if five salespeople are kept on the showroom floor each day? [*Note:* A measure of the reliability of these predictions will be discussed in Section 11.7.]

11.9. Find the least squares line to describe the relationship between a company's sales and the total sales for a particular industry. The data are shown in the table. Plot the data points and graph the least squares line as a check on your calculations.

YEAR	COMPANY SALES y, millions of dollars	INDUSTRY SALES x, millions of dollars
1972	0.5	10
1973	1.0	12
1974	1.0	13
1975	1.4	15
1976	1.3	14
1977	1.6	15

11.10. An appliance company is interested in relating the sales rate of 17 inch color television sets to the price per set. To do this, the company randomly selected 15 weeks in the past year and recorded the number of sets sold per week and the price of the set at the time it was sold. The data are shown in the table.

WEEK	NUMBER OF 17 INCH COLOR TELEVISION SETS SOLD PER WEEK y	PRICE x, dollars
1	55	350
2	54	360
3	25	385
4	18	400
5	51	370
6	20	390
7	45	375
8	19	390
9	20	400
10	45	340
11	50	350
12	35	335
13	30	330
14	30	325
15	53	365

a. Find the least squares line relating y to x.
b. Plot the data and graph the least squares line as a check on your calculations.

**11.3
RANDOM ERROR
COMPONENT**

Recall that the hypothesized model relating the firm's sales revenue y to the advertising dollars x is

$$y = \beta_0 + \beta_1 x + \varepsilon$$

and that the least squares estimate of the deterministic component of the model $\beta_0 + \beta_1 x$ is

$$\hat{y} = \hat{\beta}_0 + \hat{\beta}_1 x = -.1 + .7x$$

Now we turn our attention to the random component ε of the probabilistic model and its relation to the errors of estimating β_0 and β_1. In particular, we will see how the probability distribution of ε determines how well the model describes the true relationship between the dependent variable y and the independent variable x.

Although we will estimate the variance of the distribution of ε for a specific problem, we will make four basic assumptions about the general form of the probability distribution of ε.

Assumption 1. The mean of the probability distribution of ε is zero. That is, the average of the errors over an infinitely long series of experiments is zero for each setting of the independent variable x.

Assumption 2. The variance of the probability distribution of ε is constant for all settings of the independent variable x. For our straight-line model, this assumption means that the variance of ε is equal to a constant, say σ^2, for all values of x.

Assumption 3. The probability distribution of ε is normal.

Assumption 4. The errors associated with any two different observations are independent. That is, the error associated with one value of y has no effect on the errors associated with other y values.

The implications of the first three assumptions can be seen in Figure 11.5, which shows distributions of errors for three particular values of x, namely x_1, x_2, and x_3. Note that the relative frequency distributions of the errors are normal, with a mean of zero, and a constant variance σ^2 (all the distributions shown have the same amount of spread or variability). The straight line shown in Figure 11.5 is the mean value of

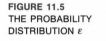

$E(\varepsilon|x) = 0$

$Var(\varepsilon) = \sigma^2$

$\varepsilon_i \sim N(0, \sigma)$

$Cov(\varepsilon_i, \varepsilon_j) = 0$

where's

$Cov(X, \varepsilon) = 0$?

FIGURE 11.5
THE PROBABILITY
DISTRIBUTION ε

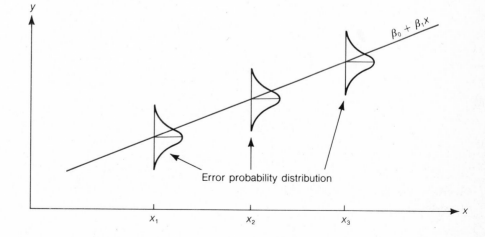

Error probability distribution

y for a given value of *x*. We will denote this mean value as $E(y)$. Then, the line of means is given by the equation

$$E(y) = \beta_0 + \beta_1 x$$

Various techniques exist for checking the validity of these assumptions, and there are remedies to be applied when they appear to be invalid. Most of these are beyond the scope of this text, but we will mention a few in later chapters. In actual practice, the assumptions need not hold exactly in order for the results of a least squares analysis to be valid. They will be satisfied adequately for many applications encountered in business.

If we knew σ^2, the assumptions stated above would completely describe the probability distribution of ε. Therefore, the remaining task to be accomplished in this section is the estimation of σ^2, the variance of ε. To do this, we make use of the SSE for the least squares model, i.e.,

$$SSE = \sum (y_i - \hat{y}_i)^2$$

The estimator s^2 of σ^2 is calculated by dividing the SSE by the number of degrees of freedom associated with the error component. We use 2 df to estimate the *y*-intercept and slope in the straight-line model, leaving $(n - 2)$ df for the error variance estimation.

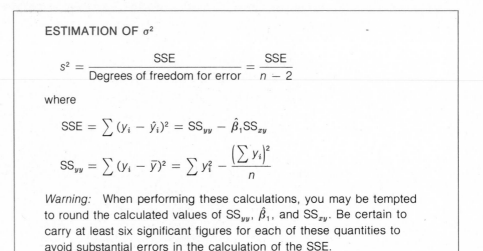

ESTIMATION OF σ^2

$$s^2 = \frac{SSE}{\text{Degrees of freedom for error}} = \frac{SSE}{n - 2}$$

where

$$SSE = \sum (y_i - \hat{y}_i)^2 = SS_{yy} - \hat{\beta}_1 SS_{xy}$$

$$SS_{yy} = \sum (y_i - \bar{y})^2 = \sum y_i^2 - \frac{\left(\sum y_i\right)^2}{n}$$

Warning: When performing these calculations, you may be tempted to round the calculated values of SS_{yy}, $\hat{\beta}_1$, and SS_{xy}. Be certain to carry at least six significant figures for each of these quantities to avoid substantial errors in the calculation of the SSE.

In the advertising–sales example, we previously calculated SSE = 1.10 for the least squares line $\hat{y} = -.1 + .7x$. Recalling that there were $n = 5$ data points, we have $(n - 2)$ or $5 - 2 = 3$ df for estimating σ^2. Thus,

$$s^2 = \frac{SSE}{n - 2} = \frac{1.10}{3} = .367$$

is the estimated variance, and

$$s = \sqrt{.367} = .61$$

is the estimated standard deviation of ε.

You may be able to obtain an intuitive feeling for s by recalling the interpretation given to a standard deviation in Chapter 4 and remembering that the least squares line estimates the mean value of y for a given value of x. Since s measures the spread of the distribution of y values about the least squares line, we should not be surprised to find that most of the observations lie within $2s$ or $2(.61) = 1.22$ of the least squares line. For this simple example (only five data points), all five data points fall within $2s$ of the least squares line. As you will subsequently see, we will use s to evaluate the error of prediction when the least squares line is used to predict a value of y to be observed for a given value of x.

EXERCISES

11.11. Suppose you fit a least squares line to nine data points and calculate the SSE to be .219. Find s^2, the estimator of σ^2 and the variance of the random error term ε.

11.12. Calculate the SSE and s^2 for the least squares lines plotted in:

    a. Exercise 11.6   b. Exercise 11.7
    c. Exercise 11.8   d. Exercise 11.9
    e. Exercise 11.10

11.13. An electronics dealer believes that there is a positive linear relationship between the number of hours of quadraphonic programming on a city's FM stations and sales of quadraphonic systems. Records for the dealer's sales during the last 6 months and the amount of quadraphonic programming for the corresponding months are given in the table.

MONTH	AVERAGE AMOUNT OF QUADRAPHONIC PROGRAMMING x, hours	NUMBER OF QUADRAPHONIC SYSTEMS SOLD y
1	33.6	7
2	36.3	10
3	38.7	13
4	36.6	11
5	39.0	14
6	38.4	18

    a. Fit a least squares line to the data.
    b. Plot the data and graph the least squares line as a check on your calculations.
    c. Calculate the SSE and s^2.

11.14. A company keeps extensive records on its new salespeople on the premise that sales should increase with experience. A random sample of seven new salespeople produced the data on experience and sales shown in the table.

MONTHS ON JOB x	MONTHLY SALES y, thousands of dollars
2	2.4
4	7.0
8	11.3
12	15.0
1	0.8
5	3.7
9	12.0

a. Fit a least squares line to the data.
b. Plot the data and graph the least squares line.
c. Predict the sales that a new salesperson would be expected to generate after 6 months on the job. After 9 months.
d. Calculate the SSE and s^2.

11.4
ASSESSING THE UTILITY OF THE MODEL: MAKING INFERENCES ABOUT THE SLOPE β_1

Refer again to the data of Table 11.1 and suppose that the appliance store's sales revenue is **completely unrelated** to the advertising expenditure. What could be said about the values of β_0 and β_1 in the hypothesized probabilistic model

$$y = \beta_0 + \beta_1 x + \varepsilon$$

if x contributes no information for the prediction of y? The implication is that the mean of y, i.e., the deterministic part of the model $E(y) = \beta_0 + \beta_1 x$, does not change as x changes. In the straight-line model, this means that the true slope, β_1, is equal to zero. Therefore, to test the null hypothesis that x contributes no information for the prediction of y against the alternative hypothesis that these variables are linearly related with a slope differing from zero, we test

$$H_0: \quad \beta_1 = 0 \qquad H_a: \quad \beta_1 \neq 0$$

If the data support the alternative hypothesis, we will conclude that x does contribute information for the prediction of y using the straight-line model [although the true relationship between $E(y)$ and x could be more complex than a straight line]. Thus, to some extent, this is a test of the utility* of the hypothesized model.

The appropriate test statistic is found by considering the sampling distribution of $\hat{\beta}_1$, the least squares estimator of the slope β_1.

---

*We are using the word *utility* in Chapters 11–13 in a literal sense. It should not be confused with the more technical business usage in risk analysis.

FIGURE 11.6
SAMPLING
DISTRIBUTION OF $\hat{\beta}_1$

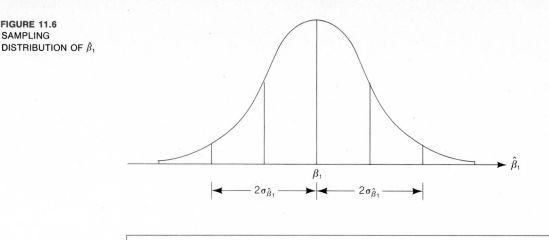

SAMPLING DISTRIBUTION OF $\hat{\beta}_1$
If we make the four assumptions about ε (see Section 11.3), the sampling distribution of the least squares estimator of slope, $\hat{\beta}_1$, will be normal, with mean β_1 (the true slope) and standard deviation

$$\sigma_{\hat{\beta}_1} = \frac{\sigma}{\sqrt{SS_{xx}}}$$ See Figure 11.6.

Since σ will usually be unknown, the appropriate test statistic will generally be a Student's t statistic formed as follows:

$$t = \frac{\hat{\beta}_1 - \text{Hypothesized value of } \beta_1}{s_{\hat{\beta}_1}}$$ where $s_{\hat{\beta}_1} = \frac{s}{\sqrt{SS_{xx}}}$

$$= \frac{\hat{\beta}_1 - 0}{s/\sqrt{SS_{xx}}}$$

Note that we have substituted the estimator s for σ, and then formed $s_{\hat{\beta}_1}$ by dividing s by $\sqrt{SS_{xx}}$. The number of degrees of freedom associated with this t statistic is the same as the number of degrees of freedom associated with s. Recall that this will be $(n - 2)$ df when the hypothesized model is a straight line (see Section 11.3).

The setup of our test of the utility of the model is summarized below.

A TEST OF MODEL UTILITY

$$H_0: \ \beta_1 = 0 \qquad H_a: \ \beta_1 \neq 0$$

Test statistic: $\quad t = \dfrac{\hat{\beta}_1}{s_{\hat{\beta}_1}} = \dfrac{\hat{\beta}_1}{s/\sqrt{SS_{xx}}}$

Assumptions: The four assumptions about ε listed in Section 11.3

Rejection region: $t < -t_{\alpha/2, n-2}$ $\qquad$ or $\qquad$ $t > t_{\alpha/2, n-2}$

FIGURE 11.7
REJECTION REGION
AND CALCULATED
t VALUE FOR
TESTING WHETHER
THE SLOPE $\beta_1 = 0$

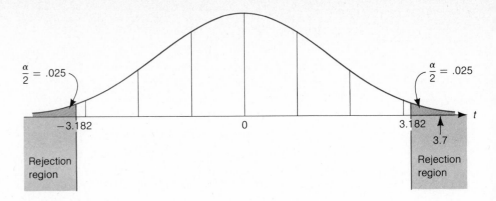

For the advertising–sales example, we will choose $\alpha = .05$ and, since $n = 5$, our rejection region is

$$t < -t_{.025, 5-2} = -3.182$$

$$t > \quad t_{.025, 3} \quad = 3.182$$

We previously calculated $\hat{\beta}_1 = .7$, $s = .61$, and $SS_{xx} = 10$. Thus,

$$t = \frac{\hat{\beta}_1}{s / \sqrt{SS_{xx}}} = \frac{.7}{.61 / \sqrt{10}} = \frac{.7}{.19} = 3.7$$

Since this calculated *t* value falls in the upper-tail rejection region (see Figure 11.7), we reject the null hypothesis and conclude that the slope β_1 is not zero. The sample evidence indicates that *x* contributes information for the prediction of *y* using a linear model for the relationship between sales revenue and advertising.

What conclusion can be drawn if the calculated *t* value does not fall in the rejection region? We know from previous discussions of the philosophy of hypothesis testing that such a *t* value does *not* lead us to accept the null hypothesis. That is, we do not conclude that $\beta_1 = 0$. Additional data might indicate that β_1 differs from zero, or a more complex relationship may exist between *x* and *y*, requiring the fitting of a model other than the straight-line model. We will discuss several such models in Chapter 12.

Another way to make inferences about the slope of β_1 is to estimate it using a confidence interval. This interval is formed as shown below.

A 100(1 − α) PERCENT CONFIDENCE INTERVAL FOR THE SLOPE β_1

$$\hat{\beta}_1 \pm t_{\alpha/2, n-2} s_{\hat{\beta}_1}$$

where

$$s_{\hat{\beta}_1} = \frac{s}{\sqrt{SS_{xx}}}$$

For the advertising–sales example, a 95% confidence interval for the slope β_1 is

$$\hat{\beta}_1 \pm t_{.025,3}s_{\hat{\beta}_1} = .7 \pm 3.182\left(\frac{s}{\sqrt{SS_{xx}}}\right)$$

$$= .7 \pm 3.182\left(\frac{.61}{\sqrt{10}}\right) = .7 \pm .61$$

Thus, we estimate that the interval from .09 to 1.31 includes the slope parameter β_1.

Since all the values in this interval are positive, it appears that β_1 is positive and that the mean of y, $E(y)$, increases as x increases. However, the rather large width of the confidence interval reflects the small number of data points (and, consequently, a lack of information) in the experiment. We would expect a narrower interval if the sample size were increased.

EXERCISES

11.15. Do the data provide sufficient evidence to indicate that β_1 differs from zero for the least squares analyses in the following exercises (use $\alpha = .05$)?

    a.   Exercise 11.6   b.   Exercise 11.7
    c.   Exercise 11.8   d.   Exercise 11.9
    e.   Exercise 11.10

11.16. Do the data in Exercise 11.13 provide sufficient evidence to indicate that sales, y, tend to increase as the number of hours of programming, x, increases (i.e., that $\beta_1 > 0$)? Test using $\alpha = .10$.

11.17. Do the data in Exercise 11.14 support the theory that sales increase as experience of a salesperson increases? Test using $\alpha = .05$.

11.18. A local brewery is interested in determining whether a linear relationship exists between the amount it spends on television advertising and total sales. The data listed in the table is available.

MONTH	SALES Thousands of dollars	TELEVISION ADVERTISING EXPENDITURES Thousands of dollars
January	50	0.5
February	90	0.9
March	30	0.4
April	90	0.7
May	91	1.1
June	95	0.75
July	95	0.8

    a.   Find the least squares line for the given data. Plot the data on a scattergram and graph the line as a check on your calculations.

    b.   Letting $\alpha = .05$, test the null hypothesis that $\beta_1 = 0$. What alternative hypothesis would you select for this test? Draw appropriate conclusions concerning the adequacy of a linear model to describe the relationship between sales and television advertising expenditures.

c. Construct a 90% confidence interval for the slope parameter in the hypothesized linear model.

d. Interpret the confidence interval and explain what it tells you about the relationship between sales and television advertising expenditure.

11.19. Buyers are often influenced by bulk advertising of a particular product. For example, suppose you have a product that sells for 25¢. If it is advertised at 2/50¢, 3/75¢, or 4/$1, some people may think they are getting a bargain. To test this theory, a store manager advertised an item for equal periods of time at five different bulk rates and observed the data listed in the table. Do the data provide sufficient evidence to indicate that sales increase as the number in the bulk increases?

ADVERTISED NUMBER IN BULK SALE	VOLUME SOLD
x	y
1	27
2	36
3	34
4	63
5	52

11.20. A large car rental agency sells its cars after using them for a year. Among the records kept for each car are mileage and maintenance costs for the year. To evaluate the performance of a particular car model in terms of maintenance costs, the agency wants to use a 95% confidence interval to estimate the mean increase in maintenance costs for each additional 1,000 miles driven. Assume the relationship between maintenance cost and miles driven is linear.

CAR	MILES DRIVEN x, thousands	MAINTENANCE COST y, dollars
1	54	326
2	27	159
3	29	202
4	32	200
5	28	181
6	36	217

Use these data to accomplish the objective of the rental agency.

11.5 CORRELATION: ANOTHER MEASURE OF THE UTILITY OF THE MODEL

The claim is often made that the crime rate and the unemployment rate are "highly correlated." Another popular belief is that the GNP and the rate of inflation are "correlated." Some people even believe that the Dow Jones Industrial Average and the lengths of fashionable skirts are "correlated." In this section, we will discuss the concept of correlation.

Note that the computational formula for the correlation coefficient r given in Definition 11.2 involves the same quantities that were used in computing the least squares prediction equation. In fact, it can be shown that r measures the strength of the linear

FIGURE 11.8
VALUES OF r AND
THEIR IMPLICATIONS

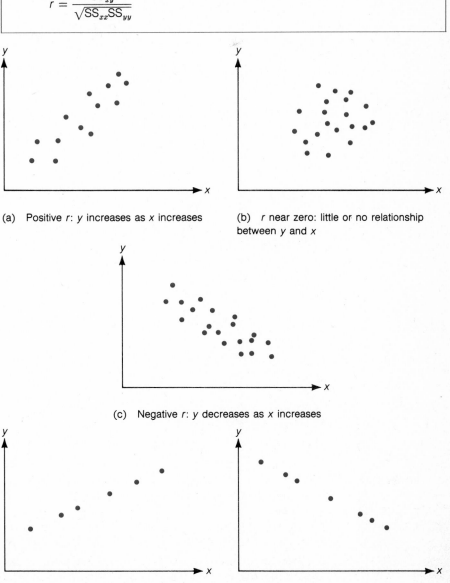

(a) Positive r: y increases as x increases

(b) r near zero: little or no relationship between y and x

(c) Negative r: y decreases as x increases

(d) $r = 1$: a perfect positive relationship between y and x

(e) $r = -1$: a perfect negative relationship between y and x

relationship between x and y, just as the least squares slope $\hat{\beta}_1$, does. However, unlike the slope, the correlation coefficient r is **scaleless**. The value of r is always between -1 and $+1$, no matter what the units of x and y are.

A value of r near or equal to zero implies little or no linear relationship between y and x. In contrast, the closer r approaches 1 or -1, the stronger the linear relationship between y and x. And, if $r = 1$ or $r = -1$, all the points fall exactly on the least squares line. Positive values of r imply that y increases as x increases; negative values imply that y decreases as x increases. Each of these situations is portrayed in Figure 11.8.

EXAMPLE 11.1   A firm wants to know the correlation between the size of its sales force and its yearly sales revenue. The records for the past 10 years are examined, and the results listed in Table 11.5 are obtained. Calculate the coefficient of correlation, r, for this data.

TABLE 11.5

YEAR	NUMBER OF SALESPEOPLE x	SALES y, hundred thousand dollars
1967	15	1.35
1968	18	1.63
1969	24	2.33
1970	22	2.41
1971	25	2.63
1972	29	2.93
1973	30	3.41
1974	32	3.26
1975	35	3.63
1976	38	4.15

Solution   We need to calculate SS_{xy}, SS_{xx}, and SS_{yy}.

$$SS_{xy} = \sum x_i y_i - \frac{\left(\sum x_i\right)\left(\sum y_i\right)}{10} = 800.62 - \frac{(268)(27.73)}{10} = 57.456$$

$$SS_{xx} = \sum x_i^2 - \frac{\left(\sum x_i\right)^2}{10} = 7,668 - \frac{(268)^2}{10} = 485.6$$

$$SS_{yy} = \sum y_i^2 - \frac{\left(\sum y_i\right)^2}{10} = 83.8733 - \frac{(27.73)^2}{10} = 6.97801$$

Then, the coefficient of correlation is

$$r = \frac{SS_{xy}}{\sqrt{SS_{xx}SS_{yy}}} = \frac{57.456}{\sqrt{(485.6)(6.97801)}} = \frac{57.456}{58.211} = .99$$

Thus, the size of the sales force and sales revenue are very highly correlated—at least over the past 10 years. The implication is that a strong positive linear relation-

FIGURE 11.9
SCATTERGRAM FOR
EXAMPLE 11.1

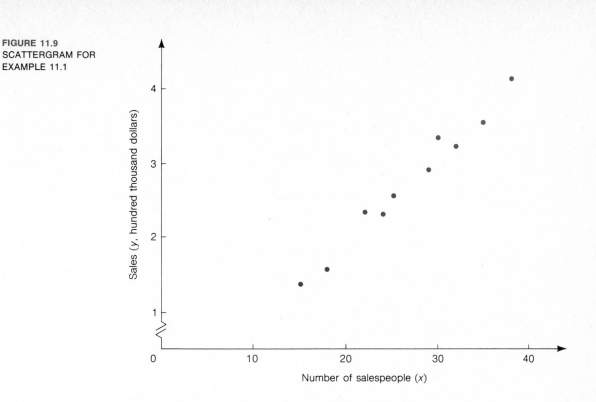

ship exists between these variables (see Figure 11.9). We must be careful, however, not to jump to any unwarranted conclusions. For instance, the firm may be tempted to conclude that the best thing it can do to increase sales is to hire a large number of new salespeople. The implication of such a conclusion is that there is a causal relationship between the two variables. However, high correlation does not imply causality. The fact is, many things have probably contributed both to the increase in the size of the sales force and to the increase in sales revenue. The firm's expertise has undoubtedly grown, the economy has inflated (so that 1976 dollars are not worth as much as 1967 dollars), and perhaps the scope of products and services sold by the firm has widened. We must be careful not to infer a causal relationship on the basis of high sample correlation. The only safe conclusion when a high correlation is observed in the sample data is that a linear trend may exist between x and y.

Keep in mind that the correlation coefficient r measures the correlation between x values and y values in the sample, and that a similar linear coefficient of correlation exists for the population from which the data points were selected. The population correlation coefficient is denoted by the symbol ρ (rho). As you might expect, ρ is estimated by the corresponding sample statistic, r. Or, rather than estimating ρ, we might want to test the hypothesis H_0: $\rho = 0$ against H_a: $\rho \neq 0$, i.e., test the hypothesis that x contributes no information for the prediction of y using the straight-line model against the alternative that the two variables are at least linearly related.

However, we have already performed this *identical* test in Section 11.4 when we tested H_0: $\beta_1 = 0$ against H_a: $\beta_1 \neq 0$. When we tested the null hypothesis H_0: $\beta_1 = 0$ in connection with the advertising–sales example, the data led to a rejection of the hypothesis at the $\alpha = .05$ level. This implies that the null hypothesis of a zero linear correlation between the two variables (advertising and sales) can also be rejected at the $\alpha = .05$ level. The only real difference between the least squares slope $\hat{\beta}_1$ and the coefficient of correlation r is the measurement scale. Therefore, the information they provide about the utility of the least squares model is to some extent redundant. For this reason, we will use the slope to make inferences about the existence of a positive or negative linear relationship between two variables.

11.6 COEFFICIENT OF DETERMINATION

Another way to measure the contribution of x in predicting y is to consider how much the errors of prediction of y were reduced by using the information provided by x. If you had not used x, the best prediction for any value of y would be $\bar{y}$, and the sum of squares of the deviations of the y values about $\bar{y}$ is the familiar

$$SS_{yy} = \sum (y_i - \bar{y})^2$$

On the other hand, if we use x to predict y, the sum of squares of the deviations of the y values about the least squares line is

$$SSE = \sum (y_i - \hat{y})^2$$

Then, the drop in the sum of squares of deviations that can be attributed to x, expressed as a proportion of SS_{yy}, is

$$\frac{SS_{yy} - SSE}{SS_{yy}}$$

It can be shown that this quantity is equal to the square of the simple linear coefficient of correlation.

> DEFINITION 11.3
> The square of the coefficient of correlation is called the coefficient of determination. It represents the proportion of the sum of squares of deviations of the y values about their mean that can be attributed to a linear relation between y and x.
>
> $$r^2 = \frac{SS_{yy} - SSE}{SS_{yy}} = 1 - \frac{SSE}{SS_{yy}}$$

Note that r^2 is always between 0 and 1, because r is between -1 and $+1$. Thus, an r^2 of .60 means that the sum of squares of deviations of the y values about their mean has been reduced 60% by the use of the linear predictor $\hat{y}$.

EXAMPLE 11.2   Calculate the coefficient of determination for the advertising–sales example. The data are repeated in Table 11.6 for convenience.

TABLE 11.6

ADVERTISING EXPENDITURE x, hundreds of dollars	SALES REVENUE y, thousands of dollars
1	1
2	1
3	2
4	2
5	4

Solution   We first calculate

$$SS_{yy} = \sum y_i^2 - \frac{\left(\sum y_i\right)^2}{5} = 26 - \frac{(10)^2}{5}$$

$$= 26 - 20 = 6$$

From previous calculations,

$$SSE = \sum (y_i - \hat{y}_i)^2 = 1.10$$

Then, the coefficient of determination is given by

$$r^2 = \frac{SS_{yy} - SSE}{SS_{yy}} = \frac{6.0 - 1.1}{6.0} = \frac{4.9}{6.0}$$

$$= .82$$

So we know that the use of the advertising expenditure x to predict y, using the least squares line

$$\hat{y} = -.1 + .7x$$

reduces the total sum of squares of deviations of the five sample y values about their mean by 82%.

CASE STUDY 11.1   As evidenced by the cost overruns of public building projects, the initial estimate of the ultimate cost of a structure is often rather poor. These estimates usually rely on a precise definition of the proposed building in terms of working drawings and specifications. However, cost estimators do not take random error into account, so that no measure of reliability is possible for their deterministic estimates. Crandall and Cedercreutz (1976) propose the use of a probabilistic model to make cost estimates. They use regression models to relate cost to independent variables like volume, amount of glass, floor area, etc. Crandall and Cedercreutz's rationale for choosing this approach is that "one of the principal merits of the least squares regression

FIGURE 11.10
SIMPLE LINEAR
MODEL RELATING
COST TO FLOOR AREA

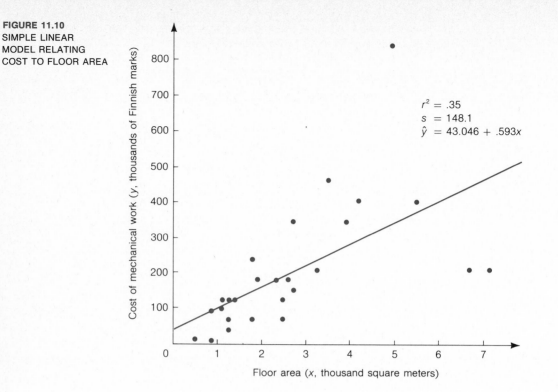

$r^2 = .35$
$s = 148.1$
$\hat{y} = 43.046 + .593x$

Cost of mechanical work (y, thousands of Finnish marks)

Floor area (x, thousand square meters)

model, for the purpose of preliminary cost estimating, is the method of dealing with anticipated error.'' They go on to point out that when random error is anticipated, "statistical methods, such as regression analysis, attack the problem head on.''

Crandall and Cedercreutz initially focused on the cost of mechanical work (heating, ventilating, and plumbing), since this part of the total cost is generally difficult to predict. Conventional cost estimates rely heavily on the amount of ductwork and piping used in construction, but this information is not precisely known until too late to be of use to the cost estimator. One of several models discussed was a simple linear model relating mechanical cost to floor area. Based upon the data associated with twenty-six factory and warehouse buildings, the least squares prediction equation given in Figure 11.10 was found. It was concluded that floor area and mechanical cost are linearly related, since the t statistic (for testing H_0: $\beta_1 = 0$) was found to equal 3.61, which is significant with an α as small as .002. Thus, floor area should be useful when predicting the mechanical cost of a factory or warehouse. In addition, the regression model enables the reliability of the predicted cost to be assessed.

The value of the coefficient of determination, r^2, was found to be .35. This tells us that only 35% of the variation among mechanical costs is accounted for by the differences in floor areas. Since there is only one independent variable in the model, this relatively small value of r^2 should not be too surprising. If other variables related to mechanical cost were included in the model, they would probably account for a significant portion of the remaining 65% of the variation in mechanical cost not explained by floor area. In the next chapter we discuss this important aspect of relating a response to more than one independent variable.

EXERCISES

11.21. Find the correlation coefficient and the coefficient of determination for the sample data listed in the table and interpret your results.

YEAR	NUMBER OF EIGHTEEN HOLE AND LARGER GOLF COURSES IN THE UNITED STATES	UNITED STATES DIVORCE RATE PER 1,000 POPULATION
1960	2,725	2.2
1965	3,769	2.5
1970	4,845	3.5
1972	5,385	4.1
1975	6,282	4.8

Source: United States Bureau of the Census, *Statistical Abstracts of the United States 1976.*

11.22. Find the correlation coefficient and the coefficient of determination for the sample data listed in the table and interpret your results.

YEAR	GROSS NATIONAL PRODUCT Billions of 1972 dollars	NEW HOUSING STARTS Thousands
1960	736.8	1,296
1965	925.9	1,510
1970	1,075.3	1,469
1973	1,235.0	2,057
1974	1,214.0	1,352
1975	1,191.7	1,171

Source: United States Bureau of the Census, *Statistical Abstracts of the United States 1976.*

11.23. Data on monthly sales, y, price per unit during the month, x_1, and amount spent on advertising, x_2, for a product are shown in the table for a 5 month period. Based on this sample, which variable—price or advertising expenditure—appears to provide more information about sales? Explain.

MONTH	TOTAL MONTHLY SALES y, thousands of dollars	PRICE PER UNIT x_1, dollars	AMOUNT SPENT ON ALL FORMS OF ADVERTISING x_2, hundreds of dollars
June	40	0.85	6.0
July	50	0.76	5.0
August	55	0.75	8.0
September	30	1.00	7.5
October	45	0.80	5.5

11.24. In analyzing the costs of construction, labor and material costs are two basic components. Changes in the component costs, of course, will lead to changes in total construction costs.

    a. Use the data in the table to find a measure of the importance of the materials component. Do this by determining the fraction of reduction in the variability of the construction cost index that can be explained by a linear relationship between the construction cost index and the material cost index.

    b. Do the data provide sufficient evidence to indicate a nonzero correlation between y and x?

MONTH	CONSTRUCTION COST* y	INDEX OF ALL CONSTRUCTION MATERIALS[†] x
January	193.2	180.0
February	193.1	181.7
March	193.6	184.1
April	195.1	185.3
May	195.6	185.7
June	198.1	185.9
July	200.9	187.7
August	202.7	189.6

*Source: United States Department of Commerce, Bureau of the Census.

[†] Source: United States Department of Labor, Bureau of Labor Statistics. Tables were given in Tables E-1 (p. 43) and E-2 (p. 44), respectively, in *Construction Review*, United States Department of Commerce, Oct. 1976, 22 (8).

11.25.

TOTAL OUTPUT y	TOTAL VARIABLE COST x, dollars
10	10
15	12
20	20
20	21
25	22
30	20
30	19

Use the method of least squares and the sample data in the table to model the relationship between the number of items produced by a particular manufacturing process and the total variable cost involved in production. Find the coefficient of determination and explain its significance in the context of this problem.

**11.7
USING THE
MODEL FOR
ESTIMATION
AND
PREDICTION**

If we are satisfied that a useful model has been found to describe the relationship between sales revenue and advertising, we are ready to accomplish the original objectives for building the model: using it to estimate or to predict sales on the basis of advertising dollars spent.

The most common uses of a probabilistic model can be divided into two categories. The first is the use of the model for estimating the mean value of y, $E(y)$, for a specific value of x. For our example, we may want to estimate the mean sales revenue for *all* months during which \$400 ($x = 4$) is expended on advertising. The second use of the model entails predicting a particular y value for a given x. That is, if we decide to expend \$400 next month, we want to predict the firm's sales revenue for that month.

In the case of estimating a mean value of y, we are attempting to estimate the mean result of a very large number of experiments at the given x value. In the second case, we are trying to predict the outcome of a single experiment at the given x value. In which of these model uses do you expect to have more success, i.e., which value, the mean or individual value of y, can we estimate (or predict) with more accuracy?

Before answering this question, we first consider the problem of choosing an estimator (or predictor) of the mean (or individual) y value. We will use the least squares model

$$\hat{y} = \hat{\beta}_0 + \hat{\beta}_1 x$$

**FIGURE 11.11
ESTIMATED MEAN
VALUE AND PREDICTED
INDIVIDUAL VALUE
OF SALES REVENUE, y,
FOR $x = 4$**

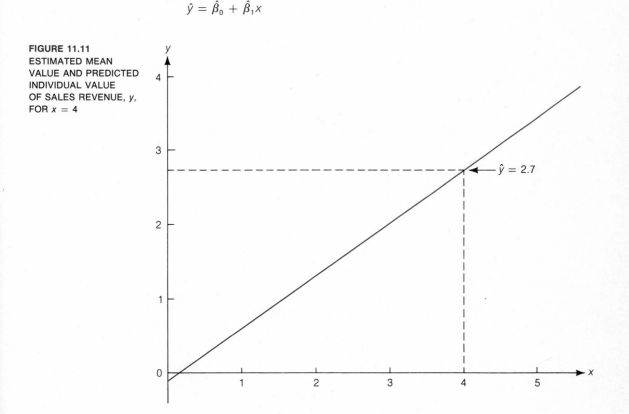

to estimate both the mean value of y and predict a particular value of y for a given value of x. For our example, we found

$$\hat{y} = -.1 + .7x$$

so that the estimated mean value of sales revenue for all months when $x = 4$ (advertising $= \$400$) is

$$\hat{y} = -.1 + .7(4) = 2.7$$

or $2,700 (the units of y are thousands of dollars). The identical value is used to predict the y value when $x = 4$. That is, both the estimated *and* the predicted value of y equal $\hat{y} = 2.7$ when $x = 4$, as shown in Figure 11.11.

The difference in these two model uses lies in the relative accuracy of the estimate and the prediction. These accuracies are best measured by the repeated sampling errors of the least squares line when it is used as an estimator and as a predictor, respectively. These errors are given below.

SAMPLING ERRORS FOR THE ESTIMATOR OF THE MEAN OF y AND THE PREDICTOR OF AN INDIVIDUAL y

1. The standard deviation of the sampling distribution of the estimator $\hat{y}$ of the mean value of y at a fixed x is

$$\sigma_{\hat{y}} = \sigma \sqrt{\frac{1}{n} + \frac{(x - \bar{x})^2}{SS_{xx}}}$$

where σ is the standard deviation of the random error ε.

2. The standard deviation of the prediction error for the predictor $\hat{y}$ of an individual y value at a fixed x is

$$\sigma_{(y - \hat{y})} = \sigma \sqrt{1 + \frac{1}{n} + \frac{(x - \bar{x})^2}{SS_{xx}}}$$

where σ is the standard deviation of the random error ε.

The true value of σ will rarely be known. Thus, we estimate σ by s and calculate the estimation and prediction intervals as shown below.

A $100(1 - \alpha)$ PERCENT CONFIDENCE INTERVAL FOR THE MEAN VALUE OF y AT A FIXED x

$$\hat{y} \pm t_{\alpha/2, n-2} \,(\text{Estimated standard deviation of } \hat{y})$$

or

$$\hat{y} \pm t_{\alpha/2, n-2}\, s \sqrt{\frac{1}{n} + \frac{(x - \bar{x})^2}{SS_{xx}}}$$

> **A 100(1 − α) PERCENT PREDICTION INTERVAL FOR AN INDIVIDUAL y AT A FIXED x**
>
> $$\hat{y} \pm t_{\alpha/2, n-2} \; [\text{Estimated standard deviation of } (y - \hat{y})]$$
>
> or
>
> $$\hat{y} \pm t_{\alpha/2, n-2} \; s \sqrt{1 + \frac{1}{n} + \frac{(x - \bar{x})^2}{SS_{xx}}}$$

EXAMPLE 11.3

Find a 95% confidence interval for mean monthly sales when the appliance store spends $400 on advertising.

Solution

For a $400 advertising expenditure, $x = 4$ and the confidence interval for the mean value of y is

$$\hat{y} \pm t_{\alpha/2, n-2} s \sqrt{\frac{1}{n} + \frac{(x - \bar{x})^2}{SS_{xx}}}$$

or

$$\hat{y} \pm t_{.025,3} s \sqrt{\frac{1}{5} + \frac{(4 - \bar{x})^2}{SS_{xx}}}$$

Recall that $\hat{y} = 2.7$, $s = .61$, $\bar{x} = 3$ and $SS_{xx} = 10$. From Table V of Appendix B, $t_{.025,3} = 3.182$. Thus, we have

$$2.7 \pm (3.182)(.61) \sqrt{\frac{1}{5} + \frac{(4 - 3)^2}{10}} = 2.7 \pm (3.182)(.61)(.55)$$

$$= 2.7 \pm 1.1$$

We estimate that the interval from $1,600 to $3,800 encloses the mean sales revenue when the store expends $400 a month on advertising. Note that we used a small amount of data for purposes of illustration in fitting the least squares line and that the interval would probably be narrower if a larger amount of data had been employed.

EXAMPLE 11.4

Predict the monthly sales for next month if a $400 expenditure is to be made on advertising. Use a 95% prediction interval.

Solution

To predict the sales for a particular month for which $x = 4$, we calculate the 95% prediction interval as

$$\hat{y} \pm t_{\alpha/2, n-2} s \sqrt{1 + \frac{1}{n} + \frac{(x - \bar{x})^2}{SS_{xx}}} = 2.7 \pm (3.182)(.61) \sqrt{1 + \frac{1}{5} + \frac{(4 - 3)^2}{10}}$$

$$= 2.7 \pm (3.182)(.61)(1.14) = 2.7 \pm 2.2$$

FIGURE 11.12
A 95% CONFIDENCE
INTERVAL FOR
MEAN SALES AND A
PREDICTION INTERVAL
FOR SALES WHEN
$x = 4$

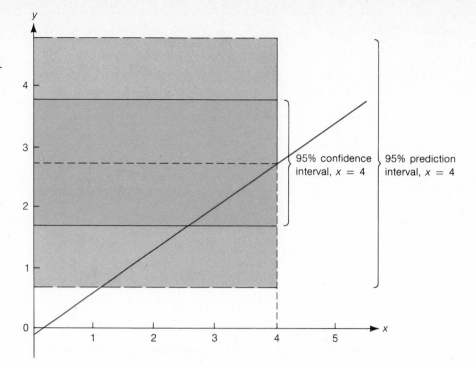

Therefore, we predict that the sales next month will fall in the interval from $500 to $4,900. As in the case for the confidence interval for the mean value of y, the prediction interval for y is quite large. This is because we have chosen a simple example (only five data points) to fit the least squares line. The width of the prediction interval could be reduced by using a larger number of data points.

FIGURE 11.13
ERROR OF ESTIMATING
THE MEAN VALUE
OF y FOR A GIVEN
VALUE OF x

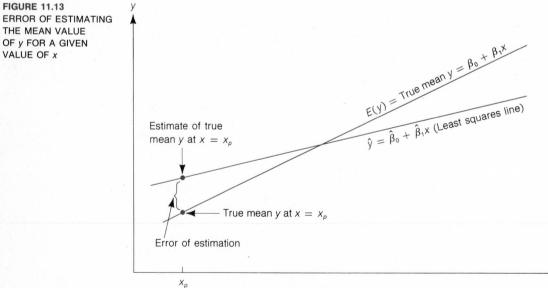

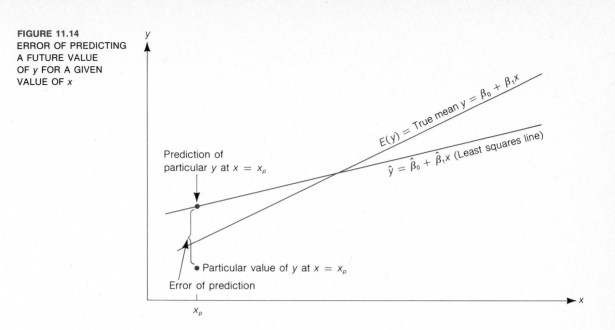

A comparison of the confidence interval for the mean value of y and the prediction interval for some future value of y for a $400 advertising expenditure ($x = 4$) is illustrated in Figure 11.12. It is important to note that the prediction interval for an individual value of y will always be wider than the confidence interval for a mean value of y. You can see this by examining the formulas for the two intervals and you can see it in Figure 11.12.

The error in estimating the mean value of y, $E(y)$, for a given value of x, say x_p, is the distance between the least squares line and the true line of means, $\beta_0 + \beta_1 x$. This error, shown in Figure 11.13, will take its smallest value when $x = \bar{x}$. The farther x lies from $\bar{x}$, the larger will be the error of estimation. In contrast, the error in predicting some future value of y is the sum of the two errors—the error of estimating the mean of y, $E(y)$, shown in Figure 11.13, plus the random error ε that is a component of the value of y to be predicted (see Figure 11.14). Consequently, the error of predicting a particular value of y will usually be larger than the error of estimating the mean value of y for a given value of x.

EXERCISES

11.26. Refer to Exercise 11.9. Find a 95% confidence interval for the mean yearly company sales when industry sales are $11 million.

11.27. Refer to Exercise 11.18. Television advertising next month will be $750.

  a. Find a 90% prediction interval for sales next month.
  b. Find a 90% confidence interval for average (mean) monthly sales when television advertising is $750 per month.
  c. Compare and comment on the sizes of the intervals in parts a and b.
  d. Could you reduce the size of either or both intervals by increasing your sample size? Explain.

11.28. Explain why for a given x value, the prediction interval for an individual y value will always be wider than the confidence interval for a mean value of y.

11.29. Explain why the confidence interval of the mean value of y for a given x value gets wider the farther x is from $\bar{x}$. What are the implications of this phenomenon for estimation and prediction?

11.30. Refer to Exercise 11.20. Find a 90% confidence interval for the mean maintenance cost per rental car during the first year if it is driven 35,000 miles.

11.31. In planning for an initial orientation meeting with new accounting majors, the chairman of the Accounting Department wants to emphasize the importance of doing well in the major courses in order to get better-paying jobs after graduation. To support this point, the chairman plans to show that there is a strong positive correlation between starting salaries for recent accounting graduates and their grade-point averages in the major courses. Records for seven of last year's accounting graduates are selected at random and given in the table.

GRADE-POINT AVERAGE IN MAJOR COURSES x	STARTING SALARY y, thousands of dollars
2.58	11.5
3.27	13.8
3.85	14.5
3.50	14.2
3.33	13.5
2.89	11.6
2.23	10.6

a. Find the least squares prediction equation.
b. Plot the data and graph the line as a check on your calculations.
c. Find a 95% prediction interval for a graduate whose grade-point average is 3.2.
d. What is the mean starting salary for graduates with grade-point averages equal to 3.0? Use a 95% confidence interval.

**11.8
SIMPLE LINEAR
REGRESSION:
AN EXAMPLE**

In the previous sections we have presented the basic elements necessary to fit and use a straight-line regression model. In this final section we will assemble these elements by applying them in an example.

Suppose a fire insurance company wants to relate the amount of fire damage in major residential fires to the distance between the residence and the nearest fire station. The study is to be conducted in a large suburb of a major city; a sample of fifteen recent fires in this suburb is selected. The amount of damage, y, and the distance, x, between the fire and the nearest fire station is recorded for each fire. The results are given in Table 11.7.

TABLE 11.7 FIRE DAMAGE DATA	DISTANCE FROM FIRE STATION x, miles	FIRE DAMAGE y, thousands of dollars
	3.4	26.2
	1.8	17.8
	4.6	31.3
	2.3	23.1
	3.1	27.5
	5.5	36.0
	0.7	14.1
	3.0	22.3
	2.6	19.6
	4.3	31.3
	2.1	24.0
	1.1	17.3
	6.1	43.2
	4.8	36.4
	3.8	26.1

Step 1. First, we hypothesize a model to relate fire damage, y, to the distance from the nearest fire station, x. We will hypothesize a straight-line probabilistic model:

$$y = \beta_0 + \beta_1 x + \varepsilon$$

Step 2. Next, we use the data to estimate the unknown parameters in the deterministic component of the hypothesized model. We make some preliminary calculations:

$$SS_{xx} = \sum x_i^2 - \frac{\left(\sum x_i\right)^2}{15} = 196.16 - \frac{(49.2)^2}{15}$$

$$= 196.160 - 161.376 = 34.784$$

$$SS_{yy} = \sum y_i^2 - \frac{\left(\sum y_i\right)^2}{15} = 11{,}376.48 - \frac{(396.2)^2}{15}$$

$$= 11{,}376.480 - 10{,}464.963 = 911.517$$

$$SS_{xy} = \sum x_i y_i - \frac{\left(\sum x_i\right)\left(\sum y_i\right)}{15} = 1{,}470.65 - \frac{(49.2)\,(396.2)}{15}$$

$$= 1{,}470.650 - 1{,}299.536 = 171.114$$

Then the least squares estimates of the slope β_1 and intercept β_0 are

$$\hat{\beta}_1 = \frac{SS_{xy}}{SS_{xx}} = \frac{171.114}{34.784} = 4.919$$

$$\hat{\beta}_0 = \bar{y} - \hat{\beta}_1 \bar{x} = \frac{396.2}{15} - 4.919\left(\frac{49.2}{15}\right)$$

$$= 26.413 - (4.919)(3.28) = 26.413 - 16.134$$

$$= 10.279$$

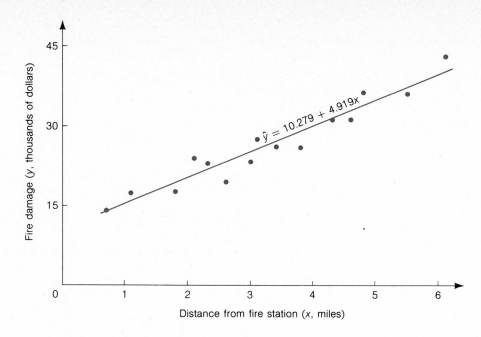

FIGURE 11.15
LEAST SQUARES
MODEL FOR THE
FIRE DAMAGE DATA

And the least squares equation is

$$\hat{y} = 10.279 + 4.919x$$

This prediction equation is graphed in Figure 11.15, along with a plot of the data points.

Step 3. Now, we specify the probability distribution of the random error component ε. The assumptions about the distribution will be identical to those listed in Section 11.3 Although we know that these assumptions are not completely satisfied (they rarely are for any practical problem), we are willing to assume they are approximately satisfied for this example. We have to estimate the variance, σ^2, of ε, so we calculate

$$SSE = \sum (y_i - \hat{y}_i)^2 = SS_{yy} - \hat{\beta}_1 SS_{xy}$$

where the last expression represents a shortcut formula for SSE. Thus,

$$SSE = 911.517 - (4.919)(171.114)$$
$$= 911.517 - 841.709766 = 69.807234^*$$

To estimate σ^2, we divide SSE by the degrees of freedom available for error, $n - 2$. Thus,

$$s^2 = \frac{SSE}{n - 2} = \frac{69.807234}{15 - 2} = 5.3698$$
$$s = \sqrt{5.3698} = 2.32$$

*The values for SS_{yy}, $\hat{\beta}_1$, and SS_{xy} used to calculate SSE are exact for this example. For other problems where rounding is necessary, at least six significant figures should be carried for these quantities. Otherwise, the calculated value of SSE may be substantially in error.

Step 4. We can now check the utility of the hypothesized model, that is, whether x really contributes information for the prediction of y using the straight-line model. First test the null hypothesis that the slope β_1 is zero, i.e., that there is no linear relationship between fire damage and the distance from the nearest fire station. We test

$$H_0: \quad \beta_1 = 0 \qquad H_a: \quad \beta_1 \neq 0$$

Test statistic: $\quad t = \dfrac{\hat{\beta}_1 - 0}{s_{\hat{\beta}_1}} = \dfrac{\hat{\beta}_1}{s/\sqrt{SS_{xx}}}$

Assumptions: Those made about ε in Section 11.3

For $\alpha = .05$, we will reject H_0 if

$$t > t_{\alpha/2, n-2} \qquad \text{or} \qquad t < -t_{\alpha/2, n-2}$$

where for $n = 15$ we find $t_{.025, 13} = 2.160$. We then calculate the t statistic:

$$t = \frac{\hat{\beta}_1}{s_{\hat{\beta}_1}} = \frac{\hat{\beta}_1}{s/\sqrt{SS_{xx}}} = \frac{4.919}{2.32/\sqrt{34.784}} = \frac{4.919}{.393}$$

$$= 12.5$$

This large t value leaves little doubt that mean fire damage and distance between the fire and the fire station are at least linearly related, with mean fire damage increasing as the distance increases.

We gain additional information about the relationship by forming a confidence interval for the slope β_1. A 95% confidence interval is

$$\hat{\beta}_1 \pm t_{.025, 13} s_{\hat{\beta}_1} = 4.919 \pm (2.160)(.393)$$

$$= 4.919 \pm .849 = (4.070, 5.768)$$

We estimate that the interval from \$4,070 to \$5,768 encloses the mean increase (β_1) in mean fire damage per additional mile distance from the fire station.

Another measure of the utility of the model is the coefficient of correlation r. We have

$$r = \frac{SS_{xy}}{\sqrt{SS_{xx} SS_{yy}}} = \frac{171.114}{\sqrt{(34.784)(911.517)}}$$

$$= \frac{171.114}{178.062} = .96$$

The high correlation confirms our conclusion that β_1 differs from zero; it appears that fire damage and distance from the fire station are highly correlated.

The coefficient of determination is

$$r^2 = (.96)^2 = .92$$

which implies that 92% of the sum of squares of deviations of the y values about $\bar{y}$ is explained by the linear distance x between the fire and the fire station. All signs point to a strong relationship between x and y.

Step 5. We are now prepared to use the least squares model. Suppose the insurance company wants to predict the fire damage if a major residential fire were to occur 3.5 miles from the nearest fire station. The predicted value is

$$\hat{y} = \hat{\beta}_0 + \hat{\beta}_1 x = 10.279 + (4.919)(3.5)$$
$$= 10.279 + 17.216 = 27.5$$

(we round to the nearest tenth to be consistent with the units of the original data in Table 11.7). If we want a 95% prediction interval, we calculate

$$\hat{y} \pm t_{.025,13}s\sqrt{1 + \frac{1}{n} + \frac{(x - \bar{x})^2}{SS_{xx}}} = 27.5 \pm (2.16)(2.32)\sqrt{1 + \frac{1}{15} + \frac{(3.5 - 3.28)^2}{34.784}}$$
$$= 27.5 \pm (2.16)(2.32)\sqrt{1.0681}$$
$$= 27.5 \pm 5.2 = (22.3, 32.7)$$

The model yields a 95% prediction interval for fire damage in a major residential fire 3.5 miles from the nearest station of $22,300 to $32,700.

One caution before closing: We would not use this prediction model to make predictions for homes less than 0.7 mile or more than 6.1 miles from the nearest fire station. A look at the data in Table 11.7 reveals that all the x values fall between 0.7 and 6.1. It is dangerous to use the model to make predictions outside the region in which the sample data fall. A straight line might not provide a good model for the relationship between the mean value of y and the value of x when stretched over a wider range of x values.

SUMMARY

We have introduced an extremely useful tool in this chapter—the method of least squares for fitting a prediction equation to a set of data. This procedure, along with associated statistical tests and estimations, is called a regression analysis. In five steps we showed how to use sample data to build a model relating a dependent variable y to a single independent variable x.

1. The first step is to hypothesize a probabilistic model. In this chapter, we confined our attention to the straight-line model, $y = \beta_0 + \beta_1 x + \varepsilon$.

2. The second step is to use the method of least squares to estimate the unknown parameters in the deterministic component, $\beta_0 + \beta_1 x$. The least squares estimates yield a model $\hat{y} = \hat{\beta}_0 + \hat{\beta}_1 x$ with a sum of squared errors (SSE) that is smaller than any other straight-line model.

3. The third step is to specify the probability distribution of the random error component, ε.

4. The fourth step is to assess the utility of the hypothesized model. Included here are making inferences about the slope β_1, calculating the coefficient of correlation, r, and calculating the coefficient of determination, r^2.

5. Finally, if we are satisfied with the model, we are prepared to use it. We used the model to estimate the mean y value, $E(y)$, for a given x value and to predict an individual y value for a specific value of x.

The following two chapters will develop more fully the concepts introduced in this chapter.

SUPPLEMENTARY EXERCISES

11.32.

MONTH	UNITED STATES CONSUMER PURCHASES OF ORANGES y, thousands of boxes	PRICE PER BOX x, dollars
October	6,100	6.20
November	6,800	6.05
December	8,400	6.20
January	6,000	8.10
February	5,800	8.70
March	5,500	8.75
April	4,400	9.40
May	4,000	9.75

a. Construct a scattergram of the data.

b. Find the least squares line for the data and plot it on your scattergram. The least squares line may be viewed as an estimate of the short-run demand function for oranges.

c. Define β_1 in the context of this problem.

d. Test the hypothesis that the price per box of oranges contributes no information for the prediction of the number of boxes consumed when a linear model of short-run demand is used (let $\alpha = .05$). Draw the appropriate conclusions.

e. Find a 90% confidence interval for β_1. Interpret your results.

f. Find the coefficient of correlation for the given data.

g. Find the coefficient of determination for the linear model of demand you constructed in part b. Interpret your result.

h. Given the price per box of oranges is $8.00, find a 90% prediction interval for the number of boxes that will be consumed.

i. Find a 95% confidence interval for the expected number of boxes that will be consumed at a price of $8.00 per box.

11.33. a. Find the correlation coefficient and coefficient of determination for the data in the table at the top of page 330 and interpret your results.

b. Do the data provide sufficient evidence to indicate correlation between x and y?

YEAR	PASSENGERS CARRIED BY SCHEDULED AIR CARRIERS IN THE UNITED STATES y, millions	PASSENGERS CARRIED BY RAILROADS IN THE UNITED STATES x, millions
1950	19	488
1955	42	433
1960	62	327
1965	103	306
1970	169	289
1974	208	275

Source: United States Bureau of the Census, *Statistical Abstracts of the United States 1976.*

11.34. The data in the table give the market share for a product as a function of television advertising expenditures.

MONTH	MARKET SHARE y, %	TELEVISION ADVERTISING EXPENDITURE x, thousands of dollars
January	15	23
March	17	25
May	13	21
July	14	24
September	16	26

a. Use the methods of this chapter to find the least squares line relating market share to television advertising expenditure. Plot the data and graph the least squares line as a check on your calculations.

b. Do the data provide sufficient evidence to indicate that x contributes information for the prediction of y? Test using $\alpha = .10$.

c. Find a 95% confidence interval for β_1 and interpret your result.

d. Find a 90% confidence interval from the expected market share when $25,000 is spent on television advertising.

e. Find a 95% prediction interval for the market share that will be obtained when $23,000 is spent in television advertising.

11.35. A large supermarket chain has its own store brand for many grocery items. These tend to be priced lower than other brands. For a particular item, the chain wants to study the effect of varying the price for the major competing brand on the sales of the store brand item, while the prices for the store brand and all other brands are held fixed. The experiment is conducted at one of the chain's stores over a 7 week period and the results are shown in the table at the top of page 331.

a. Find the least squares line relating store brand sales, y, to major competitor's price, x.

b. Plot the data and graph the line as a check on your calculations.

c. Does x contribute information for the prediction of y?

d. Calculate r and r^2 and interpret their values.

WEEK	MAJOR COMPETITOR'S PRICE x, cents	STORE BRAND SALES y
1	37	122
2	32	107
3	29	99
4	35	110
5	33	113
6	31	104
7	35	116

e. Find a 90% confidence interval for mean store brand sales when the competitor's price is 33¢.

f. Suppose you were to set the competitor's price at 33¢. Find a 90% prediction interval for next week's sales.

11.36. As a result of the increase in the number of suburban shopping centers, many center-city stores are suffering financially. A downtown department store thinks that increased advertising might help lure more shoppers into the area. To study the effect of advertising on sales, records were obtained for several mid-year months during which the store varied advertising expenditures.

a. Estimate the coefficient of correlation between sales and advertising expenditures.

b. Do the data provide sufficient evidence to indicate a correlation between sales, y, and advertising expense, x?

ADVERTISING EXPENSE x, thousands of dollars	SALES y, thousands of dollars
0.9	30
1.1	34
0.8	32
1.2	37
0.7	31

11.37. As part of the first-year evaluation for new salespeople, a large food-processing firm projects the second-year sales for each salesperson based on his/her sales for the first year.

FIRST-YEAR SALES x, thousands of dollars	SECOND-YEAR SALES y, thousands of dollars
75.2	99.3
91.7	125.7
100.3	136.1
64.2	108.6
81.8	102.0
110.2	153.7
77.3	108.8
80.1	105.4

a. Use the data in the table on eight salespeople for this firm to fit a simple linear prediction model for second-year sales based on the first year's sales. Assume the data have been adjusted in terms of a base year to discount inflation effects.

b. Plot the data and graph the line as a check on your calculations.

c. Do the data provide sufficient information to indicate that x contributes information for the prediction of y?

d. Calculate r^2 and interpret its value.

e. If a salesperson has first-year sales of $90,000, find a 90% prediction interval for next year's sales.

11.38. In placing a weekly order, a concessionaire that provides services at a baseball stadium must know what size crowd is expected during the coming week in order to know how much food, etc., to order. Since advanced ticket sales give an indication of expected attendance, food needs might be predicted on the basis of the advanced sales.

a. Use the data in the table from 7 previous weeks of home games to develop a simple linear model for hot dogs purchased as a function of advanced ticket sales.

b. Plot the data and graph the line as a check on your calculations.

HOT DOGS PURCHASED DURING WEEK y, thousands	ADVANCED TICKET SALES FOR WEEK x, thousands
39.1	54.0
35.9	48.1
20.8	28.8
42.4	62.4
46.0	64.4
40.7	59.5
29.9	42.3

c. Do the data provide sufficient information to indicate that advanced ticket sales provide information for the prediction of hot dog demand?

d. Calculate r^2 and interpret its value.

e. Find a 90% confidence interval for the mean number of hot dogs purchased when the advance ticket sales equal 50,000.

f. If the advanced ticket sales this week equal 55,000, find a 90% prediction interval for the number of hot dogs that will be purchased this week at the game.

11.39. A certain manufacturer evaluates the sales potential for a product in a new marketing area by selecting several stores within the area to sell the product on a trial basis for a 1 month period. The sales figures for the trial period are then used to project sales for the entire area. [*Note:* The same number of trial stores are used each time.]

a. Use the data in the table to develop a simple linear model for predicting first-month sales for the entire area based on sales during the trial period.
b. Plot the data and graph the line as a check on your calculations.

TOTAL SALES DURING TRIAL PERIOD x, hundreds of dollars	TOTAL SALES FOR FIRST MONTH FOR ENTIRE AREA y, hundreds of dollars
16.8	48.2
14.0	46.8
18.3	54.3
22.1	59.7
14.9	48.3
23.2	67.5

c. Do the data provide sufficient evidence to indicate that total sales during the trial period contribute information for predicting total sales during the first month?
d. Use a 90% prediction interval to predict total sales for the first month for the entire area if the trial sales equal $2,000.

11.40. The management of a manufacturing firm is considering the possibility of setting up its own market research department rather than continuing to use the services of a market research firm. The management wants to know what salary should be paid to a market researcher, based on years of experience. An independent consultant checks with several other firms in the area and obtains the information shown in the table on market researchers.

ANNUAL SALARY y, thousands of dollars	EXPERIENCE x, years
16.3	2
16.2	1.5
25.0	11
29.1	15
25.4	9
21.9	6

a. Fit a least squares line to the data.
b. Plot the data and graph the line as a check on your calculations.
c. Calculate r and r^2. Explain how these values measure the utility of the model.
d. Estimate the mean annual salary of a market researcher with 8 years of experience. Use a 90% confidence interval.
e. Predict the salary of a market researcher with 7 years of experience using a 90% prediction interval.

11.41. Although the income tax system is structured so that people with higher incomes should pay taxes at a higher percentage of their incomes, there are many loopholes and tax shelters available for individuals with higher incomes. A sample of seven individual 1976 tax returns gave the data listed in the table on income and percent taxes paid.

INDIVIDUAL	GROSS INCOME x, thousands of dollars	TAXES PAID y, percentage of total income
1	35.8	16.7
2	80.2	21.4
3	14.9	15.2
4	7.3	10.1
5	9.1	12.2
6	150.7	19.6
7	25.9	17.3

a. Fit a least squares line to the data.
b. Plot the data and graph the line as a check on your calculations.
c. Calculate r and r^2 and interpret them.
d. Find a 90% confidence interval for the mean percent taxes paid for individuals with gross incomes of $70,000.

11.42. A tire company sells five different kinds of automobile tires. The more expensive tires are the best in terms of toughness, durability, and mileage guarantee, but they are not in great demand because of their high prices. The data in the table represent the total number of sales for a 1 year period for tires sold at five different prices.

TIRE COST x, dollars	NUMBER SOLD y, units of 100
20	13
35	57
45	85
60	43
70	17

a. Fit a least squares line to the data.
b. Plot the data and graph the line as a check on your calculations.
c. Test H_0: $\beta_1 = 0$ using a two-tailed test at $\alpha = .05$. Does nonrejection of H_0 imply no relationship between tire price and sales volume?

ON YOUR OWN . . .

The Gross National Product (GNP) is one of the nation's best-known economic indicators. Many economists have developed models to forecast future values of the GNP. There are surely a large number of variables that should be included if an accurate prediction is to be made. For the moment, however, consider the simple case of choosing one important variable to include in a simple straight-line model for GNP.*

First, list three independent variables, x_1, x_2, and x_3, that you think might be (individually) strongly related to the GNP. Next, obtain ten yearly values (preferably the last ten) of the three independent variables and the GNP.

a. Use the least squares formulas given in this chapter to fit three straight-line models—one for each independent variable—for predicting the GNP.

b. Interpret the sign of the estimated slope coefficient $\hat{\beta}_1$ in each case, and test the utility of the model by testing H_0: $\beta_1 = 0$ against H_a: $\beta_1 \neq 0$.

c. Calculate the coefficient of determination, r^2, for each model. Which of the independent variables predicts the GNP best over the 10 sample years when a straight-line model is used? Is this variable necessarily best in general (i.e., for all years)? Explain.

REFERENCES

Chou, Ya-lun. *Statistical analysis with business and economic applications.* 2d ed. New York: Holt, Rinehart, and Winston, 1975. Chapter 17.

Crandall, J. S., & Cedercreutz, M. "Preliminary cost estimates for mechanical work." *Building Systems Design,* Oct.–Nov. 1976, *73,* 35–51.

Draper, N., & Smith, H. *Applied regression analysis.* New York: Wiley, 1966. Chapter 1.

Miller, R. B., & Wichern, D. W. *Intermediate business statistics: Analysis of variance, regression, and time series.* New York: Holt, Rinehart, and Winston, 1977. Chapter 5.

Neter, J., & Wasserman, W. *Applied linear statistical models.* Homewood, Ill.: Richard Irwin, 1974. Chapters 2–6.

---

*The assumption that the random errors are independent is debatable for time series data. For the purposes of illustration, we will assume they are approximately independent. The problem of dependent errors is discussed in Chapter 14.

WHERE WE'VE BEEN . . .

In Chapter 11 we demonstrated how to model the relationship between a dependent variable y and an independent variable x using a straight line. We fit the straight line to the data points, used r and r^2 to measure the strength of the relationship between y and x, and used the resulting prediction equation to estimate the mean value of y or to predict some future value of y for a given value of x.

WHERE WE'RE GOING . . .

This chapter will convert the basic concept of Chapter 11 into a powerful estimation and prediction device by modeling the mean value of y as a function of two or more independent variables. This will enable you to model a response y (say, the assessed value of a house) as a function of quantitative variables (such as floor space, age of the house, etc.) or as a function of qualitative variables (such as type of construction, location, etc.). As in the case of a simple linear regression, a multiple regression analysis will include fitting the model to a data set, testing the utility of the model, and using it for the estimation of the mean value of y for given values of the independent variables.
We will also use the model to predict some particular value of y to be observed in the future.

12
MULTIPLE REGRESSION

Most practical applications of regression analysis utilize models that are more complex than the simple straight-line model. For example, a realistic probabilistic model for monthly sales revenue would include more than just the advertising expenditure discussed in Chapter 11 in order to provide a good predictive model for sales. Factors such as season, inventory on hand, sales force, and productivity are a few of the many variables that might influence sales. Thus, we would want to incorporate these and other potentially important independent variables into the model if we need to make accurate predictions.

Probabilistic models that include terms involving x^2, x^3 (or higher-order terms), or more than one independent variable are called **multiple regression models**. The general form of these models is

$$y = \beta_0 + \beta_1 x_1 + \beta_2 x_2 + \cdots + \beta_k x_k + \varepsilon$$

The dependent variable y is now written as a function of k independent variables, $x_1, x_2, \ldots, x_k$. The random error term is added to make the model probabilistic rather than deterministic. The value of the coefficient β_i determines the contribution of the independent variable x_i, and β_0 is the y-intercept. The coefficients $\beta_0, \beta_1, \ldots, \beta_k$ will usually be unknown, since they represent population parameters.

At first glance it might appear that the regression model shown above would not allow for anything other than straight-line relationships between y and the independent variables, but this is not true. Actually, $x_1, x_2, \ldots, x_k$ can be functions of variables as long as the functions do not contain unknown parameters. For example, the dollar sales, y, in new housing in a region could be a function of the independent variables

$x_1 =$ Mortgage interest rate

$x_2 =$ (Mortgage interest rate)$^2 = x_1^2$

$x_3 =$ Unemployment rate in the region

and so on. You could even insert a cyclical term (if it would be useful) of the form $x_4 = \sin t$, where t is a time variable. The multiple regression model is quite versatile and can be made to model many different types of response variables.

The same steps we followed in developing a straight-line model are applicable to the multiple regression model.

Step 1. First, hypothesize the form of the model. This involves the choice of the independent variables to be included in the model.

Step 2. Next, estimate the unknown parameters $\beta_0, \beta_1, \ldots, \beta_k$.

Step 3. Then, specify the probability distribution of the random error component, ε, and estimate its variance, σ^2.

Step 4. The fourth step is to check the utility of the model.

Step 5. Finally, use the fitted model to estimate the mean value of y or to predict a particular value of y for given values of the independent variables.

The initial step—hypothesizing the form of the model—is the subject of Chapter 13. In this chapter we will assume that the form of the model is known, and we will discuss steps 2–5 for a given model.

CASE STUDY 12.1   Towers, Perrin, Forster & Crosby (TPF&C), an international management consulting firm, has developed a unique and interesting application of multiple regression analysis. Many firms are interested in evaluating their management salary structure, and TPF&C uses multiple regression models to accomplish this salary evaluation. The Compensation Management Service, as TPF&C calls it, measures both the internal and external consistency of a company's pay policies to determine whether they reflect the management's intent.

The dependent variable y used to measure executive compensation is annual salary. The independent variables used to explain salary structure include the executive's age, education, rank, and bonus eligibility; number of employees under the executive's direct supervision; as well as variables that describe the company for which the executive works, such as annual sales, profit, and total assets.

The initial step in developing models for executive compensation is to obtain a sample of executives from various client firms, which TPF&C calls the Compensation Data Bank.

The data for these executives are used to estimate the model coefficients (the β parameters) and these estimates are then substituted into the linear model to form a prediction equation. To predict a particular executive's compensation, TPF&C substitutes into the prediction equation the values of the independent variables that pertain to the executive (the executive's age, rank, etc.). This application of multiple regression analysis will be developed more fully in Section 12.6.

**12.1
FITTING
THE MODEL:
LEAST SQUARES
APPROACH**

The method of fitting multiple regression models is identical to that of fitting the simple straight-line model: the method of least squares. That is, we choose the estimated model

$$\hat{y} = \hat{\beta}_0 + \hat{\beta}_1 x_1 + \cdots + \hat{\beta}_k x_k$$

that minimizes

$$SSE = \sum (y_i - \hat{y}_i)^2$$

As in the case of the simple linear model, the sample estimates $\hat{\beta}_0, \hat{\beta}_1, \ldots, \hat{\beta}_k$ will be obtained as a solution of a set of simultaneous linear equations.*

The primary difference between fitting the simple and multiple regression models is computational difficulty. The $(k + 1)$ simultaneous linear equations that must be solved to find the $(k + 1)$ estimated coefficients $\hat{\beta}_0, \hat{\beta}_1, \ldots, \hat{\beta}_k$ are difficult (sometimes physically impossible) to solve with a pocket or desk calculator. Consequently, we resort to the use of computers. Many computer packages have been developed to fit a multiple regression model by the method of least squares. We will present output from one of the more popular computer packages instead of presenting the tedious hand calculations required to fit the models. The computer output we will use is from the Statistical Analysis System (SAS). Since the regression output of the SAS

---

*Students who are familiar with the calculus should note that $\hat{\beta}_0, \hat{\beta}_1, \ldots, \hat{\beta}_k$ are the solutions to the set of equations $\partial SSE/\partial \beta_0 = 0$, $\partial SSE/\partial \beta_1 = 0$, $\ldots$, $\partial SSE/\partial \beta_k = 0$. The solution is usually given in matrix form, but we will not present the details here.

is similar to that of most other package regression programs, you should have little trouble interpreting regression output from other packages.

To illustrate, suppose we think that monthly electrical usage, y, in all-electric homes is related to the size, x, of the home, by the model

$$y = \beta_0 + \beta_1 x + \beta_2 x^2 + \varepsilon$$

To estimate the unknown parameters β_0, β_1, and β_2, values of y and x were collected for each of ten homes during a particular month. The data are shown in Table 12.1.

TABLE 12.1

SIZE OF HOME x, square feet	MONTHLY USAGE y, kilowatt-hours
1,290	1,182
1,350	1,172
1,470	1,264
1,600	1,493
1,710	1,571
1,840	1,711
1,980	1,804
2,230	1,840
2,400	1,956
2,930	1,954

FIGURE 12.1
SCATTERGRAM OF THE HOME SIZE–ELECTRICAL USAGE DATA

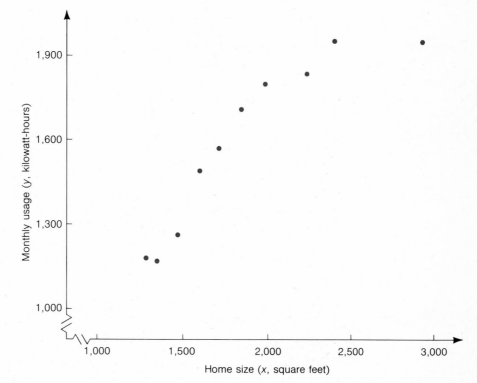

Notice that we include a term involving x^2 in the model above because we expect curvature in the graph of the response model relating x to y. The term involving x^2 is called a **quadratic** term. Figure 12.1 illustrates that the electrical usage appears to increase in a curvilinear manner with the size of the home. This provides some support for the inclusion of the quadratic term x^2 in the model.

Part of the output from the SAS multiple regression routine for the data in Table 12.1 is reproduced in Figure 12.2. The least squares estimates of the β parameters appear in the column labeled ESTIMATE. You can see that $\hat{\beta}_0 = -1,216.1$, $\hat{\beta}_1 = 2.3989$, and $\hat{\beta}_2 = -.00045$. Therefore, the equation that minimizes the SSE for this data is

$$\hat{y} = 1,216.1 + 2.3989x - .00045x^2$$

The minimum value of the SSE, 15,332.6, also appears in the printout. [*Note:* Much detail on the printout has not yet been discussed. We will continue throughout this chapter to shade the aspects of the printout that are under discussion.]

Note that the graph of the multiple regression model (Figure 12.3, a response curve) provides a good fit to the data of Table 12.1. Furthermore, the small value of $\hat{\beta}_2$ does *not* imply that the curvature is insignificant, since the numerical value of $\hat{\beta}_2$ is dependent upon the scale of the measurements. We will test the contribution of the quadratic coefficient $\hat{\beta}_2$ in Section 12.3.

The ultimate goal of this multiple regression analysis is to use the fitted model to predict electrical usage, y, for a home of a specific size (area), x. And, of course, we will want to give a prediction interval for y so that we will know how much faith we can place in the prediction. That is, if the prediction model is used to predict electrical usage, y, for a given size of home, x, what will be the error of prediction? To answer this question, we need to estimate σ^2, the variance of ε.

FIGURE 12.2

OUTPUT FROM THE SAS FOR THE HOME SIZE–ELECTRICAL USAGE DATA

SOURCE	DF	SUM OF SQUARES	MEAN SQUARE	F VALUE	PR > F
MODEL	2	831069.54637065	415534.77318533	189.71	0.0001
ERROR	7	15332.55362935	2190.36480419		STD DEV
CORRECTED TOTAL	9	846402.10000000		R-SQUARE	46.8013333
				0.981885	

PARAMETER	ESTIMATE	T FOR HO: PARAMETER = 0	PR > |T|	STD ERROR OF ESTIMATE
INTERCEPT	−1216.14388700	−5.01	0.0016	242.80636850
X	2.39893018	9.76	0.0001	0.24583560
X∗X	−0.00045004	−7.62	0.0001	0.00005908

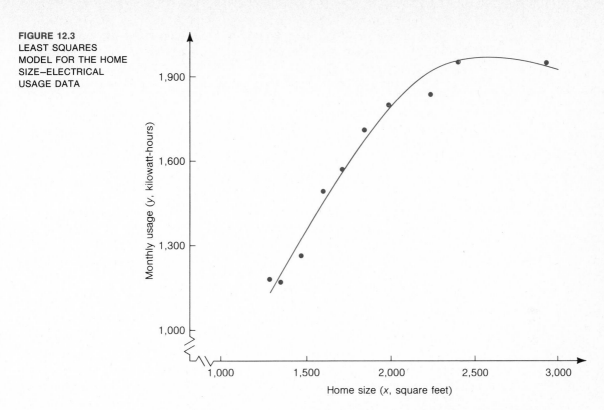

FIGURE 12.3
LEAST SQUARES
MODEL FOR THE HOME
SIZE–ELECTRICAL
USAGE DATA

12.2
ESTIMATION
OF σ^2, THE
VARIANCE OF ε

The specification of the probability distribution of the random error component, ε, of the multiple regression model follows the same general outline as for the straight-line model. We assume that ε is normally distributed with mean zero and constant variance σ^2 for all settings of the independent variables $x_1, x_2, \ldots, x_k$. Furthermore, the errors are assumed to be independent. Given these assumptions, the remaining task in specifying the probability distribution of ε is to estimate σ^2.

For example, in the quadratic model describing electrical usage as a function of home size, we found a minimum SSE = 15,332.6. We now want to use this quantity to estimate the variance of ε. Recall that the estimator for the straight-line model was $s^2 = \text{SSE}/(n - 2)$ and note that the denominator is $n -$ (Number of estimated β parameters), which is $n - (2)$ in the straight-line model. Since we must estimate one more parameter, β_2, for the quadratic model $y = \beta_0 + \beta_1 x + \beta_2 x^2 + \varepsilon$, the estimator of σ^2 is

$$s^2 = \frac{\text{SSE}}{n - 3}$$

That is, the denominator becomes $(n - 3)$ because there are now three β parameters in the model.

The numerical estimate for this example is

$$s^2 = \frac{\text{SSE}}{10 - 3} = \frac{15,332.6}{7} = 2,190.36$$

In many computer printouts and textbooks, s^2 is called the **Mean Square for Error**, or MSE. This estimate of σ^2 is shown in the column title MEAN SQUARE in the SAS printout in Figure 12.2.

For the general multiple regression model

$$y = \beta_0 + \beta_1 x_1 + \beta_2 x_2 + \cdots + \beta_k x_k + \varepsilon$$

we must estimate the $(k + 1)$ parameters $\beta_0, \beta_1, \beta_2, \ldots, \beta_k$. Thus, the estimator of σ^2 is the SSE divided by the quantity $n -$ (Number of estimated β parameters).

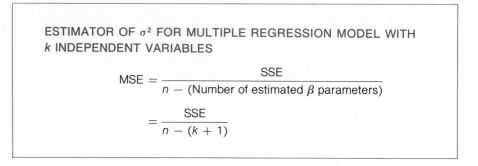

ESTIMATOR OF σ^2 FOR MULTIPLE REGRESSION MODEL WITH k INDEPENDENT VARIABLES

$$\text{MSE} = \frac{\text{SSE}}{n - (\text{Number of estimated } \beta \text{ parameters})}$$

$$= \frac{\text{SSE}}{n - (k + 1)}$$

We will use the estimator of σ^2 both to check the utility of the model (Sections 12.3 and 12.4) and to provide a measure of the reliability of predictions and estimates when the model is used for those purposes (Section 12.5). Thus, you can see that the estimation of σ^2 plays an important part in the development of a regression model.

**12.3
ESTIMATING
AND TESTING
HYPOTHESES
ABOUT THE
β PARAMETERS**

Sometimes the individual β parameters in a model have particular practical significance and we want to estimate their values or test hypotheses about them. For example, if electrical usage, y, is related to home size, x, by the straight-line relationship

$$y = \beta_0 + \beta_1 x + \varepsilon$$

β_1 has a very practical interpretation. That is, you saw in Chapter 11 that β_1 is the mean increase in electrical usage, y, for a 1 unit increase in home size, x.

As proposed in the preceding sections, suppose the electrical usage, y, is related to home size, x, by the quadratic model

$$y = \beta_0 + \beta_1 x + \beta_2 x^2 + \varepsilon$$

Then the mean value of y for a given value of x is

$$E(y) = \beta_0 + \beta_1 x + \beta_2 x^2$$

What is the practical interpretation of β_2? As noted earlier, the parameter β_2 measures the curvature in this response curve. That is, it would not be surprising to observe the electrical usage, y, rise almost proportional to home size, x. Then, eventually, as the size of the home increases, the increase in electrical usage for a 1 unit increase in home size might begin to decrease. Thus, a forecaster of electrical usage would want to determine whether curvature actually was present in the response curve, or, equivalently, the forecaster would want to test the null hypothesis

$$H_0: \quad \beta_2 = 0 \quad \text{(No curvature in the response curve)}$$

against the alternative hypothesis

$$H_a: \quad \beta_2 < 0 \quad \text{(Downward curvature exists in the response curve)}$$

A test of this hypothesis can be performed using either a Student's t test or an F test. We will commence by explaining the t test.

The t test utilizes a test statistic that is analogous to that used to make inferences about the slope of the simple straight-line model (Section 11.4). The t statistic is formed by dividing the sample estimate $\hat{\beta}_2$ of the population coefficient β_2 by the estimated standard deviation of the repeated sampling distribution of $\hat{\beta}_2$.

$$\text{Test statistic:} \quad t = \frac{\hat{\beta}_2}{s_{\hat{\beta}_2}}$$

We use the symbol $s_{\hat{\beta}_2}$ to represent the estimated standard deviation of $\hat{\beta}_2$. The formula for computing $s_{\hat{\beta}_2}$ is very complex and its presentation is beyond the scope of this text,* but this will not cause difficulty. Most computer packages list the estimated standard deviation $s_{\hat{\beta}_i}$ for each of the estimated model coefficients $\hat{\beta}_i$. In addition, they usually give the calculated t values for each coefficient in the model.

The rejection region for the test is found in exactly the same way as the rejection regions for the t tests in Chapters 9–11. That is, we consult Table V of Appendix B to obtain an upper-tail value of t. This is a value t_α such that $P(t > t_\alpha) = \alpha$. We can then use this value to construct rejection regions for either one- or two-tailed tests. To illustrate, in the electrical usage example, the error degrees of freedom is $(n - 3) = 7$, the denominator of the estimate of σ^2. Then the rejection region (shown in Figure 12.4) for a one-tailed test with $\alpha = .05$ is

$$\text{Rejection region:} \quad t < -t_{\alpha, n-3}$$
$$t < -1.895$$

---

*Because most of the formulas in a multiple regression analysis are so complex, the only reasonable way to present them is by using matrix algebra. We do not assume a prerequisite of matrix algebra for this text and, in any case, we think the formulas can be omitted in an introductory course without serious loss. They are programmed into almost all standard multiple regression computer packages and are presented in some of the texts listed in the references.

FIGURE 12.4
REJECTION REGION
FOR TEST OF $\hat{\beta}_2$

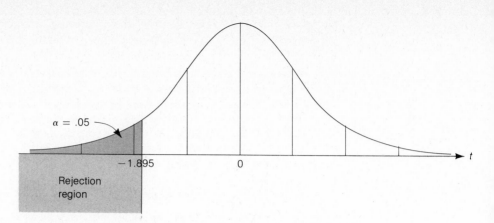

$\alpha = .05$

-1.895

0

t

Rejection
region

FIGURE 12.5
OUTPUT FROM THE SAS

SOURCE	DF	SUM OF SQUARES	MEAN SQUARE	F VALUE	PR > F
MODEL	2	831069.54637065	415534.77318533	189.71	0.0001
ERROR	7	15332.55362935	2190.36480419		STD DEV
CORRECTED TOTAL	9	846402.10000000		R-SQUARE	46.8013333
				0.981885	

PARAMETER	ESTIMATE	T FOR HO: PARAMETER = 0	PR > |T|	STD ERROR OF ESTIMATE
INTERCEPT	−1216.14388700	−5.01	0.0016	242.80636850
X	2.39893018	9.76	0.0001	0.24583560
X*X	−0.00045004	−7.62	0.0001	0.00005908

In Figure 12.5 we again show a portion of the SAS printout for the electrical usage example. The following quantities are shaded:

1. The estimated coefficients, $\hat{\beta}_0$, $\hat{\beta}_1$, and $\hat{\beta}_2$.
2. The SSE.
3. The MSE (estimate of the variance of ε, σ^2).

The estimated standard deviations for the model coefficients appear under the column labeled STD ERROR OF ESTIMATE. The t statistics for testing the null hypothesis that the true coefficients are equal to zero appear under the column headed T FOR HO: PARAMETER = 0. The t value corresponding to the test of the null hypothesis

H_0: $\beta_2 = 0$ is the last one in the column, i.e., $t = -7.62$. Since this value is less than -1.895, we conclude that the quadratic term $\beta_2 x^2$ makes an important contribution to the prediction model of electrical usage.

The SAS printout shown in Figure 12.5 also lists the two-tailed significance levels for each t value. These values appear under the column headed PR > |T|. The significance level .0001 corresponds to the quadratic term, and this implies that we would reject H_0: $\beta_2 = 0$ in favor of H_a: $\beta_2 \neq 0$ at any α level larger than .0001. Since our alternative was one-sided, H_a: $\beta_2 < 0$, the α value is half that given in the printout, i.e., $\alpha = \frac{1}{2}(.0001) = .00005$. Thus, there is very strong evidence that the mean electrical usage increases more slowly per square foot for large houses than for small houses.

We can also form a confidence interval for the parameter β_2 as follows:

$$\hat{\beta}_2 \pm t_{\alpha/2, n-3} s_{\hat{\beta}_2} = -.000450 \pm (2.365)(.0000591)$$

or, $(-.000590, -.000310)$. Note that the t value 2.365 corresponds to $\alpha/2 = .025$ and $(n - 3) = 7$ df. This interval constitutes a 95% confidence interval for β_2, and can be used to estimate the rate of curvature in mean electrical usage as home size is increased. Note that all values in the interval are negative, reconfirming the conclusion of our test.

Testing an hypothesis about a single β parameter that appears in any multiple regression model is accomplished in exactly the same manner as described for the quadratic electrical usage model. The form of the t test is shown below.

TEST OF AN INDIVIDUAL PARAMETER COEFFICIENT IN THE MULTIPLE REGRESSION MODEL (TWO-TAILED)

$$y = \beta_0 + \beta_1 x_1 + \beta_2 x_2 + \cdots + \beta_k x_k + \varepsilon$$

H_0: $\beta_i = 0$ H_a: $\beta_i \neq 0$

Test statistic: $t = \dfrac{\hat{\beta}_i}{s_{\hat{\beta}_i}}$

Assumptions: See Section 11.3 for the assumptions about the probability distribution of the random error component ε

Rejection region: $t > t_{\alpha/2, n-(k+1)}$ or $t < -t_{\alpha/2, n-(k+1)}$

where

n = Number of observations

k = Number of independent variables in the model

EXAMPLE 12.1

A collector of antique grandfather clocks knows that the price received for the clocks increases with the age of the clocks. In addition, the collector hypothesizes that the auction price of the clocks will increase as the number of bidders increases. Thus, the following model is hypothesized:

$$y = \beta_0 + \beta_1 x_1 + \beta_2 x_2 + \varepsilon$$

where

$\quad y = $ Auction price

$\quad x_1 = $ Age of clock (years)

$\quad x_2 = $ Number of bidders

TABLE 12.2
AUCTION PRICE DATA

AGE x_1	NUMBER OF BIDDERS x_2	AUCTION PRICE y
127	13	1235
115	12	1080
127	7	845
150	9	1522
156	6	1047
182	11	1979
156	12	1822
132	10	1253
137	9	1297
113	9	946
137	15	1713
117	11	1024
137	8	1147
153	6	1092
117	13	1152
126	10	1336
170	14	2131
182	8	1550
162	11	1884
184	10	2041
143	6	854
159	9	1483
108	14	1055
175	8	1545
108	6	729
179	9	1792
111	15	1175
187	8	1593
111	7	785
115	7	744
194	5	1356
168	7	1262

A sample of thirty-two auction prices of grandfather clocks, along with their age and the number of bidders, is given in Table 12.2. The model $y = \beta_0 + \beta_1 x_1 + \beta_2 x_2 + \varepsilon$ is fit to this data, and a portion of the SAS printout is shown in Figure 12.6. Test the hypothesis that the auction price increases as the number of bidders increases, i.e., $\beta_2 > 0$. Use $\alpha = .05$.

FIGURE 12.6
SAS PRINTOUT FOR EXAMPLE 12.1

SOURCE	DF	SUM OF SQUARES	MEAN SQUARE	F VALUE	PR > F
MODEL	2	4277159.70740504	2138579.85170252	120.65	0.0001
ERROR	29	514034.51534496	17725.32811534		STD DEV
CORRECTED TOTAL	31	4791194.21875000	R-SQUARE		133.13650181
			0.892713		

PARAMETER	ESTIMATE	T FOR HO: PARAMETER = 0	PR > |T|	STD ERROR OF ESTIMATE
INTERCEPT	−1336.72205214	−7.71	0.0001	173.35612607
X1	12.73619884	14.11	0.0001	0.90238049
X2	85.81513260	9.86	0.0001	8.70575681

Solution   The hypothesis of interest concerns the parameter β_2. Specifically,

$$H_0: \quad \beta_2 = 0$$

$$H_a: \quad \beta_2 > 0$$

Test statistic: $t = \dfrac{\hat{\beta}_2}{s_{\hat{\beta}_2}}$

Rejection region: For $\alpha = .05, \quad t > t_{.05, 29}$

where $n = 32$, $k = 2$ and $t_{.05, 29} = 1.699$. The calculated t value, $t = 9.86$, is indicated in Figure 12.7. This value exceeds 1.699 and therefore falls in the rejection region. Thus, the collector can conclude that the mean auction price of the clocks increases as the number of bidders increases.

Note that the values $\hat{\beta}_1 = 12.74$ and $\hat{\beta}_2 = 85.82$ (shaded in Figure 12.6) are easily interpreted. We estimate that the mean auction price increases $12.74 per year of age of the clock, and the mean price increases by $85.82 per additional bidder.

FIGURE 12.7
REJECTION REGION
FOR H_0: $\beta_2 = 0$

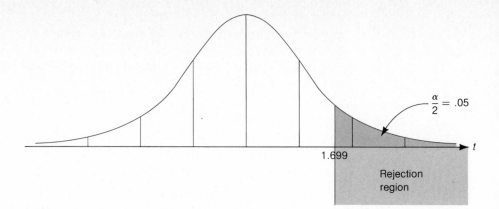

Be careful not to try to interpret the estimated intercept $\hat{\beta}_0 = -1{,}336.72$ in the same way as we interpreted $\hat{\beta}_1$ and $\hat{\beta}_2$. You might think that this implies a negative price for clocks 0 years of age with 0 bidders. However, these zeros are meaningless numbers in this example, since the ages range from 108 to 194 and the number of bidders ranges from 6 to 15. Interpretations of the models that use values of the independent variables outside their sampled ranges can be very misleading.

Some computer programs use the F test to test hypotheses concerning the individual β parameters, because the square of a Student's t with ν (Greek nu) degrees of freedom is equal to an F statistic with 1 df in the numerator and ν df in the denominator. If you conduct a two-tailed t test and reject the hypothesis if $t > t_{\alpha/2}$ or $t < -t_{\alpha/2}$, the corresponding F test will imply rejection if the computed value of F (which is equal to the square of the computed t statistic) is larger than F_α. Thus,

$$t^2_{\alpha/2} = F_\alpha$$

As an example, when we tested the curvature parameter, β_2, in the quadratic model relating electrical usage to home size, the computed t value was -7.62 (see Figure 12.5). The equivalent F test yields a value $F = t^2 = (-7.62)^2 = 58.06$. And the upper-tail rejection region for a two-tailed test with $\alpha = .05$ is

$$F > F_{.05,1,n-(k+1)} = F_{.05,1,7}$$
$$F > 5.59$$

Note that the F value, 5.59, is equal to the square of 2.365, the value of t that corresponds to $t_{.025,7}$. You can see that the conclusion is the same no matter which test statistic is used: There is very strong evidence that curvature is present in the model.

EXERCISES

12.1. How is the number of independent variables in a regression model related to the degrees of freedom available for estimating σ^2, the variance of ε?

12.2. An employer has found that factory workers who are with the company longer tend to invest more in a company investment program per year than workers with less time with the company. The following model is believed to be adequate in modeling the relationship of annual amount invested, y, to years working for the company, x:

$$y = \beta_0 + \beta_1 x + \beta_2 x^2 + \varepsilon$$

The employer checks the records for a sample of fifty factory employees for a previous year, and fits the above model to get $\hat{\beta}_2 = .0015$ and $s_{\hat{\beta}_2} = .000712$. The basic shape of a quadratic model depends upon whether $\beta_2 < 0$ or $\beta_2 > 0$. Test to see whether the employer can conclude that $\beta_2 > 0$. Use $\alpha = .05$.

12.3. To project personnel needs for the Christmas shopping season, a department store wants to project sales for the season. The sales for the previous Christmas season are an indication of what to expect for the current season. However, the projection should also reflect the current economic environment by taking into consideration sales for a more recent period. The following model might be appropriate:

$$y = \beta_0 + \beta_1 x_1 + \beta_2 x_2 + \varepsilon$$

where

$x_1 = $ Previous Christmas sales

$x_2 = $ Sales for August of current year

$y = $ Sales for upcoming Christmas

(All units are in thousands of dollars.) Data for 10 previous years were used to fit the prediction equation, and the following were calculated:

$$\hat{\beta}_1 = .62 \qquad s_{\hat{\beta}_1} = .273$$
$$\hat{\beta}_2 = .55 \qquad s_{\hat{\beta}_2} = .181$$

Use these results to determine whether there is evidence to indicate that the mean sales this Christmas depend upon this year's August sales.

**12.4
CHECKING THE
UTILITY OF A
MODEL: R^2 AND
THE ANALYSIS
OF VARIANCE
F TEST**

Conducting t tests on each β parameter in a model is *not* a good way to determine whether a model is contributing information for the prediction of y. If we were to conduct a series of t tests to determine whether the independent variables are contributing to the predictive relationship, we would be very likely to make one or more errors in deciding which terms to retain in the model and which to exclude. For example, even if all the β parameters (except β_0) are equal to zero, $100(\alpha)$ percent of the time you will reject the null hypothesis and conclude that some β parameter differs from zero. Thus, in multiple regression models for which a large number of independent variables are being considered, conducting a series of t tests may include a large number of insignificant variables and exclude some useful ones. If we want to test the utility of a multiple regression model, we will need a global test (one that encompasses all the β parameters). We would also like to find some statistical quantity that measures how well the model fits the data.

We commence with the easier problem—finding a measure of how well a linear model fits a set of data. For this we use the multiple regression equivalent of r^2, the coefficient of determination for the straight-line model (Chapter 11). Thus, we define the multiple coefficient of determination, R^2, as

$$R^2 = 1 - \frac{\sum (y_i - \hat{y}_i)^2}{\sum (y_i - \bar{y})^2} = 1 - \frac{SSE}{SS_{yy}}$$

where $\hat{y}_i$ is the predicted value of y_i for the model. Just as for the simple linear model, R^2 represents the fraction reduction in the sample variation of the y values (measured by SS_{yy}) that is attributable to the regression model. Thus, $R^2 = 0$ implies a complete lack of fit of the model to the data, and $R^2 = 1$ implies a perfect fit, with the model passing through every data point. In general, the larger the value of R^2, the better the model fits the data.

To illustrate, the value $R^2 = .982$ for the electrical usage example is indicated in a reprint of the SAS computer printout (Figure 12.8). This very high value of R^2 implies that using the independent variable home size in a quadratic model results in a 98.2% reduction in the total **sample** variation (measured by SS_{yy}) of electrical usage, y. Thus, R^2 is a sample statistic that tells how well the model fits the data, and thereby represents a measure of the utility of the entire model.

FIGURE 12.8
SAS PRINTOUT FOR ELECTRICAL USAGE EXAMPLE

SOURCE	DF	SUM OF SQUARES	MEAN SQUARE	F VALUE	PR > F
MODEL	2	831069.54637065	415534.77318533	189.71	0.0001
ERROR	7	15332.55362935	2190.36480419		STD DEV
CORRECTED TOTAL	9	846402.10000000		R-SQUARE	46.8013333
				0.981885	

PARAMETER	ESTIMATE	T FOR HO: PARAMETER = 0	PR > |T|	STD ERROR OF ESTIMATE
INTERCEPT	−1216.14388700	−5.01	0.0016	242.80636850
X	2.39893018	9.76	0.0001	0.24583560
X*X	−0.00045004	−7.62	0.0001	0.00005908

The fact that R^2 is a sample statistic implies that it can be used to make inferences about the utility of the entire model for predicting the population of y values at each setting of the independent variables. In particular, for the electrical usage data, the test

H_0: $\beta_1 = \beta_2 = 0$

H_a: At least one of the coefficients is nonzero

would formally test the global utility of the model. The test statistic used to test this null hypothesis is

Test statistic: $\quad F = \dfrac{R^2/k}{(1 - R^2)/[n - (k + 1)]}$

where n is the number of data points and k is the number of parameters in the model not including β_0. As we discussed in Section 10.3, F will have the F probability distribution with k degrees of freedom in the numerator and $[n - (k + 1)]$ degrees of freedom in the denominator. The tail values of the F distribution are given in Tables VI and VII of Appendix B.

The F test statistic becomes large as the coefficient of determination, R^2, becomes large. To determine how large F must be before we can conclude at a given significance level that the model is useful for predicting y, we set up the rejection region as follows:

Rejection region: $\quad F > F_{\alpha,k,n-(k+1)}$

For the electrical usage example ($n = 10$, $k = 2$, $n - (k + 1) = 7$, and $\alpha = .05$), we will reject H_0: $\quad \beta_1 = \beta_2 = 0$ if

$F > F_{.05,2,7}$

or

$F > 4.74$

From the computer printout (Figure 12.8), we find that the computed F is 189.71. Since this value greatly exceeds the tabulated value of 4.74, we conclude that at least one of the model coefficients β_1 and β_2 is nonzero. Therefore, this global F test indicates that the quadratic model $y = \beta_0 + \beta_1 x + \beta_2 x^2 + \varepsilon$, is useful for predicting electrical usage.

EXAMPLE 12.2   Refer to Example 12.1, in which an antique collector modeled the auction price, y, of grandfather clocks as a function of the age of the clock, x_1, and the number of bidders, x_2. The hypothesized model was

$y = \beta_0 + \beta_1 x_1 + \beta_2 x_2 + \varepsilon$

FIGURE 12.9
SAS PRINTOUT FOR EXAMPLE 12.2

SOURCE	DF	SUM OF SQUARES	MEAN SQUARE	F VALUE	PR > F
MODEL	2	4277159.70740504	2138579.85170252	120.65	0.0001
ERROR	29	514034.51534496	17725.32811534		STD DEV
CORRECTED TOTAL	31	4791194.21875000	R-SQUARE		133.13650181
			0.892713		

PARAMETER	ESTIMATE	T FOR HO: PARAMETER = 0	PR > |T|	STD ERROR OF ESTIMATE
INTERCEPT	−1336.72205214	−7.71	0.0001	173.35612607
X1	12.73619884	14.11	0.0001	0.90238049
X2	85.81513260	9.86	0.0001	8.70575681

A sample of thirty-two observations was obtained, with the results summarized in the SAS printout repeated here in Figure 12.9.

Discuss the coefficient of determination, R^2, for this example and then conduct the global F test of model utility at the $\alpha = .05$ level of significance.

Solution

The R^2 value is .89 (see Figure 12.9). This implies that the least squares model has reduced the total variation SS_{yy} of auction prices by 89%. We now test

H_0: $\beta_1 = \beta_2 = 0$ [*Note:* $k = 2$.]

H_a: At least one of the two model coefficients is nonzero

Test statistic: $F = \dfrac{R^2/k}{(1 - R^2)/[n - (k + 1)]}$

Rejection region: $F > F_{\alpha, k, n-(k+1)}$

For this example, $n = 32$, $k = 2$, and $n - (k + 1) = 32 - 3 = 29$. Then, for $\alpha = .05$, we will reject H_0: $\beta_1 = \beta_2 = 0$ if $F > F_{.05,2,29}$, i.e., if $F > 3.33$. The computed value of the F test statistic is 120.65 (see Figure 12.9). Since this value of F falls in the rejection region ($F = 120.65$ greatly exceeds $F_{.05,2,29} = 3.33$), the data provide strong evidence that at least one of the model coefficients is nonzero. The model appears to be useful for predicting auction prices.

Can we be sure that the best prediction model has been found if the global F test indicates a model is useful? Unfortunately, we cannot. There is no way of knowing whether the addition of other independent variables will further improve the utility of the model, as the following example indicates.

EXAMPLE 12.3

Refer to Examples 12.1 and 12.2. Suppose the collector, having observed many auctions, believes that the rate of increase of the auction price with age will be driven upward by a large number of bidders. Thus, instead of a relationship like that shown

FIGURE 12.10
EXAMPLES OF
NO INTERACTION AND
INTERACTION MODELS

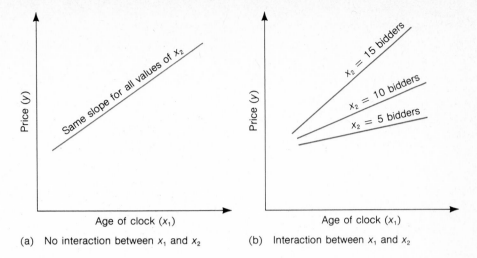

(a) No interaction between x_1 and x_2

(b) Interaction between x_1 and x_2

in Figure 12.10(a), in which the rate of increase in price with age is the same for any number of bidders, the collector believes the relationship is like that shown in Figure 12.10(b). Note that as the number of bidders increases from five to fifteen, the slope of the price versus age line increases. When the slope of the relationship between y and one independent variable (x_1) depends on the value of a second independent variable (x_2), as is the case here, we say that x_1 and x_2 interact.[*] The model that includes interaction is written

$$y = \beta_0 + \beta_1 x_1 + \beta_2 x_2 + \beta_3 x_1 x_2 + \varepsilon$$

Note that the increase in the mean price, $E(y)$, for each 1 year increase in age, x_1, is no longer given by the constant β_1, but is now $\beta_1 + \beta_3 x_2$. That is, the amount $E(y)$ increases for each 1 unit increase in x_1 is dependent on the number of bidders, x_2. Thus, the two variables x_1 and x_2 interact to affect y.

The thirty-two data points listed in Table 12.2 were used to fit the model with interaction. A portion of the SAS printout is shown in Figure 12.11.

Test the hypothesis that the price–age slope increases as the number of bidders increases, i.e., that age and number of bidders, x_2, interact positively.

Solution

The model is

$$y = \beta_0 + \beta_1 x_1 + \beta_2 x_2 + \beta_3 x_1 x_2 + \varepsilon$$

and the hypothesis of interest to the collector concerns the parameter β_3. Specifically,

$H_0: \quad \beta_3 = 0 \qquad H_a: \quad \beta_3 > 0$

Test statistic: $\quad t = \dfrac{\hat{\beta}_3}{s_{\hat{\beta}_3}}$

Rejection region: For $\quad \alpha = .05, \quad t > t_{.05, n - (k + 1)}$

[*] A more complete discussion of interaction is given in Chapter 13.

FIGURE 12.11
PORTION OF THE SAS PRINTOUT FOR THE MODEL WITH INTERACTION

SOURCE	DF	SUM OF SQUARES	MEAN SQUARE	F VALUE	PR > F
MODEL	3	4572547.98717668	1524182.66239223	195.19	0.0001
ERROR	28	218646.23157332	7808.79398476		STD DEV
CORRECTED TOTAL	31	4791194.21875000		R-SQUARE	88.36738077
				0.954365	

PARAMETER	ESTIMATE	T FOR HO: PARAMETER = 0	PR > |T|	STD ERROR OF ESTIMATE
INTERCEPT	322.75435309	1.10	0.2806	293.32514660
X1	0.87328775	0.43	0.6688	2.01965115
X2	−93.40991991	−3.14	0.0039	29.70767946
X1*X2	1.29789828	6.15	0.0001	0.21102602

where $n = 32$, $k = 3$, and $t_{.05, 28} = 1.701$. [*Note:* Remember, $(k + 1) = 4$ is the number of parameters in the regression model.]

The t value corresponding to $\hat{\beta}_3$ is indicated in Figure 12.11. The value, $t = 6.15$, exceeds 1.701 and therefore falls in the rejection region. Thus, the collector can conclude that the rate of change of the mean price of the clocks with age increases as the number of bidders increases, i.e., x_1 and x_2 interact. Thus, it appears that the interaction term should be included in the model.

One note of caution: Although the coefficient of x_2 is negative ($\hat{\beta}_2 = -93.41$), this does *not* imply that auction price decreases as the number of bidders increases. Since interaction is present, the rate of change (slope) of mean auction price with the number of bidders *depends on* x_1, the age of the clock. Thus, for example, the estimated rate of change of y with x_2 for a 150 year old clock is

$$\text{Estimated } x_2 \text{ slope} = \hat{\beta}_2 + \hat{\beta}_3 x_1 = -93.41 + 1.30(150)$$
$$= 101.60$$

In other words, we estimate that the auction price of a 150 year old clock will *increase* by about $101.60 for every additional bidder. Although this rate of increase will vary as x_1 is changed, it will remain positive for the range of values of x_1 included in the sample. Extreme care is needed in interpreting the signs and sizes of coefficients in a multiple regression model.

If, after conducting all relevant tests of model utility, we are satisfied with the model, then we want to use it for the estimation of the mean value of y for a given value of x and for the prediction of y. This is the subject of Section 12.5.

12.4. In hopes of increasing the company's share of the fine food market, researchers for a meat-processing firm that prepares meats for exclusive restaurants are working to improve the quality of its hickory-smoked hams. One of their studies concerns the effect of time spent in the smokehouse on the flavor of the ham. Hams that were in the smokehouse for varying amounts of time were each subjected to a taste test by a panel of ten food experts. The following model was thought to be appropriate by the researchers:

$$y = \beta_0 + \beta_1 t + \beta_2 t^2 + \varepsilon$$

where

$y =$ Mean of the taste scores for the ten experts
$t =$ Time in the smokehouse (hours)

Assume the least squares model estimated using a sample of twenty hams is

$$y = 20.3 + 5.2t - .0025t^2$$

and that $s_{\hat{\beta}_2} = .0011$. The coefficient of determination is $R^2 = .79$.

a. Is there evidence to indicate that the overall model is useful? Test at $\alpha = .05$.

b. Is there evidence to indicate the quadratic term is important in this model? Test at $\alpha = .05$.

12.5. Because the coefficient of determination R^2 always increases when a new independent variable is added to the model, it is tempting to include many variables in a model to force R^2 to be near 1. However, doing so reduces the degrees of freedom available for estimating σ^2, which adversely affects our ability to make reliable inferences. As an example, suppose you want to use eighteen economic indicators to predict next year's GNP. You fit the model

$$y = \beta_0 + \beta_1 x_1 + \beta_2 x_2 + \cdots + \beta_{17} x_{17} + \beta_{18} x_{18} + \varepsilon$$

where $y =$ GNP and $x_1, x_2, \ldots, x_{18}$ are indicators. Only 20 years of data ($n = 20$) are used to fit the model, and you obtain $R^2 = .95$. Test to see whether this impressive looking R^2 is large enough for you to infer that this model is useful, i.e., that at least one term in the model is important for predicting GNP. Use $\alpha = .05$.

12.6. A utility company of a major city gave the average utility bills listed in the table at the top of page 356 for a standard-size home during the last year.

a. Plot the points in a scattergram.

b. Use the methods of Chapter 11 to fit the model

$$y = \beta_0 + \beta_1 x + \varepsilon$$

What do you conclude about the utility of this model?

c. Hypothesize another model that might better describe the relationship between the average utility bill and average temperature. If you have access to a computer package, fit the model and test its utility.

MONTH	AVERAGE MONTHLY TEMPERATURE x, °F	AVERAGE UTILITY BILL y, dollars
January	38	99
February	45	91
March	49	78
April	57	61
May	69	55
June	78	63
July	84	80
August	89	95
September	79	65
October	64	56
November	54	74
December	41	93

12.5

USING THE MODEL FOR ESTIMATION AND PREDICTION

In Section 11.7 we discussed the use of the least squares line for estimating the mean value of y, $E(y)$, for some value of x, say $x = x_p$. We also showed how to use the same fitted model to predict, when $x = x_p$, some value of y to be observed in the future. Recall that the least squares line yielded the same value for both the estimate of $E(y)$ and the prediction of some future value of y. That is, both are the result of substituting x_p into the prediction equation $\hat{y}_p = \hat{\beta}_0 + \hat{\beta}_1 x_p$ and calculating $\hat{y}$. There the equivalence ends. The confidence interval for the mean $E(y)$ was narrower than the prediction interval for y, because of the additional uncertainty attributable to the random error ε when predicting some future value of y.

These same concepts carry over to the multiple regression model. For example, suppose we want to estimate the mean electrical usage for a given home size, say $x_p = 1,500$ square feet. Assuming the quadratic model represents the true relationship between electrical usage and home size, we want to estimate

$$E(y) = \beta_0 + \beta_1 x_p + \beta_2 x_p^2$$
$$= \beta_0 + \beta_1(1,500) + \beta_2(1,500)^2$$

Substituting into the least squares prediction equation, the estimate of $E(y)$ is

$$\hat{y} = \hat{\beta}_0 + \hat{\beta}_1(1,500) + \hat{\beta}_2(1,500)^2$$
$$= -1,216.144 + 2.3989(1,500) - .00045004(1,500)^2$$
$$= 1,369.7$$

To form a confidence interval for the mean, we need to know the standard deviation of the sampling distribution for the estimator $\hat{y}$. For multiple regression models, the form of this standard deviation is rather complex. However, the SAS regression package allows us to obtain the confidence intervals for mean values of y at any given setting of the independent variables. This portion of the SAS output for the electrical usage example is shown in Figure 12.12. The mean value and corresponding 95%

FIGURE 12.12
SAS PRINTOUT FOR
ESTIMATED MEAN
VALUE AND
CORRESPONDING
CONFIDENCE INTERVAL
FOR x = 1,500

x	PREDICTED VALUE	LOWER 95% CL FOR MEAN	UPPER 95% CL FOR MEAN
1500	1369.66088739	1324.98831001	1414.33346477

confidence interval for $x = 1,500$ are shown in the columns labeled PREDICTED VALUE, LOWER 95% CL FOR MEAN, and UPPER 95% CL FOR MEAN. Note that

$$\hat{y} = 1,369.7$$

which agrees with our earlier calculation. The 95% confidence interval for the true mean of y is shown to be 1,325.0 to 1,414.3 (see Figure 12.13).

If we were interested in predicting the electrical usage for a particular 1,500 square foot home, $\hat{y} = 1,369.7$ would be used as the predicted value. However, the prediction interval for a particular value of y will be wider than the confidence interval for the mean value. This is reflected by the printout shown in Figure 12.14, which gives the predicted values of y and corresponding 95% prediction intervals for each predicted

FIGURE 12.13
CONFIDENCE INTERVAL
FOR MEAN
ELECTRICAL USAGE

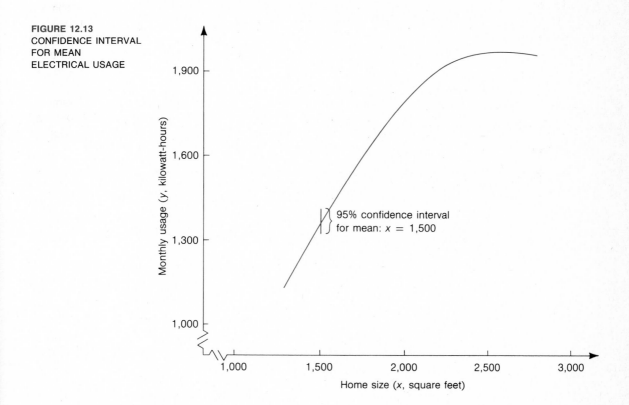

FIGURE 12.14
SAS PRINTOUT FOR
PREDICTED VALUE
AND CORRESPONDING
PREDICTION INTERVAL
FOR x = 1,500

x	PREDICTED VALUE	LOWER 95% CL INDIVIDUAL	UPPER 95% CL INDIVIDUAL
1500	1369.66088739	1250.31627944	1489.00549533

value. The last predicted value is for x = 1,500, and the prediction interval extends from 1,250.3 to 1,489.0. This interval is shown in Figure 12.15.

Unfortunately, not all computer packages have the capability to produce confidence intervals for means and prediction intervals for particular y values. This is a rather serious oversight, since the estimation of mean values and the prediction of particular values represent the culmination of our model building efforts: using the model to make inferences about the dependent variable y.

FIGURE 12.15
PREDICTION INTERVAL FOR
ELECTRICAL USAGE

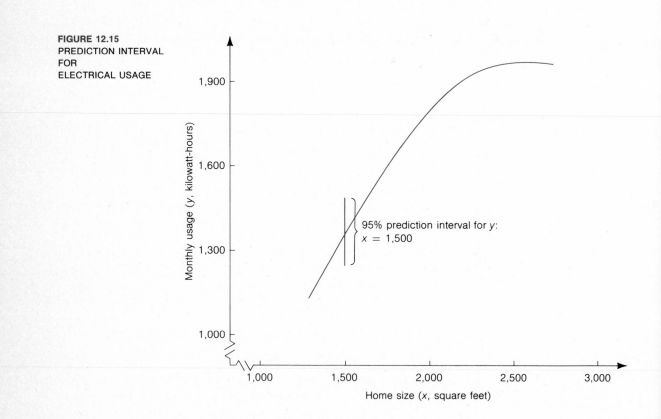

12.6 MULTIPLE REGRESSION: AN EXAMPLE

Let us return to the executive compensation example introduced in Case Study 12.1. Recall that the management consultant firm of Towers, Perrin, Forster & Crosby (TPF&C) uses a multiple regression model to project executive salaries. Suppose the list of independent variables given in Table 12.3 is to be used to build a model for the salaries of corporate executives.

TABLE 12.3
LIST OF INDEPENDENT VARIABLES FOR EXECUTIVE COMPENSATION EXAMPLE

INDEPENDENT VARIABLE	DESCRIPTION
x_1	Years of experience
x_2	Years of education
x_3	1 if male; 0 if female
x_4	Number of employees supervised
x_5	Corporate assets (millions of dollars)
x_6	x_1^2
x_7	$x_3 x_4$

Step 1. The first step is to hypothesize a model relating executive salary to the independent variables listed above. TPF&C have found that executive compensation models that use the logarithm of salary as the dependent variable provide better predictive models than those using the salary as the dependent variable. This is probably because salaries tend to be incremented in *percentages* rather than dollar values. When a dependent variable undergoes percentage changes as the independent variables are varied, the logarithm of the dependent variable will be more suitable as a dependent variable. The model we propose is

$$y = \beta_0 + \beta_1 x_1 + \beta_2 x_2 + \beta_3 x_3 + \beta_4 x_4 + \beta_5 x_5 + \beta_6 x_6 + \beta_7 x_7 + \varepsilon$$

where $y = $ log (Executive salary), $x_6 = x_1^2$ (quadratic term in years of experience), and $x_7 = x_3 x_4$ (cross product or interaction term between sex and number of employees supervised). The variable x_3 is a **dummy** variable; it is used to describe an independent variable that is not measured on a numerical scale, but instead is qualitative (categorical) in nature. Sex is such a variable, since its values, male and female, are categories rather than numbers. Thus, we assign the value $x_3 = 1$ if the executive is male, $x_3 = 0$ if the executive is female. For more detail on the use and interpretation of dummy variables, see Chapter 13. The interaction term $x_3 x_4$ accounts for the fact that the relationship between the number of employees supervised, x_4, on corporate salary is dependent on sex, x_3. For example, as the number of supervised employees increases, a woman's salary (with all other factors being equal) might rise more rapidly than a man's. This concept (interaction) is also explained in more detail in Chapter 13.

Step 2. Now, we estimate the model coefficients $\beta_0, \beta_1, \ldots, \beta_7$. Suppose that a sample of 100 executives is selected, and the variables y and $x_1, x_2, \ldots, x_7$ are recorded (or, in the case of x_6 and x_7, calculated). The sample is then used as input

FIGURE 12.16
SAS PRINTOUT FOR EXECUTIVE COMPENSATION EXAMPLE

SOURCE	DF	SUM OF SQUARES	MEAN SQUARE	F VALUE	PR > F
MODEL	7	27.06425564	3.85632223	1819.30	0.0001
ERROR	92	0.19551523	0.00212517		STD DEV
CORRECTED TOTAL	99	27.25977087		R-SQUARE	0.0460995
				0.992828	

PARAMETER	ESTIMATE	T FOR HO: PARAMETER = 0	PR > |T|	STD ERROR OF ESTIMATE
INTERCEPT	8.87878688	192.49	0.0001	0.04612667
X1 (EXPERIENCE)	0.04460301	26.83	0.0001	0.00166257
X2 (EDUCATION)	0.03326230	12.31	0.0001	0.00270306
X3 (SEX)	0.11892473	6.89	0.0001	0.01724977
X4 (EMPLOYEES SUPERVISED)	0.00033216	19.97	0.0001	0.00001664
X5 (ASSETS)	0.00201021	73.25	0.0001	0.00002744
X6 (= X1*X1)	−0.00071702	−15.11	0.0001	0.00004746
X7 (= X3*X4)	0.00031244	16.16	0.0001	0.00001933

for SAS regression routine; the output is shown in Figure 12.16. The least squares model is

$$\hat{y} = 8.88 + .045x_1 + .033x_2 + .119x_3 + .00033x_4$$
$$+ .0020x_5 - .00072x_6 + .00031x_7$$

Step 3. The next step is to specify the probability distribution of ε, the random error component. We assume that ε is normally distributed, with a mean of zero and a constant variance σ^2. Furthermore, we assume that the errors are independent. The estimate of the variance σ^2 is given in the SAS printout as

$$s^2 = \text{MSE} = \frac{\text{SSE}}{n - (k + 1)} = \frac{\text{SSE}}{100 - (7 + 1)}$$
$$= 0.0021$$

Step 4. We now want to see how well the model predicts salaries. First, note that $R^2 = .993$. This implies that 99.3% of the variation in y (the logarithm of salaries) for these 100 sampled executives is accounted for by the model. The significance of this can be tested:

H_0: $\beta_1 = \beta_2 = \cdots = \beta_7 = 0$

H_a: At least one of the model coefficients is nonzero

Test statistic: $F = \dfrac{R^2/k}{(1 - R^2)/[n - (k + 1)]}$

Rejection region: For $\alpha = .05$, $F > F_{.05, k, n - (k + 1)}$

where from Table VI of Appendix B, $F_{.05,7,92} \simeq 2.1$. The test statistic is given on the SAS printout. Since $F = 1,819.3$ exceeds the tabulated value of F, we conclude that the model does contribute information for predicting executive salaries. It appears that at least one or more of the β parameters in the model differs from zero.

We may be particularly interested in whether this data provides evidence that the mean salaries of executives increase as the asset value of the company increases, when all other variables (experience, education, etc.) are held constant. Putting it another way, we may want to know whether the data provide sufficient evidence to show that $\beta_5 > 0$. We use the following test:

$$H_0: \quad \beta_5 = 0 \qquad H_a: \quad \beta_5 > 0$$

$$\text{Test statistic:} \quad t = \frac{\hat{\beta}_5}{s_{\hat{\beta}_5}}$$

For $\alpha = .05$, $n = 100$, $k = 7$, and $n - (k + 1) = 92$, we will reject H_0 if $t > t_{.05,92}$, where (because the degrees of freedom of t are so large) $t_{.05,92} \approx z_{.05} = 1.645$. Thus, we reject if

$$t > 1.645$$

The t value is indicated in Figure 12.16. The value corresponding to the independent variable x_5 is 73.25. Since this value exceeds 1.645, we find evidence that the mean salaries of executives do depend on the firm's assets.

Step 5. The culmination of the modeling effort is to use the model for estimation and/or prediction. Suppose a firm is trying to determine fair compensation for an executive with the characteristics shown in Table 12.4. The least squares model can be used to obtain a predicted value for the logarithm of salary. That is,

$$\hat{y} = \hat{\beta}_0 + \hat{\beta}_1(12) + \hat{\beta}_2(16) + \hat{\beta}_3(0) + \hat{\beta}_4(400) + \hat{\beta}_5(160.1) + \hat{\beta}_6(144) + \hat{\beta}_7(0)$$

**TABLE 12.4
VALUES OF
INDEPENDENT
VARIABLES FOR
AN EXECUTIVE**

$x_1 = 12$ years of experience
$x_2 = 16$ years of education
$x_3 = 0$ (female)
$x_4 = 400$ employees supervised
$x_5 = \$160.1$ million (the firm's asset value)
$x_6 = x_1^2 = 144$
$x_7 = x_3 x_4 = 0$

This predicted value is given in Figure 12.17, a partial reproduction of the SAS regression printout for this problem: $\hat{y} = 10.298$. The 95% prediction interval is also given: from 10.203 to 10.392. To predict the salary of an executive with these characteristics we take the antilog of these values. That is, the predicted salary is $e^{10.298} = \$29,700$ (rounded to the nearest hundred) and the 95% prediction interval is from $e^{10.203}$ to $e^{10.392}$ (or from \$27,000 to \$32,600). Thus, an executive with the characteristics in Table 12.4 should be paid between \$27,000 and \$32,600 to be consistent with the sample data.

FIGURE 12.17
SAS PRINTOUT FOR EXECUTIVE COMPENSATION PROBLEM

							PREDICTED VALUE	LOWER 95% CL INDIVIDUAL	UPPER 95% CL INDIVIDUAL
X1	X2	X3	X4	X5	X6	X7			
12	16	0	400	160.1	144	0	10.29766682	10.20298295	10.39235070

SUMMARY

We have discussed some of the methodology of multiple regression analysis, a technique for modeling a dependent variable y as a function of several independent variables $x_1, x_2, \ldots, x_k$. The steps we follow in constructing and using multiple regression models are much the same as those for the simple straight-line models:

1. The form of the probabilistic model is hypothesized.
2. The model coefficients are estimated using least squares.
3. The probability distribution of ε is specified and σ^2 is estimated.
4. The utility of the model is checked.
5. If the model is deemed useful, it may be used to make estimates and to predict values of y to be observed in the future.

We have covered steps 2–5 in Chapter 12, assuming that the model was specified. Chapter 13 is devoted to model construction—step 1.

We stress that this is not intended to be a complete coverage of multiple regression analysis. Whole texts have been devoted to this topic. However, we have presented the core necessary for a basic understanding of multiple regression. If you are interested in a more extensive coverage, consult the references at the end of this chapter.

SUPPLEMENTARY EXERCISES

12.7. After a regression model is fit to a set of data, a confidence interval for the mean value of y at a given setting of the independent variables will *always* be narrower than the corresponding prediction interval for a particular value of y at the same setting of the independent variables. Why?

12.8. Before accepting a job, a computer at a major university estimates the cost of running the job in order to see if the user's account contains enough money to cover the cost. As part of the job submission, the user must specify estimated values for two variables—central processing unit (CPU) time and lines printed. While the CPU time required and the lines printed do not account for the complete cost of the run, it is thought that knowledge of their values should allow a good prediction of job cost. The following model is proposed to explain the relationship of CPU time and lines printed to job cost:

$$E(y) = \beta_0 + \beta_1 x_1 + \beta_2 x_2 + \beta_3 x_1 x_2$$

where

PORTION OF THE SAS PRINTOUT FOR EXERCISE 12.8

SOURCE	DF	SUM OF SQUARES	MEAN SQUARE	F VALUE	PR > F
MODEL	3	43.25090461	14.41696820	84.96	0.0001
ERROR	16	2.71515039	0.16969690		STD DEV
CORRECTED TOTAL	19	45.96605500		R-SQUARE	0.41194283
				0.940931	

PARAMETER	ESTIMATE	T FOR HO: PARAMETER = 0	PR > |T|	STD ERROR OF ESTIMATE
INTERCEPT	0.04564705	0.22	0.8313	0.21082636
X1	0.00078505	5.80	0.0001	0.00013537
X2	0.23737262	7.50	0.0001	0.03163301
X1 * X2	-0.00003809	-2.99	0.0086	0.00001273

X1	X2	PREDICTED VALUE	LOWER 95% CL FOR MEAN	UPPER 95% CL FOR MEAN
4.2	2000	8.38574865	7.32284845	9.44864885

y = Job cost

x_1 = Lines printed

x_2 = CPU time

Records from twenty previous runs were used to fit this model.

a. Identify the least squares model that was fit to the data.

b. What are the values of SSE and s^2 (estimate of σ^2) for the data?

c. What do we mean by the statement: This value of SSE (see part b) is minimum?

12.9. Refer to Exercise 12.8, and the portion of the SAS printout shown.

a. Is there evidence that the model is useful (as a whole) for predicting job cost? Test at α = .05.

b. Is there evidence that the variables x_1 and x_2 interact to affect y? Test at α = .01.

c. What assumptions are necessary for the validity of the tests conducted in parts a and b?

12.10. Refer to Exercise 12.8 and the portion of the SAS printout shown. Use a 95% confidence interval to estimate the mean cost of computer jobs that require 4.2 seconds of CPU time and print 2,000 lines.

12.11. Most companies institute rigorous safety programs in order to assure employee safety. Suppose that accident reports over the last year at a company are sampled, and the number of hours the employee had worked before the accident occurred, x, and the amount of time the employee lost from work, y, are recorded. A quadratic model is proposed to investigate a fatigue hypothesis that more serious accidents occur near the end of workdays than near the beginning. Thus, the proposed model is

$$E(y) = \beta_0 + \beta_1 x + \beta_2 x^2$$

A total of sixty accident reports are examined and part of the computer printout appears as shown.

SOURCE	DF	SUM OF SQUARES	MEAN SQUARE	F VALUE
MODEL	2	112.110	56.055	1.28
ERROR	57	2496.201	43.793	R-SQUARE
TOTAL	59	2608.311		.0430

a. Do these data support the fatigue hypothesis? Use $\alpha = .05$ to test this hypothesis by testing whether the proposed model is useful in predicting the lost work time, y.

b. Does the result of the test in part a necessarily mean that no fatigue factor exists? Explain.

12.12. Refer to Exercise 12.11. Suppose the company persists in using the quadratic model despite its apparent lack of utility. The fitted model is

$$\hat{y} = 12.3 + 0.25x - .0033x^2$$

where $\hat{y}$ is the predicted time lost (days) and x is the number of hours worked prior to an accident.

a. Use the model to predict the number of days missed by an employee who has an accident after 6 hours of work.

b. Suppose the 95% confidence interval for the estimated mean in part a is (1.35, 26.01). What is the interpretation of this interval? Does this interval reconfirm your conclusion about this model in Exercise 12.11?

12.13. A company that relies on door-to-door sales wants to determine the relationship, if any, between the proportion of customers who buy its product, y, and two independent variables: price, x_1, and years of experience of the salesperson, x_2. Twenty salespeople employed by the company are randomly assigned to sell the products, five to each of four prices, ranging from $1.98 to $5.98. Each salesperson makes a sales presentation to thirty prospects, and the percentage of sales is recorded. The twenty observations (five salespeople for each of four prices) are used to fit the model

$$y = \beta_0 + \beta_1 x_1 + \beta_2 x_2 + \varepsilon$$

The least squares model is

$$\hat{y} = -.30 - .010x_1 + .10x_2$$

with $s_{\hat{\beta}_1} = .0030$, $s_{\hat{\beta}_2} = .025$, and $R^2 = .86$.

    a.   Interpret the values of $\hat{\beta}_1$ and $\hat{\beta}_2$.

    b.   Test the null hypothesis, H_0: $\beta_1 = \beta_2 = 0$, that the model is not useful for predicting y. Use $\alpha = .05$.

    c.   Do the data support the research hypothesis that as the price of the product is increased the mean proportion of buyers will decrease?

    d.   Is there evidence that as the experience of the salesperson increases the mean proportion of buyers increases?

12.14. Refer to Exercise 12.13. Suppose it is claimed that the least squares model cannot be correct, since the value of $\hat{\beta}_0 = -.30$, and a negative proportion of buyers is clearly impossible. How do you refute this argument?

12.15. To increase the motivation and productivity of workers, an electronics manufacturer decides to experiment with a new pay incentive structure at one of two plants. The experimental plan will be tried at plant A for 6 months, while workers at plant B will remain on the original pay plan. To evaluate the effectiveness of the new plan, the average assembly time for part of an electronic system was measured for employees at both plants at the beginning and end of the 6 month period. Suppose the following model was proposed:

$$y = \beta_0 + \beta_1 x_1 + \beta_2 x_2 + \varepsilon$$

where

    y = Assembly time (hours) at end of 6 month period

    x_1 = Assembly time (hours) at beginning of 6 month period

$$x_2 = \begin{cases} 1 & \text{if plant A} \\ 0 & \text{if plant B} \end{cases} \text{ (dummy variable)}$$

A sample of $n = 42$ observations yielded

$$\hat{y} = 0.11 + 0.98x_1 - 0.53x_2$$

where

$$s_{\hat{\beta}_1} = .231 \qquad s_{\hat{\beta}_2} = .48$$

Test to see whether, after allowing for the effect of initial assembly time, plant A had a lower mean assembly time than plant B. Use $\alpha = .01$. [*Note:* When the (0, 1) coding is used to define a dummy variable, the coefficient of the variable represents the difference between the mean response at the two levels represented by the variable. Thus, the coefficient β_2 is the difference in mean assembly time between plant A and plant B at the end of the 6 month period, and $\hat{\beta}_2$ is the sample estimator of that difference.]

12.16. The Environmental Protection Agency (EPA) wants to model the gas mileage ratings, y, of automobiles as a function of their engine size, x. A quadratic model,

$$y = \beta_0 + \beta_1 x + \beta_2 x^2$$

is proposed. A sample of fifty engines of varying sizes is selected and the miles per gallon rating of each is determined. The least squares model is

$$\hat{y} = 51.3 - 10.1x + 0.15x^2$$

The size, x, of the engine is measured in hundreds of cubic inches. Also, $s_{\hat{\beta}_2} = .0037$ and $R^2 = .93$.

    a. Sketch this model between $x = 1$ and $x = 4$.
    b. Is there evidence that the quadratic term in the model is contributing to the prediction of the miles per gallon rating, y? Use $\alpha = .05$.
    c. Use the model to estimate the mean miles per gallon rating for all cars with 350 cubic inch engines ($x = 3.5$).
    d. Suppose a 95% confidence interval for the quantity estimated in part c is (17.2, 18.4). Interpret this interval.
    e. Suppose you purchase an automobile with a 350 cubic inch engine and determine that the miles per gallon rating is 14.7. Is the fact that this value lies outside the confidence interval given in part d surprising? Explain.

12.17. To determine whether extra personnel are needed for the day, the owners of a water adventure park would like to find a model that would allow them to predict the day's attendance each morning before opening based on the day of the week and weather conditions. The model is of the form

$$E(y) = \beta_0 + \beta_1 x_1 + \beta_2 x_2 + \beta_3 x_3$$

where

    y = Daily admissions

$$x_1 = \begin{cases} 1 & \text{if weekend} \\ 0 & \text{otherwise} \end{cases} \quad \text{(dummy variable)}$$

$$x_2 = \begin{cases} 1 & \text{if sunny} \\ 0 & \text{if overcast} \end{cases} \quad \text{(dummy variable)}$$

    x_3 = Predicted daily high temperature ($^\circ$F)

After taking 30 days of data, the following least squares model is obtained:

$$\hat{y} = -105 + 25x_1 + 100x_2 + 10x_3$$

with

$$s_{\hat{\beta}_1} = 10, \, s_{\hat{\beta}_2} = 30, \text{ and } s_{\hat{\beta}_3} = 4. \text{ Also, } R^2 = .65.$$

a. Interpret the model coefficients.

b. Is there sufficient evidence to conclude that this model is useful in the prediction of daily attendance? Use $\alpha = .05$.

c. Is there sufficient evidence to conclude that mean attendance increases on weekends? Use $\alpha = .10$.

d. Use the model to predict the attendance on a sunny weekday with a predicted high temperature of 95°F.

e. Suppose the 90% prediction interval for part d is (645, 1,245). Interpret this interval.

12.18. Refer to Exercise 12.17. The owners of the water adventure park are advised that the prediction model could probably be improved if interaction terms were added. In particular, it is thought that the *rate* of increase in mean attendance with increases in predicted high temperature will be greater on weekends than on weekdays. The following model is therefore proposed:

$$E(y) = \beta_0 + \beta_1 x_1 + \beta_2 x_2 + \beta_3 x_3 + \beta_4 x_1 x_3$$

The same 30 days of data as were used in Exercise 12.17 are again used to obtain the least squares model

$$\hat{y} = 250 - 700x_1 + 100x_2 + 5x_3 + 15x_1 x_3$$

with

$$s_{\hat{\beta}_2} = 3.0 \text{ and } R^2 = .96.$$

a. Graph the predicted day's attendance, y, against the day's predicted high temperature, x_3, for a sunny weekday and for a sunny weekend day. Graph both on the same paper for x_3 between 70°F and 100°F. Note the increase in slope for the weekend day.

b. Do the data indicate that the interaction term is a useful addition to the model? Use $\alpha = .05$.

c. Use this model to predict the attendance for a sunny weekday with a predicted high temperature of 95°F.

d. Suppose the 90% prediction interval for part c is (800, 850). Compare this with the prediction interval for the model without interaction in Exercise 12.17, part e. Do the relative widths of the confidence intervals support or refute your conclusion about the utility of the interaction term (part b)?

12.19. Refer to Exercise 12.18. The owners, noting that the coefficient $\hat{\beta}_1 = -700$, conclude the model is ridiculous, because it seems to imply that the mean attendance will be 700 less on weekends than on weekdays. Refute their argument.

12.20. Many students must work parttime to help finance their college education. A survey of 100 students was completed at a university to see if the number of hours worked per week, x, was affecting their grade-point averages, y. A quadratic model was proposed:

$$y = \beta_0 + \beta_1 x + \beta_2 x^2 + \varepsilon$$

The 100 observations yielded the least squares model

$$\hat{y} = 2.8 - .005x - .0002x^2$$

with $R^2 = .12$.

    a. Do these statistics indicate that the model is useful in explaining grade-point averages? Use $\alpha = .05$.

    b. Interpret the value $R^2 = .12$. Do you think the relationship between x and y is strong? Would you expect to be able to predict grade-point averages precisely (narrow prediction interval) if you knew how many hours students work per week?

12.21. Recent increases in gasoline prices have increased interest in modes of transportation other than the automobile. A metropolitan bus company wants to know if changes in numbers of bus riders are related to changes in gasoline prices. By using information contained in the company files and gasoline price information obtained from fuel distributors, the company planned to fit the following model:

$$y = \beta_0 + \beta_1 x_1 + \beta_2 x_2 + \beta_3 x_1 x_2 + \varepsilon$$

where

    x_1 = Average wholesale price for regular gas in a given month

$$x_2 = \begin{cases} 1 & \text{if the bus travels a city route only} \\ 0 & \text{if the bus travels a suburb–city route} \end{cases}$$

    y = Total number of riders in a bus over the month

    a. For the above model, how would you test to see if the relationship between gasoline price and the mean number of riders is different for the two different types of bus routes?

    b. Suppose 12 months of data are kept, and the least squares model is

$$\hat{y} = 500 + 50x_1 + 5x_2 - 10x_1 x_2$$

Graph the predicted relationship between numbers of riders and gas price for city buses and for suburb–city buses. Compare the slopes.

    c. If $s_{\hat{\beta}_3} = 3.0$, do the data indicate that gas price affects the number of riders differently for city and suburb buses? Use $\alpha = .05$.

12.22. During the winter months a sample of 100 homes is taken to obtain information concerning the relationship between kilowatt usage, y, and total window and glass area, x (measured as a percentage of the total wall area). The correlation coefficient for the data was equal to .24. Test to see whether the data indicate that some relationship exists between y and x. Use $\alpha = .05$. [*Hint:* Use the methods of Section 12.4.]

ON YOUR OWN . . .

[*Note:* The use of a computer is required for this study.]

This is a continuation of the "On Your Own" presented in Chapter 11, in which you selected three independent variables as predictors of the Gross National Product, and obtained 10 years of data for each. Now fit the multiple regression model (use an available computer package, if possible)

$$y = \beta_0 + \beta_1 x_1 + \beta_2 x_2 + \beta_3 x_3 + \varepsilon$$

where

$y = $ Gross National Product

$x_1 = $ First variable you chose

$x_2 = $ Second variable you chose

$x_3 = $ Third variable you chose

a. Compare the coefficients $\hat{\beta}_1$, $\hat{\beta}_2$, and $\hat{\beta}_3$ to their corresponding slope coefficients in the Chapter 11 "On Your Own," where you fit three separate straight-line models. How do you account for the differences?

b. Calculate the coefficient of determination R^2, and conduct the F test of the null hypothesis H_0: $\beta_1 = \beta_2 = \beta_3 = 0$. What is your conclusion?

If the independent variables you chose are themselves highly correlated, you may encounter some results that are difficult to explain. For example, the coefficients $\hat{\beta}_1$, $\hat{\beta}_2$, and $\hat{\beta}_3$ may assume signs that run counter to what you expected. Or you may get a highly significant F value in part b, but the individual t statistics for x_1, x_2, and x_3 may all be nonsignificant. This phenomenon— a high correlation between the independent variables in a regression model—is known as **multicollinearity**. We will discuss it in more detail in Chapter 13.

REFERENCES

Chou, Ya-lun. *Statistical analysis with business and economic applications.* 2d ed. New York: Holt, Rinehart, and Winston, 1975. Chapter 18.

Hamburg, M. *Statistical analysis for decision making.* 2d ed. New York: Harcourt Brace Jovanovich, 1977. Chapter 9.

Miller, R. B., & Wichern, D. W. *Intermediate business statistics: Analysis of variance, regression, and time series.* New York: Holt, Rinehart, and Winston, 1977. Chapters 6–8.

Neter, J. & Wasserman, W. *Applied linear statistical models.* Homewood, Ill.: Richard Irwin, 1974. Chapter 7.

Winkler, R. L., & Hays, W. L. *Statistics: Probability, inference, and decision.* 2d ed. New York: Holt, Rinehart, and Winston, 1975. Chapter 10.

One of the most important topics in applied statistics, regression analysis, was presented in Chapters 11 and 12. Simple linear regression, using a straight line to model the relationship between the mean of a population and a single independent variable, was the topic of Chapter 11. Multiple regression, relating a population mean to any number of qualitative or quantitative independent variables, was the topic of Chapter 12. In both chapters we learned how to fit regression models to a set of data and how to use the model to estimate the mean value of y or to predict a future value of y for a given value of x.

WHERE WE'RE GOING . . .

Chapters 11 and 12 discussed, in general, how to use regression analysis to solve business problems. But an important problem was circumvented—the selection of a model that is appropriate for the given data. No matter how much you know about regression analysis, or how well you can fit a model to a set of data and interpret the results, the information will be of little value if you choose an ill-fitting model to relate the mean value of y to the independent variables. How to choose a reasonable model and how to use the data to modify and improve it, is called model building. This is the topic of Chapter 13.

13

MODEL BUILDING

We have emphasized in both Chapters 11 and 12 that the first step in the construction of a regression model is to hypothesize the form of the deterministic portion of the probabilistic model. This **model building,** or model construction, stage is the key to the success (or failure) of the regression analysis. If the hypothesized model does not reflect, at least approximately, the true nature of the relationship between the mean response $E(y)$ and the independent variables $x_1, x_2, \ldots, x_k$, the modeling effort will usually be unrewarded.

By model building, we mean writing a model that will provide a good fit to a set of data and that will give good estimates of the mean value of y and good predictions of future values of y for given values of the independent variables. To illustrate, several years ago, a nationally recognized educational research group issued a report concerning the variables related to academic achievement for a certain type of college student. The researchers selected a random sample of students and recorded a measure of academic achievement, y, at the end of the senior year along with data on an extensive list of independent variables, $x_1, x_2, \ldots, x_k$, that they thought were related to y. They fit the model

$$E(y) = \beta_0 + \beta_1 x_1 + \beta_2 x_2 + \cdots + \beta_k x_k$$

to their data, analyzed the results, and reached the conclusion that none of the independent variables are ''significantly related'' to y. The **goodness of fit** of the model, measured by the coefficient of determination R^2, was not particularly good and t tests on individual parameters did not lead to rejection of the null hypothesis that these parameters equaled zero.

How could the researchers have reached the conclusion that there is no significant relationship, when it is evident to the average person, just as a matter of experience, that some of the independent variables studied are related to academic achievement? For example, achievement on a college mathematics placement test should be related to achievement in college mathematics. Certainly, many other variables will affect achievement—motivation, environmental conditions, etc.—but generally speaking, there will be a positive correlation between entrance achievement test scores and college academic achievement. So, what went wrong with the educational researchers' study?

Although you can never discard the possibility of computing error as a reason for erroneous answers, most likely the difficulties in the results of the educational study were caused by the use of an improperly constructed model. For example, the model

$$E(y) = \beta_0 + \beta_1 x_1 + \beta_2 x_2 + \cdots + \beta_k x_k$$

assumes that the independent variables $x_1, x_2, \ldots, x_k$ affect mean achievement $E(y)$ independently of each other.* Thus, if you hold all the other independent variables constant and only vary x_1, $E(y)$ will increase by the amount β_1 for every unit increase in x_1. A 1 unit change in each of the other independent variables will increase $E(y)$ by the value of the β parameter for that variable.

---

*Keep in mind that we are discussing the deterministic portion of the model and that the word *independent* is used in a mathematical rather than in a probabilistic sense.

Do the assumptions implied by the model agree with your knowledge about academic achievement? First, is it reasonable to assume that the effect of time spent on study is independent of native intellectual ability? We think not. No matter how much effort some students invest in a particular subject, their rate of achievement is low. For others, it may be high. Therefore, assuming that these two variables—effort and native intellectual ability—affect $E(y)$ independently of each other is likely to be an erroneous assumption. Second, is it reasonable to expect that 1 unit increases in a variable, say x_5, will always produce increases of β_5 in $E(y)$? The increases in $E(y)$ for a 1 unit increase in x_5 might increase or decrease depending on the value of x_5 (for example, the law of diminishing returns). Consequently, it is quite likely that the assumption of a constant rate of increase in $E(y)$ for 1 unit increases in the independent variables will not be satisfied.

Clearly, the model

$$E(y) = \beta_0 + \beta_1 x_1 + \beta_2 x_2 + \cdots + \beta_k x_k$$

was a poor choice in view of the researchers' prior knowledge of some of the variables involved. Terms have to be added to the model to account for interrelationships between the independent variables and for curvature in the response function. Failure to include needed terms causes inflated values of the SSE, nonsignificance in statistical tests, and, often, erroneous practical conclusions.

In this chapter we discuss the most difficult part of a multiple regression analysis, the formulation of a good model for $E(y)$.

13.1
THE TWO TYPES OF INDEPENDENT VARIABLES: QUANTITATIVE AND QUALITATIVE

In Chapter 2 we defined two types of variables that may arise in business applications: quantitative and qualitative. In a regression analysis the dependent variable will always be quantitative, but the independent variable may be either quantitative or qualitative. As you will see, the way an independent variable enters the model depends on its type.

DEFINITION 13.1
A **quantitative** independent variable is one that assumes numerical values corresponding to the points on a line. An independent variable that is not quantitative is called **qualitative**.

The Gross National Product, prime interest rate, number of defects in a product, and kilowatt hours of electricity used per day are all examples of quantitative independent variables. On the other hand, suppose that three different styles of packaging, A, B, and C, are used by a manufacturer. This independent variable is qualitative, since it is not measured on a numerical scale. Certainly, the style of packaging is an independent variable that may affect sales of a product, and we would want to include it in a model describing the product's sales, y.

> **DEFINITION 13.2**
> The different intensity settings of an independent variable are called its levels.

For a quantitative independent variable, the levels correspond to the numerical values it assumes. For example, if the number of defects in a product ranges from 0 to 3, the independent variable assumes four levels: 0, 1, 2, and 3.

The levels of a qualitative variable are not numerical. They can only be defined by describing them. For example, the independent variable for the style of packaging was observed at three levels: A, B, and C.

EXAMPLE 13.1   In Chapter 12 we considered the problem of predicting executive salaries as a function of several independent variables. Consider the following four independent variables that may affect executive salaries:

a. Number of years of experience
b. Sex of the employee
c. Firm's net asset value
d. Rank of the employee

For each of these independent variables, give its type and describe the nature of the levels you would expect to observe.

Solution   **a.** The independent variable for the number of years of experience is quantitative, since its values are numerical. We would expect to observe levels ranging from 0 to 40 (approximately) years.
b. The independent variable for sex is qualitative, since its levels can only be described by the nonnumerical labels "female" and "male."
c. The independent variable for the firm's net asset value is quantitative, with a very large number of possible levels corresponding to the range of dollar values representing various firms' net asset values.
d. Suppose the independent variable for the rank of the employee is observed at three levels: supervisor, assistant vice president, and vice president. Since we cannot assign a realistic measure of relative importance to each position, rank is a qualitative independent variable.

Quantitative independent variables are treated differently in regression modeling than are qualitative variables. In the next section, we will begin our discussion of how quantitative variables are used.

EXERCISES   **13.1.**   Companies keep personnel files on their employees that contain important information on each individual's background. These data could be used to predict employee performance ratings. Identify the independent variables listed below as qualitative or quantitative. For qualitative variables, suggest several levels that might be observed. For quantitative variables, give a range of values (levels) for which the variable might be observed.

    a. Age
    b. Years of experience with the company
    c. Highest educational degree
    d. Job classification
    e. Marital status
    f. Religious preference
    g. Salary
    h. Sex

13.2. Which of the assumptions about ε (Section 11.3) prohibit the use of a qualitative variable as a dependent variable?

13.2
MODELS FOR A SINGLE QUANTITATIVE INDEPENDENT VARIABLE

To write a prediction equation that provides a good model for a response (one that will eventually yield good predictions), we have to know how the response might vary as the levels of an independent variable change. Then we have to know how to write a mathematical equation to model it. To illustrate (with a simple example), suppose we want to model corporate profit, y, as a function of the single independent variable x, the amount of capital invested. It may be that corporate profit, y, increases in a straight line as the amount of capital invested, x, varies from \$1 to 2 million, as shown in Figure 13.1(a). If this were the entire range of x values for which you wanted to predict y, the model

$$E(y) = \beta_0 + \beta_1 x$$

would be appropriate.

FIGURE 13.1
MODELING CORPORATE PROFIT, y, AS A FUNCTION OF CAPITAL INVESTED, x

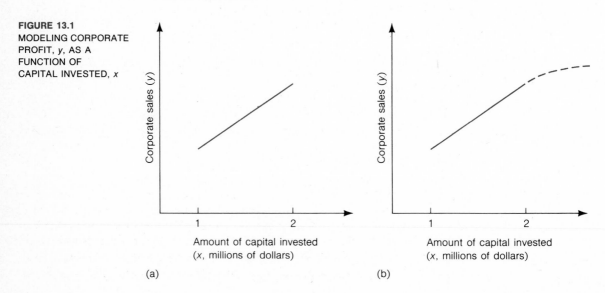

(a)
(b)

Amount of capital invested
(x, millions of dollars)

Amount of capital invested
(x, millions of dollars)

Now, suppose you want to expand the range of values of x to $x = \$3$ or 4 million of capital investment. Will the straight-line model

$$E(y) = \beta_0 + \beta_1 x$$

be satisfactory? Perhaps, but making this assumption could be risky. As the amount of capital invested, x, is increased, sooner or later the point of diminishing returns will be reached. That is, the unit increase in profit for a unit increase in capital invested will decrease, as shown by the dashed line in Figure 13.1(b). To produce this type of curvature, you need to know the relationship between models and graphs, and how types of terms will change the shape of the curve.

A response that is a function of a single quantitative independent variable can often be modeled by the first few terms of a polynomial. The equation for a polynomial of order p in one independent variable x is shown below.

FORMULA FOR A pTH-ORDER POLYNOMIAL FOR ONE INDEPENDENT VARIABLE

$$E(y) = \beta_0 + \beta_1 x + \beta_2 x^2 + \beta_3 x^3 + \cdots + \beta_p x^p$$

where p is an integer and $\beta_0, \beta_1, \ldots, \beta_p$ are unknown parameters that must be estimated.

As we mentioned in Chapters 11 and 12, a first-order polynomial in x (i.e., $p = 1$),

$$E(y) = \beta_0 + \beta_1 x$$

graphs as a straight line. A second-order polynomial model ($p = 2$), called a quadratic, is given by the equation below.

A QUADRATIC MODEL FOR ONE INDEPENDENT VARIABLE

$$E(y) = \beta_0 + \beta_1 x + \beta_2 x^2$$

where β_0, β_1, and β_2 are known parameters that must be estimated.

Graphs of two quadratic models are shown in Figure 13.2. The quadratic model is the equation of a parabola that opens either upward, as in Figure 13.2(a), or downward, as in Figure 13.2(b). (If the coefficient of x^2 is positive, it opens upward; if it is negative, it opens downward.) The parabola may be shifted upward or downward, left or right. The least squares procedure only uses the portion of the parabola that is needed to model the data. For example, if you fit a parabola to the data points shown in Figure 13.3, the portion shown as a solid curve passes through the data points. The outline of the unused portion of the parabola is indicated by a dashed curve.

FIGURE 13.2
GRAPHS FOR TWO
SECOND-ORDER
POLYNOMIAL MODELS

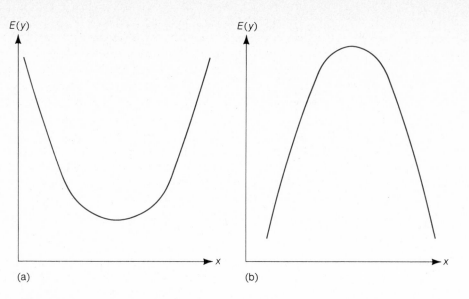

(a)   (b)

Figure 13.3 illustrates an important limitation on the use of prediction equations—the model is valid only over the range of x values that were used to fit the model. For example, the response might rise, as shown in the figure, until it reaches a plateau. The quadratic model might fit the data very well over the range of x values shown in Figure 13.3, but would provide a very poor fit if data were collected in the region where the parabola turns downward.

**FIGURE 13.3
EXAMPLE OF THE
USE OF A QUADRATIC
MODEL**

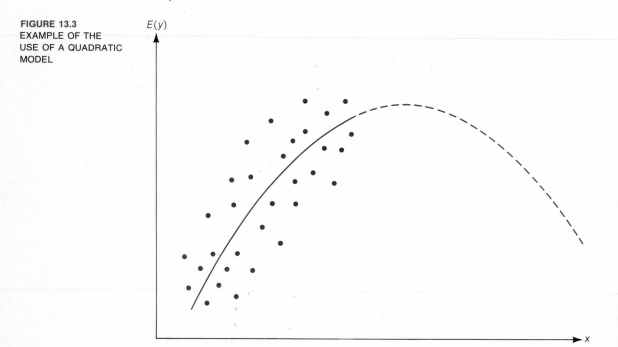

How do you decide the order of the polynomial you should use to model a response that is a function of one quantitative independent variable? You may have a rough idea as to how the response will behave as the level of the independent variable is increased. In addition, you might use the following information. The graphs of most responses as a function of an independent variable x are, in general, curvilinear. Nevertheless, if the rate of curvature of the response curve is very small over the range of x that is of interest to you, a straight line might provide an excellent fit to the response data and function as a very useful prediction equation. If the curvature is not (or may not be) slight, you should try a second-order model. Third- or higher-order models would only be used where you expect more than one reversal in the direction of the curve. These situations are rare, except where the response is a function of time. Models for forecasting over time are presented in Chapter 14.

EXAMPLE 13.2   Power companies have to be able to predict the peak power load at their various stations in order to operate effectively. The peak power load is the maximum amount of power that must be generated each day in order to meet demand.

Suppose a power company located in the southern part of the United States decides to model daily peak power load, y, as a function of the daily high temperature, x, and the model is to be constructed for the summer months when demand is greatest. Although we would expect the peak power load to increase as the high temperature increases, the *rate* of increase in $E(y)$ might also increase as x increases. That is, a 1 unit increase in high temperature from 100 to 101 °F might result in a larger increase in power demand than would a 1 unit increase from 80 to 81 °F. Therefore, we postulate the quadratic model

$$E(y) = \beta_0 + \beta_1 x + \beta_2 x^2$$

and we expect β_2 to be positive.

A random sample of 25 summer days is selected, and the data are shown in Table 13.1. Fit a quadratic model using this data, and test the hypothesis that the power load increases at an increasing *rate* with temperature, i.e., that $\beta_2 > 0$.

TABLE 13.1
POWER LOAD DATA

TEMPERATURE °F	PEAK LOAD Megawatts	TEMPERATURE °F	PEAK LOAD Megawatts	TEMPERATURE °F	PEAK LOAD Megawatts
94	136.0	106	178.2	76	100.9
96	131.7	67	101.6	68	96.3
95	140.7	71	92.5	92	135.1
108	189.3	100	151.9	100	143.6
67	96.5	79	106.2	85	111.4
88	116.4	97	153.2	89	116.5
89	118.5	98	150.1	74	103.9
84	113.4	87	114.7	86	105.1
90	132.0				

FIGURE 13.4
PORTION OF THE SAS PRINTOUT FOR THE QUADRATIC MODEL OF EXAMPLE 13.2

SOURCE	DF	SUM OF SQUARES	MEAN SQUARE	F VALUE	PR > F
MODEL	2	15011.77199776	7505.88599888	259.69	0.0001
ERROR	22	635.87840224	28.90356374		STD DEV
CORRECTED TOTAL	24	15647.65040000		R-SQUARE	5.37620347
				0.959363	

PARAMETER	ESTIMATE	T FOR H0: PARAMETER = 0	PR > |T|	STD ERROR OF ESTIMATE
INTERCEPT	385.04809323	6.98	0.0001	55.17243578
TEMP	−8.29252680	−6.38	0.0001	1.29904502
TEMP * TEMP	0.05982337	7.93	0.0001	0.00754855

FIGURE 13.5
PLOT OF THE
OBSERVATIONS AND
THE QUADRATIC
LEAST SQUARES FIT

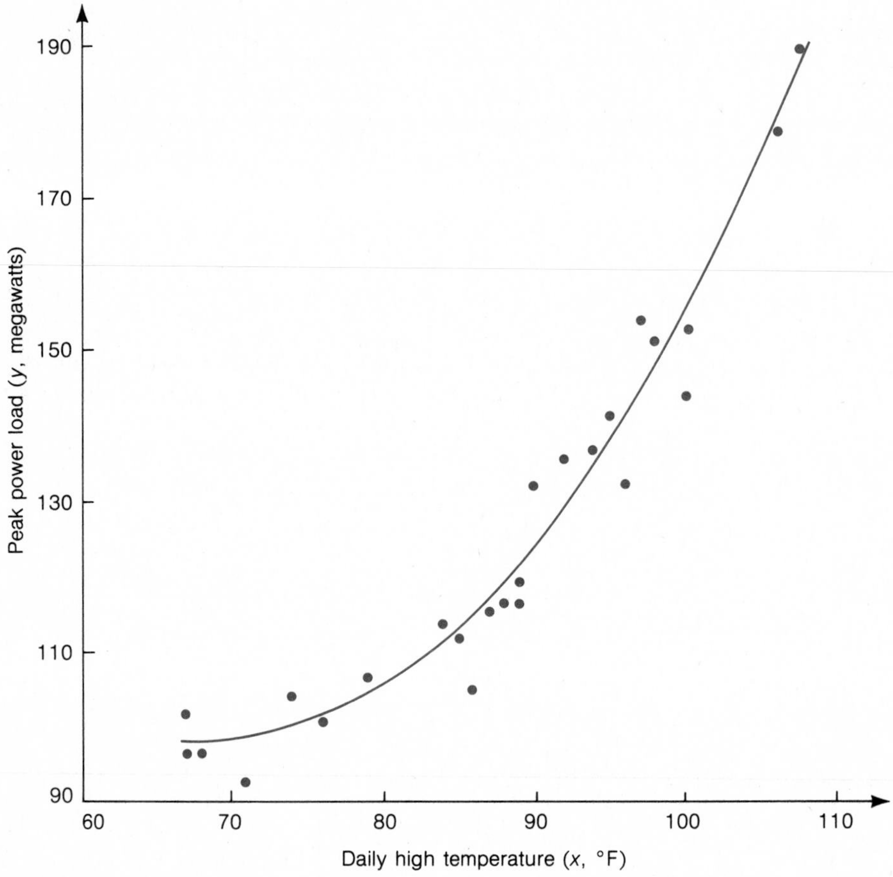

Solution

The SAS printout shown in Figure 13.4 gives the least squares fit of the quadratic model using the data in Table 13.1. The prediction equation is

$$\hat{y} = 385.048 - 8.293x + .05982x^2$$

A plot of this equation and the observed values is given in Figure 13.5.

We now test to see whether the sample value, $\hat{\beta}_2 = .05982$, is large enough to conclude *in general* that the power load increases at an increasing rate with temperature:

$$H_0: \quad \beta_2 = 0 \qquad H_a: \quad \beta_2 > 0$$

Test statistic: $\quad t = \dfrac{\hat{\beta}_2}{s_{\hat{\beta}_2}}$

For $\alpha = .05$, $n = 25$, $k = 2$, and $n - (k + 1) = 22$, we reject if

$$t > t_{.05,22}$$

where $t_{.05,22} = 1.717$ (from Table V of Appendix B). From Figure 13.4, the calculated value of t is 7.93. Since this value exceeds $t_{.05,22} = 1.717$, we reject H_0 and conclude that the mean power load increases at an increasing rate with temperature.

EXERCISES

13.3. A company is considering having the employees on its assembly line work 4 days for 10 hours each instead of 5 days for 8 hours. The management is concerned that the effect of fatigue due to longer afternoons of work might increase assembly times to an unsatisfactory level. An experiment with the 4 day week is planned in which time studies will be conducted on some of the workers during the afternoons. It is believed that an adequate model of the relationship between assembly time, y, and time since lunch, x, should allow for the average assembly time to decrease for a while after lunch (as workers get back in the groove) before it starts to increase as the workers become tired. Write a model to relate $E(y)$ and x that would reflect the management's belief, and sketch the hypothesized shape of the model.

13.4. Underinflated or overinflated tires can increase tire wear and decrease gas mileage. A new tire was tested for wear at different pressures with the results shown in the table.

PRESSURE x, pounds per square inch	MILEAGE y, thousands
30	29
31	32
32	36
33	38
34	37
35	33
36	26

a. Plot the data on a scattergram.
b. If you were only given the information for $x = 30, 31, 32, 33$, what kind of model would you suggest? For $x = 33, 34, 35, 36$? For all the data?

13.3
FIRST-ORDER MODELS FOR TWO OR MORE QUANTITATIVE INDEPENDENT VARIABLES

Like models for a single independent variable, models for two or more independent variables are classified as first-order, second-order, etc. Unfortunately, we cannot graph the response because the plot is in a multidimensional space. For example, with one quantitative independent variable, x, the response y traces a curve. But for two quantitative independent variables, x_1 and x_2, the plot of y traces a surface over the x_1, x_2-plane (see Figure 13.6). For three or more quantitative independent variables, the response traces a surface in a four- or higher-dimensional space. For these, we can construct two-dimensional contour curves for one independent variable or three-dimensional plots of response surfaces for two independent variables for fixed levels of the remaining independent variables, but this is the best we can do in providing a graphic description of a response.

A **first-order model** in k quantitative variables is a first-order polynomial in k independent variables. (See the box at the top of page 381.) For $k = 1$, the graph is a straight line. For $k = 2$, the response surface is a plane (usually tilted) over the x_1, x_2-plane.

FIGURE 13.6
A RESPONSE SURFACE FOR TWO QUANTITATIVE INDEPENDENT VARIABLES

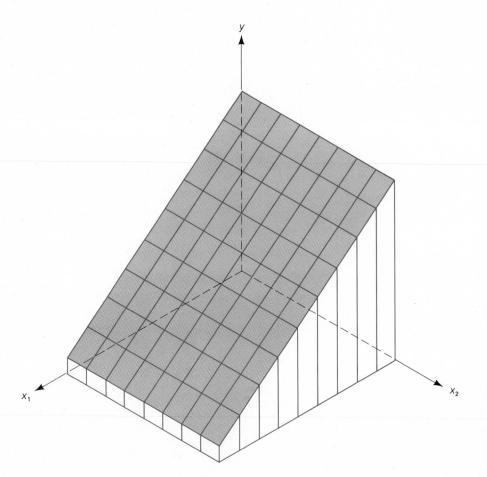

If we use a first-order polynomial to model a response, we are assuming that there is no curvature in the response surface and that the variables affect the response independently of each other. For example, suppose the true relationship between the mean response and the independent variables x_1 and x_2 is given by the equation

$$E(y) = 1 + 2x_1 + x_2$$

The response surface (a plane) corresponding to this equation is shown in Figure 13.7. The graphs of this expression for $x_2 = 1$, 2, and 3 (called contour lines), are

FIGURE 13.7
THE PLANE
$E(y) = 1 + 2x_1 + x_2$

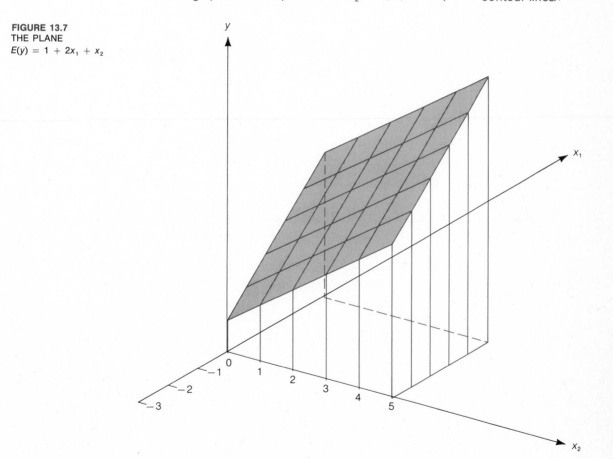

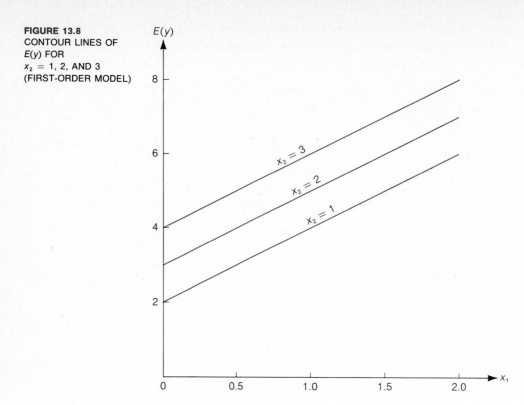

shown in Figure 13.8. You can see that when you substitute $x_2 = 1$ into the model, you obtain

$$E(y) = 1 + 2x_1 + x_2$$
$$= 1 + 2x_1 + 1$$
$$= 2 + 2x_1$$

For $x_2 = 2$,

$$E(y) = 1 + 2x_1 + 2$$
$$= 3 + 2x_1$$

And for $x_3 = 3$, $E(y) = 4 + 2x_1$. In other words, regardless of the value of x_2, $E(y)$ graphs as a straight line. Changing x_2 only changes the y-intercept (the constant in the equation). Consequently, assuming that a first-order model will adequately model a response is equivalent to assuming that a 1 unit change in one independent variable will have the same effect on the mean value of y regardless of the levels of the other independent variables. That is, **the contour lines will be parallel.**

Except in cases where the ranges of levels for all independent variables are very small, the implication of no curvature in the response surface and the independence of variable effects on the response restrict the applicability of first-order models.

13.4
SECOND-ORDER MODELS WITH TWO OR MORE QUANTITATIVE INDEPENDENT VARIABLES

Second-order models with two or more independent variables permit curvature in the response surface. One important type of second-order term is interaction between two variables. To see the effect of interaction on the model, consider the two-variable model

$$E(y) = \beta_0 + \beta_1 x_1 + \beta_2 x_2 + \beta_3 x_1 x_2$$

The term $\beta_3 x_1 x_2$ is called the interaction term, and it permits the contour lines to be nonparallel. For example, suppose the true equation of the response surface is

$$E(y) = 1 + 2x_1 + x_2 - x_1 x_2$$

We graph the contour lines of this response for $x_2 = 1$, 2, and 3 in Figure 13.9. Note that when we substitute $x_2 = 1$ into the model, we get

$$
\begin{aligned}
E(y) &= 1 + 2x_1 + x_2 - x_1 x_2 \\
&= 1 + 2x_1 + 1 - x_1(1) \\
&= 2 + x_1
\end{aligned}
$$

For $x_2 = 2$,

$$
\begin{aligned}
E(y) &= 1 + 2x_1 + 2 - x_1(2) \\
&= 3
\end{aligned}
$$

FIGURE 13.9
CONTOUR LINES OF $E(y)$ FOR $x_2 = 1$, 2, AND 3 (FIRST-ORDER PLUS INTERACTION)

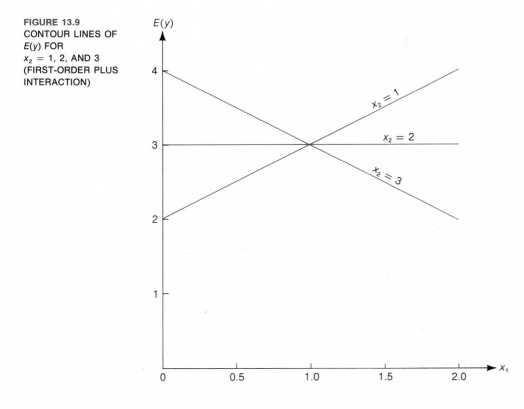

And for $x_2 = 3$, $E(y) = 4 - x_1$. Thus, when interaction is present in the model, both the y-intercept and the slope change as x_2 changes. Consequently, the contour lines are not parallel. The presence of an interaction term implies that the effect of a 1 unit change in one independent variable will depend on the level of the other independent variable. In our example (Figure 13.9), a 1 unit change in x_1 produces a 1 unit change in $E(y)$ when $x_2 = 1$, but a 1 unit change in x_1 produces *no* change in $E(y)$ when $x_2 = 2$ (i.e., the slope is zero).

We can introduce even more flexibility into a model by the addition of quadratic terms. The *complete* second-order model includes the constant β_0, all linear (first-order) terms, all two-variable interactions, and all quadratic terms. This complete second-order model for two quantitative independent variables is shown below.

COMPLETE SECOND-ORDER MODEL FOR $k = 2$ QUANTITATIVE INDEPENDENT VARIABLES

$$E(y) = \beta_0 + \beta_1 x_1 + \beta_2 x_2 + \beta_3 x_1 x_2 + \beta_4 x_1^2 + \beta_5 x_2^2$$

where $\beta_0, \beta_1, \ldots, \beta_5$ are unknown parameters that must be estimated.

FIGURE 13.10
CONTOURS OF
$E(y)$ FOR
$x_2 = 1, 2,$ AND 3
(COMPLETE SECOND-ORDER MODEL)

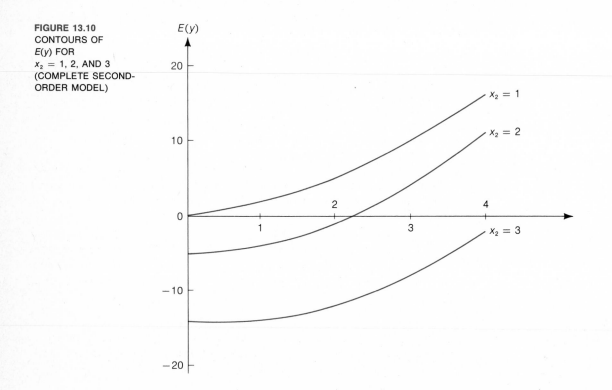

CHAPTER 13   MODEL BUILDING

The interaction term $\beta_3 x_1 x_2$ still implies that the contours of $E(y)$ for various values of x_2 will not be parallel. The quadratic terms $\beta_4 x_1^2$ and $\beta_5 x_2^2$ imply that the contours will be curvilinear. For example, suppose the complete second-order model relating $E(y)$ to x_1 and x_2 is

$$E(y) = 1 + 2x_1 + x_2 - x_1 x_2 + x_1^2 - 2x_2^2$$

Then the contours of $E(y)$ for $x_2 = 1$, 2, and 3 are shown in Figure 13.10. When we substitute $x_2 = 1$ into the model, we get

$$\begin{aligned} E(y) &= 1 + 2x_1 + x_2 - x_1 x_2 + x_1^2 - 2x_2^2 \\ &= 1 + 2x_1 + 1 - x_1(1) + x_1^2 - 2(1)^2 \\ &= x_1 + x_1^2 \end{aligned}$$

For $x_2 = 2$,

$$\begin{aligned} E(y) &= 1 + 2x_1 + 2 - x_1(2) + x_1^2 - 2(2)^2 \\ &= -5 + x_1^2 \end{aligned}$$

And $x_2 = 3$, $E(y) = -14 - x_1 + x_1^2$.

The complete second-order model for $k = 3$ independent variables is shown below.

A COMPLETE SECOND-ORDER MODEL FOR $k = 3$ INDEPENDENT VARIABLES

$$\begin{aligned} E(y) = \beta_0 &+ \beta_1 x_1 + \beta_2 x_2 + \beta_3 x_3 \\ &+ \beta_4 x_1 x_2 + \beta_5 x_1 x_3 + \beta_6 x_2 x_3 \\ &+ \beta_7 x_1^2 + \beta_8 x_2^2 + \beta_9 x_3^2 \end{aligned}$$

where $\beta_0, \beta_1, \beta_2, \ldots, \beta_9$ are unknown parameters that must be estimated.

This second-order model in $k = 3$ independent variables demonstrates how you would write a second-order model for any number of independent variables. Always include the constant β_0 and then all first-order terms corresponding to $x_1, x_2, \ldots$. Then add the interaction terms for all pairs of independent variables, $x_1 x_2$, $x_1 x_3$, $x_2 x_3, \ldots$. Finally, include the quadratic terms $x_1^2, x_2^2, \ldots$.

For $k = 3$ or more quantitative independent variables, the response traces a surface in a $(k + 1)$-dimensional space, which is impossible to visualize. In spite of this handicap, the prediction equation can still tell us much about the phenomenon being studied.

EXAMPLE 13.3   Many companies manufacture products that are at least partially chemically produced (e.g., steel, paint, gasoline). In many instances, the quality of the finished product is a function of the temperature and pressure at which the chemical reactions take place.

Suppose you wanted to model the quality, y, of a product as a function of the temperature, x_1, and the pressure, x_2, at which it is produced. Four inspectors independently assign a quality score between 0 and 100 to each product, and then the quality, y, is calculated by averaging the four scores. An experiment is conducted by varying temperature between 80 and 100°F and pressure between 50 and 60 pounds per square inch. The resulting data are given in Table 13.2. Fit a complete second-order model to this data and sketch the response surface.

TABLE 13.2
TEMPERATURE, PRESSURE, AND QUALITY OF THE FINISHED PRODUCT

x_1, °F	x_2, pounds per square inch	y	x_1, °F	x_2, pounds per square inch	y	x_1, °F	x_2, pounds per square inch	y
80	50	50.8	90	50	63.4	100	50	46.6
80	50	50.7	90	50	61.6	100	50	49.1
80	50	49.4	90	50	63.4	100	50	46.4
80	55	93.7	90	55	93.8	100	55	69.8
80	55	90.9	90	55	92.1	100	55	72.5
80	55	90.9	90	55	97.4	100	55	73.2
80	60	74.5	90	60	70.9	100	60	38.7
80	60	73.0	90	60	68.8	100	60	42.5
80	60	71.2	90	60	71.3	100	60	41.4

Solution

The complete second-order model is

$$E(y) = \beta_0 + \beta_1 x_1 + \beta_2 x_2 + \beta_3 x_1^2 + \beta_4 x_2^2 + \beta_5 x_1 x_2$$

The data in Table 13.2 were used to fit this model, and a portion of the SAS output is shown in Figure 13.11.

FIGURE 13.11
PORTION OF THE SAS PRINTOUT FOR EXAMPLE 13.3

SOURCE	DF	SUM OF SQUARES	MEAN SQUARE	F VALUE	PR > F
MODEL	5	8402.26453714	1680.45290743	596.32	0.0001
ERROR	21	59.17842582	2.81802028		STD DEV
CORRECTED TOTAL	26	8461.44296296		R-SQUARE	1.67869601
				0.993006	

PARAMETER	ESTIMATE	T FOR HO: PARAMETER = 0	PR > |T|	STD ERROR OF ESTIMATE
INTERCEPT	−5127.89907417	−46.49	0.0001	110.29601483
X1	31.09638889	23.13	0.0001	1.34441322
X2	139.74722222	44.50	0.0001	3.14005411
X1＊X1	−0.13338889	−19.46	0.0001	0.00685325
X2＊X2	−1.14422222	−41.74	0.0001	0.02741299
X1＊X2	−0.14550000	−15.01	0.0001	0.00969196

FIGURE 13.12
PLOT OF SECOND-
ORDER LEAST
SQUARES MODEL FOR
EXAMPLE 13.3

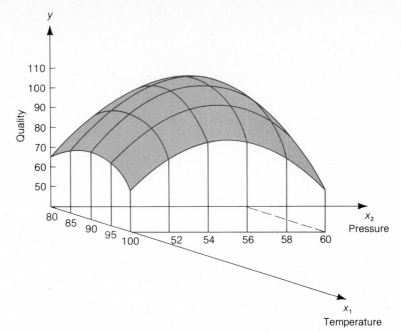

The least squares model is

$$\hat{y} = -5{,}127.90 + 31.10x_1 + 139.75x_2 - .133x_1^2 - 1.14x_2^2 - .146x_1x_2$$

A three-dimensional graph of this prediction model is shown in Figure 13.12. Note that the mean quality seems to be greatest for temperatures of about 85–90°F and for pressures of about 55–57 pounds per square inch.[*] Further experimentation in these ranges might lead to a more precise determination of the optimal temperature–pressure combination.

A look at the coefficient of determination, $R^2 = .993$, and the corresponding F value for the entire model, $F = 596.32$ (in Figure 13.11) leaves little doubt that the complete second-order model is useful for explaining mean quality as a function of temperature and pressure. This, of course, will not always be the case. The additional complexity of second-order models is only worthwhile if a better model results. We will discuss the statistical evaluation of these models in Section 13.8.

EXERCISES

13.5. Some corporations, instead of owning a fleet of cars, rent cars from a rental agency. A corporation may do this because it is sometimes more economical to rent new cars for a year than to buy new cars each year. A major rental agency wants to

---

[*]Students with knowledge of the calculus should note that we can solve for the exact temperature and pressure that maximize quality in the least squares model by solving $\partial\hat{y}/\partial x_1 = 0$ and $\partial\hat{y}/\partial x_2 = 0$ for x_1 and x_2. These estimated optimal values are $x_1 = 86.25°$F and $x_2 = 55.58$ pounds per square inch. Remember, however, that these only represent sample estimates of the coordinates for the optimal value.

develop a model that will allow it to estimate the average annual cost to the prospective customer of renting cars, y, as a function of two independent variables:

x_1 = Number of cars rented

x_2 = Average number of miles driven per car during year (in thousands)

a. Identify the independent variables as quantitative or qualitative.
b. Write the first-order model for $E(y)$.
c. Write the first-order model plus interaction for $E(y)$. Graph $E(y)$, the mean cost, versus x_2, the average mileage driven, as you would expect it to appear between x_1 and x_2.
d. Write the complete second-order model for $E(y)$.

13.6. Refer to Exercise 13.5. Suppose the model from part c is fit, with the following result:

$$\hat{y} = 1 + .05x_1 + x_2 + .05x_1x_2$$

(The units of $\hat{y}$ are thousands of dollars.) Graph the estimated cost $\hat{y}$ as a function of the average number of miles driven, x_1, over the range $x_1 = 10$ to $x_1 = 50$ (10–50 thousand miles) for $x_2 = 1$, 5, and 10. Do these functions agree (approximately) with the graphs you drew for Exercise 13.5, part c?

13.7. Refer to Exercise 13.5. Suppose an additional independent variable is considered:

x_3 = Average yearly gas price

a. Write the first-order model plus interaction for $E(y)$ as a function of x_1, x_2, and x_3.
b. Write the complete second-order model for $E(y)$ as a function of x_1, x_2, and x_3.

**13.5
MODELS FOR
ONE
QUALITATIVE
INDEPENDENT
VARIABLE**

Suppose we want to write a model for the mean profit, $E(y)$, per sales dollar of a construction company as a function of the sales engineer who estimates and bids on a job (for purposes of explanation, we will ignore other independent variables that might affect the response). Further, suppose there are three sales engineers, Jones, Smith, and Adams. Then Sales engineers is a single qualitative variable set at three levels corresponding to Jones, Smith, and Adams. Note that with a qualitative independent variable, we cannot attach a quantitative meaning to a given level. All we can do is describe it.

To simplify our notation, let μ_A be the mean profit per sales dollar for Jones, and let μ_B and μ_C be the corresponding mean profits for Smith and Adams. Our objective is to write a single prediction equation that will give the mean value of y for the three sales engineers. This can be done as follows:

$$E(y) = \beta_0 + \beta_1x_1 + \beta_2x_2$$

where

$$x_1 = \begin{cases} 1 & \text{if Smith is the sales engineer} \\ 0 & \text{if Smith is not the sales engineer} \end{cases}$$

$$x_2 = \begin{cases} 1 & \text{if Adams is the sales engineer} \\ 0 & \text{if Adams is not the sales engineer} \end{cases}$$

The variables x_1 and x_2 are not meaningful independent variables as for the case of the models for quantitative independent variables. Instead, they are dummy (or indicator) variables that make the model function. To see how they work, let $x_1 = 0$ and $x_2 = 0$. This condition will apply when we are seeking the mean response for Jones (neither Smith nor Adams will be the sales engineer; hence, it must be Jones). Then the mean value of y when Jones is the sales engineer is

$$\mu_A = E(y) = \beta_0 + \beta_1(0) + \beta_2(0) = \beta_0$$

This tells us that the mean profit per sales dollar for Jones is β_0. Or, it means that $\beta_0 = \mu_A$.

Now suppose we want to represent the mean response, $E(y)$, when Smith is the sales engineer. Checking the dummy variable definitions, we see that we should let $x_1 = 1$ and $x_2 = 0$:

$$\mu_B = E(y) = \beta_0 + \beta_1 x_1 + \beta_2 x_2 = \beta_0 + \beta_1(1) + \beta_2(0) = \beta_0 + \beta_2$$

or, since $\beta_0 = \mu_A$,

$$\mu_B = \mu_A + \beta_1$$

Then it follows that the interpretation of β_1 is

$$\beta_1 = \mu_B - \mu_A$$

which is the difference in the mean profit per sales dollar for Jones and Smith.

Finally, if we want the mean value of y when Adams is the sales engineer, we let $x_1 = 0$ and $x_2 = 1$:

$$\mu_C = E(y) = \beta_0 + \beta_1(0) + \beta_2(1) = \beta_0 + \beta_2$$

or, since $\beta_0 = \mu_A$,

$$\mu_C = \mu_A + \beta_2$$

Then it follows that the interpretation of β_2 is

$$\beta_2 = \mu_C - \mu_A$$

Note that we were able to describe three levels of the qualitative variable with only two dummy variables. This is because the mean of the base level (Jones, in this case) is accounted for by the intercept β_0.

Now, carefully examine the model for a single qualitative independent variable at three levels, because we will use exactly the same pattern for any number of levels. Also, the interpretation of the parameters will always be the same.

One level is selected as the base level (we used Jones as level A). Then, for the one–zero system of coding,* for the dummy variables,

$$\mu_A = \beta_0$$

The coding for all dummy variables is as follows: To represent the mean value of y for a particular level, let that dummy variable equal 1; otherwise, the dummy variable is set equal to 0. Using this system of coding,

$$\mu_B = \beta_0 + \beta_1$$
$$\mu_C = \beta_0 + \beta_2$$

Because $\mu_A = \beta_0$, any other model parameter will represent the difference in means for that level and the base level:

$$\beta_1 = \mu_B - \mu_A$$
$$\beta_2 = \mu_C - \mu_A$$

PROCEDURE FOR WRITING A MODEL FOR ONE QUALITATIVE INDEPENDENT VARIABLE AT k LEVELS

$$E(y) = \beta_0 + \beta_1 x_1 + \beta_2 x_2 + \cdots + \beta_{k-1} x_{k-1}$$

where x_i is the dummy variable for level i and

$$x_i = \begin{cases} 1 & \text{if } E(y) \text{ is the mean for level } i \\ 0 & \text{otherwise} \end{cases}$$

Then, for this system of coding

$$\mu_A = \beta_0$$
$$\mu_B = \beta_0 + \beta_1$$
$$\mu_C = \beta_0 + \beta_2$$
$$\mu_D = \beta_0 + \beta_3$$
$$\vdots$$

Also, note that

$$\beta_1 = \mu_B - \mu_A$$
$$\beta_2 = \mu_C - \mu_A$$
$$\beta_3 = \mu_D - \mu_A$$
$$\vdots$$

---

*We do not have to use a one–zero system of coding for the dummy variables. Any two-value system will work, but the interpretation given to the model parameters will depend on the code. Using the one–zero system makes the model parameters easy to interpret.

Thus, we can use least squares to fit predictive models in which the response y is a function of quantitative or qualitative variables. The interpretation of the parameters will differ for the two types of variables, but the objective is the same no matter what type of variable is used—to obtain a good prediction model for y.

13.6 MODELS FOR TWO OR MORE QUALITATIVE INDEPENDENT VARIABLES

We will demonstrate how to write a model for two or more qualitative independent variables and then explain how to use this technique to write models for any number of qualitative independent variables.

Let us return to the example used in Section 13.5, where we wrote a model for the mean profit per sales dollar, $E(y)$, as a function of one qualitative independent variable, Sales engineers. Now suppose that the mean profit is also a function of the state in which the construction job is located, because of tax differences, different labor conditions, etc. Assume that the company operates in two states. Then we will have a second qualitative independent variable, State, which will be observed at two levels. To simplify our notation, we will change the symbols for the three levels of sales engineers from A, B, C to E_1, E_2, E_3, and we will let S_1 and S_2 represent the two states in which the company operates. The six population means of profit per sales dollar measurements (measurements of y) are symbolically represented by the six cells in the two-way table shown in Table 13.3. Each μ subscript corresponds to one sales engineer–state combination.

TABLE 13.3
TABLE SHOWING THE SIX COMBINATIONS OF SALES ENGINEER AND STATE

		STATE	
		S_1	S_2
SALES ENGINEER	E_1	μ_{11}	μ_{12}
	E_2	μ_{21}	μ_{22}
	E_3	μ_{31}	μ_{32}

First we will write a model in its simplest form—where the two qualitative variables affect the response independently of each other. To write the model for a mean profit, $E(y)$, we start with a constant β_0 and then add *two* dummy variables for the three levels of sales engineers in the manner explained in Section 13.5. These terms, which are called the main effect terms for variable E, account for the effect of E on $E(y)$ when E and S affect $E(y)$ independently. Then,

$$E(y) = \beta_0 + \overbrace{\beta_1 x_1 + \beta_2 x_2}^{\text{Main effect terms for } E}$$

where

$$x_1 = \begin{cases} 1 & \text{if } E_2 \text{ was the sales engineer} \\ 0 & \text{if not} \end{cases}$$

$$x_2 = \begin{cases} 1 & \text{if } E_3 \text{ was the sales engineer} \\ 0 & \text{if not} \end{cases}$$

Now let level S_1 be the base level of the State variable. Since there are two levels of S, we will need only one dummy variable to include the state in the model:

$$E(y) = \beta_0 + \overbrace{\beta_1 x_1 + \beta_2 x_2}^{\substack{\text{Main effect} \\ \text{terms for } E}} + \overbrace{\beta_3 x_3}^{\substack{\text{Main effect} \\ \text{term for } S}}$$

where the dummy variables x_1 and x_2 are defined on page 391 and

$$x_3 = \begin{cases} 1 & \text{if } S_2 \text{ was the state} \\ 0 & \text{if } S_1 \text{ (base level) was the state} \end{cases}$$

If you check the model, you will see that by assigning specific values to x_1, x_2, and x_3, you create a model for the mean value of y corresponding to one of the cells of Table 13.3. We will illustrate with two examples.

EXAMPLE 13.4

Give the values of x_1, x_2, and x_3 and the model for the mean profit per sales dollar, $E(y)$, when E_1 is the sales engineer and S_1 is the state in which the job is located.

Solution

Checking the coding system, you will see that E_1 and S_1 occur when $x_1 = x_2 = x_3 = 0$. Then,

$$\begin{aligned} E(y) &= \beta_0 + \beta_1 x_1 + \beta_2 x_2 + \beta_3 x_3 \\ &= \beta_0 + \beta_1(0) + \beta_2(0) + \beta_3(0) \\ &= \beta_0 \end{aligned}$$

Therefore, the mean value of y at levels E_1 and S_1, which we represent as μ_{11}, is

$$\mu_{11} = \beta_0$$

EXAMPLE 13.5

Give the values of x_1, x_2, and x_3 and the model for the mean profit per sales dollar, $E(y)$, when E_3 is the sales engineer and S_2 is the state.

Solution

Checking the coding system, you will see that for levels E_3 and S_2,

$$x_1 = 0 \qquad x_2 = 1 \qquad x_3 = 1$$

Then, the mean profit per sales dollar when E_3 is the sales engineer and S_2 is the state, represented by the symbol μ_{32} (see Table 13.3), is

$$\begin{aligned} \mu_{32} = E(y) &= \beta_0 + \beta_1 x_1 + \beta_2 x_2 + \beta_3 x_3 \\ &= \beta_0 + \beta_1(0) + \beta_2(1) + \beta_3(1) \\ &= \beta_0 + \beta_2 + \beta_3 \end{aligned}$$

Note that we assumed that the qualitative independent variables for sales engineers and state affected the mean response, $E(y)$, independently of each other. This model is called a main effects model. Changing the level of one qualitative variable will have the same effect on $E(y)$ for any level of the second qualitative variable. In other words, the effect of one qualitative variable on $E(y)$ is independent (in a mathematical sense) of the level of the second qualitative variable.

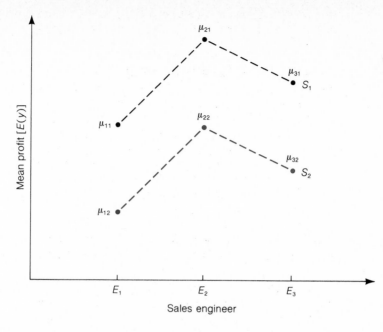

FIGURE 13.13
MAIN EFFECTS MODEL:
MEAN RESPONSE AS A
FUNCTION OF E AND S
WHEN E AND S
AFFECT $E(y)$
INDEPENDENTLY

When two independent variables affect the mean response independently of each other, you may obtain the pattern shown in Figure 13.13. Note that the difference in mean profit between any two sales engineers (levels of E) is the same, *regardless* of the state in which the job is located. That is, the main effects model assumes the effect of sales engineers on profit is the same in both states.

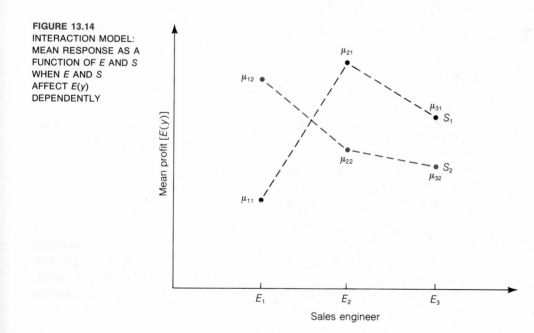

FIGURE 13.14
INTERACTION MODEL:
MEAN RESPONSE AS A
FUNCTION OF E AND S
WHEN E AND S
AFFECT $E(y)$
DEPENDENTLY

If E and S do not affect $E(y)$ independently of each other, then the response function might appear as shown in Figure 13.14. Note the difference between the mean response functions for Figures 13.13 and 13.14. When E and S affect the mean response in a dependent manner (Figure 13.14), the response functions differ for each state. This means that you cannot study the effect of one variable on $E(y)$ without considering the level of the other. When this situation occurs, we say that the qualitative independent variables interact. In this example, interaction might be expected if one sales engineer tends to develop a knack for bidding on jobs in state S_1, while another becomes adept at bidding in state S_2.

When qualitative independent variables interact, the model for $E(y)$ must be constructed so that it is able (if necessary) to give a different mean value, $E(y)$, for every cell in Table 13.3. We do this by adding interaction terms to the main effects model. These terms will involve all possible two-way cross products of the two E dummy variables, x_1, and x_2, with the one S dummy variable, x_3.

AN INTERACTION MODEL FOR TWO QUALITATIVE INDEPENDENT VARIABLES, ONE AT THREE LEVELS AND THE OTHER AT TWO LEVELS

$$E(y) = \beta_0 + \underbrace{\beta_1 x_1 + \beta_2 x_2}_{\substack{\text{Main effect}\\\text{terms for } E}} + \underbrace{\beta_3 x_3}_{\substack{\text{Main effect}\\\text{term for } S}} + \underbrace{\beta_4 x_1 x_3 + \beta_5 x_2 x_3}_{\substack{\text{Interaction}\\\text{terms}}}$$

where the dummy variables x_1, x_2, and x_3 are defined in the same way as for the main effects model.

Note that when E and S interact, the model contains six parameters (including β_0). This will make it possible, by assigning the various combinations of values to the dummy variables x_1, x_2, and x_3, to give six different values for $E(y)$ that will correspond to the six cells of Table 13.3.

EXAMPLE 13.6

In Example 13.4 we gave the mean response when E_1 was the sales engineer and S_1 was the state, where we assumed that E and S affected $E(y)$ independently (no interaction). Now give the value of $E(y)$ for the model where E and S are assumed to affect $E(y)$ dependently (i.e., E and S interact).

Solution

When E and S interact,

$$E(y) = \beta_0 + \beta_1 x_1 + \beta_2 x_2 + \beta_3 x_3 + \beta_4 x_1 x_3 + \beta_5 x_2 x_3$$

For levels E_1 and S_1, we have agreed (according to our system of coding) to let $x_1 = x_2 = x_3 = 0$. Substituting into the equation for $E(y)$, we have

$$E(y) = \beta_0$$

(the same as for the main effects model).

EXAMPLE 13.7	In Example 13.5 we gave the mean response for sales engineer E_3 and state S_2 when E and S affected $E(y)$ independently. Now assume that E and S interact and write a model for $E(y)$ when E_3 is the sales engineer and S_2 is the state.

Solution

When E and S interact,

$$E(y) = \beta_0 + \beta_1 x_1 + \beta_2 x_2 + \beta_3 x_3 + \beta_4 x_1 x_3 + \beta_5 x_2 x_3$$

To model $E(y)$ for E_3 and S_2, we set $x_1 = 0$, $x_2 = 1$, and $x_3 = 1$:

$$E(y) = \beta_0 + \beta_1(0) + \beta_2(1) + \beta_3(1) + \beta_4(0)(1) + \beta_5(1)(1)$$
$$= \beta_0 + \beta_2 + \beta_3 + \beta_5$$

This is the model for the value of μ_{32} in Table 13.3. Note the difference in $E(y)$ for the model assuming independence between E and S versus this one, which assumes interaction between E and S. The difference is β_5.

EXAMPLE 13.8

The profit per sales dollar, y, for the six combinations of sales engineers and states is shown in Table 13.4. Note that the number of construction jobs per combination varies from one for levels (E_1, S_2) to three for levels (E_1, S_1). A total of twelve jobs are sampled.

a. Assume the interaction between E and S is negligible. Fit the model for $E(y)$ with interaction terms omitted.

b. Fit the complete model for $E(y)$ allowing for the fact that interactions might occur.

c. Estimate the mean profit for jobs bid by sales engineer E_3 in state S_2 using the prediction equation $\hat{y}$ for each of the two models in parts a and b. Then calculate the sample mean for this cell of Table 13.4. Explain the discrepancy between the sample mean for levels (E_3, S_2) and the estimate(s) obtained from one or both of the two prediction equations.

TABLE 13.4
PROFIT DATA FOR COMBINATIONS OF SALES ENGINEERS AND STATES

		STATE	
		S_1	S_2
	E_1	$0.065	
		0.073	$0.036
		0.068	
SALES ENGINEER	E_2	0.078	0.050
		0.082	0.043
	E_3	0.048	0.061
		0.046	0.062

Solution

a. The SAS printout for the main effects model

$$E(y) = \beta_0 + \underbrace{\beta_1 x_1}_{\substack{E \\ \text{main effect}}} + \underbrace{\beta_2 x_2 + \beta_3 x_3}_{\substack{S \\ \text{main effect}}}$$

FIGURE 13.15
SAS PRINTOUT FOR MAIN EFFECTS MODEL OF EXAMPLE 13.8

SOURCE	DF	SUM OF SQUARES	MEAN SQUARE	F VALUE	PR > F
MODEL	3	0.00085826	0.00028609	1.51	0.2838
ERROR	8	0.00151241	0.00018905		STD DEV
CORRECTED TOTAL	11	0.00237067		R-SQUARE	0.01374959
				0.362032	

PARAMETER	ESTIMATE	T FOR HO: PARAMETER = 0	PR > |T|	STD ERROR OF ESTIMATE
INTERCEPT	0.06445455	8.98	0.0001	0.00718049
X1	0.00670455	0.67	0.5190	0.00994093
X2	−0.00229545	−0.23	0.8232	0.00994093
X3	−0.01581818	−1.91	0.0928	0.00829131

X1	X2	X3	PREDICTED VALUE	LOWER 95% CL FOR MEAN	UPPER 95% CL FOR MEAN
0	1	1	0.04634091	0.02782807	0.06485375

is given in Figure 13.15. The least squares prediction equation is

$$\hat{y} = .0645 + .0067x_1 - .00230x_2 - .0158x_3$$

b. The complete model SAS printout is given in Figure 13.16. Recall that the complete model is

$$E(y) = \beta_0 + \beta_1 x_1 + \beta_2 x_2 + \beta_3 x_3 + \beta_4 x_1 x_3 + \beta_5 x_2 x_3$$

The least squares prediction equation is

$$\hat{y} = .0687 + .0113x_1 - .0217x_2 - .0327x_3 - .0008x_1 x_3 + .0472x_2 x_3$$

c. To get the estimated mean response for cell (E_3, S_2), we put $x_1 = 0$, $x_2 = 1$, and $x_3 = 1$. Then, for the main effects model, we find

$$\hat{y} = .0645 + .0067(0) - .0023(1) - .0158(1)$$

$$= .0464$$

The 95% confidence interval for the true mean profit per sales dollar (shown in Figure 13.15) is (.0278, .0649).

For the complete model, we find

$$\hat{y} = .0687 + .0113(0) - .0217(1) - .0327(1) - .0008(0)(1) + .0472(1)(1)$$

$$= .0615$$

The 95% confidence interval for the true mean profit (shown in Figure 13.16) is (.0557, .0673).

The mean for the cell (E_3, S_2) in Table 13.4 is

$$\bar{y}_{32} = \frac{.061 + .062}{2} = .0615$$

which is precisely what is estimated by the complete (interaction) model. However, the main effects model yields a different estimate, .0464. The reason for the discrepancy is that the main effects model assumes the two qualitative independent variables affect $E(y)$ independently. In contrast, the complete model contains six parameters $(\beta_0, \beta_1, \ldots, \beta_5)$ to describe the six cell populations, so that each population cell mean will be estimated by its sample mean. Thus, the complete model estimate for any cell mean is equal to the observed (sample) mean for that cell.

Example 13.8 demonstrates an important point. If we were to ignore the least squares analysis and calculate the six sample means of Table 13.4 directly, we would obtain exactly the same estimates of $E(y)$ as would be obtained by a least squares analysis for the case where the interaction between E and S is assumed to exist. We would not obtain the same estimates if the model assumes interaction does not exist.

Also, the estimates of means raise important questions that we will learn how to answer in Section 13.8. Do the data provide sufficient evidence to indicate that E

FIGURE 13.16

SAS PRINTOUT FOR COMPLETE MODEL (INCLUDES INTERACTION) OF EXAMPLE 13.8

SOURCE	DF	SUM OF SQUARES	MEAN SQUARE	F VALUE	PR > F
MODEL	5	0.00230300	0.00046060	40.84	0.0001
ERROR	6	0.00006767	0.00001128		STD DEV
CORRECTED TOTAL 11		0.00237067		R-SQUARE	0.00335824
				0.971457	

PARAMETER	ESTIMATE	T FOR HO: PARAMETER = 0	PR > |T|	STD ERROR OF ESTIMATE
INTERCEPT	0.06866667	35.42	0.0001	0.00193888
X1	0.01133333	3.70	0.0101	0.00306564
X2	−0.02166667	−7.07	0.0004	0.00306564
X3	−0.03266667	−8.42	0.0002	0.00387776
X1*X3	−0.00083333	−0.16	0.8763	0.00512980
X2*X3	0.04716667	9.19	0.0001	0.00512980

X1	X2	X3	X1*X3	X2*X3	PREDICTED VALUE	LOWER 95% CL FOR MEAN	UPPER 95% CL FOR MEAN
0	1	1	0	1	0.06150000	0.05568948	0.06731052

FIGURE 13.17
GRAPH OF
SAMPLE MEANS FOR
PROFIT EXAMPLE

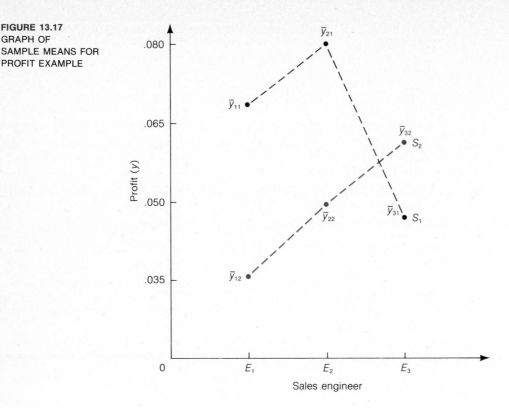

and S interact? For our example, does the contribution to mean profit per sales dollar for a job in one state depend on which sales engineer estimated and bid the job? The plot of all six sample means shown in Figure 13.17 seems to indicate interaction, since engineers E_1 and E_2 appear to operate more effectively in state S_1, while the mean profit of E_3 is higher in state S_2. The question of whether these sample facts can be reliably generalized to conclusions about the populations is considered in Section 13.8.

Models for three or more qualitative variables are constructed in a manner similar to that shown for two variables. Remember, if you do not include interaction among the variables, you are implicitly assuming that the variables affect the response independently of one another.

EXERCISES

13.8. The manager of a supermarket wants to model the total weekly sales of beer, y, as a function of brand. (This model will enable the manager to plan the store's inventory.) The market carries three brands, B_1, B_2, and B_3.

a. What type of independent variable is Brand of beer?

b. Write the model relating mean weekly beer sales, $E(y)$, as a function of brand of beer. Be sure to explain any dummy variables you use.

c. Interpret the parameters (β's) of your model in part b.

d. In terms of the model parameters, what is the mean weekly sales for brand B_3?

13.9. Refer to Exercise 13.8. Suppose the manager uses brand B_1 as the base level and obtains the model

$$\hat{y} = 450 + 60x_1 - 30x_2$$

where

$$x_1 = \begin{cases} 1 & \text{if brand } B_2 \\ 0 & \text{otherwise} \end{cases}$$

$$x_2 = \begin{cases} 1 & \text{if brand } B_3 \\ 0 & \text{otherwise} \end{cases}$$

    a. What is the difference between the estimated mean* weekly sales for brands B_2 and B_1?

    b. What is the estimated mean* weekly sales for brand B_2?

13.10. Due to the increase in gasoline prices, many service stations are offering self-service gasoline at reduced prices. Suppose an oil company wants to model the mean monthly gasoline sales, $E(y)$, of its affiliated stations as a function of the type of gasoline purchased—regular, premium, or lead-free—and of the type of service—self-service or full-service.

    a. How many dummy variables will be needed to describe each of the qualitative variables—type of gasoline and type of service?

    b. Write the main effects model relating $E(y)$ to the type of gasoline and the type of service. Be sure to code the dummy variables.

    c. Write a model $E(y)$ that includes interaction between the type of gasoline and the type of service.

    d. Do you think interaction would be important in this model? A sketch of the mean sales you might expect to see will help you decide.

13.11. Suppose the interaction model of Exercise 13.10, part c, is used, and the following least squares model is obtained (units of sales, y, are millions of dollars):

$$\hat{y} = 4 - 2x_1 - x_2 - x_3 + 2x_1x_3 + 3x_2x_3$$

where

$$x_1 = \begin{cases} 1 & \text{if premium} \\ 0 & \text{otherwise} \end{cases}$$

$$x_2 = \begin{cases} 1 & \text{if lead-free} \\ 0 & \text{otherwise} \end{cases}$$

$$x_3 = \begin{cases} 1 & \text{if full-service} \\ 0 & \text{if self-service} \end{cases}$$

    a. What is the estimate of mean sales for lead-free gasoline at the full-service pumps?

*We would generally form confidence intervals for the true means in order to assess the reliability of these estimates. Our objective in these exercises is to develop the ability to use the models to obtain the estimates. The corresponding confidence intervals can be obtained using the methods of Chapter 12.

b. What is the estimated difference between mean sales of regular gasoline at full-service and self-service pumps?

c. To see the effects of interaction, compare the difference between the regular self-service and full-service mean sales to the difference between the premium self-service and full-service mean sales.

13.7 MODELS FOR BOTH QUANTITATIVE AND QUALITATIVE INDEPENDENT VARIABLES

Perhaps the most interesting data analysis problems are those that involve both quantitative and qualitative independent variables. For example, suppose profit per mean sales of the construction company is a function of one qualitative independent variable, Sales engineers, at levels E_1, E_2, and E_3, and one quantitative independent variable, Size of the contract. The company might be expected to make more profit per sales dollar on small jobs than on very large jobs due to increased competition for the larger jobs. We will proceed to build a model in stages, showing graphically the interpretation that we would give to the model at each stage. This will help you see the contribution of various terms in the model.

At first we assume the qualitative independent variable has no effect on the response (i.e., the mean contribution to the response is the same for all three sales engineers), but the size of the construction job is related to mean profit per sales dollar, $E(y)$. Then, one response curve, which might appear as shown in Figure 13.18, would be sufficient to characterize $E(y)$ for all three sales engineers. The following second-order model would likely provide a good approximation to $E(y)$:

$$E(y) = \beta_0 + \beta_1 x_1 + \beta_2 x_1^2$$

where x_1 is the size of the construction job in millions of dollars. This model has some distinct disadvantages. If differences in mean profit exist for the three sales engineers,

FIGURE 13.18
MODEL FOR $E(y)$ AS A FUNCTION OF JOB SIZE

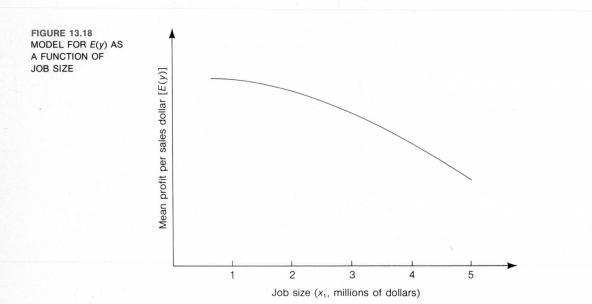

they cannot be detected (because the model does not contain any parameters representing differences among sales engineers). Also, the differences would inflate the SSE associated with the fitted model and consequently would increase errors of estimation and prediction.

The next stage in developing a model for $E(y)$ is to assume the qualitative independent variable, Sales engineers, does affect mean profit, but the effect on $E(y)$ is independent of job size. In other words, the assumption is that the two independent variables do not interact. This model is obtained by adding main effect terms to the second-order model we used in the first stage. Therefore, using the methods of Sections 13.5 and 13.6, we choose E_1 as the base level and add two terms to the model corresponding to levels E_2 and E_3:

$$E(y) = \beta_0 + \beta_1 x_1 + \beta_2 x_1^2 + \beta_3 x_2 + \beta_4 x_3$$

where

$$x_1 = \text{Job size}$$

$$x_2 = \begin{cases} 1 & \text{if } E_2 \\ 0 & \text{if not} \end{cases}$$

$$x_3 = \begin{cases} 1 & \text{if } E_3 \\ 0 & \text{if not} \end{cases}$$

What effect do these terms have on the graph for the response curve(s)? Suppose we want to model $E(y)$ for level E_1. Then we let $x_2 = 0$ and $x_3 = 0$. Substituting into the model equation, we have

$$E(y) = \beta_0 + \beta_1 x_1 + \beta_2 x_1^2 + \beta_3(0) + \beta_4(0)$$
$$= \beta_0 + \beta_1 x_1 + \beta_2 x_1^2$$

which would graph as a second-order curve similar to the one shown in Figure 13.18.

Now suppose that either of the other two sales engineers bids a job, for example, E_2. Then $x_2 = 1$, $x_3 = 0$, and

$$E(y) = \beta_0 + \beta_1 x_1 + \beta_2 x_1^2 + \beta_3(1) + \beta_4(0)$$
$$= (\beta_0 + \beta_3) + \beta_1 x_1 + \beta_2 x_1^2$$

This is the equation of exactly the same parabola that we obtained for sales engineer E_1 except that the y-intercept has changed from β_0 to $(\beta_0 + \beta_3)$. Similarly, the response curve for E_3 is

$$E(y) = (\beta_0 + \beta_4) + \beta_1 x_1 + \beta_2 x_1^2$$

Therefore, the three response curves for levels E_1, E_2, and E_3 (shown in Figure 13.19) are identical except that they are shifted vertically upward or downward in relation to each other. The curves depict the situation when the two independent variables do not interact; that is, the effect of job size on mean profit is the same regardless of the sales engineer, and the contribution of the sales engineers to mean profit is the same for all job sizes (the relative distances between the curves is constant).

FIGURE 13.19
MODEL FOR $E(y)$ AS
A FUNCTION OF
SALES ENGINEERS
AND JOB SIZE
(NO INTERACTION)

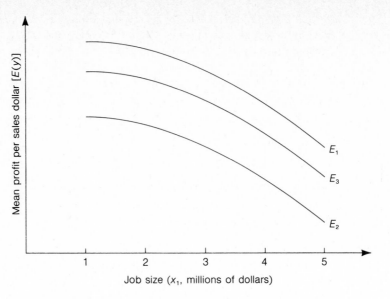

This noninteractive second-stage model has drawbacks similar to those of the simple first-stage model. It is highly unlikely that the response curves for the three sales engineers would be identical except for differing y-intercepts. Because the model does not contain parameters that measure interaction between the job size and the sales engineers, we cannot test to see if a relationship exists. Also, if interaction does exist, it will cause the SSE for the fitted model to be inflated and will consequently increase the errors of estimating model parameters and $E(y)$.

This leads us to the final stage of the model building process—adding interaction terms to allow the three response curves to differ:

$$E(y) = \beta_0 + \overbrace{\beta_1 x_1 + \beta_2 x_1^2}^{\substack{\text{Main effect} \\ \text{terms for} \\ \text{job size}}} + \overbrace{\beta_3 x_2 + \beta_4 x_3}^{\substack{\text{Main effect} \\ \text{terms for} \\ \text{sales engineers}}}$$

$$+ \overbrace{\beta_5 x_1 x_2 + \beta_6 x_1 x_3 + \beta_7 x_1^2 x_2 + \beta_8 x_1^2 x_3}^{\text{Interaction terms}}$$

where

$$x_1 = \text{Job size}$$

$$x_2 = \begin{cases} 1 & \text{if } E_2 \\ 0 & \text{if not} \end{cases}$$

$$x_3 = \begin{cases} 1 & \text{if } E_3 \\ 0 & \text{if not} \end{cases}$$

Notice that this model graphs as three different second-order curves. If E_1 is the sales engineer, we substitute $x_2 = x_3 = 0$ into the formula for $E(y)$, and all but the first three terms equal zero. The result is

$$E(y) = \beta_0 + \beta_1 x_1 + \beta_2 x_1^2$$

If E_2 is the sales engineer, $x_2 = 1$, $x_3 = 0$, and

$$\begin{aligned} E(y) &= \beta_0 + \beta_1 x_1 + \beta_2 x_1^2 + \beta_3(1) + \beta_4(0) + \beta_5 x_1(1) + \beta_6 x_1(0) \\ &\quad + \beta_7 x_1^2(1) + \beta_8 x_1^2(0) \\ &= (\beta_0 + \beta_3) + (\beta_1 + \beta_5)x_1 + (\beta_2 + \beta_7)x_1^2 \end{aligned}$$

The y-intercept, the coefficient of x_1, and the coefficient of x_1^2 differ from the corresponding coefficients in $E(y)$ at level E_1. Finally, when E_3 is the sales engineer, $x_2 = 0$, $x_3 = 1$, and the result is

$$E(y) = (\beta_0 + \beta_4) + (\beta_1 + \beta_6)x_1 + (\beta_2 + \beta_8)x_1^2$$

A graph of the model for $E(y)$ might appear as shown in Figure 13.20. Compare this figure with Figure 13.18, where we assumed the response curves were identical for all three sales engineers, and with Figure 13.19, where we assumed no interaction between the independent variables. Note that in Figure 13.20 the second-order curves may be completely different.

Now that you know how to write a model for two independent variables—one qualitative and one quantitative—we ask a question. Why do it? Why not write a separate second-order model for each level of E where $E(y)$ is a function of only job size? One reason we wrote the single model representing all three response curves is so that we can test to determine whether the curves *are* different. For

FIGURE 13.20
GRAPH OF $E(y)$ AS A FUNCTION OF SALES ENGINEERS AND JOB SIZE (INTERACTION)

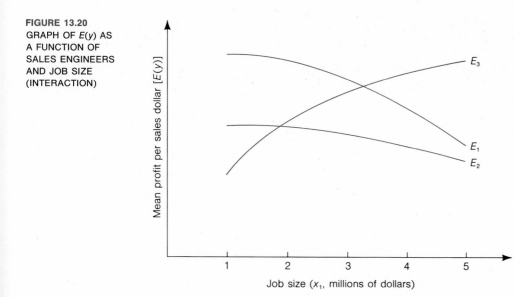

example, we might want to know whether the contribution of the sales engineers depends on the job size. Thus, one sales engineer might be especially good on small jobs, but poor on large jobs. The reverse might be true for one of the other two sales engineers. The hypothesis that the independent variables Sales engineers and Job size affect the response independently of one another (a case of no interaction) is equivalent to testing the hypothesis that $\beta_5 = \beta_6 = \beta_7 = \beta_8 = 0$ [i.e., that the model in Figure 13.19 adequately characterizes $E(y)$]. We will give a test for this hypothesis in Section 13.8. **A second reason for writing a single model is that we obtain a pooled estimate of σ^2, the variance of the random error component ε.** If the variance of ε is truly the same for each sales engineer, the pooled estimate is superior to calculating three separate estimates by fitting a separate model for each sales engineer.

In conclusion, suppose you want to write a model for $E(y)$ where you have several quantitative and qualitative independent variables. Proceed in exactly the same manner as for two independent variables, one qualitative and one quantitative. First, write the first-stage model (using the method of Section 13.4) that you want to use to model the quantitative independent variables. Then introduce the main effect and interaction terms for the qualitative independent variables. This gives a second-stage model that represents a set of identically shaped response surfaces, one corresponding to each combination of levels of the qualitative independent variables. If you could imagine surfaces in a multidimensional space, their appearance would be analogous to the response curves of Figure 13.19. To complete the model, add all cross product terms, pairing one term of the quantitative portion of the model with one term from the qualitative portion.

EXERCISES

13.12. Researchers for a dog food company have developed a new puppy food that they hope will compete with the major brands. One premarketing test involved the comparison of the new food with that of two competitors in terms of weight gain. Fifteen 8 week old German Shepherd puppies, each from a different litter, were divided into three groups of five puppies each. Each group was fed one of the three brands of food.

a. Set up a model that assumes the initial weight, x_1, is linearly related to final weight, y, but does not allow for differences among the three brands; i.e., assume the response curve is the same for the three brands of dog food. Sketch the response curve as it might appear.

b. Set up a model that assumes the effect of initial weight is linearly related to final weight, and allows the intercept of the line to differ for the three brands. In other words, assume the initial weight and brand both affect final weight, but in an independent fashion. Sketch typical response curves.

c. Now write the main effects plus interaction model. For this model we assume the initial weight is linearly related to final weight, but both the slope and the intercept of the line depend upon the brand. Sketch typical response curves.

13.13. A company is studying three different safety programs in an attempt to reduce the number of work-hours lost due to accidents. Each program is to be tried at three of the company's nine factories, and the plan is to monitor the lost work-hours, y, for a 1 year period beginning 6 months after the new safety program is instituted.

    a. Write a main effects model relating $E(y)$ to the lost work-hours, x_1, the year before the plan is instituted and to the type of program that is instituted.

    b. In terms of the model parameters from part a, what hypothesis would you test to determine whether the mean work-hours lost differs for the three safety programs?

13.14. An equal rights group has charged that women are being discriminated against in terms of the salary structure in a state university system. It is thought that a complete second-order model will be adequate to describe the relationship between salary and years of experience for both groups. A sample is to be taken from the records for faculty members (all of equal status) within the system and the following model is to be fit:*

$$E(y) = \beta_0 + \beta_1 x_1 + \beta_2 x_2 + \beta_3 x_1 x_2 + \beta_4 x_2^2$$

where

    $y = $ Annual salary (in thousands of dollars)

$$x_1 = \begin{cases} 1 & \text{if female} \\ 0 & \text{if male} \end{cases}$$

    $x_2 = $ Experience (years)

    a. What hypothesis would you test to determine whether the *rate* of increase of mean salary with experience is different for males and females?

    b. What hypothesis would you test to determine whether there are differences in mean salaries that are attributable to sex?

13.8
MODEL
BUILDING:
TESTING
PORTIONS OF
A MODEL

In Section 13.6 we constructed models for the mean profit per sales dollar of a construction job as a function of two qualitative variables, the sales engineer, E, and the state in which the job was located, S. The main effects model was

$$\overset{\text{Main effect}}{\overbrace{}}\ \overset{\text{Main effect}}{\overbrace{}}$$
$$\qquad\quad \overset{\text{for } E}{\overbrace{}}\quad \overset{\text{for } S}{\overbrace{}}$$
$$E(y) = \beta_0 + \overbrace{\beta_1 x_1 + \beta_2 x_2} + \overbrace{\beta_3 x_3}$$

Recall that E was observed at three levels and S at two levels, necessitating two and one dummy variables, respectively. If we assume that the sales engineer and state affect profit in a dependent way, the interaction model is appropriate:

$$\overset{\text{Main effect}}{\overbrace{}}\ \overset{\text{Main effect}}{\overbrace{}}$$
$$\qquad\quad \overset{\text{for } E}{\overbrace{}}\quad \overset{\text{for } S}{\overbrace{}}\quad \overset{\text{Interaction terms}}{\overbrace{}}$$
$$E(y) = \beta_0 + \overbrace{\beta_1 x_1 + \beta_2 x_2} + \overbrace{\beta_3 x_3} + \overbrace{\beta_4 x_1 x_3 + \beta_5 x_2 x_3}$$

---

*In practice, we would include other variables in the model. We include only two here to simplify the exercise.

We will call the interaction model the **complete model**, and the main effects model the **reduced model**. Now, suppose we wanted to use some data to test which of these models is more appropriate. This can be done by testing the hypothesis that the β parameters for the interaction terms equal zero:

$$H_0: \quad \beta_4 = \beta_5 = 0$$

$$H_a: \quad \text{At least one interaction } \beta \text{ parameter differs from zero}$$

In Section 11.4 we presented the t test for a single coefficient, and in Section 12.4 we gave the F test for *all* the β parameters (except β_0) in the model. We now need a test for *some* of the β parameters in the model. The test procedure is intuitive: First, we use the method of least squares to fit the main effects model, and calculate the corresponding sum of squares for error, SSE_1 (the sum of squares of the deviations between observed and predicted y values). Next, we fit the interaction model, and calculate its sum of squares for error, SSE_2. Then, we compare SSE_1 to SSE_2 by calculating the difference $SSE_1 - SSE_2$. If the interaction terms contribute to the model, then SSE_2 should be much smaller than SSE_1, and the difference $SSE_1 - SSE_2$ will be large. That is, the larger the difference, the greater the weight of evidence that the variables Sales engineer and State interact to affect the mean profit per sales dollar in the construction job.

The sum of squares for error will always decrease when new terms are added to the model. The question is whether this decrease is large enough to conclude that it is due to more than just an increase in the number of model terms and to chance. To test the null hypothesis that the interaction terms β_4 and β_5 simultaneously equal

FIGURE 13.21
REJECTION REGION FOR THE F TEST
$H_0: \quad \beta_4 = \beta_5 = 0$

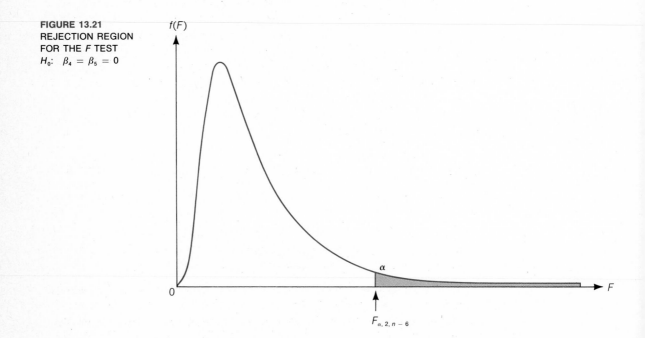

zero, we use an F statistic calculated as follows:

$$F = \frac{(SSE_1 - SSE_2)/2}{SSE_2/[n - (5 + 1)]}$$

$$= \frac{\text{Drop in SSE/Number of } \beta \text{ parameters being tested}}{s^2 \text{ for complete model}}$$

When the assumptions listed in Section 11.3 about the error term ε are satisfied and the β parameters for interaction are all zero (H_0 is true), this F statistic has an F distribution with $\nu_1 = 2$ and $\nu_2 = n - 6$ degrees of freedom. Note that ν_1 is the number of β parameters being tested and ν_2 is the number of degrees of freedom associated with s^2 in the complete model.

If the interaction terms *do* contribute to the model (H_a is true), we expect the F statistic to be large. Thus, we use a one-tailed test and reject H_0 when F exceeds some critical value, F_α, as shown in Figure 13.21.

EXAMPLE 13.9

In Example 13.8 we fit both the main effects and the interaction model for a set of $n = 12$ data points relating profit per sales dollar to Sales engineer and State. Referring to the printouts shown in Figures 13.15 and 13.16, we find the following:

Main effects model: $SSE_1 = .00151241$

Interaction model: $SSE_2 = .00006767$

Test the hypothesis that the interaction terms do not contribute to the model.

Solution

The test statistic is

$$F = \frac{(SSE_1 - SSE_2)/2}{SSE_2/(12 - 6)} = \frac{(.00151241 - .00006767)/2}{.00006767/6}$$

$$= \frac{.00072237}{.00001128} = 64.04$$

The critical value of F for $\alpha = .05$, $\nu_1 = 2$, and $\nu_2 = 6$ is found in Table VI of Appendix B to be

$$F_{.05,2,6} = 5.14$$

Since the calculated $F = 64.04$ greatly exceeds 5.14, we are quite confident in concluding that the interaction terms contribute to the prediction of y, profit per sales dollar. They should be retained in the model.

The F test can be used to determine whether *any* set of terms should be included in a model by testing the null hypothesis that a particular set of β parameters simultaneously equal zero. For example, we may want to test to determine whether a set of quadratic terms for quantitative variables or a set of main effect terms for a qualitative variable should be included in a model. The *F* test appropriate for testing the null hypothesis that all of a set of β parameters are equal to zero is summarized below.

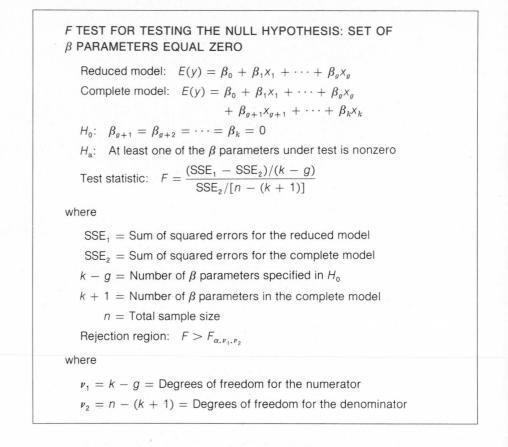

F TEST FOR TESTING THE NULL HYPOTHESIS: SET OF β PARAMETERS EQUAL ZERO

Reduced model: $E(y) = \beta_0 + \beta_1 x_1 + \cdots + \beta_g x_g$

Complete model: $E(y) = \beta_0 + \beta_1 x_1 + \cdots + \beta_g x_g$
$$+ \beta_{g+1} x_{g+1} + \cdots + \beta_k x_k$$

H_0: $\beta_{g+1} = \beta_{g+2} = \cdots = \beta_k = 0$

H_a: At least one of the β parameters under test is nonzero

Test statistic: $F = \dfrac{(SSE_1 - SSE_2)/(k - g)}{SSE_2/[n - (k + 1)]}$

where

$SSE_1 =$ Sum of squared errors for the reduced model

$SSE_2 =$ Sum of squared errors for the complete model

$k - g =$ Number of β parameters specified in H_0

$k + 1 =$ Number of β parameters in the complete model

$n =$ Total sample size

Rejection region: $F > F_{\alpha, \nu_1, \nu_2}$

where

$\nu_1 = k - g =$ Degrees of freedom for the numerator

$\nu_2 = n - (k + 1) =$ Degrees of freedom for the denominator

EXERCISES

13.15. An insurance company is experimenting with three different training programs, *A*, *B*, and *C*, for their salespeople. The following main effects model is proposed:

$$E(y) = \beta_0 + \beta_1 x_1 + \beta_2 x_2 + \beta_3 x_3$$

where

$y =$ Monthly sales (in thousands of dollars)

$x_1 =$ Number of months experience

$x_2 = \begin{cases} 1 & \text{if training program } B \text{ was used} \\ 0 & \text{otherwise} \end{cases}$

$x_3 = \begin{cases} 1 & \text{if training program } C \text{ was used} \\ 0 & \text{otherwise} \end{cases}$

Training program *A* is the base level.

a. What hypothesis would you test to determine whether the mean monthly sales differ for salespeople trained by the three programs?

b. After experimenting with fifty salespeople over a 5 year period, the complete model is fit, with the result

$$\hat{y} = 10 + .5x_1 + 1.2x_2 - .4x_3 \qquad SSE = 140.5$$

Then the reduced model $E(y) = \beta_0 + \beta_1 x_1$ is fit to the same data, with the result

$$\hat{y} = 11.4 + .4x_1 \qquad SSE = 183.2$$

Test the hypothesis you formulated in part a. Use $\alpha = .05$.

13.16. Refer to Exercise 13.13, in which a company tested three safety programs, A, B, and C, each at three of the company's nine factories. The proposed complete model is

$$E(y) = \beta_0 + \beta_1 x_1 + \beta_2 x_2 + \beta_3 x_3$$

where

$y =$ Total work-hours lost due to accidents for a 1 year period beginning 6 months after the plan is instituted

$x_1 =$ Total work-hours lost due to accidents during the year before the plan was instituted

$x_2 = \begin{cases} 1 & \text{if program } B \text{ is in effect} \\ 0 & \text{otherwise} \end{cases}$

$x_3 = \begin{cases} 1 & \text{if program } C \text{ is in effect} \\ 0 & \text{otherwise} \end{cases}$

After the programs have been in effect for 18 months, the complete model is fit to the $n = 9$ data points, with the result

$$\hat{y} = -2.1 + .88x_1 - 150x_2 + 35x_3 \qquad SSE = 1,527.27$$

Then the reduced model $y = \beta_0 + \beta_1 x_1$ is fit, with the result

$$\hat{y} = 15.3 + .84x_1 \qquad SSE = 3,113.14$$

Test to see whether the mean work-hours lost differ for the three programs. Use $\alpha = .05$.

13.17. Refer to Exercise 13.14, in which a model was proposed for testing salary discrimination against women in a state university system. The model is

$$E(y) = \beta_0 + \beta_1 x_1 + \beta_2 x_2 + \beta_3 x_1 x_2 + \beta_4 x_2^2$$

where

$y =$ Annual salary (in thousands of dollars)

$x_1 = \begin{cases} 1 & \text{if female} \\ 0 & \text{if male} \end{cases}$

$x_2 =$ Experience (years)

Below is a portion of the computer printout that results from fitting this model to a sample of 200 faculty members in the university system:

SOURCE	DF	SUM OF SQUARES	MEAN SQUARE
MODEL	4	2351.70	587.92
ERROR	195	783.90	4.02
TOTAL	199	3135.60	R-SQUARE
			0.7500

The reduced model $E(y) = \beta_0 + \beta_2 x_2 + \beta_4 x_2^2$ is fit to the same data and the resulting computer printout is partially reproduced below:

SOURCE	DF	SUM OF SQUARES	MEAN SQUARE
MODEL	2	2340.37	1170.185
ERROR	197	795.23	4.04
TOTAL	199	3135.60	R-SQUARE
			0.7464

Do these data provide sufficient evidence to support the claim that the mean salary of faculty members is dependent upon sex? Use $\alpha = .05$.

13.9 MODEL BUILDING: STEPWISE REGRESSION

The problem of predicting executive salaries was discussed in Chapter 12. Perhaps the biggest problem in building a model to describe executive salaries is choosing the important independent variables to be included in the model. The list of potentially important independent variables is extremely long, and we need some objective method of screening out those that are not important.

The problem of deciding which of a large set of independent variables to include in a model is common. Trying to determine which variables influence the profit of a firm, affect product quality, or are related to the state of the economy are only a few examples.

A systematic approach to building a model with a large number of independent variables is difficult because the interpretation of multivariable interactions and higher-order polynomials is tedious. We therefore turn to a screening procedure known as stepwise regression.

The most commonly used stepwise regression procedure, available in most popular computer packages, works as follows: The user first identifies the response, y, and the set of potentially important independent variables, $x_1, x_2, \ldots, x_k$, where k will generally be large. (Note that this set of variables could include both first- and higher-order terms. However, we may often include only the main effects of both quantitative variables (linear terms) and qualitative variables (dummy variables), since the inclusion of interactions and quadratic terms will greatly increase the number of independent variables.) The response and independent variables are then entered into the computer, and the stepwise procedure begins.

Step 1. The computer fits all possible one-variable models of the form

$$E(y) = \beta_0 + \beta_1 x_i$$

to the data. For each model, the test of the null hypothesis

$$H_0: \quad \beta_1 = 0$$

against the alternative hypothesis

$$H_a: \quad \beta_1 \neq 0$$

is conducted using the t (or the equivalent F) test for a single β parameter. The independent variable that produces the largest (absolute) t value is declared the best one-variable predictor of y.* Call this independent variable x_1.

Step 2. The stepwise program now begins to search through the remaining $(k - 1)$ independent variables for the best two-variable model of the form

$$E(y) = \beta_0 + \beta_1 x_1 + \beta_2 x_i$$

This is done by fitting all two-variable models containing x_1 and each of the other $(k - 1)$ options for the second variable x_i. The t values for the test $H_0: \quad \beta_2 = 0$ are computed for each of the $(k - 1)$ models (corresponding to the remaining independent variables x_i, $i = 2, 3, \ldots, k$), and the variable having the largest t is retained. Call this variable x_2.

At this point, some computer packages diverge in methodology. The better packages now go back and check the t value of $\hat{\beta}_1$ after $\hat{\beta}_2 x_2$ has been added to the model. If the t value has become nonsignificant at some specified α level (say $\alpha = .10$), the variable x_1 is removed and a search is made for the independent variable with a β parameter that will yield the most significant t value in the presence of $\hat{\beta}_2 x_2$. Other packages do not recheck $\hat{\beta}_1$, but proceed directly to step 3.

The reason the t value for x_1 may change from step 1 to step 2 is that the meaning of the coefficient β_1 may change. In step 2, we are approximating a complex response surface in two variables with a plane. The best fitting plane may yield a differ-

*Note that the variable with the largest t value will also be the one with the largest Pearson product moment correlation, r (Section 11.5), with y.

ent value for β_1 than that obtained in step 1. Thus, both the value of $\hat{\beta}_1$ and, therefore, its significance will usually change from step 1 to step 2. For this reason, the computer packages that recheck the t values at each step are preferred.

Step 3. The stepwise procedure now checks for a third independent variable to include in the model with x_1 and x_2. That is, we seek the best model of the form

$$E(y) = \beta_0 + \beta_1 x_1 + \beta_2 x_2 + \beta_3 x_i$$

To do this, we fit all the $(k - 2)$ models using x_1, x_2, and each of the $(k - 2)$ remaining variables, x_i, as a possible x_3. The criterion is again to include the independent variable with the largest t value. Call this best third variable x_3.

The better programs now recheck the t values corresponding to the x_1 and x_2 coefficients, replacing the variables that have t values that have become nonsignificant. This procedure is continued until no further independent variables can be found that yield significant t values (at the specified α level) in the presence of the variables already in the model.

The result of the stepwise procedure is a model containing only the main effects with t values that are significant at the specified α level. Thus, in most practical situations, only several of the large number of independent variables will remain. However, it is very important *not* to jump to the conclusion that all the independent variables important for predicting y have been identified or that the unimportant independent variables have been eliminated. Remember, the stepwise procedure is only using **sample estimates** of the true model coefficients (β's) to select the important variables. An extremely large number of single β parameter t tests have been conducted, and the probability is very high that one or more errors have been made in including or excluding variables. That is, we have very probably included some unimportant independent variables in the model (Type I errors) and eliminated some important ones (Type II errors).

There is a second reason why we might not have arrived at a good model. When we choose the variables to be included in the stepwise regression, we may often omit high-order terms (to keep the number of variables manageable). Consequently, we may have initially omitted several important terms from the model. Thus, we should recognize stepwise regression for what it is: an objective screening procedure.

Now, we will consider interactions and quadratic terms (for quantitative variables) among variables screened by the stepwise procedure. It would be best to develop this response surface model with a second set of data independent of that used for the screening, so the results of the stepwise procedure can be partially verified with new data. However, this is not always possible, because in many business modeling situations only a small amount of data is available.

Remember, do not be deceived by the impressive looking t values that result from the stepwise procedure—it has only retained the independent variables with the largest t values. Also, be certain to consider second-order terms in systematically developing the prediction model. The main effects model given by the stepwise procedure may be greatly improved by the addition of interaction and quadratic terms.

EXAMPLE 13.10

In Section 12.6 we fit a multiple regression model for executive salaries as a function of experience, education, sex, etc. A preliminary step in the construction of this model was the determination of the most important independent variables. Ten independent variables were considered, as shown in Table 13.5. It would be very difficult to construct a second-order model with ten independent variables. Therefore, use the sample of 100 executives from Section 12.6 to decide which of the ten variables should be included in the construction of the final model for executive salaries.

TABLE 13.5
INDEPENDENT VARIABLES IN THE EXECUTIVE SALARY EXAMPLE

INDEPENDENT VARIABLE	DESCRIPTION
x_1	Experience (years)—quantitative
x_2	Education (years)—quantitative
x_3	Sex (1 if male, 0 if female)—qualitative
x_4	Number of employees supervised—quantitative
x_5	Corporate assets (millions of dollars)—quantitative
x_6	Board member (1 if yes, 0 if no)—qualitative
x_7	Age (years)—quantitative
x_8	Company profits (past 12 months, millions of dollars)—quantitative
x_9	Has international responsibility (1 if yes, 0 if no)—qualitative
x_{10}	Company's total sales (past 12 months, millions of dollars)—quantitative

Solution

We will use stepwise regression with the main effects of the ten independent variables to identify the most important variables. The dependent variable y is the natural logarithm of the executive salaries. The SAS stepwise regression printout is shown in Figure 13.22. Note that the first variable included in the model is x_4, the Number of employees supervised by the executive. At the second step, x_5, Corporate assets, enters the model. At the sixth step, x_6, a dummy variable for the qualitative variable Board member or not, is brought into the model. However, because the significance (.2295) of the F statistic (SAS uses the $F = t^2$ statistic in the stepwise procedure rather than the t statistic) for x_6 is above the preassigned $\alpha = .10$, x_6 is then removed from the model. Thus, at step 7 the procedure indicates that the five-variable model including x_1, x_2, x_3, x_4, and x_5 is best. That is, none of the other independent variables can meet the $\alpha = .10$ criterion for admission to the model.

Thus, in our final modeling effort (Section 12.6) we concentrated on these five independent variables, and determined that several second-order terms were important in the prediction of executive salaries.

FIGURE 13.22
STEPWISE REGRESSION PRINTOUT FOR EXAMPLE 13.10

STEP 1
VARIABLE X4 ENTERED   R-SQUARE = 0.42071677

	DF	SUM OF SQUARES	MEAN SQUARE	F	PROB>F
REGRESSION	1	11.46854285	11.46864285	71.17	0.0001
ERROR	98	15.79112802	0.16113396		
TOTAL	99	27.25977087			

	B VALUE	STD ERROR		F	PROB>F
INTERCEPT	10.20077500				
X4 (EMPLOYEES SUPERVISED)	0.00057284	0.00006790		71.17	0.0001

STEP 2
VARIABLE X5 ENTERED   R-SQUARE = 0.78299675

	DF	SUM OF SQUARES	MEAN SQUARE	F	PROB>F
REGRESSION	2	21.34431198	10.67215599	175.00	0.0001
ERROR	97	5.91545889	0.06098411		
TOTAL	99	27.25977087			

	B VALUE	STD ERROR		F	PROB>F
INTERCEPT	9.87702903				
X4 (EMPLOYEES SUPERVISED)	0.00058353	0.00004178		195.06	0.0001
X5 (ASSETS)	0.00183730	0.00014438		161.94	0.0001

STEP 3
VARIABLE X1 ENTERED   R-SQUARE = 0.89667614

	DF	SUM OF SQUARES	MEAN SQUARE	F	PROB>F
REGRESSION	3	24.44318616	8.14772872	277.71	0.0001
ERROR	96	2.81658471	0.02933942		
TOTAL	99	27.25977087			

	B VALUE	STD ERROR		F	PROB>F
INTERCEPT	9.66449288				
X1 (EXPERIENCE)	0.01870784	0.00182032		105.62	0.0001
X4 (EMPLOYEES SUPERVISED)	0.00055251	0.00002914		359.59	0.0001
X5 (ASSETS)	0.00191195	0.00010041		362.60	0.0001

STEP 4

VARIABLE X3 ENTERED   R-SQUARE = 0.94815717

	DF	SUM OF SQUARES	MEAN SQUARE	F	PROB>F
REGRESSION	4	25.84654710	6.46163678	434.37	0.0001
ERROR	95	1.41322377	0.01487604		
TOTAL	99	27.25977087			

	B VALUE	STD ERROR	F	PROB>F
INTERCEPT	9.40077349			
X1 (EXPERIENCE)	0.02074868	0.00131310	249.68	0.0001
X3 (SEX)	0.30011726	0.03089939	94.34	0.0001
X4 (EMPLOYEES SUPERVISED)	0.00055288	0.00002075	710.15	0.0001
X5 (ASSETS)	0.00190876	0.00007150	712.74	0.0001

STEP 5

VARIABLE X2 ENTERED   R-SQUARE = 0.96039323

	DF	SUM OF SQUARES	MEAN SQUARE	F	PROB>F
REGRESSION	5	26.18009940	5.23601988	455.87	0.0001
ERROR	94	1.07967147	0.01148587		
TOTAL	99	27.25977087			

	B VALUE	STD ERROR	F	PROB>F
INTERCEPT	8.85387930			
X1 (EXPERIENCE)	0.02141724	0.00116047	340.61	0.0001
X2 (EDUCATION)	0.03315807	0.00615303	29.04	0.0001
X3 (SEX)	0.31927842	0.02738298	135.95	0.0001
X4 (EMPLOYEES SUPERVISED)	0.00056061	0.00001829	939.84	0.0001
X5 (ASSETS)	0.00193684	0.00006304	943.98	0.0001

(continued)

FIGURE 13.22 (continued)

STEP 6

VARIABLE X6 ENTERED   R-SQUARE = 0.96100666

	DF	SUM OF SQUARES	MEAN SQUARE	F	PROB>F
REGRESSION	6	26.19682148	4.36613691	382.00	0.0001
ERROR	93	1.06294939	0.01142956		
TOTAL	99	27.25977087			

	B VALUE	STD ERROR	F	PROB>F
INTERCEPT	8.87509152			
X1 (EXPERIENCE)	0.02133460	0.00115963	338.48	0.0001
X2 (EDUCATION)	0.03272195	0.00614851	28.32	0.0001
X3 (SEX)	0.31093801	0.02817264	121.81	0.0001
X4 (EMPLOYEES SUPERVISED)	0.00055820	0.00001835	925.32	0.0001
X5 (ASSETS)	0.00193764	0.00006289	949.31	0.0001
X6 (BOARD)	0.0386226	0.03196369	1.46	0.2295

STEP 7

VARIABLE X6 REMOVED   R-SQUARE = 0.96039323

	DF	SUM OF SQUARES	MEAN SQUARE	F	PROB>F
REGRESSION	5	26.18009940	5.23601988	455.87	0.0001
ERROR	94	1.07967147	0.01148587		
TOTAL	99	27.25977087			

	B VALUE	STD ERROR	F	PROB>F
INTERCEPT	8.85387930			
X1 (EXPERIENCE)	0.02141724	0.00116047	340.61	0.0001
X2 (EDUCATION)	0.03315807	0.00615303	29.04	0.0001
X3 (SEX)	0.31927842	0.02738298	135.95	0.0001
X4 (EMPLOYEES SUPERVISED)	0.00056061	0.00001829	939.84	0.0001
X5 (ASSETS)	0.00193684	0.00006304	943.98	0.0001

New factors and a lack of knowledge about the importance of factors that affect value continue to complicate the job of the rural appraiser. In order to provide knowledge on the subject, this article reports on and evaluates a study in which multiple linear regression equations were used to evaluate and quantify factors affecting value . . . . It is believed that the findings obtained with these equations, and the relationships they indicate, will be of value to the appraiser.

The authors of this statement, James O. Wise and H. Jackson Dover (1974), use stepwise regression to identify a number of important factors (variables) that can be used to predict rural property values. They obtained their results by analyzing a sample of 105 cases from seven counties in the state of Georgia. A part of their findings are duplicated in Table 13.6. The variable names are listed in the order in which the stepwise regression procedure identified their importance, and the t values found at each step are given for each variable. Note that both qualitative and quantitative variables have been included. Since each qualitative variable is at two levels, only one main effect term could be included in the model for each factor.

TABLE 13.6
STEPWISE
REGRESSION
ANALYSIS OF
PRICE PER ACRE

VARIABLE NAME	t VALUES
Residential land (yes–no)	10.466
Seedlings and saplings (number)	6.692
Percent ponds (percent)	4.141
Distance to state park (miles)	3.985
Branches or springs (yes–no)	3.855
Site index (ratio)	3.160
Size (acres)	1.142
Farm land (yes–no)	2.288

Since there were 105 cases used in the study, a large number of degrees of freedom are associated with each t statistic (first 103, then 102, etc.). Thus, we should compare the value of the test statistic to a corresponding z value (1.645 for $\alpha = .10$ and the two-sided alternative hypothesis H_a: $\beta_i \neq 0$) when we judge the importance of each variable. Although Wise and Dover (1974) imply that the variable Size is important, we might not include it, since the t value is only 1.142.

Finally, we have now only isolated a set of important variables. We still must decide exactly how each should be entered into our prediction equation, remembering that interactions and quadratic terms often improve the model.

13.10 MODEL BUILDING: SOME PROBLEMS

There are several problems you should be aware of when constructing a prediction model for some response y. A few of the most important will be discussed in this section.

Problem 1: parameter estimability

Suppose you want to fit a model relating a firm's monthly profit, y, to the advertising expenditure, x. We propose the first-order model

$$E(y) = \beta_0 + \beta_1 x$$

FIGURE 13.23
PROFIT AND
ADVERTISING
EXPENDITURE DATA:
3 MONTHS

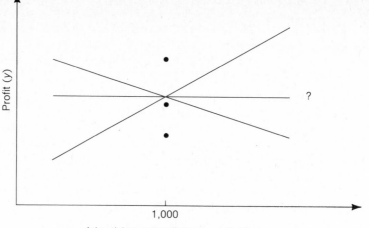

Advertising expenditure (x, dollars)

Now, suppose we have 3 months of data, and the firm spent $1,000 on advertising during each month. The data are shown in Figure 13.23. You can see the problem: The parameters of the line cannot be estimated when all the data are concentrated at a single x value. Recall that it takes two points (x values) to fit a straight line. Thus, the parameters are not **estimable** when only one x value is observed.

A similar problem would occur if we attempted to fit the quadratic model

$$E(y) = \beta_0 + \beta_1 x + \beta_2 x^2$$

to a set of data for which only one *or two* different x values were observed (see Figure 13.24). At least three different x values must be observed before a quadratic model can be fit to a set of data (that is, before all three parameters are estimable). In general, the number of levels of x must be one more than the order of the polynomial in x that you want to fit.

Since most business variables are not controlled by the researcher, the independent variables will almost always be observed at a sufficient number of levels to permit estimation of the model parameters. However, when the computer program you use suddenly refuses to fit a model, the problem is probably inestimable parameters.

Problem 2: multicollinearity

Often, two or more of the independent variables used in the model for $E(y)$ will contribute redundant information. That is, the independent variables will be correlated with each other. For example, suppose we want to construct a model to predict the gasoline mileage rating of a truck as a function of its load, x_1, and the horsepower, x_2, of its engine. In general, you would expect heavy loads to require greater horsepower and to result in lower mileage ratings. Thus, although both x_1 and x_2 contribute information for the prediction of mileage rating, some of the information is overlapping, because x_1 and x_2 are correlated.

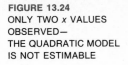

FIGURE 13.24
ONLY TWO x VALUES
OBSERVED—
THE QUADRATIC MODEL
IS NOT ESTIMABLE

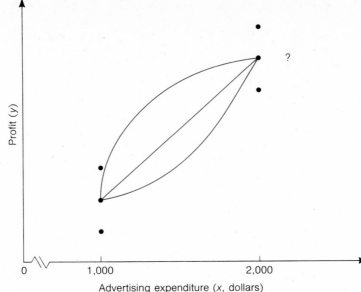

If the model

$$E(y) = \beta_0 + \beta_1 x_1 + \beta_2 x_2$$

were fit to a set of data, we might find that the t values for both $\hat{\beta}_1$ and $\hat{\beta}_2$ (the least squares estimates) are nonsignificant. However, the F test for H_0: $\beta_1 = \beta_2 = 0$ would probably be highly significant. The tests may seem to be contradictory, but really they are not. The t tests indicate that the contribution of one variable, say $x_1 =$ Load, is not significant **after the effect of** $x_2 =$ **Horsepower** has been discounted (because x_2 is also in the model). The significant F test, on the other hand, tells us that at least one of the two variables is making a contribution to the prediction of y (i.e., either β_1, β_2, or both differ from 0). In fact, both are probably contributing, but the contribution of one overlaps with that of the other.

When highly correlated independent variables are present in a regression model, the results are confusing. The researcher may want to include only one of the variables in the final model. One way of deciding which one to include is by using stepwise regression. Generally, only one of a set of multicollinear independent variables will be included in a stepwise regression model, since at each step every variable is tested in the presence of all the variables already in the model. For example, if at one step the variable truck load is included as a significant variable in the prediction of the mileage rating, the variable horsepower will probably never be added in a future step. Thus, if a set of independent variables is thought to be multicollinear, some screening by stepwise regression may be helpful.

Problem 3: prediction outside the experimental region
By the late 1960's many research economists had developed highly technical models to relate the state of the economy to various economic indices and other

FIGURE 13.25
USING A REGRESSION
MODEL OUTSIDE THE
EXPERIMENTAL
REGION

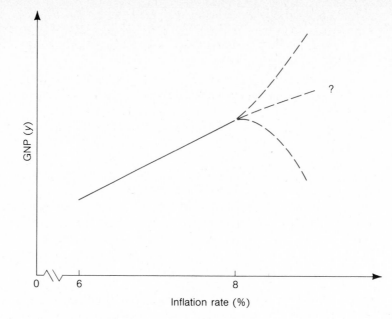

independent variables. Many of these models were multiple regression models, where, for example, the dependent variable y might be next year's growth in GNP and the independent variables might include this year's rate of inflation, this year's Consumer Price Index, etc. In other words, the model might be constructed to predict next year's economy using this year's knowledge.

Unfortunately, these models were almost unanimously unsuccessful in predicting the recession in the early 1970's. What went wrong? Well, one of the problems was that the regression models were used to predict y for values of the independent variables that were outside the region in which the model was developed. For example, the inflation rate in the late 1960's, when the models were developed, ranged from 6 to 8%. When the double-digit inflation of the early 1970's became a reality, some researchers attempted to use the same models to predict the growth in GNP 1 year hence. As you can see in Figure 13.25, the model may be very accurate for predicting y when x is in the range of experimentation, but the use of the model outside that range is a dangerous practice.

Problem 4: correlated errors

Another problem associated with using a regression model to predict an economic variable y based on independent variables $x_1, x_2, \ldots, x_k$ arises from the fact that the data are frequently **time series**. That is, the values of both the dependent and independent variables are observed sequentially over a period of time. The observations tend to be correlated over time, which in turn often causes the prediction errors of the regression model to be correlated. Thus, the assumption of independent errors is violated, and the model tests and prediction intervals are no longer valid.

The solution to this problem is to construct a **time series model;** this will be the subject of Chapter 14.

Although this chapter on model building covered many topics, only experience can make you competent in this fascinating area of statistics. Successful model building requires a delicate blend of knowledge of the process being modeled, geometry, and formal statistical testing.

The first step is to identify the response variable y and the set of independent variables. Each independent variable is then classified as either quantitative or qualitative, and dummy variables are defined to represent the qualitative independent variables. If the total number of independent variables is large, you may want to use stepwise regression to screen out those that do not seem important for the prediction of y.

When the number of independent variables is manageable, the model builder is ready to begin a systematic effort. At least second-order models, those containing two-way interactions and quadratic terms in the quantitative variables, should be considered. Remember that a model with no interaction terms implies that each of the independent variables affects the response independently of the other independent variables. Quadratic terms add curvature to the contour curves when $E(y)$ is plotted as a function of the independent variable. The F test for testing a set of β parameters aids in deciding the final form of the prediction model.

Many problems can arise in regression modeling, and the intermediate steps are often tedious and frustrating. However, the end result of a careful and determined modeling effort is very rewarding—you will have a better understanding of the process and a predictive model for the dependent variable y.

SUPPLEMENTARY EXERCISES

13.18. An appliance store is interested in modeling the total sales of television sets sold per month as a function of the following independent variables: (1) warranty period, (2) color or black-and-white, (3) solid-state or tube, (4) picture tube size, (5) brand (the store carries three brands).

    a. Determine whether each of the independent variables is quantitative or qualitative. If it is quantitative, give the approximate range of levels you might expect to observe. If it is qualitative, give the number of levels and define dummy variables to describe each variable.

    b. Write a main effects model to relate $E(y)$, the mean monthly sales for televisions sold, as a function of the five independent variables.

    c. It is believed that the mean sales will be greater for larger picture tubes than for smaller picture tubes, but the rate of increase will depend on the brand. Why doesn't the main effects model in part b incorporate this belief? How can it be incorporated into the model?

13.19. To model the relationship between y, a dependent variable, and x, an independent variable, a researcher has taken one measurement on y at each of five different x values. Drawing on his mathematical expertise, the researcher realizes that he can fit the fourth-order polynomial model

$$E(y) = \beta_0 + \beta_1 x + \beta_2 x^2 + \beta_3 x^3 + \beta_4 x^4$$

and it will pass exactly through all five points, yielding SSE = 0. The researcher, delighted with the "excellent" fit of the model, eagerly sets out to use it to make inferences. What problems will he encounter in attempting to make inferences?

13.20. To make a product more appealing to the consumer, an automobile manufacturer is experimenting with a new type of paint that is supposed to help the car maintain its new car look. The durability of this paint depends on the length of time the car body is in the oven after it has been painted. In the initial experiment, three groups of ten car bodies each were baked for three different lengths of time—12, 24, and 36 hours—at the standard temperature setting. Then, the paint finish of each of the thirty cars was analyzed to determine a durability rating, y.

    a. Write a quadratic model relating the mean durability, $E(y)$, to the length of baking.

    b. Could a cubic model be fit to these data? Explain.

13.21. Refer to Exercise 13.20. Suppose the Research and Development Department develops three new types of paint to be tested. Thus, ninety cars are to be tested—thirty for each type of paint—in the manner described in Exercise 13.20. Write the complete second-order model for $E(y)$ as a function of the type of paint and bake time.

13.22. One factor that must be considered in developing a shipping system that is beneficial to both the customer and the seller is time of delivery. A manufacturer of farm equipment can ship its products by either rail or truck. Quadratic models are thought to be adequate in relating time of delivery to distance traveled for both modes of transportation. Consequently, it has been suggested that the following model be fit:

$$E(y) = \beta_0 + \beta_1 x_1 + \beta_2 x_2 + \beta_3 x_1 x_2 + \beta_4 x_2^2$$

where

    $y = $ Shipping time

$$x_1 = \begin{cases} 1 & \text{if rail} \\ 0 & \text{if truck} \end{cases}$$

    $x_2 = $ Distance to be shipped

    a. What hypothesis would you test to determine whether the data indicate that the quadratic distance term is useful in the model, i.e., whether curvature is present in the relationship between mean delivery time and distance?

    b. What hypothesis would you test to determine whether there is a difference in mean delivery time by rail and by truck?

13.23. Refer to Exercise 13.22. Suppose the complete second-order model is fit to a total of fifty observations on delivery time. The sum of squared errors is SSE $=$ 226.12. Then, the reduced model

$$E(y) = \beta_0 + \beta_2 x_2 + \beta_4 x_2^2$$

is fit to the same data, and SSE $=$ 259.34. Test to see whether the data indicate that the mean delivery time differs for rail and truck deliveries.

13.24. A company wants to model the total weekly sales, y, of its product as a function of packaging and location. Two types of packaging, P_1 and P_2, are used in each of four locations, L_1, L_2, L_3, and L_4.

  a. Write a main effects model to relate $E(y)$ to packaging and location. What implicit assumption are we making about the interrelationships between sales, packaging, and location when we use this model?

  b. Now write a model for $E(y)$ that includes interaction between packaging and location. How many parameters are in this model (remember to include β_0)? Compare this number to the number of packaging–location combinations being modeled.

13.25. Refer to Exercise 13.24. Suppose the main effects and interaction models are fit for forty observations on weekly sales. The SSE's are

SSE for main effects model $= 422.36$

SSE for interaction model $= 346.65$

  a. Determine whether these data indicate that the interaction between location and packaging is important in estimating mean weekly sales. Use $\alpha = .05$.

  b. What implications does your conclusion in part a have for the company's marketing strategy?

13.26. Many companies must accurately estimate their costs before a job is begun in order to acquire a contract and make a profit. For example, a heating and plumbing contractor may base cost estimates for new homes on the total area of the house, the number of baths in the plans, and whether central air conditioning is to be installed.

  a. Write a main effects model relating the mean cost of material and labor, $E(y)$, to the area, number of baths, and central air conditioning variables.

  b. Write a complete second-order model for the mean cost as a function of the same three variables.

  c. How would you test the hypothesis that the second-order terms are useful for predicting mean cost?

13.27. Refer to Exercise 13.26. The contractor samples twenty-five recent jobs and fits both the complete second-order model (part b) and the reduced main effects model (part a), so that a test can be conducted to determine whether the additional complexity of the second-order model is necessary. The resulting SSE and R^2 are

	SSE	R^2
Main effects	8.548	.950
Second-order	6.133	.964

  a. Is there sufficient evidence to conclude that the second-order terms are important for predicting the mean cost?

  b. Suppose the contractor decides to use the main effects model to predict costs. Use the global F test (Section 12.4) to determine whether the main effects model is useful for predicting costs.

ON YOUR OWN . . .

We continue our "On Your Own" theme from Chapters 11 and 12. Remember that you selected three independent variables related to the annual GNP. Now, increase your list of three variables to include approximately ten that you feel would be useful in predicting the GNP. Obtain data for as many years as possible for the new list of variables and the GNP. With the aid of a computer analysis package, employ a stepwise regression program to choose the important variables among those you have listed. To test your intuition, list the variables in the order you think they will be selected before you conduct the analysis. How does your list compare with the stepwise regression results?

After the group of ten variables has been narrowed to a smaller group of variables by the stepwise analysis, try to improve the model by including interactions and quadratic terms. Be sure to consider the meaning of each interaction or quadratic term before adding it to the model—a quick sketch can be very helpful. See if you can systematically construct a useful model for predicting the GNP. You might want to hold out the last several years of data to test the predictive ability of your model after it is constructed. (As noted in Section 13.9, the same data to construct *and* to evaluate predictive ability can lead to invalid statistical tests and a false sense of security.)

REFERENCES

Draper, N., & Smith, H. *Applied regression analysis.* New York: Wiley, 1966.

Graybill, F. A. *Theory and application of the linear model.* North Scituate, Mass.: Duxbury, 1976.

Mendenhall, W. *Introduction to linear models and the design and analysis of experiments.* Belmont, Ca.: Wadsworth, 1968.

Wise, J. O., & Dover, H. J. "An evaluation of a statistical method of appraising rural property." *Appraisal Journal,* Jan. 1974, *42,* 103–113.

In Chapters 11, 12, and 13 we discussed the construction, estimation, and use of regression models. We saw that regression models provide very powerful tools for analyzing and exploiting the relationships between variables. However, when the data are collected sequentially over time, the assumption of independent random errors—the key to regression models—is probably not true.

In this chapter we consider data that are collected sequentially over time and, thus, are usually correlated. Time series models are constructed to describe these data and to use the correlated structure to make forecasts, or predictions, of future values. The probabilistic nature of the time series models allows us to assess the reliability of the forecasts.

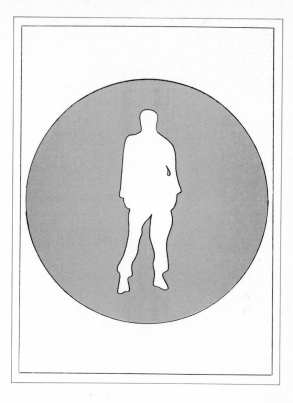

14

TIME SERIES ANALYSIS AND FORECASTING

If you turn to the financial section of a newspaper, you are very likely to see a graph of the Dow Jones Average* over the past several months or years. The Dow Jones Average is a number based upon the daily stock prices of thirty large corporations listed on the New York Stock Exchange and is calculated at the close of each day's trading. Many people believe that the Dow Jones Average characterizes the present status of the stock market, which explains the predisposition of the news media to report it and graph its values. Numerical variables that, like the Dow Jones Average, are calculated, measured, or observed sequentially on a regular chronological basis, are called time series. The rate of inflation, Consumer Price Index, balance of trade, Wholesale Price Index, and annual profit of a firm are just a few other examples of business and economic time series.

The values of a time series may be plotted on the y-axis, with time as the x-axis, to provide an easily understood summary of the past and present values of the series. The graphical display is one of several descriptive techniques applicable to time series. We will present some useful methods for describing time series in Sections 14.1 and 14.2.

In many practical applications of time series to business problems, the objective is to forecast (predict) some future value or values of the series. For example, an investor may want to use the past and present values of the Dow Jones Average to forecast its value 6 months from now. Since significant amounts of money may be riding on the accuracy of the forecast, the investor would require some measure of the forecast's reliability. Forecasting and measuring the reliability of forecasts requires the use of inferential techniques. The construction of probabilistic models for time series and the use of these models for forecasting is discussed in Section 14.3.

14.1
INDEX NUMBERS

"The Consumer Price Index rose to 167.2 in March, an increase of 1.2 over the previous month. Government officials attribute this increase primarily to an increase in food prices." This news report is typical of what is heard each month when the latest Consumer Price Index is released to the news media. Several questions come to mind. How is the Consumer Price Index (CPI) computed? How should the CPI be interpreted? To whom is the CPI important, and why?

In general, index numbers are expressed as percentages. The general form for calculating the index I at time t is

$$I_t = 100 \frac{X_t}{X_{t_0}}$$

where X represents the time series variable being indexed, measured at two times, t_0 and t. Time t_0 is called the base period, and time t is the time at which the index is being computed. The quantity X_t might be a single time series, like the price of silver, in which case the index I_t is called a simple index number. On the other hand, X_t may be a composite of several time series, like a combination of wholesale prices of manufactured goods. Then, I_t is a composite index number.

---

*We are referring to the Dow Jones Industrial Average.

To construct either a simple or a composite index, the base period must be chosen (i.e., the time t_0 upon which the index I_t is to be based). The base period may be a month, a year, or several consecutive years. The objective is to choose a period during which price levels are "normal," although defining price normality is a complex, if not impossible, problem. Most indices use a base period of at least 1 year so that minor price fluctuations tend not to be reflected in the base price. Furthermore, the base period is usually chosen to be in the relatively recent past, so that the index does not lose its significance over time. Most base periods are shifted forward in time every 10 years or so.

EXAMPLE 14.1

The price of silver (dollars per ounce) is shown in Table 14.1 for the years 1960–1976. Using 1967 as a base period, as many current indices do, calculate and graph the simple index number for the price of silver for the period 1960–1976.

TABLE 14.1
SILVER PRICES (DOLLARS PER OUNCE) FROM 1960 TO 1976

YEAR	PRICE	YEAR	PRICE
1960	$0.914	1969	$1.791
1961	0.924	1970	1.771
1962	1.085	1971	1.546
1963	1.279	1972	1.684
1964	1.293	1973	2.558
1965	1.293	1974	4.708
1966	1.293	1975	4.419
1967	1.550	1976	4.353
1968	2.145		

Solution

Let X_t be the price of silver in year t. Then, using the base period $t_0 = 1967$, we have $X_{t_0} = 1.550$. Thus, we calculate

$$I_{1960} = (100)\frac{I_{1960}}{I_{1967}} = (100)\frac{0.914}{1.550} = 59.0$$

$$I_{1961} = (100)\frac{I_{1961}}{I_{1967}} = (100)\frac{0.924}{1.550} = 59.6$$

and so forth. The complete silver price index for 1960–1976 is shown in Table 14.2 and the graph is given in Figure 14.1.

TABLE 14.2
SIMPLE INDEX NUMBERS FOR SILVER PRICES FROM 1960 TO 1976

YEAR	INDEX	YEAR	INDEX
1960	59.0	1969	115.6
1961	59.6	1970	114.3
1962	70.0	1971	99.7
1963	82.5	1972	108.6
1964	83.4	1973	165.0
1965	83.4	1974	303.7
1966	83.4	1975	285.1
1967	100.0	1976	280.8
1968	138.4		

FIGURE 14.1
GRAPH OF SILVER PRICE INDEX, 1960–1976

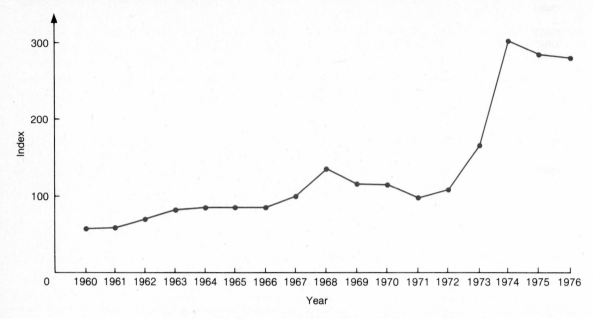

Note that the index makes it easy to identify the highly inflationary period beginning in 1973. This is one of the primary values of simple indices—they make price fluctuations and trends easier to identify and compare.

The construction of a composite index is complicated by the necessity of choosing a method of combining, or *aggregating*, the commodities that compose the index. The simplest method of combining commodity prices is to sum them at times t_0 and t to form the values X_{t_0} and X_t, respectively. Thus, if the index consists of r commodities with prices P_{1t}, P_{2t}, . . . , P_{rt} at time t, we calculate

$$X_t = \sum P_{it} = \text{Sum of the commodity prices at time } t$$

$$X_{t_0} = \sum P_{it_0} = \text{Sum of the commodity prices at time } t_0$$

Then the index I_t is calculated just as before:

$$I_t = (100)\frac{X_t}{X_{t_0}}$$

A composite index based upon simple addition of the commodity prices is called a *simple composite index*.

EXAMPLE 14.2   The total annual profits (in billions of dollars) of all manufacturing corporations in the United States are given from 1960 to 1976 in Table 14.3. Note that this time series is the aggregate of profits for all manufacturing corporations. Calculate and graph the simple composite index for this series, using the base period $t_0 = 1972$.

TABLE 14.3
TOTAL ANNUAL PROFIT
(BILLIONS OF DOLLARS)
OF ALL
MANUFACTURING
CORPORATIONS,
1960–1976

YEAR	TOTAL PROFIT	YEAR	TOTAL PROFIT
1960	15,198	1969	33,248
1961	15,311	1970	28,572
1962	17,719	1971	31,038
1963	19,483	1972	36,467
1964	23,211	1973	48,259
1965	27,521	1974	58,747
1966	30,937	1975	49,135
1967	29,008	1976	64,348
1968	32,069		

Solution

Since the "commodity prices" in this example are the profits of manufacturing corporations, the numbers in Table 14.3 represent the sum of these profits, or

$$X_t = \sum P_{it}$$

where P_{it} is the profit of the ith manufacturer during year t. The simple composite index is then calculated as follows:

$$I_{1960} = (100)\frac{X_{1960}}{X_{1972}} = (100)\frac{15,198}{36,467} = 41.7$$

$$I_{1961} = (100)\frac{X_{1961}}{X_{1972}} = (100)\frac{15,311}{36,467} = 42.0$$

and so forth. The simple composite index is given for 1960–1976 in Table 14.4 and a graph of the index is shown in Figure 14.2.

TABLE 14.4
SIMPLE COMPOSITE
INDEX FOR TOTAL
ANNUAL PROFIT OF
MANUFACTURING
CORPORATIONS,
1960–1976

YEAR	INDEX	YEAR	INDEX
1960	41.7	1969	91.2
1961	42.0	1970	78.4
1962	48.6	1971	85.1
1963	53.4	1972	100.0
1964	63.6	1973	132.3
1965	75.5	1974	161.1
1966	84.8	1975	134.7
1967	79.5	1976	176.5
1968	87.9		

Using a later base period (1972) allows us to measure the inflationary jump from 1973 to 1974 even more accurately than we did before. The 1973 index value of 132.3 represents a 32.3% increase in annual profits in 1 year, and an increase of about the same percentage (using 1972 as the base) occurred in the following year.

Although it is easy to compute, the simple composite index has a major drawback. Commodities with high prices exert a greater influence on the index than those with

FIGURE 14.2
GRAPH OF TOTAL ANNUAL PROFIT INDEX, 1960–1976

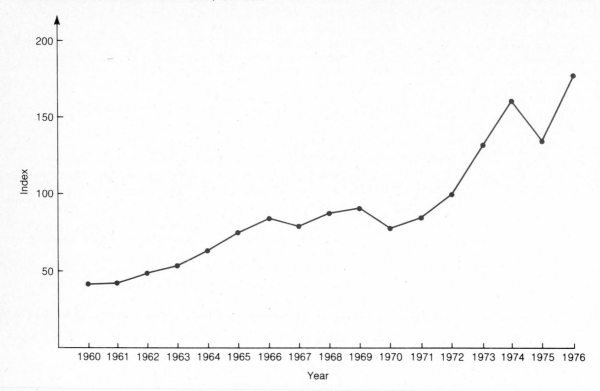

low prices. The index therefore depends on the quantity of each commodity that is included. A more objective measure of composite prices is the **weighted composite index**. The commodity prices are weighted before being summed, where the weights are multipliers chosen to reflect the relative importance of each commodity. If the weights for the r commodities at time t are W_{1t}, W_{2t}, . . . , W_{rt}, then

$$X_t = \sum W_{it} P_{it}$$
$$X_{t_0} = \sum W_{it_0} P_{it_0}$$

The formula for the index is unchanged:

$$I_t = 100 \frac{X_t}{X_{t_0}}$$

Even the weighted composite index is not a panacea. The choice of weights is intended to reflect the relative importance of each commodity, but there is an element of subjectivity in their selection. In addition, the import of the weights may change as the prices of the commodities change over time. A composite index that uses the original base period weights for the calculations is called a **Laspeyres Index**. One that uses weights computed for the period at which the index is being calculated is called a **Paasche Index**. We will not detail the specifics of their calculation here (the interested reader should consult the references at the end of the chapter).

CASE STUDY 14.1   Earlier this month, the United Steelworkers Union signed a remarkable labor contract with aluminum producers. The pact provides for a pension plan with a partial escalator, figured at 65% of the annual rise in the cost of living as measured by the Consumer Price Index, which is compiled monthly by the Bureau of Labor Statistics.

The revolutionary agreement, certain to affect bargaining in other organized industries, again shows that the CPI has become a potent economic force in its own right. With inflation spiraling upward at a fantastic clip, the index is now more than a simple measure of events; it is a mover and a shaper as well.

This was the lead-in to an article by Eric Aiken (1974). You can see that the CPI represents a very influential time series index. And Aiken's conjecture was correct: Many labor contracts now have escalator clauses tied to the CPI.

The CPI is based on a weighted average of prices of 398 items, called the **market basket**. Among the items in the market basket are meat, soap, shirts, appliances, doctor's fees, and funerals. The 398 items are intended to represent purchases of middle-income city dwellers, so the index is not designed to reflect consumer tendencies of professionals, farm residents, or the wealthy. The list of items is rarely changed, and therefore quickly becomes an outdated representation of buying trends, even for the middle-income city dweller.

Prices of the market basket items are determined by sampling approximately 18,000 retail stores in fifty-six cities on a regular basis (food items monthly, others quarterly except in the five largest metropolitan areas, where all items are priced monthly). The prices are then weighted by estimated importance to consumers and by the population of the area from which they are obtained. The result is a weighted sum of prices, which makes the CPI a weighted composite index.

The weights used to compute the CPI are determined by a survey of buying patterns in the United States. The results of the 1972–1973 survey have just recently been compiled; however, the CPI is still computed (as of this writing) using the 1960–1961 weights. The base period used is usually 1967, although some use 1972. The yearly CPI is given in Table 14.5 for the period 1960–1976 using 1967 as the base period and a graph is shown in Figure 14.3.

TABLE 14.5
CONSUMER PRICE
INDEX, 1960–1976

YEAR	CPI	YEAR	CPI
1960	88.7	1969	109.8
1961	89.6	1970	116.3
1962	90.6	1971	121.3
1963	91.7	1972	125.3
1964	92.9	1973	133.1
1965	94.5	1974	147.7
1966	97.2	1975	161.2
1967	100.0	1976	170.5
1968	104.2		

A common interpretation for the 1976 CPI of 170.5 is that in 1976 it cost approximately $170.50 to purchase the same goods and services that could have been purchased for $100 in 1967. However, as Aiken (1974) notes, there are those "who persist in using it [the CPI] for purposes for which it was never designed. They might,

FIGURE 14.3
CONSUMER PRICE INDEX, 1960–1976

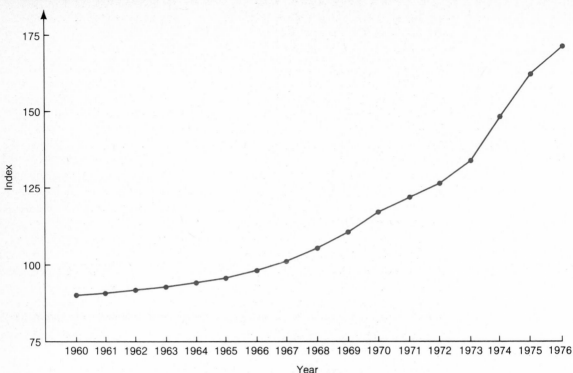

however, respond as did the habitual gambler who defended his play at a crooked roulette table on the grounds it was the only wheel in town.''

Index numbers provide useful **descriptive** summaries of economic activity. Their true meaning at any point in time is open to debate, but their proliferation leaves little doubt that many people find them valuable. However, there is a danger of using index numbers for more than they are intended. Specifically, attempts to use index numbers to make inferences about future economic events often prove fruitless. One problem is that no measure of reliability can be assigned to the inference unless a time series model is constructed to describe the sequence of index numbers.

EXERCISES

14.1. A stock you are interested in buying has had the yearly closing prices shown in the table between 1965 and 1976. Using 1967 as the base period, calculate the simple index for this stock's price between 1965 and 1976.

YEAR	STOCK PRICE	YEAR	STOCK PRICE
1965	$30.125	1971	49.125
1966	25.500	1972	38.750
1967	32.000	1973	22.250
1968	38.375	1974	28.750
1969	42.500	1975	43.000
1970	47.125	1976	52.875

14.2. The GNP is the sum of several components. One of these is personal consumption expenditures, which is itself the sum of durable goods, nondurable goods, and services.

BILLIONS OF DOLLARS

YEAR	DURABLE GOODS	NONDURABLE GOODS	SERVICES
1961	41.6	155.3	138.1
1962	46.7	161.6	147.0
1963	51.4	167.1	156.1
1964	56.3	176.9	167.1
1965	62.8	188.6	178.7
1966	67.7	204.7	192.4
1967	69.6	212.6	208.1
1968	80.0	230.4	225.6
1969	85.5	247.0	247.2
1970	84.9	264.7	269.1
1971	97.1	277.7	293.4
1972	111.2	299.3	322.4
1973	122.9	334.4	351.3
1974	121.9	375.7	388.3
1975	131.7	409.1	432.4
1976	156.5	440.4	482.8

a. Using these three component values for the years 1961–1976, construct a simple composite index for personal consumption, using 1967 as the base year.

b. Suppose we wanted to update the index by making 1974 the base year. Can you do this by using only the index values you calculated in part a, without referring to the original data?

14.3. Refer to Exercise 14.2. Graph the personal consumption expenditure index for the years 1961–1976, first using 1967 as the base year and then using 1974 as the base year. What effect does changing the base year have on the graph of this index?

14.2

DESCRIPTIVE COMPONENTS OF A TIME SERIES

In describing the nature of a time series, X_t, researchers often write X_t as the sum of four other component time series:

$$X_t = T_t + C_t + S_t + R_t$$

where

T_t = Secular trend

C_t = Cyclical effect

S_t = Seasonal effect

R_t = Residual effect

The secular trend, T_t, also known as the long-term trend, is a time series that describes the long-term movements of X_t. For example, if you want to characterize the secular trend of the production of automobiles since 1930, you would show T_t as an upward moving time series over the period 1930 to the present. This does not imply that the automobile production series has always moved upward from month to month and year to year, but it does mean the long-term trend has been an increasing one over that period of time.

The cyclical effect, C_t, generally describes fluctuations of the time series about the secular trend that are attributable to business and economic conditions at the time. For example, the closing day's Dow Jones Average over the past 30 years is given in Table 14.6. You can see in Figure 14.4 that it has a generally increasing secular trend.* However, during periods of recession, the Dow Jones Average tends to lie below the secular trend, while in times of general economic expansion, it lies above the long-term trend line.

YEAR	DJA	YEAR	DJA	YEAR	DJA
1947	181.16	1957	435.69	1967	905.11
1948	177.30	1958	583.65	1968	943.75
1949	200.13	1959	679.36	1969	800.36
1950	235.41	1960	615.89	1970	838.92
1951	269.23	1961	731.14	1971	884.76
1952	291.90	1962	652.10	1972	950.71
1953	280.90	1963	762.95	1973	923.88
1954	404.39	1964	874.13	1974	759.37
1955	488.40	1965	969.26	1975	802.49
1956	499.47	1966	785.69	1976	974.92

TABLE 14.6
DOW JONES AVERAGE (DJA), 1947–1976

The seasonal effect, S_t, describes the fluctuations in the time series that recur during specific portions of each year. (Thus, S_t is useful only when X_t is observed more often than yearly.) For example, quarterly power loads for a utility company located in the southern part of the United States are given in Table 14.7, with a graph in Figure 14.5. Note that the values of X_t tend to be highest in the summer months (quarter III) with another smaller peak in the winter months (quarter I), as shown in Figure 14.5. The spring and fall (quarters II and IV) seasonal effect is negative, meaning that the series tends to lie below the long-term trend line during those months.

TABLE 14.7
QUARTERLY POWER LOADS FOR A SOUTHERN UTILITY COMPANY, 1973–1976

YEAR	QUARTER	POWER LOAD Megawatts	YEAR	QUARTER	POWER LOAD Megawatts
1973	I	103.5	1975	I	144.5
	II	94.7		II	137.1
	III	118.6		III	159.0
	IV	109.3		IV	149.5
1974	I	126.1	1976	I	166.1
	II	116.0		II	152.5
	III	141.2		III	178.2
	IV	131.6		IV	169.0

*The secular trend shown in Figure 14.4 is a 7 point moving average, which we will subsequently explain.

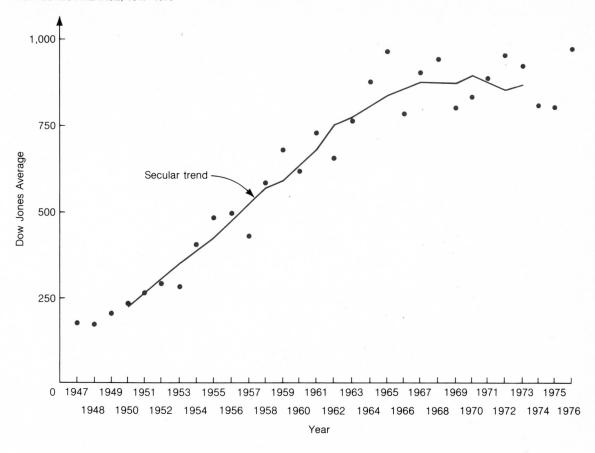

FIGURE 14.4
DOW JONES AVERAGE, 1947–1976

The **residual effect**, R_t, is what remains of X_t after the secular, cyclical, and seasonal components have been removed. Part of the residual effect may be attributable to unpredictable rare events (earthquake, presidential assassination, people landing on the moon, etc.), and part to the randomness of human actions. In any case, the presence of the residual component makes it impossible to forecast the future values of a time series without error. Thus, the presence of the residual effect emphasizes a point we first made in Chapter 11 in connection with regression models: No business phenomena should be described by deterministic models. All realistic business models, time series or otherwise, should include a residual component.

Various descriptive techniques are available for identifying and characterizing time series components. Probably the most popular technique is the **moving average** of X_t. The moving average, M_t, at time t is formed by averaging X_t over N adjacent time periods:

$$M_t = \frac{X_{t-m} + X_{t-m+1} + \cdots + X_t + \cdots + X_{t+m-1} + X_{t+m}}{N}$$

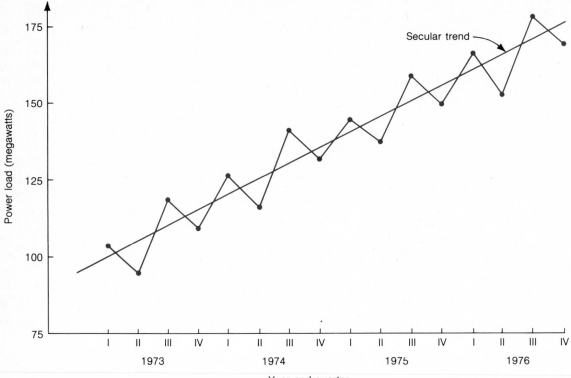

Year and quarter

where $m = (N - 1)/2$. For example, the first three values of a **5 point moving average** would be calculated as follows:

$$M_3 = \frac{X_1 + X_2 + X_3 + X_4 + X_5}{5}$$

$$M_4 = \frac{X_2 + X_3 + X_4 + X_5 + X_6}{5}$$

$$M_5 = \frac{X_3 + X_4 + X_5 + X_6 + X_7}{5}$$

Note that the $(N - 1)/2 = 2$ points on each end will be lost in forming the moving average.

A moving average aids in identifying the secular trend of a time series, because the averaging tends to modify the effects of short-term variation. For example, consider a 7 point moving average for the 30 years of Dow Jones Averages given in Table 14.8. The first value of M_t corresponds to 1950, and we find

TABLE 14.8
DOW JONES AVERAGE AND ITS 7 POINT MOVING AVERAGE, 1947–1976

| | | 7 POINT MOVING | | | 7 POINT MOVING |
YEAR	DJA	AVERAGE	YEAR	DJA	AVERAGE
1947	181.16	—	1962	652.10	754.98
1948	177.30	—	1963	762.95	770.17
1949	200.13	—	1964	874.13	811.48
1950	235.41	233.72	1965	969.26	841.86
1951	269.23	265.61	1966	785.69	863.04
1952	291.90	310.05	1967	905.11	873.89
1953	280.90	352.81	1968	943.75	875.41
1954	404.39	381.42	1969	800.36	872.76
1955	488.40	426.34	1970	838.92	892.50
1956	499.47	481.69	1971	884.76	871.68
1957	435.69	529.55	1972	950.71	851.50
1958	583.64	576.23	1973	923.88	876.44
1959	679.36	599.61	1974	759.37	—
1960	615.89	637.25	1975	802.49	—
1961	731.14	699.89	1976	974.92	—

$$M_{1950} = \frac{X_{1947} + X_{1948} + X_{1949} + X_{1950} + X_{1951} + X_{1952} + X_{1953}}{7}$$

$$= 233.72$$

To find M_{1951}, we use the relationship

$$M_{t+1} = M_t + \frac{X_{t+m+1} - X_{t-m}}{N}$$

or, in this case, with $t = 1951$, $N = 7$, and $m = (N - 1)/2 = 3$, so,

$$M_{1951} = M_{1950} + \frac{(X_{1954} - X_{1947})}{7} = 233.72 + \frac{404.39 - 181.16}{7}$$

$$= 265.61$$

This process is continued until we calculate M_{1973}. All values of the Dow Jones Average and its 7 point moving average are shown in Table 14.8. The graphs of both the Dow Jones Average and its 7 point moving average are shown in Figure 14.4. The plot of the moving average clearly depicts the long-term trend of the Dow Jones Average. The choice of $N = 7$ was arbitrary. We usually will try several values, in a search for one that yields a smooth series M_t, but is not so large that many points at each end of the series are lost.

The moving average is also useful for identifying cylical and seasonal effects. If we examine the difference $(X_t - M_t)$ between the time series and its moving average, we can identify periods of time during which short-term variations occur. For example, in Figure 14.4 you can identify the recessionary periods as clusters of Dow Jones Average values all lying below the 7 point moving average values. Cylical periods of economic expansion can be similarly identified as clusters of observed Dow Jones Average values lying above the 7 point moving average.

To use the moving average for identification of seasonal effects, we usually work with quarterly or monthly data. For quarterly data, a 4 point moving average is often used to average out the quarterly seasonal effects. (Since $N = 4$ is even, we must average successive values of M_t before they can be associated with specific quarters. We will not go into more detail here.) The difference $(X_t - M_t)$ for each quarter indicates the size and direction of the seasonal effect for that quarter. For example, consider the quarterly power load series in Table 14.9. The time series and 4 point moving average are shown in the table, and a graph of each is shown in Figure 14.6. The pronounced seasonal effect, primarily attributable to temperature differences, is clearly indicated by the positive and negative differences between X_t and M_t.

TABLE 14.9
QUARTERLY
POWER LOADS
AND A 4 POINT
MOVING AVERAGE

YEAR	QUARTER	POWER LOAD X_t	4 POINT MOVING AVERAGE M_t	$P_t = (100)\dfrac{X_t}{M_t}$
1973	I	103.5		
	II	94.7		
	III	118.6	109.3	109
	IV	109.3	114.8	95
1974	I	126.1	120.4	105
	II	116.0	126.0	92
	III	141.2	131.1	108
	IV	131.6	136.0	97
1975	I	144.5	141.0	102
	II	137.1	145.4	94
	III	159.0	150.3	106
	IV	149.5	154.9	97
1976	I	166.1	159.2	104
	II	152.5	162.3	94
	III	178.2		
	IV	169.0		

Some analysts calculate the percentage

$$P_t = (100)\frac{X_t}{M_t}$$

to represent a quarterly seasonal index. When the percentage P_t exceeds 100, the indication is a positive seasonal effect, while a value of P_t less than 100 would imply a negative seasonal effect. Of course, P_t would not be free of cyclical and residual effects (or even all secular trends), so care must be taken in interpreting P_t. One method of further eliminating effects that are not seasonal is to average all first-quarter values of P_t to get an overall first-quarter seasonal index, and then repeat this process for the other three quarters. This is called the ratio-to-moving average method of measuring seasonal variation. We show the percentages P_t for the power load data

FIGURE 14.6
QUARTERLY POWER LOADS AND 4 POINT MOVING AVERAGE

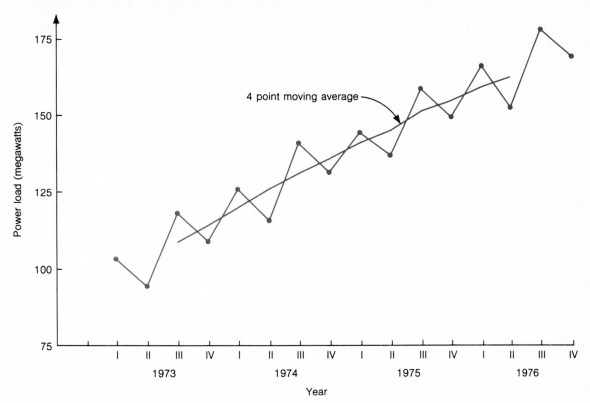

in Table 14.9. The average first-quarter percentage is

$$R_{\text{I}} = \frac{P_{1974,\text{I}} + P_{1975,\text{I}} + P_{1976,\text{I}}}{3} = \frac{105 + 102 + 104}{3}$$

$$= 104$$

The other three quarters' ratio-to-moving average figures are $R_{\text{II}} = 93$, $R_{\text{III}} = 108$, and $R_{\text{IV}} = 96$. The implication is that for this 3 year period, power loads are about 4% and 8% higher than the secular trend in quarters I and III (summer and winter), respectively, and about 7% and 4% lower than the secular trend in quarters II and IV (spring and fall), respectively.

In addition to moving averages, there are several other methods of smoothing a time series to identify the various long-term and short-term effects. Among these is exponential smoothing, a method that forms a weighted average of X_t with all the previous values of X_t in the data set. The effect and purpose of exponential smoothing is much the same as for the moving average, so we will not give the mathematical details. The interested reader should consult the references at the end of the chapter.

The primary uses of smoothing techniques are to provide a pictorial description of the time series secular trend and to aid in the identification of cyclical and seasonal effects. Although some analysts attempt to project a moving average into future time periods graphically, the reliability of a forecast obtained in this way is unknown, which makes its use for decision-making purposes very risky. To assess the reliability of forecasts, we must first construct a time series model.

EXERCISES

14.4. The Federal Reserve Board Index of Quarterly Output is an industrial production index. Using the values of this index for 1961–1975, calculate moving averages for $N = 3$, 5, and 7, and graph them (use 1967 as the base year). Which moving average series most clearly depicts the long-term trend of the index? For the moving average series chosen, examine $X_t - M_t$. Do there appear to be any cyclical effects?

YEAR	INDEX	YEAR	INDEX
1961	66.7	1969	110.7
1962	72.2	1970	106.6
1963	76.5	1971	106.8
1964	81.7	1972	115.2
1965	89.2	1973	125.6
1966	97.9	1974	124.8
1967	100.0	1975	117.8
1968	105.7		

14.5. Using the data in Exercise 14.2, plot on a large sheet of graph paper the three component series—durable goods, nondurable goods, and services—with the personal consumption expenditure series. Visually compare the trends in the three component series with each other and with the total series. Which of the component series has a trend that most resembles the trend for the personal consumption expenditure (total) series? If the resemblance is quite strong, what might this tell you about the importance of this component in evaluating changes in personal consumption expenditures?

14.6. The table represents the quarterly sales index of a particular brand of calculator from a campus bookstore. The quarters are based on an academic year, so the first quarter represents fall, the second winter, the third spring, and the fourth summer.

YEAR	FIRST QUARTER	SECOND QUARTER	THIRD QUARTER	FOURTH QUARTER
1972	252	160	438	398
1973	376	216	464	429
1974	425	318	523	496
1975	456	398	593	576
1976	526	498	636	640

a. Plot the time series.
b. Construct a 5 point moving average, and then compute the ratio of each of the time series values to the corresponding moving average value at that time. Does this ratio reveal a seasonal pattern?

14.3

TIME SERIES MODELS: REGRESSION AND AUTOREGRESSION

Suppose a firm is interested in forecasting its sales revenues for each of the next 5 years. To make such forecasts and assess their reliability, a time series model must be constructed. The yearly sales data for the firm's 35 years of operation is given in Table 14.10. A plot of the data (Figure 14.7) reveals a linearly increasing trend, so that the model

$$E(X_t) = \beta_0 + \beta_1 t$$

seems plausible for the secular trend. Fitting the model by least squares (see Section 11.2), we find the least squares model

$$\hat{X}_t = \hat{\beta}_0 + \hat{\beta}_1 t = .4015 + 4.2956t$$

with

$$SSE = 1,345.45$$

This least squares line is shown in Figure 14.7 and the SAS printout is given in Figure 14.8. We can now forecast sales for the 36th through the 40th year of operation. The forecasts of sales and the corresponding 95% prediction intervals are shown in the printout. For example, for $t = 36$, we have

$$\hat{X}_{36} = 155.0$$

with the 95% prediction interval (141.3, 168.8). Similarly, we can obtain the forecasts and prediction intervals for the years 37–40. The observed sales, forecast sales, and prediction intervals are shown in Figure 14.9. Although it is not easily perceptible in the figure, the prediction intervals widen as we attempt to forecast further into the future (see the printout, Figure 14.8). This agrees with the intuitive notion that short-term forecasts should be more reliable than long-term forecasts.

TABLE 14.10

A FIRM'S YEARLY SALES REVENUE (THOUSANDS OF DOLLARS)

t	X_t	t	X_t
1	4.8	19	94.2
2	4.0	20	85.4
3	5.5	21	86.2
4	15.6	22	89.9
5	23.1	23	89.2
6	23.3	24	99.1
7	31.4	25	100.3
8	46.0	26	111.7
9	46.1	27	108.2
10	41.9	28	115.5
11	45.5	29	119.2
12	53.5	30	125.2
13	48.4	31	136.3
14	61.6	32	146.8
15	65.6	33	146.1
16	71.4	34	151.4
17	83.4	35	150.9
18	93.6		

FIGURE 14.7
PLOT OF SALES DATA

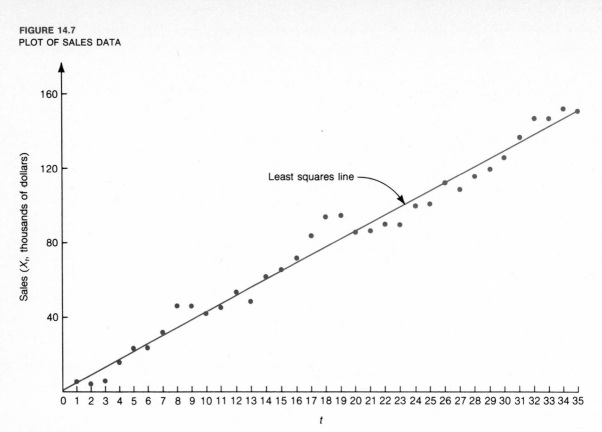

FIGURE 14.8
SAS PRINTOUT FOR LEAST SQUARES FIT (STRAIGHT LINE) TO X_t = SALES

SOURCE	DF	SUM OF SQUARES	MEAN SQUARE	F VALUE	PR > F
MODEL	1	65875.20816807	65875.20816807	1615.72	0.0001
ERROR	33	1345.45354622	40.77131958		STD DEV
CORRECTED TOTAL	34	67220.66171429		R-SQUARE	6.38524233
				0.979985	

PARAMETER	ESTIMATE	T FOR HO: PARAMETER = 0	PR > |T|	STD ERROR OF ESTIMATE
INTERCEPT	0.40151261	0.18	0.8567	2.20570829
T	4.29563025	40.20	0.0001	0.10686692

T	PREDICTED VALUE	LOWER 95% CL INDIVIDUAL	UPPER 95% CL INDIVIDUAL
36	155.04420168	141.30017574	168.78822762
37	159.33983193	145.53232286	173.14734101
38	163.63546218	149.76135290	177.50957147
39	167.93109244	153.98731054	181.87487434
40	172.22672269	158.21024159	186.24320379

There are two problems with forecasting time series using a least squares model.

Problem 1

We are using the least squares model to forecast values outside the region of observation of the independent variable, t. That is, we are forecasting for values of t between 36 and 40, but the observed sales are for t values between 1 and 35. As we noted in Chapters 11–13, it is extremely risky to use a least squares regression model for prediction outside the experimental region.

Problem 1 obviously cannot be avoided. Since forecasting always involves predictions about the future values of a time series, some or all of the independent variables will probably be outside the region of observation on which the model was developed. It is important that the forecaster recognize the dangers of this type of prediction. If underlying conditions change drastically after the model is estimated (e.g., if federal price controls are imposed on the firm's products during the 36th year of operation), the forecasts and their confidence intervals are probably useless.

FIGURE 14.9
OBSERVED
(YEARS 1–35) AND
FORECAST
(YEARS 36–40)
SALES USING THE
STRAIGHT-LINE MODEL

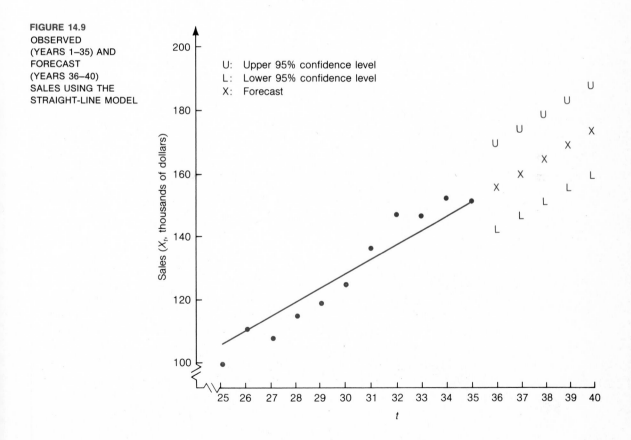

Problem 2

Although the straight-line model may adequately describe the secular trend of the sales, we have not attempted to build any cyclical effects into the model. Thus, the effect of inflationary and recessionary periods will be to increase the error of the forecasts, because the model does not anticipate such periods.

Fortunately, the forecaster often has more control over problem 2. In forming the prediction intervals for the forecasts we made the standard regression assumptions (Chapters 11 and 12) about the random error component of the model. We assume the errors have zero mean, constant variance, normal probability distributions, and are *independent*. The latter assumption is very dubious in time series models, especially in the presence of short-term trends. Often, if a year's value lies above the secular trend line, the next year's value has a tendency to be above the line also. That is, the errors tend to be correlated (see Figure 14.7).

We can take advantage of the correlated errors that may result from cyclical effects by modeling the random component of the time series model. For example, we might model X_t, the firm's sales, as

$$X_t = \beta_0 + \beta_1 t + Y_t$$

where Y_t is the random component of the model. We now postulate a **first-order autoregressive model** for the correlated error term Y_t:

$$Y_t = \phi Y_{t-1} + \varepsilon_t$$

where ϕ is a constant coefficient less than 1 in absolute value, and ε_t is a zero mean, constant variance, normally distributed, and *independent* time series (called **white noise** by time series analysts). This model for Y_t implies that the values of Y_t are correlated over time. The correlation of Y_t with its own past values is called **autocorrelation**. For example, the autocorrelation between Y_t and Y_{t-d} (that is, the present random component and the one d time units in the past) is plotted for $d = 1, 2, \ldots,$ 5 in Figure 14.10 for $\phi = .5$. Note that the neighboring values of Y_t ($d = 1$) have the highest correlation, and the correlation dies out rapidly as the distance d between time points is increased.* This positive correlation between near neighbors of Y_t implies cyclic departures from the regression model.

In summary, the pair of models

$$X_t = \beta_0 + \beta_1 t + Y_t$$
$$Y_t = \phi Y_{t-1} + \varepsilon_t$$

provides a more flexible and, hopefully, a more realistic description of the yearly sales of the firm. However, for this additional flexibility, we must estimate one more parameter, ϕ. This is accomplished by a modification of the least squares technique, the details of which are beyond the scope of this text. The SAS printout that results

---

*The autoregressive model is called a **stationary model** because the autocorrelation function depends only on the distance, d, between the Y values, and not on the time, t. We usually assume that the random component Y_t of the model is stationary.

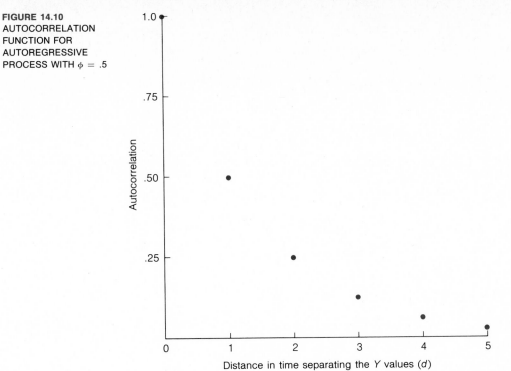

Distance in time separating the Y values (d)

from using this modified least squares technique to fit the pair of models to the sales revenue data in Table 14.10 is shown in Figure 14.11. The fitted models are

$$\hat{X}_t = .4058 + 4.2959t + \hat{Y}_t$$

$$\hat{Y}_t = .5896Y_{t-1}$$

with

$$SSE = 877.69$$

Note that the SSE has been reduced from 1,345.45 for the least squares fit to 877.69 for the pair of models shown above. Thus, we expect our forecasts to be more reliable for the straight-line–autoregressive models.

To obtain the forecasts for years 36–40, we find

$$\hat{Y}_{35} = X_{35} - [.4058 + 4.2959(35)] = 150.9 - 150.7623 = .1377$$

We use the estimated value of $\hat{Y}_{35} = .1377$ to obtain

$$\hat{Y}_{36} = \hat{\phi}\hat{Y}_{35} = (.5896)(.1377) = .0812$$

and then

$$\hat{X}_{36} = \hat{\beta}_0 + \hat{\beta}_1(36) + \hat{Y}_{36}$$
$$= .4058 + (4.2959)(36) + .0812 = 155.2$$

FIGURE 14.11

SAS PRINTOUT FOR STRAIGHT-LINE–AUTOREGRESSIVE MODELS FIT TO SALES DATA

	DF	SUM OF SQUARES	MEAN SQUARE	F RATIO	APPROX PROB
REGRESS	1	66342.9763	66342.9763	2494.43	.0001
ERROR	33	877.6854	26.5965		
TOTAL	34	67220.6617		R-SQUARE = .9869	

VARIABLE	B VALUE	STD DEVIATION	T RATIO	APPROX PROB
INTERCEPT	0.40575698772	3.93594906111	0.103	0.9185
T	4.29593038119	0.18693269351	22.981	0.0001

ESTIMATES OF THE AUTOREGRESSIVE PARAMETERS

LAG	COEFFICIENT	STD DEVIATION	T RATIO
1	0.58962415	0.136522	−4.318880

FIGURE 14.12
FORECASTS AND CONFIDENCE INTERVALS FOR YEARS 36–40 USING STRAIGHT-LINE–AUTOREGRESSIVE MODELS

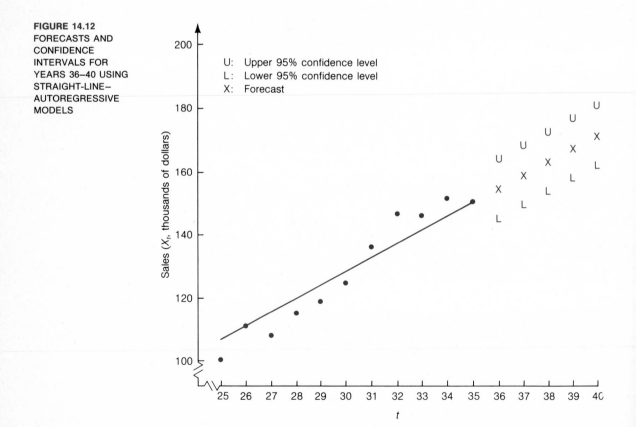

U: Upper 95% confidence level
L: Lower 95% confidence level
X: Forecast

Approximate 95% prediction limits are (144.8, 165.5). Note that this interval is narrower than the interval we obtained for the same forecast using the least squares model, (141.3, 168.8). The procedure for forecasting X_{37} to X_{40} is similar, and the entire set of forecasts and approximate prediction limits are shown in Figure 14.12.

A comparison of Figures 14.9 and 14.12 reveals that the prediction intervals are somewhat narrower when the autoregressive model is used for the random component. It appears that the autoregressive model for Y_t helps identify the short-term cyclic effects on sales, thereby making the forecasts more reliable.

The type of modeling exemplified by the straight-line—autoregressive models for the sales data is useful for many business variables. First, a model is postulated for the deterministic component to describe the secular trend and, if the data is monthly or quarterly, the seasonal effect. Then, the random component is modeled to describe the cyclical effects. The autoregressive model is useful for this random component, with the general form

$$Y_t = \phi_1 Y_{t-1} + \phi_2 Y_{t-2} + \cdots + \phi_p Y_{t-p} + \varepsilon_t$$

which is called an autoregressive model of order p. The name autoregressive comes from the fact that Y_t is regressed on its own past values. As the order p is increased, more complex autocorrelation functions can be modeled. There are several other types of models that can be used for the random component, but the autoregressive model is very flexible and seems to receive more application in business forecasting than the others.

When data is collected on a monthly or quarterly basis, the time series may contain seasonal effects. Regression models for describing seasonal time series will often contain trigonometric terms. For example, the model of a monthly series with mean $E(X_t)$ might be

$$E(X_t) = \beta_0 + \beta_1\left(\cos\frac{2\pi}{12}t\right) + \beta_2\left(\sin\frac{2\pi}{12}t\right)$$

**FIGURE 14.13
A SEASONAL
TIME SERIES MODEL**

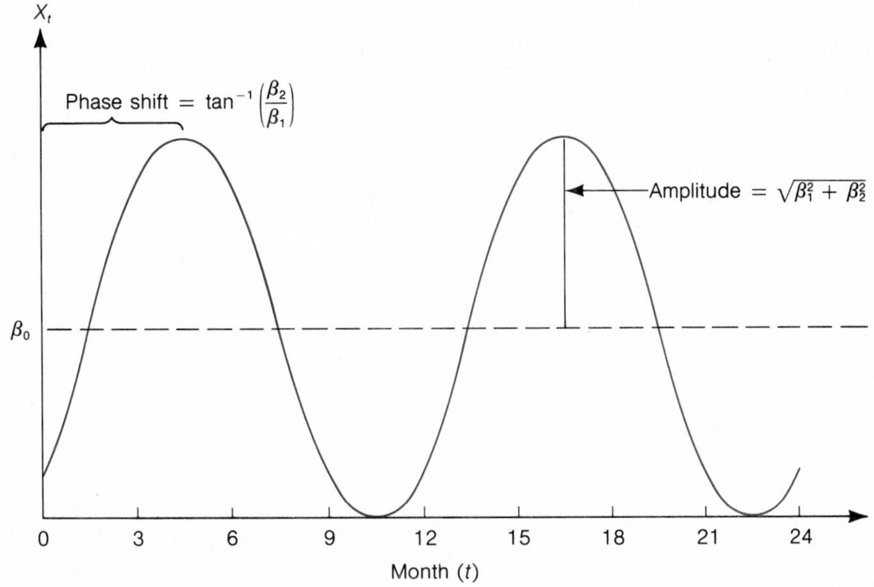

This model would appear as shown in Figure 14.13. Note that the model is cyclic, with a period of 12 months. That is, the mean $E(X_t)$ completes a cycle every 12 months and then repeats the same cycle over the next 12 months. Thus, the expected peaks and valleys of the series remain the same from year to year. The coefficients β_1 and β_2 determine the amplitude and phase shift of the model. The amplitude is the magnitude of the seasonal effect, while the phase shift locates the peaks and valleys in time. For example, if we assume month 1 is January, the mean of the time series depicted in Figure 14.13 has a peak each April and a valley each October.

If the data are quarterly, we can treat the season as a qualitative independent variable, and write the model

$$E(X_t) = \beta_0 + \beta_1 S_1 + \beta_2 S_2 + \beta_3 S_3$$

where

$$S_1 = \begin{cases} 1 & \text{if Season} = \text{Spring (II)} \\ 0 & \text{otherwise} \end{cases}$$

$$S_2 = \begin{cases} 1 & \text{if Season} = \text{Summer (III)} \\ 0 & \text{otherwise} \end{cases}$$

$$S_3 = \begin{cases} 1 & \text{if Season} = \text{Fall (IV)} \\ 0 & \text{otherwise} \end{cases}$$

FIGURE 14.14
SEASONAL MODEL FOR QUARTERLY DATA USING DUMMY VARIABLES

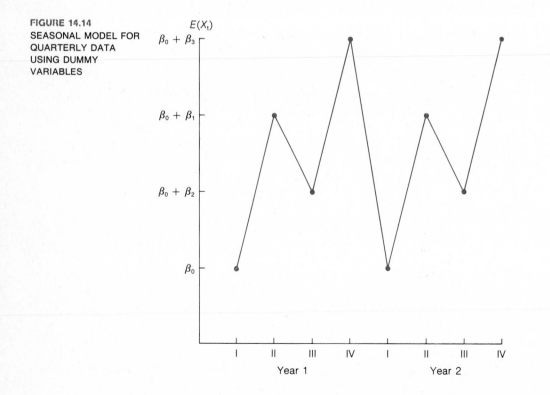

Thus, S_1, S_2, and S_3 are dummy variables that describe the four levels of Season, letting Season = Winter (I) be the base level (see Chapter 13 for a discussion of modeling with qualitative variables). The β coefficients determine the mean value of X_t for each season, as shown in Figure 14.14. Note that for the dummy variable model and the trigonometric model we assume the seasonal effects are approximately the same from year to year. If they tend to increase or decrease with time, an inter-action of the seasonal effect with time may be necessary. (An example will be given in Section 14.4.)

We can now describe a general approach for constructing a time series model:

1. Construct a model for the secular and seasonal components of the model. This model may be a regression model consisting of a polynomial in t for the secular trend (usually a straight-line or quadratic model) and trigonometric terms or dummy variables for the seasonal effects. The model may also include as independent variables other time series. For example, last year's rate of inflation may be used as a predictor of this year's GNP.

2. Next, construct a model for the random component (cyclical and residual effects) of the model. The autoregressive model is very useful for this aspect of time series modeling.

3. The two components are then combined so that the model can be used for fore-casting. Prediction intervals are calculated to measure the reliability of the forecasts.

14.4 TIME SERIES MODELING: AN EXAMPLE

Critical water shortages can have dire consequences for both business and private sectors of communities. Forecasting water usage months in advance is essential to avoid such shortages.

Suppose a community has monthly water usage records over the past 15 years. A plot of the last 6 years of the time series X_t is shown in Figure 14.15. We want to use time series modeling techniques to model the secular, seasonal, and cyclic com-ponents of this time series. Note that both an increasing secular trend and a seasonal pattern appear in Figure 14.15. The water usage seems to peak during the summer months and decline during the winter months. Thus, we might propose the following model for the secular and seasonal components:

$$E(X_t) = \beta_0 + \beta_1 t + \beta_2 \left(\cos \frac{2\pi}{12} t \right) + \beta_3 \left(\sin \frac{2\pi}{12} t \right)$$

Since the amplitude of the seasonal effect, i.e., the magnitude of the peaks and valleys, appears to increase with time, we include in the model an interaction between time and the trigonometric components, to get

$$E(X_t) = \beta_0 + \beta_1 t + \beta_2 \left(\cos \frac{2\pi}{12} t \right) + \beta_3 \left(\sin \frac{2\pi}{12} t \right) + \beta_4 t \left(\cos \frac{2\pi}{12} t \right) + \beta_5 t \left(\sin \frac{2\pi}{12} t \right)$$

The model for the random component Y_t must allow for short-term cyclic effects. For example, in an especially hot summer, if the water usage, X_t, exceeds the ex-pected usage, $E(X_t)$, for July, we would expect the same thing to happen in August.

FIGURE 14.15
WATER USAGE TIME SERIES

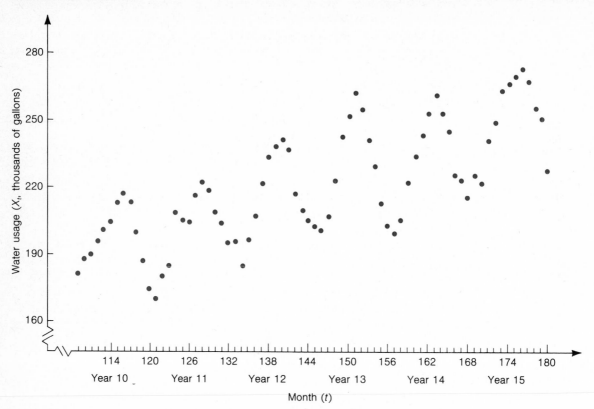

Thus, we propose a first-order* autoregressive model for the random component:

$$Y_t = \phi Y_{t-1} + \varepsilon_t$$

We now fit the models to the time series X_t. The SAS output is shown in Figure 14.16. The estimated models are given by

$$\hat{X}_t = 100.083 + .826t - 10.801\left(\cos\frac{2\pi}{12}t\right) - 7.086\left(\sin\frac{2\pi}{12}t\right)$$

$$- .0556t\left(\cos\frac{2\pi}{12}t\right) - .0296t\left(\sin\frac{2\pi}{12}t\right)$$

$$\hat{Y}_t = .6617Y_{t-1}$$

with MSE = 23.135. The R^2 value of .99 indicates that the model provides a good fit to the data.

We now use the models to forecast water usage for the next 12 months. The forecast for 1 month ahead is made by finding that the last residual value is $\hat{Y}_{180} = -1.3247$, so that

*A more complex time series model may be more appropriate. We use the simple first-order autoregressive model so you can follow the modeling process more easily.

FIGURE 14.16

SAS PRINTOUT FOR WATER USAGE MODEL

ESTIMATES OF THE AUTOREGRESSIVE PARAMETERS

LAG	COEFFICIENT	STD DEVIATION	T RATIO
1	−0.66167894	0.055886	−11.839831

	DF	SUM OF SQUARES	MEAN SQUARE	F RATIO	APPROX PROB
REGRESS	5	373452.958	74690.592	3228.47	.0001
ERROR	174	4025.513	23.135		
TOTAL	179	377478.471		R-SQUARE = .9893	

VARIABLE	B VALUE	STD DEVIATION	T RATIO	APPROX PROB
INTERCEPT	100.083218977	2.07617706007	48.206	0.0001
T	0.826274293	0.01979498750	41.742	0.0001
CS	−10.801144	1.85586558083	−5.820	0.0001
SN	−7.0857642	1.89574083666	−3.738	0.0003
CST	−0.055634923	0.01771077652	−3.141	0.0020
SNT	−0.029630055	0.01820045673	−1.628	0.1053

$$\hat{Y}_{181} = (.6617)(-1.3247) = -.8766$$

Then,

$$\hat{X}_{181} = \hat{\beta}_0 + \hat{\beta}_1(181) + \hat{\beta}_2\left(\cos\frac{2\pi}{12}181\right) + \hat{\beta}_3\left(\sin\frac{2\pi}{12}181\right)$$

$$+ \hat{\beta}_4 t\left(\cos\frac{2\pi}{12}181\right) + \hat{\beta}_5 t\left(\sin\frac{2\pi}{12}181\right) + \hat{Y}_{181} = 227.9$$

Approximate 95% prediction bounds on this forecast are given by $\pm 2\sqrt{\text{MSE}} = \pm 2\sqrt{23.135} = \pm 9.6$.[*] That is, we expect our forecast for 1 month ahead to be within 9,600 gallons of the actual water usage. This forecasting process is then repeated for the next 11 months. The forecasts and their bounds are shown in Figure 14.17. Also shown are the actual values of water usage during year 16. Note that the forecast prediction intervals widen as we attempt to forecast further into the future. This property of the prediction intervals makes long-term forecasts very unreliable.

We have barely scratched the surface of time series modeling. The variety and complexity of available techniques is overwhelming. However, if we have convinced you that time series modeling is a useful and powerful tool for business forecasting, we have accomplished our purpose. The successful construction of time series models requires much experience, and like regression modeling, entire texts are devoted to the subject (see the references at the end of the chapter).

[*]We are ignoring the errors in the parameter estimates in calculating the forecast reliability. These errors should be small for a series of this length.

FIGURE 14.17
FORECASTS OF
WATER USAGE

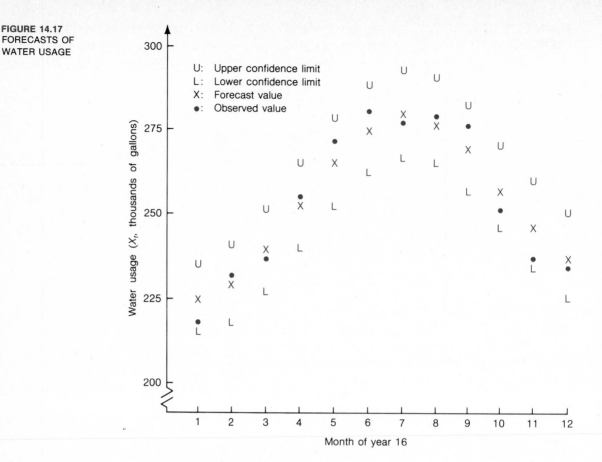

We conclude with a warning. Many oversimplified forecasting methods have been proposed. They usually consist of graphical extensions of a secular trend or seasonal pattern to future time periods. Although such pictorial techniques are easy to understand and therefore are intuitively appealing, they should be avoided. There is no measure of reliability for these forecasts, and thus the risk associated with making decisions based on them is very high.

SUMMARY

Time series modeling plays an important role in business forecasting. Some models, like index numbers and moving averages, are purely descriptive. Other models are probabilistic and therefore useful for inferential purposes. An example is a combination of a regression model for the secular and seasonal components, coupled with an autoregressive model for the cyclic component.

The forecaster should be very careful to distinguish between descriptive and inferential time series models. If descriptive models are used to project future values of the series, no assessment of forecast reliability is possible. Only when a probabilistic model is constructed can a prediction interval be used to evaluate the reliability of the forecast.

14.7. List and describe the four components of a business time series.

14.8. Why is the choice of the base period important when computing an index?

14.9. What is the difference between a simple composite index and a weighted composite index?

14.10. What are the effects of choosing the length of a moving average to be a large rather than a small number?

14.11. What do we mean when we say that a time series is autocorrelated? Why is a regression model alone inadequate when the random component of a business time series is autocorrelated?

14.12. The United States Balance of International Payments is an indicator of the country's economic status in the world economy. A table of its values from 1965 to 1975 is given here.

**BALANCE ON GOODS AND SERVICES
(MILLIONS OF DOLLARS)**

YEAR	BALANCE	YEAR	BALANCE
1965	7,140	1971	−237
1966	4,552	1972	−5,930
1967	4,380	1973	4,177
1968	1,620	1974	3,574
1969	1,020	1975	16,316
1970	2,966		

a. Calculate a simple international payments index by using 1970 as a base year.

b. Do the two negative values of the index have a meaningful interpretation?

14.13. Refer to Exercise 14.12. Calculate a 3 point moving average for the United States Balance of International Payments and graph it. Is there any apparent secular trend?

14.14. Sometimes consideration of how a time series is derived will give some insight as to what might be the form of an appropriate model for the series. For example, one business indicator is the Business Inventory–Sales Ratio, in which a measure of total yearly business inventories is divided by total yearly sales. Values for 1961–1975 are given in the table. Would you expect to find a secular trend in this time series? Graph the series values for 1961–1975. Does the graph tend to support your answer to the above question?

YEAR	BUSINESS INVENTORY–SALES RATIO	YEAR	BUSINESS INVENTORY–SALES RATIO
1961	1.54	1969	1.57
1962	1.51	1970	1.64
1963	1.49	1971	1.61
1964	1.47	1972	1.53
1965	1.45	1973	1.46
1966	1.47	1974	1.50
1967	1.57	1975	1.60
1968	1.55		

14.15. Refer to Exercise 14.14. Calculate and graph a 3 point moving average for the Business Inventory—Sales Ratio. What does this reveal about the secular trend of the time series?

14.16. An indicator of industrial activity is new plant and equipment expenditures. Quarterly figures for new plant and equipment expenditures from 1973 to 1976 are given in the table.

NEW PLANT AND EQUIPMENT EXPENDITURES
(ALL INDUSTRY TOTAL, UNADJUSTED SEASONALLY)

YEAR	QUARTER	BILLIONS OF DOLLARS
1973	I	21.50
	II	24.73
	III	25.04
	IV	28.48
1974	I	24.10
	II	28.16
	III	28.23
	IV	31.92
1975	I	25.82
	II	28.43
	III	27.79
	IV	30.74
1976	I	25.87
	II	29.70
	III	30.41
	IV	34.52

a. Graph both the time series values and a 4 point moving average for the time series on the same paper. [*Note:* You will have to average consecutive values of the moving average in order to associate a value with one of the time series values.] What model would you recommend for the secular trend over the time period shown?

b. Compute the ratio-to-moving average for the series, i.e., the ratios of each time series value to the corresponding moving average value for the same time period. Is any seasonal component evident?

14.17. The data in the table represent the percentages of imports of all new car sales in the United States from 1967 to 1977.

YEAR	PERCENTAGE X_t	YEAR	PERCENTAGE X_t
1967	9.3	1973	13.7
1968	10.5	1974	14.3
1969	10.9	1975	18.4
1970	13.6	1976	13.5
1971	13.6	1977	17.5
1972	13.4		

a. Use the methods given in Chapter 11 to fit the model

$$E(X_t) = \beta_0 + \beta_1 t$$

To simplify calculations, let $t = 1$ in 1967, $t = 2$ in 1968, etc.

b. Plot the least squares model from part a and then extend the line to forecast the percentage of imports of new car sales from 1978 to 1990 (i.e., for $t = 12, \ldots, 24$). How reliable do you think these forecasts are?

c. What basic precept of regression analysis is violated by the forecasting technique used in part b?

ON YOUR OWN . . .

Find a time series (preferably a yearly one) that is of interest to you. Try to obtain at least 20 years of data for the series.

a. Compute a simple index for the series, using at least two different base periods.

b. Compute 3, 5, and 7 point moving averages for the time series. Try to identify the secular trend—if one exists.

c. By comparing the observed values of the time series to the 5 point moving average, try to identify cyclical periods of the series. Can you ascribe a cause (recession, inflation, etc.) to these periods?

REFERENCES

Aiken, E. "Whose cost-of-living?" *Barrons,* Feb. 25, 1974.

Box, G. E. P., & Jenkins, G. M. *Time series analysis, forecasting and control.* San Francisco: Holden-Day, 1970.

Brillinger, D. R. *Time series data analysis and theory.* New York: Holt, Rinehart, and Winston, 1975.

Hamburg, M. *Statistical analysis for decision making.* 2d ed. New York: Harcourt Brace Jovanovich, 1977. Chapter 10.

Miller, R. B., & Wichern, D. W. *Intermediate business statistics: Analysis of variance, regression and time series.* New York: Holt, Rinehart, and Winston, 1977. Chapters 9–11.

Nelson, C. R. *Applied time series analysis for managerial forecasting.* San Francisco: Holden-Day, 1973.

Neter, J., Wasserman, W., & Whitmore, G. A. *Fundamental statistics for business and economics,* 4th ed. Boston: Allyn and Bacon, 1973. Chapters 28–32.

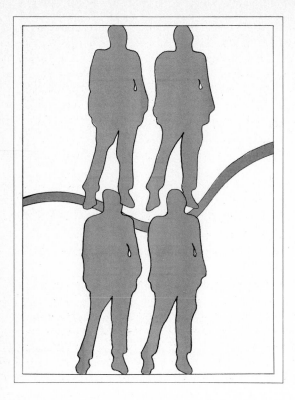

As we have seen in preceding chapters, the solutions of many business problems are based on inferences about population means. Methods for estimating and testing hypotheses about a single mean and the comparison of two means were presented in Chapters 9 and 10. Chapters 11–13 dealt with linear models for estimating the mean value of a response using regression models, and Chapter 14 treated the special case where the response measurements represent a time series.

WHERE WE'RE GOING . . .

This chapter extends the methods of Chapters 9–13 for the comparison of more than two means. We will use sampling procedures that are analogous to the independent sampling and paired difference designs of Chapter 10.

15

ANALYSIS
OF
VARIANCE

In Chapter 10 we learned how to compare the means of two populations using independent random samples (Section 10.2) and the paired difference design (Section 10.4). But most experiments tend to be more complex, often involving the comparison of more than two populations using a variety of sampling schemes (called experimental designs). Therefore, this chapter presents an extension of the methodology of Chapter 10 to the comparison of two or more population means using the independent sampling design and a design analogous to the paired difference design.*

Recall that an independent sampling design for comparing the means of 3, 4, or, in general, k populations, is one in which you select independent random samples from each of the k populations.

DEFINITION 15.1
An independent sampling design (often called a completely randomized design) is one in which independent random samples are drawn from each of the populations.

To illustrate, suppose a consumer group wants to compare the mean gas mileage for four different compact car models using an independent sampling design. The experimental units are cars and the measurements are the miles per gallon ratings for cars driven over a 1,000 mile course. Each car is assigned a different driver, and the contribution of the driver to a car's rating is inseparable from the contribution of the car. Consequently, the variability in the miles per gallon rating due to the driver contributes to the experimental error.

A particular car model identifies one of the four populations of measurements that is of interest to the consumer group. For example, suppose four models are identified as A, B, C, and D, and one of the models, call it model A, is a Ford Pinto. Then the consumer group might define the population of measurements for population A as the miles per gallon ratings for every Ford Pinto manufactured in 1977, and the populations associated with models B, C, and D can be defined in a similar manner. If a random sample of cars (say fifteen) is randomly and independently selected from each population, then the consumer group is using an independent sampling design.

As noted in Chapter 10, a paired difference design for comparing two population means often provides more information because it makes a comparison of observations from two populations (call them A and B) between pairs of matched (or similar) experimental units. For example, if you were comparing the miles per gallon ratings for two car models, measurements would vary substantially for the same model

---

*From Chapter 13 you will see that the populations can be viewed as the levels of one qualitative independent variable or the combination of levels of two or more qualitative independent variables. Therefore, all the data described in this chapter can be analyzed using a multiple regression analysis. The advantages of using the analysis of variance procedure described here are: (1) it is easier to understand and (2) the computations are relatively simple and can be performed on a desk calculator.

FIGURE 15.1
A RANDOMIZED BLOCK
DESIGN FOR
COMPARING FOUR
CAR MODELS

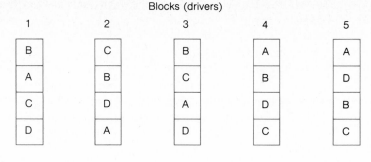

because of the difference in the driving habits of the drivers. To remove this source of variation, you could pair an A and a B car and assign both cars to a *single* driver. The driver would drive both cars and obtain the ratings for each. By taking the difference between these measurements for all driver pairs, you would cancel out the variation among drivers.

The extension of the paired difference design to a combination of more than two means implies that larger groups of experimental units are matched. To compare the means for the four car models, you would use matched groups of four experimental units. You could have each driver drive four cars, one of each model type. The matched group of four experimental units (matched on drivers) is called a block and the resulting design, employing a number of blocks, is called a randomized block design. For example, a randomized block design using five blocks (drivers) to compare the four car models (A, B, C, and D) is shown in Figure 15.1. The word randomized in the phrase randomized block design implies that the cars should be driven by each driver in a random sequence. This is done to eliminate any bias that might result from a particular position in the block. For example, driver 1 would drive the four car models in the sequence B, A, C, D.

Because the analysis of variance first achieved importance in agricultural experimentation, the terminology of the subject has an agricultural flavor. Most agricultural experiments involve the treatment of experimental units in two or more different ways and then a comparison of the means of the populations of measurements corresponding to the different treatments. For example, they might compare the yield of plots of corn treated with four different types of fertilizer, say A, B, C, and D. The four fertilizer types would be called *treatments.* Similarly, they might compare the gain in the weight of pigs fed on four different diets, A, B, C, and D. Again, the diets are called *treatments,* and the objective of the experiment is to compare the means of the populations of measurements corresponding to the four treatments.

Now, if we try to apply this line of thought to the comparison of car models, we see that it is impossible to apply a treatment to a car and have it result in a model A, B, C, or D type of car. Nevertheless, in the terminology of the analysis of variance, model types are called *treatments.* Thus, saying that we want to compare the means for four treatments is equivalent to saying that we want to compare the means for four populations. Using this terminology, we would define a randomized block design as follows:

DEFINITION 15.2
A randomized block design is a design devised to compare the means for k treatments utilizing matched blocks of k experimental units. Each treatment appears once in every block.

**15.1
COMPARING
MORE THAN TWO
POPULATION
MEANS:
THE COMPLETELY
RANDOMIZED
DESIGN**

The completely randomized design makes use of independent random samples to compare more than two population means. If we assume there are k population means to be compared, the notation for the completely randomized design would appear as shown in Table 15.1.

To decide whether a difference exists among the treatment means $\mu_1, \mu_2, \ldots, \mu_k$, we examine the spread (or variation) among the sample means. The greater the variation, the greater will be the evidence to indicate differences among $\mu_1, \mu_2, \ldots, \mu_k$. This variation, measured by a weighted sum of squares of deviations of the sample means $\bar{x}_1, \bar{x}_2, \ldots, \bar{x}_k$ about the overall mean $\bar{\bar{x}}$, is called the sum of squares for treatments and is given by the expression

$$SST = \sum n_i(\bar{x}_i - \bar{\bar{x}})^2$$

Note that each squared distance between the sample mean and the overall mean is multiplied by a weight, the sample size n_i. Also, note that the SST is large when the sample means are very different.

**TABLE 15.1
SUMMARY NOTATION
FOR A COMPLETELY
RANDOMIZED DESIGN**

POPULATIONS (TREATMENTS)				
	1	2	3	. . . k
MEAN	μ_1	μ_2	μ_3	. . . μ_k
VARIANCE	σ_1^2	σ_2^2	σ_3^2	. . . σ_k^2
INDEPENDENT RANDOM SAMPLES				
	1	2	3	. . . k
SAMPLE SIZE	n_1	n_2	n_3	. . . n_k
SAMPLE TOTALS	T_1	T_2	T_3	. . . T_k
SAMPLE MEANS	$\bar{x}_1$	$\bar{x}_2$	$\bar{x}_3$	. . . $\bar{x}_k$

Total number of measurements $= n = n_1 + n_2 + n_3 + \cdots + n_k$

Sum of all n measurements $= \sum x_i$

Mean of all n measurements $= \bar{\bar{x}}$

Sum of squares of all n measurements $= \sum x_i^2$

FIGURE 15.2
DOT DIAGRAMS FOR
TWO SAMPLES
(NO EVIDENCE OF A
DIFFERENCE BETWEEN
POPULATION MEANS)

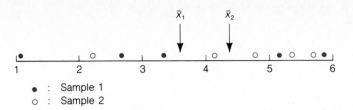

$\bullet$: Sample 1
$\circ$: Sample 2

Now, suppose we want to test the null hypothesis that the k treatment means are equal, i.e.,

$$H_0: \quad \mu_1 = \mu_2 = \cdots = \mu_k$$

versus the alternative

$$H_a: \quad \text{At least two of the treatment means differ}$$

The value of the SST will help us decide which hypothesis to accept. Large values of the SST will show support for the alternative hypothesis. That is, if the sum of squared differences between the sample means and the overall mean is large, we will tend to believe that the population means differ.

How large must the SST be before we accept H_a? We will compare this measure of variability between sample means to a measure of the variability of the experimental units themselves, i.e., the within-sample variability.

You can see how this principle works by comparing the dot diagrams for two samples as shown in Figure 15.2. Five observations for sample 1 and five for sample 2 are shown. The locations of the sample means are indicated by the two arrows. Do you think the data provide sufficient evidence to indicate a difference in the corresponding population means μ_1 and μ_2? In our opinion, the difference between $\bar{x}_1$ and $\bar{x}_2$ is not large enough to indicate a difference between μ_1 and μ_2. This is because the difference between sample means is small in relation to the variability within the sample observations.

Now look at two more samples of $n_1 = n_2 = 5$ measurements, as shown in Figure 15.3. The data appear to give clear evidence of a difference between μ_1 and μ_2, because the difference between the sample means, $\bar{x}_1$ and $\bar{x}_2$, is large in comparison with the variability within the sample observations.

To measure the within-sample variability, we pool the within-sample sum of squared deviations about the mean:

$$\text{SSE} = \sum_{i=1}^{n_1} (x_{1i} - \bar{x}_1)^2 + \sum_{i=1}^{n_2} (x_{2i} - \bar{x}_2)^2 + \cdots + \sum_{i=1}^{n_k} (x_{ki} - \bar{x}_k)^2$$

FIGURE 15.3
DOT DIAGRAMS FOR
TWO SAMPLES
(EVIDENCE OF A
DIFFERENCE BETWEEN
POPULATION MEANS)

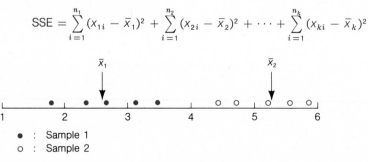

$\bullet$: Sample 1
$\circ$: Sample 2

where x_{1i} is the ith measurement in sample 1, x_{2i} is the ith measurement in sample 2, etc. We use **SSE** to denote the **sum of squared errors**; this is the same concept used in the least squares approach to fitting models (Chapters 11 and 12). As with regression models, the SSE measures unexplained variability. But in this case it measures variability unexplained by the differences between the sample means. That is, the SSE is a pooled measure of the variability within the k samples.*

We now want to compare the variability between treatment means (SST) to the within-sample variability (SSE). The first step is to divide each sum of squares by its degrees of freedom, to obtain **mean squares**. We have $(k - 1)$ degrees of freedom for treatments—one for each of the k treatment means minus one for the estimation of the overall mean. Thus, we calculate

$$MST = \frac{SST}{k - 1}$$

where MST denotes **mean square for treatments**.

The degrees of freedom for error equals $(n - k)$, one for each of the n measurements minus one for estimating each of the k treatment means. Thus, we calculate

$$MSE = \frac{SSE}{n - k}$$

where MSE denotes **mean square for error**.

TEST TO COMPARE k TREATMENT MEANS FOR A COMPLETELY RANDOMIZED DESIGN

H_0: $\mu_1 = \mu_2 = \cdots = \mu_k$

H_a: At least two treatment means differ

Test statistic: $F = \dfrac{MST}{MSE}$

Assumptions: 1. All k population probability distributions are normal.
  2. The k population variances are equal.

Rejection region: $F > F_{\alpha, (k-1), (n-k)}$, where $(k - 1)$ is the numerator degrees of freedom associated with the MST, and $(n - k)$ is the denominator degrees of freedom associated with the MSE

---

*This is an extension of the pooled estimator of σ^2 discussed in Chapter 10. For the two-sample case,

$$s_p^2 = \frac{\sum_{i=1}^{n_1} (x_{1i} - \bar{x}_1)^2 + \sum_{i=1}^{n_2} (x_{2i} - \bar{x}_2)^2}{n_1 + n_2 - 2}$$

The numerator of s_p^2 is the SSE.

We now compare the two sources of variability—the source due to differences between the sample (treatment) means and the source due to within-sample differences among experimental units—by forming an F statistic:

$$F = \frac{\text{MST}}{\text{MSE}}$$

Large values of the F statistic indicate that the differences between the sample means are large, and therefore support the alternative hypothesis that the population means differ. The test, with necessary assumptions, is summarized at the bottom of page 461. Because the F statistic involves a comparison of two sources of variation, this procedure for comparing two or more population means is usually referred to as an **analysis of variance**, or **ANOVA**.

EXAMPLE 15.1   Suppose a large chain of department stores wants to compare the mean dollar amounts owed by its delinquent credit card customers in three different annual income groups: under $12,000, $12,000–$25,000, and over $25,000. A sample of ten customers with delinquent accounts is to be selected from each group and the amount owed by each recorded.

  Set up the test to compare the population mean amounts owed by the three groups. (We will give the data and perform the test in a later example.)

Solution   We will test the null hypothesis that the mean amount owed by each income group is the same. Denoting the mean amounts owed by the low-, middle-, and high-income groups by μ_1, μ_2, and μ_3, respectively, we will test

   H_0: $\mu_1 = \mu_2 = \mu_3$
   H_a: At least two of the mean amounts differ

The test statistic compares the variability between the sample mean amounts due to the within-sample variability, i.e.,

   Test statistic: $F = \dfrac{\text{MST}}{\text{MSE}}$

   Assumptions: 1. The amounts due for each of the three income groups have (at least approximately) a normal distribution.
        2. The variances of the distributions of amounts due are the same for the three income groups.

  Rejection region: There are three treatments (the income groups) being compared, so the treatment degrees of freedom is $(k - 1) = (3 - 1) = 2$. There are $n = 30$ measurements in the combined samples, so the error degrees of freedom is $(n - k) = (30 - 3) = 27$. Using $\alpha = .05$, we will reject the null hypothesis that the true means are the same if

   $F > F_{.05,2,27}$

where from Table VI, Appendix B, $F_{.05,2,27} = 3.35$. This rejection region is shown in

FIGURE 15.4
REJECTION REGION
FOR EXAMPLE 15.1:
NUMERATOR df = 2,
DENOMINATOR df = 27

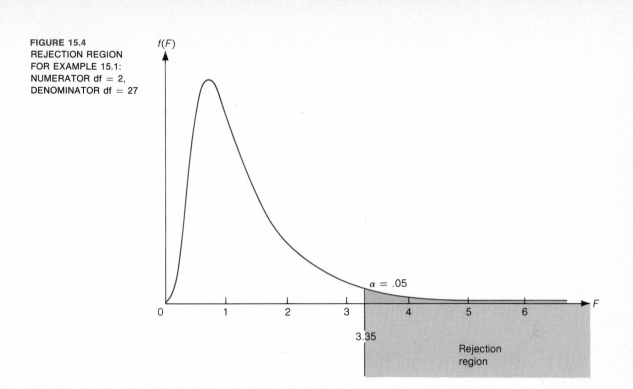

Figure 15.4. Once the test is set up, we are prepared to collect samples, perform the calculations, and state conclusions.

Although the sums of squares, SST and SSE, can be calculated by the formulas given earlier in this section, simpler computing formulas are available. Much of the theory and computation of analysis of variance rests on the concept of **partitioning the sum of squares of deviations** of all of the x values about the overall mean:

$$SS(Total) = \sum (x_i - \bar{\bar{x}})^2$$

This is called the total sum of squares. The meaning of the partitioning is diagrammed in Figure 15.5.

FIGURE 15.5
PARTITIONING OF
THE TOTAL SUM OF
SQUARES FOR THE
COMPLETELY
RANDOMIZED DESIGN

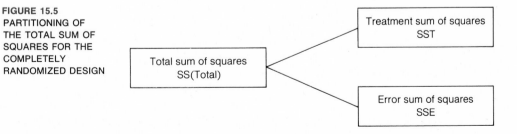

The computational simplification offered by the partitioning is that the SSE can be computed by subtraction, i.e.,

$$SSE = SS(Total) - SST$$

We present the computational formulas that lead to the calculation of the F statistic below.

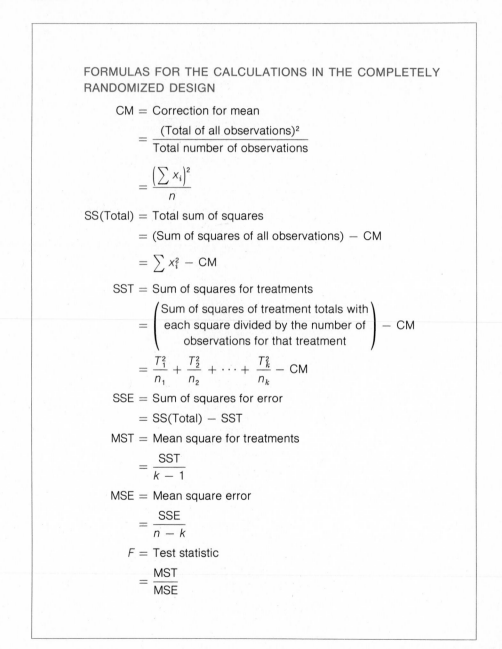

FORMULAS FOR THE CALCULATIONS IN THE COMPLETELY RANDOMIZED DESIGN

CM = Correction for mean

$$= \frac{(Total\ of\ all\ observations)^2}{Total\ number\ of\ observations}$$

$$= \frac{\left(\sum x_i\right)^2}{n}$$

$SS(Total)$ = Total sum of squares

$$= (Sum\ of\ squares\ of\ all\ observations) - CM$$

$$= \sum x_i^2 - CM$$

SST = Sum of squares for treatments

$$= \left(\begin{array}{c} Sum\ of\ squares\ of\ treatment\ totals\ with \\ each\ square\ divided\ by\ the\ number\ of \\ observations\ for\ that\ treatment \end{array}\right) - CM$$

$$= \frac{T_1^2}{n_1} + \frac{T_2^2}{n_2} + \cdots + \frac{T_k^2}{n_k} - CM$$

SSE = Sum of squares for error

$$= SS(Total) - SST$$

MST = Mean square for treatments

$$= \frac{SST}{k - 1}$$

MSE = Mean square error

$$= \frac{SSE}{n - k}$$

F = Test statistic

$$= \frac{MST}{MSE}$$

EXAMPLE 15.2

Refer to Example 15.1, in which we set up a test to compare the mean indebtedness of delinquent credit card holders in three different income classes. The data for this experiment are given in Table 15.2. Perform the calculations of the F statistic and state a conclusion.

TABLE 15.2
INCOME CLASS:
DOLLARS OWED

UNDER $12,000	$12,000–$25,000	OVER $25,000
$148	$513	$335
76	264	643
393	433	216
520	94	536
236	535	128
134	327	723
55	214	258
166	135	380
415	280	594
153	304	465
TOTALS $2,296	$3,099	$4,278

Solution

From the table, the totals for the three samples are $T_1 = \$2,296$, $T_2 = \$3,099$, and $T_3 = \$4,278$.

$$\sum x_i = T_1 + T_2 + T_3 = 9,673$$

$$\sum x_i^2 = (148)^2 + (76)^2 + \cdots + (465)^2 = 4,088,341$$

Then, following the order of calculations listed earlier, we find

$$CM = \frac{\left(\sum x_i\right)^2}{n} = \frac{(9,673)^2}{30} = 3,118,897.633$$

$$SS(Total) = \sum x_i^2 - CM$$

$$= 4,088,341 - 3,118,897.633$$

$$= 969,443.367$$

$$SST = \frac{T_1^2}{n_1} + \frac{T_2^2}{n_2} + \frac{T_3^2}{n_3} - CM$$

$$= \frac{(2,296)^2}{10} + \frac{(3,099)^2}{10} + \frac{(4,278)^2}{10} - 3,118,897.633$$

$$= 3,317,670.1 - 3,118,897.633 = 198,772.467$$

$$SSE = SS(Total) - SST = 969,443.367 - 198,772.467$$

$$= 770,670.9$$

$$MST = \frac{SST}{k-1} = \frac{198,772.467}{2} = 99,386.234$$

$$MSE = \frac{SSE}{n-k} = \frac{770,670.9}{27} = 28,543.367$$

Finally, the F statistic is

$$F = \frac{MST}{MSE} = \frac{99,386.234}{28,543.367} = 3.48$$

This calculated F exceeds the tabulated value (the value that locates the rejection region; see Example 15.1) $F_{.05,2,27} = 3.35$. Therefore, we conclude at the $\alpha = .05$ level of significance that the mean indebtedness of the delinquent credit card holders differs for the three income groups.

The results of an analysis of variance are often summarized in tabular form. The general form of an ANOVA table for a completely randomized design is shown in Table 15.3. Source refers to the source of variation, and for each source, df refers to the degrees of freedom, SS to the sum of squares, MS to the mean squares, and F to the F statistic comparing the treatment mean square to the error mean square. Table 15.4 is the ANOVA summary table corresponding to the analysis of variance data for Examples 15.1 and 15.2.

TABLE 15.3
ANOVA SUMMARY TABLE FOR A COMPLETELY RANDOMIZED DESIGN

SOURCE	df	SS	MS	F
Treatments	$k - 1$	SST	MST	MST/MSE
Error	$n - k$	SSE	MSE	
Totals	$n - 1$	SS (Total)		

TABLE 15.4
ANOVA SUMMARY TABLE FOR EXAMPLES 15.1 AND 15.2

SOURCE	df	SS	MS	F
Income group	2	198,772.467	99,386.234	3.48
Error	27	770,670.900	28,543.367	
Totals	29	969,443.367		

Because the completely randomized design involves the selection of independent random samples, we can find a confidence interval for a single treatment mean using the method of Section 9.3 or for the difference between two treatment means using the methods of Section 10.2. The estimate of σ^2 will be based on the pooled sum of squares within all k samples; that is,

$$MSE = s^2 = \frac{SSE}{n - k}$$

This is the same quantity that is used as the denominator for the analysis of variance F test. The formulas for the confidence intervals of Chapters 9 and 10 are reproduced at the top of page 467.

CONFIDENCE INTERVALS FOR MEANS

Single treatment mean (say, treatment i): $\bar{x}_i \pm t_{\alpha/2,n-k} \dfrac{s}{\sqrt{n_i}}$

Difference between two treatment means (say, treatments i and j):

$$(\bar{x}_i - \bar{x}_j) \pm t_{\alpha/2,n-k}\, s \sqrt{\dfrac{1}{n_i} + \dfrac{1}{n_j}}$$

where $s = \sqrt{\text{MSE}}$ and $t_{\alpha/2,n-k}$ is the tabulated value of t (Table V, Appendix B) that locates $\alpha/2$ in the upper tail of the t distribution and has $(n - k)$ degrees of freedom (the degrees of freedom associated with error in the ANOVA).

EXAMPLE 15.3

Refer to Example 15.2 and find a 95% confidence interval for the mean indebtedness of people with incomes less than $12,000 per year.

Solution

From Table 15.4,

$$\text{MSE} = 28{,}543.367$$

Then,

$$s = \sqrt{\text{MSE}} = \sqrt{28{,}543.367} = 168.9$$

The sample mean indebtedness for those with income levels under $12,000 is

$$\bar{x}_1 = \frac{T_1}{n_1} = \frac{2{,}296}{10} = 229.6$$

The tabulated value, $t_{.025}$, for 27 df (the same as for MSE) is 2.052. So, a 95% confidence interval for μ_1, the mean indebtedness of people with incomes less than $12,000, is

$$\bar{x}_1 \pm t_{\alpha/2} \frac{s}{\sqrt{n_1}} = 229.6 \pm 2.052\left(\frac{168.9}{\sqrt{10}}\right)$$

or (120.0, 339.2).

Note that this confidence interval is quite wide—probably too wide to be of any practical value. The reason why the interval is so wide can be seen in the large amount of variation within each income class. For example, the indebtedness for people with incomes under $12,000 varies from $55 to $520. Consequently, if you want to obtain a more accurate estimate of treatment means with a narrower confidence interval, you will have to select larger samples of people from within each income class.

EXAMPLE 15.4   Find a 95% confidence interval for the difference in mean indebtedness between the people with incomes under $12,000 and those with incomes over $25,000.

Solution   The mean of the sample for people with incomes over $25,000 is

$$\bar{x}_3 = \frac{T_3}{n_3} = \frac{4{,}278}{10} = 427.8$$

and, from Example 15.3, $\bar{x}_1 = 229.6$. The tabulated t value, $t_{.025,27}$ is the same as for Example 15.3, namely 2.052. Then, the 95% confidence interval for $(\mu_3 - \mu_1)$, the difference in mean indebtedness between the two groups, is

$$(\bar{x}_3 - \bar{x}_1) \pm t_{.025,27} \, s\sqrt{\frac{1}{n_3} + \frac{1}{n_1}}$$

$$= (427.8 - 229.6) \pm (2.052)(168.9)\sqrt{\frac{1}{10} + \frac{1}{10}}$$

or (43.2, 353.2).

As for the confidence interval for a single mean, the confidence interval for the difference $(\mu_3 - \mu_1)$ is very wide. This is due to the excessive within-sample variation. To obtain a narrower confidence interval, the sample sizes for the three income groups must be increased. However, the fact that the interval contains only positive numbers means we can conclude, with 95% confidence, that the mean indebtedness of those with incomes over $25,000 exceeds the mean indebtedness of those with incomes less than $12,000.

CASE STUDY 15.1   In the late 1960's there was considerable discussion in business literature concerning college student attitudes toward the business community. Leslie M. Dawson (1969) states:

> It is not surprising that the possibility of hostile student attitudes toward business has become a source of great concern. A loss of faith in the viability of our business system and institutions on the part of college youth, leading to widespread aversion to business careers, could well sap the strength of our nation . . . . While we need the brightest and best of our young people in fields such as government, education, and science, we also need them in business if we are to endure as an industrial power of the first order.

Since many college graduates with negative attitudes toward business are eventually employed by the business community, Dawson decided to investigate the relationship between business employees' proficiency and their attitudes toward business. A total of 152 employees were divided into four **job performance rating categories** based upon ratings by immediate superiors, using a uniform rating scale. The employees were then administered a questionnaire to obtain a quantitative measure of their attitudes toward business. This constitutes completely randomized design, with the four different rating categories representing the **treatments**.

An analysis of variance of the data indicated a difference in the mean **attitude scores** of the four job rating categories at the $\alpha = .05$ level of significance. This points out a need to investigate further the nature of relationships that may exist between employees' attitudes and job performance. The information could then be used to institute programs for college students (such as parttime jobs) that may influence their attitudes toward business. The results might also be used to aid business in hiring graduating college students. As Dawson says, the study indicates a need "for greater efforts by businessmen and educators alike to encourage students to think more positively about business."

15.1. Most new products are test marketed in several locations, frequently using different advertising techniques.* Suppose the following table represents the number of sales for a new product at each of three locations during each of the last 4 months:

	LOCATION	
I	II	III
456	441	501
421	419	467
397	415	520
419	420	493

a. Treat this as a completely randomized design and test to see whether there is a difference in mean sales at the three locations. Use $\alpha = .05$.

b. Suppose you want to estimate the difference in the mean sales between locations I and III. Find a 90% confidence interval for $(\mu_I - \mu_{III})$.

15.2. A company that employs a large number of salespeople is interested in learning which of the salespeople sell the most: those strictly on commission, those with a fixed salary, or those with a reduced fixed salary plus a commission. The previous month's records for a sample of salespeople are inspected and the amount of sales (in dollars) is recorded for each, as shown in the table.

COMMISSIONED	FIXED SALARY	COMMISSION PLUS SALARY
$425	$420	$430
507	448	492
450	437	470
483	432	501
466	444	
492		

a. Do the data provide sufficient evidence to indicate a difference in the mean sales for the three types of compensation? Use $\alpha = .05$.

b. Use a 90% confidence interval to estimate the mean sales for salespeople who receive a commission plus salary.

c. Use a 90% confidence interval to estimate the difference in mean sales between salespeople on commission plus salary versus those on fixed salary.

*For an example of test marketing, see Klompmaker et al. (1976).

15.3. One of the selling points of golf balls is their durability. An independent testing laboratory is commissioned to compare the durability of three different brands of golf balls. Balls of each type will be put into a machine that hits the balls with the same force that a golfer does on the course. The number of hits required until the outer covering is cracked is recorded for each ball, with the results given in the table. Ten balls from each manufacturer are randomly selected for testing.

| | BRAND | |
A	B	C
310	261	233
235	219	289
279	263	301
306	247	264
237	288	273
284	197	208
259	207	245
273	221	271
219	244	298
301	228	276

a. Is there evidence that the mean durabilities of the three brands differ? Use $\alpha = .05$.

b. Estimate the difference between the mean durability of brands A and C using a 99% confidence interval.

15.4. What assumptions are necessary for the validity of the F test in a completely randomized design?

15.2
RANDOMIZED
BLOCK DESIGN

The randomized block design employs groups of homogeneous experimental units (matched as closely as possible) to compare the means of the populations associated with k treatments. Suppose there are b blocks of relatively homogeneous

FIGURE 15.6
GENERAL FORM OF THE RANDOMIZED BLOCK DESIGN (TREATMENT i IS DENOTED BY T_i)

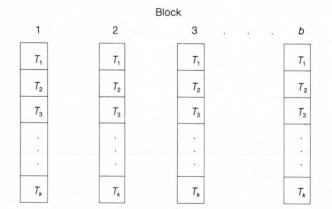

experimental units. Since each treatment must be represented in each block, the blocks will each contain k experimental units, which will be randomly assigned to the k treatments. The general format of the randomized block design is shown in Figure 15.6. Although we show the treatments in order within the blocks, in practice they would be assigned to the experimental units in a random order (thus the name *randomized block design*). The notation for the results of a randomized block experiment is summarized in Table 15.5.

We are interested in using the randomized block design to test the same null hypothesis as we tested using the completely randomized design, i.e.,

H_0: $\mu_1 = \mu_2 = \cdots = \mu_k$

H_a: At least two treatment means differ

TABLE 15.5
NOTATION FOR THE
RESULTS OF
A RANDOMIZED
BLOCK EXPERIMENT

	TREATMENT 1	TREATMENT 2 . . .	TREATMENT k
SAMPLE SIZE	b	b . . .	b
TOTALS	T_1	T_2 . . .	T_k
	BLOCK 1	BLOCK 2 . . .	BLOCK b
SAMPLE SIZE	k	k . . .	k
TOTALS	B_1	B_2 . . .	B_k

Total number of observations $= bk = n$

Sum of all observations $= \sum x_i$

Sum of squares of all observations $= \sum x_i^2$

The test statistic is also identical to that used for the completely randomized design:

Test statistic: $F = \dfrac{\text{MST}}{\text{MSE}}$

The numerator of the F statistic, MST (mean square for treatments), is computed exactly as it was for the completely randomized design. However, the denominator, MSE (mean square for error), is computed differently. This is most easily seen from Figure 15.7, which illustrates the partitioning of the total sum of squares about the overall mean, SS(Total). Note that the SS(Total) is now partitioned into three parts. The SSE for the completely randomized experiment has been subdivided into two parts —the sum of squares for blocks, SSB, and the sum of squares for error, the SSE for the randomized block design. (We use the same symbol, SSE, for the sum of squares for error in both designs, although their computational formulas differ.)

Figure 15.7 may help you understand how a randomized block design works. Since

$$\text{SS(Total)} = \text{SSB} + \text{SST} + \text{SSE}$$

it follows that the SSE for this design is

$$\text{SSE} = \text{SS(Total)} - \text{SST} - \text{SSB}$$

In other words, the SSE will equal the sum of squares for error for the completely

FIGURE 15.7
PARTITIONING OF
THE TOTAL SUM OF
SQUARES FOR THE
RANDOMIZED
BLOCK DESIGN

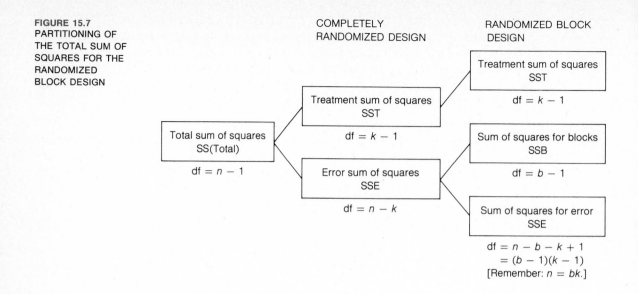

randomized design [SS(Total) − SST] *minus* SSB. Thus, the randomized block design permits us to remove the variation between blocks from within-sample variation and, hopefully, will decrease the MSE. Remember, the smaller the value of the MSE (which appears in the denominator of the *F* statistic), the more likely it is that we will detect a difference between the treatment means.

The test for treatment differences using the randomized block design is summarized below.

TEST TO COMPARE k TREATMENT MEANS: RANDOMIZED BLOCK DESIGN

H_0: $\mu_1 = \mu_2 = \cdots = \mu_k$

H_a: At least two treatment means differ

Test statistic: $F = \dfrac{\text{MST}}{\text{MSE}}$

Assumptions: 1. The probability distributions of observations corresponding to all the block–treatment combinations are normal.
2. The variances of all the probability distributions are equal.

Rejection region: $F > F_{\alpha,(k-1),(n-b-k+1)}$, where $(k - 1)$ is the numerator degrees of freedom and $(n - b - k + 1)$ is the denominator degrees of freedom

---

EXAMPLE 15.5

A study was conducted in a large city following the dramatic increase in coffee prices during the final quarter of 1976. The objective was to compare the mean supermarket prices of the four leading brands at the end of the year. Ten supermarkets in the city were selected, and the price per pound was recorded for each brand. Set up the test of the null hypothesis that the mean prices of the four brands sold in the city were the same at the end of the year. Use $\alpha = .05$.

Solution

We would expect prices to be more homogeneous within a store than between stores. In other words, the experimental units—the 1 pound cans of coffee—will be more homogeneous (with respect to price) within stores. The stores, then, act as blocks and the coffee brands act as treatments.

Denote the true mean prices of the four brands as μ_1, μ_2, μ_3, and μ_4. Then the elements of the test are:

H_0: $\mu_1 = \mu_2 = \mu_3 = \mu_4$

H_a: At least two brands have different mean prices

Test statistic: $F = \dfrac{\text{MST}}{\text{MSE}}$

Assumptions: 1. The probability distributions of coffee prices corresponding to all the supermarket–brand combinations are normal.

2. The variances of the probability distributions are equal.

Rejection region: Since we have $k = 4$ treatments (brands) and $b = 10$ blocks (stores), we use a tabulated F value with $k - 1 = 4 - 1 = 3$ df in the numerator, and $n - b - k + 1 = (4)(10) - 10 - 4 + 1 = 27$ df in the denominator. Then, for $\alpha = .05$, we will reject H_0 if $F > F_{.05,3,27}$, where (from Table VI, Appendix B) $F_{.05,3,27} = 2.96$.

The formulas needed for the analysis of a randomized block design are presented on page 474.

EXAMPLE 15.6

The data (and totals) for the coffee price study described in Example 15.5 are given in Table 15.6. Calculate the F statistic. Do the data provide sufficient evidence to indicate a difference in the mean prices for the four brands of coffee?

Solution

Following the order of calculations just listed, we have:

$$\sum x_i^2 = (2.43)^2 + (2.48)^2 + \cdots + (2.36)^2$$
$$= 242.0966$$

$$\text{CM} = \frac{\left(\sum x_i\right)^2}{n} = \frac{(98.36)^2}{40} = 241.86724$$

$$\text{SS(Total)} = \sum x_i^2 - \text{CM} = 242.0966 - 241.86724$$
$$= .22936$$

FORMULAS FOR THE CALCULATIONS IN THE RANDOMIZED BLOCK DESIGN

CM = Correction for mean

$$= \frac{(\text{Total of all observations})^2}{\text{Total number of observations}}$$

$$= \frac{\left(\sum x_i\right)^2}{n}$$

$SS(\text{Total})$ = Total sum of squares

$$= (\text{Sum of squares of all observations}) - CM$$

$$= \sum x_i^2 - CM$$

SST = Sum of squares for treatments

$$= \left(\begin{array}{l}\text{Sum of squares of treatment totals with} \\ \text{each square divided by } b, \text{ the number of} \\ \text{observations for that treatment}\end{array}\right) - CM$$

$$= \frac{T_1^2}{b} + \frac{T_2^2}{b} + \cdots + \frac{T_k^2}{b} - CM$$

SSB = Sum of squares for blocks

$$= \left(\begin{array}{l}\text{Sum of squares for block totals with} \\ \text{each square divided by } k, \text{ the number} \\ \text{of observations in that block}\end{array}\right) - CM$$

$$= \frac{B_1^2}{k} + \frac{B_2^2}{k} + \cdots + \frac{B_b^2}{k} - CM$$

SSE = Sum of squares for error

$$= SS(\text{Total}) - SST - SSB$$

MST = Mean square for treatments

$$= \frac{SST}{k - 1}$$

MSB = Mean square for blocks

$$= \frac{SSB}{b - 1}$$

MSE = Mean square for error

$$= \frac{SSE}{n - k - b + 1}$$

F = Test statistic

$$= \frac{MST}{MSE}$$

SUPERMARKET	BRAND				TOTALS
	A	B	C	D	
1	$2.43	$2.47	$2.47	$2.41	9.78
2	2.48	2.52	2.53	2.48	10.01
3	2.38	2.44	2.42	2.35	9.59
4	2.40	2.47	2.46	2.39	9.72
5	2.35	2.42	2.44	2.32	9.53
6	2.43	2.49	2.47	2.42	9.81
7	2.55	2.62	2.64	2.56	10.37
8	2.41	2.49	2.47	2.39	9.76
9	2.53	2.60	2.59	2.49	10.21
10	2.35	2.43	2.44	2.36	9.58
TOTALS	24.31	24.95	24.93	24.17	98.36

TABLE 15.6
PRICE PER POUND OF COFFEE

$$SST = \frac{T_1^2}{10} + \frac{T_2^2}{10} + \frac{T_3^2}{10} + \frac{T_4^2}{10} - CM$$

$$= \frac{(24.31)^2}{10} + \frac{(24.95)^2}{10} + \frac{(24.93)^2}{10} + \frac{(24.17)^2}{10} - 241.86724$$

$$= 241.91724 - 241.86724 = .05000$$

$$SSB = \frac{B_1^2}{4} + \frac{B_2^2}{4} + \cdots + \frac{B_{10}^2}{4} - CM$$

$$= \frac{(9.78)^2}{4} + \frac{(10.01)^2}{4} + \cdots + \frac{(9.58)^2}{4} - 241.86724$$

$$= 242.04175 - 241.86724$$

$$= .17451$$

$$SSE = SS(Total) - SST - SSB$$

$$= .22936 - .05 - .17451$$

$$= .00485$$

$$MST = \frac{SST}{k-1} = \frac{.05}{3} = .016667$$

$$MSB = \frac{SSB}{b-1} = \frac{.17451}{9} = .019390$$

$$MSE = \frac{SSE}{n-k-b+1} = \frac{.00485}{27} = .00017963$$

$$F = \frac{MST}{MSE} = \frac{.016667}{.00017963} = 92.8$$

Since the calculated $F = 92.8$ greatly exceeds the tabulated value of $F_{.05,3,27} = 2.96$, there is very strong evidence that the means for the populations of prices of the four coffee brands differ.

The ANOVA summary table for a randomized block analysis would appear as shown in Table 15.7. Table 15.8 is the ANOVA table for the data analysis in Example 15.6.

TABLE 15.7
ANOVA SUMMARY TABLE FOR A RANDOMIZED BLOCK DESIGN

SOURCE	df	SS	MS	F
Treatment	$k - 1$	. SST	MST	MST/MSE
Blocks	$b - 1$	SSB	MSB	
Error	$n - k - b + 1$	SSE	MSE	
Totals	$n - 1$	SS(Total)		

TABLE 15.8
ANOVA TABLE FOR EXAMPLE 15.6

SOURCE	df	SS	MS	F
Treatment	9	.05000	.016667	92.8
Block	3	.17451	.019390	
Error	27	.00485	.00017963	
Totals	39	.22936		

The formula for the confidence interval for the difference between a pair of treatment means is identical to the formula presented in Section 10.2 except for the estimate of σ^2, which is

$$s^2 = MSE = \frac{SSE}{n - k - b + 1}$$

This quantity appears in the ANOVA table. The formula for the confidence interval is shown below.

100$(1 - \alpha)$ PERCENT CONFIDENCE INTERVAL FOR THE DIFFERENCE IN A PAIR OF TREATMENT MEANS (SAY, $\mu_i - \mu_j$)

$$(\bar{x}_i - \bar{x}_j) \pm t_{\alpha/2, n-k-b+1} \, s \sqrt{\frac{1}{b} + \frac{1}{b}}$$

or $(\bar{x}_i - \bar{x}_j) \pm t_{\alpha/2, n-k-b+1} \, s \sqrt{\frac{2}{b}}$

where b is the number of blocks and $t_{\alpha/2}$ is the tabulated value of t (Table V, Appendix B) that locates $\alpha/2$ in the upper tail of the t distribution.

EXAMPLE 15.7   Refer to the coffee brand price data in Example 15.6 and find a 90% confidence interval for the difference in the mean price of brand A versus brand B.

Solution   From Example 15.6, the sample means for brands A and B (identified as 1 and 2, respectively) are:

$$\bar{x}_1 = \frac{T_1}{b} = \frac{24.31}{10} = \$2.431$$

$$\bar{x}_2 = \frac{T_2}{b} = \frac{24.95}{10} = \$2.495$$

From Table V, Appendix B, $t_{.05,27} = 1.703$, and from Table 15.8, we have

$$s^2 = MSE = .00017963$$

$$s = .0134$$

Then, the 90% confidence interval for $(\mu_1 - \mu_2)$ is

$$(\bar{x}_1 - \bar{x}_2) \pm t_{.05}\, s\sqrt{\frac{2}{b}}$$

Substituting into the formula, we get

$$(2.431 - 2.495) \pm (1.703)(.0134)\sqrt{\frac{2}{10}}$$

or $(-.074, -.054)$. Thus, we estimate the mean price of brand B to exceed the mean price for A by as little as $0.054 or as much as $0.074.

We can also conduct a test of an hypothesis to determine whether the differences exist among block means. This test will help to decide whether blocking was success-

---

TEST TO COMPARE b BLOCK MEANS: RANDOMIZED BLOCK DESIGN

H_0:   The b block means are equal

H_a: At least two block means differ

Test statistic: $F = \dfrac{MSB}{MSE}$

Assumptions: Same as for the test of treatment means.

Rejection region: The numerator degrees of freedom is $(b - 1)$, the number of blocks minus one. The denominator degrees of freedom is $n - k - b + 1 = 27$. We will reject H_0 if $F > F_{\alpha,(b-1),(n-k-b+1)}$.

---

ful in reducing the experimental error. That is, if the block means differ, we know the experimental units are indeed more homogeneous within blocks than between blocks, and the use of the randomized block experiment is justified. Such information is useful if similar experiments are to be conducted.

The test setup for block means is very similar to that for treatment means. We compare the variation among blocks, as measured by the mean square for blocks (MSB), to the variation due to error, as measured by the mean square for error (MSE). The test is summarized at the bottom of page 477.

EXAMPLE 15.8

Refer to Examples 15.5 and 15.6, in which we used a randomized block design to compare the mean prices of four brands of coffee. The blocks were supermarkets in a large city. Test the null hypothesis that the block means are the same, i.e., that the average price of coffee is the same for the ten supermarkets. Use $\alpha = .05$.

Solution

The test for comparing the block means is

H_0: Mean coffee prices are the same for all ten supermarkets

H_a: Mean coffee prices differ for at least two supermarkets

Test statistic: $F = \dfrac{\text{MSB}}{\text{MSE}}$

Assumptions: Same as for the test comparing the mean prices of the four coffee brands (Example 15.5).

Rejection region: The numerator and denominator degrees of freedom for the F statistic are $b - 1 = 10 - 1 = 9$ and $n - k - b + 1 = 27$, respectively. Then the rejection region is $F > F_{.05,9,27}$, where (from Table VI, Appendix B) $F_{.05,9,27} = 2.25$.

We have previously calculated MSB and MSE in Example 15.6. Substituting these values into the F statistic, we have

$$F = \frac{\text{MSB}}{\text{MSE}} = \frac{.019390}{.00017963} = 107.9$$

Since the calculated F greatly exceeds the tabulated F value, we have conclusive evidence that the means of coffee prices differ among the ten supermarkets. The decision to use a randomized block design was wise. Blocking had the effect of reducing the SSE and increasing the amount of information in the experiment. Future price comparison studies might benefit from this information. Table 15.9 is the complete ANOVA summary table for this experiment.

TABLE 15.9
COMPLETE ANOVA
SUMMARY TABLE FOR
EXAMPLE 15.8

SOURCE	df	SS	MS	F
Treatment	9	.05000	.016667	92.8
Block	3	.17451	.019390	107.9
Error	27	.00485	.00017963	
Totals	39	.22936		

We conclude this section with a caution: The result of the test for the equality of block means must be interpreted with care, especially when the calculated value of the F test statistic does not fall in the rejection region. This does not necessarily imply that the block means are the same, i.e., that blocking is unimportant. Reaching this conclusion would be equivalent to accepting the null hypothesis, a practice we have carefully avoided due to the unknown probability of committing a Type II error (that is, of accepting H_0 when H_a is true). In other words, even when a test for block differences is inconclusive, we may still want to use the randomized block design in similar future experiments. If the experimenter believes that the experimental units are more homogeneous within blocks than among blocks, he or she should use the randomized block design regardless of whether or not the test comparing the block means shows them to be different.

EXERCISES

15.5. A food chain sells a particular item at all its stores. Each store carries three brands, two of which are economy brands. The management decides to discontinue selling one of the economy brands. It has decided to look at the "turn time" of each brand, i.e., the time between successive purchases of the same brand. Five of the stores in the chain are selected, and an employee in each store records the turn time (in minutes) for each brand:

STORE	ECONOMY BRAND	
	I	II
1	4.1	3.9
2	5.2	5.1
3	5.0	5.0
4	4.9	4.7
5	6.1	5.9

a. Is there a difference in the mean turn times for the two economy brands? Use $\alpha = .05$.

b. What is the purpose of the blocks in this experiment? That is, why is the mean square for blocks so large?

c. Recall that a randomized block design with $k = 2$ treatments is a paired difference experiment (Chapter 10). Analyze the data as a paired difference experiment using a t test to compare the treatment means. Test using $\alpha = .05$.

d. Compare the computed F and t values from parts a and c, and verify that $F = t^2$. Also verify that for the rejection region values of F and t, $F_\alpha = t^2_{\alpha/2}$ and, hence, the F test (of the randomized block analysis and the t test (of the paired difference analysis) are equivalent tests for $k = 2$ treatments.

15.6. A restaurant chain operates three restaurants in a city: one serves Italian food, one Tyrolean food, and one Spanish food. To compare the current mean sales of the restaurants, the management recorded the weekly sales at each restaurant over a particular 6 week period. The sales (in thousands of dollars) are shown in the table.

WEEK	ITALIAN	TYROLEAN	SPANISH
1	11.9	12.1	12.9
2	10.7	11.4	11.4
3	9.6	10.6	10.3
4	11.1	12.2	12.3
5	9.2	9.9	10.0
6	8.8	10.1	10.4

a.   Do the data provide sufficient information to indicate a difference in the mean profit levels for the three restaurants?

b.   Suppose the management wants to estimate the difference in mean profit levels between the Italian and Spanish restaurants. Estimate using a 90% confidence interval.

15.7.   A construction firm employs three cost estimators. Usually, only one estimator works on each potential job, but it is advantageous to the company if the estimators are consistent enough so that it does not matter which of the three estimators is assigned to a particular job. To check on the consistency of the estimators, several jobs are selected and all three estimators are asked to make estimates. The estimates for each job by each estimator are given in the table.

ESTIMATES (IN THOUSANDS OF DOLLARS)

JOB	ESTIMATOR		
	A	B	C
1	27.3	26.5	28.2
2	66.7	67.3	65.9
3	104.8	102.1	100.8
4	87.6	85.6	86.5
5	54.5	55.6	55.9
6	58.7	59.2	60.1

a.   Do these estimates provide sufficient evidence that the means for the estimators differ? Use $\alpha = .05$.

b.   Present the complete ANOVA summary table for this experiment.

c.   Use a 90% confidence interval to estimate the difference between the mean responses given by estimators B and C.

15.8.   What assumptions are necessary for the validity of the F test in a randomized block design?

SUMMARY

This chapter presents an extension of the independent sampling and paired difference experiments to allow for the comparison of two or more means. The independent sampling design (or completely randomized design) uses independent samples from each of k populations to compare their means. The randomized block design, like the paired difference design, uses relatively homogeneous blocks of experimental units, with each treatment randomly assigned to one experimental unit in each block to compare the treatment means.

For both designs, the comparison of population (or treatment) means is made by comparing the sample variation between the treatment means, as measured by the mean square for treatments (MST), to the variation attributable to differences between experimental units, as measured by the mean square for error (MSE). If the ratio of MST to MSE is large, we conclude that a difference exists between some of the means of the k populations.

Unfortunately, most of the data of interest in business research cannot be collected according to a preconceived plan (or design). For example, economic data are studied, but researchers generally have little or no control over the method of collecting such data. Where you can design your experiment, knowledge of the principles exemplified by the completely randomized and randomized block designs should be helpful. If you would like to study other types of experimental designs, consult the references at the end of this chapter.

SUPPLEMENTARY EXERCISES

15.9. Higher wholesale beef prices over the past few years have resulted in the sale of ground beef with higher fat content in an attempt to keep retail prices down. Four different supermarket chains were chosen, and four 1 pound packages of ground beef were randomly selected from each. The percentage of fat content was measured for each package, with the results shown in the table.

| | SUPERMARKET | | |
A	B	C	D
22	25	30	18
20	27	20	20
23	24	23	17
25	24	27	17

a. What type of experimental design does this represent?

b. Do the data provide evidence at the $\alpha = .05$ level that the mean percentage of fat content differs for the four supermarket chains?

c. Use a 90% confidence interval to estimate the mean percentage of fat content per pound at supermarket C.

15.10. A company is planning to market a new cereal, with one of three possible package designs. To determine which has the most appeal, five stores are supplied

| STORE | DESIGN | | |
	A	B	C
1	101	111	100
2	98	102	105
3	121	120	114
4	132	140	127
5	95	98	94

with all three package designs. All packages are priced the same, so that if any design outsells the others, it will be due primarily to visual attractiveness. The cereal is on the market for several months, and the number of sales for each design at each store is recorded in the table.

    a.   Test to see whether there are differences in the mean number of sales for the three designs.

    b.   Give statistical justification as to why (or why not) blocking was necessary in this experiment.

    c.   What assumptions were necessary for the validity of the test you conducted in part a?

15.11. One important consideration in determining which location is best for a new retail business is the amount of traffic that passes the location each business day. Counters are placed at each of four locations on the 5 weekdays, and the number of cars passing each location is recorded in the table.

DAY	LOCATION			
	I	II	III	IV
1	453	482	444	395
2	500	605	505	490
3	392	400	383	390
4	441	450	429	405
5	427	431	440	430

    a.   What type of design does this represent?

    b.   Is there evidence of a difference in the mean number of cars per day at the four locations?

    c.   Estimate the difference between the mean numbers of cars that pass locations I and III each weekday.

15.12. Several companies are experimenting with the concept of paying production workers (generally paid by the hour) on a salary basis. It is believed that absenteeism and tardiness will increase under this plan, yet some companies feel that the working environment and overall productivity will improve. Fifty production workers under the salary plan are monitored at company A, and likewise, fifty under the hourly plan at company B. The number of work-hours missed due to tardiness or absenteeism over a 1 year period is recorded for each worker. The results are partially summarized in the table.

SOURCE	df	SS	MS	F
Company		3,237.2		
Error	—	16,167.7		
Totals	99			

a. Fill in the missing information above.

b. Is there evidence at the $\alpha = .05$ level of significance that the mean number of hours missed differs for employees of the two companies?

c. Is there sufficient information given to form a confidence interval for the difference between the mean number of hours missed at the two companies?

15.13. Due to increased energy shortages and costs, utility companies are stressing ways in which home and apartment utility bills can be cut. One utility company reached an agreement with the owner of a new apartment complex to conduct a test of energy saving plans for apartments. The tests were to be conducted before the apartments were rented. Four apartments were chosen that were identical in size, amount of shade, and direction faced. Four plans were to be tested, one on each apartment. The thermostat was set at 75°F in each apartment and the monthly utility bill was recorded for each of the 3 summer months. The results are listed in the table.

MONTH	TREATMENT			
	1	2	3	4
June	$74.44	$68.75	$71.34	$65.47
July	86.96	73.47	83.62	72.33
August	82.00	71.23	79.98	70.87

Treatment 1: No insulation
Treatment 2: Insulation in walls and ceilings
Treatment 3: No insulation—awnings for windows
Treatment 4: Insulation and awnings for windows

a. Is there evidence that the mean monthly utility bills differ for the four treatments? Use $\alpha = .01$.

b. Is there evidence that blocking is important, i.e., that the mean bills differ for the 3 months? Use $\alpha = .05$.

c. To see whether awnings on the windows help reduce costs, place a 95% confidence interval on the difference in the means of treatments 2 and 4.

15.14. From time to time, one branch office of a company must make shipments to a certain branch office in another state. There are three package delivery services between the two cities where the branch offices are located. Since the price structures for the three delivery services are quite similar, the company wants to compare

SHIPMENT	CARRIER		
	I	II	III
1	15.2	16.9	17.1
2	14.3	16.4	16.1
3	14.7	15.9	15.7
4	15.1	16.7	17.0
5	14.0	15.6	15.5

the delivery times. The company plans to make several different types of shipments to its branch office. To compare the carriers, each shipment will be sent in triplicate, one with each carrier. The results listed in the table are the delivery times in hours.

a. Is there evidence that the mean delivery times differ for the three companies? Use $\alpha = .05$.

b. Use a 99% confidence interval to estimate the difference between the mean delivery time for carriers I and II.

c. What assumptions are necessary for the validity of the procedures you used in parts a and b?

15.15. A fast-food chain expects mean gross sales of $800,000 per year per franchise. A random sampling of the chain's stores was selected in Los Angeles, Miami, and Chicago, and the results are given in the table.

GROSS SALES (IN UNITS OF $100,000)

MIAMI	LOS ANGELES	CHICAGO
8.7	8.7	7.8
7.4	8.0	7.6
7.9	9.0	6.9
8.0	8.3	5.7
8.5	9.0	
7.9		

a. Is there evidence that the mean gross sales for stores in this chain differ in these three cities? Use $\alpha = .01$.

b. Form a 90% confidence interval for the mean gross sales of the Miami stores in this fast food chain.

15.16. Psychologists have studied the effect of the working environment or surroundings on the quality or quantity of work done. Many businesses have music piped into the work area to improve the work environment. An experiment is performed to determine which type of music is best suited for a particular company. Three types of music—country, rock, and classical—are tried, each on four randomly selected workdays. The productivity is measured by recording the number of items produced on each of the days. The results are shown in the table.

COUNTRY	ROCK	CLASSICAL
857	791	824
801	753	847
795	781	881
842	776	865

Based on this information can we conclude that the mean number of items produced differ for the three types of music?

15.17. A corporation manages a very large number of stores, which it classifies into three geographical divisions. Three stores are randomly selected from each division and a study is made to determine the mean inflation rate for the items in inventory. The inflation rate is recorded in the table as a percent change in price over a year's time.

	DIVISION	
I	II	III
1.1	1.4	0.4
0.9	1.6	0.3
0.8	1.0	0.5

    a.   Is there sufficient evidence to indicate that the inflation rate differs for the stores in different divisions?

    b.   In division I, the numbers 1.1, 0.9, and 0.8 represent a sample from what population?

15.18. One indicator of employee morale is the length of time employees stay with a company. A large corporation has three factories located in similar areas of the country. While the corporation management attempts to maintain uniformity in management, working conditions, employee relations, etc., at its various factories, it realizes that differences may exist between the various factories. To study this phenomenon, employee records are randomly selected at each of the three factories and the length of employee service with the company is recorded. The following is a summary of the data:

FACTORY	1	2	3
NUMBER IN SAMPLE	15	21	17
SST = 421.74	SSE = 3574.06		

Is there evidence of a difference in mean length of service at the three factories? Use $\alpha = .05$.

15.19. England has experimented with different 40 hour work weeks to maximize production and minimize expenses. A factory tested a 5 day week (8 hours per day), a 4 day week (10 hours per day), and a $3\frac{1}{3}$ day week (12 hours per day), with the

8 HOUR DAY	10 HOUR DAY	12 HOUR DAY
87	75	95
96	82	76
75	90	87
90	80	82
72	73	65
86		

weekly production results shown in the table (in thousands of dollars worth of items produced).

    a.   What type of experimental design was employed here?

    b.   Construct an ANOVA summary table for this experiment.

    c.   Is there evidence that the mean productivity differs for the three lengths of workdays?

15.20. Refer to Exercise 15.19. Form a 90% confidence interval for the mean weekly productivity when 12 hour workdays are used.

15.21. Mileage tests were performed to compare three different brands of regular gas. Four different automobiles were used in the experiment, and each brand of gas was used in each car until the mileage was determined. The results are shown in the table.

MILES PER GALLON

| BRAND | AUTOMOBILE | | | |
	1	2	3	4
A	20.2	18.7	19.7	17.9
B	19.7	19.0	20.3	19.0
C	18.3	18.5	17.9	21.1

    a.   Is there evidence of a difference in the mean mileage rating among the three brands of gasoline? Use $\alpha = .05$.

    b.   Construct the ANOVA summary table for this experiment.

    c.   Is there evidence of a difference in the mean mileage for the four models, i.e., is blocking important in this type of experiment? Use $\alpha = .05$.

15.22. Refer to Exercise 15.21. Form a 99% confidence interval for the difference between the mileage ratings of brands B and C.

15.23. To reduce the time spent in transferring materials from one location to another, three methods have been devised. With no previous information available on the effectiveness of these three approaches, a study is performed. Each approach is tried several times, and the amount of time to completion (in hours) is recorded in the table.

| METHOD | | |
A	B	C
8.2	7.9	7.1
7.1	8.1	7.4
7.8	8.3	6.9
8.9	8.5	6.8
8.8	7.6	
	8.5	

    a.   What type of experimental design was used?

    b.   Is there evidence that the mean time to completion of the task differs for the three methods? Use $\alpha = .01$.

    c.   Form a 95% confidence interval for the mean time to completion for method B.

15.24. Methods of displaying goods can have an effect on their sales. The manager of a large produce market would like to try three different display types for a certain fruit. The locations for the three displays are chosen in a way that the manager thinks each display type will be equally accessible to the customers. The three displays will be set up for five 1 week periods. Between each of these periods will be a 2 week period when a standard display is used. For each of the 5 experimental weeks, the sales (in dollars) of the fruit from each display is determined, with the results shown in the table.

PERIOD	DISPLAY		
	A	B	C
1	$125	$153	$108
2	137	135	113
3	110	122	105
4	119	133	112
5	141	144	136

a. Is there evidence of a difference in mean sales for the three types of display? Use $\alpha = .05$.

b. Do the data indicate that the use of weeks as blocks was necessary? Test at the $\alpha = .05$ level.

c. Construct the ANOVA summary table for this experiment.

15.25. Refer to Exercise 15.24. Use a 95% confidence interval to estimate the differences between the mean sales for displays A and C.

15.26. In hopes of attracting more riders, a city transit company plans to have express bus service from a suburban terminal to the downtown business district. These buses will travel along a major city street where there are numerous traffic lights that will affect travel time. The city decides to perform a study of the effect of four different plans (a special bus lane, traffic signal progression, etc.) on the travel times for the buses. Travel times (in minutes) are measured for several weekdays during a morning rush-hour trip while each plan was in effect. The results are recorded in the table.

	PLAN		
1	2	3	4
27	25	34	30
25	28	29	33
29	30	32	31
26	27	31	
	24	36	

a. What type of experimental design was employed?

b. Is there evidence of a difference in the mean travel times for the four plans? Use $\alpha = .01$.

c. Form a 95% confidence interval for the difference between plan 1 (express lane) and plan 3 (a control—no special travel arrangements).

15.27. To be able to provide its clients with comparative information on two large suburban residential communities, a realtor wants to know the average home value in each community. Eight homes are selected at random within each community and are appraised by the realtor. The appraisals are given in the table (in thousands of dollars). Can you conclude that the average home value is different in the two communities? You have three ways of analyzing this problem:

COMMUNITY	
A	B
43.5	73.5
49.5	62.0
38.0	47.5
66.5	36.5
57.5	44.5
32.0	56.0
67.5	68.0
71.5	63.5

a. Use the two-sample t statistic (Section 10.2) to test H_0: $\mu_A = \mu_B$.

b. Consider the regression model

$$y = \beta_0 + \beta_1 x + \varepsilon$$

where

$$x = \begin{cases} 1 & \text{if community B} \\ 0 & \text{if community A} \end{cases}$$

y = Appraised price

Since $\beta_1 = \mu_B - \mu_A$, testing H_0: $\beta_1 = 0$ is equivalent to testing H_0: $\mu_A = \mu_B$. Use the partial reproduction of the SAS printout shown here to test H_0: $\beta_1 = 0$. Use $\alpha = .05$.

PORTION OF THE SAS PRINTOUT FOR EXERCISE 15.27

SOURCE	DF	SUM OF SQUARES	MEAN SQUARE	F VALUE	PR > F
MODEL	1	40.64062500	40.64062500	0.21	0.6501
ERROR	14	2648.71875000	189.19419643		STD DEV
CORRECTED TOTAL 15		2689.35937500		R-SQUARE	13.75478813
				0.015112	

PARAMETER	ESTIMATE	T FOR HO: PARAMETER = 0	PR > |T|	STD ERROR OF ESTIMATE
INTERCEPT	53.25000000	10.95	0.0001	4.86305198
X1	3.18750000	0.46	0.6501	6.87739406

c. Use the ANOVA method to test H_0: $\mu_A = \mu_B$. Use $\alpha = .05$.

Using the results of the three tests above, verify that the tests are the equivalent (for this special case, $k = 2$) of the completely randomized design in terms of the test statistic value and rejection region. For the three methods used, what are the advantages and disadvantages (limitations) of using each in analyzing results for this type of experimental design?

ON YOUR OWN . . .

Due to ever-increasing food costs, consumers are becoming more discerning in their choice of supermarkets. It usually is more convenient to shop at only one market, as opposed to buying different items at different markets. Thus it would be useful to compare the mean food expenditure for a market basket of food items from store to store. Since there is a great deal of variability in the prices of products sold at any supermarket, we will consider an experiment that blocks on products.

Choose three (or more) supermarkets in your area that you want to compare; then choose approximately ten (or more) food products you typically purchase. For each food item, record the price each store charges in the following manner:

FOOD ITEM 1	FOOD ITEM 2 . . .	FOOD ITEM 10
Price store 1	Price store 1 . . .	Price store 1
Price store 2	Price store 2 . . .	Price store 2
Price store 3	Price store 3 . . .	Price store 3

Use the data you obtain to test

H_0: Mean expenditures at the stores are the same

H_a: Mean expenditures for at least two of the stores are different

Also, test to determine whether blocking on food items is advisable in this kind of experiment. Fully interpret the results of your analysis.

REFERENCES

Dawson, L. M. "Campus attitudes toward business." *Business Topics,* Summer 1969, *17*, 36–46.
Klompmaker, J. E., Hughes, G. D., & Haley, R. I. "Test marketing in new products development." *Harvard Business Review,* May–June 1976, 128.
Mendenhall, W. *Introduction to linear models and the design and analysis of experiments.* Belmont, Ca.: Wadsworth, 1968. Chapter 8.
Miller, R. B., & Wichern, D. W. *Intermediate business statistics: Analysis of variance, regression, and time series.* New York: Holt, Rinehart, and Winston, 1977. Chapter 4.
Neter, J., & Wasserman, W. *Applied linear statistical models.* Homewood, Ill.: Richard Irwin, 1974.
Scheffé, H. *The analysis of variance.* New York: Wiley, 1959.

NONPARAMETRIC STATISTICS

WHERE WE'VE BEEN . . .

Chapters 9, 10, and 15 presented techniques for making inferences about the mean of a single population and for comparing the means of two or more populations. Chapters 11–13 treated multiple regression—the problem of relating the mean of a population of y values to a set of independent variables $x_1, x_2, \ldots, x_k$. Most of the techniques discussed in Chapters 9–15 are based on the assumption that the sampled populations have probability distributions that are approximately normal with equal variances. But how can you analyze data that evolve from populations that do not satisfy these assumptions? Or, how can you make comparisons between populations when you cannot assign specific values to your measurements?

WHERE WE'RE GOING . . .

In this chapter, we present statistical techniques for comparing two or more populations that are based on an ordering of the sample measurements according to their relative magnitudes. These techniques, which require few assumptions concerning the nature of the probability distributions of the populations, are called nonparametric statistics. The statistical tests presented in this chapter apply to the same experimental designs as those covered in the introduction to an analysis of variance (Chapter 15). Thus, we will present nonparametric statistical techniques for comparing two or more populations using either a completely randomized or a randomized block design.

The *t* and *F* tests for comparing two or more populations (Chapters 10 and 15) are unsuitable for some types of business data. These data fall into two categories: The first are data sets that do not satisfy the assumptions upon which the *t* and *F* tests are based. For both tests, we assume that the random variables being measured have normal probability distributions with equal variances. Yet in practice, the observations from one population may exhibit much greater variability than those from another, or the probability distributions may be decidedly nonnormal. For example, the distribution might be very flat, peaked, or strongly skewed to the right or left. When any of the assumptions required for the *t* and *F* tests are seriously violated, the computed *t* and *F* statistics may not follow the standard *t* and *F* distributions. If this is true, the tabulated values of *t* and *F* (Tables V–VII, Appendix B) are not applicable, the correct value of α for the test is unknown, and the *t* and *F* tests are of dubious value.

The second type of data for which the *t* and *F* tests are inappropriate are responses that are not susceptible to measurement but can be **ranked in order of magnitude**. For example, if we want to compare the managerial ability of two executives based on subjective evaluations of trained observers, despite the fact that we cannot give an exact value to the managerial ability of a single executive, we may be able to decide that executive A has more ability than executive B. If executives A and B are evaluated by each of ten observers, we have the standard problem of comparing the probability distributions for two populations of ratings, one for executive A and one for B. But the *t* test of Chapter 10 would be inappropriate, because the only data that can be recorded are preferences; i.e., each observer decides that either A is better than B or vice versa.

Consider another example of this type of data. Most firms that plan to market a new product nationally first test the product in a few cities or regions to determine its acceptability. For a food product this may entail taste tests in which consumers rank the new product in order of preference with respect to one or more currently popular brands. A consumer probably has a preference for each product, but the strength of the preference is difficult, if not impossible, to measure. Consequently, the best we can do is to have each consumer examine the new product along with a few established products, and rank them according to preference: 1 for the most preferred, 2 for second, etc.

The **nonparametric** counterparts of the *t* and *F* tests compare the probability distributions of the sampled populations, rather than specific parameters of these populations (such as the means or variances). For example, nonparametric tests can be used to compare the probability distribution of the strengths of preferences for a new product to the probability distributions of the strengths of preferences for the currently popular brands. If it can be inferred that the distribution of the new product lies above (to the right of) the others (see Figure 16.1), the implication is that the new product tends to be more preferred than the currently popular products. Such an inference might lead to a decision to market the product nationally.

Many nonparametric methods use the **relative ranks** of the sample observations, rather than their actual numerical values. These tests are particularly valuable when we are unable to obtain numerical measurements of some phenomena but are able to rank them in comparison to each other. Statistics based on ranks of measurements

FIGURE 16.1
PROBABILITY
DISTRIBUTIONS OF
STRENGTHS OF
PREFERENCE
MEASUREMENTS
(NEW PRODUCT IS
PREFERRED)

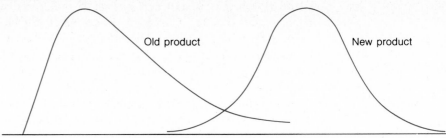

Strength of preference measurements

are called rank statistics. In Sections 16.1 and 16.3, we will present rank statistics for comparing two probability distributions using independent samples. In Sections 16.2 and 16.4, the matched-pairs and randomized block design are used to make nonparametric comparisons of populations. Finally, in Section 16.5 we present a nonparametric measure of correlation between two variables—Spearman's rank correlation coefficient.

16.1
COMPARING TWO POPULATIONS: WILCOXON RANK SUM TEST FOR INDEPENDENT SAMPLES

Suppose two independent random samples are to be used to compare two populations and the *t* test of Chapter 10 is inappropriate for making the comparison. Either we are unwilling to make assumptions about the form of the underlying probability distributions, or we are unable to obtain exact values of the sample measurements but can rank them in order of magnitude. For either of these situations, the Wilcoxon rank sum test (developed by Frank Wilcoxon) can be used to test an hypothesis that the probability distributions associated with the two populations are equivalent.

For example, suppose six economists who work for the federal government and seven university economists are randomly selected, and each is asked to predict next year's percentage change in cost of living as compared with this year's figure. The objective of the study is to compare the government economists' predictions to those of the university economists. The data are shown in Table 16.1.

The two populations of predictions are those obtained from *all* government and *all* university economists. To compare their probability distributions, we first rank the sample observations as though they were all drawn from the same population. That is, we pool the measurements from both samples, and then rank the measurements from the smallest (a rank of 1) to the largest (a rank of 13). The ranks of the economists' predictions are indicated in Table 16.1.

TABLE 16.1
PERCENTAGE COST OF LIVING CHANGE, AS PREDICTED BY GOVERNMENT AND UNIVERSITY ECONOMISTS

GOVERNMENT ECONOMIST		UNIVERSITY ECONOMIST	
Prediction	Rank	Prediction	Rank
3.1	4	4.4	6
4.8	7	5.8	9
2.3	2	3.9	5
5.6	8	8.7	11
0.0	1	6.3	10
2.9	3	10.5	12
		10.8	13

The test statistic for the Wilcoxon test is based on the totals of the ranks for each of the two samples, that is, on the **rank sums**. If the two rank sums are nearly equal, the implication is that there is no evidence that the probability distributions from which the samples were drawn are different. On the other hand, if the two rank sums are very different, the implication is that the two samples may have come from different populations.

In the economists' predictions example, we arbitrarily denote the rank sum for government economists by T_A and that for university economists by T_B. Then

$$T_A = 4 + 7 + 2 + 8 + 1 + 3 = 25$$
$$T_B = 6 + 9 + 5 + 11 + 10 + 12 + 13 = 66$$

The sum of T_A and T_B will always equal $n(n + 1)/2$, where $n = n_1 + n_2$. So, for this example, $n_1 = 6$, and $n_2 = 7$, and

$$T_A + T_B = \frac{13(13 + 1)}{2} = 91,$$

Since $T_A + T_B$ is fixed, a small value for T_A implies a large value for T_B (and vice versa) and a large difference, $T_A - T_B$. Therefore, the smaller the value of one of the rank sums, the greater will be the evidence to indicate that the samples were selected from different populations.

Values that locate the rejection region for the rank sum associated with the smaller sample are given in Table VIII, Appendix B. A partial reproduction of this table is shown in Figure 16.2. The columns of the table represent n_1, the first sample size, and the rows represent n_2, the second sample size. **The T_L and T_U entries in the table begin the lower and upper regions, respectively, for the rank sum associated with the sample that has fewer measurements.** If the sample sizes n_1 and n_2 are the same, either rank sum may be used as the test statistic. To illustrate, suppose $n_1 = 8$ and $n_2 = 10$. For a two-tailed test with $\alpha = .05$, we consult part a of the table and find that the null hypothesis will be rejected if the rank sum of sample 1 (the sample with fewer measurements), T, is less than or equal to $T_L = 54$ *or* greater than or equal to $T_U = 98$. The two-tailed Wilcoxon rank sum test is summarized on page 494.

FIGURE 16.2
REPRODUCTION OF PART OF TABLE VIII, APPENDIX B

a. $\alpha = .025$ one-tailed; $\alpha = .05$ two-tailed

n_2 \ n_1	3		4		5		6		7		8		9		10	
	T_L	T_U	T_L	T_U	T_L	T_U	T_L	T_U	T_L	T_U	T_L	T_U	T_L	T_U	T_L	T_U
3	5	16	6	18	6	21	7	23	7	26	8	28	8	31	9	33
4	6	18	11	25	12	28	12	32	13	35	14	38	15	41	16	44
5	6	21	12	28	18	37	19	41	20	45	21	49	22	53	24	56
6	7	23	12	32	19	41	26	52	28	56	29	61	31	65	32	70
7	7	26	13	35	20	45	28	56	37	68	39	73	41	78	43	83
8	8	28	14	38	21	49	29	61	39	73	49	87	51	93	54	98
9	8	31	15	41	22	53	31	65	41	78	51	93	63	108	66	114
10	9	33	16	44	24	56	32	70	43	83	54	98	66	114	79	131

EXAMPLE 16.1

Test the null hypothesis that the university economists' predictions of next year's percentage change in cost of living tend to be higher than the government economists'. Conduct the test using the data in Table 16.1 and $\alpha = .05$.

Solution

H_0:   The probability distributions corresponding to the government and
university economists' predictions of inflation rate are identical

H_a: The probability distribution for the university economists' predictions
lies above (to the right of) that for the government economists'
predictions

Test statistic: Since fewer government economists ($n_1 = 6$) than university economists ($n_2 = 7$) were sampled, the test statistic is T_A, the rank sum of the government economists predictions.

Rejection region: Since the test is one-sided, we consult part b of Table VIII for the rejection region corresponding to $\alpha = .05$. We will reject only for $T_A \leq T_L$, the lower value from Table VIII, since we are specifically testing that the distribution of government economists' predictions lies *below* the distribution of university economists' predictions, as shown in Figure 16.3. Thus, we will reject if $T_A \leq 30$.

Since T_A, the rank sum of the government economists' predictions in Table 16.1, is 25, it is in the rejection region (see Figure 16.3). Therefore, we can conclude that the university economists' predictions tend, in general, to exceed the government economists' predictions.

Occasionally some measurements in the two samples will be tied (i.e., have equal values). When this occurs, we assign the average of the ranks that would be assigned to the measurements if they were unequal but occurred in successive order. For example, if the third- and fourth-ranked measurements were equal, both would receive a rank of 3.5.

---

*Another statistic used for comparing two populations based on independent random samples is the Mann–Whitney U statistic.   The U statistic is a simple function of the rank sums. It can be shown that the Wilcoxon rank sum test and the Mann–Whitney U test are equivalent.

FIGURE 16.3
ALTERNATIVE
HYPOTHESIS AND
REJECTION REGION
FOR EXAMPLE 16.1

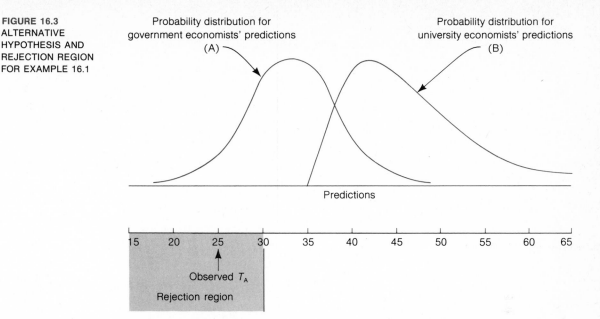

EXERCISES

16.1. The owner of a restaurant recently fired the restaurant manager and hired a new one because of the number of customer complaints that were made. The owner decided to wait 3 months before evaluating the new manager. Then, the number of complaints for each of the next 5 weeks were recorded and compared with the number of complaints per week for the last 5 weeks that the previous manager had worked. The results are given in the table.

NUMBER OF COMPLAINTS

PREVIOUS MANAGER	PRESENT MANAGER
9	8
12	11
10	7
14	5
15	13

Have things improved under the new manager?

16.2. A realtor wants to determine whether a difference exists between home prices in two subdivisions. Six homes from subdivision A and eight homes from subdivision B are sampled, and the prices (in thousands of dollars) are recorded in the table at the top of page 496.

    a. Use the two-sample t test to compare the population mean price per house of the two subdivisions. What assumptions are necessary for the validity of this procedure? Do you think they are reasonable in this case?
    b. Use the Wilcoxon rank sum test to see whether there is a difference in the probability distributions of house prices in the two subdivisions.

16.1 COMPARING TWO POPULATIONS: WILCOXON RANK SUM TEST FOR INDEPENDENT SAMPLES   **495**

SUBDIVISION	
A	B
43	57
48	39
42	55
60	52
39	88
47	46
	41
	64

16.2 COMPARING TWO POPULATIONS: WILCOXON RANK SUM TEST FOR THE PAIRED DIFFERENCE DESIGN

Nonparametric techniques can also be employed to compare two probability distributions when a paired difference design is used. For example, for some paper products, softness of the paper is an important consideration in determining consumer acceptance. One method of determining softness is to have judges give a sample of the products a softness rating. Suppose each of ten judges is given a sample of two products that a company wants to compare. Each judge rates the softness of each product on a scale from 1 to 10, with higher ratings implying a softer product. The results of the experiment are shown in Table 16.2.

TABLE 16.2

JUDGE	PRODUCT		DIFFERENCE	ABSOLUTE VALUE OF DIFFERENCE	RANK OF ABSOLUTE VALUE
	A	B	(A − B)		
1	6	4	2	2	5
2	8	5	3	3	7.5
3	4	5	−1	1	2
4	9	8	1	1	2
5	4	1	3	3	7.5
6	7	9	−2	2	5
7	6	2	4	4	9
8	5	3	2	2	5
9	6	7	−1	1	2
10	8	2	6	6	10

T_A = Sum of positive ranks = 46
T_B = Sum of negative ranks = 9

Since this is a paired difference experiment, we analyze the differences between the measurements (see Section 10.4). However, the nonparametric approach requires that we calculate the ranks of the absolute values of the differences between the measurements, i.e., the ranks of the differences after removing any minus signs. Note that tied absolute differences are assigned the average of the ranks they would receive if they were unequal but successive measurements. After the absolute differences are ranked, the sum of the ranks of the positive differences, T_A, and the sum of the ranks of the negative differences, T_B, are computed.

FIGURE 16.4
REPRODUCTION OF
PART OF
TABLE IX, APPENDIX B

ONE-TAILED	TWO-TAILED	n = 5	n = 6	n = 7	n = 8	n = 9	n = 10
$\alpha = .05$	$\alpha = .10$	1	2	4	6	8	11
$\alpha = .025$	$\alpha = .05$		1	2	4	6	8
$\alpha = .01$	$\alpha = .02$			0	2	3	5
$\alpha = .005$	$\alpha = .01$				0	2	3
		n = 11	n = 12	n = 13	n = 14	n = 15	n = 16
$\alpha = .05$	$\alpha = .10$	14	17	21	26	30	36
$\alpha = .025$	$\alpha = .05$	11	14	17	21	25	30
$\alpha = .01$	$\alpha = .02$	7	10	13	16	20	24
$\alpha = .005$	$\alpha = .01$	5	7	10	13	16	19
		n = 17	n = 18	n = 19	n = 20	n = 21	n = 22
$\alpha = .05$	$\alpha = .10$	41	47	54	60	68	75
$\alpha = .025$	$\alpha = .05$	35	40	46	52	59	66
$\alpha = .01$	$\alpha = .02$	28	33	38	43	49	56
$\alpha = .005$	$\alpha = .01$	23	28	32	37	43	49
		n = 23	n = 24	n = 25	n = 26	n = 27	n = 28
$\alpha = .05$	$\alpha = .10$	83	92	101	110	120	130
$\alpha = .025$	$\alpha = .05$	73	81	90	98	107	117
$\alpha = .01$	$\alpha = .02$	62	69	77	85	93	102
$\alpha = .005$	$\alpha = .01$	55	61	68	76	84	92

We are now prepared to test the nonparametric hypothesis:

H_0: The probability distributions of the ratings for products A and B are identical

H_a: The probability distributions of the ratings differ for the two products

Test statistic: $T =$ Smaller of the positive and negative rank sums T_A and T_B

The smaller the value of T, the greater will be the evidence to indicate that the two probability distributions differ. The rejection region for T can be determined by consulting Table IX, Appendix B. A portion of the table is shown in Figure 16.4. This table gives a value T_0 for each value of n, the number of matched pairs. The values of T_0 are tabulated for both a one- and a two-tailed test. For a two-tailed test with $\alpha = .05$, we will reject H_0 if $T \leq T_0$. The rejection region for the judges' ratings in Table 16.2 is the value indicated for $n = 10$ pairs of observations. This value of T_0 is 8. Therefore, the rejection region for the test (see Figure 16.5) is

Rejection region: $T \leq 8$ for $\alpha = .05$

FIGURE 16.5
REJECTION REGION
FOR
PAIRED DIFFERENCE
EXPERIMENT

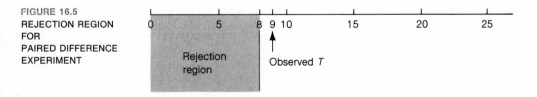

Since the smaller rank sum for the paper data, $T = 9$, does not fall within the rejection region, the experiment has not provided sufficient evidence to indicate that the two paper products differ with respect to their softness ratings at the $\alpha = .05$ level.

Note that if a significance level of $\alpha = .10$ had been used, the rejection region would be $T \leq 11$. Then we would reject H_0. In other words, the samples do provide evidence that the probability distributions of the softness ratings differ at the $\alpha = .10$ significance level.

The Wilcoxon rank sum test for a paired difference experiment is summarized below.

SUMMARY OF WILCOXON RANK SUM TEST FOR A PAIRED DIFFERENCE EXPERIMENT (TWO-TAILED)

H_0: The probability distributions corresponding to the two populations are identical

H_a: The probability distributions corresponding to the two populations differ

Test statistic: T, the smaller of the positive and negative rank sums, T_A and T_B

Rejection region: $T \leq T_0$, where T_0 is found in Table IX for the significance level α

Table IX in Appendix B can also be used to conduct a one-tailed test of the hypothesis that the probability distributions associated with the two populations are identical.

EXAMPLE 16.2   Suppose the United States Consumer Product Safety Commission wants to test the hypothesis that New York City electrical contractors are more likely to install unsafe electrical outlets in urban homes than in suburban homes. A pair of homes, one urban and one suburban and both serviced by the same electrical contractor, is chosen for each of ten randomly selected electrical contractors. A commission inspector assigns each of the twenty homes a safety rating between 1 and 10, with

TABLE 16.3
ELECTRICAL SAFETY RATINGS FOR TEN PAIRS OF NEW YORK CITY HOMES

ELECTRICAL CONTRACTOR	URBAN HOME	SUBURBAN HOME
1	7	9
2	4	5
3	8	8
4	9	8
5	3	6
6	6	10
7	8	9
8	10	8
9	9	4
10	5	9

the higher numbers implying safer electrical conditions. The results are shown in Table 16.3. Use the Wilcoxon rank sum test to determine whether the hypothesis that the probability distribution for the ratings of suburban homes lies above that for urban homes is supported by these data at the $\alpha = .05$ level.

Solution

The null and alternative hypotheses are

H_0: The probability distributions of home electrical ratings are identical for urban and suburban homes

H_a: The electrical ratings for suburban homes tend to exceed those for urban homes

These hypotheses can be tested for the data in Table 16.3 using the Wilcoxon paired difference rank sum test. Since a paired difference design was used (the homes were selected in urban–suburban pairs so that the electrical contractor was the same for both), we first calculate the difference between the ratings for each pair of homes, and then rank the absolute values of the differences (see Table 16.4). Note that one pair of ratings were the same (both 8), and the resulting zero difference contributes to neither the positive nor the negative rank sum. Thus, we eliminate this pair from the calculation of the test statistic.

TABLE 16.4
DIFFERENCES IN RATINGS AND THE RANKS OF THEIR ABSOLUTE VALUES

RATING		DIFFERENCE	RANK OF ABSOLUTE DIFFERENCE
Urban	Suburban	(Urban − Suburban)	
7	9	−2	4.5
4	5	−1	2
8	8	0	(Eliminated)
9	8	1	2
3	6	−3	6
6	10	−4	7.5
8	9	−1	2
10	8	2	4.5
9	4	5	9
5	9	−4	7.5
		Positive rank sum = $T_A = 15.5$	

FIGURE 16.6
THE RESEARCH HYPOTHESIS FOR EXAMPLE 16.2; WE EXPECT T_A = POSITIVE RANK SUM TO BE SMALL

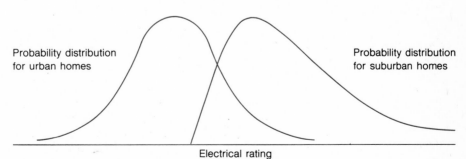

Probability distribution for urban homes

Probability distribution for suburban homes

Electrical rating

Test statistic: T_A, the positive rank sum

In Table 16.4 we compute the urban minus suburban rating differences, and if the research hypothesis is true, we expect most of these differences to be negative. Or, in other words, we expect the *positive* rank sum T_A to be small if the research hypothesis is true (see Figure 16.6).

Rejection region: For $\alpha = .05$, from Table IX, we use $n = 9$ (remember, one pair of observations was eliminated) to find the rejection region for this one-tailed test:

$$T_A \leq 8$$

Since the computed value $T_A = 15.5$ exceeds the critical value of 8, we conclude that this sample provides insufficient evidence at the $\alpha = .05$ level to support the research hypothesis. We *cannot* conclude on the basis of this sample information that suburban homes have safer electrical outlets than urban homes.

EXERCISES

16.3. A food vending company currently uses vending machines made by two different manufacturers. Before purchasing new machines, the company wants to compare the two types in terms of reliability. Records for 7 weeks are given in the table; the data indicate the number of breakdowns per week for each type of machine. The company has the same number of machines of each type. Are there differences in the probability distributions of the number of breakdowns for the two machine types? Use $\alpha = .05$.

| | MACHINE TYPE | |
WEEK	A	B
1	14	12
2	17	13
3	10	14
4	15	12
5	14	9
6	9	11
7	12	11

16.4. Economic indices provide measures of economic change. The June 1977 issue of *U.S. News and World Report* listed the Index of Business Activity for May 1977 and May 1976 in order to provide a means for measuring economic change over the year:

	MAY 1977	MAY 1976
Steel products	99.3	106.4
Automobile products	123.9	118.7
Crude petroleum products	91.0	93.2
Lumber products	117.1	112.6
Freight products	84.8	82.2
Electric power products	169.5	167.0

a. Conduct a paired difference t test to compare the mean values of these indices for the month of May in 1976 and 1977. Use $\alpha = .05$. What assumptions are necessary for the validity of this procedure? Why might these assumptions be doubtful?

b. Use the Wilcoxon paired difference rank test to determine whether these data provide evidence that the probability distributions of the economic indices have changed. Use $\alpha = .05$.

16.3
KRUSKAL–WALLIS H TEST FOR A COMPLETELY RANDOMIZED DESIGN

Recall that a completely randomized design is one in which *independent* random samples are selected from each of k populations to be compared (Section 15.1). In Chapter 15 we used an analysis of variance and the F test to compare the means of the k populations (assuming the populations have normal probability distributions with equal variances). We now present a nonparametric technique that requires no assumptions concerning the population probability distributions to compare the k populations.

For example, suppose you want to compare the numbers of employees in companies representing each of three different business classifications: agriculture, manufacturing, and service. You sample ten companies from each type, and record the number of employees in each sampled business (see Table 16.5). You can see that the assumptions necessary for a parametric comparison of the means are doubtful for these data; the probability distributions are very likely to be skewed to the right, as indicated by the presence of some extremely large values. In addition, the variability in number of employees may not be constant for the different classifications. We therefore base our comparison on the rank sums for the classifications. The ranks are computed for each observation according to the relative magnitude of the measurements **when all k samples are combined** (see Table 16.5). Note that ties are handled in the usual manner, by assigning the average value of the ranks to each of the tied observations.

We test

H_0: All three populations have identical probability distributions

H_a: At least two of the three populations have different probability distributions

Denoting the three sample rank sums by R_1, R_2, and R_3, the **test statistic** is given by

$$H = \frac{12}{n(n+1)} \sum_{j=1}^{k} \frac{R_j^2}{n_j} - 3(n+1)$$

where n_j is the number of measurements in the jth sample and n is the **total sample size** $(n = n_1 + n_2 + \cdots + n_k)$. For the data in Table 16.5, we have $n_1 = n_2 = n_3 = 10$, and $n = 30$. The rank sums are $R_1 = 120$, $R_2 = 210.5$, and $R_3 = 134.5$. Thus,

$$H = \frac{12}{30(31)} \left[\frac{(120)^2}{10} + \frac{(210.5)^2}{10} + \frac{(134.5)^2}{10} \right] - 3(31)$$

$$= 99.097 - 93 = 6.097$$

TABLE 16.5
NUMBER OF
EMPLOYEES IN
THIRTY DIFFERENT
COMPANIES

AGRICULTURE	RANK	MANUFACTURING	RANK	SERVICE	RANK
10	5	244	25	17	9.5
350	27	93	19	249	26
4	2	3,532	30	38	15
26	13	17	9.5	5	3
15	8	526	29	101	20
106	21	133	22	1	1
18	11	14	7	12	6
23	12	192	23	233	24
62	17	443	28	31	14
8	4	69	18	39	16
$R_1 = 120$		$R_2 = 210.5$		$R_3 = 134.5$	

If the null hypothesis is true, the distribution of H in repeated sampling is approximately a χ^2 (chi square) distribution. This approximation for the sampling distribution of H is adequate as long as each of the k sample sizes exceeds five (see the

FIGURE 16.7
SEVERAL
χ^2 PROBABILITY
DISTRIBUTIONS

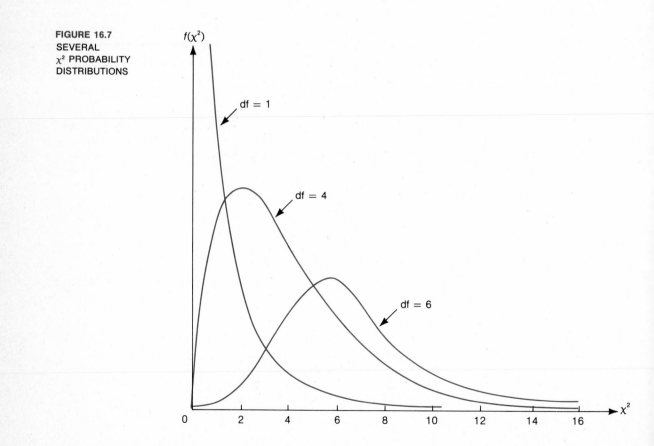

references for more detail). The χ^2 probability distribution is characterized by a single parameter, called the **degrees of freedom associated with the distribution**. Several χ^2 probability distributions with different degrees of freedom are shown in Figure 16.7. The degrees of freedom corresponding to the approximate sampling distribution of H will always be one less than the number of probability distributions being compared, $(k - 1)$. Because large values of H support the research hypothesis that the populations have different probability distributions, the rejection region for the test will be located in the upper tail of the χ^2 distribution, as shown in Figure 16.8.

For the data of Table 16.5, the approximate distribution of the test statistic H is a χ^2 with $(k - 1) = 2$ df. To determine how large H must be before we will reject the null hypothesis, we consult Table X in Appendix B; part of this table is shown in Figure 16.8. Entries in the table give an upper-tail value of χ^2, call it χ_α^2, such that $P(\chi^2 > \chi_\alpha^2) = \alpha$. The columns of the table identify the value of α associated with the tabulated value of χ_α^2, and the rows correspond to the degrees of freedom. Thus, for

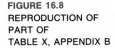

FIGURE 16.8
REPRODUCTION OF
PART OF
TABLE X, APPENDIX B

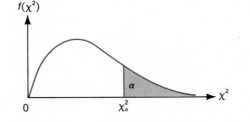

DEGREES OF FREEDOM	$\chi_{.100}^2$	$\chi_{.050}^2$	$\chi_{.025}^2$	$\chi_{.010}^2$	$\chi_{.005}^2$
1	2.70554	3.84146	5.02389	6.63490	7.87944
2	4.60517	5.99147	7.37776	9.21034	10.5966
3	6.25139	7.81473	9.34840	11.3449	12.8381
4	7.77944	9.48773	11.1433	13.2767	14.8602
5	9.23635	11.0705	12.8325	15.0863	16.7496
6	10.6446	12.5916	14.4494	16.8119	18.5476
7	12.0170	14.0671	16.0128	18.4753	20.2777
8	13.3616	15.5073	17.5346	20.0902	21.9550
9	14.6837	16.9190	19.0228	21.6660	23.5893
10	15.9871	18.3070	20.4831	23.2093	25.1882
11	17.2750	19.6751	21.9200	24.7250	26.7569
12	18.5494	21.0261	23.3367	26.2170	28.2995
13	19.8119	22.3621	24.7356	27.6883	29.8194
14	21.0642	23.6848	26.1190	29.1413	31.3193
15	22.3072	24.9958	27.4884	30.5779	32.8013
16	23.5418	26.2962	28.8454	31.9999	34.2672
17	24.7690	27.5871	30.1910	33.4087	35.7185
18	25.9894	28.8693	31.5264	34.8053	37.1564
19	27.2036	30.1435	32.8523	36.1908	38.5822

FIGURE 16.9
REJECTION REGION
FOR THE COMPARISON
OF THREE
PROBABILITY
DISTRIBUTIONS

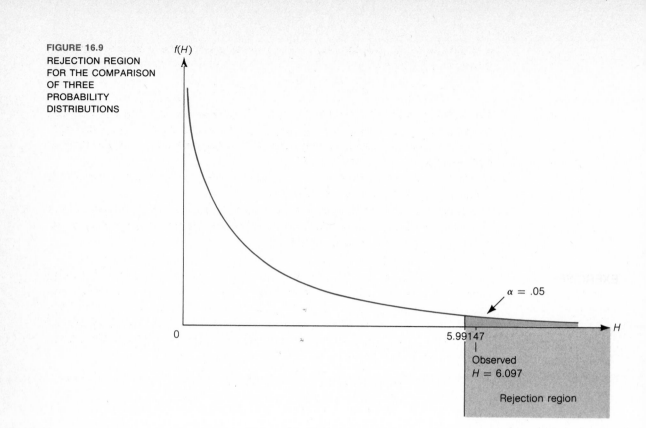

KRUSKAL–WALLIS H TEST FOR COMPARING k PROBABILITY
DISTRIBUTIONS

H_0: The k probability distributions are identical

H_a: At least two of the k probability distributions differ

Test statistic: $H = \dfrac{12}{n(n+1)} \displaystyle\sum_{j=1}^{k} \dfrac{R_j^2}{n_j} - 3(n+1)$

where

n_j = Number of measurements in sample j

R_j = Rank sum for sample j, where the rank of each measurement
      is computed according to its relative magnitude in the totality of
      data for the k samples

n = Total sample size = $n_1 + n_2 + \cdots + n_k$

Rejection region: $H > \chi_\alpha^2$ with $(k-1)$ degrees of freedom

$\alpha = .05$ and df = 2, we can reject the null hypothesis that the three probability distributions are the same if

$$H > \chi^2_{.05,2} \qquad \text{where} \qquad \chi^2_{.05,2} = 5.99147$$

The rejection region is pictured in Figure 16.9. Since the calculated $H = 6.097$ exceeds the critical value of 5.99147, we conclude that at least two of the three probability distributions describing the number of employees for the three sampled business types differ.

The Kruskal–Wallis H test for comparing more than two probability distributions is summarized at the bottom of page 504.

Note that we can use the Wilcoxon rank sum test to compare the separate pairs of populations if the Kruskal–Wallis H test supports the research hypothesis that some of the probability distributions differ.

EXERCISES

16.5. A large charitable fund-raising organization attempts to use civic pride to increase contributions during its annual drive. Contribution records are selected randomly at the organization offices in each of four cities within the same state. The amount of each contribution for those selected are given in the table. Is there evidence of differences among the probability distributions of the amounts contributed for each of the four cities? Use $\alpha = .10$.

AMOUNT CONTRIBUTED (IN DOLLARS)

CITY 1	CITY 2	CITY 3	CITY 4
75	65	15	45
20	30	25	30
30	45	10	25
45	50	35	60
25	35	5	55
	70		

16.6. Three different brands of magnetron tubes (the key components in microwave ovens) were subjected to stressful testing, and the number of hours each operated without repair was recorded. Although these times do not represent typical life lengths, they do indicate how well the tubes can withstand extreme stress:

	BRAND	
A	B	C
36	49	71
48	33	31
5	60	140
67	2	59
53	55	42

a. Use the F test for a completely randomized design (Chapter 15) to test the hypothesis that the mean length of life under stress is the same for the three brands. Use $\alpha = .05$. What assumptions are necessary for the validity of this procedure? Is there any reason to doubt these assumptions?

b.   Use the Kruskal–Wallis H test to determine whether evidence exists to conclude that the probability distributions of length of life under stress differ for the three brands. Use $\alpha = .05$.

16.4
THE FRIEDMAN
F_r TEST FOR
A RANDOMIZED
BLOCK DESIGN

In Section 15.2 we used relatively homogeneous blocks of experimental units to compare k population means. However, for the randomized block design (like the completely randomized design), we must assume that the k populations have normal probability distributions and that their variances are equal. No assumptions are required for the nonparametric counterpart, the Friedman F_r test, to compare the k probability distributions.

For example, suppose a marketing firm wants to compare the relative effectiveness of three different modes of advertising: direct-mail, newspaper ads, and magazine ads. For fifteen clients, all three modes are used over a 1 year period, and the marketing firm records the year's percentage response to each type of advertising. That is, the firm divides the number of responses to a particular type of advertising by the total number of potential customers reached by the advertisements of that type. The results are shown in Table 16.6.

The fifteen companies act as blocks in this experiment, since we would expect the percentage responses to depend on the nature of the products of the company, its size, etc. Thus, we rank the observations within each company (block), and then compute the rank sums for each of the three types of advertising (treatments).

The null and alternative hypotheses are

H_0:   The probability distributions of the response rates are identical for the three modes of advertising

H_a: At least two of the three probability distributions differ

The Friedman F_r test statistic is based on the rank sums:

$$F_r = \frac{12}{bk(k + 1)} \sum_{j=1}^{k} R_j^2 - 3b(k + 1)$$

where b is the number of blocks, k is the number of treatments, and R_j is the jth rank sum. For the data in Table 16.6,

$$F_r = \frac{12}{(15)(3)(4)}(R_1^2 + R_2^2 + R_3^2) - (3)(15)(4)$$

$$= \frac{12}{(15)(3)(4)}[(20)^2 + (39)^2 + (31)^2] - (3)(15)(4)$$

$$= 192.13 - 180 = 12.13$$

As for the Kruskal–Wallis H statistic, the χ^2 distribution with $(k - 1)$ degrees of freedom provides an approximation to the sampling distribution of F_r. We assume the approximation is adequate if either b (the number of blocks) or k (the number of

TABLE 16.6	COMPANY	DIRECT-MAIL	RANK	NEWSPAPER	RANK	MAGAZINE	RANK
PERCENT RESPONSE TO THREE TYPES OF ADVERTISING FOR FIFTEEN DIFFERENT COMPANIES	1	7.3	1	15.7	3	10.1	2
	2	9.4	2	18.3	3	8.2	1
	3	4.3	1	11.2	3	5.1	2
	4	11.3	2	19.1	3	6.5	1
	5	3.3	1	9.2	3	8.7	2
	6	4.2	1	10.5	3	6.0	2
	7	5.9	1	8.7	2	12.3	3
	8	6.2	1	14.3	3	11.1	2
	9	4.3	2	3.1	1	6.0	3
	10	10.0	1	18.8	3	12.1	2
	11	2.2	1	5.7	2	6.3	3
	12	6.3	2	20.2	3	4.3	1
	13	8.0	1	14.1	3	9.1	2
	14	7.4	2	6.2	1	18.1	3
	15	3.2	1	8.9	3	5.0	2
			$R_1 = 20$		$R_2 = 39$		$R_3 = 31$

treatments) exceeds five. Then, for the advertising example, we use $\alpha = .10$ to form the rejection region:

Rejection region: $F_r > \chi^2_{.10}$, with $k - 1 = 2$ df

Consulting Table X in Appendix B, we find that $\chi^2_{.10}$ based on 2 df is 4.60517. Consequently, we will reject H_0 if $F_r > 4.60517$ (see Figure 16.10). Since the calculated $F_r = 12.13$ exceeds the critical value of 4.60517, we conclude that the response rate probability distributions differ for the three modes of advertising.

The Friedman F_r test for randomized block designs is summarized below.

FRIEDMAN F_r TEST FOR A RANDOMIZED BLOCK DESIGN

H_0: The probability distributions for the k treatments are identical

H_a: At least two of the probability distributions differ

Test statistic: $F_r = \dfrac{12}{bk(k + 1)} \sum_{j=1}^{k} R_j^2 - 3b(k + 1)$

where

$b =$ Number of blocks

$k =$ Number of treatments

$R_j =$ Rank sum of the jth treatment, where the rank of each measurement is computed relative to its position *within its own block*

Rejection region: $F_r > \chi^2_\alpha$ with $(k - 1)$ degrees of freedom

---

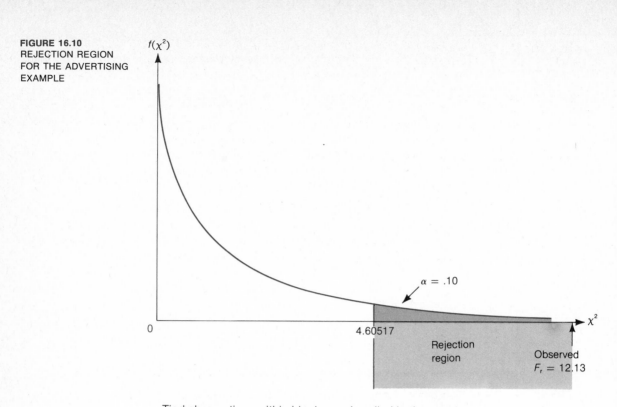

FIGURE 16.10
REJECTION REGION
FOR THE ADVERTISING
EXAMPLE

$f(\chi^2)$

0

$\alpha = .10$

4.60517

χ^2

Rejection
region

Observed
$F_r = 12.13$

Tied observations within blocks are handled in the usual manner by assigning the average value of the rank to each of the tied observations.

The Wilcoxon rank sum test for paired difference designs (Section 16.2) can be used to compare the pairs of treatments if the F_r statistic supports the research hypothesis that some of the probability distributions differ.

CASE STUDY 16.1

Since consumers' images reflect to some extent actions taken by marketers in dealing with many marketing variables, it is frequently desirable to determine if these images have patterns.

McClure (1971) studied the pattern of consumers' images of three appliances. Five attributes—price, looks, need for repair, ease of use, and familiarity—were examined for each of two brands. For example, a consumer was asked to rank brand A's refrigerators, ranges, and automatic clothes washers in terms of the attribute "ease of use." McClure states:

> Conceptually, it was an investigation of the "halo effect" . . . which refers to the individual's supposed tendency to imbue his evaluations of specific characteristics of an appliance with the same direction of general feeling expressed about the brand. The halo effect would be considered operative to the extent that the individual's general image of Brand X influences his rating of an individual appliance of that brand when asked to evaluate it.

Responses of 282 female heads of households were obtained in a large midwestern city. For each of the ten responses (five attributes for two brands) a Friedman two-way analysis of variance was conducted, with the three types of appliances representing the treatments and the 282 consumers acting as blocks. A significant value of the test statistic F_r would indicate consistent ranking of the three appliances by the 282 subjects for the attribute, i.e., that the probability distributions of ranks given the three appliances differ. A small value of F_r would lend credence to the hypothesis that the rankings are randomly performed, i.e., that they have approximately the same probability distributions. McClure found that the rank probability distributions differ for all attributes except "price" for brand A (at the $\alpha = .10$ level); brand A refrigerators consistently tend to obtain the highest ranking. However, brand B has no such clear pattern, with only the "familiarity" rankings showing significant differences. The subjects seemed to be most familiar with the brand B clothes washer, but could not agree on the ranking of the other attributes.

McClure concluded his article:

Many marketing researchers have not been aware of the Friedman two-way analysis of variance by ranks. However, it has potential for use in situations common to many consumer surveys in which sets of ordinal [rank] data are generated by each respondent.

EXERCISES

16.7. In recent years, domestic car manufacturers have devoted more attention to the small car market. To compare the popularity of four domestic small cars within a city, a local trade organization obtained the information given in the table from four car dealers—one dealer for each of the four car makes. Is there evidence of differences among the probability distributions of the number of cars sold for each type? Use $\alpha = .10$.

NUMBER OF SMALL CARS SOLD

MONTH	MAKE OF CAR			
	A	B	C	D
1	9	17	14	8
2	10	20	16	9
3	13	15	19	12
4	11	12	19	11
5	7	18	13	8

16.8. One of the byproducts of inflationary times is increased replacement costs of materials. The June 20, 1977 issue of *Business Week* gave a table of ratios of current replacement costs to historical costs in four categories for three well-known pharmaceutical companies. Use Friedman's test to determine whether evidence exists to indicate that the inflationary effects have been felt to different extents by the companies.

	GROSS ASSETS	NET ASSETS	DEPRECIATION	INVENTORY
Bristol-Myers	1.62	1.58	1.64	1.03
Eli-Lilly	1.74	1.41	1.57	1.00
Pfizer	1.84	1.85	1.67	1.16

16.5
SPEARMAN'S
RANK
CORRELATION
COEFFICIENT

When economic conditions are favorable, many banks advertise special loan rates for new cars, appliances, etc., to attract customers. Suppose a bank wants to determine whether to aim its advertising at a broad spectrum of potential borrowers or to concentrate on a specific income group. It randomly samples ten noncommercial customers from recent files and ascertains the present income of each and the total amount each has borrowed over the past 3 years (excluding mortgages and business loans). The data are shown in Table 16.7.

TABLE 16.7

CUSTOMER	INCOME	RANK	TOTAL BORROWED	RANK
1	$14,800	5	$4,300	7
2	8,900	1	4,800	8
3	83,600	10	500	2
4	22,100	8	3,300	5
5	18,200	7	5,500	9
6	13,700	4	3,700	6
7	41,800	9	0	1
8	9,300	2	3,200	4
9	12,700	3	6,100	10
10	16,100	6	1,800	3

One method of determining whether a correlation exists between income and amount borrowed is to calculate the Pearson product moment correlation, r (Section 11.5). However, to make an inference about the population correlation ρ (Greek rho), we must assume that the two random variables, income and amount borrowed, are normally distributed. This assumption is usually doubtful for incomes, since they tend to have a relative frequency distribution that is heavily skewed to the right (Figure 16.11). Although the modal income (that with the largest relative frequency) is rela-

FIGURE 16.11
TYPICAL RELATIVE
FREQUENCY
DISTRIBUTION
OF INCOMES

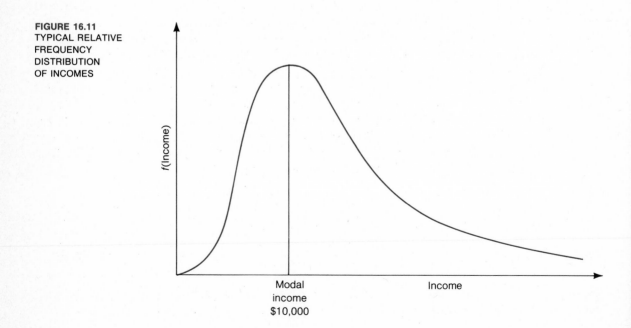

tively low, there are enough individuals with high incomes to make the distribution asymmetric.

Thus, we turn to a nonparametric approach to correlation, which does not require underlying normal distributions. This nonparametric method, like those in the previous sections of this chapter, uses the ranks of the measurements to determine a measure of correlation.

SPEARMAN'S RANK CORRELATION COEFFICIENT

$$r_s = \frac{SS_{uv}}{\sqrt{SS_{uu}SS_{vv}}}$$

where

$$SS_{uv} = \sum (u_i - \bar{u})(v_i - \bar{v}) = \sum u_i v_i - \frac{\left(\sum u_i\right)\left(\sum v_i\right)}{n}$$

$$SS_{uu} = \sum (u_i - \bar{u})^2 = \sum u_i^2 - \frac{\left(\sum u_i\right)^2}{n}$$

$$SS_{vv} = \sum (v_i - \bar{v})^2 = \sum v_i^2 - \frac{\left(\sum v_i\right)^2}{n}$$

u_i = Rank of the ith measurement in sample 1

v_i = Rank of the ith measurement in sample 2

n = Number of pairs of measurements (number of measurements in each sample)

Note that the definition of Spearman's rank correlation coefficient is identical to the definition of Pearson's r (see page 311), except that Spearman's r_s uses ranks. You can use the following shortcut formula for calculating r_s if there are no ties. The shortcut formula will also provide a satisfactory approximation to r_s when the number of ties is small relative to the number of pairs.

SHORTCUT FORMULA FOR r_s

$$r_s = 1 - \frac{6 \sum d_i^2}{n(n^2 - 1)}$$

where

$d_i = u_i - v_i$ (difference in the ranks of the ith measurement for sample 1 and sample 2)

EXAMPLE 16.3

Calculate Spearman's rank correlation coefficient, r_s, for the bank customer data in Table 16.7.

Solution

The ranks are reproduced in Table 16.8, along with the difference, d_i, for each pair of measurements. Then,

TABLE 16.8

CUSTOMER	INCOME RANK u_i	TOTAL BORROWED RANK v_i	DIFFERENCE $d_i = u_i - v_i$	DIFFERENCE SQUARED d_i^2
1	5	7	-2	4
2	1	8	-7	49
3	10	2	8	64
4	8	5	3	9
5	7	9	-2	4
6	4	6	-2	4
7	9	1	8	64
8	2	4	-2	4
9	3	10	-7	49
10	6	3	3	9
				Total = 260

$$r_s = 1 - \frac{6 \sum d_i^2}{n(n^2 - 1)} = 1 - \frac{6(260)}{10(100 - 1)} = 1 - 1.576 = -.576$$

The sign of r_s indicates the nature of the relationship between the two variables. Positive values indicate a tendency for the variables to increase together, and negative values indicate a tendency for one variable to increase while the other decreases. However, because only the ranks are used in calculating r_s, we cannot tell what the magnitudes of the changes are.

The strength of the relationship between the ranks is indicated by the numerical size of r_s. Since r_s is really a Pearson product moment correlation of the ranks, it must lie between -1 and $+1$. Recall that a 0 correlation implies no relationship, while -1 and $+1$ correlations imply perfect negative and positive relationships, respectively. In Example 16.3 we obtained $r_s = -.576$. Is this different enough from 0 to conclude that the variables are negatively related in the population?

If we define ρ_s as the population Spearman rank correlation coefficient, this question can be answered by conducting the test

H_0: $\rho_s = 0$ (no population correlation between ranks)

H_a: $\rho_s \neq 0$ (there is a population correlation between ranks)

Test statistic: r_s, the sample Spearman rank correlation coefficient

To determine a rejection region, we consult Table XI in Appendix B, which is partially reproduced in Figure 16.12. Note that the left-hand column gives values of n, the number of pairs of measurements. The entries in the table are values for an upper-tail rejection region, since only positive values are given. Thus, for $n = 10$ and $\alpha = .05$, the value .564 is the beginning of the upper-tailed rejection region, so that $P(r_s > .564) = .05$ when H_0: $\rho_s = 0$ is true. That is, we expect to see r_s exceed .564 only 5% of the time when there is really no relationship between the variables. The two-tailed rejection region is $r_s > .564$ or $r_s < -.564$, and the α value is therefore double the table value: $\alpha = 2(.05) = .10$. Thus, we have

Rejection region: $\alpha = .10$ $r_s < -.564$ or $r_s > .564$

FIGURE 16.12
REPRODUCTION OF
PART OF
TABLE XI, APPENDIX B

n	$\alpha = .05$	$\alpha = .025$	$\alpha = .01$	$\alpha = .005$
5	.900	—	—	—
6	.829	.886	.943	—
7	.714	.786	.893	—
8	.643	.738	.833	.881
9	.600	.683	.783	.833
10	.564	.648	.745	.794
11	.523	.623	.736	.818
12	.497	.591	.703	.780
13	.475	.566	.673	.745
14	.457	.545	.646	.716
15	.441	.525	.623	.689
16	.425	.507	.601	.666
17	.412	.490	.582	.645
18	.399	.476	.564	.625
19	.388	.462	.549	.608
20	.377	.450	.534	.591

Since the calculated value from Example 16.3 is $r_s = -.576$, which is less than $-.564$, we reject H_0 at the .10 level of significance. We can conclude that bank customers at lower income levels tend to borrow more than those at higher income levels. Therefore, the bank would be wise to aim its loan advertising at those in the middle- and lower-income groups, unless it wants to attempt to entice those who rarely borrow to become customers, in which case higher-income groups should be the target.

A summary of Spearman's nonparametric test for correlation is summarized below.

SPEARMAN'S NONPARAMETRIC TEST FOR RANK CORRELATION (TWO-TAILED)

H_0: $\rho_s = 0$ H_a: $\rho_s \neq 0$

Test statistic: $r_s = \dfrac{SS_{uv}}{\sqrt{SS_{uu}SS_{vv}}}$

where

d_i = Difference between ranks of the ith pairs of measurements

n = Number of pairs of measurements

Rejection region: $r_s > r_{s,\alpha/2,n}$ or $r_s < -r_{s,\alpha/2,n}$

where $r_{s,\alpha/2,n}$ is the value from Table XI corresponding to the upper-tail area $\alpha/2$ and n pairs of measurements.

EXAMPLE 16.4

Manufacturers of perishable foods often use preservatives to retard spoilage. One concern is that using too much preservative will change the flavor of the food. Suppose an experiment is conducted using samples of a food product with varying amounts of preservative added. The length of time until the food shows signs of spoiling and a taste rating are recorded for each sample. The taste rating is the average rating for three tasters, each of whom rate each sample on a scale from 1 (good) to 5 (bad). Twelve sample measurements are shown in Table 16.9. Use a nonparametric test to find out whether the spoilage times and taste ratings are negatively correlated. Use $\alpha = .05$.

TABLE 16.9
DATA FOR
EXAMPLE 16.4

SAMPLE	TIME UNTIL SPOILAGE (Days)	RANK	TASTE RATING	RANK
1	30	2	4.3	11
2	47	5	3.6	7.5
3	26	1	4.5	12
4	94	11	2.8	3
5	67	7	3.3	6
6	83	10	2.7	2
7	36	3	4.2	10
8	77	9	3.9	9
9	43	4	3.6	7.5
10	109	12	2.2	1
11	56	6	3.1	5
12	70	8	2.9	4

[*Note:* Tied measurements are assigned the average of the ranks that would be given the measurements if they were different but consecutive.]

Solution

The test is one-tailed, with

$$H_0: \quad \rho_s = 0 \qquad H_a: \quad \rho_s < 0$$

Test statistic:* $\quad r_s = 1 - \dfrac{6 \sum d_i^2}{n(n^2 - 1)}$

Rejection region: For $\alpha = .05$ and $n = 12$, $r_s < -r_{s,\alpha,n}$, where from Table XI, $-r_{s,.05,12} = -.497$. [*Note:* The value of α need not be doubled since the test is one-tailed.]

The first step in the computation of r_s is to sum the squares of the differences between ranks:

$$\sum d_i^2 = (2 - 11)^2 + (5 - 7.5)^2 + \cdots + (8 - 4)^2 = 536.5$$

Then

$$r_s = 1 - \frac{6(536.5)}{12(144 - 1)} = -.876$$

Since $-.876 < -.497$, we reject H_0 and conclude that the preservative does affect the taste of this food adversely.

---

*The shortcut formula is not exact when there are tied measurements, but it is a good approximation when the total number of ties is not large relative to n.

16.9. Many large businesses send representatives to college campuses to conduct job interviews. To aid the interviewer, one company decides to study the correlation between the strength of an applicant's references (the company requires three references) and the performance of the applicant on the job. Eight recently hired employees are sampled, and independent evaluations of both references and job performance are made on a scale from 1 to 20. The scores are given in the table.

EMPLOYEE	REFERENCES	JOB PERFORMANCE
1	18	20
2	14	13
3	19	16
4	13	9
5	16	14
6	11	18
7	20	15
8	9	12

a. Compute Spearman's rank correlation coefficient for these data.

b. Is there evidence that strength of references and job performance are positively correlated? Use $\alpha = .05$.

16.10. A large manufacturing firm wants to determine whether a relationship exists between the number of work-hours an employee misses per year and the employee's annual wages. A sample of fifteen employees produced the data in the table. Do these data provide evidence that the work-hours missed are related to annual wages? Use $\alpha = .05$.

EMPLOYEE	WORK-HOURS MISSED	ANNUAL WAGES (Thousands of dollars)
1	49	12.8
2	36	14.5
3	127	8.3
4	91	10.2
5	72	10.0
6	34	11.5
7	155	8.8
8	11	17.2
9	191	7.8
10	6	15.8
11	63	10.8
12	79	9.7
13	43	12.1
14	57	21.2
15	82	10.9

We have presented several useful **nonparametric techniques** for comparing two or more populations. Nonparametric techniques are useful when the underlying assumptions for their parametric counterparts are not justified or when it is impossible to assign specific values to the observations. Nonparametric methods provide more general comparisons of populations than parametric methods, because they compare the probability distributions of the populations rather than specific parameters.

Rank sums are the primary tools of nonparametric statistics. The **Wilcoxon rank sum statistic** can be used to compare two populations for either an independent sampling experiment or a **paired difference experiment**. The Kruskal–Wallis H **test** is applied when comparing k populations using a **completely randomized design**. The **Friedman F_r test** is used to compare k populations when a **randomized block design** is conducted.

The strength of nonparametric statistics lies in their general applicability. Few restrictive assumptions are required, and they may be used for observations that can be ranked but not be exactly measured. Therefore, nonparametric tests provide very useful sets of statistical tests to use in conjunction with the parametric tests of Chapters 9, 10, and 15.

16.11. A national clothing store franchise operates two stores in one city—one urban and one suburban. To stock the stores with clothing suited to the customers' needs, a survey is conducted to determine the incomes of the customers. Ten customers in each store are offered significant discounts if they will reveal the annual income of their household. The results are listed in the table (in thousands of dollars). Is there evidence that the probability distributions of the customers' incomes differ for the two stores? Use $\alpha = .05$.

STORE 1	STORE 2
18.8	12.3
27.9	19.2
12.2	6.3
85.3	24.5
13.1	11.0
29.5	10.3
16.3	15.6
22.1	9.8
15.7	8.6
24.0	19.3

16.12. Suppose a company wants to study how personality relates to leadership. Four supervisors with different types of personalities are selected. Several employees are then selected from the group supervised by each, and these employees are asked to rate the leader of their group on a scale from 1 to 20 (20 signifies highly favorable). The resulting data are shown in the table. Is there evidence to indicate that the probability distribution of ratings differs for the four supervisors? Use $\alpha = .05$.

| | SUPERVISOR | | |
I	II	III	IV
20	17	16	8
19	11	15	12
20	13	13	10
18	15	18	14
17	14	11	9
	16		10

16.13. Refer to Exercise 16.12. Suppose the company is particularly interested in comparing the ratings of the personality types represented by supervisors I and III. Make this comparison using $\alpha = .05$.

16.14. A union wants to determine the preferences of its members before negotiating with management. Ten union members are randomly selected, and an extensive questionnaire is completed by each member. The responses to the various aspects of the questionnaire will enable the union to rank in order of importance the items to be negotiated. The rankings are shown in the table. Is there evidence that the distributions of preferences differ among the four items? Use $\alpha = .05$.

PERSON	MORE PAY	JOB STABILITY	FRINGE BENEFITS	SHORTER HOURS
1	2	1	3	4
2	1	2	3	4
3	4	3	2	1
4	1	4	2	3
5	1	2	3	4
6	1	3	4	2
7	2.5	1	2.5	4
8	3	1	4	2
9	1.5	1.5	3	4
10	2	3	1	4

16.15. An insurance company wants to determine whether a relationship exists between the number of claims filed by owners of family policies and the annual incomes of the families. A random sample of ten policies is selected, with the results listed in the table on page 518. Is there evidence of a relationship between the number of claims filed and the incomes of the family policyholders? Use $\alpha = .10$.

FAMILY	CLAIMS (3 year period)	ANNUAL INCOME (Thousands of dollars, averaged over 3 years)
1	5	14.5
2	1	9.6
3	9	62.5
4	0	22.5
5	4	10.3
6	7	16.2
7	0	8.1
8	2	21.2
9	6	17.1
10	3	12.3

16.16. The trend among doctors in some areas of the country is to form a group practice. By combining treatment resources, doctors hope to be more efficient. One doctor who recently joined a group family practice wants to compare the distribution of the number of patients he treated during a day when he was an individual practitioner with the distribution after joining the group practice. Records were checked for 8 days before and 8 days after, with the results listed in the table. Use the Wilcoxon rank sums test to determine whether these samples indicate that the doctor tends to treat more patients per day now than before. Use $\alpha = .05$.

NUMBER OF PATIENTS TREATED PER DAY

BEFORE	AFTER
26	28
25	30
27	27
26	31
24	29
20	23
22	28
21	29

16.17. In recent years, many magazines have been forced to raise their prices because of increased postage, printing, and paper costs. Because magazines are now more expensive, some households may be subscribing to fewer magazines than they did 3 years ago. Ten households were selected at random, and the number of magazines subscribed to 3 years ago and now was determined. The results are listed in the table. Does this sample provide sufficient evidence to indicate that households tend to subscribe to fewer magazines now than they did 3 years ago? Use $\alpha = .05$.

NUMBER OF MAGAZINE SUBSCRIPTIONS

HOUSEHOLD	3 YEARS AGO	NOW
1	8	4
2	3	5
3	6	4
4	3	3
5	10	5
6	6	5
7	4	3
8	2	2
9	9	6
10	8	2

16.18. A hotel had a problem with people reserving rooms for a weekend and then not honoring their reservations (no-shows). As a result, the hotel developed a new reservation and deposit plan that it hoped would reduce the number of no-shows. One year after the new policy was initiated, the management evaluated its effect in comparison with the old policy. Compare the records given in the table for the ten nonholiday weekends preceding the institution of the new policy and the ten nonholiday weekends preceding the evaluation time. Has the situation improved under the new policy? Test at $\alpha = .05$.

NUMBER OF NO-SHOWS

BEFORE	AFTER
10	4
5	3
3	8
6	5
7	6
11	4
8	2
9	5
6	7
5	1

16.19. A clothing manufacturer employs five inspectors, who provide quality control of workmanship. Every item of clothing produced carries with it the number of the inspector who checked it. Thus, the company can evaluate an inspector by keeping records of the number of complaints received about products bearing his or her inspection number. Records for 6 months are given in the table on page 520. Are there differences among the inspectors in terms of the probability distributions of the number of complaints? Use $\alpha = .10$.

NUMBER OF RETURNS

MONTH	I	II	III	IV	V
1	8	10	7	6	9
2	5	7	4	12	12
3	5	8	6	10	6
4	9	6	8	10	13
5	4	13	3	7	15
6	4	8	2	6	9

16.20. Refer to Exercise 16.19. Use the Wilcoxon paired rank sums test to determine whether evidence exists to indicate that the performances of inspectors I and IV differ. Use $\alpha = .05$.

16.21. A savings and loan association is considering three locations in a large city as potential office sites. The company has hired a marketing firm to compare the incomes of people living in the area surrounding each location. The market researchers interview ten households chosen at random in each area to determine the type of job, length of employment, etc., of those in the households who work. This information will enable them to estimate the annual income of each household. The results in the table are obtained. Is there evidence of differences in the income distributions for the three locations? Use $\alpha = .05$.

ESTIMATED ANNUAL INCOME (THOUSANDS OF DOLLARS)

LOCATION 1	LOCATION 2	LOCATION 3
14.3	19.3	14.5
15.5	25.5	9.3
12.1	30.2	17.2
8.3	52.1	13.2
20.5	28.6	12.6
16.2	22.2	18.3
23.5	83.5	23.3
14.7	27.9	16.7
18.0	21.2	20.0
15.1	24.0	15.2

16.22. Refer to Exercise 16.21. Use the Wilcoxon rank sum test to compare the probability distributions of incomes in locations 1 and 2. Use $\alpha = .05$.

16.23. A manufacturer wants to determine whether the number of defectives produced by its employees tends to increase as the day progresses. Unknown to the employees, a complete inspection is made of every item that was produced on one day, and the hourly fraction defective is recorded. The resulting data are given in the table. Do they provide evidence that the fraction defective increases as the day progresses? Test at the $\alpha = .05$ level.

HOUR	FRACTION DEFECTIVE
1	.02
2	.05
3	.03
4	.08
5	.06
6	.09
7	.11
8	.10

16.24. A businesswoman who is looking for a new investment considers a certain suburban community to be a good location for a new restaurant. She decides to survey some residents in the area to see what type of restaurant would be preferred. Ten people are chosen at random and each is asked to estimate how many times in the past 6 months he or she has eaten in each of three types of restaurants—fast-food, family menu, and smorgasbord. The businesswoman then ranks the numbers for each person to obtain a preference ranking. The results are shown in the table. Is there evidence of differences among the probability distributions of preferences for the three restaurant types? Use $\alpha = .05$.

PERSON	PREFERENCE RANKING OF RESTAURANT TYPE		
	Fast-food	Family menu	Smorgasbord
1	1	2.5	2.5
2	2	1	3
3	3	2	1
4	3	1	2
5	3	1	2
6	2	3	1
7	1.5	1.5	3
8	1	2	3
9	3	1	2
10	3	2	1

16.25. For many years, the Girl Scouts of America have sold cookies using various sales techniques. One troop experimented with several techniques, and reported the number of sales per girl listed in the table. Is there evidence that the probability distributions of number of sales differs for the four techniques? Use $\alpha = .10$.

DOOR-TO-DOOR	TELEPHONE	GROCERY STORE STAND	DEPARTMENT STORE STAND
47	63	113	25
93	19	50	36
58	29	68	21
37	24	37	27
62	33	39	18
		77	31

16.26. Refer to Exercise 16.25. Compare the probability distributions of number of sales for the door-to-door and grocery store stand techniques. Use $\alpha = .05$.

16.27. Performance in a personal interview often determines whether a candidate is offered a job. Suppose the personnel director of a company interviewed six potential job applicants without knowing anything about their backgrounds, and then rated them on a scale from 1 to 10. Independently, the director's supervisor made an evaluation of the background qualifications of each candidate on the same scale. The results are shown in the table. Is there evidence that candidates' qualification scores are related to their interview performance? Use $\alpha = .10$.

CANDIDATE	QUALIFICATIONS	INTERVIEW PERFORMANCE
1	10	8
2	8	9
3	9	10
4	4	5
5	5	3
6	6	6

16.28. Two car-rental companies have long waged an advertising war. An independent testing agency is hired to compare the number of rentals at one major airport. After 10 days, the agency has the data listed in the table. At this point, can either car-rental company claim to be number one at this airport? Use $\alpha = .05$.

DAY	RENTAL COMPANY A	B
1	29	22
2	26	29
3	19	30
4	28	25
5	27	26
6	16	20
7	35	30
8	43	45
9	29	38
10	32	40

16.29. The health food business has boomed in recent years. Suppose three different health food diets are compared by placing eight overweight individuals on each diet for 6 weeks. The values in the table represent the weight losses (in pounds) of the twenty-four individuals. Can we conclude that the probability distributions of the weight losses differ for the three diets? Use $\alpha = .05$.

	DIET	
A	B	C
11	0	3
19	4	7
23	19	8
7	15	11
2	8	9
13	11	10
20	14	16
22	17	5

16.30. Refer to Exercise 16.29. Compare the weight loss distributions for diets A and B using $\alpha = .10$.

ON YOUR OWN . . .

In Chapters 15 and 16 we have discussed two methods of analyzing a randomized block design. When the populations have normal probability distributions and their variances are equal, we can employ the analysis of variance described in Chapter 15. Otherwise, we can use the Friedman F_r test.

In the "On Your Own" section of Chapter 15, we asked you to conduct a randomized block design to compare supermarket prices, and to use an analysis of variance to interpret the data. Now use the Friedman F_r test to compare the supermarket prices.

How do the results of the two analyses compare? How can you explain the similarity (or lack of similarity) between the two results?

REFERENCES

Gibbons, J. D. *Nonparametric statistical inference.* New York: McGraw-Hill, 1971.
Hollander, M., & Wolfe, D. A. *Nonparametric statistical methods.* New York: Wiley, 1973.
McClure, P. "Analyzing consumer image data using the Friedman two-way analysis of variance by ranks." *Journal of Marketing Research,* Aug. 1971, *8,* 370–371.
Siegel, S. *Nonparametric statistics for the behavioral sciences.* New York: McGraw-Hill, 1956.
Winkler, R. L., & Hays, W. L. *Statistics: Probability, inference and decision.* 2d ed. New York: Holt, Rinehart, and Winston, 1975. Chapter 12.

WHERE WE'VE BEEN . . .

The preceding chapters have presented statistical methods for analyzing many types of business data. Chapters 9–15 were appropriate for populations of data on quantitative random variables that were independent and had (at least approximately) normal probability distributions with a common variance. Nonparametric statistical procedures were presented in Chapter 16 to compare two or more populations when the assumptions of normality or common variance were likely to be violated or when the responses could only be ranked according to their relative magnitudes.

WHERE WE'RE GOING . . .

The methods of this chapter are also regarded as nonparametric. They are appropriate for a type of data that is common in business but does not fit the mold (the assumptions) of the preceding chapters. We refer to count or classificatory data. For example, a brokerage company might want to investigate the relationship between customer stock preferences (common, preferred, mutual fund, etc.) and customer occupations. To do this, the company would sample its customers and count the number in each preference–occupation category. Then, the data would be used to make inferences about the proportions of people in the population categories. Problems of this type, as well as others that involve count data, will be the topic of Chapter 17.

17

CONTINGENCY TABLES: THE ANALYSIS OF COUNT DATA

Many business experiments consist of enumerating the number of occurrences of some event. For example, we may count the number of defectives during a particular shift at a manufacturing plant, or the number of consumers who choose each of three brands of coffee, or the number of sales made by each of five automobile salespeople during the month of June.

In some instances, the objective of collecting the count data is to analyze the distribution of the counts in the various **classes or cells**. For example, we may want to estimate the proportion of smokers who prefer each of three different brands of cigarettes by counting the number in a sample of smokers who buy each brand. We will say that count data classified on a single scale has a **one-dimensional classification**. The analysis of one-dimensional count data is discussed in Section 17.1.

In many instances the objective of collecting the count data is to determine the relationship between two different methods of classifying the data. For example, we may be interested in knowing whether the size and model of the automobile purchased by new car buyers are related. Or, the relationship between the shift and the number of defectives produced in a plant could be of interest. When count data are classified in a **two-dimensional** table, we call the result a **contingency table**. The analysis of general contingency tables is discussed in Section 17.2. In Section 17.3 we consider some special cases of contingency table analyses.

17.1 ONE-DIMENSIONAL COUNT DATA: MULTINOMIAL DISTRIBUTION

Consumer-preference surveys can be valuable aids in making marketing decisions. Suppose a large supermarket chain conducts a consumer-preference survey by recording the brand of bread purchased by customers in its stores. Assume the chain carries three brands of bread, two major brands and its own store brand. The brand preferences of a random sample of 150 buyers are observed, and the resulting count data appear in Table 17.1. Do you think these data indicate that a preference exists for any of the brands?

TABLE 17.1
CONSUMER-PREFERENCE SURVEY

BRAND NAME A	BRAND NAME B	STORE BRAND
61	53	36

To answer this question, we have to know the underlying probability distribution of these count data. This distribution, called the **multinomial probability distribution,** is an extension of the binomial distribution (Section 6.4). The properties of the multinomial distribution are shown below.

PROPERTIES OF THE MULTINOMIAL PROBABILITY DISTRIBUTION

1. The experiment consists of n identical trials.
2. There are k possible outcomes to each trial.
3. The probabilities of the k outcomes, denoted by $p_1, p_2, \ldots, p_k$, remain the same from trial to trial; where $p_1 + p_2 + \cdots + p_k = 1$.
4. The trials are independent.
5. The random variables of interest are the counts in each of the k cells, denoted by $n_1, n_2, \ldots, n_k$.

You can see that the properties of the multinomial experiment closely resemble those of the binomial experiment and that, in fact, a binomial experiment is a multinomial experiment for the special case where $k = 2$.

In most practical applications involving a multinomial experiment, the true values of the k outcome probabilities, $p_1, p_2, \ldots, p_k$, will be unknown. The objective will therefore be to make inferences about these probabilities.

Note that the consumer-preference survey given in Table 17.1 satisfies the multinomial conditions. Suppose we want to test the null hypothesis that there is no preference for any of the three brands versus the research hypothesis that a preference exists for one or more of the brands. Then, letting

p_1 = Proportion of all customers who prefer brand name A

p_2 = Proportion of all customers who prefer brand name B

p_3 = Proportion of all customers who prefer the store brand

we want to test

$$H_0: \quad p_1 = p_2 = p_3 = \frac{1}{3} \quad \text{(no preference)}$$

$$H_a: \quad \text{At least one of the proportions exceeds } \frac{1}{3} \quad \text{(a preference exists)}$$

If the null hypothesis is true and $p_1 = p_2 = p_3 = \frac{1}{3}$, then we expect to see approximately $\frac{1}{3}$ of the customers in the sample purchase each brand. Or, more formally, the expected value (mean value) of the number of customers purchasing brand name A is given by

$$E(n_1) = np_1$$

and

$$E(n_1) = n\frac{1}{3} = (150)\frac{1}{3} = 50$$

Similarly, $E(n_2) = E(n_3) = 50$ if no preference exists.

The following test statistic measures the degree of agreement between the data and the null hypothesis:

$$X^2 = \frac{[n_1 - E(n_1)]^2}{E(n_1)} + \frac{[n_2 - E(n_2)]^2}{E(n_2)} + \frac{[n_3 - E(n_3)]^2}{E(n_3)}$$

$$= \frac{(n_1 - 50)^2}{50} + \frac{(n_2 - 50)^2}{50} + \frac{(n_3 - 50)^2}{50}$$

Note that the farther the observed numbers n_1, n_2, and n_3 are from their expected value (50), the larger X^2 will become. That is, large values of X^2 imply that the null hypothesis is false.

We have to know the distribution of X^2 in repeated sampling before we can decide whether the data indicate that a preference exists. When H_0 is true, X^2 can be shown

**FIGURE 17.1
REJECTION REGION
FOR CONSUMER-
PREFERENCE SURVEY**

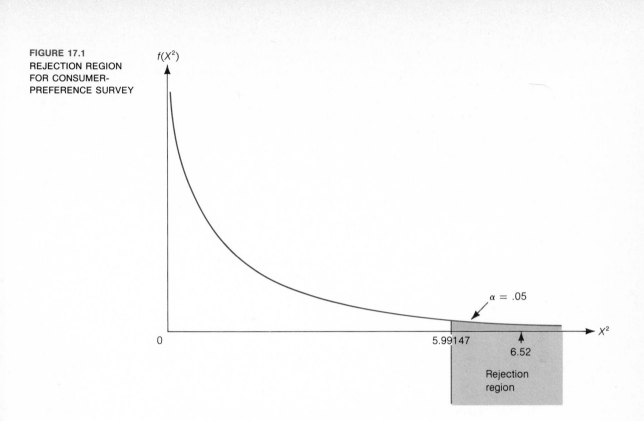

to have approximately a χ^2 distribution with $(k - 1)$ degrees of freedom.* The χ^2 distribution was first introduced in Section 16.3, and the critical values are given in Table X of Appendix B. For the consumer-preference survey in Table 17.1, we have the following rejection region: For $\alpha = .05$ and $k - 1 = 3 - 1 = 2$ df, we will reject H_0 if

$$X^2 > \chi^2_{.05,2}$$

This value of χ^2 (found in Table X) is 5.99147. See Figure 17.1. The computed value of the test statistic is

$$X^2 = \frac{(n_1 - 50)^2}{50} + \frac{(n_2 - 50)^2}{50} + \frac{(n_3 - 50)^2}{50}$$

$$= \frac{(61 - 50)^2}{50} + \frac{(53 - 50)^2}{50} + \frac{(36 - 50)^2}{50} = 6.52$$

Since the computed $X^2 = 6.52$ exceeds the critical value of 5.99147, we conclude at the $\alpha = .05$ level of significance that there does exist a customer preference for one or more of the brands of bread.

*The derivation of the degrees of freedom for X^2 involves the number of linear restrictions imposed on the count data. We will simply give the degrees of freedom for each usage of X^2, and refer the interested reader to the references at the end of the chapter for more detail.

The general form for a test of an hypothesis concerning multinomial probabilities is shown below.

A TEST OF AN HYPOTHESIS ABOUT MULTINOMIAL PROBABILITIES

H_0: $p_1 = p_{1,0}, p_2 = p_{2,0}, \ldots, p_k = p_{k,0}$, where $p_{1,0}, p_{2,0}, \ldots, p_{k,0}$ represent the hypothesized values of the multinomial probabilities

H_a: At least one of the multinomial probabilities does not equal its hypothesized value

Test statistic: $X^2 = \sum_{i=1}^{k} \dfrac{[n_i - E(n_i)]^2}{E(n_i)}$

where $E(n_i) = np_{i,0}$, the expected number of outcomes of type i under H_0. The total sample size is n.

Rejection region: $X^2 > \chi^2_{\alpha, k-1}$

EXAMPLE 17.1

A large firm has established what it hopes is an objective system of deciding on annual pay increases for its employees. The system is based on a series of evaluation scores determined by the supervisors of each employee. Employees with scores above 80 receive a merit pay increase, those with scores between 50 and 80 receive the standard increase, while those below 50 receive no increase. The firm designed the plan with the objective that on the average 25% of its employees would receive merit increases, 65% would receive standard increases, and 10% would receive no increase.

After 1 year of operation using the new plan, the distribution of pay increases for the 600 company employees was shown in Table 17.2. Test at the $\alpha = .01$ level to see whether these data indicate that the distribution of pay increases differs significantly from the proportions established by the firm.

TABLE 17.2
DISTRIBUTION OF PAY INCREASES

NO INCREASE	STANDARD INCREASE	MERIT INCREASE
42	365	193

Solution

Define

p_1 = Proportion of employees who receive no pay increase

p_2 = Proportion of employees who receive a standard increase

p_3 = Proportion of employees who receive a merit increase

Then the null hypothesis representing the firm's design is

H_0: $p_1 = .10, p_2 = .65, p_3 = .25$

and the alternative is

H_a: The proportions differ from the firm's proposed plan

Test statistic: $X^2 = \sum \dfrac{[n_i - E(n_i)]^2}{E(n_i)}$

where

$$E(n_1) = np_{1,0} = 600(.10) = 60$$
$$E(n_2) = np_{2,0} = 600(.65) = 390$$
$$E(n_3) = np_{3,0} = 600(.25) = 150$$

Rejection region: For $\alpha = .01$ and $k - 1 = 2$, reject H_0 if $X^2 > \chi^2_{.01,2}$, where (from Table X, Appendix B) $\chi^2_{.01,2} = 9.21034$. We now calculate the test statistic:

$$X^2 = \frac{(42 - 60)^2}{60} + \frac{(365 - 390)^2}{390} + \frac{(193 - 150)^2}{150} = 19.32$$

Since this value exceeds the table value of χ^2 (9.21034), the data provide strong evidence ($\alpha = .01$) that the company's pay plan is not working as planned.

By focusing on one particular outcome of a multinomial experiment, we can use the methods developed in Section 9.4 for a binomial proportion to establish a confidence interval for any one of the multinomial probabilities.* For example, if we want a 95% confidence interval for the proportion of the company's employees who will receive merit increases under the new system, we calculate

$$\hat{p}_3 \pm 1.96\sigma_{\hat{p}_3} = \hat{p}_3 \pm 1.96\sqrt{\frac{\hat{p}_3(1 - \hat{p}_3)}{n}} \quad \left(\text{where } \hat{p}_3 = \frac{n_3}{n} = \frac{193}{600} = .32 \right)$$

$$\approx .32 \pm 1.96\sqrt{\frac{(.32)(1 - .32)}{600}} = .32 \pm .04$$

Thus, we estimate that between 28% and 36% of the firm's employees will qualify for merit increases under the new plan. It appears that the firm will have to raise the requirements for merit increases in order to achieve the stated goal of a 25% employee qualification rate.

EXERCISES

17.1. After purchasing a policy from one life insurance company, a person has a certain period of time in which the policy can be cancelled without financial obligation. An insurance company is interested in seeing whether those who cancel a policy during this time period are as likely to be in one policy-size category as another. Records for 250 people who cancelled policies during this period were selected at random from company files with the results shown in the table. Is there sufficient

*Note that focusing on one outcome has the effect of lumping the other $(k - 1)$ outcomes into a single group. Thus, we obtain, in effect, two outcomes—or a binomial experiment.

evidence to conclude that the cancelled policies are not distributed equally among the five policy-size categories? Use $\alpha = .05$.

NUMBER OF PEOPLE CANCELLING PER POLICY-SIZE CATEGORY

SIZE OF POLICY (THOUSANDS OF DOLLARS)				
10	15	20	25	30
31	39	67	54	59

17.2. Supermarket chains often carry products with their own brand labels, and usually price them at a lower level than the nationally known brands. A supermarket conducted a taste test to determine whether there was a difference in taste among the four brands of ice cream it carried: a local brand (A) and three national brands (B, C, D). A sample of 200 people participated, and they indicated the following preferences:

	BRAND		
A	B	C	D
39	57	55	49

Is there evidence of a difference in preference for the four brands? Test at $\alpha = .05$.

17.3. Most companies target their advertising at specific income groups. To provide information to advertisers about its readers' incomes, a magazine decides to conduct a survey. A previous survey had indicated that 25% of the readers earned less than $15,000 per year, 60% earned from $15,000 to $25,000 per year, and 15% earned more than $25,000 per year. For the 6,478 people who responded to the latest survey, the income category breakdown was as follows:

INCOME CATEGORY	Less than $15,000	$15,000–25,000	More than $25,000
NUMBER OF RESPONDENTS	1,653	3,946	879

Do these new survey results indicate that the proportions of the readership in the three categories has changed since the previous survey?

**17.2
CONTINGENCY
TABLES**

The energy shortage has made many consumers more aware of the size of the automobiles they purchase. Suppose an automobile manufacturer who is interested in determining the relationship between the size and manufacturer of newly purchased automobiles randomly samples 1,000 recent buyers of American-made cars. The manufacturer classifies each buyer with respect to the size and make of the purchased automobile. The data are shown in Table 17.3, which is an example of a contingency table. Contingency tables consist of **multinomial count data classified on two scales, or dimensions.**

Let the probabilities for the multinomial experiment in Table 17.3 be those shown in Table 17.4. Thus, p_{11} is the probability that a new car buyer purchases a small car of make A. Note the probability totals, called **marginal probabilities,** for each row and column. The marginal probability p_1 is the probability that a small car is purchased, and the marginal probability p_A is the probability that a car of make A is purchased.

TABLE 17.3

	MANUFACTURER				TOTALS
	A	B	C	D	
SMALL	157	65	181	10	413
INTERMEDIATE	126	82	142	46	396
LARGE	58	45	60	28	191
TOTALS	341	192	383	84	1,000

TABLE 17.4
PROBABILITIES
FOR CONTINGENCY
TABLE 17.3

	MANUFACTURER				TOTALS
	A	B	C	D	
SMALL	p_{11}	p_{12}	p_{13}	p_{14}	p_1
INTERMEDIATE	p_{21}	p_{22}	p_{23}	p_{24}	p_2
LARGE	p_{31}	p_{32}	p_{33}	p_{34}	p_3
TOTALS	p_A	p_B	p_C	p_D	1

Suppose we want to know whether the two classifications, manufacturer and size, are dependent. That is, if we know which size car a buyer will choose, does that information give us a clue about the make of car the buyer will choose? In a probabilistic sense we know (Chapter 5) that independence of events A and B implies that $P(AB) = P(A)P(B)$. Similarly, in the contingency table analysis, if the two classifications are independent, the probability that an item is classified in any particular cell of the table is the product of the corresponding marginal probabilities. Thus, under the hypothesis of independence, in Table 17.4 we must have

$$p_{11} = p_1 p_A \qquad p_{12} = p_1 p_B$$

and so forth.

To test the hypothesis of independence, we use the same reasoning employed in the one-dimensional tests of Section 17.1. First, we calculate the expected, or mean, count in each cell by noting that the expected count in the upper left-hand corner of the table is just the total number of multinomial trials, n, times the probability, p_{11}. Then

$$E(n_{11}) = np_{11}$$

and, if the classifications are independent,

$$E(n_{11}) = np_1 p_A$$

We can estimate p_1 and p_A by the sample proportions $\hat{p}_1 = n_1/n$ and $\hat{p}_A = n_A/n$.

Thus, the estimate of the expected value $\hat{E}(n_{11})$ is

$$\hat{E}(n_{11}) = n\left(\frac{n_1}{n}\right)\left(\frac{n_A}{n}\right) = \frac{n_1 n_A}{n}$$

Similarly,

$$\hat{E}(n_{12}) = \frac{n_1 n_B}{n}$$

$$\vdots \qquad \vdots$$

$$\hat{E}(n_{34}) = \frac{n_3 n_D}{n}$$

Using the data in Table 17.3, we find

$$\hat{E}(n_{11}) = \frac{n_1 n_A}{n} = \frac{(413)(341)}{1,000} = 140.833$$

$$\hat{E}(n_{12}) = \frac{n_1 n_B}{n} = \frac{(413)(192)}{1,000} = 79.296$$

$$\vdots \qquad \vdots \qquad \vdots \qquad \vdots$$

$$\hat{E}(n_{34}) = \frac{n_3 n_D}{n} = \frac{(191)(84)}{1,000} = 16.044$$

The observed data and the estimated expected values are shown in Table 17.5.

TABLE 17.5
OBSERVED AND
ESTIMATED EXPECTED
(IN PARENTHESES)
COUNTS

| | MANUFACTURER | | | |
	A	B	C	D
SMALL	157	65	181	10
	(140.833)	(79.296)	(158.179)	(34.692)
INTERMEDIATE	126	82	142	46
	(135.036)	(76.032)	(151.668)	(33.264)
LARGE	58	45	60	28
	(65.131)	(36.672)	(73.153)	(16.044)

We now use the X^2 statistic to compare the observed and expected (estimated) counts in each cell of the contingency table:

$$X^2 = \frac{[n_{11} - \hat{E}(n_{11})]^2}{\hat{E}(n_{11})} + \frac{[n_{12} - \hat{E}(n_{12})]^2}{\hat{E}(n_{12})} + \cdots + \frac{[n_{34} - \hat{E}(n_{34})]^2}{\hat{E}(n_{34})}$$

$$= \sum_{i=1}^{3}\sum_{j=1}^{4} \frac{[n_{ij} - \hat{E}(n_{ij})]^2}{\hat{E}(n_{ij})}$$

Substituting the data of Table 17.5 into this expression,

$$X^2 = \frac{(157 - 140.833)^2}{140.833} + \frac{(65 - 79.296)^2}{79.296} + \cdots + \frac{(28 - 16.044)^2}{16.044} = 45.81$$

Large values of X^2 imply that the observed and expected counts do not closely agree, and therefore imply that the hypothesis of independence is false. To determine how large X^2 must be before it is too large to be attributed to chance, we make use of the fact that the sampling distribution of X^2 is approximately a χ^2 probability distribution when the classifications are independent.

In almost all contingency table analyses the appropriate degrees of freedom will be $(r-1)(c-1)$, where r is the number of rows and c is the number of columns in the table.

For the size and make of automobiles example, the degrees of freedom for χ^2 is $(r-1)(c-1) = (3-1)(4-1) = 6$. Then, for $\alpha = .05$, we reject the hypothesis of independence when

$$X^2 > \chi^2_{.05,6} = 12.5916$$

Since the computed $X^2 = 45.81$ exceeds the value 12.5916, we conclude that the size and make of a car selected by a purchaser are dependent events.

The general form of a contingency table is shown in Table 17.6. Note that the observed count in the (ij) cell is denoted by n_{ij}, the ith row total is r_i, the jth column total is c_j, and the total sample size is n. Using this notation, we give the general form of the contingency table test for independent classifications below.

TABLE 17.6
GENERAL $r \times c$
CONTINGENCY TABLE

		COLUMN 1	COLUMN 2	. . .	COLUMN c	ROW TOTALS
ROW	1	n_{11}	n_{12}	. . .	n_{1c}	r_1
	2	n_{21}	n_{22}	. . .	n_{2c}	r_2
	:	:	:		:	:
	r	n_{r1}	n_{r2}	. . .	n_{rc}	r_r
COLUMN TOTALS		c_1	c_2	. . .	c_c	n

GENERAL FORM OF A CONTINGENCY TABLE ANALYSIS: A TEST FOR INDEPENDENCE

H_0: The two classifications are independent

H_a: The two classifications are dependent

Test statistic: $\displaystyle X^2 = \sum_{i=1}^{r} \sum_{j=1}^{c} \frac{[n_{ij} - \hat{E}(n_{ij})]^2}{\hat{E}(n_{ij})}$

where

$$\hat{E}(n_{ij}) = \frac{r_i c_j}{n}$$

Rejection region: $X^2 > \chi^2_{\alpha,(r-1)(c-1)}$

EXAMPLE 17.2   A large brokerage firm wants to determine whether its affluent customers get better service from their brokers than lower-income customers. A sample of 500 customers is selected, and each customer is asked to rate his or her broker. The results are shown in Table 17.7. Test to see whether there is evidence that broker rating and customer income are dependent. Use $\alpha = .10$.

Solution   The first step is to calculate estimated expected cell frequencies under the assumption that the classifications are independent. Thus,

$$\hat{E}(n_{11}) = \frac{r_1 c_1}{n} = \frac{(153)(176)}{500} = 53.856$$

$$\hat{E}(n_{12}) = \frac{r_1 c_2}{n} = \frac{(153)(217)}{500} = 66.402$$

and so forth. All the estimated expected counts are shown in Table 17.7.

TABLE 17.7
OBSERVED AND
ESTIMATED EXPECTED
(IN PARENTHESES)
COUNTS FOR
EXAMPLE 17.2

| | | CUSTOMER'S INCOME | | | TOTALS |
		Under $20,000	$20,000–$50,000	Over $50,000	
	Outstanding	48 (53.856)	64 (66.402)	41 (32.742)	153
BROKER RATING	Average	98 (94.336)	120 (116.312)	50 (57.352)	268
	Poor	30 (27.808)	33 (34.286)	16 (16.906)	79
TOTALS		176	217	107	500

We are now ready to conduct the test for independence:

H_0: The rating a customer gives his or her broker is independent of the customer's income

H_a: Broker rating and customer income are dependent

Test statistic: $X^2 = \sum_{i=1}^{3} \sum_{j=1}^{3} \frac{[n_{ij} - \hat{E}(n_{ij})]^2}{\hat{E}(n_{ij})}$

Rejection region: For $\alpha = .10$ and $(r - 1)(c - 1) = (2)(2) = 4$ df, reject H_0 if

$$X^2 > X^2_{.10, 4}$$

where $X^2_{.10, 4} = 7.77944$.
The calculated value of X^2 is

$$X^2 = \frac{(48 - 53.856)^2}{53.856} + \frac{(64 - 66.402)^2}{66.402} + \frac{(16 - 16.906)^2}{16.906}$$

$$= 4.28$$

Since $X^2 = 4.28$ does not exceed the critical value, 7.77944, there is insufficient evidence at the $\alpha = .10$ level to conclude that broker rating and customer income are dependent. This survey does not support the firm's research hypothesis that affluent customers get better broker service than lower-income customers.

CASE STUDY 17.1   In their article ''Deceived Respondents: Once Bitten, Twice Shy,'' Sheets et al. (1974) explore a situation sometimes encountered by marketing research personnel:

> For some time, people engaged in marketing and other field-based research have had to contend with the consequences of a fairly widely used ploy in the direct selling field: gaining a potential customer's attention and interest by requesting cooperation in some sort of false survey. Despite the efforts of the American Association for Public Opinion Research, the American Marketing Association, and other groups, and regardless of Federal Trade Commission orders, this gambit is still in use, although perhaps somewhat modified.

The authors hypothesized that a previous exposure to a false survey will increase the probability that a person will refuse to respond in a legitimate survey. They conducted an experiment in which 104 individuals were asked to cooperate in a marketing research study. The fifty-four people who agreed to participate were then given a low-key sales presentation for a fictitious encyclopedia. Between 2 and 4 days later, forty-nine of the original fifty-four participants (five were not available) and seventy completely new individuals were interviewed. Each group was asked the same opening question. The results of this survey are presented in Table 17.8.

TABLE 17.8
EXPERIMENTAL AND
CONTROL GROUP
WILLINGNESS
TO PARTICIPATE IN
TRUE MARKET
RESEARCH

	EXPERIMENTAL	CONTROL	TOTALS
CONSENT	12	36	48
REFUSED	37	34	71
TOTALS	49	70	119

A χ^2 test was used to analyze these count data. The χ^2 test statistic is found to be 8.691, significant at the $\alpha = .005$ level. This indicates dependence of the refusal·rate on previous exposure to false surveys. The interpretation given to these data by Sheets et al. (1974) is:

> The findings indicate support for the hypothesis: false market surveys have a deleterious effect upon respondent willingness to cooperate in subsequent market research studies. By inference, households that have been previously exposed to false research are half again as likely to refuse to cooperate in legitimate field research as those who have not. The implication for field researchers is either to stay away from areas that have had recent, heavy, direct, sales efforts or to plan for higher refusal rates in such areas.

EXERCISES   17.4.   A study was conducted to help determine who takes advantage of sales and specials at food stores that advertise in newspapers. Shoppers were asked whether they usually check the advertisements before shopping and which of the following income brackets they fit into: annual income below $5,000, between $5,000 and $10,000, between $10,000 and $15,000, between $15,000 and $20,000, or over $20,000. The data are given in the table on page 536. Test to see whether the proportion of shoppers who watch the advertisements depends on income level. Use $\alpha = .10$.

	INCOME (THOUSANDS OF DOLLARS)				
	Less than 5	5–10	10–15	15–20	Over 20
NUMBER OF YES RESPONSES	33	62	31	14	6
NUMBER OF NO RESPONSES	3	8	19	15	14

17.5. One criterion used to evaluate employees in the assembly section of a large factory is the number of defective pieces per 1,000 parts produced. The quality control department wants to find out whether there is a relationship between years of experience and defect rate. Since the job is rather repetitious, after the initial training period, any improvement due to a learning effect might be offset by a decrease in the motivation of a worker. A defect rate is calculated for each worker for a yearly evaluation. The results for 100 workers are given in the table. Is there evidence of a relationship between defect rate and years of experience? Use $\alpha = .05$.

		YEARS OF EXPERIENCE (AFTER TRAINING PERIOD)		
		1	2–5	5–10
	High	6	9	9
DEFECT RATE	Average	9	19	23
	Low	7	8	10

17.6. An insurance company that sells hospitalization policies wants to know whether there is a relationship between the amount of hospitalization coverage a person has and the length of stay in the hospital. Records are selected at random at a large hospital by hospital personnel, and the information on length of stay and hospitalization coverage is given to the insurance company. The results are summarized in the table. Can you conclude that there is a relationship between length of stay and hospitalization coverage? Use $\alpha = .01$.

		LENGTH OF STAY IN HOSPITAL (DAYS)			
		5 or under	6–10	11–15	Over 15
	Under 25%	26	30	6	5
HOSPITALIZATION COVERAGE OF COSTS	25–50%	21	30	11	7
	51–75%	25	25	45	9
	Over 75%	11	32	17	11

17.3 CONTINGENCY TABLES WITH FIXED MARGINAL TOTALS

Suppose a national college placement firm wants to determine whether the job performance of college graduates is related to the region of the country in which the graduate attended college. The firm randomly selects 800 of last year's graduates who are currently employed, 200 from each of four regions: northeast (NE), southeast (SE), northwest (NW), southwest (SW). Then the employer of each graduate is contacted, and a rating of the employee's job performance is obtained. The results are shown in Table 17.9. The only difference between this contingency table and those in the previous section is that the row totals in Table 17.9 are all determined before the experiment is conducted, whereas, in Section 17.2 the marginal totals were not known until after the experiment was run. Fortunately, this fact does not affect the analysis. Thus, in order to test for dependence between job performance of college graduates and the region in which they attended college, we proceed as follows:

H_0: Job performance and region are independent

H_a: Job performance and region are related

Test statistic: $X^2 = \sum_{i=1}^{4} \sum_{j=1}^{3} \frac{[n_{ij} - \hat{E}(n_{ij})]^2}{\hat{E}(n_{ij})}$

TABLE 17.9
RESULTS OF JOB PERFORMANCE BY REGION

		JOB PERFORMANCE RATING			TOTALS
		Unsatisfactory	Satisfactory	Outstanding	
REGION	NE	21 (16.75)	121 (134.75)	58 (48.5)	200
	NW	18 (16.75)	133 (134.75)	49 (48.5)	200
	SE	10 (16.75)	147 (134.75)	43 (48.5)	200
	SW	18 (16.75)	138 (134.75)	44 (48.5)	200
TOTALS		67	539	194	800

Rejection region: For $\alpha = .05$ and $(r - 1)(c - 1) = 6$ df, we will reject H_0 if

$$X^2 > \chi^2_{.05,6}$$

where

$$\chi^2_{.05,6} = 12.5916$$

We calculate the estimated expected counts exactly as in Section 17.2:

$$\hat{E}(n_{11}) = \frac{r_1 c_1}{n} = \frac{(200)(67)}{800} = 16.75$$

$$\hat{E}(n_{12}) = \frac{r_1 c_2}{n} = \frac{(200)(539)}{800} = 134.75$$

and so forth. The estimated expected counts are shown in parentheses in Table 17.9. Then,

$$X^2 = \frac{(21 - 16.75)^2}{16.75} + \frac{(121 - 134.75)^2}{134.75} + \cdots + \frac{(44 - 48.5)^2}{48.5}$$

$$= 9.51$$

Since $X^2 = 9.51$ does not exceed the critical value of 12.5916, the placement firm cannot conclude at the $\alpha = .05$ level that job performance rating and region of college training are related.

<table>
<tr><td>

**17.4
CAUTION**

</td><td>

Because the X^2 statistic for testing hypotheses about multinomial probabilities is one of the most widely applied statistical tools, it is also one of the most abused statistical procedures. The user should always be certain that the experiment satisfies the properties of the multinomial experiment given in Section 17.1.* Furthermore, the user should be certain that the sample is drawn from the correct population—that is, from the population about which the inference is to be made. If in Section 17.3 the placement firm had chosen 200 graduates from one college in each region, no valid inference could be made about the entire region. We would obtain a comparison of four colleges, not four regions.

The use of the χ^2 probability distribution as an approximation to the sampling distribution for X^2 should be avoided when the expected counts are very small. The approximation can become very poor when these expected counts are small, and thus the true level may be very different from the tabled value. As a rule of thumb, an expected cell count of at least five will mean that the χ^2 probability distribution can be used to determine an approximate critical value.

Finally, if the X^2 value does not exceed the established critical value of χ^2, *do not accept* the hypothesis of independence. You would be risking a Type II error (accepting H_0 when it is false), and the probability β of committing such an error is unknown. The usual alternative hypothesis is that the classifications are dependent. Because there are literally an infinite number of ways two classifications can be dependent, it is difficult to calculate one or even several values of β to represent such a broad research hypothesis. Therefore, we avoid concluding that two classifications are independent, even when X^2 is small.

</td></tr>
<tr><td>

SUMMARY

</td><td>

The use of count data to test hypotheses about multinomial probabilities represents a very useful statistical technique. In a one-dimensional table we can use count data to test the hypothesis that the multinomial probabilities are equal to specified values. In the two-dimensional contingency table, we can test the independence of the two classifications. And these by no means exhaust the uses of the χ^2 statistic. Many other applications can be found in the references at the end of this chapter.

Caution should be exercised to avoid misuse of the χ^2 procedure. The experiment must be multinomial,* and the expected counts should not be too small if the χ^2 critical value is used. Also, the X^2 statistic should not always be viewed as the final answer. If two classifications are found to be dependent, many measures of association exist for quantifying the nature and strength of their dependence (see the references).

</td></tr>
</table>

*When the row (or column) totals are fixed, each row (or column) represents a separate multinomial experiment.

17.7. A restaurateur who owns restaurants in four cities is considering the possibility of building separate dining rooms for nonsmokers to accommodate customers who wish to dine in a smokefree environment. Since this would involve significant expense, the restaurateur plans to survey the customers at each restaurant and ask them the following question: "Would you be more comfortable dining here if there were a separate dining room for nonsmokers only?" Suppose seventy-five people were randomly selected and surveyed at each restaurant with the results shown in the table. Is there sufficient evidence to indicate that customer preferences are different for the four restaurants? Use $\alpha = .10$.

		ANSWERS TO QUESTION		
		Yes	No	It makes no difference
RESTAURANT	1	38	32	5
	2	42	26	7
	3	35	34	6
	4	37	30	8

17.8. A study was done on the accuracy of newspaper advertisements by the twenty-one food stores in a southeastern city. On each of 4 days, eight items were randomly selected from the advertisements for each store and the actual price was compared to the advertised price. Each of the stores was classified as one of the following types: national, regional chain A, regional chain B, regional chain C, or independent. Values in the table represent the number of items that were correctly and incorrectly priced.

TYPE OF CHAIN	NUMBER CORRECTLY PRICED	NUMBER INCORRECTLY PRICED
National chain	89	71
Regional chain A	53	107
Regional chain B	43	85
Regional chain C	32	96
Independent	41	55

a. Determine whether these data provide sufficient evidence to conclude that the proportion of correctly priced items differs from chain to chain. Use $\alpha = .10$.

b. Use a 95% confidence interval to estimate the proportion of correctly priced items in the stores in the national chain category.

17.9. Despite a good winning percentage, a certain major league baseball team has not drawn as many fans as one would expect. In hopes of finding ways to increase attendance, the management plans to interview fans who come to the games to find out why they come. One thing that the management might want to know is whether there are differences in support for the team among various age groups. Suppose the information in the table was collected during interviews with fans selected at random. Can you conclude that there is a relationship between age and number of games attended per year? Use $\alpha = .05$.

		NUMBER OF GAMES ATTENDED PER YEAR		
		1 or 2	3–5	Over 5
	Under 20	78	107	17
AGE OF FAN	21–30	147	87	13
	31–40	129	86	19
	41–55	55	103	40
	Over 55	23	74	22

17.10. If a company can identify times of day when accidents are most likely to occur, extra precautions can be instituted during those times. A random sampling of the accident report records over the last year at a plant gives the frequency of occurrence of accidents at the different hours of the workday. Can it be concluded from the data in the table that the proportions of accidents are different for the four time periods?

HOURS	1–2	3–4	5–6	7–8
NUMBER OF ACCIDENTS	31	28	45	47

17.11. An appliance store is having a sale and wants to determine which modes of advertising are effective. A survey of the customers who know about the sale reveals the breakdown given in the table. Is there evidence that the proportions of customers who learned about the sale differ for the four modes of advertising? Use $\alpha = .05$.

TELEVISION	NEWSPAPER	RADIO	WORD OF MOUTH
53	36	32	48

17.12. Refer to Exercise 17.11. Estimate the proportion who learn about the sale by word of mouth. Use a 90% confidence interval.

17.13. Employee integrity is important to the success of all businesses. Suppose an industrial security firm wants to conduct a study of criminal cases involving stolen company money in which employees have been found guilty. Among the data they record are the employee's salary (wages) and the amount of money stolen from the company for 400 recent cases. Does this information provide evidence of a relationship between employee income and amount stolen? Use $\alpha = .05$.

| | | AMOUNT STOLEN (THOUSANDS OF DOLLARS) | | | |
		Under 5	5–10	11–20	Over 20
INCOME OF EMPLOYEE (THOUSANDS OF DOLLARS)	Under 15	46	39	17	5
	15–25	78	79	61	19
	Over 25	5	14	25	12

17.14. A local bank plans to offer a special service to its young customers. To determine their economic interests, a survey of 100 people under 30 years of age is conducted. Each person is asked to identify his or her top two financial priorities from the six choices below:

FIRST PRIORITY	SECOND PRIORITY	NUMBER OF RESPONSES
Buy a car	Go on a trip	15
Car	Save money	14
Save	Car	22
Save	Trip	23
Trip	Car	10
Trip	Save	16
		100

Use the χ^2 test to determine whether the proportion of responses is the same for all six pairs of priorities. Test at $\alpha = .10$.

17.15. Along with the technological age comes the problem of workers being replaced by machines. A labor management organization wants to study the problem of workers displaced by automation within three industries. Case reports for 100 workers whose loss of job is directly attributable to technological advances are selected within each industry. For each worker selected it is determined whether he or she was given another job within the same company, found a job with another company in the same industry, found a job in a new industry, or has been unemployed for longer than 6 months. The results are given in the table. Does the plight of automation-displaced workers depend on the industry? Use $\alpha = .01$.

CURRENT STATUS OF AUTOMATION-DISPLACED WORKERS

		SAME COMPANY	NEW COMPANY (Same industry)	NEW INDUSTRY	UNEMPLOYED
INDUSTRY	A	62	11	20	7
	B	45	8	38	9
	C	68	19	8	5

17.16. Refer to Exercise 17.15. Estimate the difference between the proportions of displaced workers who find work in another industry for industries A and C. Use a 95% confidence interval.

17.17. A corporation owns several convenience stores that are open 24 hours a day. It is interested in knowing whether there is a relationship between the time of day and the size of purchase. One of its stores is selected at random to be involved in a study. Store records are collected over a period of several weeks and then 300 purchases are randomly selected. Since the register also prints the time of the purchase, this random selection procedure yields both amount and time of purchase. The information is summarized in the table. Is there a relationship between time and size of purchase? Use $\alpha = .05$.

		SIZE OF PURCHASE		
		$2 or less	$2.01–$7	Over $7
	8 AM–4 PM	65	38	14
TIME OF PURCHASE	4 PM–12 midnight	61	49	10
	12 midnight–8 AM	29	27	7

17.18. Refer to Exercise 17.17. Use a 90% confidence interval to estimate the difference between the proportions of customers who spend $2 or less for the periods 8 AM–4 PM and 12 midnight–8 AM.

17.19. A city has three television stations. Each station has its own evening news program from 6:00 to 6:30 PM every weekday. An advertising firm wants to know whether there is an unequal breakdown of the evening news audience among the three stations. One hundred people are selected at random from those who watch the evening news on one of these three stations. Each is asked to specify which news program he or she watches. Do the results in the table provide sufficient evidence to indicate that the three stations do not have equal shares of the evening news audience? Use $\alpha = .05$.

STATION	1	2	3
NUMBER OF VIEWERS	35	43	22

17.20. Several life insurance firms have policies geared to college students. To get more information about this group, a major insurance firm interviewed college students to find out the type of life insurance owned, if any. The following table was produced after surveying 1,600 students:

	OWNED A TERM POLICY	OWNED A WHOLE-LIFE POLICY	NO INSURANCE
Females	116	27	676
Males	215	33	533

Is there evidence that the life insurance situation of students depends on their sex?

17.21. Refer to Exercise 17.20. Estimate the difference in the proportions of female and male college students who own no life insurance.

17.22. A statistical analysis is to be done on a set of data consisting of 1,000 monthly salaries. The analysis requires the assumption that the sample was drawn from a normal distribution. A preliminary test, called the χ^2 *goodness of fit test,* can be used to help determine whether it is plausible to assume that the sample is from a normal distribution. Suppose the mean and standard deviation of the 1,000 salaries are $900 and $50, respectively. Using the standard normal tables, we can approximate the probabilities of being in the intervals listed in the table. The third column represents the expected number of the 1,000 salaries to be found in each interval if the sample was drawn from a normal distribution with $\mu = 900$ and $\sigma = 50$. Suppose the last column contains the actual observed frequencies in the sample. Large differences between the observed and expected frequencies cast doubt on the normality assumption.

INTERVAL	PROBABILITY	EXPECTED FREQUENCY	OBSERVED FREQUENCY
Less than $800	.023	23	26
$800–$850	.136	136	146
$850–$900	.341	341	361
$900–$950	.341	341	311
$950–$1,000	.136	136	143
Above $1,000	.023	23	13

a. Compute the X^2 statistic based upon the observed and expected frequencies—just as you would in a contingency table analysis.
b. Find the tabulated χ^2 value when $\alpha = .05$ and there are 3 df (there are 3 df associated with this X^2 statistic).
c. Based upon the X^2 statistic and the tabulated χ^2 value, is there evidence that the salary distribution is nonnormal?

ON YOUR OWN . . .

Market researchers rely on surveys to estimate the proportions of the consumer market that prefer various brands of a product. Choose a product with which you are familiar, and guesstimate the proportion of consumers you think favor the major brands of the product. (Choose a product for which there are at least three major brands sold in the same store.)

Now go to a store that carries these brands, and observe how many consumers purchase each brand. Be sure to observe long enough so that at least five (and preferably at least ten) purchases of each brand have been made. Also, quit sampling after a predetermined length of time or after a predetermined number of total purchases, rather than at some arbitrary time, which could bias your results.

Use the count data to test the null hypothesis that the true proportions of consumers who favor each brand equal your presampling guesstimates of the proportions. Would failure to reject this null hypothesis imply that your guesstimates are correct?

REFERENCES

Neter, J., Wasserman, W., & Whitmore, G. A. *Fundamental statistics for business and economics.* 4th ed. Boston: Allyn and Bacon, 1973. Chapter 19.

Sheets, T., Radlinski, A., Kohne, J., & Brunner, G. A. "Deceived respondents: Once bitten, twice shy." *Public Opinion Quarterly,* 1974, *18,* 261–263.

Siegel, S. *Nonparametric statistics for the behavioral sciences.* New York: McGraw-Hill, 1956. Chapter 9.

Winkler, R. L., & Hays, W. L. *Statistics: Probability, inference and decision,* 2d ed. New York: Holt, Rinehart, and Winston, 1975. Chapter 12.

APPENDIX

A

BASIC
COUNTING RULES

Simple events associated with many experiments have identical characteristics. If you can develop a counting rule to count the number of simple events for such an experiment, it can be used to aid in the solution of many probability problems. For example, many experiments involve sampling n elements from a population of N. Then, as explained in Section 5.1, we can use the formula

$$\binom{N}{n} = \frac{N!}{n!(N-n)!}$$

to find the number of different samples of n elements that could be selected from the total of N elements. This gives the number of simple events for the experiment.

Here, we give you a few useful counting rules. You should learn the characteristics of the situation to which each rule applies. Then, when working a probability problem, carefully examine the experiment to see whether you can use one of the rules.

Learning how to decide whether a particular counting rule applies to an experiment takes patience and practice. If you want to develop this skill, try to use the rules to solve some of the exercises in Chapter 5. You will also find large numbers of exercises in the texts listed in the references at the end of Chapter 5. Proofs of the rules below can be found in the text by W. Feller listed in the references to Chapter 5.

1. **Multiplicative Rule:** You have k sets of different elements, n_1 in the first set, n_2 in the second set, . . . , and n_k in the kth set. Suppose you want to form a sample of k elements by taking one element from each of the k sets. The number of different samples that can be formed is the product

$$n_1 \cdot n_2 \cdot n_3 \cdots n_k$$

EXAMPLE A.1

If a product can be shipped by four different airlines and each airline can ship via three different routes, how many ways can you ship the product?

Solution

A method of shipment corresponds to a pairing of one airline and one route. Therefore, $k = 2$, the number of airlines is $n_1 = 4$, the number of routes is $n_2 = 3$, and the number of ways to ship the product is $n_1 \cdot n_2 = (4)(3) = 12$.

How the multiplicative rule works can be seen by using a **decision tree**. The airline choice is shown by three branching lines in Figure A.1.

FIGURE A.1
DECISION TREE FOR
EXAMPLE A.1

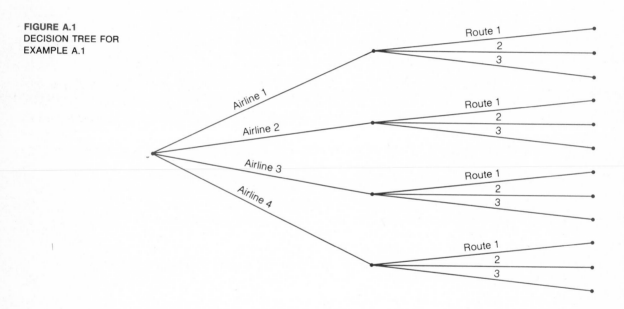

EXAMPLE A.2

You have twenty candidates for three different executive positions, E_1, E_2, and E_3. How many different ways could you fill the positions?

Solution

For this example, there are $k = 3$ sets of elements:

    Set 1:   The candidate available to fill position E_1

    Set 2:   The candidates remaining (after filling E_1) that are available to fill E_2

    Set 3:   The candidates remaining (after filling E_1 and E_2) that are available to fill E_3

The numbers of elements in the sets are $n_1 = 20$, $n_2 = 19$, $n_3 = 18$. Thus, the number of different ways to fill the three positions is $n_1 \cdot n_2 \cdot n_3 = (20)(19)(18) = 6{,}840$.

2. **Partitions Rule:** You have a single set of N distinctly different elements and you want to partition them into k sets, the first set containing n_1 elements, the second containing n_2 elements, . . . , and the kth containing n_k elements. The number of different partitions is

$$\frac{N!}{n_1!n_2!\cdots n_k!} \qquad \text{where} \qquad n_1 + n_2 + n_3 + \cdots + n_k = N$$

EXAMPLE A.3

You have twelve construction workers and you want to assign three to job 1, four to job 2, and five to job 3. How many different ways could you make this assignment?

Solution

For this example, $k = 3$ (corresponding to the $k = 3$ job sites), $N = 12$, and $n_1 = 3$, $n_2 = 4$, $n_3 = 5$. Then, the number of different ways to assign the workers to the job sites is

$$\frac{N!}{n_1!n_2!n_3!} = \frac{12!}{3!4!5!} = \frac{12 \cdot 11 \cdot 10 \cdots 3 \cdot 2 \cdot 1}{(3 \cdot 2 \cdot 1)(4 \cdot 3 \cdot 2 \cdot 1)(5 \cdot 4 \cdot 3 \cdot 2 \cdot 1)}$$

$$= 27{,}720$$

3. **Combinations Rule:** The combinations rule given in Chapter 5 is a special case ($k = 2$) of the partitions rule. That is, sampling is equivalent to partitioning a set of N elements into $k = 2$ groups—elements that appear in the sample and those that do not. Let $n_1 = n$, the number of elements in the sample, and $n_2 = N - n$, the number of elements remaining. Then the number of different samples of n elements that can be selected from N is

$$\frac{N!}{n_1!n_2!} = \frac{N!}{n!(N - n)!} = \binom{N}{n}$$

This formula was given in Section 5.1.

EXAMPLE A.4

How many samples of four firemen can be selected from a group of ten?

Solution

$N = 10$, $n = 4$; then,

$$\binom{N}{n} = \binom{10}{4} = \frac{10!}{4!6!} = \frac{10 \cdot 9 \cdot 8 \cdots 3 \cdot 2 \cdot 1}{(4 \cdot 3 \cdot 2 \cdot 1)(6 \cdot 5 \cdots 2 \cdot 1)}$$

$$= 210$$

APPENDIX
B
TABLES

TABLE I
RANDOM NUMBERS

ROW \ COLUMN	1	2	3	4	5	6	7	8	9	10	11	12	13	14
1	10480	15011	01536	02011	81647	91646	69179	14194	62590	36207	20969	99570	91291	90700
2	22368	46573	25595	85393	30995	89198	27982	53402	93965	34095	52666	19174	39615	99505
3	24130	48360	22527	97265	76393	64809	15179	24830	49340	32081	30680	19655	63348	58629
4	42167	93093	06243	61680	07856	16376	39440	53537	71341	57004	00849	74917	97758	16379
5	37570	39975	81837	16656	06121	91782	60468	81305	49684	60672	14110	06927	01263	54613
6	77921	06907	11008	42751	27756	53498	18602	70659	90655	15053	21916	81825	44394	42880
7	99562	72905	56420	69994	98872	31016	71194	18738	44013	48840	63213	21069	10634	12952
8	96301	91977	05463	07972	18876	20922	94595	56869	69014	60045	18425	84903	42508	32307
9	89579	14342	63661	10281	17453	18103	57740	84378	25331	12566	58678	44947	05585	56941
10	85475	36857	53342	53988	53060	59533	38867	62300	08158	17983	16439	11458	18593	64952
11	28918	69578	88231	33276	70997	79936	56865	05859	90106	31595	01547	85590	91610	78188
12	63553	40961	48235	03427	49626	69445	18663	72695	52180	20847	12234	90511	33703	90322
13	09429	93969	52636	92737	88974	33488	36320	17617	30015	08272	84115	27156	30613	74952
14	10365	61129	87529	85689	48237	52267	67689	93394	01511	26358	85104	20285	29975	89868
15	07119	97336	71048	08178	77233	13916	47564	81056	97735	85977	29372	74461	28551	90707
16	51085	12765	51821	51259	77452	16308	60756	92144	49442	53900	70960	63990	75601	40719
17	02368	21382	52404	60268	89368	19885	55322	44819	01188	65255	64835	44919	05944	55157
18	01011	54092	33362	94904	31273	04146	18594	29852	71585	85030	51132	01915	92747	64951
19	52162	53916	46369	58586	23216	14513	83149	98736	23495	64350	94738	17752	35156	35749
20	07056	97628	33787	09998	42698	06691	76988	13602	51851	46104	88916	19509	25625	58104
21	48663	91245	85828	14346	09172	30168	90229	04734	59193	22178	30421	61666	99904	32812
22	54164	58492	22421	74103	47070	25306	76468	26384	58151	06646	21524	15227	96909	44592
23	32639	32363	05597	24200	13363	38005	94342	28728	35806	06912	17012	64161	18296	22851
24	29334	27001	87637	87308	58731	00256	45834	15398	46557	41135	10367	07684	36188	18510
25	02488	33062	28834	07351	19731	92420	60952	61280	50001	67658	32586	86679	50720	94953

TABLE I CONTINUED

COLUMN ROW	1	2	3	4	5	6	7	8	9	10	11	12	13	14
26	81525	72295	04839	96423	24878	82651	66566	14778	76797	14780	13300	87074	79666	95725
27	29676	20591	68086	26432	46901	20849	89768	81536	86645	12659	92259	57102	80428	25280
28	00742	57392	39064	66432	84673	40027	32832	61362	98947	96067	64760	64584	96096	98253
29	05366	04213	25669	26422	44407	44048	37937	63904	45766	66134	75470	66520	34693	90449
30	91921	26418	64117	94305	26766	25940	39972	22209	71500	64568	91402	42416	07844	69618
31	00582	04711	87917	77341	42206	35126	74087	99547	81817	42607	43808	76655	62028	76630
32	00725	69884	62797	56170	86324	88072	76222	36086	84637	93161	76038	65855	77919	88006
33	69011	65795	95876	55293	18988	27354	26575	08625	40801	59920	29841	80150	12777	48501
34	25976	57948	29888	88604	67917	48708	18912	82271	65424	69774	33611	54262	85963	03547
35	09763	83473	73577	12908	30883	18317	28290	35797	05998	41688	34952	37888	38917	88050
36	91576	42595	27958	30134	04024	86385	29880	99730	55536	84855	29080	09250	79656	73211
37	17955	56349	90999	49127	20044	59931	06115	20542	18059	02008	73708	83517	36103	42791
38	46503	18584	18845	49618	02304	51038	20655	58727	28168	15475	56942	53389	20562	87338
39	92157	89634	94824	78171	84610	82834	09922	25417	44137	48413	25555	21246	35509	20468
40	14577	62765	35605	81263	39667	47358	56873	56307	61607	49518	89656	20103	77490	18062
41	98427	07523	33362	64270	01638	92477	66969	98420	04880	45585	46565	04102	46880	45709
42	34914	63976	88720	82765	34476	17032	87589	40836	32427	70002	70663	88863	77775	69348
43	70060	28277	39475	46473	23219	53416	94970	25832	69975	94884	19661	72828	00102	66794
44	53976	54914	06990	67245	68350	82948	11398	42878	80287	88267	47363	46634	06541	97809
45	76072	29515	40980	07391	58745	25774	22987	80059	39911	96189	41151	14222	60697	59583
46	90725	52210	83974	29992	65831	38857	50490	83765	55657	14361	31720	57375	56228	41546
47	64364	67412	33339	31926	14883	24413	59744	92351	97473	89286	35931	04110	23726	51900
48	08962	00358	31662	25388	61642	34072	81249	35648	56891	69352	48373	45578	78547	81788
49	95012	68379	93526	70765	10592	04542	76463	54328	02349	17247	28865	14777	62730	92277
50	15664	10493	20492	38391	91132	21999	59516	81652	27195	48223	46751	22923	32261	85653
51	16408	81899	04153	53381	79401	21438	83035	92350	36693	31238	59649	91754	72772	02338
52	18629	81953	05520	91962	04739	13092	97662	24822	94730	06496	35090	04822	86774	98289
53	73115	35101	47498	87637	99016	71060	88824	71013	18735	20286	23153	72924	35165	43040
54	57491	16703	23167	49323	45021	33132	12544	41035	80780	45393	44812	12515	98931	91202
55	30405	83946	23792	14422	15059	45799	22716	19792	09983	74353	68668	30429	70735	25499
56	16631	35006	85900	98275	32388	52390	16815	69298	82732	38480	73817	32523	41961	44437
57	96773	20206	42559	78985	05300	22164	24369	54224	35083	19687	11052	91491	60383	19746
58	38935	64202	14349	82674	66523	44133	00697	35552	35970	19124	63318	29686	03387	59846
59	31624	76384	17403	53363	44167	64486	64758	75366	76554	31601	12614	33072	60332	92325
60	78919	19474	23632	27889	47914	02584	37680	20801	72152	39339	34806	08930	85001	87820
61	03931	33309	57047	74211	63445	17361	62825	39908	05607	91284	68833	25570	38818	46920
62	74426	33278	43972	10119	89917	15665	52872	73823	73144	88662	88970	74492	51805	99378

63	09066	00903	20795	95452	92648	45454	09552	88815	16553	51125	79375	97596	16296	66092
64	42238	12426	87025	14267	20979	04508	64535	31355	86064	29472	47689	05974	52468	16834
65	16153	08002	26504	41744	81959	65642	74240	56302	00033	67107	77510	70625	28725	34191
66	21457	40742	29820	96783	29400	21840	15035	34537	33310	06116	95240	15957	16572	06004
67	21581	57802	02050	89728	17937	37621	47075	42080	97403	48626	68995	43805	33386	21597
68	55612	78095	83197	33732	05810	24813	86902	60397	16489	03264	88525	42786	05269	92532
69	44657	66999	99324	51281	84463	60563	79312	93454	68876	25471	93911	25650	12682	73572
70	91340	84979	46949	81973	37949	61023	43997	15263	80644	43942	89203	71795	99533	50501
71	91227	21199	31935	27022	84067	05462	35216	14486	29891	68607	41867	14951	91696	85065
72	50001	38140	66321	19924	72163	09538	12151	06878	91903	18749	34405	56087	82790	70925
73	65390	05224	72958	28609	81406	39147	25549	48542	42627	45233	57202	94617	23772	07896
74	27504	96131	83944	41575	10573	08619	64482	73923	36152	05184	94142	25299	84387	34925
75	37169	94851	39117	89632	00959	16487	65536	49071	39782	17095	02330	74301	00275	48280
76	11508	70225	51111	38351	19444	66499	71945	05422	13442	78675	84081	66938	93654	59894
77	37449	30362	06694	54690	04052	53115	62757	95348	78662	11163	81651	50245	34971	52924
78	46515	70331	85922	38329	57015	15765	97161	17869	45349	61796	66345	81073	49106	79860
79	30986	81223	42416	58353	21532	30502	32305	86482	05174	07901	54339	58861	74818	46942
80	63798	64995	46583	09785	44160	78128	83991	42865	92520	83531	80377	35909	81250	54238
81	82486	84846	99254	67632	43218	50076	21361	64816	51202	88124	41870	52689	51275	83556
82	21885	32906	92431	09060	64297	51674	64126	62570	26123	05155	59194	52799	28225	85762
83	60336	98782	07408	53458	13564	59089	26445	29789	85205	41001	12535	12133	14645	23541
84	43937	46891	24010	25560	86355	33941	25786	54990	71899	15475	95434	98227	21824	19585
85	97656	63175	89303	16275	07100	92063	21942	18611	47348	20203	18534	03862	78095	50136
86	03299	01221	05418	38982	55758	92237	26759	86367	21216	98442	08303	56613	91511	75928
87	79626	06486	03574	17668	07785	76020	79924	25651	83325	88428	85076	72811	22717	50585
88	85636	68335	47539	03129	65651	11977	02510	26113	99447	68645	34327	15152	55230	93448
89	18039	14367	61337	06177	12143	46609	32989	74014	64708	00533	35398	58408	13261	47908
90	08362	15656	60627	36478	65648	16764	53412	09013	07832	41574	17639	82163	60859	75567
91	79556	29068	04142	16268	15387	12856	66227	38358	22478	73373	88732	09443	82558	05250
92	92608	82674	27072	32534	17075	27698	98204	63863	11951	34648	88022	56148	34925	57031
93	23982	25835	40055	67006	12293	14827	23235	35071	99704	37543	11601		35503	85171
94	09915	96306	05908	97901	28395	14186	00821	80703	70426	75647	76310	88717	37890	40129
95	59037	33300	26695	62247	69927	76123	50842	43834	86654	70959	79725	93872	28117	19233
96	42488	78077	69882	61657	34136	79180	97526	43092	04098	73571	80799	76536	71255	64239
97	46764	86273	63003	93017	31204	36692	40202	35275	57306	55543	53203	18098	47625	88684
98	03237	45430	55417	63282	90816	17349	88298	90183	36600	78406	06216	95787	42579	90730
99	86591	81482	52667	61582	14972	90053	89534	76036	49199	43716	97548	04379	46370	28672
100	38534	01715	94964	87288	65680	43772	39560	12918	62738	19636	51132	25739	62947	

Source: Abridged from W. H. Beyer, Ed., *Handbook of Tables for Probability and Statistics*, 2d ed. (Cleveland: The Chemical Rubber Company), 1968. Reproduced by permission of the publisher.

TABLE II
BINOMIAL PROBABILITIES

Tabulated values are $\sum\limits_{x=0}^{k} p(x)$. (Computations are rounded at the third decimal place.)

a. $n = 5$

k	0.01	0.05	0.10	0.20	0.30	0.40	0.50	0.60	0.70	0.80	0.90	0.95	0.99
0	.951	.774	.590	.328	.168	.078	.031	.010	.002	.000	.000	.000	.000
1	.999	.977	.919	.737	.528	.337	.188	.087	.031	.007	.000	.000	.000
2	1.000	.999	.991	.942	.837	.683	.500	.317	.163	.058	.009	.001	.000
3	1.000	1.000	1.000	.993	.969	.913	.812	.663	.472	.263	.081	.023	.001
4	1.000	1.000	1.000	1.000	.998	.990	.969	.922	.832	.672	.410	.226	.049

b. $n = 10$

k	0.01	0.05	0.10	0.20	0.30	0.40	0.50	0.60	0.70	0.80	0.90	0.95	0.99
0	.904	.599	.349	.107	.028	.006	.001	.000	.000	.000	.000	.000	.000
1	.996	.914	.736	.376	.149	.046	.011	.002	.000	.000	.000	.000	.000
2	1.000	.988	.930	.678	.383	.167	.055	.012	.002	.000	.000	.000	.000
3	1.000	.999	.987	.879	.650	.382	.172	.055	.011	.001	.000	.000	.000
4	1.000	1.000	.998	.967	.850	.633	.377	.166	.047	.006	.000	.000	.000
5	1.000	1.000	1.000	.994	.953	.834	.623	.367	.150	.033	.002	.000	.000
6	1.000	1.000	1.000	.999	.989	.945	.828	.618	.350	.121	.013	.001	.000
7	1.000	1.000	1.000	1.000	.998	.988	.945	.833	.617	.322	.070	.012	.000
8	1.000	1.000	1.000	1.000	1.000	.998	.989	.954	.851	.624	.264	.086	.004
9	1.000	1.000	1.000	1.000	1.000	1.000	.999	.994	.972	.893	.651	.401	.096

c. $n = 15$

k	0.01	0.05	0.10	0.20	0.30	0.40	0.50	0.60	0.70	0.80	0.90	0.95	0.99
0	.860	.463	.206	.035	.005	.000	.000	.000	.000	.000	.000	.000	.000
1	.990	.829	.549	.167	.035	.005	.000	.000	.000	.000	.000	.000	.000
2	1.000	.964	.816	.398	.127	.027	.004	.000	.000	.000	.000	.000	.000
3	1.000	.995	.944	.648	.297	.091	.018	.002	.000	.000	.000	.000	.000
4	1.000	.999	.987	.836	.515	.217	.059	.009	.001	.000	.000	.000	.000
5	1.000	1.000	.998	.939	.722	.403	.151	.034	.004	.000	.000	.000	.000
6	1.000	1.000	1.000	.982	.869	.610	.304	.095	.015	.001	.000	.000	.000
7	1.000	1.000	1.000	.996	.950	.787	.500	.213	.050	.004	.000	.000	.000
8	1.000	1.000	1.000	.999	.985	.905	.696	.390	.131	.018	.000	.000	.000
9	1.000	1.000	1.000	1.000	.996	.966	.849	.597	.278	.061	.002	.000	.000
10	1.000	1.000	1.000	1.000	.999	.991	.941	.783	.485	.164	.013	.001	.000
11	1.000	1.000	1.000	1.000	1.000	.998	.982	.909	.703	.352	.056	.005	.000
12	1.000	1.000	1.000	1.000	1.000	1.000	.996	.973	.873	.602	.184	.036	.000
13	1.000	1.000	1.000	1.000	1.000	1.000	1.000	.995	.965	.833	.451	.171	.010
14	1.000	1.000	1.000	1.000	1.000	1.000	1.000	1.000	.995	.965	.794	.537	.140

d. $n = 20$

k \ p	0.01	0.05	0.10	0.20	0.30	0.40	0.50	0.60	0.70	0.80	0.90	0.95	0.99
0	.818	.358	.122	.002	.001	.000	.000	.000	.000	.000	.000	.000	.000
1	.983	.736	.392	.069	.008	.001	.000	.000	.000	.000	.000	.000	.000
2	.999	.925	.677	.206	.035	.004	.000	.000	.000	.000	.000	.000	.000
3	1.000	.984	.867	.411	.107	.016	.001	.000	.000	.000	.000	.000	.000
4	1.000	.997	.957	.630	.238	.051	.006	.000	.000	.000	.000	.000	.000
5	1.000	1.000	.989	.804	.416	.126	.021	.002	.000	.000	.000	.000	.000
6	1.000	1.000	.998	.913	.608	.250	.058	.006	.000	.000	.000	.000	.000
7	1.000	1.000	1.000	.968	.772	.416	.132	.021	.001	.000	.000	.000	.000
8	1.000	1.000	1.000	.990	.887	.596	.252	.057	.005	.000	.000	.000	.000
9	1.000	1.000	1.000	.997	.952	.755	.412	.128	.017	.001	.000	.000	.000
10	1.000	1.000	1.000	.999	.983	.872	.588	.245	.048	.003	.000	.000	.000
11	1.000	1.000	1.000	1.000	.995	.943	.748	.404	.113	.010	.000	.000	.000
12	1.000	1.000	1.000	1.000	.999	.979	.868	.584	.228	.032	.000	.000	.000
13	1.000	1.000	1.000	1.000	1.000	.994	.942	.750	.392	.087	.002	.000	.000
14	1.000	1.000	1.000	1.000	1.000	.998	.979	.874	.584	.196	.011	.000	.000
15	1.000	1.000	1.000	1.000	1.000	1.000	.994	.949	.762	.370	.043	.003	.000
16	1.000	1.000	1.000	1.000	1.000	1.000	.999	.984	.893	.589	.133	.016	.000
17	1.000	1.000	1.000	1.000	1.000	1.000	1.000	.996	.965	.794	.323	.075	.001
18	1.000	1.000	1.000	1.000	1.000	1.000	1.000	.999	.992	.931	.608	.264	.017
19	1.000	1.000	1.000	1.000	1.000	1.000	1.000	1.000	.999	.988	.878	.642	.182

TABLE II
CONTINUED

e. $n = 25$

k \ p	0.01	0.05	0.10	0.20	0.30	0.40	0.50	0.60	0.70	0.80	0.90	0.95	0.99
0	.778	.277	.072	.004	.000	.000	.000	.000	.000	.000	.000	.000	.000
1	.974	.642	.271	.027	.002	.000	.000	.000	.000	.000	.000	.000	.000
2	.998	.873	.537	.098	.009	.000	.000	.000	.000	.000	.000	.000	.000
3	1.000	.966	.764	.234	.033	.002	.000	.000	.000	.000	.000	.000	.000
4	1.000	.993	.902	.421	.090	.009	.000	.000	.000	.000	.000	.000	.000
5	1.000	.999	.967	.617	.193	.029	.002	.000	.000	.000	.000	.000	.000
6	1.000	1.000	.991	.780	.341	.074	.007	.000	.000	.000	.000	.000	.000
7	1.000	1.000	.998	.891	.512	.154	.022	.001	.000	.000	.000	.000	.000
8	1.000	1.000	1.000	.953	.677	.274	.054	.004	.000	.000	.000	.000	.000
9	1.000	1.000	1.000	.983	.811	.425	.115	.013	.000	.000	.000	.000	.000
10	1.000	1.000	1.000	.994	.902	.586	.212	.034	.002	.000	.000	.000	.000
11	1.000	1.000	1.000	.998	.956	.732	.345	.078	.006	.000	.000	.000	.000
12	1.000	1.000	1.000	1.000	.983	.846	.500	.154	.017	.000	.000	.000	.000
13	1.000	1.000	1.000	1.000	.994	.922	.655	.268	.044	.002	.000	.000	.000
14	1.000	1.000	1.000	1.000	.998	.966	.788	.414	.098	.006	.000	.000	.000
15	1.000	1.000	1.000	1.000	1.000	.987	.885	.575	.189	.017	.000	.000	.000
16	1.000	1.000	1.000	1.000	1.000	.996	.946	.726	.323	.047	.000	.000	.000
17	1.000	1.000	1.000	1.000	1.000	.999	.978	.846	.488	.109	.002	.000	.000
18	1.000	1.000	1.000	1.000	1.000	1.000	.993	.926	.659	.220	.009	.000	.000
19	1.000	1.000	1.000	1.000	1.000	1.000	.998	.971	.807	.383	.033	.001	.000
20	1.000	1.000	1.000	1.000	1.000	1.000	1.000	.991	.910	.579	.098	.007	.000
21	1.000	1.000	1.000	1.000	1.000	1.000	1.000	.998	.967	.766	.236	.034	.000
22	1.000	1.000	1.000	1.000	1.000	1.000	1.000	1.000	.991	.902	.463	.127	.002
23	1.000	1.000	1.000	1.000	1.000	1.000	1.000	1.000	.998	.973	.729	.358	.026
24	1.000	1.000	1.000	1.000	1.000	1.000	1.000	1.000	1.000	.996	.928	.723	.222

TABLE III
EXPONENTIALS

λ	$e^{-\lambda}$	λ	$e^{-\lambda}$	λ	$e^{-\lambda}$	λ	$e^{-\lambda}$
0.00	1.000000	2.60	.074274	5.10	.006097	7.60	.000501
0.10	.904837	2.70	.067206	5.20	.005517	7.70	.000453
0.20	.818731	2.80	.060810	5.30	.004992	7.80	.000410
0.30	.740818	2.90	.055023	5.40	.004517	7.90	.000371
0.40	.670320	3.00	.049787	5.50	.004087	8.00	.000336
0.50	.606531	3.10	.045049	5.60	.003698	8.10	.000304
0.60	.548812	3.20	.040762	5.70	.003346	8.20	.000275
0.70	.496585	3.30	.036883	5.80	.003028	8.30	.000249
0.80	.449329	3.40	.033373	5.90	.002739	8.40	.000225
0.90	.406570	3.50	.030197	6.00	.002479	8.50	.000204
1.00	.367879	3.60	.027324	6.10	.002243	8.60	.000184
1.10	.332871	3.70	.024724	6.20	.002029	8.70	.000167
1.20	.301194	3.80	.022371	6.30	.001836	8.80	.000151
1.30	.272532	3.90	.020242	6.40	.001661	8.90	.000136
1.40	.246597	4.00	.018316	6.50	.001503	9.00	.000123
1.50	.223130	4.10	.016573	6.60	.001360	9.10	.000112
1.60	.201897	4.20	.014996	6.70	.001231	9.20	.000101
1.70	.182684	4.30	.013569	6.80	.001114	9.30	.000091
1.80	.165299	4.40	.012277	6.90	.001008	9.40	.000083
1.90	.149569	4.50	.011109	7.00	.000912	9.50	.000075
2.00	.135335	4.60	.010052	7.10	.000825	9.60	.000068
2.10	.122456	4.70	.009095	7.20	.000747	9.70	.000061
2.20	.110803	4.80	.008230	7.30	.000676	9.80	.000056
2.30	.100259	4.90	.007447	7.40	.000611	9.90	.000050
2.40	.090718	5.00	.006738	7.50	.000553	10.00	.000045
2.50	.082085						

TABLE IV
NORMAL CURVE AREAS

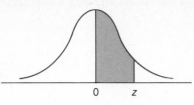

z	.00	.01	.02	.03	.04	.05	.06	.07	.08	.09
0.0	.0000	.0040	.0080	.0120	.0160	.0199	.0239	.0279	.0319	.0359
0.1	.0398	.0438	.0478	.0517	.0557	.0596	.0636	.0675	.0714	.0753
0.2	.0793	.0832	.0871	.0910	.0948	.0987	.1026	.1064	.1103	.1141
0.3	.1179	.1217	.1255	.1293	.1331	.1368	.1406	.1443	.1480	.1517
0.4	.1554	.1591	.1628	.1664	.1700	.1736	.1772	.1808	.1844	.1879
0.5	.1915	.1950	.1985	.2019	.2054	.2088	.2123	.2157	.2190	.2224
0.6	.2257	.2291	.2324	.2357	.2389	.2422	.2454	.2486	.2517	.2549
0.7	.2580	.2611	.2642	.2673	.2704	.2734	.2764	.2794	.2823	.2852
0.8	.2881	.2910	.2939	.2967	.2995	.3023	.3051	.3078	.3106	.3133
0.9	.3159	.3186	.3212	.3238	.3264	.3289	.3315	.3340	.3365	.3389
1.0	.3413	.3438	.3461	.3485	.3508	.3531	.3554	.3577	.3599	.3621
1.1	.3643	.3665	.3686	.3708	.3729	.3749	.3770	.3790	.3810	.3830
1.2	.3849	.3869	.3888	.3907	.3925	.3944	.3962	.3980	.3997	.4015
1.3	.4032	.4049	.4066	.4082	.4099	.4115	.4131	.4147	.4162	.4177
1.4	.4192	.4207	.4222	.4236	.4251	.4265	.4279	.4292	.4306	.4319
1.5	.4332	.4345	.4357	.4370	.4382	.4394	.4406	.4418	.4429	.4441
1.6	.4452	.4463	.4474	.4484	.4495	.4505	.4515	.4525	.4535	.4545
1.7	.4554	.4564	.4573	.4582	.4591	.4599	.4608	.4616	.4625	.4633
1.8	.4641	.4649	.4656	.4664	.4671	.4678	.4686	.4693	.4699	.4706
1.9	.4713	.4719	.4726	.4732	.4738	.4744	.4750	.4756	.4761	.4767
2.0	.4772	.4778	.4783	.4788	.4793	.4798	.4803	.4808	.4812	.4817
2.1	.4821	.4826	.4830	.4834	.4838	.4842	.4846	.4850	.4854	.4857
2.2	.4861	.4864	.4868	.4871	.4875	.4878	.4881	.4884	.4887	.4890
2.3	.4893	.4896	.4898	.4901	.4904	.4906	.4909	.4911	.4913	.4916
2.4	.4918	.4920	.4922	.4925	.4927	.4929	.4931	.4932	.4934	.4936
2.5	.4938	.4940	.4941	.4943	.4945	.4946	.4948	.4949	.4951	.4952
2.6	.4953	.4955	.4956	.4957	.4959	.4960	.4961	.4962	.4963	.4964
2.7	.4965	.4966	.4967	.4968	.4969	.4970	.4971	.4972	.4973	.4974
2.8	.4974	.4975	.4976	.4977	.4977	.4978	.4979	.4979	.4980	.4981
2.9	.4981	.4982	.4982	.4983	.4984	.4984	.4985	.4985	.4986	.4986
3.0	.4987	.4987	.4987	.4988	.4988	.4989	.4989	.4989	.4990	.4990

Source: Abridged from Table I of A. Hald, *Statistical Tables and Formulas* (New York: John Wiley & Sons, Inc.), 1952. Reproduced by permission of A. Hald and the publisher.

TABLE V
CRITICAL VALUES OF *t*

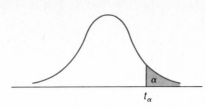

DEGREES OF FREEDOM	$t_{.100}$	$t_{.050}$	$t_{.025}$	$t_{.010}$	$t_{.005}$
1	3.078	6.314	12.706	31.821	63.657
2	1.886	2.920	4.303	6.965	9.925
3	1.638	2.353	3.182	4.541	5.841
4	1.533	2.132	2.776	3.747	4.604
5	1.476	2.015	2.571	3.365	4.032
6	1.440	1.943	2.447	3.143	3.707
7	1.415	1.895	2.365	2.998	3.499
8	1.397	1.860	2.306	2.896	3.355
9	1.383	1.833	2.262	2.821	3.250
10	1.372	1.812	2.228	2.764	3.169
11	1.363	1.796	2.201	2.718	3.106
12	1.356	1.782	2.179	2.681	3.055
13	1.350	1.771	2.160	2.650	3.012
14	1.345	1.761	2.145	2.624	2.977
15	1.341	1.753	2.131	2.602	2.947
16	1.337	1.746	2.120	2.583	2.921
17	1.333	1.740	2.110	2.567	2.898
18	1.330	1.734	2.101	2.552	2.878
19	1.328	1.729	2.093	2.539	2.861
20	1.325	1.725	2.086	2.528	2.845
21	1.323	1.721	2.080	2.518	2.831
22	1.321	1.717	2.074	2.508	2.819
23	1.319	1.714	2.069	2.500	2.807
24	1.318	1.711	2.064	2.492	2.797
25	1.316	1.708	2.060	2.485	2.787
26	1.315	1.706	2.056	2.479	2.779
27	1.314	1.703	2.052	2.473	2.771
28	1.313	1.701	2.048	2.467	2.763
29	1.311	1.699	2.045	2.462	2.756
∞	1.282	1.645	1.960	2.326	2.576

Source: From M. Merrington, "Table of Percentage Points of the *t*-Distribution," *Biometrika*, 1941, *32*, 300. Reproduced by permission of E. S. Pearson.

TABLE VI

PERCENTAGE POINTS OF THE F DISTRIBUTION, $\alpha = .05$

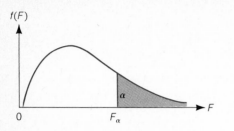

ν_2	NUMERATOR DEGREES OF FREEDOM								
ν_1	1	2	3	4	5	6	7	8	9
1	161.4	199.5	215.7	224.6	230.2	234.0	236.8	238.9	240.5
2	18.51	19.00	19.16	19.25	19.30	19.33	19.35	19.37	19.38
3	10.13	9.55	9.28	9.12	9.01	8.94	8.89	8.85	8.81
4	7.71	6.94	6.59	6.39	6.26	6.16	6.09	6.04	6.00
5	6.61	5.79	5.41	5.19	5.05	4.95	4.88	4.82	4.77
6	5.99	5.14	4.76	4.53	4.39	4.28	4.21	4.15	4.10
7	5.59	4.74	4.35	4.12	3.97	3.87	3.79	3.73	3.68
8	5.32	4.46	4.07	3.84	3.69	3.58	3.50	3.44	3.39
9	5.12	4.26	3.86	3.63	3.48	3.37	3.29	3.23	3.18
10	4.96	4.10	3.71	3.48	3.33	3.22	3.14	3.07	3.02
11	4.84	3.98	3.59	3.36	3.20	3.09	3.01	2.95	2.90
12	4.75	3.89	3.49	3.26	3.11	3.00	2.91	2.85	2.80
13	4.67	3.81	3.41	3.18	3.03	2.92	2.83	2.77	2.71
14	4.60	3.74	3.34	3.11	2.96	2.85	2.76	2.70	2.65
15	4.54	3.68	3.29	3.06	2.90	2.79	2.71	2.64	2.59
16	4.49	3.63	3.24	3.01	2.85	2.74	2.66	2.59	2.54
17	4.45	3.59	3.20	2.96	2.81	2.70	2.61	2.55	2.49
18	4.41	3.55	3.16	2.93	2.77	2.66	2.58	2.51	2.46
19	4.38	3.52	3.13	2.90	2.74	2.63	2.54	2.48	2.42
20	4.35	3.49	3.10	2.87	2.71	2.60	2.51	2.45	2.39
21	4.32	3.47	3.07	2.84	2.68	2.57	2.49	2.42	2.37
22	4.30	3.44	3.05	2.82	2.66	2.55	2.46	2.40	2.34
23	4.28	3.42	3.03	2.80	2.64	2.53	2.44	2.37	2.32
24	4.26	3.40	3.01	2.78	2.62	2.51	2.42	2.36	2.30
25	4.24	3.39	2.99	2.76	2.60	2.49	2.40	2.34	2.28
26	4.23	3.37	2.98	2.74	2.59	2.47	2.39	2.32	2.27
27	4.21	3.35	2.96	2.73	2.57	2.46	2.37	2.31	2.25
28	4.20	3.34	2.95	2.71	2.56	2.45	2.36	2.29	2.24
29	4.18	3.33	2.93	2.70	2.55	2.43	2.35	2.28	2.22
30	4.17	3.32	2.92	2.69	2.53	2.42	2.33	2.27	2.21
40	4.08	3.23	2.84	2.61	2.45	2.34	2.25	2.18	2.12
60	4.00	3.15	2.76	2.53	2.37	2.25	2.17	2.10	2.04
120	3.92	3.07	2.68	2.45	2.29	2.17	2.09	2.02	1.96
∞	3.84	3.00	2.60	2.37	2.21	2.10	2.01	1.94	1.88

DENOMINATOR DEGREES OF FREEDOM

Source: From M. Merrington and C. M. Thompson, "Tables of Percentage Points of the Inverted Beta (F)-Distribution," *Biometrika*, 1943, *33*, 73–88. Reproduced by permission of the *Biometrika* Trustees.

ν_2 \ ν_1	NUMERATOR DEGREES OF FREEDOM									
	10	12	15	20	24	30	40	60	120	∞
1	241.9	243.9	245.9	248.0	249.1	250.1	251.1	252.2	253.3	254.3
2	19.40	19.41	19.43	19.45	19.45	19.46	19.47	19.48	19.49	19.50
3	8.79	8.74	8.70	8.66	8.64	8.62	8.59	8.57	8.55	8.53
4	5.96	5.91	5.86	5.80	5.77	5.75	5.72	5.69	5.66	5.63
5	4.74	4.68	4.62	4.56	4.53	4.50	4.46	4.43	4.40	4.36
6	4.06	4.00	3.94	3.87	3.84	3.81	3.77	3.74	3.70	3.67
7	3.64	3.57	3.51	3.44	3.41	3.38	3.34	3.30	3.27	3.23
8	3.35	3.28	3.22	3.15	3.12	3.08	3.04	3.01	2.97	2.93
9	3.14	3.07	3.01	2.94	2.90	2.86	2.83	2.79	2.75	2.71
10	2.98	2.91	2.85	2.77	2.74	2.70	2.66	2.62	2.58	2.54
11	2.85	2.79	2.72	2.65	2.61	2.57	2.53	2.49	2.45	2.40
12	2.75	2.69	2.62	2.54	2.51	2.47	2.43	2.38	2.34	2.30
13	2.67	2.60	2.53	2.46	2.42	2.38	2.34	2.30	2.25	2.21
14	2.60	2.53	2.46	2.39	2.35	2.31	2.27	2.22	2.18	2.13
15	2.54	2.48	2.40	2.33	2.29	2.25	2.20	2.16	2.11	2.07
16	2.49	2.42	2.35	2.28	2.24	2.19	2.15	2.11	2.06	2.01
17	2.45	2.38	2.31	2.23	2.19	2.15	2.10	2.06	2.01	1.96
18	2.41	2.34	2.27	2.19	2.15	2.11	2.06	2.02	1.97	1.92
19	2.38	2.31	2.23	2.16	2.11	2.07	2.03	1.98	1.93	1.88
20	2.35	2.28	2.20	2.12	2.08	2.04	1.99	1.95	1.90	1.84
21	2.32	2.25	2.18	2.10	2.05	2.01	1.96	1.92	1.87	1.81
22	2.30	2.23	2.15	2.07	2.03	1.98	1.94	1.89	1.84	1.78
23	2.27	2.20	2.13	2.05	2.01	1.96	1.91	1.86	1.81	1.76
24	2.25	2.18	2.11	2.03	1.98	1.94	1.89	1.84	1.79	1.73
25	2.24	2.16	2.09	2.01	1.96	1.92	1.87	1.82	1.77	1.71
26	2.22	2.15	2.07	1.99	1.95	1.90	1.85	1.80	1.75	1.69
27	2.20	2.13	2.06	1.97	1.93	1.88	1.84	1.79	1.73	1.67
28	2.19	2.12	2.04	1.96	1.91	1.87	1.82	1.77	1.71	1.65
29	2.18	2.10	2.03	1.94	1.90	1.85	1.81	1.75	1.70	1.64
30	2.16	2.09	2.01	1.93	1.89	1.84	1.79	1.74	1.68	1.62
40	2.08	2.00	1.92	1.84	1.79	1.74	1.69	1.64	1.58	1.51
60	1.99	1.92	1.84	1.75	1.70	1.65	1.59	1.53	1.47	1.39
120	1.91	1.83	1.75	1.66	1.61	1.55	1.50	1.43	1.35	1.25
∞	1.83	1.75	1.67	1.57	1.52	1.46	1.39	1.32	1.22	1.00

DENOMINATOR DEGREES OF FREEDOM

TABLE VII
PERCENTAGE POINTS OF THE F DISTRIBUTION, α = .01

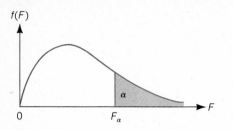

ν₁	NUMERATOR DEGREES OF FREEDOM								
ν₂	1	2	3	4	5	6	7	8	9
1	4,052	4,999.5	5,403	5,625	5,764	5,859	5,928	5,982	6,022
2	98.50	99.00	99.17	99.25	99.30	99.33	99.36	99.37	99.39
3	34.12	30.82	29.46	28.71	28.24	27.91	27.67	27.49	27.35
4	21.20	18.00	16.69	15.98	15.52	15.21	14.98	14.80	14.66
5	16.26	13.27	12.06	11.39	10.97	10.67	10.46	10.29	10.16
6	13.75	10.92	9.78	9.15	8.75	8.47	8.26	8.10	7.98
7	12.25	9.55	8.45	7.85	7.46	7.19	6.99	6.84	6.72
8	11.26	8.65	7.59	7.01	6.63	6.37	6.18	6.03	5.91
9	10.56	8.02	6.99	6.42	6.06	5.80	5.61	5.47	5.35
10	10.04	7.56	6.55	5.99	5.64	5.39	5.20	5.06	4.94
11	9.65	7.21	6.22	5.67	5.32	5.07	4.89	4.74	4.63
12	9.33	6.93	5.95	5.41	5.06	4.82	4.64	4.50	4.39
13	9.07	6.70	5.74	5.21	4.86	4.62	4.44	4.30	4.19
14	8.86	6.51	5.56	5.04	4.69	4.46	4.28	4.14	4.03
15	8.68	6.36	5.42	4.89	4.56	4.32	4.14	4.00	3.89
16	8.53	6.23	5.29	4.77	4.44	4.20	4.03	3.89	3.78
17	8.40	6.11	5.18	4.67	4.34	4.10	3.93	3.79	3.68
18	8.29	6.01	5.09	4.58	4.25	4.01	3.84	3.71	3.60
19	8.18	5.93	5.01	4.50	4.17	3.94	3.77	3.63	3.52
20	8.10	5.85	4.94	4.43	4.10	3.87	3.70	3.56	3.46
21	8.02	5.78	4.87	4.37	4.04	3.81	3.64	3.51	3.40
22	7.95	5.72	4.82	4.31	3.99	3.76	3.59	3.45	3.35
23	7.88	5.66	4.76	4.26	3.94	3.71	3.54	3.41	3.30
24	7.82	5.61	4.72	4.22	3.90	3.67	3.50	3.36	3.26
25	7.77	5.57	4.68	4.18	3.85	3.63	3.46	3.32	3.22
26	7.72	5.53	4.64	4.14	3.82	3.59	3.42	3.29	3.18
27	7.68	5.49	4.60	4.11	3.78	3.56	3.39	3.26	3.15
28	7.64	5.45	4.57	4.07	3.75	3.53	3.36	3.23	3.12
29	7.60	5.42	4.54	4.04	3.73	3.50	3.33	3.20	3.09
30	7.56	5.39	4.51	4.02	3.70	3.47	3.30	3.17	3.07
40	7.31	5.18	4.31	3.83	3.51	3.29	3.12	2.99	2.89
60	7.08	4.98	4.13	3.65	3.34	3.12	2.95	2.82	2.72
120	6.85	4.79	3.95	3.48	3.17	2.96	2.79	2.66	2.56
∞	6.63	4.61	3.78	3.32	3.02	2.80	2.64	2.51	2.41

DENOMINATOR DEGREES OF FREEDOM

Source: From M. Merrington and C. M. Thompson, "Tables of Percentage Points of the Inverted Beta (F)-Distribution," *Biometrika*, 1943, *33*, 73–88. Reproduced by permission of the *Biometrika* Trustees.

v_2 \ v_1	NUMERATOR DEGREES OF FREEDOM									
	10	12	15	20	24	30	40	60	120	∞
1	6,056	6,106	6,157	6,209	6,235	6,261	6,287	6,313	6,339	6,366
2	99.40	99.42	99.43	99.45	99.46	99.47	99.47	99.48	99.49	99.50
3	27.23	27.05	26.87	26.69	26.60	26.50	26.41	26.32	26.22	26.13
4	14.55	14.37	14.20	14.02	13.93	13.84	13.75	13.65	13.56	13.46
5	10.05	9.89	9.72	9.55	9.47	9.38	9.29	9.20	9.11	9.02
6	7.87	7.72	7.56	7.40	7.31	7.23	7.14	7.06	6.97	6.88
7	6.62	6.47	6.31	6.16	6.07	5.99	5.91	5.82	5.74	5.65
8	5.81	5.67	5.52	5.36	5.28	5.20	5.12	5.03	4.95	4.86
9	5.26	5.11	4.96	4.81	4.73	4.65	4.57	4.48	4.40	4.31
10	4.85	4.71	4.56	4.41	4.33	4.25	4.17	4.08	4.00	3.91
11	4.54	4.40	4.25	4.10	4.02	3.94	3.86	3.78	3.69	3.60
12	4.30	4.16	4.01	3.86	3.78	3.70	3.62	3.54	3.45	3.36
13	4.10	3.96	3.82	3.66	3.59	3.51	3.43	3.34	3.25	3.17
14	3.94	3.80	3.66	3.51	3.43	3.35	3.27	3.18	3.09	3.00
15	3.80	3.67	3.52	3.37	3.29	3.21	3.13	3.05	2.96	2.87
16	3.69	3.55	3.41	3.26	3.18	3.10	3.02	2.93	2.84	2.75
17	3.59	3.46	3.31	3.16	3.08	3.00	2.92	2.83	2.75	2.65
18	3.51	3.37	3.23	3.08	3.00	2.92	2.84	2.75	2.66	2.57
19	3.43	3.30	3.15	3.00	2.92	2.84	2.76	2.67	2.58	2.49
20	3.37	3.23	3.09	2.94	2.86	2.78	2.69	2.61	2.52	2.42
21	3.31	3.17	3.03	2.88	2.80	2.72	2.64	2.55	2.46	2.36
22	3.26	3.12	2.98	2.83	2.75	2.67	2.58	2.50	2.40	2.31
23	3.21	3.07	2.93	2.78	2.70	2.62	2.54	2.45	2.35	2.26
24	3.17	3.03	2.89	2.74	2.66	2.58	2.49	2.40	2.31	2.21
25	3.13	2.99	2.85	2.70	2.62	2.54	2.45	2.36	2.27	2.17
26	3.09	2.96	2.81	2.66	2.58	2.50	2.42	2.33	2.23	2.13
27	3.06	2.93	2.78	2.63	2.55	2.47	2.38	2.29	2.20	2.10
28	3.03	2.90	2.75	2.60	2.52	2.44	2.35	2.26	2.17	2.06
29	3.00	2.87	2.73	2.57	2.49	2.41	2.33	2.23	2.14	2.03
30	2.98	2.84	2.70	2.55	2.47	2.39	2.30	2.21	2.11	2.01
40	2.80	2.66	2.52	2.37	2.29	2.20	2.11	2.02	1.92	1.80
60	2.63	2.50	2.35	2.20	2.12	2.03	1.94	1.84	1.73	1.60
120	2.47	2.34	2.19	2.03	1.95	1.86	1.76	1.66	1.53	1.38
∞	2.32	2.18	2.04	1.88	1.79	1.70	1.59	1.47	1.32	1.00

DENOMINATOR DEGREES OF FREEDOM

TABLE VIII
CRITICAL VALUES OF
T_L AND T_U FOR THE
WILCOXON RANK
SUM TEST:
INDEPENDENT
SAMPLES

Test statistic is rank sum associated with smaller sample (if equal sample sizes, either rank sum can be used).

a. $\alpha = .025$ one-tailed; $\alpha = .05$ two-tailed

n_2 \ n_1	3 T_L	3 T_U	4 T_L	4 T_U	5 T_L	5 T_U	6 T_L	6 T_U	7 T_L	7 T_U	8 T_L	8 T_U	9 T_L	9 T_U	10 T_L	10 T_U
3	5	16	6	18	6	21	7	23	7	26	8	28	8	31	9	33
4	6	18	11	25	12	28	12	32	13	35	14	38	15	41	16	44
5	6	21	12	28	18	37	19	41	20	45	21	49	22	53	24	56
6	7	23	12	32	19	41	26	52	28	56	29	61	31	65	32	70
7	7	26	13	35	20	45	28	56	37	68	39	73	41	78	43	83
8	8	28	14	38	21	49	29	61	39	73	49	87	51	93	54	98
9	8	31	15	41	22	53	31	65	41	78	51	93	63	108	66	114
10	9	33	16	44	24	56	32	70	43	83	54	98	66	114	79	131

b. $\alpha = .05$ one-tailed; $\alpha = .10$ two-tailed

n_2 \ n_1	3 T_L	3 T_U	4 T_L	4 T_U	5 T_L	5 T_U	6 T_L	6 T_U	7 T_L	7 T_U	8 T_L	8 T_U	9 T_L	9 T_U	10 T_L	10 T_U
3	6	15	7	17	7	20	8	22	9	24	9	27	10	29	11	31
4	7	17	12	24	13	27	14	30	15	33	16	36	17	39	18	42
5	7	20	13	27	19	36	20	40	22	43	24	46	25	50	26	54
6	8	22	14	30	20	40	28	50	30	54	32	58	33	63	35	67
7	9	24	15	33	22	43	30	54	39	66	41	71	43	76	46	80
8	9	27	16	36	24	46	32	58	41	71	52	84	54	90	57	95
9	10	29	17	39	25	50	33	63	43	76	54	90	66	105	69	111
10	11	31	18	42	26	54	35	67	46	80	57	95	69	111	83	127

Source: From F. Wilcoxon and R. A. Wilcox, ''Some Rapid Approximate Statistical Procedures,'' 1964, 20–23. Reproduced with the permission of R. A. Wilcox and the Lederle Laboratories.

TABLE IX
CRITICAL VALUES OF T_0 IN THE WILCOXON PAIRED DIFFERENCE SIGNED-RANKS TEST

ONE-TAILED	TWO-TAILED	$n = 5$	$n = 6$	$n = 7$	$n = 8$	$n = 9$	$n = 10$
$\alpha = .05$	$\alpha = .10$	1	2	4	6	8	11
$\alpha = .025$	$\alpha = .05$		1	2	4	6	8
$\alpha = .01$	$\alpha = .02$			0	2	3	5
$\alpha = .005$	$\alpha = .01$				0	2	3
		$n = 11$	$n = 12$	$n = 13$	$n = 14$	$n = 15$	$n = 16$
$\alpha = .05$	$\alpha = .10$	14	17	21	26	30	36
$\alpha = .025$	$\alpha = .05$	11	14	17	21	25	30
$\alpha = .01$	$\alpha = .02$	7	10	13	16	20	24
$\alpha = .005$	$\alpha = .01$	5	7	10	13	16	19
		$n = 17$	$n = 18$	$n = 19$	$n = 20$	$n = 21$	$n = 22$
$\alpha = .05$	$\alpha = .10$	41	47	54	60	68	75
$\alpha = .025$	$\alpha = .05$	35	40	46	52	59	66
$\alpha = .01$	$\alpha = .02$	28	33	38	43	49	56
$\alpha = .005$	$\alpha = .01$	23	28	32	37	43	49
		$n = 23$	$n = 24$	$n = 25$	$n = 26$	$n = 27$	$n = 28$
$\alpha = .05$	$\alpha = .10$	83	92	101	110	120	130
$\alpha = .025$	$\alpha = .05$	73	81	90	98	107	117
$\alpha = .01$	$\alpha = .02$	62	69	77	85	93	102
$\alpha = .005$	$\alpha = .01$	55	61	68	76	84	92
		$n = 29$	$n = 30$	$n = 31$	$n = 32$	$n = 33$	$n = 34$
$\alpha = .05$	$\alpha = .10$	141	152	163	175	188	201
$\alpha = .025$	$\alpha = .05$	127	137	148	159	171	183
$\alpha = .01$	$\alpha = .02$	111	120	130	141	151	162
$\alpha = .005$	$\alpha = .01$	100	109	118	128	138	149
		$n = 35$	$n = 36$	$n = 37$	$n = 38$	$n = 39$	
$\alpha = .05$	$\alpha = .10$	214	228	242	256	271	
$\alpha = .025$	$\alpha = .05$	195	208	222	235	250	
$\alpha = .01$	$\alpha = .02$	174	186	198	211	224	
$\alpha = .005$	$\alpha = .01$	160	171	183	195	208	
		$n = 40$	$n = 41$	$n = 42$	$n = 43$	$n = 44$	$n = 45$
$\alpha = .05$	$\alpha = .10$	287	303	319	336	353	371
$\alpha = .025$	$\alpha = .05$	264	279	295	311	327	344
$\alpha = .01$	$\alpha = .02$	238	252	267	281	297	313
$\alpha = .005$	$\alpha = .01$	221	234	248	262	277	292
		$n = 46$	$n = 47$	$n = 48$	$n = 49$	$n = 50$	
$\alpha = .05$	$\alpha = .10$	389	408	427	446	466	
$\alpha = .025$	$\alpha = .05$	361	379	397	415	434	
$\alpha = .01$	$\alpha = .02$	329	345	362	380	398	
$\alpha = .005$	$\alpha = .01$	307	323	339	356	373	

Source: From F. Wilcoxon and R. A. Wilcox, "Some Rapid Approximate Statistical Procedures," 1964, 28. Reproduced with the permission of R. A. Wilcox and the Lederle Laboratories.

TABLE X
CRITICAL VALUES OF χ^2

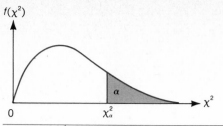

DEGREES OF FREEDOM	$\chi^2_{.995}$	$\chi^2_{.990}$	$\chi^2_{.975}$	$\chi^2_{.950}$	$\chi^2_{.900}$
1	0.0000393	0.0001571	0.0009821	0.0039321	0.0157908
2	0.0100251	0.0201007	0.0506356	0.102587	0.210720
3	0.0717212	0.114832	0.215795	0.351846	0.584375
4	0.206990	0.297110	0.484419	0.710721	1.063623
5	0.411740	0.554300	0.831211	1.145476	1.61031
6	0.675727	0.872085	1.237347	1.63539	2.20413
7	0.989265	1.239043	1.68987	2.16735	2.83311
8	1.344419	1.646482	2.17973	2.73264	3.48954
9	1.734926	2.087912	2.70039	3.32511	4.16816
10	2.15585	2.55821	3.24697	3.94030	4.86518
11	2.60321	3.05347	3.81575	4.57481	5.57779
12	3.07382	3.57056	4.40379	5.22603	6.30380
13	3.56503	4.10691	5.00874	5.89186	7.04150
14	4.07468	4.66043	5.62872	6.57063	7.78953
15	4.60094	5.22935	6.26214	7.26094	8.54675
16	5.14224	5.81221	6.90766	7.96164	9.31223
17	5.69724	6.40776	7.56418	8.67176	10.0852
18	6.26481	7.01491	8.23075	9.39046	10.8649
19	6.84398	7.63273	8.90655	10.1170	11.6509
20	7.43386	8.26040	9.59083	10.8508	12.4426
21	8.03366	8.89720	10.28293	11.5913	13.2396
22	8.64272	9.54249	10.9823	12.3380	14.0415
23	9.26042	10.19567	11.6885	13.0905	14.8479
24	9.88623	10.8564	12.4011	13.8484	15.6587
25	10.5197	11.5240	13.1197	14.6114	16.4734
26	11.1603	12.1981	13.8439	15.3791	17.2919
27	11.8076	12.8786	14.5733	16.1513	18.1138
28	12.4613	13.5648	15.3079	16.9279	18.9392
29	13.1211	14.2565	16.0471	17.7083	19.7677
30	13.7867	14.9535	16.7908	18.4926	20.5992
40	20.7065	22.1643	24.4331	26.5093	29.0505
50	27.9907	29.7067	32.3574	34.7642	37.6886
60	35.5346	37.4848	40.4817	43.1879	46.4589
70	43.2752	45.4418	48.7576	51.7393	55.3290
80	51.1720	53.5400	57.1532	60.3915	64.2778
90	59.1963	61.7541	65.6466	69.1260	73.2912
100	67.3276	70.0648	74.2219	77.9295	82.3581

Source: From C. M. Thompson, "Tables of the Percentage Points of the χ^2-Distribution," *Biometrika*, 1941, *32*, 188–189. Reproduced by permission of E. S. Pearson.

DEGREES OF FREEDOM	$\chi^2_{.100}$	$\chi^2_{.050}$	$\chi^2_{.025}$	$\chi^2_{.010}$	$\chi^2_{.005}$
1	2.70554	3.84146	5.02389	6.63490	7.87944
2	4.60517	5.99147	7.37776	9.21034	10.5966
3	6.25139	7.81473	9.34840	11.3449	12.8381
4	7.77944	9.48773	11.1433	13.2767	14.8602
5	9.23635	11.0705	12.8325	15.0863	16.7496
6	10.6446	12.5916	14.4494	16.8119	18.5476
7	12.0170	14.0671	16.0128	18.4753	20.2777
8	13.3616	15.5073	17.5346	20.0902	21.9550
9	14.6837	16.9190	19.0228	21.6660	23.5893
10	15.9871	18.3070	20.4831	23.2093	25.1882
11	17.2750	19.6751	21.9200	24.7250	26.7569
12	18.5494	21.0261	23.3367	26.2170	28.2995
13	19.8119	22.3621	24.7356	27.6883	29.8194
14	21.0642	23.6848	26.1190	29.1413	31.3193
15	22.3072	24.9958	27.4884	30.5779	32.8013
16	23.5418	26.2962	28.8454	31.9999	34.2672
17	24.7690	27.5871	30.1910	33.4087	35.7185
18	25.9894	28.8693	31.5264	34.8053	37.1564
19	27.2036	30.1435	32.8523	36.1908	38.5822
20	28.4120	31.4104	34.1696	37.5662	39.9968
21	29.6151	32.6705	35.4789	38.9321	41.4010
22	30.8133	33.9244	36.7807	40.2894	42.7956
23	32.0069	35.1725	38.0757	41.6384	44.1813
24	33.1963	36.4151	39.3641	42.9798	45.5585
25	34.3816	37.6525	40.6465	44.3141	46.9278
26	35.5631	38.8852	41.9232	45.6417	48.2899
27	36.7412	40.1133	43.1944	46.9630	49.6449
28	37.9159	41.3372	44.4607	48.2782	50.9933
29	39.0875	42.5569	45.7222	49.5879	52.3356
30	40.2560	43.7729	46.9792	50.8922	53.6720
40	51.8050	55.7585	59.3417	63.6907	66.7659
50	63.1671	67.5048	71.4202	76.1539	79.4900
60	74.3970	79.0819	83.2976	88.3794	91.9517
70	85.5271	90.5312	95.0231	100.425	104.215
80	96.5782	101.879	106.629	112.329	116.321
90	107.565	113.145	118.136	124.116	128.299
100	118.498	124.342	129.561	135.807	140.169

TABLE XI
CRITICAL VALUES OF
SPEARMAN'S RANK
CORRELATION
COEFFICIENT

The α values correspond to a one-tailed test of H_0: $\rho_s = 0$. The value should be doubled for two-tailed tests.

n	$\alpha = .05$	$\alpha = .025$	$\alpha = .01$	$\alpha = .005$
5	.900	—	—	—
6	.829	.886	.943	—
7	.714	.786	.893	—
8	.643	.738	.833	.881
9	.600	.683	.783	.833
10	.564	.648	.745	.794
11	.523	.623	.736	.818
12	.497	.591	.703	.780
13	.475	.566	.673	.745
14	.457	.545	.646	.716
15	.441	.525	.623	.689
16	.425	.507	.601	.666
17	.412	.490	.582	.645
18	.399	.476	.564	.625
19	.388	.462	.549	.608
20	.377	.450	.534	.591
21	.368	.438	.521	.576
22	.359	.428	.508	.562
23	.351	.418	.496	.549
24	.343	.409	.485	.537
25	.336	.400	.475	.526
26	.329	.392	.465	.515
27	.323	.385	.456	.505
28	.317	.377	.448	.496
29	.311	.370	.440	.487
30	.305	.364	.432	.478

Source: From E. G. Olds, "Distribution of Sums of Squares of Rank Differences for Small Samples," *Annals of Mathematical Statistics,* 1938, 9. Reproduced with the permission of the Editor, *Annals of Mathematical Statistics.*

ANSWERS
TO
SELECTED EXERCISES

CHAPTER 2

2.1. **a.** Qualitative   **b.** Quantitative   **c.** Quantitative   **d.** Qualitative   **e.** Quantitative
2.2. **a.** Qualitative   **b.** Quantitative   **c.** Qualitative
2.3. **a.** Quantitative   **b.** Quantitative   **c.** Quantitative   **d.** Qualitative
2.13. **a.** Qualitative   **b.** Quantitative   **c.** Quantitative

CHAPTER 3

3.1. 38.625, 39.5   **3.3.** 98.2, 85   **3.5.** **b.** 483.98, 466, each number is a mode
3.6. **c.** 35.3667, 32.5, 28

CHAPTER 4

4.1. **a.** 5, 43.1, 6.57   **b.** 9.5, 9.85, 3.14
4.2. **a.** 25, 175, 625   **b.** 10, 44, 100   **c.** 216, 20,160, 46,656   **d.** -10, 30, 100
e. 10, 100, 100

4.3. a. 5, 12.5, 3.536   **b.** 2, 6, 2.449   **c.** 54, 2,832, 53.22   **d.** -2, 2.5, 1.581
e. 2, 20, 4.472

4.4. a. 3, 7, 2.646   **b.** 2, 4.4, 2.098   **c.** 8, 18.67, 4.320   **d.** 4.75, 12.92, 3.594

4.5. a. 10, 91.5, 9.566   **b.** 52, 3,336, 57.76   **c.** -2, 1.6, 1.265   **d.** 0.333, 0.0587, 0.242

4.6. 10, 32, 5.657   **4.8: b.** 20, 4.276, 2.068   **d.** 76.7%, 96.7%, 100%

4.9. $R = 25 - 16 = 9$, $s \approx \frac{9}{4}$

4.10. 3,100–3,150; 3,075–3,175; 3,050–3,200; at least 0%, 75%, 88.9%, respectively (or approx. 68%, 95%, 100% if data are considered mound-shaped)

4.11. a. 147   **b.** $s^2 = 12,039.9$, $s = 109.7$ **d.** 70%, 95%, 100%

4.12. $R = 410 - 0 = 410$, $s \approx \frac{410}{4} = 102.5$ **4.13.** Approx. 68%, 95%, 100%, respectively

4.14. a. 23.76, 6.607, 2.570   **c.** 68%, 96%, 100%   **4.15.** $R = 30 - 19 = 11$, $s \approx \frac{11}{4} = 2.75$

4.16. $R = 900 - 50 = 850$, $s \approx \frac{850}{4} = 212.5$ **4.17.** Approx. 2.5%, 2.5%, 0%

4.18. $R = 92 - 60 = 32$, $s \approx \frac{32}{4} = 8$ **4.20.** Median

4.21. a. $z = -2$, sample   **b.** $z = 0.5$, population   **c.** $z = -3$, population   **d.** $z = 0$, sample

4.22. 96% of the 500 largest industrial corporations had sales less than Westinghouse Electric

4.23. a. $z = 3$ **b.** 3   **c.** Yes, most receipts should be within 3 standard deviations of the mean

4.24. More than 90% of the 500 corporations had sales higher than Northwestern

4.25. a. At most 25%; at most 100%; at most 11.1%   **b.** $z = 1.5$, 1.5

4.26. a. 12.73   **b.** 0.079, 0.845, -0.664, -0.053, 0, -0.573 **c.** Same as in part b

4.27. a. 68%, 100%   **b.** 31   **c.** First store, 2.5% versus 0% probability

4.28. a. 2.5%, 16%, 0%   **b.** 3.5   **c.** Over $190, 2.5% versus 0% probability

4.29. a. 142, 20, 400   **b.** 554, 46, 2,116   **c.** 185, -1, 1   **d.** 10,001, 101, 10,201

4.30. a. 15.5, 3.937   **b.** 32.7, 5.718   **c.** 36.97, 6.080   **d.** 2,483.6, 49.84

4.31. a. 7.929   **b.** 3.898   **c.** 8.905

4.32. a. 5, 4.637, 21.5   **b.** 16.75, 6.021, 36.25   **c.** 4.857, 5.460, 29.81   **d.** 4, 0, 0

4.33. a. 5.5, 0.548, 0.3   **b.** -0.667, 2.582, 6.667   **c.** 0.55, 0.3, 0.09

4.37. a. At least 0%   **b.** At most $\frac{1}{4} = 25\%$ **4.38. a.** Approx. 68%   **b.** Approx. 2.5%

4.39. a. $\bar{x} = 5.1$, median $= 5.5$, mode $= 6$, $R = 9$, $s^2 = 7.433$, $s = 2.726$ **4.40.** $s \approx \frac{9}{4} = 2.25$

4.42. $\bar{x} = 0.0795$, $s = 0.0154$, $s^2 = 0.00024$ **4.43.** At least 0%; at least 75%; at least 88.9%; 14, 20, 20

4.44. $z = 1.331$ **4.46.** $s \approx 30,000/4 = 7,500$

4.47. Over $120,000 since $z = 1.33$, while $z = -2.67$ for $90,000

4.48. Possible but not likely since $160,000 has a $z = 6.67$

4.49. 34% of the world's 130 largest cities have fewer people than Philadelphia   **4.50.** At least $\frac{8}{9} = 88.9\%$

4.51. Approx. 2.5%; approx. 50%

4.52. a. Invalid—does not prove conclusively, only with a high degree of certainty (at best)
b. Invalid—$4,000 is not typical since $z = -3.5$
c. Valid—if μ were smaller and/or σ larger, $4,000 in sales would not be as rare an outcome
d. Valid—$4,000 in sales could be a rare event   **e.** Invalid—at most $\frac{1}{9}$
f. Invalid—if σ were smaller than $6,000, then $4,000 in sales would be less likely, i.e., $z < -3.5$ (see part b)

4.53. $z = 2.5$ **4.54.** $y = 25,000 + (2.5)(6,000) = 40,000$

4.55. a. $R = 10$ **b.** $R = 13$ **c.** $R = 11$ **d.** $R = 0$

4.56. Highest total profit $8,000; lowest $4,000; $R = 4,000$ **4.57.** No information; $V = 0$ for all data sets

4.58. a. $z = -3.0$ **b.** Approx. 0%   **c.** 90 or above since $z = 2.0$; thus, approx. 2.5% score 90 or above

4.59. a. At least $\frac{3}{4} = 75\%$ **b.** At least $\frac{8}{9} = 88.9\%$ **c.** At least $1.25/2.25 = 55.6\%$

4.60 a. August: $R = 11$ while June: $R = 10$; June: $s^2 = 17.48$ while August: $s^2 = 11.9$; s^2, since R is affected by extreme values (i.e., 11 in August is relatively high)   **b.** $s^2 = 17.48$, no effect   **c.** $s^2 = 157.3 = 9(17.48)$; s^2 is multiplied by the square of the constant

CHAPTER 5

5.2. $P(A) = .16, P(B) = .64$ **5.3.** $P(A) = \frac{1}{6}, P(B) = \frac{5}{6}$ **5.4.** $P(A) = .25, P(B) = .15, P(C) = .60$

5.8. **a.** $\frac{6}{8}$ **b.** 0   **c.** $\frac{3}{8}$ **d.** 0

5.9. **a.** (1, R), (1, S), (1, E), (2, R), (2, S), (2, E), (3, R), (3, S), (3, E)   **b.** Sample space   **c.** $P(C) = .46$

5.10. **a.** (I, ES), (I, WS), (I, EZ), (OS, ES), (OS, WS), (OS, EZ)   **b.** Sample space   **c.** $P(A) = .86$

d. $P(B) = .14$ **e.** $P(C) = .30$ **f.** $P(D) = .25$ **g.** $P(E) = .45$

5.12. **a.** .48, .52, .16, .26, .35, .23   **b.** 1   **c.** .05   **d.** .05   **e.** 0   **f.** 0

5.14. **a.** .70, .41, .18, .16   **b.** .74   **c.** .59   **d.** .37   **e.** .11

5.15. **b.** $P(A^c) = .30$ **c.** $P(B^c) = .59$ **d.** .41   **e.** .96

5.17. **a.** .76   **b.** .03   **c.** .62   **d.** 0   **e.** 0

5.19. **a.** .35   **b.** .35   **c.** 0   **d.** .49   **e.** .55   **f.** 0

5.20. **b.** .55   **c.** .86   **d.** 0   **e.** .70   **f.** 1.0

5.21. **a.** $\frac{7}{8}$ **b.** $\frac{3}{8}$ **c.** $\frac{7}{8}$ **d.** $\frac{3}{8}$ **e.** 0   **f.** $\frac{4}{8}$

5.22 **a.** $\frac{3}{7}$ **b.** $\frac{3}{4}$ **c.** $\frac{3}{4}$ **5.23.** $P(R|S) = 0, P(S|R) = 0$

5.24. Independent since $P(A|B) = P(A) = \frac{1}{2}$ **5.25.** .005   **5.26.** **a.** 55%, 15%   **b.** .5

5.27. **a.** $\frac{25}{44} = .568$ **b.** $\frac{6}{25} = .24$ **5.28.** $\frac{15}{20} = .75$ **5.29.** 1.0

5.30. Dependent, $P(A|B) = .625 \neq P(A) = .44$ **5.31.** **a.** .30   **b.** $\frac{10}{55} = .182$ **c.** $\frac{25}{30} = .833$

5.32. $\frac{40}{45} = .889$ **5.33.** .25   **5.34.** Dependent, $P(A|B) = .111 \neq P(A) = .3$

5.35. Dependent since C and D are mutually exclusive events   **5.37.** $\frac{10}{16}, \frac{14}{16}, \frac{6}{16}, \frac{8}{16}, 1, \frac{8}{14}$

5.38. Probabilities do not sum to 1, $\frac{11}{16}, \frac{14}{16}, \frac{5}{16}, \frac{9}{16}, 1, \frac{9}{14}$ **5.39.** **c.** .25, .20, .10, .05, .15, .25, respectively

5.41. **a.** .60   **b.** .05   **c.** .70   **d.** 0   **e.** 1   **5.46.** .28, since $P(A^c) = 1 - P(A)$

5.48. **a.** $\frac{30}{45} = .667$ **b.** 1   **5.50.** 54   **5.51.** **a.** $\frac{2}{54} = .037$ **b.** $\frac{50}{54} = .926$

5.52. $\frac{25}{45} = .556$ **5.55.** $50/1{,}000 = .05$ **5.56.** **a.** $14/.52 = .269$ **b.** $.05/.16 = .313$

5.57. Dependent events since A and B are mutually exclusive

5.58. **a.** $.06/.14 = .429$ **b.** $.06/.25 = .24$ **c.** $.20/.86 = .233$ **d.** $.35/.40 = .875$

5.61. $.4/.8 = .5$ **5.63.** **a.** $\frac{1}{3}$ **b.** $\frac{1}{3}$ **c.** $\frac{1}{6}$ **d.** $\frac{1}{6}$

5.64. **a.** $\frac{6}{30} = .2$ **b.** $\frac{6}{29} = .207$ **c.** $\frac{552}{870} = .634$ **5.65.** .79

CHAPTER 6

6.3. **a.** Continuous   **b.** Discrete   **c.** Discrete   **d.** Continuous   **e.** Discrete

6.7. **a.**

x	1	2	3	4	5	6
$p(x)$	$\frac{1}{6}$	$\frac{1}{6}$	$\frac{1}{6}$	$\frac{1}{6}$	$\frac{1}{6}$	$\frac{1}{6}$

6.8.

x	0	1	2
$p(x)$	$\frac{4}{9}$	$\frac{4}{9}$	$\frac{1}{9}$

6.9. **b.** .41   **c.** .17

6.10.

x	0	1	2
$p(x)$	.2	.3	.5

6.11. **a.** 5.1   **6.12.** **a.** 1.5   **6.13.** $\mu = 0$ **6.14.** Yes, $\mu = \$11{,}500$

6.15. **a.** $\mu = 3.58, \sigma^2 = 3.814, \sigma = 1.953, \mu \pm 2\sigma$ is $-.326$ to 7.486   **b.** .95

6.16. $\sigma^2 = 3.96, \sigma = 1.990, \mu \pm 2\sigma$ is -3.98 to 3.98, .90

6.17. **a.** 114.4   **b.** 1,000.6   **c.** 31.63   **d.** $\mu \pm 2\sigma$ is 51.2 to 177.7

6.21. **a.** 10   **b.** 20   **c.** 1   **6.22.**

x	0	1	2	3	4	5
$p(x)$	.328	.409	.205	.051	.007	.000

6.23. **a.** .375   **b.** .001   **c.** .49

6.24. **a.**

x	0	1	2	3	4	5
$p(x)$	.168	.360	.309	.132	.029	.002

b. $\mu = 1.5, \sigma^2 = 1.05$

c. $\mu \pm 2\sigma$ is $-.549$ to 3.549   **d.** .969

6.25. **a.**

x	0	1	2	3	4	5	6
$p(x)$	.016	.094	.234	.313	.234	.094	.016

b. $\mu = 3$, $\sigma^2 = 1.5$

c. $\mu \pm 2\sigma$ is .551 to 5.449 **d.** .969

6.26. **a.** .344 **b.** .891 **c.** .344

6.27. **a.** .127 **b.** .485 **c.** 1.0 **d.** .996 **e.** .001 **f.** .003 **6.28.** .009

6.29. .098 **6.30.** $\mu = 0.5$, $\sigma = .707$; no, 4 is 4.95 standard deviations away from μ

6.31. **a.** 0 **b.** .000 **c.** .000 **d.** .098 **e.** .873 **f.** 1.0

6.32. **a.** 0 **b.** .000 **c.** .000 **d.** .234 **e.** .966 **f.** 1.0

6.33. $\mu = 48$, $\sigma = 6.5$, 31 is -2.62 standard deviations away from μ

6.35. **a.** .857 **b.** .007 **c.** .632 **d.** .000

6.36. **a.**

x	0	1	2	3	4	5	6	7	8	9
$p(x)$	.135	.271	.271	.180	.090	.036	.012	.003	.001	.000

b. $\mu = 2$, $\sigma = 1.414$, $\mu \pm 2\sigma$ is $-.828$ to 4.828 **c.** .947

6.37. **a.**

x	0	1	2	3	4	5	6	7	8	9
$p(x)$	.007	.034	.084	.140	.176	.176	.146	.104	.065	.036

b. $\mu = 5$, $\sigma = 2.236$, $\mu \pm 2\sigma$ is .528 to 9.472 **c.** .961

6.38. .193, .660 **6.39.** .090, .91 **6.40.** .080; no **6.41.** $\sigma = 2$; not likely; .003

6.42. $p(0) = .277$, $p(1) = .365$, $p(2) = .231$ from binomial table; $p(0) = .287$, $p(1) = .358$, $p(2) = .224$ using Poisson approximation

6.43. .632 **6.45.** **a.** $^4/_{20}$ **b.** 0 **c.** $^4/_{20}$ **d.** 0

6.46. **a.** 0 **b.** $^1/_{12}$ **c.** $^1/_3$ **d.** $^1/_6$

6.47. **a.**

x	1	2	3	4	5
$p(x)$	$^1/_{42}$	$^5/_{21}$	$^{10}/_{21}$	$^5/_{21}$	$^1/_{42}$

b. $\mu = 3$, $\sigma^2 = ^2/_3$ **c.** $\mu \pm 2\sigma$ is 1.37 to 4.63 **d.** $^{40}/_{42}$

6.48. **a.**

x	3	4	5	6	7
$p(x)$	$^{35}/_{495}$	$^{175}/_{495}$	$^{210}/_{495}$	$^{70}/_{495}$	$^5/_{495}$

b. $\mu = ^{14}/_3$, $\sigma = .841$ **c.** $\mu \pm 2\sigma$ is 2.98 to 6.35

d. $^{490}/_{495} = .990$

6.49. **a.** 0 **b.** $^{175}/_{495}$ **c.** $^{210}/_{495}$ **d.** $^{285}/_{495}$ **e.** 0 **f.** 0 **6.50.** $^1/_{20}$, $^1/_{20}$, $^{10}/_{20}$

6.51. $^1/_{10}$, $^7/_{10}$ **6.52.** $^1/_4$ **6.53.** $^6/_{10}$, $^1/_{14}$

6.55. **a.** .09 **b.** .0729 **c.** .271 **d.** .6561 **e.** .1 **f.** .9

6.56. **a.**

x	1	2	3	4	5	6	7
$p(x)$	.4	.24	.144	.086	.052	.031	.019

b. $\mu = 2.5$, $\sigma^2 = 3.75$, $\mu \pm 2\sigma$ is -1.37 to 6.37 **c.** .953

6.57. .0819 **6.58.** .081, .10 **6.59.** .343 **6.60.** **a.** .243 **b.** .156 **c.** .360

6.61. **a.** $^9/_{15}$ **b.** $^1/_{10}$ **c.** $^{12}/_{35}$ **6.62.** **a.** .128 **b.** .0625 **c.** .09

6.63. **a.** .1804 **b.** .0153 **c.** .0758

6.64. **a.** Discrete **b.** Continuous **c.** Continuous **d.** Continuous **6.65.** 22,250

6.66. .401 **6.67.** .512 **6.68.** .4019, .1608 **6.69.** \$33,333.33 **6.70.** $^{11}/_{12}$, $^1/_{30}$

6.71. .0996, .0738 **6.72.** .1024 **6.73.** .042 **6.74.** .051 **6.75.** $^4/_7$, $^{11}/_{14}$

6.76. .0315, .1067 **6.77.** .343 **6.78.** .0039 **6.79.** .657, .027 **6.80.** .1715

6.81. **a.** .1494 **b.** .2240 **c.** .0498 **d.** .1008 **e.** .4232 **f.** .8009

6.82. **a.** .16 **b.** .3904 **c.** .36 **d.** .0819 **e.** .4096 **f.** .4419

6.83. **a.**

x	1	2	3	4	5	6	7
$p(x)$	.5	.25	.125	.0625	.0313	.0156	.0078

b. $\mu = 2$, $\sigma = 1.414$, $\mu \pm 2\sigma$ is $-.828$ to 4.828 **c.** .9375

6.84. .265, .1755 **6.85.** .346, .683 **6.86.** 4.664%

CHAPTER 7

7.1. **a.** .4772   **b.** .4332   **c.** .4987   **d.** .1915
7.2. **a.** .6826   **b.** .9544   **c.** .3830   **d.** .9974
7.3. **a.** .7745   **b.** .4649   **c.** .1359   **d.** .9319   **e.** Approx. .3085   **f.** .6687
7.4. **a.** .0228   **b.** .0228   **c.** .0250   **d.** .5   **e.** .3085   **f.** .0250
7.5. **a.** .6826   **b.** .950   **c.** .90   **d.** .9974
7.6. **a.** 1.645   **b.** 1.96   **c.** -1.96 **d.** 2.0
7.7. **a.** -1.0 **b.** 0   **c.** 1.5   **d.** -4 **e.** 4   **f.** .4
7.8. **a.** 4 below the mean   **b.** .5 above the mean   **c.** 0   **d.** 6 above
7.9. **a.** -3 **b.** 1.96   **c.** 1.645   **d.** 1.0   **e.** $-.15$
7.10. **a.** .9544   **b.** .1587   **c.** .1587   **d.** .8185   **e.** .1498   **f.** .9974
7.11. .5, .0062   **7.12.** 2.07%   **7.13.** .2843, .0228   **7.14.** 473
7.15. **a.** 7,666.5   **b.** .4562   **7.16.** **a.** 50%   **b.** 4.75%   **c.** 32.987
7.17. **a.** $f(x) = \frac{1}{20}$ $(10 \leq x \leq 30)$ **b.** $\mu = 20$, $\sigma^2 = 33.33$ **c.** $\mu \pm 2\sigma$ is 8.45 to 31.55
7.18. **a.** .25   **b.** .5   **c.** .5   **d.** .2   **e.** 0   **f.** .4   **g.** 0
7.19. **a.** $f(x) = 1$ $(1 \leq x \leq 2)$ **b.** $\mu = 1.5$, $\sigma^2 = \frac{1}{12} = .083$
7.20. **a.** Continuous; it can assume any value in the interval 6.5 to 7.5
c. $\mu = 7$, $\sigma = 1/\sqrt{12} = .289$, $\mu \pm 2\sigma$ is 6.423 to 7.577
7.21. **a.** .5   **b.** 1.0   **c.** .25   **d.** .25   **e.** 0   **f.** .75   **7.22.** $(.25)^6 = .0002$
7.23. **b.** $\mu = .03$, $\sigma^2 = .00013$ **c.** .0069 to .0531   **d.** .04
7.24. **a.** .03   **b.** .02   **c.** .018   **d.** .01   **e.** .5
7.26. **a.** .1353   **b.** .3679   **c.** .0003   **d.** .6065
7.27. **a.** .9502   **b.** .9975   **c.** .7769   **d.** .5276   **7.28.** $\mu = \frac{1}{3}$, $\sigma^2 = \frac{1}{9}$, .9502
7.29. .2231   **7.30.** **a.** 10   **b.** .7534   **c.** .1353   **7.31.** .1353, .3935   **7.32.** .1248
7.33. **a.** .2212   **b.** .0024   **c.** .0821
7.37. **a.** Yes   **b.** $\mu = 10$, $\sigma^2 = 5$ **c.** .456   **d.** Approx. .4557
7.38. **a.** .586, approx. .5793   **b.** .268, approx. .2709   **c.** .034, approx. .0329
7.39. **a.** Approx. 1.0   **b.** Approx. .0031   **c.** Approx. .5557   **7.40.** Approx. .0559
7.41. Approx. .2104   **7.42.** Approx. 0   **7.43.** **a.** Approx. .0516   **b.** Approx. .8324
7.44. **a.** Approx. .0885   **b.** Approx. .7123   **7.45.** **a.** Approx. .1762   **b.** Not likely; $z = 3.42$
7.46. **a.** $f(x) = \frac{1}{80}$ $(20 \leq x \leq 100)$ **b.** $\mu = 60$, $\sigma = 23.09$ **c.** $\mu \pm 2\sigma$ is 13.8 to 106.2
d. .375   **e.** .125   **f.** 1.0   **g.** .5774   **h.** 0
7.47. **a.** .2212   **b.** .7788   **c.** 0   **d.** .8647   **e.** .3181
7.48. **a.** .95   **b.** .90   **c.** .9974   **d.** .9759   **e.** .1574   **f.** .9319
7.49. **a.** .3085   **b.** .6915   **c.** .9938   **d.** .3983
7.50. **a.** 0   **b.** .05   **c.** .44   **d.** -1.09
7.51. **a.** .3085   **b.** .1587   **c.** .1359   **d.** .6915   **e.** 0   **f.** .9938
7.52. **a.** Approx. .9441   **b.** Approx. .5557   **c.** Approx. .0031   **d.** Approx. .8426
7.53. .0122, .0062   **7.54.** **a.** .1469   **b.** $(.1469)^2$ **7.55.** Approx. .1446
7.56. **a.** .095   **b.** .9987   **c.** .3085   **7.57.** .6065, .6321   **7.58.** Approx. 1.0; approx. .6618
7.59. .6886   **7.60.** .0721   **7.61.** .1056
7.62. **a.** Approx. .488   **b.** .0968   **c.** Approx. .8926   **7.63.** **a.** .6065   **b.** .5940
7.64. **a.** .1922   **b.** .4681   **c.** $(.4681)^3$
7.65. **a.** .0548   **b.** .6006   **c.** .3446   **d.** \$6,503.80   **7.66.** **a.** .2033   **b.** \$12,800
7.67. $P(x \geq 400 | p \leq .2) \approx 0$

CHAPTER 8

8.1. **b.** 4.68 **c.** 7.931 **d.** 4.780, 1.642 **8.2.** **b.** 4.84, 1.313 **8.3.** **b.** 4.68, .8270

8.4. **a.** $\mu_{\bar{x}} = 6$, $\sigma_{\bar{x}} = .3536$ **b.** .5222 **c.** .0793 **d.** Less spread

8.5. **a.** Approx. normal, $\mu_{\bar{x}} = 400$, $\sigma_{\bar{x}} = 11.86$ **b.** .0174, .5 **8.7.** .3830 **8.8.** .0228

8.9. **a.** .2514

8.10. **a.** 45; $\{(1, 2), (1, 3), \ldots, (9, 10)\}$ **b.** $\{(1, 4), (1, 5), \ldots, (8, 10)\}$; $^{21}/_{45}$

c. $P(0) = ^{3}/_{45}$, $P(1) = ^{21}/_{45}$, $P(2) = ^{21}/_{45}$

8.11. **a.** $\mu \pm 1.342$ **b.** Approx. .0026 **8.12.** .0668

8.13. 60,000 to 75,000, $\sigma_B = 1,666.7$, $\mu_A = 22,500$, $\mu_B = 45,000$, 61,910 to 73,090

8.14. **b.** Normal by the central limit theorem **c.** .3147

CHAPTER 9

9.1. In repeated sampling, 95% of all such confidence intervals contain μ **9.2.** 28.2 ± 1.96

9.3. 20.3 ± .548 **9.4.** 75 ± 5.152

9.11. **a.** .025 **b.** .05 **c.** .005 **d.** .0985 **e.** .10 **f.** .01

9.12. $z = -2.67$; no **9.13.** $z = 2.0$; yes **9.14.** $z = -3.16$; yes **9.15.** $z = 3.53$; yes

9.17. **a.** 2.262 **b.** 3.747 **c.** −2.861 **d.** −1.796 **9.18.** $t = -3.0$; yes

9.19. 19.7 ± .186 **9.20.** $t = 2.667$; yes **9.21.** 4.16 ± .103 **9.22.** $t = -4.193$; yes

9.23. 49.7 ± .124 **9.24.** 6.38 ± 3.74 **9.25.** 4.17 ± 2.85 **9.26.** **a.** $t = -1.35$; no

9.27. The mean of the sampling distribution of $\hat{p}$ is p **9.28.** .45 ± .122 **9.29.** .9 ± .0494

9.30. .055 ± .0202 **9.31.** .06 ± .02 **9.32.** $z = -1.03$; no **9.33.** $z = .976$; no

9.34. .0833 ± .0242 **9.35.** 2,401 **9.36.** 55 **9.37.** 97 **9.38.** 457

9.39. **a.** −1.321 **b.** 9.925 **c.** 2.447 **d.** 2.807

9.41. **a.** 12.2 ± 1.645 **b.** 166 **c.** $z = 1.3$; no **9.42.** .04 ± .0222 **9.43.** 1,476

9.44. **a.** .075 ± .0365 **b.** $z = 1.622$, reject H_0 **9.45.** 667 **9.46.** **a.** $z = 1.414$; no

9.47. .273 ± .0276 **9.48.** $z = 1.071$; no **9.49.** 65

CHAPTER 10

10.2. $z = -4.22$; yes **10.3.** −1.1 ± .429 **10.4.** **b.** $z = 4.27$; yes **10.5.** 1.9 ± .872

10.6. $z = 2.77$; yes **10.7.** The two samples were randomly and independently selected

10.8. $z = 2.17$; yes

10.9. Populations have equal variances and approximately normal distributions; samples are random and independent

10.12. $t = 2.099$; no **10.13.** 4 ± 3.304 **10.14.** $t = 7.521$; yes **10.15.** 105 ± 13.96

10.16. **a.** $s_1^2 = 88.62$, $s_2^2 = 68.49$ **c.** $t = .605$; no **10.17.** **b.** $t = 1.535$; no

10.19. **a.** 3.73 **b.** 3.09 **c.** 4.68 **d.** 3.85 **10.20.** $F = 1.170$; do not reject H_0

10.21. $F = 1.110$; do not reject H_0 **10.22.** $F = 2.626$; reject H_0; assembly line 1 **10.23.** $F = 10$; yes

10.25. **a.** $t = 7.679$; yes **c.** .4167 ± .1395 **10.26.** **a.** $t = .4043$; no **b.** .4167 ± 2.296

10.27. **a.** No, same plants used twice **b.** $t = -5.880$; yes **c.** −2.2 ± .7977

10.28. **a.** 662.5 ± 995.3 **10.34.** **a.** .1732 ± .0076 **b.** .0756 ± .0064 **c.** .0977 ± .0099

10.35. $z = 19.33$; yes, B **10.36.** Less likely   **10.37. a.** $.17 \pm .0353$ **10.38.** $z = 7.915$; yes

10.40. $z = .881$; do not reject H_0 **10.41. a.** $n_1 = n_2 = 769$ **b.** Yes; $n = 385$

10.42. $n = 34$ (95% confidence level)   **10.43.** $n_1 = 260, n_2 = 520$ **10.45. a.** $t = 1.064$; do not reject H_0

10.46. $F = 1.21$; do not reject H_0 **10.47.** $n_1 = n_2 = 542$ **10.48.** $n_1 = n_2 = 195$

10.49. $t = -4.022$; reject H_0 **10.50.** $z = 1.680$; yes   **10.51.** $.4 \pm .6134$; yes

10.52. a. $-.0913 \pm .0518$ **b.** $.308 \pm .0405$ **10.53.** $z = -3.979$; yes, for $\alpha = .05$

10.54. a. $t = -2.085$; no, for $\alpha = .05$ **10.55.** $n_1 = n_2 = 193$

10.56. $t = 2.269$; yes   **b.** Paired design   **10.57.** 9.9 ± 8.937 **10.58.** $.0309 \pm .0341$

10.59. $z = -1.308$; do not reject H_0 **10.60. a.** -177 ± 79.02 **10.61.** $F = 2.788$; no

10.62. a. $-\$1,141.7 \pm \$2,018.8$ **b.** No   **10.63.** $z = -2,934$; reject H_0 **10.64.** $-.0467 \pm .0839$

10.65. a. $t = -1.383$; no, for $\alpha = .05$ **10.66.** $F = 1.817$; do not reject H_0 for $\alpha = .10$

10.67. $n_1 = n_2 = 70$

CHAPTER 11

11.2. $\beta_0 = 1, \beta_1 = 1$

11.3. a. $\beta_0 = 2, \beta_1 = 2$ **b.** $\beta_0 = 4, \beta_1 = 1$ **c.** $\beta_0 = -2, \beta_1 = 4$ **d.** $\beta_0 = -4, \beta_1 = -1$

11.5. a. $\beta_1 = 2, \beta_0 = 3$ **b.** $\beta_1 = 1, \beta_0 = 1$ **c.** $\beta_1 = 3, \beta_0 = -2$ **d.** $\beta_1 = 5, \beta_0 = 0$

e. $\beta_1 = -2, \beta_0 = 4$ **11.6. a.** $\hat{\beta}_0 = 0, \hat{\beta}_1 = .8571$ **11.7. a.** $\hat{\beta}_0 = 2, \hat{\beta}_1 = -1.2$

11.8. b. $\hat{\beta}_0 = -.125, \hat{\beta}_1 = 3.125$ **d.** 15.5 **11.9.** $\hat{\beta}_0 = -1.430, \hat{\beta}_1 = .1947$

11.10. a. $\hat{y} = 133.1 - .2647x$ **11.11.** $.0313$

11.12. a. $1.143, .2857$ **b.** $1.60, .5333$ **c.** $11.0, 3.667$ **d.** $.0395, .0099$ **e.** $2,235.9, 171.99$

11.13. a. $\hat{y} = -45.78 + 1.562x$ **c.** $SSE = 19.60, s^2 = 4.90$

11.14. a. $\hat{y} = -.2462 + 1.315x$ **c.** $7.645, 11.59$ **d.** $SSE = 12.44, s^2 = 2.487$

11.15. a. $t = 6.708$; yes   **b.** $t = -5.196$; yes   **c.** $t = 8.506$; yes   **d.** $t = 8.056$; yes

e. $t = -1.919$; no   **11.16.** $t = 3.233$; yes   **11.17.** $t = 8.122$; yes

11.18. a. $\hat{y} = 10.39 + 90.92x$ **b.** $H_a: \beta_1 > 0, t = 3.182$; reject H_0 **c.** 90.92 ± 57.58

11.19. $\hat{\beta}_1 = 7.70, t = 2.556$; yes $(\alpha = .05)$ **11.20.** 5.638 ± 1.448 **11.21.** $r = .9836, r^2 = .9675$

11.22. $r = .3142, r^2 = .0987$ **11.23.** $r_1 = -.9674, r_2 = -.1105$; x_1

11.24. a. $r^2 = .8089$ **b.** $t = 5.039$; yes $(\alpha = .05)$ **11.25.** $\hat{y} = 7.319 + .4851x, r^2 = .5921$

11.26. $.7115 \pm .1778$ **11.27. a.** 78.58 ± 35.56 **b.** 78.58 ± 12.60 **11.30.** 217.9 ± 10.35

11.31. a. $\hat{y} = 4.554 + 2.671x$ **c.** 13.10 ± 1.189 **d.** $12.57 \pm .4260$

11.32. b. $\hat{y} = 11,898.8 - 763.1x$ **d.** $t = -3.944$; reject H_0 **e.** -763.1 ± 375.9

f. $r = -.8495$ **g.** $r^2 = .7216$ **h.** $5,793.9 \pm 1,609.3$ **i.** $5,793.9 \pm 677.2$

11.33. a. $r = -.8516, r^2 = .7253$ **b.** $t = -3.250$; yes $(\alpha = .05)$

11.34. a. $\hat{y} = -1.081 + .6757x$ **b.** $t = 2.5$; yes   **c.** $.6757 \pm .860$

d. 15.81 ± 1.334 **e.** 14.46 ± 3.689

11.35. a. $\hat{y} = 22.32 + 2.650x$ **c.** $t = 6.280$; yes $(\alpha = .05)$ **d.** $r = .9421, r^2 = .8875$

e. 109.8 ± 2.155 **f.** 101.8 ± 6.648

11.36. a. $r = .8429$ **b.** $t = 2.713$; yes $(\alpha = .05$, one-tailed test$)$

11.37. a. $\hat{y} = 18.22 + 1.166x$ **c.** $t = 4.967$; yes $(\alpha = .05)$ **d.** $r^2 = .8044$ **e.** 123.2 ± 19.09

11.38. a. $\hat{y} = 2.084 + .6682x$ **c.** $t = 16.28$; yes $(\alpha = .05)$ **d.** $.9815$ **e.** $35.49 \pm .9787$

f. 38.83 ± 2.766 **11.39. a.** $\hat{y} = 16.28 + 2.078x$ **c.** $t = 6.672$; yes $(\alpha = .05)$ **d.** 57.84 ± 6.146

11.40. a. $\hat{y} = 15.11 + .9720x$ **c.** $r = .9815, r^2 = .9634$ **d.** $22.88 \pm .9793$ **e.** 21.91 ± 2.574

11.41. a. $\hat{y} = 13.48 + .0560x$ **c.** $r = .7402, r^2 = .5479$ **d.** 17.40 ± 2.474

11.42. a. $\hat{y} = 44.17 - .0255x$ **c.** $t = -.0294$; do not reject H_0

CHAPTER 12

12.2. $t = 2.107$; reject H_0 **12.3.** $t = 3.039$; reject H_0 ($\alpha = .05$)

12.4. **a.** $F = 31.98$; yes   **b.** $t = -2.273$; yes   **12.5.** $F = 1.056$; do not reject H_0

12.6. **b.** $\hat{y} = 95.75 - .3199x$ **c.** Quadratic model

12.8. **a.** $\hat{y} = .0456 + .00079x_1 + .2374x_2 - .00004x_1x_2$ **b.** SSE $= 2.715$, $s^2 = .1697$

12.9. **a.** $F = 84.96$; yes   **b.** $t = -2.99$; yes   **12.10.** 7.323 to 9.449

12.11. **a.** $F = 1.28$; do not reject H_0 **12.12.** **a.** 13.68

12.13. **b.** $F = 52.21$; reject H_0 **c.** $t = -3.333$; yes ($\alpha = .05$)   **d.** $t = 4$; yes ($\alpha = .05$)

12.15. $t = -1.104$; do not reject H_0 **12.16.** **b.** $t = 40.54$; yes   **c.** 17.79

12.17. **b.** $F = 16.1$; yes   **c.** $t = 2.5$; yes   **d.** 945

12.18. **b.** $t = 5$; yes   **c.** 825   **d.** Support

12.19. The estimate of the difference in mean attendance between weekends and weekdays is $15x_3 = 700$

12.20. **a.** $F = 6.614$; yes   **12.21.** **a.** Test $H_0: \beta_2 = \beta_3 = 0$ **c.** $t = -3.333$; yes

12.22. $F = 5.990$; reject H_0

CHAPTER 13

13.2. The assumption of normality   **13.3.** $E(y) = \beta_0 + \beta_1x + \beta_2x^2$, where $\beta_2 > 0$

13.4. **b.** Linear; linear; quadratic

13.5. **a.** Both are quantitative   **b.** $E(y) = \beta_0 + \beta_1x_1 + \beta_2x_2$ **c.** Include $\beta_3x_1x_2$

d. Include $\beta_4x_1^2 + \beta_5x_2^2$

13.7. **a.** $E(y) = \beta_0 + \beta_1x_1 + \beta_2x_2 + \beta_3x_3 + \beta_4x_1x_2 + \beta_5x_1x_3 + \beta_6x_2x_3$ **b.** Include $\beta_7x_1^2 + \beta_8x_2^2 + \beta_9x_3^2$

13.9. **a.** 60   **b.** 510

13.10. **a.** 3   **b.** $E(y) = \beta_0 + \beta_1x_1 + \beta_2x_2 + \beta_3x_3$, where x_1, x_2, and x_3 are defined in Exercise 13.11

c. Include $\beta_4x_1x_3 + \beta_5x_2x_3$ **d.** Yes   **13.11.** **a.** 5   **b.** -1 **c.** -1 versus 1

13.12. **a.** $E(y) = \beta_0 + \beta_1x_1$ **b.** Include $\beta_2x_2 + \beta_3x_3$ **c.** Include $\beta_4x_1x_2 + \beta_5x_1x_3$

13.13. **a.** $E(y) = \beta_0 + \beta_1x_1 + \beta_2x_2 + \beta_3x_3$ **b.** $H_0: \beta_2 = \beta_3 = 0$

13.14. **a.** $H_0: \beta_3 = 0$ **b.** $H_0: \beta_1 = \beta_3 = 0$ **13.15.** **a.** $H_0: \beta_2 = \beta_3 = 0$ **b.** $F = 6.99$; reject H_0

13.16. $F = 2.596$; do not reject H_0 **13.17.** $F = 1.409$; do not reject H_0

13.18. **a.** 1, quantitative, 0–4 years; 2, qualitative, 2 levels; 3, qualitative, 2 levels; 4, quantitative, 6–24 inches; 5, qualitative, 3 levels   **b.** $E(y) = \beta_0 + \beta_1x_1 + \beta_2x_2 + \beta_3x_3 + \beta_4x_4 + \beta_5x_5 + \beta_6x_6$

c. No interaction terms; include $\beta_7x_4x_5 + \beta_8x_4x_6$ **13.19.** No estimate of σ^2

13.20. **a.** $E(y) = \beta_0 + \beta_1x + \beta_2x^2$ **b.** No, need at least four different baking times

13.21. $E(y) = \beta_0 + \beta_1x_1 + \beta_2x_2 + \beta_3x_3 + \beta_4x_1x_2 + \beta_5x_1x_3 + \beta_6x_1^2$

13.22. **a.** $H_0: \beta_4 = 0$ **b.** $H_0: \beta_1 = \beta_3 = 0$ **13.23.** $F = 3.306$; reject H_0 ($\alpha = .05$)

13.24. **a.** $E(y) = \beta_0 + \beta_1x_1 + \beta_2x_2 + \beta_3x_3 + \beta_4x_4$; no interaction   **b.** Include $\beta_5x_1x_2 + \beta_6x_1x_3 + \beta_7x_1x_4$

13.25. **a.** $F = 2.33$; do not reject H_0

13.26. **a.** $E(y) = \beta_0 + \beta_1x_1 + \beta_2x_2 + \beta_3x_3$ **b.** Include $\beta_4x_1x_2 + \beta_5x_1x_3 + \beta_6x_2x_3 + \beta_7x_1^2 + \beta_8x_2^2$

c. $H_0: \beta_4 = \beta_5 = \beta_6 = \beta_7 = \beta_8 = 0$; use F test   **13.27.** **a.** $F = 1.26$; no   **b.** $F = 133$; reject H_0 ($\alpha = .01$)

CHAPTER 14

14.1.

1965	1966	1967	1968	1969	1970	1971	1972	1973	1974	1975	1976
94.1	79.7	100	119.9	132.8	147.3	153.5	121.1	69.5	89.8	134.4	165.2

14.2.

1961	1962	1963	1964	1965	1966	1967	1968	1969	1970	1971	1972	1973
68.33	72.47	76.40	81.64	87.72	94.80	100.0	109.32	118.23	126.19	136.28	149.48	164.92

1974	1975	1976
180.69	198.49	220.21

b. Use $I_t^* = \dfrac{I_t}{I_{74}}$

14.4.

	1961	1962	1963	1964	1965	1966	1967	1968	1969	1970	1971	1972	1973	1974	1975
3	—	71.8	76.8	82.5	89.6	95.7	101.2	105.5	107.7	108.0	109.5	115.9	121.9	122.7	—
N 5	—	—	77.3	83.5	89.1	94.9	100.7	104.2	106.0	109.0	113.0	115.8	118.0	—	—
7	—	—	—	83.5	89.0	94.5	98.8	102.4	106.1	110.1	113.6	115.4	—	—	—

14.6. b. Moving average (100 × Ratio)

1972	—	(—)	—	(—)	324.8	(134.9)	317.6	(125.3)
1973	378.4	(99.4)	376.6	(57.4)	382.0	(121.5)	370.4	(115.8)
1974	431.8	(98.4)	438.2	(72.6)	443.6	(117.9)	438.2	(113.2)
1975	493.2	(92.5)	503.8	(79.0)	509.8	(116.3)	518.2	(111.2)
1976	565.8	(93.0)	575.2	(86.6)	—	(—)	—	(—)

14.12. a.

1965	1966	1967	1968	1969	1970	1971	1972	1973	1974	1975
240.7	153.5	147.7	54.6	34.4	100	−8.0	−199.9	140.8	120.5	550.1

14.13.

1965	1966	1967	1968	1969	1970	1971	1972	1973	1974	1975
—	5,357.3	3,517.3	2,340.0	1,868.7	1,249.7	−1,067.0	−663.0	607.0	8,022.3	—

14.15.

1961	1962	1963	1964	1965	1966	1967	1968	1969	1970	1971	1972	1973	1974	1975
—	1.513	1.490	1.470	1.463	1.497	1.530	1.563	1.587	1.607	1.593	1.533	1.497	1.520	—

14.16. a.
MOVING AVERAGES

	I	II	III	IV
1973	—	—	25.56	26.02
1974	26.84	27.67	28.32	28.57
1975	28.55	28.34	28.20	28.37
1976	28.85	29.65	—	—

b.
RATIO-TO-MOVING AVERAGE

	I	II	III	IV
1973	—	—	99.13	109.45
1974	89.79	101.77	99.68	111.73
1975	90.44	100.32	98.55	108.35
1976	89.67	100.17	—	—
R_i	89.97	100.75	99.12	109.84

14.17. a. $\hat{y} = 9.318 + .7x$

b.

t	12	13	14	15	16	17	18	19	20	21	22	23	24
$\hat{y}$	17.72	18.42	19.12	19.82	20.52	21.22	21.92	22.62	23.32	24.02	24.72	25.42	26.12

c. You should not predict outside the experimental region

15.1. **a.** $F = 16.95$; reject H_0 **b.** -72 ± 26.08
15.2. **a.** $F = 3.168$; no **b.** 473.3 ± 22.93 **c.** 37.05 ± 30.76
15.3. **a.** $F = 3.529$; yes **b.** 4.5 ± 37.09
15.5. **a.** $F = 12.25$; yes **c.** $t = 3.5$; reject H_0 **d.** $12.25 = (3.5)^2$, $7.71 = (2.776)^2$
15.6. **a.** $F = 25.24$; yes **b.** $-1 \pm .2733$

15.7. **a.** $F = .3381$; no **b.**

SOURCE	df	SS	MS	F
Treatment	2	.9411	.4706	.3381
Block	5	10,240.	2,048.	1,471.
Error	10	13.92	1.392	
Total	17	10,254.9		

c. $-.1833 \pm 1.234$

15.9. **a.** Completely randomized **b.** $F = 6.301$; yes **c.** 25 ± 2.343
15.10. **a.** $F = 3.638$; do not reject H_0 $(\alpha = .05)$ **b.** $F = 46.85$
15.11. **a.** Randomized block **b.** $F = 3.884$; yes $(\alpha = .05)$ **c.** 2.4 ± 33.48 (95% confidence)
15.12. **a.** df: 1, 98; MS: 3,237.2, 164.98; $F = 19.62$ **b.** Yes **c.** No, need the sample means
15.13. **a.** $F = 22.23$; yes **b.** $F = 20.45$; yes **c.** 1.593 ± 4.088
15.14. **a.** $F = 83.82$; yes **b.** $-1.64 \pm .4877$ **15.15.** **a.** $F = 7.613$; yes **b.** $8.067 \pm .4491$
15.16. $F = 10.66$; yes $(\alpha = .05)$ **15.17.** **a.** $F = 15.58$; yes $(\alpha = .05)$ **15.18.** $F = 2.950$; no

15.19. **a.** Completely randomized **b.**

SOURCE	df	SS	MS	F
Treatment	2	57.60	28.80	.3375
Error	13	1,109.33	85.33	
Total	15	1,166.93		

c. $F = .3375$; no

15.20. 81 ± 7.316

15.21. **a.** $F = .1925$; no **b.**

SOURCE	df	SS	MS	F
Treatment	2	.6317	.3158	.1925
Block	3	.8558	.2853	.1739
Error	6	9.8417	1.6403	
Total	11	11.3292		

c. $F = .1739$; no

15.22. $.55 \pm 3.357$ **15.23.** **a.** Completely randomized **b.** $F = 7.025$; yes **c.** $8.15 \pm .449$

15.24. **a.** $F = 9.747$; yes **b.** $F = 4.881$; yes **c.**

SOURCE	df	SS	MS	F
Treatment	2	1,277.2	638.60	9.747
Block	4	1,279.1	319.78	4.881
Error	8	524.1	65.52	
Total	14	3,080.4		

15.25. 11.6 ± 11.80 **15.26.** **a.** Completely randomized **b.** $F = 7.793$ **c.** -5.65 ± 3.250
15.27. **a.** $t = .4635$ **b.** $t = .46$; reject if $|t| > 2.145$ or $t^2 > (2.145)^2 = 4.6$
c. $F = .2148 = (.4635)^2$, reject if $F > 4.6$

CHAPTER 16

16.1. $T_A = 35$; no evidence ($\alpha = .05$)

16.2. **a.** $t = -1.258$; independent samples from normally distributed populations with equal variances

b. $T_A = 37.5$; do not reject H_0 ($\alpha = .05$)   **16.3.** $T_B = 8$; no evidence

16.4. **a.** $t = .4776$; do not reject H_0; differences in indices are distributed normally   **b.** $T_B = 7$; do not reject H_0

16.5. $H = 7.971$; yes

16.6. **a.** $F = 1.326$; do not reject H_0; life lengths for the three brands are distributed normally with equal variances

b. $H = 1.22$; do not reject H_0 **16.7.** $F_r = 12.3$; yes   **16.8.** $F_r = 6.5$; reject H_0 ($\alpha = .05$)

16.9. **a.** .4524   **b.** No   **16.10.** $r_s = -.8536$; yes   **16.11.** $T_A = 135$; yes

16.12. $H = 14.61$; yes   **16.13.** $T_{III} = 16.5$; reject H_0 **16.14.** $F_r = 6.21$; no   **16.15.** $r_s = .4091$; no

16.16. $T_{After} = 94.5$; reject H_0 **16.17.** $T_B = 3.5$; yes   **16.18.** $T_{After} = 77.5$, yes

16.19. $F_r = 11.77$; yes   **16.20.** $T_A = 2.5$; do not reject H_0 **16.21.** $H = 16.39$; yes

16.22. $T_1 = 59$, reject H_0 **16.23.** $r_s = .9286$; yes   **16.24.** $F_r = 1.55$; no   **16.25.** $H = 12.79$; yes

16.26. $T_A = 28.5$; do not reject H_0 **16.27.** $r_s = .7714$; no   **16.28.** $T_A = 17.5$; no

16.29. $H = 3.225$; no   **16.30.** $T_B = 58$; do not reject H_0

CHAPTER 17

17.1. $X^2 = 17.36$; yes   **17.2.** $X^2 = 3.92$; no   **17.3.** $X^2 = 10.44$; yes ($\alpha = .05$)

17.4. $X^2 = 43.72$; reject H_0 **17.5.** $X^2 = 1.351$; no   **17.6.** $X^2 = 40.70$; yes   **17.7.** $X^2 = 2.601$; no

17.8. **a.** $X^2 = 33.67$; reject H_0 **b.** $.5563 \pm .077$ **17.9.** 103.1; yes

17.10. $X^2 = 7.384$; no ($\alpha = .05$)   **17.11.** $X^2 = 6.929$; no   **17.12.** $.2840 \pm .0571$

17.13. $X^2 = 38.68$; yes   **17.14.** $X^2 = 7.4$; do not reject H_0 **17.15.** $X^2 = 31.86$; yes

17.16. $.12 \pm .0947$ **17.17.** $X^2 = 3.132$; no evidence   **17.18.** $.0952 \pm .1280$

17.19. $X^2 = 6.74$; yes   **17.20.** $X^2 = 46.25$; yes ($\alpha = .05$)   **17.21.** $.1429 \pm .0417$ (95% confidence)

17.22. **a.** $X^2 = 9.647$ **b.** $\chi^2_{.05,3} = 7.8147$ **c.** Yes

INDEX

This book was typeset in Vega Light by Typothetae, and printed by Halliday
  Lithograph
Phyllis Niklas was the editor and production coordinator
Janet Bollow was the designer
Technical art was prepared by Boardworks
Nan Golub created the artwork that appears on the cover, on chapter opening
  pages, and accompanying On Your Own sections